KING GEORGE THE FIFTH
His Life and Reign

KING GEORGE V
June 4, 1933

KING GEORGE
THE FIFTH

His Life and Reign

by

HAROLD NICOLSON

CONSTABLE & CO LTD
LONDON

LONDON

PUBLISHED BY

Constable and Company Ltd.

10 ORANGE STREET, W.C.2

First published August 1952
Second impression August 1952
Third impression August 1952
Fourth impression 1953
Fifth impression March 1970

ISBN *0 09 453181 1*

PRINTED IN GREAT BRITAIN BY COMPTON PRINTING LTD.

LONDON & AYLESBURY

AUTHOR'S NOTE

WHEN, in June 1948, I was invited to undertake this work, I was told that, after King George's death, it had been decided that his biography should be written in two separate instalments and entrusted to two different authors.

The first instalment was to be a portrait of the man himself; it was to describe his *private* life and to give a picture of his homes, friendships, occupations, tastes and hobbies. This task was entrusted to Mr John Gore, who brought to his work the application of a trained scholar, the liveliness of an alert mind, great gifts of selection and arrangement, and the agreeable virtues of tact and taste. His book was published by John Murray in 1941 under the title *King George V. A Personal Memoir*.

My own task, as the author chosen for the second instalment, was to chronicle King George's *public* life and to examine his attitude towards the successive political issues of his reign. To attempt a comprehensive history of those years of transition would, I soon realised, throw the biography out of scale. With many of the major events of his reign, King George was only indirectly concerned: to have identified him directly with these events would have been to falsify proportions, and to confuse what I anticipated would prove this book's most useful theme. My desire was to suggest some answer to the two questions: 'How does a Monarchy function in a modern State?' and 'To what extent were the powers and influence of the Monarchy diminished or increased during the twenty five years of King George's reign?'

The relevant papers in the Royal Archives at Windsor, to which, by gracious permission of His late Majesty I was accorded unrestricted access, fall into six main categories:

(1) Papers dealing with King George's childhood and education. They include letters from Mr Dalton to the Prince of Wales and Queen Victoria, reports from tutors and instructors, letters from naval commandants etc.

(2) King George's own diaries. These run without intermission from May 3 1880 to January 17 1936. Even when he was ill he would dictate his daily entry to Queen Mary or one of his nurses. The diaries fall into three divisions: (a) a small pocket engagement book for the year 1878, begun on July 30 and given up three days later: (b) a section from May 3, 1880 to January 1, 1881 written on loose sheets torn from

an engagement block: (c) a section from January 1, 1881 to December 31, 1886, written in the ordinary diaries provided by stationers which have subsequently been bound up together: and (d) the main diary running from January 1, 1887 to the end, written carefully on specially prepared paper and filling twenty five large volumes bound in Morocco and to be opened only by a small gold key.

(3) Letters from and to Queen Victoria, King Edward and Queen Alexandra, King George and Queen Olga of Greece, Prince George of Greece, the Duke of York, the Duke of Gloucester and the Duke of Kent. These personal letters are either bound or filed in strict chronological sequence and bear no registration numbers. They can, however, be readily identified by their dates.

(4) The main files, comprising the official correspondence, minutes and memoranda. These are contained in canvas boxes labelled by the initial letters A. B. C etc, according to subject. In these boxes will be found the letters addressed to Ministers by the King's Private Secretaries and the records of his audiences and interviews.

I have been through all these papers myself: the only section for which I obtained assistance was that dealing with ecclesiastical preferments and honours. In sorting out these dull but numerous documents, I had the valuable help of Miss M. Alcock, formerly Private Secretary to Lord Stamfordham.

(5) Cabinet documents, minutes and memoranda.

(6) Reports sent to the King daily when the House of Commons was in session by the Prime Minister or Leader of the House. These reports deal with the general feeling of the House, the effect of individual speeches, and the personality of old or young politicians. They were of great value to the King as giving him information and suggestions that were not to be found in Hansard. These daily reports were composed in No. 10 Downing Street and are vivacious, and even jocose, in style. They were of course revised and signed by the Prime Minister or Leader of the House before being sent off to the Palace. This curious custom was abandoned after July, 1936 by command of King Edward VIII.

The note references in the text are of two sorts. Numerals (1, 2, 3, etc.) indicate substantive notes which will be found at the bottom of the page. The small letters (*a, b, c, d*, etc.) indicate sources, a full list of which will be found at the end of the book in Appendix III. The latter are intended for students only, and I apologize to the ordinary reader if their frequency and typographical ugliness cause irritation.

The habit possessed by eminent Englishmen and Scotsmen of frequently altering their own names is one that may trouble the reader, especially the foreign reader. Mr A of one chapter becomes Sir Charles A. in the next; three chapters further on he emerges as Viscount B; and as we read further, he enters again, disguised as the

Earl of C. I have dealt harshly with this problem, calling people by the names they possessed at the date of which I am writing.

I have been fortunate in having known personally the political figures whom I describe. The survivors of that generation have been kind in recalling for me fond memories of the past, and even in checking passages in this book dealing with events with which they were directly concerned. I had intended to include a nominal list of all those to whom I felt myself under obligation. When, however, I saw the list in type, it appeared to me pretentious and indiscreet. I trust that all those eminent persons who gave me their time and attention will realize that it is certainly not owing to lack of gratitude that I have omitted my list of benefactors.

Some names must, however, be mentioned. To Sir Alan Lascelles, the King's Private Secretary and Keeper of the Royal Archives, I am indebted for much friendly guidance; I am also obliged to his predecessors, Lord Hardinge of Penshurst and Lord Wigram. Miss Daisy Bigge, daughter of Lord Stamfordham, has been so kind as to allow me to use some letters from and to her father. Sir Owen Morshead, Librarian at Windsor Castle, has been at my side to advise, to encourage and to warn. To Miss Mary Mackenzie, Registrar of the King's Archives, and to her ever kindly staff, my debt is great. Her detailed knowledge, her gift for decyphering illegible handwritings, her patience, calm and unfailing encouragement, have sustained me through many a dark day, when the North East wind howled along the Thames valley and my light was low. My own secretary, Miss Elvira Niggeman, never abated for one instant the gay efficiency with which she copied documents that she knew I should never use, or typed draft Chapters which she knew would be frequently revised. And finally I am indebted to my publishers, Messrs Constable, and to the printers, Messrs Robert MacLehose, for the great trouble they have taken with the proofs and final production.

H. N.

Sissinghurst

ACKNOWLEDGMENTS

For permission to use copyright material, the author wishes to express his gratitude to:

Messrs Chatto & Windus for extracts from *Dawson of Penn*, by Francis Watson.

Miss Sara Eakins Black and Messrs Hurst & Blackett Ltd for extract from *King's Nurse, Beggar's Nurse*, by Sister Catherine Black.

Messrs Cassell & Co. Ltd for extract from *Politics from Inside*, by Sir Austen Chamberlain.

Messrs Macmillan & Co. Ltd for extract from *Henry Ponsonby*, by Lord Ponsonby.

The Hon. Margaret Bigge and Messrs John Murray (Publishers) Ltd for a letter from Sir Arthur Bigge to the Master of Elibank, taken from *Master and Brother*, by Colonel the Hon. Arthur Murray.

Messrs Hutchinson & Co. (Publishers) Ltd and Messrs Rupert Crew Ltd, for two extracts from *Memoirs* by the Rt Hon. J. R. Clynes.

CONTENTS

Contents

Contents

Contents

Contents

Contents

Contents

LIST OF ILLUSTRATIONS

(The photographs facing pages 72 and 73 are taken from Queen Victoria's albums at Windsor. That of Lord Stamfordham facing page 264 has been provided by his daughter, Miss Margaret Bigge. All the other photographs come from Queen Mary's private albums and are published by gracious permission)

KING GEORGE V

His Life and Reign

CHAPTER

CHILDHOOD

1865–1879

Prince George born in London June 3, 1865—The problem of his name—
Queen Victoria's suggestions—His mother—His father—Sandringham and Abergeldie—Charles Fuller—The Rev. John Dalton—
Early lessons—Francis and Charlotte Knollys—His grandmother,
the Queen—Suggestion that Prince Eddy should accompany him to
the *Britannia*—Queen Victoria's objections—Life in the *Britannia*—
Prince George leaves the *Britannia* July 1879.

(1)

PRINCE GEORGE was born at Marlborough House, London, at
1.30 a.m. on the morning of June 3, 1865. He was the second son of
Albert Edward, Prince of Wales (subsequently King Edward VII)
and of Alexandra, daughter of Christian IX, King of Denmark.[1]

At 3.30 a.m. on that morning of June 3, Queen Victoria was
awakened at Windsor Castle by two telegrams from the Prince of
Wales announcing the birth of a second son. The customary dis-
cussion arose as to the names by which the boy should be known.
The Prince had suggested that he should be christened *George
Frederick*:

[1] King Christian IX (1818–1906) was a younger son of William, Duke
of Schleswig-Holstein-Sonderburg-Glücksburg. In 1842 he married
Louise, daughter of William, Landgraf of Hesse-Cassel, whose mother
was next-of-kin to King Frederick VII of Denmark. When it became clear
that King Frederick would remain childless, the representatives of the
Great Powers met in London and, by the Protocol of May 1852, designated
Prince Christian as King Frederick's heir. On the latter's death, in
November 1863, he ascended the throne of Denmark as King Christian
IX.

His eldest son succeeded him in 1906 as King Frederick VIII (1843–
1912). His second son, William (1845–1913), became King of the Hellenes
in 1863. His eldest daughter, Alexandra (1844–1925), became Queen of
England. His second daughter, Dagmar, became Empress of Russia. His
third daughter, Thyra, became Duchess of Cumberland.

He and Queen Louise figure in the royal correspondence as 'Apapa'
and 'Amama'.

3

'As to the names of the young gentleman,' he wrote to Queen Victoria on June 11, 1865, 'we had both for some time settled that, if we had another boy, he should be called *George*, as we like the name and it is an English one.' 'I fear,' the Queen replied on June 13, 'I cannot admire the names you propose to give the Baby. I had hoped for some fine old name. Frederick is, however, the best of the two, and I hope you will *call* him so. *George* only came in with the Hanoverian family.

'However, if the dear child grows up good and wise, I shall not mind what his name is. Of course you will add *Albert* at the end, like your brothers, as you know we settled *long ago* that *all* dearest Papa's *male* descendants should bear *that* name, to mark *our line*, just as I wish all the girls to have Victoria after theirs.

'I lay great stress on this; and it is done in a great many families.'

'We are sorry', the Prince of Wales replied to the Queen on June 16, 'to hear that you don't like the names that we propose to give our little boy, but they are names that we like and have decided on for some time.'

The christening took place at St. George's Chapel, Windsor, on July 7. Among the sponsors were the King of Hanover, the Queen of Denmark, Princess Alice of Hesse, the Duchess of Cambridge and the Prince of Leiningen. Lords Palmerston and Granville were present as Ministers in attendance. The baptism was administered by the Archbishop of Canterbury, assisted by the Bishops of London, Oxford and Worcester. The programme of the ceremony has been preserved: the central passage runs as follows:

'When the Archbishop of Canterbury commences the prayer *Almighty and Ever Living God*, the Countess of Macclesfield will place the Infant Prince in the arms of the Queen, who will hand His Royal Highness to the Archbishop and receive the Prince from His Grace when His Royal Highness has been baptised.'

He was in this manner christened *George Frederick Ernest Albert*. But to his family thereafter he was always known as 'Georgy' or 'Georgie'.

(2)

His mother, Alexandra Princess of Wales, was a woman of intense, and even exclusive, family affections. Her own childhood had been spent in surroundings of extreme simplicity, whether in the little yellow palace at Copenhagen or in the beloved country home at Bernstorff. She and her sisters would do their own sewing and assist in the household chores. When in 1863, at the age of nineteen, she came to England as the bride of Queen Victoria's heir— acclaimed by the Poet Laureate as 'Sea-King's daughter from over

4

the Sea'—she immediately captured, and for ever retained, the affections of the British people by her unfading loveliness and charm. Essentially she was a simple woman. Apart from her liking for music, she possessed few intellectual or aesthetic tastes. Warmhearted and generous, retaining throughout her life the spontaneous gaiety of her girlhood, impulsive, unpunctual, unmethodical and absurdly lavish, she controlled her natural high spirits with innate dignity and instinctive tact. She preserved unclouded the candid Protestant beliefs in which she had been nurtured. The troubles of her married life (troubles which never lastingly disturbed the affection which existed between herself and her husband) and the hereditary deafness which afflicted her after her illness of 1867, confirmed her natural tendency to confine her emotional experience within a narrow domestic circle. Her devotion to her own family was passionate and possessive; like so many adoring mothers, she failed sometimes to realise that her children might one day cease to be children and might acquire interests, belongings and affections of their own.

Throughout Prince George's childhood and early boyhood the influence of his mother was predominant. She would read the Bible aloud to him and it was from her that he acquired the habit, which he never relinquished, of reading a passage from the Scriptures every day. He would sit and talk to her while her long tresses were being brushed in the morning; at night she would tuck him up in bed and receive the confidences which children will then liberate. To him she was always 'darling Motherdear'. His homesickness, when parted from her, was acute.

The affection which he felt for his father was tempered by wholesome awe. The fear of arousing his father's displeasure remained with him in adult life. Yet in the later years, when King Edward had come to take an overt pride in his son's reliability, their relationship became one of mutual confidence. Prince George's boyhood feelings of dutiful affection merged into adult loyalty and trust. King Edward was always insisting that his son should regard him as an elder brother; they held no secrets from each other; seldom has so frank and staunch a bond been forged between a Sovereign and his heir.

Prince George's childhood was boisterously happy. For most of the time the children remained at Sandringham, with occasional visits to London, Osborne and Abergeldie.[1] Their first nurse was a

[1] Prince George had two brothers and three sisters. His elder brother, Prince Albert Victor (generally known as 'Prince Eddy') was born at

5

Mrs Blackburn, generally referred to as 'Mary'. She was succeeded by a nursery governess of the name of Miss Brown. When Prince Eddy was no more than a fortnight old, a 'nursery footman' of the name of Charles Fuller was engaged as his personal attendant. Fuller was devoted to the two Princes and especially to Prince George. He served them throughout their boyhood, he went with them on their cruise round the world, he was with Prince Eddy at Cambridge. For many years he remained one of Prince George's most constant correspondents. There are letters from Fuller urging the Prince not to forget, if the weather appeared changeable, the warm waistcoat with the long sleeves; letters begging him not to smoke too much, since it would stunt his growth; a typical letter from Sandringham, dated June 20, 1883:

'It is just a week since you left us and you cannot think how much I miss your dear face, the place don't look the same.'

'My dear excellent Fuller', as Prince George called him, died of heart failure in 1901.

(3)

When Prince Eddy had reached the age of seven, and Prince George was verging upon six, it was decided that their regular education must begin. The Prince of Wales was determined that his two sons should not be subjected to the congested cramming from which he had himself suffered under the discipline inspired by Baron Stockmar. The tutor selected was the Reverend John Neale Dalton, then a young man of thirty-two and curate to Canon Prothero, rector of Whippingham near Osborne.

Mr Dalton had obtained at Cambridge a first class in theology. He was a man of character, precision and tenacity. Although his

---

Frogmore on January 8, 1864, was created Duke of Clarence and Avondale in May 1890, and died at Sandringham on January 14, 1892.

A younger brother, christened Alexander John, was born in 1871 and lived only a few hours.

His eldest sister, Princess Louise, was born in 1867, married the Duke of Fife in 1899, was declared Princess Royal in 1905, and died in 1931.

His second sister, Princess Victoria, was born in 1868 and died unmarried in December 1935.

His third sister, Princess Maud, was born in 1869, married Prince Charles of Denmark (subsequently King Haakon VII of Norway) in 1896, and died in 1938.

Tables showing Prince George's immediate relations will be found in Appendixes I and II.

6

letters to Queen Victoria and the Prince of Wales were extremely deferential, he seldom hesitated, from fear of causing irritation or provoking disapproval, to advise and to act in what he considered the best interests of his two pupils or in accordance with his own high sense of responsibility and duty. He disapproved of the lavish extravagance of Sandringham and Marlborough House. He would protest in outspoken terms against the many distractions with which the Prince and Princess of Wales were tempted to spoil their children. He would point out the harm which was being done to the rhythm of their education by the frequent and too elaborate journeyings and displacements in which their restless parents were apt to indulge. He possessed a resonant voice and much enjoyed listening to it; his handwriting was neat and scholarly; his passion for tidiness and order left an indelible impression upon Prince George's habits of thought and life. He remained tutor to one or other of the two Princes for fourteen years. Prince George's affectionate nature responded warmly to the devotion of this faithful man. Mr Dalton remained his intimate friend and counsellor until he died as Canon of Windsor in 1931 when over ninety years of age.

The time-table which Mr Dalton imposed upon his two pupils during those early years at Sandringham has been preserved. They would rise at seven and prepare their Geography and English before breakfast. At eight came a Bible or History lesson, followed by Algebra or Euclid at nine. There then ensued an hour's break for games and thereafter a French or Latin lesson until the main meal, which took place at two. The afternoon was occupied by riding or playing cricket and after tea would come English lessons, music, and preparation. The two Princes were put to bed at eight.[a]

In order to keep track of the daily progress of his pupils, Mr Dalton caused to be printed two large albums, similar to cellar books, in which he recorded their proficiency in the several subjects of the curriculum, adding each Saturday some general remarks on conduct during the week. The album entitled *Journal of Weekly Work, Prince George*, which is still preserved in the Round Tower at Windsor, bears many astringent comments in Mr Dalton's handwriting. The following extracts, covering the autumn and winter of the year 1876 may be quoted:

Week ending September 2, 1876. 'Prince G. this week has been much troubled by silly fretfulness of temper and general spirit of contradiction. Otherwise work with me has been up to the usual average.' September 23. 'Prince George has been good this week. He shows

7

however too much disposition to find fault with his brother.' October 14. 'Too fretful; and inclined to be lazy and silly this week.' November 25. 'Self-approbation enormously strong, becoming almost the only motive power in Prince George.' December 9. 'The slightest difficulty discourages him and when he frets he finds it hard to subdue himself.' December 30. 'Prince George wants application, steady application. Though he is not deficient in a wish to progress, still his sense of self-approbation is almost the only motive power in him. He has not nearly so high a sense of right and wrong for its own sake as his elder brother.'

It would be a mistake to assume from such extracts that Mr Dalton was a cantankerous pedagogue. He certainly instilled into Prince George the unwavering sense of duty which thereafter became the mainspring of his character. At the same time he felt and inspired durable affection. It is illuminating to re-read the many letters which Mr Dalton addressed to his beloved pupil over a space of almost sixty years. Here is a letter written to Prince George when he was in H.M.S. *Canada* on the North American station and when Mr Dalton, in the company of other tutors, was coaching Prince Eddy at Sandringham. It is dated July 11, 1883:

'I do long to be at sea with you again; it is frightfully dull here. I never felt so dull in my life. I shall be glad when our time is up. We miss your voice so at meals: they all sit round the table and eat and never say a syllable. I never knew such a lot. . . . Oh dear! How often my thoughts go off to you and I wish I could be, if even for a few months, with you.'

Thirty-five years passed, and here we have another letter written on the occasion of his pupil's silver wedding:

'Windsor. July 5 1918.
'Canon Dalton presents his humble duty to the King. . . . He has now had the exceptional privilege of witnessing for six and forty years, with a loyal and personal affection that has known no break or weakening, the development of a boyhood, youth and manhood, that has each, under God's guardianship and blessing, more than fulfilled the ever-cherished promise of earlier days.'

Mr Dalton's precise and conscientious tutelage was not the only instruction which the Princes at this period obtained. There was a French teacher of the name of M. Mariette, and a drawing master, Mr Weigall. 'We have just had a drawing lesson,' wrote Prince George to Queen Victoria on May 24, 1876, 'and I drew an elephant for Papa and Eddy drew a tiger.' When they were at Marlborough House a drill sergeant used to attend regularly and there were also gymnastic and fencing instructors. In the mornings, the young

Princes were subjected to the severe training of the riding school at Knightsbridge Barracks. In addition they took dancing lessons with their sisters and were coached in tennis, croquet and football. At a very early age Prince George at Sandringham was taught to shoot.

Mr Dalton was worried none the less by the confined domestic atmosphere in which they passed their days. Apart from their parents and their sisters, apart from the company of tutors, governesses, gamekeepers and servants, they had few contacts which would fit them for the outside world. They did not, at that stage, see much of their father's many friends who came to Sandringham, or consort intimately with the equerries and members of the household. There were Francis Knollys, private secretary to the Prince of Wales (who in the early days would sign his letters to them 'your sincere friend, Fookes') and his sister, Miss Charlotte Knollys, Bedchamber woman and life-long companion to the Princess.[1] Apart from them they knew scarcely anyone outside the immediate family circle.

Behind all this—behind the games with his brother and sisters, behind the sweet indulgence of his mother and his father's often alarming chaff—loomed the tremendous figure of his grandmother, the Queen.

The biographer, when introducing Queen Victoria into his narrative, finds himself at an irritating disadvantage. However seriously he may admire the massive weight of her experience, the probity of her character, the vigour of her mind and will, or the shrewdness (the often humorous shrewdness) of her understanding, he is conscious that the legend of this great woman has been distorted in the minds of modern readers by ironical presentations. The singularity of her character, the idiosyncrasies of her style, provoke amusement when amusement is not intended. To approach Queen Victoria in a mood of merriment is to ignore the seriousness of sixty years.

[1] Francis and Charlotte Knollys were the children of General Sir William Knollys, who had been attached to the Prince Consort to instruct him in his military duties and who, on the death of General Bruce in 1862, was chosen by Queen Victoria as Governor to her eldest son.

When in 1870 Mr. Fisher, Private Secretary to the Prince of Wales, resigned his appointment, the post was given to Sir William's second son Francis, then a man of thirty-three.

Sir Francis Knollys remained Private Secretary for forty-three years. After King Edward's death he acted as joint Private Secretary to King George until 1913. He was made a Baron in 1902 and a Viscount in 1911. He died in 1924 at the age of eighty-seven.

To the two Princes, the Queen was primarily a devoted grandmother, for whom they felt unawed affection and whose solicitude and kindness provided them with much excitement and constant fun. It was more rarely that they regarded her as the insistent matriarch, whose approval or disapproval conditioned their movements and entailed precautions.

Yet even as a child Prince George must have noticed that in her presence those whom he himself feared or venerated became awe-struck and diminished. The contrast between her personal homeliness and the majesty by which she was encompassed led him insensibly to look upon the Monarchy as something distinct from ordinary life, as something more ancient and durable than any political or family institution, as something sacramental, mystic and ordained.

From time to time he would be taken to see her, at Windsor, Balmoral or Osborne. His gay laughter and his garrulous questions would be hushed for a moment in those silent corridors and he would be greeted by the shy little titter with which she sought to conceal her embarrassment in the presence of children. She would send him presents on his birthdays accompanied by letters of shrewd advice:

> On June 1, 1873, she sent him a watch, 'hoping that it will serve to remind you to be very punctual in everything and very exact in all your duties. . . . I hope you will be a good, obedient, truthful boy, kind to all, humble-minded, dutiful and always trying to be of use to others! Above all, God-fearing and striving always to do His Will.'

He would acknowledge these gifts in dutiful letters, in which the spelling had been carefully corrected and of which the handwriting was clear and straight and boyish. His spelling continued to be uncertain for many years: his handwriting remained clear and straight and boyish all his life:

> 'Sandringham. Easter Monday April 17 1876.
> 'My dear Grandmama,
> 'I hope you are enjoying yourself very much in Germany as we are all doing here. I hope you found Aunt Alice and Uncle Louis and the cousins quite well at Darmstadt. I hope Aunt Vicky was quite well. Please thank Aunt Beatrice very much for that nice chocolate egg she sent me yesterday. Mama gave us some very pretty Easter eggs with lots of nice little things inside them, and ones which we had to find to the sound of music played loud when we were near and soft when we were far off. We went this morning to the farm to see some Brahmin cows which dear Papa sent home from India and we fed them with biscuits and then we went to the dairy and saw some little pats of butter made. I hope you had better weather in Germany than we have had here, we have had a great deal of snow, but it has gone away now.

'With love to you and Aunt Beatrice, I remain your affectionate grandson,

'George.'

His earlier letters to his grandmother, regular and dutiful though they were, replete though they were with punctilious enquiries regarding the health of his uncles, aunts and cousins and with precise references to the state of the weather, were not always so conventional. He and his sisters had acquired sheets of note paper on the top left-hand corner of which were painted small comic emblems. For a letter to Queen Victoria, dated December 28, 1877, thanking her for a Christmas present of spoons, he chose an emblem representing a toad sheltering from the rain under a toad-stool with the motto 'No place like home'. As the years passed, his letters to his grandmother became more appropriate and impersonal. Before she died, she came fully to appreciate his straightness and sense of duty. 'Georgie is here,' she wrote to the Duke of Connaught on June 13, 1894, 'and quite well I am thankful to say. He is a dear boy, so anxious to do right and to improve himself.'

He was certainly a solace to her in the declining years.

(4)

It had always been intended that Prince George, being the second son, should adopt the Navy as his profession. It should be borne in mind that it was not until he reached his twenty-seventh year that, with the death of his elder brother in January 1892, he came into the immediate line of succession. By that date, the fifteen years which he had spent as a serving officer in the Navy[1] had crystallised his habits and his outlook on life.

When the moment came, early in 1877, to consider his entry into the naval training ship, the *Britannia*, Mr Dalton was assailed by qualms. His first difficulty was that neither of the two Princes, in his judgement, had reached the educational standard of the average

---

[1] Prince George's career as a naval officer can be summarised as follows:

Passed examination for entry	June 5, 1877
Naval Cadet	1877–1880
Midshipman	Jan. 8, 1880
Sub-Lieutenant	June 3, 1884
Lieutenant	Oct. 8, 1885
Commander	Aug. 24, 1891
Captain	Jan. 2, 1893
Rear-Admiral	Jan. 1, 1901

private school boy of their age. His apprehensions on this score were unnecessary. Prince George at least passed the entrance examination without difficulty and in the normal way.

Mr Dalton's second anxiety was concerned with Prince Eddy, to whom, in his correspondence with Queen Victoria, he tactfully referred as 'Prince Albert Victor'. He feared that the elder Prince was not sufficiently advanced to be separated without damage from his younger brother. He was aware that the Queen desired Prince Eddy to be sent to Wellington College, an institution in which the Prince Consort had taken a special interest. Mr Dalton approached this situation with tenacious tact.

In a memorandum, dated February 11, 1877, he stressed the disadvantage of educating two boys of their age entirely in the domestic circle and without any contact with boys older than themselves. Especially was this true of Princes in their position, who were exposed to the 'quite natural excitement' continually caused by change of residence and surroundings. This had in itself rendered it impossible 'to obtain any really satisfactory result'. The difficulty of sending Prince Albert Victor to a public school, such as Wellington College, was not merely that headmasters were disinclined to make any special arrangements for his reception, but that it would be most unfortunate at this stage of his development to separate him from his younger brother. 'Prince Albert Victor', wrote Mr Dalton, 'requires the stimulus of Prince George's company to induce him to work at

Vice-Admiral	June 26, 1903
Admiral	March 1, 1907
Admiral of the Fleet	May 7, 1910

Ships

H.M.S. *Britannia*	1877–1879
H.M.S. *Bacchante*, Flying Squadron	1879–1882
H.M.S. *Canada*, North America and West Indies	1883–1884
H.M.S. *Excellent*, Portsmouth	1885
H.M.S. *Thunderer*, Mediterranean Fleet	1886–1888
H.M.S *Dreadnought*, Mediterranean Fleet	1886–1888
H.M.S. *Alexandra*, Mediterranean Fleet	1886–1888
H.M.S. *Northumberland*, Channel Fleet	1889
H.M. Torpedo Boat 79	1889
H.M.Y. *Osborne*	1889
H.M.S. *Excellent*, Portsmouth	1890
H.M.S. *Thrush*, North America and West Indies	1890–1891
H.M.S. *Melampus*, Manoeuvres	1892
H.M.S. *Crescent*	1898

all. . . . The mutual influence of their characters on one another (totally different as they are in many ways) is very beneficial. . . . Difficult as the education of Prince Albert Victor is now, it would be doubly or trebly so if Prince George were to leave him. Prince George's lively presence is his mainstay and chief incentive to exertion; and to Prince George again, the presence of his elder brother is most wholesome as a check against that tendency to self-conceit which is apt at times to show itself in him. Away from his brother, there would be a great risk of his being made too much of and treated as a general favourite.'

Mr Dalton urged therefore that Prince Albert Victor should accompany his younger brother to the *Britannia*, a course which would 'improve His Royal Highness' moral, mental and physical development'. It would provide him, so Mr Dalton affirmed, with 'physical and mental tone' and would assist him to develop 'those habits of promptitude and method, of manliness and self-reliance, in which he is now somewhat deficient'.

Queen Victoria's reply to this memorandum is dated February 15, 1877:

'I have read', she wrote, 'with the greatest care and the greatest interest Mr. Dalton's very able and sensible memorandum on the education of my dear grandsons Albert Victor and George of Wales—which in many ways resembles that of our own sons, especially the 2 eldest—and reminds me forcibly of the many proposals and plans which were brought forward and discussed for them.

'These Children have, however, the advantage of not being the Sovereign's *own* Children and therefore not born and bred in a court, which, although we always brought up ours as simply as possible, still always has one great and unavoidable disadvantage. I myself was brought up almost as a private individual, in very restricted circumstances, for which I have ever felt thankful.

'I will now, however, return to the memorandum. I quite agree with the importance and necessity of sending the 2 Boys from Home for their education, for the very objections which exist in a much greater degree with them, existed with ours, viz, the constant moving from place to place—the necessary excitement going on, which is greater than with us in *some* ways. Home influence and the Home affections should always be cultivated, but if they live with their tutor and are taught not to be ashamed of showing affection and tenderness for their Parents and Sisters and all the gentler and humanizing side of life, there will be no fear of their not retaining their love for Home. I therefore *entirely* agree in the plan of education being carried on at or near some public place of education.'

The Queen did not, however, approve of the idea of Prince

Albert Victor, her eldest grandson, being entered simultaneously as a naval cadet in the *Britannia*:

> 'Their positions,' she wrote, '(if they live) will be totally *different* and it is not intended that they should *both* enter the navy. . . . The very rough sort of life to which boys are exposed on board ship is the very thing not calculated to make a refined and amiable Prince, who in after years (if God spares him) is to ascend the throne. It would give him a very one-sided view of life which is not desirable. . . . Will a nautical education not engender and encourage national prejudices and make them think that their own Country is superior to any other? With the greatest love for and pride of one's own Country, a Prince, and especially one who is some day to be its Ruler, should not be imbued with the prejudices and peculiarities of his own Country, as George III and William IV were. Baron Stockmar, than whom *no one* gave us better and wiser advice on the education of our Children, always *dwelt* strongly on this. And *History* bears this out. Our greatest King William III, and the next to him, though not a King, but almost the same as one from the influence he exercised and the advice he gave, the Prince Consort, were *both* foreigners and this gave them a freedom from all national prejudices which is very important in Princes.'

Why, asked the Queen, could not both the boys live in some house in the vicinity of Wellington College, at least for a year and a half, and thus have all the advantages of attending a public school with none of the resultant dangers?

> 'I have', she concluded, 'a great fear of young and carefully brought up Boys mixing with older Boys and indeed with any Boys in general, for the mischief done by bad boys and the things they may hear and learn from them cannot be overrated. Our experience on this point was certainly against it. . . . Care should also be taken to prevent them merely from associating with sons of the Aristocracy; good boys, of whatever birth, should equally be allowed to associate with them to prevent the early notions of pride and superiority of position which is detrimental to young Princes, especially in these days, and which I know is so very repugnant to the Princess of Wales and also to the Prince's feelings and from which they are till now so entirely free.'

In the end the Prince of Wales was able to persuade the Queen to agree to both Princes being sent to the *Britannia* 'as an experiment'. Prince George therefore passed his examination for entry into the Navy on June 5, 1877. He joined the *Britannia*, accompanied by Prince Eddy and Mr Dalton in September of that year. They remained in the *Britannia* for nearly two years.

Apart from the fact that they had a cabin to themselves under the poop and that Mr Dalton was there to watch over them, the Princes were treated exactly as the other two hundred cadets.

14

Prince George was proficient at mathematics; in boat sailing he excelled most of the cadets of his term. Yet the contrast between the cushioned and luxurious life to which he had been accustomed and the bare boards and stiff hammocks of the *Britannia* was sharp indeed:

'It never', he recalled in after life, 'did me any good to be a Prince, I can tell you, and many was the time I wished I hadn't been. It was a pretty tough place and, so far from making any allowances for our disadvantages, the other boys made a point of taking it out of us on the grounds that they'd never be able to do it later on. There was a lot of fighting among the cadets and the rule was that if challenged you had to accept. So they used to make me go up and challenge the bigger boys—I was awfully small then—and I'd get a hiding time and again. But one day I was landed a blow on the nose which made my nose bleed badly. It was the best blow I ever took for the Doctor forbade my fighting any more.

'Then we had a sort of tuck-shop on land, up the steep hill; only we weren't allowed to bring any eatables into the ship, and they used to search you as you came aboard. Well, the big boys used to fag me to bring them back a whole lot of stuff—and I was always found out and got into trouble in addition to having the stuff confiscated. And the worst of it was, it was always *my* money; they never paid me back—I suppose they thought there was plenty more where that came from, but in point of fact we were only given a shilling a week pocket money, so it meant a lot to me, I can tell you.'[b]

The holidays would be spent at his beloved Sandringham, with occasional visits to the Isle of Wight or Scotland. It was at Osborne that, on July 30, 1878, he first began to keep a diary, recording how that day he had played croquet with Aunt Beatrice and thereafter watched a cricket match between the household and the royal yacht. This first diary ended, as is the way with diaries, on August 12 the same year. But on May 3, 1880, Prince George again began to keep a diary and from then onward he continued it without intermission until three days before his death.

For fifty-six years, in his clear handwriting, he recorded daily the moment at which he got up, the times of his meals, and the hour when he went to bed. He acquired the nautical habit of registering the direction of the wind, the condition of the barometer and the state of the weather throughout the day. He would take careful note of the places which he visited, the people whom he met, or the number of birds and other animals which he shot. Seldom did he indulge in any comment upon personal or public affairs; his diary is little more than a detailed catalogue of his engagements. He was

15

not one of those to whom the physical act of writing comes easily and with pleasure; his pen would travel slowly across the page. Yet only when he was seriously ill would he allow his mother, his sisters, or, later, his wife, to make the entries for him. His diaries swelled to twenty-four bound and locked volumes, each opening with a small golden key. They became for him part of the discipline of his life.

Prince George passed quite creditably out of the *Britannia* in July 1879,[1] being then just fourteen years of age. After a few weeks' holiday he sailed with his brother round the world on a cruise, which lasted almost exactly three years.

[1] Captain Sir Bryan Godfrey-Faussett kept a bound book in which he entered the names and subsequent careers of the fifty cadets who formed Prince George's term in the *Britannia*. By October 1935 twenty-eight of these fifty had died; seven could no longer be traced; and fourteen survived.

Of the original fifty, two reached the rank of Admiral of the Fleet, namely Lord Wester Wemyss and King George himself; three (Admiral Mark Kerr, Admiral Sir Cecil Lambert and Admiral Sir William Grant) became Admirals; six became Vice-Admirals; and four Rear-Admirals.

CHAPTER II

THE *BACCHANTE*

September 1879–August 1882

The proposal that both Princes should go together on a cruise round the world—the Cabinet object—Queen Victoria resents their interference—Doubts regarding the seaworthiness of the *Bacchante*—Sir Henry Ponsonby's dilemma—Summary of the cruise—Lord Charles Scott's instructions—the tattooing incident—Queen Victoria's anxiety regarding their social contacts—Prince George's homesickness—The *Bacchante* diverted to the Cape—the Queen's fear that the Princes may become involved in hostilities—Majuba—Cetywayo—Prince George as a midshipman—the *Bacchante* damaged in a gale—She puts into King George's Sound—the return journey—Athens and the Greek Royal Family—Back at home—Confirmation of the two Princes.

(1)

WHEN in 1879 the time approached for the Princes to leave the *Britannia*, Mr Dalton was afflicted by misgivings similar to those which had disturbed him in 1877. Whereas Prince George's development, during the two years he had spent at Dartmouth, had been 'rapid and pronounced' Prince Eddy had not been able as yet to overcome his constitutional lethargy. It had already been agreed that Prince George on leaving the *Britannia* should go to sea in a training vessel on an extended cruise round the world. Mr Dalton, in a letter of April 9, 1879, urged the Prince of Wales that Prince Eddy should accompany him on this voyage. If the elder boy were separated from his brother and sent to a public school, his backwardness might become more apparent. Moreover, whereas it would be possible carefully to select the sub-lieutenants, the midshipmen and the cadets with whom he would consort in a naval training ship, it would be difficult at a public school to isolate him from all evil associations. Mr Dalton was aware that Prince Eddy was not suited to a naval career and that a long absence in a training ship might interrupt his general education. He proposed to get over this difficulty by attaching to the two Princes Mr John Lawless, an instructor in the *Britannia*, who could teach them mathematics and navigation, and Assistant Paymaster G. F. Sceales, who had spent his youth in France and

17

who could give them special and intensive tuition in the French language.

This plan was eventually approved by the Queen and the Prince of Wales. The latter mentioned the idea to Mr W. H. Smith, the First Lord of the Admiralty, who, regarding it as hazardous to embark both Princes in the same vessel, raised the matter in Cabinet. The Prime Minister, at the request of his colleagues, telegraphed and wrote to the Queen urging her to veto the proposal:

'Lord Beaconsfield', he wrote on May 19, 1879,[a] 'must repeat that the Cabinet was strongly of opinion that the departure of the two Princes in the same ship will greatly disquiet the public mind and that if anything happened to them Your Majesty's Government would justly be called to a severe account. He cannot adequately describe the feelings of Your Majesty's Ministers on this subject.'

The Queen was angered by what she regarded as governmental intervention in a purely domestic arrangement:

'I entirely approve', she replied on the same day, 'the plans for my grandsons' journey, which should never have been brought before the Cabinet. The Prince of Wales only mentioned it to Mr Smith and was with right extremely annoyed at his doing such a thing. It was never done when the Prince of Wales and Prince Alfred went on long journeys together.'

The Prime Minister surrendered at once with grace and ingenuity:

'Lord Beaconsfield with his humble duty to Your Majesty.

'He most deeply apologizes for having, he fears, caused Your Majesty some unnecessary anxiety and trouble yesterday, respecting the cruise of the young Princes.

'The fact is, it was brought under his notice at the end of a long and exhausting Cabinet. . . . Had the matter been originally brought before his notice he should, he hopes, have given it more thought and acted with more discretion. He takes the whole blame upon himself and trusts Your Majesty will not be angry with Mr. Smith, who is inexperienced, and ought to have been guided better by Lord Beaconsfield.

'The matter ought never to have been brought before the Cabinet. Lord Beaconsfield will now withdraw the subject from the consideration of Ministers and as there are no records of the Cabinet Councils, he shall address a letter to the Lord Chancellor, taking the whole responsibility of the affair upon himself.

'It grieves him to trouble Your Majesty almost at the moment of Your Majesty's departure. It grieves him much. And yet he must congratulate the Empress of India upon the triumphant conclusion of the Afghan War.'

The project having thus been approved in principle, Mr Dalton, with his accustomed energy, flung himself upon the detailed arrangements. In consultation with naval officers of his acquaintance he went through the lists of lieutenants, sub-lieutenants, midshipmen and cadets in order to secure that the Princes should be accompanied only by shipmates of irreproachable character. The problem of the command caused him special anxiety. His own choice had been a Captain Fullerton and he was incensed when the Admiralty, without consulting his wishes, appointed Captain Lord Charles Scott. The ship chosen for the cruise was H.M.S. *Bacchante*, an unarmoured corvette of some four thousand tons. Mr Dalton was convinced that the *Bacchante* was not entirely seaworthy. He begged the Queen to insist on a frigate; she made it a condition that the *Bacchante* should undertake special trials before the two Princes embarked. The confusion and irritation which resulted is well summarised in a memorandum written at the time by Sir Henry Ponsonby, Private Secretary to the Queen:[b]

'I am much perplexed about this *Bacchante*.

1. Plan proposed to the Queen who did not at all like it.
2. Dalton sent by the Prince of Wales to urge it. Queen's objections not pressed.
3. Unanimous condemnation by the Cabinet of the plan.
4. Indignation of the Queen and Prince at their interference.
5. Cabinet say they didn't. Plan adopted.
6. Controversies on the selection of officers. The Queen supporting what she believed to be the Prince of Wales' choice. Sometimes it appeared he wished for others. Final agreement on the officers.
7. The *Bacchante* announced to be the ship. Who chose her, when and where I don't know.
8. Chorus of approbation.
9. Strong whispers against her. No stability. The Queen doubtful. The Prince of Wales doubtful. Dalton very doubtful—prefers *Newcastle*.
10. Smith (First Lord) furious, outwardly calm. Offers to turn over crew to *Newcastle*—an old ship full of bilge water. Sends report in favour of *Bacchante*.
11. Scott ordered to cruise in search of a storm so as to see if she will capsize.
12. Scott returns, says she won't. Dalton not satisfied. Wants to separate Princes.
13. Queen says this is what she first thought of but Dalton said it was impossible. Let him consult Prince and Princess of Wales.
14. Queen mentions doubts to Lord Beaconsfield.
15. B. observes he has already been snubbed—but if his advice is wanted, he will give it.
16. Knollys says that Dalton is wrong.'

Mr Dalton also was much discouraged by these controversies. On June 18, 1879, he humbly begged the Prince of Wales to relieve him of his duties. The request was not approved. It was thus with a heavy heart and with many misgivings that Mr. Dalton agreed to go. 'I wish the scheme all success,' he wrote to Sir Henry Ponsonby on June 23, 'but it is not now my device.' The *Bacchante* left Spithead for the Mediterranean on September 17, 1879.

(2)

It is not intended to recount in detail the events of the three years which Prince George spent in the *Bacchante*. Those who are specially interested in the subject can refer to the two enormous volumes of 1400 pages which Mr Dalton published on their return and which purported to be based upon the journals and letters of the two Princes.[1] There were in fact three separate cruises of varying lengths. The first lasted for seven and a half months, from September

[1] Mr Dalton's mighty work *The cruise of H.M.S. Bacchante* was well-intentioned. 'It would', he informed the Prince of Wales on May 16, 1882, 'appear in the Princes' names and would redound to their credit and to that of Your Royal Highness, I hope.'

The book was dedicated to the Queen by 'Her Majesty's affectionate and dutiful grandsons'. In his preface Mr Dalton stated that the work was based upon the diaries kept by the two Princes and upon the letters which they sent home. 'Such passages', he writes, 'as I have extracted from them I have thought it best to leave as they were first penned, however rough they might appear, rather than smooth them down in cold blood.' He adds that his own comments would be marked off in square brackets. The impression thus conveyed to the reader was that anything not in square brackets was the unedited work of the Princes themselves.

This was an incorrect impression. Not only are the Princes made to insert in their diaries long passages from the Vulgate in the original Latin, but they are also represented as being able readily to quote from Theocritus, Browning, Shakespeare, Byron, Tennyson, and the Duchess of Malfi. Typical of Mr Dalton's method is an extract, purporting to come from a diary entry by Prince George and written at Athens on May 20, 1882: 'Then into a café, where gambling is going on and there was much to remind us of Aristophanes.' It is more than doubtful whether Prince George, at the age of sixteen, had ever heard of Aristophanes. Moral maxims, which never figure in Prince George's journals, are also introduced as 'Drink and improvidence make paupers here as elsewhere'.

Those who were innocent enough to believe that they were reading the actual words of two young midshipmen must have been horrified to discover what insufferable midshipmen the two Princes were.

17, 1879 to May 2, 1880, and took them to the Mediterranean and the West Indies. The second lasted only a few weeks and was undertaken in company with the combined Channel Fleet and Reserve Squadron and took them to Bantry Bay and Vigo. The third and longest lasted from September 14, 1880, to August 5, 1882, a period of nearly two years, and took them to South America, South Africa, Australia, Japan, China, Singapore and Egypt.[1]

The instructions issued by the Admiralty to Lord Charles Scott were that Prince George should be treated 'in all respects as other midshipmen on board, with the exception of keeping Night Watch, from which he is to be excused under medical advice, as well as employment on boat service in tempestuous weather'. Prince Albert Victor, on the other hand, not being destined to become a naval officer, should be allowed more time to pursue his studies with Mr Dalton. The Queen was anxious that the two boys should not receive royal honours when visiting a foreign port; the Prince of Wales was of opinion that they should be accorded honours similar to those given to other foreign Princes, such as Prince Henry of Prussia. The matter was left to the judgement of Lord Charles Scott, who took the wise course of never advertising their presence on board, but allowing them to receive special honours when, as happened in Japan and Egypt, such courtesies appeared to be desired by the local rulers.

The Princes had been accorded a cabin on the port side under the poop; it communicated with that of Mr Dalton and contained two swinging cots and two sea chests. The Princess of Wales had presented the ship with a harmonium in an oak case and with a number of chromolithographs after Birkett Foster for the decoration of the messes. The Princes took their meals with the other midship-

---

[1] The voyages of the *Bacchante* can be summarised as follows: *First cruise, September 17, 1879, to May 2, 1880.* Spithead – Gibraltar – Port Mahon – Palermo – Gibraltar again – Madeira – Barbados – Grenada – Martinique – Jamaica – Bermuda – Spithead.

Second cruise with Channel Fleet, July 19, 1880, to August 12, 1880. Spithead – Bantry Bay – Vigo – Spithead.

Third cruise, with Lord Clanwilliam's Detached Squadron. September 14, 1880, to August 5, 1882. Spithead – Portland Roads – Ferrol – Vigo – Madeira – St Vincent – Monte Video – Buenos Aires – Falkland Islands – The Cape (from Feb. 16 to April 9, 1881) – Albany, West Australia – Adelaide – Sydney – Brisbane – Fiji – Yokohama – Shanghai – Canton – Hong Kong – Singapore – Colombo – Suez – Piraeus – Corfu – Palermo – Sardinia – Valencia – Gibraltar – Cowes.

men and cadets in the gunroom; Mr Dalton, who had been appointed honorary chaplain, messed with the Captain.[1] They continued their lessons with Mr Dalton, having additional instruction in mathematics from Mr Lawless and in French from Assistant Paymaster Sceales.

A picture of the Princes at this period is provided by Lord Napier, Governor of Gibraltar:

> 'The youngest', he wrote on November 12, 1879,[c] 'is the most lively and popular, but I think the eldest is better suited to his situation—he is shy and not demonstrative, but he does the right things as a young gentleman in a quiet way. It is well that he should be more reticent and reflective than the younger boy.'

Prince George, except in his letters and diaries, was never addicted to reticence: Prince Eddy, at least in the earlier years, spoke infrequently and in a subdued voice.

The only incident which disturbed the even current of the first cruise occurred in the West Indies. The Princes had been conducted over the Botanical Gardens in Barbados and had been encouraged to sniff the large lilies there displayed. They returned to the ship with their faces powdered with yellow pollen and a journalist who observed them telegraphed home to say that they had had themselves tattooed on the nose. The Queen and the Prince of Wales

---

[1] The *Bacchante* was fully rigged with auxiliary engines. She was 307 feet long by 45 feet broad. She carried 14 4½ ton muzzle-loading guns. Her complement was 450 officers and men, including:

Captain, Lord Charles Scott: *Commander*, Staff Commander George Hill: *Lieutenants*, Assheton Curzon Howe, Osborne, Adair, and Fisher: *Sub-Lieutenants*, Rolfe, Murray, Royds, Burrows, Moore and Henderson: *Midshipmen*, Munro, Peel, Currey, Evan-Thomas, Fitzgerald, Limpus, Christian, J. C. M. Scott, and Basset: *Naval Cadets*, Hardinge, R. E. Wemyss, Hillyard, Osborne, Prince Albert Victor and Prince George of Wales.

The Senior Midshipman, Mr E. L. Munro, was not regarded by Mr Dalton as a fitting companion for the two Princes. 'His almost feminine ways', wrote Mr Dalton, '& silly over-deference to them induced them to take liberties with him which they should not.' Mr Munro was removed from the *Bacchante* on grounds of health after the first cruise.

Of the remaining midshipmen and cadets, R. E. Wemyss became Admiral of the Fleet, John Scott became seventh Duke of Buccleuch, Hugh Evan-Thomas (whose sister Mr Dalton married) became an Admiral, Commander G. W. Hillyard survived to broadcast his reminiscences after King George's death, and Arthur Limpus became an Admiral and Adviser to the Ottoman Navy.

took the report seriously and angry telegrams were despatched. The Princess of Wales, as always, was amused:

> 'How could you', she wrote to Prince George on December 30, 1879, 'have your impudent snout tattooed? What an *object* you must look, and won't everybody stare at the ridiculous boy with an anchor on his nose! Why on earth not have put it somewhere else?'

Mr Dalton hastened to reassure the anxious father:

> 'I should wish', he wrote on January 27, 1880, 'to set Your Royal Highness' mind perfectly at rest about the "tattoeing". The Princes' noses are without any fleck, mark, scratch or spot of any kind whatever. The skin is as white as the day they left home.'

The *Bacchante* returned from her first cruise on May 2, 1880. On the day before disembarking at Spithead Mr Dalton drafted a report on the experiment for the Prince of Wales. Prince George had certainly benefited much from naval discipline, both morally and physically. His height was now 4 ft. 10 and his weight 88 pounds. He had passed his midshipman's examination with success. Prince Albert Victor, 'in spite of the kindly encouragement given him to work by his younger brother and by other of his messmates' had not made comparable progress. None the less Mr Dalton was convinced that the experiment had been a success and was positive that a more extended cruise on the part of both Princes would show equally valuable results. He was still of opinion, however, that for this longer voyage a sailing frigate would be preferable to the *Bacchante*.

After a short holiday at home and after a second short cruise to Ireland and Spain with the Channel Fleet, the Princes, before embarking on their journey round the world, joined their parents for a month at Sandringham. Queen Victoria had for some time been suggesting that the boys might be contaminated by contact with the Marlborough House set; she spoke to the Prince of Wales on the subject:

> 'We both entirely agree', he wrote to her on May 22, 1880, 'with *all* you say about our two boys. Our greatest wish is to keep them simple, pure and childlike as long as it is possible. . . . All you say, that they should avoid being mixed up with those of the so-called fashionable society, we also entirely agree in and try our utmost not to let them be with them. The older they get the more difficult we see is the problem of their education and it gives us many an anxious thought and care.'

In spite of this assurance, the Queen remained perturbed:

> 'Many affectionate thanks', she answered from Balmoral on May 26, 'for your dear letter, by which I am glad to see that you duly

appreciate the extreme importance—indeed I may say the vital importance—of the *dear Boys* being kept quiet—and above all *apart* from the society of fashionable and fast people. . . . With regard to their education, the *one* thing (after their religious education) which is of the greatest importance is now *Foreign languages*, in which they are unfortunately sadly deficient. You and your sisters spoke German and French when you were 5 or 6—and I fear they will never have this facility in speaking them.'

A few weeks later we find the Queen, on July 6,[a] recurring to this difficult theme:

'I must also return most earnestly and strongly to the *absolute necessity* of the children, all of them, *not* mixing with the society you are constantly having. They must either take their meals together *alone*, or you must breakfast and lunch *alone* with them and to this a *room* must be given up wherever you are.'

The Prince of Wales replied to this with commendable patience and dignity:

'With regard', he wrote on July 11,[e] 'to the boys mixing with what you call "fashionable society", I assure you—as I have had reason to say before—that they do not do so. And we hope and think that they are so simple and innocent that those they have come in contact with have such tact with them that they are not likely to do them any harm.'

Queen Victoria need have cherished no apprehensions. The only two people outside his immediate family who exercised any influence upon Prince George's boyhood (apart of course from Mr Dalton) were Captain Henry Stephenson and his uncle Admiral Sir Harry Keppel, 'the little Admiral'. His friendship with Oliver Montagu, generally known as 'Tut Tut', was of a later date and wholly beneficial. He never possessed any predilection for fashionable society.

(3)

On September 14, 1880, the Princes joined the *Bacchante* again for their world cruise. For the purpose of this journey the *Bacchante* had been assigned as training ship to a Detached Squadron under the command of Admiral Lord Clanwilliam. It was in company with this Squadron that they sailed to the Falklands and thereafter to the Cape, Australia and Japan.

Prince George was deeply distressed at parting from his home and family for two whole years:

'My darling Motherdear,' he wrote from Cowes on September 15, 'I miss you so very much & felt so so sorry when I had to say goodbye to you and sisters & it was dreadfully hard saying goodbye to dear

Papa & Uncle Hans.[1] It was too rough yesterday to go to sea, so we stopped in here for the night. . . . I felt so miserable yesterday saying goodbye. I shall think of you all going to Scotland tonight & I only wish we were going too. Lord Colville will take this letter & he has to go, so I must finish it. *So goodbye once more my darling Motherdear,* please give darling Papa and sisters my very best love and kisses and very much to dear Uncle Hans. I remain your very loving son Georgy. *So goodbye darling Motherdear, dearest Papa & sisters.*'

They sailed via Vigo, Madeira and St. Vincent to the River Plate. January 24, 1881, found them at the Falkland Islands, intending to round the Horn and cruise up the western coast of South America as far as the Galapagos. On January 25, however, a telegram was received from the Admiralty, instructing Lord Clanwilliam's Detached Squadron to turn eastwards immediately and to sail for the Cape.

The Boers, under the leadership of Kruger, Pretorius and Joubert, had met at Paardekraal on December 13, 1880, and repudiated the proclamation of April 1877, under which the Transvaal had been annexed to the British Crown. Three days later they proclaimed a Republic. Hostilities immediately broke out and Sir George Colley, High Commissioner for South East Africa, marched towards the Transvaal with a force of 1400 men. The Boers, on the very day that the *Bacchante* arrived at the Falkland Islands, invaded Natal and occupied Laing's Nek. The *Bacchante* reached the Cape on February 16, 1881. Ten days later Sir George Colley was defeated and killed on Majuba Hill. 'We are going to the Cape of Good Hope,' Prince George noted in his diary for January 26, 'because of the Basuter disturbances.'

The moment the Queen heard that the Detached Squadron was to be diverted to the scene of action she became alarmed lest her two grandsons might form part of some expeditionary force:

'I must earnestly protest', she telegraphed to the Prince of Wales on January 20, 1881, 'against the Princes serving with the Naval Brigade on shore at the Cape. I strongly objected to their both going to sea, but consented on the suggestion that it was necessary for their education. The proposal to send them on active service destroys the cause of my former consent, and there is no reason for and many against their incurring danger in the South African war.'

The Prince of Wales had been delighted by the idea that his sons might add to their experience by seeing a little fighting. He was hurt and irritated by the Queen's intervention. The Queen remained

[1] Queen Alexandra's uncle, Prince John of Holstein-Sonderburg-Glücksburg (1825–1911).

adamant and sent implicit instructions to the First Lord of the Admiralty that the two Princes were in no circumstances to be attached to any naval brigade:

'I am very sorry', she wrote to the Princess of Wales on February 18, 1881, 'that Bertie should have been sore about the Boys . . . The *Bacchante* going to the Cape, which was done in a hurry without due consultation with me—I *disapproved*. And feeling how valuable these 2 young lives are to the *whole Nation*, I felt *bound* to protect them against useless and unnecessary exposure in a cruel *Civil War*, for so it is, the Boers being *my subjects*, and it being a rule that Princes of the Royal Family *ought not* to be mixed up in it. In any other War, should in time there be one, (when Georgie be older) and his ship be *obliged necessarily* to take part in it, I would *quite agree* with Bertie.

'Pray show this to him, as I am sure that he and everyone else would agree in this being the *right course*.'

Prince George himself, unaware of this controversy between his father and his grandmother, regarded the war objectively. 'This is really a dredful war is it not?' he wrote to his mother from Cape Town on March 7, 1881. 'All these poor people killed & also poor General Colley.'

During the six weeks that the Detached Squadron remained at anchor in Simon's Bay, awaiting the outcome of the negotiations between Kruger and the British Government, the Princes could visit Cape Town and make a few excursions in the vicinity. 'We passed an ostridge farm', records Prince George in his diary, 'and saw a good many ostridges.' They were conducted by the Governor to visit Cetywayo.[1] 'He has got a little farm for himself,' wrote Prince George on February 26; 'we gave him each our photographs and he gave us his. He himself is eighteen stone and his wives 16 & 17 stone; there are four of them, they are very fine women, all over six feet.' Cetywayo was voluble in his expressions of loyalty to the British crown and assured the Princes that his one desire was to 'wash his spears in the blood of the Boers'.

[1] Cetywayo, King of the Zulus, was a nephew of the great Chaka. He succeeded to the throne in 1872 and organised the Zulus on a military basis. In December 1878, Sir Bartle Frere, High Commissioner of South Africa, sent him an ultimatum summoning him to disband his regiments. Cetywayo did not reply to this ultimatum, with the result that Lord Chelmsford entered Zululand on January 11, 1879, at the head of 13,000 troops. Having defeated the British at Isandhlwana, Cetywayo was himself defeated at Ulundi on July 4, 1879, and taken prisoner in the following August. He was interned near Cape Town, visited London in 1882, and was restored by Mr Gladstone in 1883. He was unable to reimpose his authority and died at Ekowe on February 8, 1884.

This opportunity was not accorded to him. Although the British public were under the impression that a fresh army under Sir Frederick Roberts was on its way to South Africa to 'avenge Majuba', Mr Gladstone was in fact in private negotiation with Kruger. On March 6, 1881, a truce was arranged, followed, on August 3, by the Convention of Pretoria, by which the Boers were granted self-government under British suzerainty. Meanwhile, on April 9, 1881, the Detached Squadron had left the Cape on their journey to Australia.

(4)

It took them five weeks of continuous sailing and steaming to cross the expanse of the Indian Ocean. Prince George, during that uninterrupted passage, was fully occupied. In the few spare moments which he could find, he read *Oliver Twist* and *Nicholas Nickleby*. He suffered much, as he always suffered, from bouts of sea-sickness. But most of his day was absorbed in study and in nautical exercises. The following extract from his diary is typical:

'April 26 1881. At sea, Cape to Australia. Got up at 6.0 o'clock & had drill. A fine day with wind right aft but not quite so cold as it has been for the last three days. Going about 6 knots. I had breakfast at 8.0. Went to school with Mr. Lawless from 9.30 to 11.45. Had dinner at 12.0. Did some French with Mr. Sceales. At 1.45 we went aloft with the ordinary seamen & boys & exercised shifting topsail. Then we did rifle and cutlass drill. Kept the 4 to 6 watch. After quarters, we exercised shifting topsails, we did it twice. Tea at 6.30. Then after tea I wrote some of my log up. Went to bed at 9.30.'

A recollection of Prince George as a cadet and midshipman was broadcast after his death by Commander Hillyard, one of the last survivors of the *Britannia* of 1877 and a messmate in the *Bacchante*[1] :

'I was shipmates for five years with our late King, when we were both youngsters. The companionship in one of Her Majesty's gunrooms in those days was of necessity a very close and intimate one. Weeks and weeks at sea, sometimes very monotonous weeks, living on food that was more than monotonous, and also exceedingly nasty. Mostly salt pork and ship's biscuits. Remember there were no comforts in those days. No such things as electrical freezing plant. So fresh vegetables, fruit and fresh provisions lasted a very, very short time after leaving harbour. Also, one got rather bored at always seeing the same old faces round the same old table, and tempers at times were apt to get a little frayed and irritable. Yet in all those years I never remember Prince George losing his temper. I certainly never had even a cross word with him. Unselfish, kindly, good-tempered, he was an ideal shipmate.

'I want you to realize that when he joined up he was only about 12½ years old, and that he actually went to sea only 14½. Yet, even at this early age he had, when in charge of one of the ship's cutters, for instance, to accept full responsibility for the lives of men. He also had to endure all the discomforts and all the hardships which were the inevitable and common lot of anyone who went to sea in those days.

'In my humble opinion the training he thus obtained in the Royal Navy, and the strict discipline to which he was subject, were tremendous factors in forming the character of the great and lovable man, and wise king he afterwards became. . . .'

The intimacies of nautical life are in any case different in kind from those forged by other associations. On the one hand, they are more physically proximate and thus more stark and less selective: on the other hand—in that, with a change of ship, the whole pattern of acquaintance has to be reformed—they are more adventitious and therefore less profound. The tendency thus arises to adopt a standardised pattern of comradeship, in which emotional relations are seldom involved. Friendliness becomes more common than friendship and general good fellowship more customary than exclusive individual affections. In the case of the two Princes this general habit of impersonal intimacy was reinforced by the presence of Mr Dalton. Anxious as he was that they should be exposed to no influence other than his own, he discouraged any close familiarity, any partial preferences, any selective fraternisation.

When four hundred miles from Australia the Squadron ran into rough weather. Heavy seas broke over the *Bacchante*, a cutter was washed away and the steering gear refused to function. Mr Dalton was much alarmed. It seemed to him that the apprehensions which he had voiced regarding the instability of the corvette were being abundantly justified. Lord Clanwilliam had been unable in the gale to retain contact with the *Bacchante*; the rest of the Detached Squadron had disappeared. Here were the two Princes, without hope of human assistance, drifting in a hurricane towards the South Pole.[1]

---

[1] This was an imaginative interpretation. The fact that it was the second cutter, which is usually hoisted on the port side, which was carried away suggests that the port side was the lee side and that the gale therefore was from the south-west. This assumption is confirmed by the rapidity with which thereafter they made King George's Sound. The rudderless *Bacchante* would therefore have drifted, had she not been repaired in time by the skill and seamanship of Lord Charles Scott and others, not towards the South Pole, but towards the coast of Australia.

Prince George's own impressions of the misfortune were more seamanlike:

'Thursday May 12 1881. At sea; blowing very hard all night. This morning at 5.0. o'clock we gave a very heavy roll & the 2nd cutter filled & was washed away and lost. A heavy sea running, 9 to 10 the force of the wind. A great many seas coming over the nettings. We tipped the 1st cutter up. We gave a heavy roll which carried away both davits & brought the cutter on to the mizzen rigging where we lashed her. We dipped the galley too, & the jollyboat, so we turned both in. We split the mainsail. Hailing in the squalls.

'Friday May 13. At sea; in the first watch we came right up in the wind in a squall and could not go off again so we treble reefed the fore & main topsails & furled the miz. tps. Blowing very hard indeed in the night. Got the screw down and tried steaming to get her head from the wind but could not. Had the morning watch. We shortened and furled sails at 7.0. Blowing 8 to 10. A heavy sea. We got her head off in the afternoon at last. . . .

'Saturday May 14. We do not yet know what is the matter with the rudder. . . .'

The rudder had in fact been torn sideways and refused to answer to the helm. Adjustments were made and Lord Charles Scott, who had no sleep for three nights, was able to turn the vessel northwards. On Sunday, May 15, they sighted Mount Gardner in Western Australia. That afternoon they anchored safely in King George's Sound, within view of the town of Albany. The Princes, much to Mr Dalton's indignation, were thereupon transferred to the *Inconstant* while the *Bacchante* was undergoing the necessary repairs.

The cruise thereafter followed its prescribed course. After visiting Sydney, they rejoined the *Bacchante* on August 2 and went in her to Brisbane, the Fiji Islands and Japan, where they were received by the Mikado. There followed visits to Hong-Kong, Shanghai, Singapore and Colombo. On March 1, 1882, the Princes landed at Suez on their return journey. They went up the Nile as far as Luxor and the month of April was spent on a tour of the Holy Land. Prince George was not impressed by the stories related to him by the local guides: 'All the places', he wrote on April 20, 1882, 'are only *said* to be the places.' At Jerusalem the two Princes camped among the olives and on this occasion they really were tattooed. 'We have been Tatoed', he wrote to his mother, 'by the same old man that tatoed Papa & the same thing too the 5 crosses. You ask Papa to show his arm.'

On May 11 they reached the Piraeus where they were welcomed

by their uncle and aunt, King George and Queen Olga, and taken for ten days up to Tatoi. Fond as he was of his uncle, the King of the Hellenes, and of his Greek cousins, it was Queen Olga especially whom he loved. 'Uncle Willy' in after years would write him long and frequent letters, containing such Danish endearments as *'gamle pølse'* or *'gamle sylte'*.[1] His cousins, Prince Nicholas and Prince George, were also frequent correspondents. But throughout his boyhood and early manhood it was Queen Olga—humorous, gifted and affectionate—who became for him almost a second mother. The parting from these beloved relations was a bitter one:

'May 20 1882. The Palace Athens. We dined at 7.0. All very sad at dinner. At 8.30. we had to say goodbye to darling Aunt Olga & cousins. We all cryed very much, we have spent such a delightful time here. We went with Uncle Willy on board the *Bacchante* in his steam launch. We talked with him in the cabin until nearly 1.0; then we had to say goodbye to him. I was so sorry, I cryed again. We then went to bed.'

Mr Dalton, for his part, was glad to see the last of Athens and Tatoi. He noted that Prince George had been 'more than usually vivacious since his stay here'. 'Late hours', he added 'are almost inevitable on shore, at any rate when they are guests in a palace; late hours, I mean, according to what they are accustomed to. Routine work for two months will do them a vast deal of good.'

On the whole he was delighted by the progress made by his younger pupil:

'Prince George's old enemy', he had reported to the Prince of Wales on January 9, 1882, 'is that nervously excitable temperament which still sometimes leads him to fret at difficulties instead of facing them, and thus "make mountains out of molehills". He is getting over this as he grows older; and now that bodily he is beginning to fill out and become physically stronger, it will I hope soon pass away.'

The *Bacchante* left the Piraeus on May 21, but spent a further five weeks visiting Mediterranean ports. At 1.0 p.m. on Friday, August 4, 1882, they sighted the coast of England. 'I was glad to see it,' Prince George enters in his diary. 'Nearly two years since I saw it last.' On Saturday, August 5, they anchored in Cowes roads, and the Prince of Wales with the Princess and their daughters came on board. Three days later they were taken up to Osborne to be welcomed by the Queen. 'Georgie', she wrote, 'is much grown. He has still the same bright, merry face as ever.'

[1] Meaning 'my dear old sausage' and 'my dear old pickled pork'.

At 4.0 p.m. that afternoon the two boys were confirmed in the Queen's presence by Archbishop Tait at Whippingham Church. Queen Victoria had already asked the Archbishop 'to point out to them both their duty to their *Sovereign and Grandmother* as well as to their *Parents*, and how responsible as Princes as well as youths their positions are'. The Archbishop in his allocution obeyed these behests. 'God grant', he said, 'that you, Sirs, may show to the world what Christian Princes ought to be.' It was almost his last allocution. Archbishop Tait died in December of that year.

On Monday, August 14, Prince George said farewell to the *Bacchante*. 'I am very sorry', he wrote 'to say goodbye to the people that I have been three years with.' The ship was paid off on August 31.

CHAPTER III

NAVAL OFFICER

1882–1892

Effect of naval training upon Prince George's character—His concept of
the duties of a seaman—And of the duties of a Prince—He goes to
Lausanne—he is separated from Prince Eddy and is appointed to the
North American Squadron—A course in gunnery—Queen Victoria's
admirable advice—Captain J. A. Fisher's eulogy—The Mediterranean Fleet—Captain Stephenson—At Malta—He grows a
beard—His continued homesickness—Miss Stonor—At Athens again
—Death of the Emperor Frederick—Torpedo Boat 79—a visit to
Berlin—H.M.S. *Thrush*—the Duke of Clarence and Princess Hélène
—Queen Victoria is anxious for Prince George to marry—the death
of the Duke of Clarence.

(1)

IT may be felt that, for a book which purports to be a political
biography, too much space has been allotted to the early years; and
that it was unnecessary to treat at such length a period which has
already been so admirably covered in Mr John Gore's *Personal
Memoir*. Yet any biography must describe the interaction between an
individual and his environment. The influence which King George
exercised during the twenty-five years of his reign was due, not to any
exceptional gifts of imagination or intellect, but to the consistency of
his principles and beliefs. It was this consistency which enabled him
throughout an angry phase of transition and disbelief, to symbolise
stability and to command universal confidence. The recurrent theme
of this biography will thus be the contrast between the simple
straightness of King George's character and the intricate political
fluctuations with which he had to cope. In order to understand his
character, it is important to realise that, in all essentials, it crystallised
in early adolescence. His temperament, his prejudices and affections,
his habits of thought and conduct, his whole outlook on life, were
formed and moulded during the years between 1877 and 1882. The
great events which happened to him in later life (the death of his
elder brother, his marriage to a woman of superior intelligence, his
accession to the throne) served only to deepen and widen furrows
which had been traced in his boyhood years. Not being an intellec-

tual, he was never variable: he remained uniform throughout his life.

It has therefore been necessary to examine in some detail the contrasting influences which, by the time he reached his seventeenth year, had produced an integrated personality. As a child he was vivacious, affectionate, inclined to self-approval and thus easily discouraged. Spoilt by his mother and intimidated by his father, surrounded by a narrow circle of mutually admiring relations, the harmony of his days constantly interrupted by displacements, he might, but for the devoted watchfulness of Mr Dalton, have surrendered too easily to the comforts of his home, the privileges of his position, or the ease of his own merriness and charm. The icy plunge into the rigours of naval discipline, the sudden fact that instead of being always saluted he had now always to salute, the harshness and dolours of the *Britannia* and the *Bacchante*, might well have lamed his self-assurance and rendered him diffident, sullen, or perplexed. The admirable thing about him was that, while retaining all the impulses and sentiments of boyhood, he so soon developed a quality more forcible than ordinary manliness—a categorical sense of duty. It was this potent quality which became the fly-wheel of his life.

The firm and simple lessons which he absorbed as a cadet and midshipman could not be better summarised than in the words which he himself used when addressing the boys of the training ship *Conway*, in July 1899. He then defined the three qualities required of a sailor as: '(1) Truthfulness, without which no man can gain the confidence of those below him; (2) Obedience, without which no man can gain the confidence of those above him; and (3) Zest, without which "no seaman is worth his salt".'

The effect upon him of his position as a Prince of the Royal House is more difficult to estimate. It is not easy for those not reared in the esoteric atmosphere of a Court to imagine by what gradations a little Prince comes to realise that he belongs to a race apart. This perplexing discovery was for Prince George rendered less personally confusing by the natural predominance of his grandmother, Queen Victoria. For him, as has been said, she was something more than the family matriarch; she was the symbol and personification of Monarchy. It seemed wholly natural to him that he, as her grandson, should in some way be gilded with the rays of this magnificent aura and should be accorded on occasions greater deference than that vouchsafed to his shipmates. The honours which were sometimes paid to him when his ship visited foreign ports never suggested any personal pre-eminence, but were always taken for granted as inevitable 'functions', which he performed (without particular pleasure or particular distaste) as part of a necessary, if irksome, routine. His only anxiety was that they should be suitably and efficiently carried out.

If, therefore, it is legitimate to assume that the main framework of his character was fixed during his five years in the *Britannia* and the *Bacchante*, then it is permissible to deal in far more summary terms with the ten further years which he spent as an active serving officer.[1]

(2)

On returning from their world voyage, the two Princes were sent for six months to Lausanne in Switzerland in order to learn French. They were accompanied by Mr Dalton, Mr Lawless and Monsieur Hua, who had been French master in the *Britannia*.[2] They stayed at the Beau Rivage at Ouchy, which Prince George pronounced to be 'a capital hotel'; they regularly visited the theatre at Lausanne and they played bezique in the evenings. It was not a lively period. 'Then we all took a good walk', Prince George noted in his diary, 'out by the cemetary & round by the town & in at 4.0.' The Princes were shy of speaking French in each other's presence and preferred, much to the distress of Mr Dalton and Monsieur Hua, to play games with the children of the English visitors to the hotel. 'Prince George', Mr Dalton reported on February 23, 1883, 'manfully does his best and is really making sound and rapid progress.' Monsieur Hua was even more eulogistic. He discovered in his younger pupil 'a remarkably spontaneous intelligence—quickly grasping some explanation or principle—but also sometimes the faults which go with these same qualities—and a momentary discouragement at meeting the first difficulty'. In spite of this intensive tuition, it cannot be said that Prince George ever became proficient in the French language; he could read and understand with ease; his accent remained British to the end.

The two Princes returned from Lausanne in May 1883, and in the

[1] The reader is referred to the abstract of Prince George's naval career which will be found in note on pp. 11–12.

[2] Monsieur Hua, a heavily bearded Frenchman, later became a master at Eton and survived to teach French to Prince George's two sons, Prince Edward (subsequently King Edward VIII) and Prince Albert (subsequently King George VI). He died in 1909.

following months they were parted for the first time in their lives. Prince Eddy remained at Sandringham with a bevy of tutors who were coaching him for Cambridge. Prince George was appointed to H.M.S. *Canada* of the West Indian and North American Squadron:

> 'My dear George,' Prince Eddy wrote to him on June 15, 1883, 'So we are at last separated for the first time and I can't tell you *how* strange it seems to be without you and how much I miss you in every-thing *all day long*.'

Prince George was now entirely on his own; there was no Prince Eddy to share his confidences, no Mr Dalton to supervise his actions and associates, no Charles Fuller to minister to his comforts. Captain Francis Durrant, who commanded H.M.S. *Canada*, was formally appointed his Governor, in a letter signed by both Queen Victoria and the Prince of Wales. 'His Royal Highness', Captain Durrant was instructed, 'will be treated in all respects and on all occasions, while on board ship, in the same manner as the other officers of his own rank with whom he is serving.' He was not to receive any special honours when visiting foreign or colonial ports, neither was he to attend 'any State receptions given in his honour'. During the year which he spent with the North American squadron he lived as any other midshipman; he slept in a hammock and had his meals in the gunroom; in the company of his fellow midshipmen he visited Niagara, Ottawa, Montreal, Quebec and Halifax. He became a Sub-Lieutenant in June 1884, and returned to England in July of that year.

The autumn of 1884 was spent at the Royal Naval College, Greenwich, and in March of 1885 he went for a gunnery course to H.M.S. *Excellent* at Portsmouth. His instructor at Greenwich, Mr J. L. Robinson, in a letter to Lawless, highly commended his 'habits of sound and honest work'. 'I only wish', he added, 'that his example in these important respects and his good sense were followed by all young officers.'

Queen Victoria was less optimistic:

> 'Avoid', she wrote to him on June 2, 1885, 'the many evil temptations wh. beset *all* young men and especially Princes. Beware of flatterers, too great love of amusement, of *races* & betting & playing high. I hear on all sides what a good steady boy you are & how you can be trusted. Still you must always be on the watch & must not fear ridicule if you do what is right. Alas! Society is very bad in these days; what is wrong is winked at, allowed even, & as for betting or anything of that kind, no end of young and older men have been ruined, parents hearts broken, & great names and Titles dragged in the dirt. It is in *your*

power to do immense good by setting an example & keeping your dear Grandpapa's name before you.

'I am afraid you will think this a long lecture, but grandmama loves you so much and is so anxious that you should be a blessing to your Parents, herself & your Country, and she cd. *not* do otherwise but write to you *as she feels.*'

His course in H.M.S. *Excellent* at Portsmouth was a great success He gained a first class in gunnery, torpedo work and seamanship, and only missed a first in pilotage by twenty marks. He was gazetted Lieutenant on October 8, 1885. Captain J. A. Fisher, commandant of H.M.S. *Excellent*, on that date addressed to Queen Victoria a most laudatory report:

'During his six months stay', he wrote, 'on board the *Excellent* under my command his attention to his work and the manner in which he has performed all his duties have been all that Your Majesty could desire. He has with great tact and good judgement, and quite of his own accord, declined many invitations, kindly meant to give him pleasure, but which would have taken him too much from his work besides bringing him more prominently into public notice than Your Majesty might have thought desirable under the circumstances. His Instructors have reported to me that his aptitude for the practical work of his profession is very good and Your Majesty may perhaps consider that this is the chief point, as it will not probably fall to his lot to write learned reports or to make mathematical investigations. His pleasant and unassuming manner has been a matter of general notice. . . .'

Lord George Hamilton, First Lord of the Admiralty, in forwarding the results of the examination to the Prince of Wales, added that 'the capacity which Prince George has shown is unusual'. The Prince of Wales was delighted. 'It shows', he wrote to his son on October 15, 'that there is no favouritism in your case.' 'Georgie', commented Queen Victoria in her diary for November 5, 1885, 'is so dear & amiable.'

(3)

The years 1886 to 1888 were spent in the Mediterranean. He served successively in H.M.S. *Thunderer*, H.M.S. *Dreadnought*, and H.M.S. *Alexandra*. His first captain was Henry Stephenson, one of his father's closest friends, and a man to whom Prince George himself was long devoted.[1] 'I feel', the Prince of Wales wrote to Captain

[1] Captain (subsequently Admiral Sir Henry) Stephenson had had an active and varied career. Born in 1842, he had served in the Crimean War, the China Expedition, the Indian Mutiny, and the Egyptian campaign against Arabi. He had also served in an Arctic expedition in 1875. He

Stephenson on January 4, 1886, 'that in entrusting my son to your care I cannot place him in safer hands, only don't *spoil him* please! Let him be treated like any other officer in the ship.'

His relaxations while serving in the Mediterranean Fleet were not different from those of any other naval officer of private means. When at Malta he could play polo on the Marsa, take long picnic rides on his horse 'Real Jam', and have a game of billiards in the evening at the Union Club in the Strada Reale. It is from this period that dates his friendship with Charles Cust, a fellow lieutenant in the *Thunderer*. His uncle, the Duke of Edinburgh,[1] was at the time Commander-in-Chief of the Mediterranean Fleet and Prince George would spend much of his spare time at San Antonio Palace with his aunt and cousins. It was his uncle who encouraged him to take up stamp-collecting, a pastime which became a constant interest to him in later life. It was in 1886 also that he first grew a beard. 'I daresay',

became Naval A.D.C. to Queen Victoria in 1888 and served as equerry to the Prince of Wales from 1878 to 1893. Eventually he became Commander-in-Chief of the Pacific Squadron and the Channel Fleet. In 1904, on his retirement from the Navy, he became Gentleman Usher of the Black Rod and died in 1919.

He had a great influence on Prince George's early life and took a great and prudent interest in his naval career. He was a nephew, on his mother's side, of Admiral of the Fleet Sir Henry Keppel (1809–1904) who, as 'the little Admiral', was one of the most intimate friends of the Royal Family.

[1] Queen Victoria's second son, Alfred Duke of Edinburgh and subsequently Duke of Saxe-Coburg-Gotha was born at Windsor in 1844. He was offered but refused the crown of Greece in 1862, and adopted a naval career. He became a captain at the age of 22, rose to command the Mediterranean Fleet and was made Admiral of the Fleet in 1893.

On the death in 1893 of his uncle, Ernest II, Duke of Saxe-Coburg-Gotha, he succeeded to the vacant Duchy and thereafter resided at Coburg until his death in July 1900.

In 1874 he married the Grand Duchess Marie, only daughter of the Emperor Alexander II of Russia. Prince George was very fond of his aunt, whom he described (Diary, February 8, 1888) as 'so kind, honest & straightforward & so true'.

They had one son and four daughters. The son, Prince Alfred, died of tuberculosis in 1899. The eldest daughter, Princess Marie ('Missy'), became Queen of Rumania and died in 1938. The second daughter, Victoria Melita ('Ducky'), married, first, the Grand Duke of Hesse and, second, the Grand Duke Cyril of Russia. The third daughter, Alexandra, married the hereditary Prince of Hohenlohe-Langenberg. The fourth daughter, Beatrice ('Baby Bee'), married the Infante Alfonso of Spain.

On his death he was succeeded as Duke of Saxe-Coburg-Gotha by Charles, son of the Duke of Albany, who was born at Claremont in 1884.

he wrote to the Queen in sending her a photograph taken at San Antonio, 'that you will think that my beard has altered me rather.' His mother was not entirely pleased:

'What I do not understand,' she wrote to him on November 21, 1886, 'is why you, you little mite, should have so much hair about you, whereas he (Prince Eddy) the biggest has none yet.'

Prince Eddy himself was more critical:

'Oh yes,' he wrote on December 27, 1886, 'I got your photos all right and thought them very good, but would have preferred you without a beard. I dare say it is more comfortable than shaving, which I now do nearly every day, but it makes you look so much older and I think you might take it off before you come home, if you feel inclined to. Old Curzon has taken off his and looks very much better.'

His family affections were enhanced rather than diminished by these separations. In the early spring of 1886 he had spent a few days alone with his father at Cannes. 'On seeing you going off', the latter wrote to him on March 5, 1886, 'by the train yesterday, I felt very sad & you could I am sure see that I had a lump in my throat when I wished you goodbye.' This letter crossed one written by Prince George:

'Hotel Royal des Etrangers. Naples
'March 7 1886.

'My dearest Papa,
  'I cannot tell you how I miss you every minute of the day, because we have been together so much lately. It was so kind of you coming all the way to Mentone to see me off the other day. I felt so very low at saying goodbye to you, but I cannot say how pleased I am that I have got such a kind & good friend as Captain Stephenson & that although now I am separated from all I love & from all my friends I still have one left in Captain Stephenson.'

This persistent tendency to homesickness was a sign of his protracted adolescence. In October 1886 we find him writing to his mother from H.M.S. *Dreadnought* at Corfu:

'You will be going to Sandringham almost at once I suppose for dear Papa's birthday. How I wish I was going to be there too, it almost makes me cry when I think of it. I wonder who will have that sweet little room of mine, you must go and see it sometimes & imagine that your little Georgie dear is living in it.'

His longing for home was, at this period, coloured by a senti-mental attraction. One of the Princess of Wales's earliest ladies-in-waiting, Mrs Francis Stonor, had died, while still comparatively young, in 1883. Her two younger children, Harry and Julie Stonor, were treated with great kindness by the Prince and Princess of Wales and frequently invited to Sandringham. Prince George, during his visits on leave to England, and again at Cannes, saw much of Julie Stonor and they exchanged warmly affectionate letters. The Prince and Princess of Wales smiled benignly on this boy and girl romance, confident that no harm could result. Their wisdom was fully justified. His affection for Miss Stonor rendered Prince George immune to any other compromising associations during the years that he was absent from home. And in 1891 she married the Marquis d'Hautpoul and remained one of the most trusted friends of the Royal Family for ever afterwards.

In June of 1887 he came on leave to attend Queen Victoria's jubilee. After paying a visit to Dublin, he had a week's yachting at Cowes. On August 4, as he noted in his diary, he sailed in the *Aline* in the company of Lady Randolph Churchill and her schoolboy son, Winston, then aged thirteen. On August 12 he left in a passenger steamer for Gibraltar where he rejoined the *Dreadnought*. During the autumn he accompanied his uncle on a cruise to Venice, the Adriatic ports and Athens. In the intervals of his naval occupations he read a quantity of novels. He mentions specifically a romance entitled *Wrong on Both Sides*. 'Such a lovely book,' he confided to his diary, 'I always cry over it.' [1] *Les Misérables* also was a book which accompanied him on many a Mediterranean cruise.

In January 1888, he was again in Athens staying for a few days at Tatoi with his uncle the King of the Hellenes and with his beloved Aunt Olga, who was always glad to welcome back 'my little sunbeam'. Queen Victoria appears to have taken some exception to these frequent visits to his Greek relations:

'Why on earth should I not?' Prince George wrote indignantly to his mother on February 2, 1888. 'Why may I not go and see Uncle Willy if you and Papa wish me to? It is the greatest bosh I ever heard.' His natural reverence for his Sovereign came immediately to check such

---

[1] The novel *Wrong on Both Sides* was written by Vin Vincent and published by Farran, Okeden & Walsh in 1885. It is composed in the revolting manner of *Little Lord Fauntleroy*. It describes how the evangelical Earl of Grantown was unable to gain the affections of his son, Viscount Tempeston, owing to the fact that the deep devotion which they potentially possessed for each other was inhibited by pride. The father was harsh on top and loving underneath; the son, although 'wild and passionate' possessed a 'warm loving heart'. The misunderstanding which arose between them led to many unhappy consequences, including the death of a young lady whose horse was frightened by a threshing machine.

audacity. 'Please', he adds, 'don't leave this letter lying about, Motherdear, as there are some things perhaps that I ought not to have said, but I always tell you everything you see Motherdear. Better burn it.'

Within a few weeks the time came round when he was again due to go home on leave, the occasion being the silver wedding of his parents:

'In about three weeks' time,' he wrote to his mother from Naples, 'I shall be leaving here for beloved old England again, it seems too delightful to be true and then in about a month's time I shall see your beloved lovely face once more. Oh! Won't I give it a great big kiss and shan't we have lots to tell one another darling Motherdear after having been separated for these long 7 months!'

The celebration of the silver wedding had been fixed for March 10, but the festivities were clouded by the death, on March 9, of the old German Emperor, William I. His successor, the Emperor Frederick III, reigned for only ninety-nine days, dying at Potsdam on June 15:

'Try, my dear Georgy,' the Prince of Wales wrote on the following day, 'never to forget Uncle Fritz. He was one of the finest and noblest characters ever known; if he had a fault, he was *too* good for this world.'

The Emperor Frederick was succeeded by his son, William II, then a young man of twenty-nine. The Princess of Wales (whose influence over her husband was much greater than is generally supposed) had never forgiven Prince Bismarck for his action in robbing her father of the Duchies of Schleswig-Holstein in 1864, and her brother-in-law, the Duke of Cumberland, of his private fortune. Her detestation of Bismarck was now transferred to the young Emperor. She was much incensed by the latter's treatment of his mother, the Empress Frederick, immediately after his accession:

'Instead', she wrote on August 12, 1888, 'of William being a comfort and support to her, he has quite gone over to Bismarck and Co. who entirely overlook and crush her. Which is too infamous.'

The relations between the Prince of Wales and his nephew, the new German Emperor, were not improved by an unfortunate incident which occurred a few weeks later. In September 1888, the Prince of Wales was paying a private visit to Vienna. The Emperor William announced his intention of arriving on an official visit and intimated that no other royal personage should be in the Austrian capital at the same time. The Emperor Francis Joseph was much embarrassed by this intimation and the Prince of Wales, in order to ease the position, went off on a journey to Rumania.

Prince George returned to England on November 17, 1888. He went down to Windsor where he found Mr Dalton married and installed as a Canon. 'They have such a nice little boy,' he wrote on December 11, 'fifteen months old.' Thereafter he proceeded to his adored Sandringham for Christmas and the New Year. The 1888 volume of his diary ends as follows:

> 'Goodbye dear old diary & don't let anyone read you. You are full now, so I shall not write in you any more.'

It was a new volume which he opened for his journal from 1889 to 1892.

(4)

After a few more weeks in the Mediterranean, Prince George returned to England in April 1889, for a further course in H.M.S. *Excellent* at Portsmouth. He at the same time attended a torpedo course in H.M.S. *Vernon*. On June 1 he was given the Freedom of the City of London:

> 'Made a speech, then drove to the Mansion House, where the Lord Mayor gave us a huge lunch. Made another speech. Was awfully nervous.'

On July 18 he commissioned Torpedo Boat No. 79, his first independent command. After taking part in the naval exercises held at Spithead in honour of William II, he went with other units of the fleet to western Ireland. The weather was stormy and he suffered much.[1] 'Up all night,' he records, 'was terribly seasick.' With the example of Nelson before him, such experiences did not damp his ardour.[a] On August 23 he succeeded in rescuing, and towing to safety, Torpedo Boat No. 41, which had broken down in Lough Swilly and was in a perilous position on a lee shore:

> 'The service', wrote Captain Fitzgerald of the *Inflexible* to the Prince of Wales, 'was not unattended by danger and required both nerve and judgement and would have reflected credit on an officer of far wider experience than His Royal Highness.'

Prince George's own comment on this incident was terse: 'It has been a most damnable day. Very tired.'

In March 1890, Prince Eddy being then in India, he accom-

[1] A naval officer, to whose flotilla T.B. 79 was attached in 1904, recalls that she shipped an unusual amount of water since her torpedo tubes were in her peak. 'We were always', he writes, 'sorry for 79 in any weather.'

panied his father on a state visit to Berlin. They arrived at the Lehrter Bahnhof on March 21, three days after the Emperor had dismissed Prince Bismarck from office. Prince George was invested by his cousin with the collar and robes of the Black Eagle and awarded the honorary command of a Prussian regiment:

> 'And so', his mother wrote to him on April 11, 'my Georgie boy has become a real live filthy bluecoated Picklehaube German soldier!!! Well, I never thought to have lived to see *that*! But never mind; as you say, it could not have been helped—it was your misfortune and not your fault—and anything was better—even my two boys being sacrificed!!!—than Papa being made a German Admiral—that I could not have survived—you would have had to look for your poor old Motherdear at the bottom of the sea, the first time he adorned himself with it!'

What Sir Sidney Lee,[b] somewhat ungenerously, calls the Prince of Wales's 'eager curiosity' led him to pay a call upon Prince Bismarck. He found the latter seething with rage and full of dire prognostications. Prince George, who accompanied his father, makes no comment on this provocative visit. 'He speaks English perfectly' was all that he recorded of the fallen Chancellor.

In May 1890, Prince George assumed command of a first-class gunboat, H.M.S *Thrush*, and was absent in her with the West Indies and North America squadron until July 1891. His brother, Prince Eddy, had by then reached the age of twenty-six and had, on May 24, 1890, been created Duke of Clarence and Avondale. Queen Victoria, not unnaturally, was anxious that he should marry. Prince George had for long held decided views upon this subject:

> 'Sisters tell me', he had written to his mother as long ago as October 21, 1886, 'that the Comte & Comtesse de Paris are coming for Papa's birthday. . . . I want to ask you something, Motherdear. Have you read that article in *Vanity Fair* of the 9th of October headed *An English Queen Consort*? If you have not, you must get it & read it. I think it is one of the best I have read & I am sure you will agree with me. Of course the first part is *stuff* (as you would say) but what it says is that all English people hope that dear Eddy will not marry a *German* but that he will marry some *English* woman, of course there is plenty of time to think of that. When I read it, it struck me as being so sensible & so true & the more I think it over the more I feel that it would be so much nicer if he married an English person. I think, Motherdear, that you think the same as I do, but I am afraid that both Grandmamma & dear Papa wish him to marry a German, but I don't know. . . . Do you remember all our talks we used to have together, before I left? And now that I am away from home I think of all these things much more than I did & I suppose it is because I am getting older too.'

Prince George showed uncanny prescience in thus coupling the Orleans family with the idea of Prince Eddy's marriage. Four years later, in September 1890, the Comte and Comtesse de Paris[1] came to stay at Abergeldie with their beautiful daughter Hélène. The latter had for more than two years been in love with the Duke of Clarence and Queen Victoria and the Prince of Wales were not in principle opposed to their becoming engaged. The Comte de Paris made it a condition however that she should change her religion only with the Pope's consent. The Pope refused to grant a dispensation and by July 1891, the project was abandoned.[c]

Meanwhile, Queen Victoria had also been urging Prince George to think of marriage. He replied to her from the *Thrush* at Jamaica on February 6, 1891:

'I quite agree with you, dearest Grandmama & understand your reasons for wishing Eddy & I to marry as soon as possible. But still I think marrying too young is a bad thing, but I don't call Eddy too young, he is 27. Then again the wife ought not to be too young; look at the poor Crown Prince Rudolph. She was certainly too young when he married her; she became very ill after her first child was born & he was naturally a very wild young man. The result was he committed suicide & killed this poor girl & brought the most terrible sorrow & shame to his poor wife & parents; that is only one instance of young marriages that I know of. . . . The one thing I never could do is to marry a person that didn't care for me. I should be miserable for the rest of my life.'

Queen Victoria remained uninfluenced by this cautionary tale. She had for some time been considering, as a suitable bride for Prince George, Princess Marie, generally known as 'Missy', eldest daughter of the Duke of Edinburgh.[2] The Princess of Wales was not in favour of such a choice, since she considered the Edinburgh girls

[1] Louis Philippe Albert d'Orléans, Comte de Paris (1838–1894), was the grandson of Louis Philippe. In 1842 on the death of his father he became heir apparent to the French throne. He married his cousin, daughter of the Duc de Montpensier. In 1873 he agreed to waive his claims to the throne of France in favour of the Comte de Chambord. With the latter's death in 1883 he became undisputed head of the House of Bourbon. He was banished from France in 1886, and took refuge in England. His elder daughter, Princess Amélie, married King Carlos of Portugal. His second daughter, Princess Hélène (b. 1871), married the Duke of Aosta in 1895. She died at Naples on January 20, 1951.

[2] Princess Marie, the eldest daughter of the Duke of Edinburgh, was born at Eastwell Park, Kent, on October 29, 1875. On January 10, 1893, she married the Crown Prince, subsequently King Ferdinand, of Rumania. She died at Sinaia on July 18, 1938.

to be noisy and pro-German. The ultimate decision was influenced by Princess Marie's German governess, a formidably anglophobe fräulein, who discouraged the proposal. Princess Marie on June 2, 1892, became engaged to Ferdinand, heir presumptive to King Carol of Rumania.

In July of 1891 Prince George, in his little gunboat the *Thrush*, returned to England after an absence on the North American station of a year and three months. He had by then been a lieutenant for six years and was already due for promotion. The Duke of Edinburgh, who felt that his own professional reputation had been damaged by preferential treatment when he was a young officer, had wisely urged that Prince George should be promoted only when his natural turn came round. It was not therefore until August 24, 1891, that he was gazetted Commander:

> 'Captain Leicester Keppel', Prince George wrote in his diary for August 12, 1891, 'came on board to inspect us. Mustered by open, Divisions, General & Fire Quarters, Man & arm boats, collision stations, out mat, drilled small arm men, made plain sail & furled, mustered bags & hammocks & inspected books.'

The *Thrush* was paid off on August 23.

(5)

After a short visit to Balmoral and Mar Lodge, Prince George crossed to Ireland where he spent a week with his brother who was at that date serving with his regiment at the Marlborough Barracks in Dublin. In the first week of November the two Princes went to Sandringham for the celebration of their father's birthday. The Princess of Wales was absent in Russia:

> 'In the autumn of the year 1891,' writes Sir Sidney Lee,[d] 'domestic considerations led the Princess, accompanied by her two unmarried daughters, to join early in October her family in Copenhagen; subsequently she accompanied the Tsar and her sister the Tsaritza to the Tsar's Crimean home at Livadia, on what promised to be a long stay. The Prince's fiftieth birthday, November 9, was thus celebrated at Sandringham in the Princess' absence. Unexpected domestic trouble was at the moment impending.'

On November 12 Prince George developed a high temperature and his father brought him up immediately to Marlborough House in order that he might receive the most expert medical attention. Typhoid was diagnosed and a telegram despatched to the Princess of Wales at Livadia. She and her daughters rushed across Europe, arriving in London on November 22. The crisis of Prince George's illness was reached on November 24 and thereafter he began to mend. In the last days of December, after seven weeks of serious illness, he was able to return to Sandringham.

On December 3, 1891, the Duke of Clarence had become engaged to Princess Mary of Teck.[1] On January 7, 1892, when at Sandringham, he fell ill with influenza. On January 13 pneumonia set in and at 9.35 on the morning of Thursday, January 14, he died.

[1] Princess Mary of Teck, generally known as 'Princess May', was the daughter of Francis Duke of Teck (1837–1900) and Mary Adelaide (1833–1897) daughter of Adolphus, Duke of Cambridge (1774–1850), son of George III.

The Duke of Teck was the son of Duke Alexander of Würtemberg and Countess Rhédey, of an Hungarian family. He was born in Vienna and served as an officer in the 7th Imperial Hussars. The Prince of Wales met him at Hanover at 1864 and invited him to England. It was there that he met Princess Mary of Cambridge whom he subsequently married.

Princess Mary of Teck, who was born in 1867, had three brothers: Prince Adolphus (Marquess of Cambridge, 1868–1927), Prince Francis (1870–1910), and Prince Alexander, Earl of Athlone (1874–   ).

CHAPTER IV

DUKE OF YORK

1892–1901

The shock of his brother's death—He is made Duke of York—Learning German at Heidelberg—He attends the Luther celebrations at Wittenberg—He begins to take an interest in politics—His engagement to Princess Mary of Teck—His family's approval—His marriage —Sandringham and York Cottage—The Duchess of York—Birth of Prince Edward—Birth of Prince Albert—His life as a country gentleman—He goes to Russia for the marriage of Nicholas II—His visit to Ireland—The South African War—The end of the Nineteenth Century—The Death of Queen Victoria.

(1)

THE death of the Duke of Clarence was the first tragedy which Prince George experienced. It left him desolate and stunned:

'I am sure', he wrote to Queen Victoria on January 18, 1892, 'no two brothers could have loved each other more than we did. Alas! it is only now that I have found out how deeply I did love him; & I remember with pain nearly every hard word & little quarrel I ever had with him & I long to ask his forgiveness, but, alas, it is too late now!'

Weakened as he had been by his own illness, the long and agonising scene in his brother's death-chamber haunted his memory and prolonged the shock. He suffered much from sleeplessness and was still only convalescent when he accompanied his parents, first to Compton Place at Eastbourne, and thereafter to Cap Martin in the south of France.

The pang of bereavement, the aching self-reproach which always accompanies such irremediable disasters, were for him intensified by the realisation that his past had been broken and his future abruptly changed. All Royal personages must experience at moments intimations of chill loneliness, of solitary isolation. Prince George was conscious that he had lost the one companion on this earth with whom his relations had been those of absolute equality. It is not surprising that, during those idle weeks on the Riviera, he should have sought to postpone the hour when he must assume the leaden cope of responsibility.[a]

46

Now that he had become his father's heir, the eventual inheritor of the Crown of England, it was felt that he should adopt some territorial title and obtain a seat in the House of Lords. At the time when it had been proposed to confer a similar dignity on Prince Eddy, Queen Victoria had expressed her preference for a name unconnected with any of her Hanoverian uncles:

'The Queen', she minuted to Sir Henry Ponsonby on March 5, 1890, 'does *not* at all wish to revive the title of York or she would have done so for her own son Alfred. Let it be Duke of Rothsay or Earl of Chester.'

None the less, in the birthday honours of May 24, 1892, Prince George was created Duke of York, Earl of Inverness and Baron Killarney. He wrote to his grandmother, expressing gratitude for this distinction and received a reply dated from Balmoral on May 27:

'I am glad that you like the title of Duke of York. I am afraid I do not, and wish you had remained as you are. A Prince *no one* else can be, whereas a Duke any nobleman can be, and many are! I am not very fond of that of York, which has not very agreeable associations.'

On June 17 he took his seat in the House of Lords, being introduced by his father and his uncle, the Duke of Connaught. 'Fancy', his mother wrote to him, 'my Georgie boy doing that and now being a grand old Duke of York!' Arrangements were also made to provide him with a personal staff. Major-General Sir Francis de Winton was chosen as Comptroller of his Household and Lieutenant Sir Charles Cust was appointed his equerry, a post which he retained for thirty-nine years. A suite of apartments, subsequently called 'York House', were assigned to him in St. James's Palace. He was allowed to use the Bachelors Cottage at Sandringham as his country residence.

So far from breaking immediately with his naval occupations, the Duke of York at the end of June took command of H.M.S *Melampus* for summer manoeuvres. The weather was rough and as usual he was extremely sea-sick; night after night he had to remain on deck and for six days he never took off his clothes:

'The Flagship', he wrote in his diary for July 27, 'made any number of mistakes & we all got anyhow. I hope I shall never be in any other manoeuvres. . . . Hate the whole thing.' 'I am over-tired,' he wrote on August 10, 'feel quite done-up.'

In September he went for a short spell to Heidelberg, in order to study the German language. He stayed at the Villa Felseck with Professor Ihne—a stout, white-haired, spectacled old man, who possessed eccentric views upon English literature and a fussy, touchy, argumentative disposition. 'Two months', the Prince of Wales had justly commented, 'is a very short time to learn a language when one is twenty seven.' The Duke of York none the less worked all morning and evening at his German grammar and in the afternoons he would visit the Castle and the University with Professor Ihne, or sit listening to the band in some beer-garden, in the company of Mr Maurice Baring.[b]

His studies were interrupted, and the tedium of the Villa Felseck relieved, when he was instructed by Queen Victoria to represent her at the golden wedding of the Grand Duke of Saxe-Weimar and thereafter at the Luther celebrations at Wittenberg. For the latter ceremony he accompanied the German Emperor in the imperial train. 'William', he wrote to his grandmother, 'was most kind & civil to me. I have never known him so nice.' The Queen was gratified by the accounts she received from her foreign informants of her grandson's conduct and bearing:

> 'George', she wrote to the Duke of Connaught, 'has made the very best impression abroad on the occasion of his visits to Weimar and Wittenberg. . . . It will do him all the good in the world.'

He was now conscious that the fifteen years which he had spent in the Navy had afforded him few opportunities to become acquainted with home politics or politicians. On his return from Germany in November 1892, he made some spasmodic attempts to remedy these defects. We find him that December dining with Lord Carrington, sitting between Mr Gladstone and Mr Asquith and having a long conversation with Mr John Morley. He began to attend parliamentary debates, both in the upper and the lower Chambers. On February 13, 1893, he heard Mr Gladstone introduce his second Home Rule Bill into the House of Commons: 'He made a beautiful speech and spoke for 2 and a quarter hours, which is wonderful for a man of 83.' From his place above the clock he listened to the Irish debate that followed. He was himself at this period obtaining further experience of public speaking. On February 6 he spoke in aid of the Society for the Prevention of Cruelty to Children and on the following day he received the Freedom of the Merchant Taylors Company and had to return a reply. 'I was horribly nervous,' he wrote, 'but got through my speeches fairly well.' On March 4 he accompanied his mother on a cruise in the Mediterranean. It was a sentimental journey. She was by then well aware that this was the last occasion on which she would have him, as a bachelor, all to herself.

(2)

For the last two years, as we have seen, Queen Victoria had been suggesting that the moment had arrived when he should marry and settle down. Her anxiety on the subject was naturally increased by the Duke of Clarence's death. 'She is', the Prince of Wales had warned him months ago,[c] 'in a terrible fuss about your marrying.' His grandmother had broached the subject with him in the previous August, and again in December, and had intimated that her most cherished desire was that he should become engaged to Princess Mary of Teck. His father was delighted by the idea; his mother (who, as has been said, took a possessive view of her children) had by then reconciled herself to the fact that he could not remain a bachelor for ever. On April 17 he left his mother at Athens and returned alone to England. On May 2 he went down to East Sheen Lodge to stay with his sister, the Duchess of Fife. On Wednesday, May 3, 1893, 'a lovely day, as hot as summer', he proposed to Princess Mary in the garden at East Sheen. Their engagement was announced on May 4.

The Times newspaper, in a sententious leading article gave expression to the general opinion:

> 'The predominant feeling, now that a sufficient interval has elapsed since the melancholy death of the Duke of Clarence, will be that this betrothal accords with the fitness of things, and, so far from offending any legitimate sentiment, is the most appropriate and delicate medicament for a wound in its nature never wholly effaceable. There is even ground for hoping that a union rooted in painful memories may prove happy beyond the common lot.'

It is strange to-day to read these hesitant prophecies—and to look back across the gulf of time to a marriage which for over forty-two years gave him both the stimulus of intelligent companionship and the repose of unruffled domestic felicity. There was no more loneliness for him thereafter; she shared all his burdens and all his confidences; she halved his sorrows and enhanced his joys.

The reaction of his family to the announcement of his betrothal was characteristic. Queen Victoria, who with her solid wisdom and shrewd insight had for long recognised the Duke's sterling qualities, was overjoyed:

> 'Let me now say', she wrote to him, 'how thankful I am that this great and so long & ardently wished for event is settled & I gladly give my consent to what I pray may be for your happiness and for the Country's good. Say everything affectionate to dear May, for whom

this must be a *trying moment* full of such mixed feelings. But she cannot find a *better* husband than you and I am sure she will be a good, devoted and useful wife to you.' 'God bless you,' she wrote again a few days later, 'beloved child, whom I have loved as my own.'

The Prince of Wales, who was much gratified by the event, expressed the not unconventional view that in gaining a daughter he had not lost a son. The Princess of Wales, as always, was more human:

'Indeed it is sad,' she had written to him on April 29, when he had parted from her at Athens, 'to think that we shall never be able to be together and travel in the same way—yet there is a bond of love between us, that of mother and child, which nothing can ever diminish or render less binding—and nobody can, or shall ever, come between me and my darling Georgie boy.'

On receiving at Malta the telegram announcing his engagement, she replied on May 6: 'With what mixed feelings I read your telegram! Well all I can say is that I pray God to give you both a long and happy life together, and that you will make up to dear May all that she lost in darling Eddy and that you will be a mutual happiness to each other, a comfort to us, and a blessing to the nation.'

The marriage was celebrated in the Chapel Royal, St. James's Palace, on July 6, 1893. Among the royal guests were the King and Queen of Denmark, Prince Henry of Prussia, Prince Albert of Belgium, and the Tsarevitch of Russia, 'whose extraordinary likeness to the Duke of York', *The Times* commented, 'may have contributed to secure for him some additional cheers'. Queen Victoria, with the Riband of the Garter slashing her black bodice with diamonds upon her head, drove to St. James's Palace in a state coach drawn by eight Hanoverian creams. The Duke of York, who was attended by his father and his uncle, the Duke of Edinburgh, wore naval uniform. After appearing with the Queen on the balcony of Buckingham Palace, he and his wife drove through crowded streets to Liverpool Street Station, pausing at Temple Bar to receive an address of congratulation from the Lord Mayor, the Aldermen and the Commons of the City of London. 'Most enormous crowds I ever saw,' the Duke noted in his diary, 'magnificent reception the whole way, it quite took one's breath away.'

The honeymoon was spent at York Cottage, Sandringham.

(3)

The Sandringham estate had been purchased in 1861 from the revenues of the Duchy of Cornwall which had accumulated during the long minority of the Prince of Wales. It belonged to Charles Spencer Cowper, who married Lady Harriet Gardiner, step-daughter to Lady Blessington and for a while the virgin bride of Alfred Count d'Orsay. The original purchase price was £220,000 and a further sum of £300,000 was expended in rendering the derelict estate one of the finest sporting and agricultural properties in the country and in constructing, in place of Mr Cowper's clumsy little house, the vast mansion which now exists.

Even when rebuilt, Sandringham House did not prove large enough to accommodate the many guests whom the Prince of Wales delighted to entertain. A small annexe was therefore erected a few hundred yards from the main building and christened 'Bachelors Cottage'. When the Prince assigned it as a residence to his son the name was changed to 'York Cottage'. It was, and remains, a glum little villa, encompassed by thickets of laurel and rhododendron, shadowed by huge Wellingtonias and separated by an abrupt rim of lawn from a pond, at the edge of which a leaden pelican gazes in dejection upon the water lilies and bamboos. The local brown stone in which the house was constructed is concealed by rough-cast which in its turn is enlivened by very imitation Tudor beams. The rooms inside, with their fumed oak surrounds, their white over-mantels framing oval mirrors, their Doulton tiles and stained glass fanlights, are indistinguishable from those of any Surbiton or Upper Norwood home. The Duke's own sitting-room, its north window blocked by heavy shrubberies, was rendered even darker by the red cloth covering which saddened the walls. Against this dismal mono-chrome (which was composed of the cloth used in those days for the trousers of the French army) hung excellent reproductions of some of the more popular pictures acquired by the Chantrey Bequest. This most undesirable residence remained his favourite home for thirty-three years. It was here that five of his six children were born.

For him Sandringham, and the Sandringham ways of life, represented the ideal of human felicity. 'Dear old Sandringham', he called it, 'the place I love better than anywhere in the world.' Here he could recapture the associations of boyhood: recalling the edge of the warren where he had shot his first rabbit; the corner of the lawn where he and his brother had discharged their arrows at a juvenile Mr Dalton, scampering for their delection like a leaping deer. It was here that, after fifteen years' absorption in the mysteries of the sea, he came to learn and love the mysteries of the soil. It was here that he experienced his greatest enjoyments and his deepest sorrow. The place was hallowed for him by familiar memories; he was a man who preferred recognition to surprise, the familiar to the strange. Compared to York Cottage, all the palaces and castles of the earth meant little more to him than a sequence of official residences. It was at Sandringham that he spent his happiest hours; to Sandringham that in later years he would escape from the burden of his official labours; at Sandringham that he died.

The lessons which he had learnt in the Navy (the categorical sense of duty, the instincts of obedience and command, the habits of responsibility, the orderliness of all his ways) were not blurred by his new life as a country gentleman, as head of a rapidly increasing family, as sportsman, agriculturalist and farmer. His temperament remained that of a naval officer, even when he became a Norfolk squire.

It may be doubted whether, in those early years of marriage, the Duchess of York fully shared his unquestioning acceptance of all that Sandringham represented. The strain imposed upon her excellent loyalty by the self-effacement, even the dependence, which her parents-in-law took so thoughtlessly for granted, has been well indicated in Mr John Gore's illuminating but tactful paragraphs:[a]

> 'The Duchess had married into a family which for years had been self-sufficient, a family which the Princess's genius for affection had turned into something that was certainly a closely guarded clique and was not far short of a mutual-admiration society. It was a family little given to intellectual pursuits, without much in the way of artistic tastes or taste, a family not easily to be converted to any other manner of life than that which they had found all-sufficing in an age wherein privilege vigorously survived.
>
> 'The Duchess was intellectually on a higher plane; she was already well educated and constantly seeking to increase her store of knowledge in many fields beyond the range of the Princess of Wales or Princess Victoria. She was full of initiative, of intellectual curiosity, of energy, which needed outlets and wider horizons. Their recreations were not hers. Their manner of life could not satisfy her ideal in the intellectual life of those days. And she was living in a small house on an estate which drew its inspiration wholly from the Prince and Princess, whereon every smallest happening or alteration was ordered and taken note of by the Prince. The very arrangements of her rooms, the planting of her small garden, were matters which required reference to Sandringham House, and the smallest innovation would be regarded with distrust. There was so much that she might usefully have done on the estate. Her ideas might have influenced a score of local institutions and increased the well-being of the neighbourhood. But such matters

were the prerogative of the Princess, whose charm and kindliness often made up for her lack of system and order.

'Sometimes the Duchess's intellectual life there may have been starved and her energies atrophied in those early years. For she came of a younger, more liberal generation, with far more serious notions of woman's spheres of usefulness, and very strong ideas of the responsibilities demanded of the first ladies in the realm. For many women, then and now, the daily call to follow the shooters, to watch the killing, however faultless, to take always a cheerful appreciative part in man-made, man-valued amusements, must have been answered at the sacrifice of many cherished, constructive and liberal ambitions. It is fair to assume that the self-effacement which conditions at Sandringham in those years demanded of a fine and energetic character must have fallen hardly on the Duchess; and fair also to suggest that the Prince and Princess might have done more to encourage her initiative and to fill her days, and with a more understanding sympathy to have alleviated the shyness with which she entered upon her ceremonial duties.'

It may have been the memory of the shy subservient years at that time imposed upon his own beloved wife that induced King George, when his younger sons in their turn came to marry, to welcome their brides into his family, not only with his accustomed cheery gusto, but with a delicate appreciation of the shyness and bewilderment which they were bound to feel.

(4)

In the Duke of York's diary for June 23, 1894, there occurs the entry: 'White Lodge, Richmond Park. At 10.0 a sweet little boy was born and weighed 8 lb. Mr Asquith, Home Secretary, came to see him.'

A difficulty immediately arose (similar to that which had occurred at the time of his own birth twenty-nine years before) in regard to the names to be accorded to the future King Edward VIII. The correspondence which ensued is significant, if only because it illustrates Queen Victoria's unfading devotion to her husband's memory, her eccentric dynastic theories, and her willingness in the last resort to subordinate to the feelings of her family her own most cherished desires.

By the hand of Sir Francis de Winton, she sent a letter to her grandson, dated Windsor Castle, June 26, 1894:

'Darling Georgie,

'The outburst of loyalty on this happy event is again most gratifying, & the way in which the papers and private people have written about it all & about me touches me deeply. Considering the many allusions to me & the future of the dear child, I am *most anxious naturally* that he should bear the name of his beloved Great Grandfather, a name which brought untold blessings to the whole Empire & that *Albert* should be his 1st name. . . . The country would expect that dear Grandpapa's name should follow mine in future to mark the Victorian Era.'

'My darling Grandmama,' he replied from White Lodge on July 1, 'Sir Francis de Winton only returned on Friday from Sandringham, when he at once gave me your dear letter & I need not tell you that I have given it my most careful consideration. You have always shown me the greatest possible kindness, dearest Grandmama, & ever since I can remember I have always tried my best to be a dutiful grandson to you & never to go against your wishes.

'Long before our dear child was born, both May & I settled that if it was a boy we should call him Edward after darling *Eddy*. *This is the dearest wish of our hearts*, dearest Grandmama, for Edward is indeed a *sacred* name to us & one which I know would have pleased *him* beyond anything; it is in loving remembrance of him and therefore *not* painful to us.

'Do not for a moment think that we do not understand your feelings about wishing him to be called after dear Grand Papa, of course we intend that one of his names *shall* be *Albert*; but we hope that you will also think of us and enter into our feelings & not press us to change our present intention.

'Both our parents have left the choice of names entirely in our hands & have not suggested anything.

'We are much distressed at not being able to meet your wishes as regards our little son's name, but we feel so strongly about it, that we are confident that when you realize how *dear and sacred* this name is to us, you, dearest Grandmama, will not cause us the *pain* we shall always feel if our little child is not called Edward.'

'Of course,' Queen Victoria replied on July 2, 'if you wish Edward to be the first name I shall not object, only I think you write as if *Edward* was the *real* name of dear Eddy, while it was *Albert Victor*. . . . My chief object and anxiety about *Albert* is that it should *mark* the Dynasty which becomes on dear Papa's succeeding me, like the Norman, Plantagenet, Tudor (fr. the grandfather of Henry VII), Stewart and finally Brunswick & all will be united in the Coburg dynasty.'

In the end the baby was christened in the drawing-room at White Lodge, with the names Edward Albert Christian George Andrew Patrick David. It was by his last name that he was thereafter known to his family.

The House of Commons passed the customary vote of congratulation on this auspicious event. The member for South West Ham,

James Keir Hardie, struck a discordant note by criticising the motion on the ground that it 'proposed to lift to an importance which it did not deserve an event of every day occurrence'. The public and the newspapers were much shocked by this unseemly intervention.

Eighteen months later, on December 14, 1895, there came another entry in the diary:

> 'A little boy was born, weighing nearly 8 lbs, at 3.40. a.m. S.T. Everything most satisfactory, both doing well. Sent a great number of telegrams, had something to eat. Went to bed at 6.45. very tired.' [1]

December 14 was not the most tactful day which the future King George VI could have chosen for his advent into a world which was so soon to become embattled, angry and disillusioned. It was the anniversary of the Prince Consort's death in 1861 and of the death of Princess Alice in 1878:

> 'The terrible anniversary', Queen Victoria wrote in her journal, 'returned for the thirty fourth time. . . . Found telegrams from Georgie and Sir J. Williams saying that dear May had been safely delivered of a son at three this morning. Georgie's first feeling was regret that this dear child should be born on such a sad day. I have a feeling it may be a blessing for the dear little boy and may be looked upon as a gift from God!'

The Prince of Wales urged him to suggest to the Queen that she should become the child's godmother and that he should be christened Albert:

> 'You might like', he wrote to the Duke on December 16, 'to call him later *Bertie*, the name I have always gone by in my family. . . . Grandmama is not the least annoyed with you about anything, but she only regretted that the little boy was born on the 14th, though we have all told her that it will dispel the gloom of that sad anniversary. She is ageing rapidly and has always been very kind and affectionate to you that I really think it would gratify her if you yourself proposed the name of *Albert* to her.'

The proposition was made and the Queen was delighted:

> 'Most gladly', she wrote, 'do I accept being Godmother to this dear little boy, born on the day his beloved Great Grandfather entered on an even greater life. He will be specially dear to me. I thank you lovingly for your kind letter & will write again soon, but I must end now to save the post. V.R.I.'

[1] The initials S.T. do not stand for 'Summer Time' but for 'Sandringham Time'. The clocks at Sandringham were always kept half an hour fast. King Edward VIII on his accession in 1936 abolished this practice.

On February 17, 1896, at the church of St Mary Magdalene, Sandringham, the child was christened Albert Frederick Arthur George.[1]

(5)

The seven and a half years between the Duke of York's marriage and the death of Queen Victoria succeeded each other with placid similitude. Apart from occasional public functions and a few official journeys, he lived the life of a private country gentleman, unostentatious, comparatively retired, almost obscure. He was not at that date accorded access to official documents or Cabinet papers. Had it not been for his frequent and intimate conversations with his father, for his occasional meetings with leading politicians, his knowledge of public affairs would have been neither wider nor deeper than that acquired by any other landowner or sportsman from a daily perusal of *The Times* newspaper. At Sandringham, when he was not out shooting, he would play with his children, read aloud to his wife, visit the farms, dairy and pheasantries, go round the kennels and stables, bicycle in the surrounding country with Sir Charles Cust or Mr Derek Keppel, skate on the lake, take his dog 'Heather' for a walk and arrange his stamps. When in London he would give dinner parties at York House, to which members of his family were invited, together with a few Ministers and diplomatists; often in the evenings he would go to the theatre or play billiards at the Marlborough Club. From time to time he and the Duchess would be invited to stay in the houses of the old and new aristocracy. There were shooting parties at Castle Rising, Elveden, Panshanger, Holkham, Wilton, Brocket, Studley Royal, Bolton Abbey, Tulchan Lodge, Gordon Castle, Drummond Castle, Drumlanrig, West Dean Park, Hall Barn and Chatsworth.

In November 1894, he went to Russia to attend the funeral of his

[1] The Duke and Duchess of York had six children: *Prince Edward* (born 1894. Subsequently Prince of Wales, King Edward VIII and Duke of Windsor. Married 1937 Mrs. Wallis Warfield). *Prince Albert* (b. 1895. Subsequently Duke of York and King George VI. Married 1923 Lady Elizabeth Bowes-Lyon). *Princess Mary* (b. 1897. Subsequently Princess Royal. Married 1922 Viscount Lascelles later Earl of Harewood). *Prince Henry* (b. 1900. Subsequently Duke of Gloucester. Married 1935 Lady Alice Montagu-Douglas-Scott). *Prince George* (b. 1902. Subsequently Duke of Kent. Married 1934 Princess Marina, daughter of Prince Nicolas of Greece. Killed on active service 1942). *Prince John* (b. 1905, d. 1919).

uncle the Tsar Alexander III and the marriage, a week later, of the new Tsar, Nicholas II, to Princess Alix of Hesse:

'I do think', he wrote to his grandmother from St. Petersburg on November 28, 'that Nicky is a very lucky man to have got such a lovely and charming wife & I must say I never saw two people more in love with each other or happier than they are. When they drove from the Winter Palace after the wedding they got a tremendous reception & ovation from the large crowds in the streets, the cheering was most hearty & reminded me of England. . . . Nicky has been kindness itself to me, he is the same dear boy he has always been to me & talks to me quite openly on every subject. . . .He does everything so quietly & naturally; everyone is struck by it & is [*sic*] very popular already.'

In August 1897, he and the Duchess paid an official visit to Ireland. He was so impressed by the loyalty manifested by the inhabitants that he urged Queen Victoria to establish a royal residence in the vicinity of Dublin. Lord Cadogan, the Lord Lieutenant, was strongly in favour of the proposal and the Cabinet approved.* The Queen refused to give her consent. The visit none the less created a valuable, if transitory, impression; it left the Duke of York with a personal affection for Ireland and the conviction (which he never relinquished) that, in spite of the politicians, there existed a sentimental bond of affection between the Irish people and the Crown:

Lord Salisbury, writing to him from Hatfield on September 9, 1897, congratulated him on the 'remarkable success' of his visit and on the 'extraordinary popularity' which he and the Duchess had gained. 'The devotion', he wrote, 'to your person which you have inspired is not only a result gratifying to yourself . . . but it will have a most valuable effect upon public feeling in Ireland, and may do much to restore the loyalty which during the last half century has been so much shaken in many districts.

'I trust it may mark the dawn of a brighter era.'*

In May 1898, Mr Gladstone died and the Duke acted as one of the pall-bearers at his funeral in Westminster Abbey. In June of that year he assumed command of H.M.S. *Crescent* for eight weeks' target practice in the Irish Channel. This was the last time that he served as an active officer in Her Majesty's Navy. He was accompanied by his old shipmate, Canon Dalton, who was happy indeed to leave the Windsor cloisters as the guest of his beloved pupil for a further spell at sea.

During that last decade of the century the Duke's attention had been drawn to certain ominous experiments in human ingenuity.

In the summer of 1895 he was shown the steam flying-machine which Mr Hiram Maxim had constructed:

> 'It made two runs for me to see. I was in it for one of them; it did lift off the ground part of the time.'

In July of 1896, Mr Bert Acres, in a tent erected in the garden of Marlborough House, displayed his 'photo-electric reproductions of real life' which he called the 'Cinematoscope'. The Duke's first reference to the internal combustion engine does not occur until June 13, 1900: 'Went in papa's new motor car. . . . The man managed it extraordinarily well.'

(5)

The nineteenth century, which had opened in stress and glory, which had rendered England the richest and most powerful country in the world, petered out in a rapid series of small shames. On October 10, 1899, the two Boer Republics, the Transvaal and the Orange Free State, declared war, invaded Natal, and almost immediately invested Mafeking, Kimberley and Ladysmith.[1] The successive defeats inflicted on the British army by the ingenious Boer commandos, culminating in the battles of Magersfontein and Colenso, shattered the accumulated self-satisfaction of the English and pro-

---

[1] The main developments in South Africa since the defeat of the British at Majuba Hill in 1881 had been as follows: In 1884 President Kruger had managed to induce Lord Derby to drop the clause in the 1881 Convention which safeguarded British suzerainty over the Transvaal. In 1886 gold was discovered on the Rand and so many foreigners or *uitlanders* flocked to the Transvaal that in a few years they outnumbered the Boers by more than four to one. President Kruger, having been unable to stop this immigration, proceeded, while taxing the foreigners, to deny them political rights. Cecil Rhodes retaliated by preparing a revolution in Johannesburg, and by sending his friend Leander Starr Jameson to invade the country. The revolution misfired and Jameson and his 600 troopers were forced to surrender to the Boer commandos at Doornkop on January 2, 1896.

President Kruger continued to make things difficult for the *uitlanders*. In June 1899 the High Commissioner, Sir Alfred Milner, held an abortive conference with the President in which he urged him to grant some at least of the more justifiable of the *uitlander* demands. This conference proved abortive and on October 9 the two Dutch Republics of the Transvaal and the Orange Free State delivered an ultimatum to the British Government demanding the withdrawal of all British troops and the submission of the dispute to arbitration. This ultimatum was rejected and on October 10, 1899, war ensued.

duced in London a black cloud of depression shot with flashes of bewildered rage. Even more perplexing to the British public was the wave of gloating animosity which suddenly swept across the Continent of Europe.

On April 4, 1900, a young man of the name of Sipido, intoxicated by the prevailing anti-British hysteria, fired his revolver at the Prince and Princess of Wales while their train was standing in the Gare du Nord at Brussels. 'I felt the ball buzzing across my eyes,' the Princess telegraphed, 'and saw him coming straight at us.' A few weeks later the Duke of York was invited by the German Emperor to attend the celebrations of the Crown Prince's coming of age:

> 'It is certainly very disagreeable to me', the Duke wrote to his mother on April 23, 1900, 'having to go to Berlin just now & in fact anywhere abroad as they apparently all hate us like poison. But William is anxious that I should be present. . . . & he is the only one who has behaved decently to us during this war & I myself am quite ready to be friends with him.'

Apart from the boos with which a few Berliners assailed some of the Duke's entourage, the visit passed without incident.

After the disaster of Spion Kop on January 26, 1900, the military situation in South Africa began to improve. On February 27, the anniversary of Majuba, Cronje surrendered to Lord Roberts and Ladysmith was relieved. On March 8 Queen Victoria paid one of her rare visits to Buckingham Palace:

> 'Between twenty & thirty thousand people', the Duke wrote in his diary for that day, 'collected outside the gates & sang songs & cheered tremendously. Before Grandmama left the dining room we pulled up the blind & made her come to the window & held candles near her so that she could be seen. The crowds cheered again and then quietly dispersed.'

(6)

'Good bye Nineteenth Century' the Duke wrote in his diary for December 31, 1900. On the night of January 17, 1901, after attending a dinner given in honour of Lord Roberts on his return from South Africa, the Duke went with his father to the Marlborough Club:

> 'When we got to the Club, Papa told me that darling Grandmama had had a slight stroke this morning. He got a cypher telegram tonight from Aunt Helena saying her condition was precarious but no immediate danger. It makes us all very anxious. . . . Grandmama has not been well for some weeks now.'

On Saturday, January 19, the reports from Osborne House were more reassuring. The Duke went down to York Cottage, but that afternoon he was urgently recalled to London. On Sunday, January 20, the German Emperor arrived from Berlin and on the early morning of Monday, January 21, the Duke accompanied the Emperor and the Prince of Wales to Osborne. The Queen was by then almost unconscious, but she rallied on the morning of Tuesday, January 22, and spoke to each of them by name. At 5.0 that evening she again became unconscious and at 6.30: 'our beloved Queen and Grandmama, one of the greatest women that ever lived, passed peacefully away.'

CHAPTER V

THE VOYAGE OF THE *OPHIR*

March–November 1901

Queen Victoria and Princess May—Walter Bagehot's *English Constitution*—
The Duke of York becomes Duke of Cornwall—Appointment of Sir
Arthur Bigge as his Private Secretary—The great value to him of Sir
Arthur Bigge's guidance and friendship—The proposed mission to
Australia to open the first Commonwealth Parliament—King
Edward's objections—Mr Balfour's letter—His staff in the *Ophir*—
Their departure on March 16—the arrival in Melbourne—The
opening ceremony—His letter to Mr Joseph Chamberlain—Visits to
New Zealand, South Africa, and Canada—Return to England—
Effect upon him of this imperial journey—The new conception of
Empire—His broadened outlook and increased self-confidence—His
Guildhall speech.

QUEEN VICTORIA was a sensible judge of human values. She had
been quick to realise that Princess May, in spite of her early diffidence
and self-effacement, was a woman of distinctive personality and one
whose range of interests, intellectual standards and refinement of
perception would be bound in the end to enlarge, deepen and enrich
her husband's mind and tastes:

> 'She strikes me', the Queen had written to the Empress Frederick on
> May 14, 1894, 'more and more as vy. clever & so sensible & right-
> minded & is a great help to Georgie. Helping him in his Speeches and
> what he has to write. They read together & he also has a Professor
> from Cambridge to read with him.'

The Professor referred to was Mr J. R. Tanner of St John's
College, an authority on naval and constitutional history, who in
March 1894, had been engaged to instruct the Duke of York in the
law and practice of the Constitution. It must be admitted that the
visits of Mr Tanner to York House are recorded with less frequency
than those of Mr Tilleard, the philatelist. Mr Tanner none the less
did succeed in inducing the Duke to read and analyse some at least
of the sparkling pages of Walter Bagehot's *English Constitution*. There
exists at Windsor a school note-book, in the opening pages of which
the Duke summarised in his own careful handwriting the precepts which Mr Bagehot, in his confident way, had laid down for the

61

instruction and guidance of our English kings. In these few notes the Duke crystallised those very conceptions of the functions and duties of a constitutional monarch which, when he came to the throne, he applied with consistent faithfulness. His summary deserves, therefore, to be quoted in its entirety:

Monarchy

'(1) The value of the Crown in its *dignified* capacity

    (a) It makes Government *intelligible* to the masses.

    (b) It makes Government *interesting* to the masses.

    (c) It *strengthens* Government with the *religious* tradition connected with the Crown.

        After the accession of George III the Hanoverian line inherited the traditional reverence of Stuart times.

    (d) The *social* value of the Crown.

        If the high social rank was to be scrambled for in the House of Commons, the number of social adventurers there would be incalculably more numerous & indefinitely more eager.

    (e) The *moral* value of the Crown.

        Great for good or evil.

        Compare the Courts of Charles II and George III in their influence on the nation.

    (f) The existence of the Crown serves to *disguise* change & therefore to deprive it of the evil consequences of revolution, e.g. The Reform Bill of 1832.

'(2) The value of the Crown in its *business* capacity. The Crown is no longer an "Estate of the Realm" or itself the executive, but the Queen nevertheless retains an immense unexhausted *influence* which goes some way to compensate for the formal *powers* which have been lost; this influence can be exercised in various ways:

    (a) In the *formation* of Ministries; especially in choosing between the Statesmen who have a claim to lead party.

    (b) During the *continuance* of Ministries. The Crown possesses *first* the right to be consulted, *second* the right to encourage & *third* the right to warn. And these rights may lead to a very important influence on the course of politics, especially as under a system of party government, the Monarch alone possesses a *continuous political experience*.

    (c) At the *break up* of a Ministry (but this can be treated best in connection with the House of Lords).

'Thus, though it would be possible to construct a system of political machinery in which there was no monarchy, yet in a State where a monarchy of the English type already exists, it is still a great political force & offers a splendid career to an

> able monarch; he is independent of parties & therefore impartial, his position ensures that his advice would be received with respect; & he is the only statesman in the country whose political experience is continuous.'

Such were the main precepts which the Duke of York derived, with the assistance of Mr Tanner, from his study of Bagehot's *English Constitution*. There are other of Mr Bagehot's apophthegms which he omitted to enter in his notebook. He makes no reference to the mystical element in Monarchy. 'Its mystery', wrote Bagehot,*ᵃ* 'is its life. We must not let in daylight upon magic.' 'Royalty', Bagehot had written,*ᵇ* 'will be strong because it appeals to diffused feeling, and Republics weak because they appeal to the understanding.' 'A *family* on the throne', wrote Bagehot,*ᶜ* 'is an interesting idea also. It brings down the pride of sovereignty to the level of petty life.' Not all of Bagehot's commentaries were so soothing. 'Theory and experience', he suggested,*ᵈ* 'both teach us that the education of a Prince can be but a poor education and that a royal family will generally have less ability than other families.' 'The occupations', he observed,*ᵉ* 'of a constitutional monarch are grave, formal, important, but never exciting; they have nothing to stir eager blood, awaken high imagination, work off wild thoughts.'

The Duke of York possessed neither an eager imagination nor wild thoughts. His faith in the principle of Monarchy was simple, devout even; but selfless. All that he aspired to do was to serve that principle with rectitude; to represent all that was most straightforward in the national character; to give to the world an example of personal probity; to advise, to encourage and to warn.

To few men has it been granted to fulfil their aspirations with such completeness.

(2)

On January 23, 1901, the day after the death of Queen Victoria, the Duke of York accompanied his father to London and attended a Privy Council in the Banqueting Hall at St. James's Palace. He was the first to swear allegiance to the new monarch:

> 'Papa made a beautiful speech in which he said that he wished to be called Edward VII. . . . I have now succeeded Papa as Duke of Cornwall.' [1]

[1] The title of 'Duke of Cornwall', together with the revenues of the Duchy, are hereditary perquisites of the heir to the throne. They derive automatically and are not conferred as the title of 'Prince of Wales' is conferred. It was not until November 9, 1901, that King Edward VII

They then returned to Osborne. 'At 4 p.m', he wrote in his diary for January 24, 'we all received Holy Communion in darling Grandmama's room, with Her lying in our midst.' That evening the Duke developed a high temperature and was too ill to attend his grandmother's funeral at Windsor. From the window of his room at Osborne he watched her coffin being carried to the sea.

One of the first and wisest of King Edward's actions was to appoint Sir Francis Knollys as his own Private Secretary and to offer to Sir Arthur Bigge[1] the post of Private Secretary to the Duke of York. For fifteen years Sir Arthur Bigge had been assistant to Sir Henry Ponsonby, the most constant, patient and humorous of Queen Victoria's servitors. On Sir Henry's death in 1895 he had succeeded him as the Queen's Principal Private Secretary. His transference to the household of the Duke of York would thus entail upon Sir Arthur Bigge a comparative decline in status and a loss of central responsibility. He was not a man to allow personal considerations to deflect the wishes of his Sovereign. He accepted the offer dutifully and remained the Duke's secretary, counsellor and friend for thirty years.

It is not possible to exaggerate the benefit which the Duke derived from the guidance and encouragement of this sagacious man. 'He taught me', his Sovereign remarked in later years, 'how to be a King.' Sir Arthur Bigge was always at hand to prompt and stimulate, to curb or to appease. He did not hesitate, when occasion required, to criticise or disapprove. He would grumble that Queen Victoria

---

conferred upon his son the title of 'Prince of Wales'. Between January 23 and November 9, his official title was thus 'Duke of Cornwall and York'.

[1] Arthur Bigge was one of the twelve children of the Rev. J. Bigge, vicar of Stamfordham in Northumberland. He was educated at Rossall and Woolwich Academy and entered the Royal Artillery. While serving in the Zulu War of 1879 he became a close friend of the Prince Imperial, but was ill with enteric when the Prince was ambushed and killed. When in 1880 the Empress Eugénie decided to visit the spot where her son had lost his life, Arthur Bigge was chosen to accompany her. Later in that year he visited the Empress at Abergeldie and was introduced by her to Queen Victoria. The Queen took an immediate liking to the young officer and appointed him a member of her household. He remained in the service of the Royal Family for fifty-one years.

From 1880 to 1895 he was assistant to Sir Henry Ponsonby. From 1895 to 1901 he was Principal Private Secretary to the Queen. From 1901 till his death in 1931 he was Private Secretary to the Duke of York, serving him both when he became Prince of Wales and King. He was created Lord Stamfordham in 1911.

was the only Monarch he had ever known who possessed a true conception of the functions of constitutional Monarchy. He would tell the Duke not to look cross or bored at public functions. 'We sailors', the Duke answered, 'never smile when on duty.' Bigge would point out that the duties of a sailor and an heir apparent were not identical. He was angry with King Edward for not at once conferring on the Duke the title of Prince of Wales. He was angry with the Duke for his passionate attachment to York Cottage, which, in Sir Arthur Bigge's opinion, was an unworthy residence for the heir to so sumptuous a throne. Some idea of the relations of trust and affection which developed between them is conveyed by the letters which the Duke addressed to him on the rare occasions when they were parted:

> 'I feel', he wrote on January 1, 1902, 'that I can always rely on you to tell me the truth, however disagreeable & that you are entirely in my confidence. To a person in my position it is of enormous help. . . . I thank you again from the bottom of my heart.' 'I fear sometimes', he wrote again on December 25, 1907, 'I have lost my temper with you & often been very rude, but I am sure you know me well enough by now to know that I did not mean it. . . . I am a bad hand at saying what I feel, but I thank God that I have a friend like you, in whom I have the fullest confidence and from whom I know on all occasions I shall get the best and soundest advice whenever I seek it.'

Fortified by the counsels and companionship of this trusted adviser, the Duke began henceforward gradually to equip himself for the responsibilities which fate had decreed.

(3)

The chronological method which has hitherto been adopted must at this stage be abandoned for more synthetic treatment. In the preceding chapters, an effort has been made to describe how a very normal, if somewhat pampered, little boy passed through the stage of merry midshipman and became a typical naval officer, with all the habits of duty and discipline, of obedience and command, which the profession of seaman necessarily inculcates. The death of his brother and his own marriage (in that the former changed his status and the latter provided a new and stimulating influence) ought to have produced a rapid expansion. No such an immediate widening of his mind or interests occurred: the quarter-deck was replaced by the coverts and marshes of Sandringham: the officer of the watch became the sporting squire. His long habituation to a confined and exclusive domestic atmosphere, the awed veneration which he felt for his father, the sentimental devotion which his mother inspired and exacted, the uncritical approval which he could always obtain from his unmarried sister Princess Victoria, all combined to retard his personal development. During the seventeen years when he was prospective or immediate heir to the throne, he remained subject, although decreasingly, to these family standards. When the King was at Windsor, he followed to Frogmore: when the King was at Balmoral, he went obediently to Abergeldie: when the King was at Sandringham, he returned to the beloved villa on the estate. It was not in England, where the part that he played was formal and subsidiary, that he acquired self-realisation; this much-needed discovery occurred overseas. It is thus of importance to examine the effect upon him of his first completely independent mission, of the journey which he undertook in 1901 to Australia, South Africa, and Canada.

In the last months of Queen Victoria's reign it had been suggested that the Duke and Duchess of York should go to Melbourne in order to open the first Parliament of the Commonwealth of Australia.[1] The Queen agreed to the proposal only on the conditions that the war in South Africa should have been brought to a successful conclusion and that the state of her own health, and that of the Prince of Wales, should be such as to warrant so prolonged an absence. Lord Salisbury was insistent. On September 18, 1900, a

[1] The idea of the federation of the seven Australasian colonies had been mooted as long ago as 1852, but was shelved owing to the refusal of New Zealand to form part of a continental union and to objections on the part of Queensland and New South Wales. Further efforts were made in 1891 to form a continental federation without New Zealand but these also proved abortive. In 1895 Mr (afterwards Sir George) Reid convened a conference of Premiers who agreed that a National Convention should be elected to draft a federal constitution for Australia. This Constitution was submitted to a referendum in the six colonies in March 1898, but was rejected by the electorate of New South Wales. At a Premier's conference held in Melbourne in January 1899, concessions were made to New South Wales and the Constitution adopted by referendum.

A Bill giving effect to this Constitution was submitted to the British Parliament and became law. On September 17, 1900, a royal proclamation was issued declaring that, 'on and after January 1st 1901, the people of New South Wales, Victoria, South Australia, Queensland, Tasmania and Western Australia should be united in a Federal Commonwealth under the name of the Commonwealth of Australia.'

The first Parliament under the Constitution was elected on March 29 and 30, 1901, and was opened by the Duke of Cornwall and York on May 9 following.

statement was issued by the Colonial Office to the effect that the Duke and Duchess of York would visit Australia in the following spring in order, in the Queen's name, to open the first Commonwealth Parliament and in order 'to signify her sense of the loyalty and devotion which have prompted the spontaneous aid so liberally offered by all the colonies in the South African war, and of the splendid gallantry of her colonial troops'.

In February 1901, after the Queen's funeral, the project was revived. King Edward did not wish, so soon after his accession, to be parted from the heir to the throne. Lord Salisbury replied that to abandon the visit would cause great disappointment in Australia and that it was politically desirable that the original plan should be adhered to. King Edward protested that 'he had only one son left out of three and he will not have his life unnecessarily endangered for any political purpose'.

This produced a cogent reply from Mr A. J. Balfour, dated from No. 10 Downing Street on February 6, 1901.¹ Mr Balfour's letter is important as containing a lucid forecast of the coming abandonment of the old colonial theory in favour of a new conception of imperial relations; a conception which acquired impetus in the thirty years to follow and in the development of which Mr Balfour himself played so important a part:

'Mr. Balfour', he wrote, 'cannot help feeling that there are on the other side reasons to be urged which touch the deepest interests of the Monarchy. The King is no longer merely King of Great Britain and Ireland and of a few dependencies whose whole value consisted in ministering to the wealth and security of Great Britain and Ireland. He is now the greatest constitutional bond uniting together in a single Empire communities of free men separated by half the circumference of the Globe. All the patriotic sentiment which makes such an Empire possible centres in him or centres chiefly in him; and everything which emphasises his personality to our kinsmen across the seas must be a gain to the Monarchy and the Empire.

'Now the present opportunity of furthering the policy thus suggested is unique. It can in the nature of things never be repeated. A great commonwealth is to be brought into existence, after infinite trouble and with the fairest prospects of success. Its citizens know little and care little for British Ministries and British party politics. But they know, and care for, the Empire of which they are members and for the Sovereign who rules it. Surely it is in the highest interests of the State that he should visually, and so to speak corporeally, associate his family with the final act which brings the new community into being; so that in the eyes of all who see it the chief actor in the ceremony, its central figure, should be the King's heir, and that

67

in the history of this great event the Monarchy of Britain and the Commonwealth of Australia should be inseparably united.

'It is a consideration of much less importance, yet one not without its weight, that the absence of the Duke of Cornwall will cause deep and widespread disappointment among all classes in the colony.'

King Edward never really cared for Mr Balfour, whose imperturbable, impersonal and indeed indiscriminate politeness, whose bland unawareness of grandeur, filled him with a certain disquiet. So peremptory an intimation could not, however, be ignored. Grudgingly he gave his consent.

For the purpose of this mission to Australia, South Africa, and Canada, the Admiralty had chartered the S.S. *Ophir* of the Orient line, a passenger steamer of some 6,900 tons, which was refitted for the occasion and painted a dazzling white. In addition to Sir Arthur Bigge, the Duke was assisted by Lord Wenlock, Sir John Anderson of the Colonial Office, and Sir Donald Mackenzie Wallace. The latter, who was given the temporary status of assistant Private Secretary, was not, either in appearance or manner, so Scottish as his name might suggest: he was a gifted linguist, a personal friend of King Edward, and had for the last eight years been Director of the Foreign Department of *The Times* newspaper. Canon Dalton, much to his satisfaction, was invited to accompany the Duke as his domestic chaplain. It was Sir Donald Mackenzie Wallace, and not Canon Dalton, who was charged with the task of recording the cruise of the *Ophir* for the instruction of posterity. Those who are interested in the details of this long itinerary[1] will find them fully recorded in the 488 pages of Sir Donald's *The Web of Empire*. The remaining members of the staff were chosen with equal felicity.[2]

[1] The tour can be summarised as follows: Leave Portsmouth, March 16 – Gibraltar – Malta – Aden – Ceylon – Singapore – Arrive Melbourne, May 6 – Brisbane – Sydney – Auckland – Wellington – Christchurch – Dunedin – Hobart – Adelaide – Albany – Perth – Mauritius – Durban – Cape Town – arrive Quebec September 16 – Montreal – Ottawa – Winnipeg – Regina – Calgary – Vancouver – Victoria B.C. – Toronto – Niagara – St. John, N.B. – Halifax – St. John's, Newfoundland – October 31 anchor in Solent – November 2 return to London.

[2] The following were attached to the Duke and Duchess of York during their mission to the Empire: Head of the Household, Lord Wenlock; Private Secretary, Sir Arthur Bigge; Assistant Private Secretary, Sir Donald Mackenzie Wallace; from the Colonial Office, Sir John Anderson; Equerries, Sir Charles Cust and Mr. Derek Keppel; Aides-de-Camp, Prince Alexander of Teck, Commander Godfrey-Faussett, Lord Crichton, the Duke of Roxburghe, Colonel Byron of the Australian Artillery, Major

Some conception of the strain imposed upon the Duke and Duchess by this eight months' voyage can be derived from the statistics which, on his return, the Duke entered in his diary. They travelled 45,000 miles, of which 33,032 were by sea and 12,000 by land. They laid 21 foundation stones, received 544 addresses, presented 4,329 medals and shook hands with 24,855 people at official receptions alone.

The Duke, as has been indicated, was a man of close sentimental affections; he felt deeply this separation from his children and parents. The King and Queen came down to Portsmouth to see them off; a farewell luncheon was given on board the *Ophir*, attended by Mr Joseph Chamberlain and other members of the Cabinet:

> 'Papa proposed our healths & wished us God speed and I answered in a few words & proposed the King and Queen. I was very much affected & could hardly speak. The leave-taking was terrible. I went back with them to the yacht when I said goodbye & broke down quite.'

On that afternoon of Saturday, March 16, the *Ophir*, attended by her escorting cruisers, steamed out of Portsmouth on her journey to the Antipodes. They reached Melbourne on May 6 and entered the city in full state. The glistening landau was drawn by four horses, mounted by bewigged postilions clad in the royal liveries of scarlet and gold. Beside the carriage rode two aides-de-camp, their helmets and cuirasses flashing in the fleeting sun. Along the route of the procession triumphal arches and high stands had been erected; the ladies of Melbourne were still dressed in deep mourning for Queen Victoria; the handkerchiefs which they waved were little spots of white against a sombre monochrome. On May 9, in a huge exhibition building, similar to the Alexandra Palace, the Duke formally inaugurated the first Commonwealth Parliament. In full naval uniform, with his cocked hat upon his head, he stepped to the front of the dais and from a printed sheet read to the assembled members and senators a message from his father, the King:

> 'His Majesty has watched with the deepest interest the social and material progress made by His people in Australia and has seen with thankfulness and heartfelt satisfaction the completion of the political union of which the Parliament is the embodiment. The King is satisfied that the wisdom and patriotism which have characterised the exercise

Bor of the Marines; Officers of the *Ophir*, Captain Winsloe and Commander R. E. Wemyss; Ladies in Waiting to the Duchess, Lady Mary Lygon, Lady Katherine Coke; Domestic Chaplain, Canon Dalton; Marine artists, Chevalier de Martino and Mr Sydney Hall; Medical attendant, Dr Manby; Barber, Mr Charles Jaschke.

69

of the wide powers of self-government hitherto enjoyed by the Colonies will continue to be displayed in the exercise of the still wider powers with which the United Commonwealth has been endowed. His Majesty feels assured that the enjoyment of these powers will, if possible, enhance the loyalty and devotion to His Throne and Empire of which the people of Australia have already given such signal proofs.'

It had been arranged that, at the termination of the speech, the Duchess should press a button which would be the signal for the Union Jack to be hoisted in every school throughout Australia. Owing to a technical mishap this symbolic ceremony was postponed until two days later. When the Duke had finished his speech the Governor-General, Lord Hopetoun, proceeded to swear in the Members.

From Melbourne the Duke and Duchess travelled to Brisbane and Sydney and thereafter to New Zealand, Tasmania, and Western Australia. Throughout the course of this Australasian journey, the Duke was much impressed by the spontaneity of the welcome he received:

> 'Putting aside', he wrote to Mr Joseph Chamberlain on June 18, 1901, 'the hackneyed phrase, which is so often used & conveys so little, I am convinced that there exists a strong feeling of loyalty to the Crown & deep attachment to the Mother Country in Australia,—which I expect you can hardly credit. Old colonists with whom I have talked admit that this spirit did not exist anything like to this extent, even a few years ago. They are good enough to attribute this partly to our having paid them this visit, but in my opinion the three great causes may be found in: the personal influence of & love for the Queen, the South African war, &, if you will allow me to say so, your own indefatigable work & sympathy for this young country. Granted this happy state of things, I feel strongly that now is the time to profit by it. Let the Mother Country on her part give to Australia her very best, whether it is in Governors, soldiers, or colonists. Australia on her side must realise that she is part & parcel of the Empire & must accept the responsibilities of that position.'[g]

Some doubt was expressed whether it would be wise for the Duke and Duchess to include a visit to South Africa, where the war was still in progress. Mr Chamberlain and Sir Alfred Milner were strongly in favour of the proposal. It would, they felt, 'have a very good political effect and would encourage the loyal party in South Africa, while its abandonment would be regarded as a triumph by the Boer press in the Colony and their supporters'.[h] The visit proved in the end a triumphant success and the Duke and Duchess were given a hearty welcome at Cape Town. Lord Kitchener came down to meet them at Durban and assured them that the war was now nearing its termination:

> 'I thought him', the Duke wrote to the King on August 18, 'looking remarkably fit & well & he has grown fat. He wished me to tell you that everybody from himself downwards is working hard to finish the war. . . . He seemed very hopeful, especially having accounted for 839 Boers last week; he does not believe that there are more than 14,000 left in the field & they must be precious short of horses. Alas! ammunition is still coming in through Lorenco Marques, in spite of what our dear good friend Soveral[1] may say to the contrary. He spoke in the highest terms of General French, who is now in command of some 20,000 troops in the Cape Colony.'

From South Africa, the Duke and Duchess sailed to Quebec. After an official visit to Montreal and Ottawa, they crossed the continent to Vancouver in the company of the Premier, Sir Wilfrid Laurier. On October 19 they rejoined the *Ophir* at Halifax and after a short visit to Newfoundland, reached Portsmouth on November 1, where they were welcomed by the King and Queen and by their own children whom they had not seen for nearly eight months. On November 2 they drove in state through the streets of London where they were given an enthusiastic reception:

> 'Most touching,' the Duke wrote in his diary. 'Got back to York House at 3.30. We do indeed feel grateful that it has pleased God to bring us home again safe and sound.'

(4)

The effect upon the Duke of York of this wide voyage was creative and lasting. Not only did it give him deeper seriousness and increased self-confidence; not only did it accustom him to being the central figure at diverse official functions; but it led him to abandon many former prejudices, to revise old ideas, and to acquire an understanding of the modern nature of Empire, of democratic imperialism, which was broader and more progressive than the assumptions by which his grandmother and his father had been guided.

The British people and politicians had tended, during the last

---

[1] *Soveral (Luiz Pinto, Marquis de, 1851-1922)* was one of King Edward's closest personal friends and Portugese Minister in London. He spent most of his diplomatic career in England, where he resided for twenty-six years. He was created a Marquis by King Carlos in February 1901. He resigned his post on the outbreak of the Portugese Revolution in October 1910 and died in Paris on October 5, 1922. He was a most affable man, kind even to the least important people, and was affectionately known to his many English friends as 'the blue monkey'.

three decades of the nineteenth century, to take their Empire for granted. It ministered to their national vanity, it gave them the small excitement of cheap colonial wars and it provided them with markets and a source of raw materials. If they differentiated at all between what they thoughtlessly conceived as the 'white' colonies and the 'black' colonies, they assumed that the latter would increasingly supply them with riches and that the former, when they came to maturity, would fall away. They were not certain even whether the 'white' colonies should be regarded as a liability or an asset, whether the cost to the British taxpayer of defending these distant dependencies, and the long line of communications which connected them with the mother-country, was worth either the effort expended, the prestige derived, or the markets offered. The 'Little Englanders' of those days were more numerous and more influential than is sometimes supposed.

The South African War (assuredly one of the most important events in British history) shattered these assumptions. It showed us that colonial wars were not always cheap or easy and that in certain circumstances great national effort would be needed to enforce our will. It created in many patriotic souls a doubt whether the old colonial theory was in every circumstance ethically justifiable. The anti-British feeling which it aroused on the Continent, while startling us out of our splendid isolation, made us all the more appreciative of the moral encouragement and the material assistance which we had received from our kinsmen overseas. In the Empire itself the humiliation and obloquy to which the Mother Country was suddenly exposed created a new sense of affection and solidarity. In this stress of doubt and emotion—doubt regarding the validity of former assumptions, doubt regarding the future requirements of our island security: emotion aroused by the new sense of kinship, by external antagonism, by wounded pride—the conception was slowly engendered of a British family of independent but like-minded nations, compacted together, not by any institutional or administrative machinery, but by the powerful ligaments of mutual commercial and strategic interest, of common sentiment, and of joint allegiance to a single Sovereign. Thirty years of effort, and further shared ordeals, were needed before Mr Balfour's early vision found its full expression in the Statute of Westminster.

The significance of the Duke of York's journey in 1901 to Australia, New Zealand, Natal, Cape Colony, Canada and Newfoundland might be under-estimated were it not related to these still

PRINCE GEORGE WITH HIS MOTHER, 1879

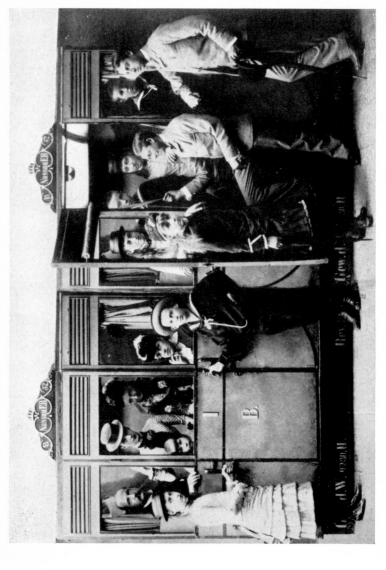

FAMILY GROUP PHOTOGRAPHED AT WIESBADEN

King George of Greece, Princess of Wales, Queen of Denmark, Queen of Greece, Prince George, Prince Eddy, with sisters and Greek cousins.

fluid transitions in the then Imperial Idea. In the Colonies the visit of the heir to the throne, coming as it did immediately after the shock occasioned by the death of Queen Victoria, identified as it was with the foundation of a great Commonwealth, did more than crystallise a transient emotion: it emphasised for these advancing peoples a new idea of Empire, founded upon a dual loyalty: loyalty in the first place to their own nation, and in the second place loyalty to the wide and powerful union between the mother-island and her now adult partners, as symbolised by a common dynasty and crown. The sentiment of solidarity was reinforced.

The Duke of York was not slow to comprehend these changed perspectives, this wider horizon. He had seen governments functioning, cabinets in office, which were composed of men of humble origins and simple education. In New Zealand he had witnessed a Welfare State in being, in which there was no poor law, in which women had been accorded the franchise, in which there was a graduated income-tax and a progressive system of social security, including old age pensions. Yet New Zealand remained for him one of the happiest memories in all his travels and the burly figure of Mr Seddon seemed to him the embodiment of practical patriotism and solid sense. His conception of democratic Monarchy as an institution, detached from politics or parties, which stood in a special and direct relation to the peoples themselves, was both widened and reinforced. He came to realise and to remember that the Empire, so far from being an assortment of geographical areas, was an association of free and rapidly expanding communities, composed of men and women of vigorous, progressive and independent minds, who were proud of both their own past and future and the shared miracle that so small an island should have engendered four young nations, set in the oceans of the world.

In the speech which, on December 5, he delivered at the Guildhall, he sought, within the conventional limits imposed upon him, to give some expression to these new ideas. He spoke with emotion of the astonishing welcome which he had received in every one of the Colonies and of the loyalty to the Mother Country of which it had been an expression. 'I appeal', he said, 'to my fellow countrymen at home to prove the strength of the attachment of the Motherland to her children by sending to them of her best.' And he concluded with the warning that, even from the commercial point of view, it was unwise to perpetuate the old lethargic habit of taking the British Empire for granted. 'I venture', he said, 'to allude to the impression

73

which seemed generally to prevail among our brethren overseas, that the Old Country must wake up if she intends to maintain her old position of pre-eminence in her Colonial trade against foreign competitors.'

This latter statement attracted much notice in the Press. The speech was much applauded and given prominence in the more popular newspapers under the headline 'Wake up England!'

The Duke in his diary refers to this speech, which had in fact for the first time brought his personality before the British public, in terms of habitual modesty:

December 5th. 'I made a long speech all about the Colonies and our memorable tour, which took 28 minutes. . . . It was a very interesting luncheon & worthy of the important occasion.'

December 6th. 'Read to May all the leading articles in the newspapers on my speech; they are very civil. . . . We received Count Metternich, the new German Ambassador.'

CHAPTER VI

PRINCE OF WALES

1901–1906

Created Prince of Wales November 9, 1901—His projected visit to Berlin
—Failure of previous attempts to reach an understanding with Germany—The Reichstag attacks on the British Army—King Edward
decides to cancel the projected visit—His letter to the German
Emperor—The visit is none the less arranged—The Prince's conversation with Prince Bülow—The origins of the Entente with France
—End of the South African War—The Coronation postponed owing
to the King's illness—The Prince's official duties—His access to
Government papers—The Dogger Bank incident—The Prince's visit
to India and Burma—Lord Curzon—The Prince's impressions of
India—His Guildhall speech.

(1)

ON November 9, 1901, King Edward, in celebration of his own
sixtieth birthday, created his son Prince of Wales:

'My dearest Georgy,' he wrote.[a] 'In making you today "Prince of
Wales and Earl of Chester" I am not only conferring on you ancient
titles which I have borne upwards of 59 years, but I wish to mark my
appreciation of the admirable manner in which you carried out the
arduous duties in the Colonies which I entrusted you with. I have but
little doubts that they will bear good fruit in the future & knit the
Colonies more than ever to the Mother Country.

'God bless you, my dear boy, & I know I can always count on your
support and assistance in the heavy duties and responsible position I
now occupy.

'Ever your devoted Papa,
'Edward R.I.'

The Prince and Princess of Wales continued to occupy York
House and did not move to Marlborough House until April 1903.
The King tried to persuade them to take over Osborne as their
country residence; the Prince was unwilling to abandon York Cottage
and Osborne was eventually transferred to the Government as a
naval college.[1]

---

[1] The Prince of Wales's household as then constituted was as follows:
Lords of the Bedchamber: Lord Wenlock and Lord Chesham. Comptroller
and Treasurer: Sir William Carington. Private Secretary: Sir Arthur
Bigge. Master of the Stables: Mr William Wentworth-Fitzwilliam.

It had been arranged that the Prince of Wales should visit Berlin on January 27, 1902, in order to congratulate the German Emperor on his forty-third birthday. The relations between England and Germany, which had once been so amicable, had by then entered upon a period of increasing strain. So long ago as November 1899, Mr Joseph Chamberlain, in a speech at Leicester, had openly advocated an alliance with Germany. Prince Bülow, the German Chancellor, had replied to this overture by stating in the Reichstag that 'the days of Germany's political and economic humility were over' and by coining the dangerous teutonic phrase: 'In the coming century, the German people will be either the hammer or the anvil.' This rebuff was followed by a decision which was bound in the end to destroy all hope of Anglo-German amity. The German Navy Bill of 1900 doubled the 1898 programme and for the first time in history created a German High Seas Fleet.

The British Government, in their desire to nip the bud of naval rivalry, decided to make a further gesture of appeasement. Profiting by the friendly impression made by the Emperor's attendance at Queen Victoria's deathbed and funeral, they suggested that formal negotiations should be opened, if not for an alliance, then at least for a settlement of all outstanding disputes. It was clearly intimated that if these renewed advances were rejected, Great Britain, who could no longer indulge in the luxury of isolation, would be forced to draw nearer to France and perhaps even to Russia. The German Government preferred to play for time. Prince Bülow, as he himself admitted,[b] was obsessed by Bismarck's dictum that Germany should never conclude any alliance in which she was not herself the dominating partner; he felt that it would be dangerous to enter into any understanding with Great Britain unless and until Germany herself possessed a powerful High Seas Fleet. Freiherr von Holstein (whose insane stratagems and obsessions proved so disastrous to German policy) was convinced that in no circumstances could Great Britain ever achieve an accommodation with France, still less with Russia. He described the British intimation as *vollständiger Schwindel* or 'utter humbug'.[c] The negotiations therefore produced no result.

On October 25, 1901, Mr Joseph Chamberlain delivered another

Equerries in Ordinary: Sir Charles Cust, Mr Derek Keppel, Lord Crichton, Commander Bryan Godfrey-Faussett. Extra Equerries: Captain Rosslyn Wemyss and Major Bor. Domestic Chaplain: Canon Dalton. At the same date Mr Henry Hansell, a Norfolk man from Magdalen College, Oxford, was appointed tutor to the young Princes.

speech, this time at Edinburgh, in which he made an incidental but tactless reference to the behaviour of the German Army in the 1870 war. This led to a renewed outburst of anti-British feeling in the German press and parliament. On January 5, 1902, Mr Chamberlain (whose utterances appear invariably to have grated upon German nerves) made a perfectly harmless speech in which he made no mention of Germany at all; the Emperor interpreted this reticence as implying that the British Government regarded Germany as a 'negligible quantity'. In replying therefore to the budget debate in the Reichstag on January 8, 1902 (scarcely a fortnight before the Prince of Wales was due to leave on his goodwill mission to Berlin), Prince Bülow took occasion to reprove Mr Chamberlain for his two speeches. He accused the British Colonial Secretary of possessing a 'crooked mind' and applied to him a phrase of Frederick the Great: 'Leave the man alone: he is biting granite.' Other speeches delivered in the Reichstag on that occasion were less temperate. Some bitter things were said, notably by the right-wing deputy Herr von Lieber-mann, about the behaviour of the British Army in South Africa. King Edward was incensed by these attacks and decided that the Prince's visit must be cancelled. On January 15 he wrote to the German Emperor as follows:[d]

'In sending my son George to Berlin to spend the anniversary of your birthday with you, I intended it as a personal mark of affection & friendship towards you, but I must confess since reading the violent speeches which have been made quite recently in the Reichstag against England, & especially against my Colonial Minister & my Army, which shows [*sic*] such a strong feeling of animosity against my Country, I think that under the circumstances it would be better for him not to go where he is liable to be insulted, or to be treated by the Public in a manner which I feel sure no one would regret more than yourself. It is very painful for me to write this, but I feel I have no other alternative.'

Lord Salisbury and his Foreign Secretary, Lord Lansdowne, were afraid that this letter would cause offence and lead to an overt and resounding breach; they would have preferred it if the Prince of Wales could have been stricken with a sudden diplomatic illness. Fortunately the German Emperor decided to ignore the letter, pretending that it had been 'mislaid'. The King was then persuaded to reconsider his former decision and to allow his son to go to Berlin.

On his arrival in the German capital, the Prince displayed initiative and tact. He did not fully share the prejudices harboured by his parents against the Emperor William, nor did the latter, in the presence of his young cousin, experience those bouts of nervous self-assertiveness which his royal uncle was apt to induce. At the *Bierabend* which followed the banquet in the *Weisse Saal*, the Prince of Wales went across to Prince Bülow, shook him warmly by the hand, and invited a frank discussion. The German Chancellor has recorded' that the Prince on this occasion struck him as 'clear-headed, sensible and manly' and that His Royal Highness listened attentively to a long 'politico-historical' discourse upon Anglo-German relations. At the conclusion of this lecture, the Prince assured the Chancellor that King Edward was as anxious as ever to maintain friendly relations between England and Germany. 'He only asks you', the Prince said, 'to avoid recriminations regarding the past and to see that the family letters written in connection with my visit here for the Kaiser's, my cousin's, birthday celebrations are not made public. We must forget the past and strive only to be friends in the future.'

The *Memoirs* of Prince Bülow, entrancing though they are, cannot always be taken as historical evidence. The Prince of Wales left no record of this important conversation. 'Had a long talk with Bülow' is all that he entered in his diary and such accounts of the interview as he may have given to the King and Lord Lansdowne on his return were not committed to writing. Yet it is evident that the Prince's refreshing friendliness on that occasion enabled the Emperor to forget his rancour for a while; to recall the happier affections of his boyhood days at Osborne or Windsor, those memories which were entwined in his emotional nature and formed a recurrent theme in his ambivalent feelings towards his mother's country.

At the conclusion of the Prince of Wales's visit, the Emperor addressed to King Edward a telegram which was amicable and sincere:

> 'Georgy left this morning for Strelitz all safe and sound and we were very sorry to have to part so soon from such a merry and genial guest. I think he has amused himself well here. Once more, best thanks for his visit.'

Something far more, however, than geniality and merriment would have been required to induce the German Government at that date either to come to a general settlement with England or to abandon their programme of naval construction. Great Britain thenceforward was obliged to adopt a different course.

Already in January 1901, Monsieur Paul Cambon, the French Ambassador in London, had tentatively suggested to Lord Lansdowne that some discussion might take place regarding French and British interests in Morocco. After the harsh rebuff given to our overtures to Germany this suggestion was revived. It was then proposed that the scope of the discussion might be enlarged to include not Morocco merely but other areas of Franco-British friction, such as Egypt, Siam, colonial frontiers in West Africa and even the Newfoundland fisheries. In February 1902, a few days only after the Prince of Wales's return from Berlin, Monsieur Cambon, after further conversations with Lord Lansdowne, addressed to the latter a private Note in which the heads of possible agreement were enumerated in detail:

> 'Next evening', Monsieur Cambon recalled many years later,¹ 'there was a big dinner at Buckingham Palace. I was placed next to King Edward who said: "Lansdowne has shown me your letter. It is excellent. We must go on. I have told the Prince of Wales about it. You can discuss it also with him."
>
> 'After dinner, the Prince of Wales, now King George, spoke to me eagerly of the letter and said: "What a good thing it would be if we could have a general agreement!" He wanted to know when it would be concluded. I told him that we could not go quite so fast as he might wish, but that with patience and goodwill it ought to be possible.'

In the spring of 1903 King Edward paid his famous visit to Paris, which was returned the following July by President Loubet and Monsieur Delcassé. By these conversations and courtesies the foundations of the Franco-British Entente were laid: but, as Monsieur Cambon had foreseen, the final agreement was not concluded until April 8, 1904.

It may be doubted whether the Prince of Wales's interest in foreign policy was at that date either so ardent or so well-informed as the French Ambassador appears to have assumed. He did not possess the cosmopolitan tastes of his father, and throughout his life he remained more closely concerned with national than with international affairs. His preoccupation with diplomacy had hitherto been confined to the uncongenial task of understanding and answering the incessant, and often querulous, letters addressed to him by his cousin, Prince George of Greece, on the affairs of Crete.¹ The

¹ The island of Crete had been in Turkish occupation since the expulsion of the Venetians in 1715. In 1878, the Powers, by the 'Pact of Halepa', obliged the Sultan to grant local autonomy under Ottoman sovereignty. The 'Pact of Halepa' was not always observed by the Sultan, and was bitterly resented by the Christian inhabitants, who desired union with Greece. Insurrections broke out in 1896 and in 1897 a Greek force

tribulations of the Greek Royal Family remained a worry to him all his life.

(2)

On May 31, 1902, peace was signed at Vereeniging and the South African war came to an end. The Coronation of King Edward had been fixed for June 26, but on June 14, while staying at the Royal Pavilion at Aldershot, the King was taken suddenly ill. He was removed to Windsor and by June 23 was well enough to travel to London. By that date the preparations for the coming Coronation had been almost completed; stands had been erected in the streets, which were already gay with garlands and Venetian masts; the prelates and Court dignitaries had held their final rehearsals in the Abbey; the first batch of foreign royalties had begun to arrive. On the afternoon of June 23 the King's symptoms returned:

> 'I don't think him at all well,' the Prince of Wales wrote, 'he suffers pain & we are getting in despair. . . . Had a long talk with Motherdear & Laking about dear Papa, who I fear is worse tonight & we are very anxious about him.' [1]

An operation for appendicitis was performed by Sir Frederick Treves on the afternoon of June 24. It was completely successful. 'I found him', wrote the Prince, on June 25, 'smoking a cigar & reading a paper. The doctors & the nurses say they never saw such a wonderful man.' By June 28 the King was declared out of danger, but meanwhile the duty of entertaining and soothing the visiting royalties and of performing such public functions as could not be cancelled had devolved upon the Prince and Princess of Wales.

landed near Canea and proclaimed the annexation of Crete to Greece. The Powers then intervened and occupied the island. By November 1898, all Turkish troops had been withdrawn and the Powers nominated Prince George of Greece, younger son of the King of the Hellenes, as High Commissioner. His position was unenviable, since he had to cope with the Moslem minority, the tutelage of the Great Powers as represented by their Admirals and Consuls-General, and an insurrectionary movement, eventually headed by Venizelos, for union with Greece. After long, arduous and quite meritorious service as High Commissioner, Prince George left the island in 1906 and was succeeded by Monsieur Zaimis. Crete was finally incorporated in Greece by the Treaty of London of 1913.

[1] Sir Francis Laking had been Physician in Ordinary to the Royal Family for many years and had attended the Duke of Clarence during his final illness. He was knighted in 1893 and made a baronet in 1902. He died in May 1914. His son, Sir Guy Laking, became Keeper of the King's Armoury and later Keeper of the London Museum.

Great public disappointment and inconvenience were caused by this last-hour postponement of the Coronation; inevitably the most pessimistic rumours spread in whispers round the world.

King Edward, however, made a rapid recovery. The Coronation, although in a curtailed form, was solemnised on August 9. It was followed by a Naval Review at Spithead. 'It was a magnificent sight,' the Prince commented, '& made me feel proud of being a sailor & an Englishman.' On the following day, August 17, Lord Kitchener introduced the Boer generals to King Edward on board the *Victoria and Albert*:

'Lord K. brought the three Boer Generals, Louis Botha, De Wet, & De la Rey, to see Papa. I was present during the interview & also shook hands with them. . . . They are fine looking men & were most civil; it was an interesting occasion.'

This audience was in truth a fitting sequel to a peace which had been honourable to both sides and an auspicious prelude to the great work of pacification, conciliation and union which Sir Alfred Milner and his young men were about to inaugurate.

The three years which intervened between the Coronation and the Prince of Wales's visit to India in October 1905, were crowded with public and representative duties. He succeeded his father as Vice-Chancellor of the University of Wales, he was elected Master of Trinity House, he was a Trustee of the British and the Natural History Museums. In May of 1903 he was invited by the Prime Minister to serve on a Royal Commission to consider food and other imports in time of war. The deliberations of this Commission, at which he was a regular attendant, lasted for two years.

In April 1904, he and the Princess paid a state visit to the Emperor Francis Joseph of Austria, and were received at Vienna with august solemnity. The protocol laid down for their reception has been preserved and reads to-day like the ceremonial ordinances of a vanished world:

'At the Bellaria: The First Grand Master of the Household and the Grand Master of the Ceremonies.
'At the Black Eagle Staircase on the First Floor: The illustrious Archduchesses, who will have been awaiting the announcement of Their Royal Highnesses' arrival in the Alexander Apartments.
'In the Pietra Dura Chamber: The Minister of the Household and the Minister for Foreign Affairs. The Marshal of the Court for Hungary and the remainder of the suites.'

On the day following their arrival the Prince and Princess were offered a 'family dinner' at the intolerable hour of 5 p.m. The officers were to be in full dress and the servants *en campagne*. This was followed at 8.30 p.m. by a Court Ball in the Hall of Ceremonies. The royal guests and the diplomatic body were to enter by the Bellaria, the other guests by the Ambassadors Staircase. The royal guests were to assemble in the Gobelins Saloon, their suites in the Rich Bedchamber, the other guests in the Hall of Ceremonies. Card tables were to be placed in the Radetzky apartments, and supper to be served in the large and small Masquerade Halls. The formal *cercle* would take place in the large hall of the Palace Library. 'My goodness!' the Prince sighed in his diary that evening, 'this Court is stiff!'

In the same month he went to Stuttgart to invest the King of Würtemberg with the Order of the Garter. In the intervals his time was fully occupied in visiting provincial cities, conferring and receiving degrees, opening docks, bridges, and hospitals, or receiving and entertaining foreign royalties and visitors of distinction. At one moment he accepted, at Mr Balfour's suggestion, the title of Lord Warden of the Cinque Ports, but thereafter resigned when he discovered that he was expected by the Courts of Brotherhood and Guestling to convene the Court of Shipway, to take the 'serement' and to preside over the Dover Harbour Board. As a relaxation from these multifarious duties, he was glad from time to time to escape to York Cottage and to the familiar coverts of 'Commodore' and 'Little Massingham'.

During his journeys to Australia and Canada he had found that he was hampered in his conversations with Dominion statesmen by lack of official information regarding government policy. Sir Arthur Bigge had been instructed to approach Sir Francis Knollys:

'I quite agree with you', the latter replied on August 20, 1901,⁹ 'that history repeats itself. The Duke of Cornwall will occasionally complain of the King for not telling him things, just as the latter complained of the Queen, and as without doubt little Prince Edward will complain in time to come of the Duke. It has been the same thing with Heirs Apparent (and generally they have had right on their side) from time immemorial and will I fear continue to be so as long as there are Monarchies.'

Sir Francis Knollys need have had no such apprehensions. King Edward had not forgotten the disadvantage from which for many years he had himself suffered in being denied access to official papers. He gave early instructions that the Prince of Wales should be shown any foreign dispatches of major importance. From 1903 onwards the Prince was also sent the daily telegram sections from the Foreign

Office and there are many references thereafter to the 'red boxes' which accumulated on his desk. He was thus able to follow, with inside information, the intricate diplomatic situation which arose in February 1904, when Great Britain's ally, Japan, declared war on France's ally, Russia. The danger of so ambiguous a position was emphasised when, on October 21, 1904, the Russian Baltic Fleet under Admiral Rozhestvensky opened fire near the Dogger Bank upon some fishing craft from Hull. The Prince was shocked by this incident:

'I was indeed thunderstruck', he wrote to the King on October 25, 'when I opened the papers yesterday morning & read the account of this outrage committed by the Russian Baltic Fleet firing on a harmless fishing fleet in the North Sea in the middle of the night. It seems impossible that individuals who call themselves sailors should do such a thing. . . . If they imagined they were Japanese destroyers, all I can say is they must have been drunk or else their nerves must be in such a state that they are not fit to go to sea in Men of War.'

The Prince of Wales's reaction to this incident, as so many of his reactions, reflected immediately and precisely the thoughts and feelings of the ordinary British citizen. Lord Lansdowne on the other hand felt that a nautical error—which, however unpardonable, was certainly not intentional—should not be allowed to involve the danger of war. The dispute was referred to arbitration, the Russian Government agreed to pay damages and public indignation was gradually allayed. A crisis by which the Entente might have been shattered from its inception was thereby averted.

(3)

It had been decided that the Prince and Princess of Wales should visit India and Burma during the winter of 1905–1906. The occasion was not in every respect auspicious. The partition of Bengal,[1] which had been carried into effect in the previous October, had created

---

[1] Lord Curzon, as Viceroy, had for long considered that the Province of Bengal was too large for administrative efficiency. His original idea had been to detach a few districts only from Eastern Bengal and to assign them to Assam. During the course of 1904 and 1905 this idea assumed far larger proportions and the eventual scheme, as put into operation in October 1905, detached from Bengal an area of 106,000 square miles, containing a population of eighteen million Moslems and twelve million Hindus.

This action, which was exploited by the Congress Party as an attack upon Bengali nationalism, caused great indignation in India, which added to the bitterness and disappointments of Lord Curzon's last months as Viceroy.

considerable indignation; and official circles were still riven by the conflict between the civilians and the military, between Lord Curzon and Lord Kitchener, which in the late summer had culminated in the Viceroy's resignation.[1]

Lord Curzon, with his exuberant zest for detail, had devoted the surplus of his astonishing energy to arranging in advance every particular of the royal tour. He was mortified by the fact that the reception and entertainment of the Prince and Princess must now devolve upon his successor, Lord Minto. On August 23, 1905, he wrote to King Edward[ʌ] saying that one of his many regrets at 'this enforced resignation—which the Viceroy consistently with self-respect could not escape'—was that it would preclude him from personally conducting the royal tour to a successful issue:

> 'I am truly grieved', he wrote to the Prince of Wales on the same day, 'that I shall not after all have the honour of being responsible for the entertainment of Your Royal Highness while in India. Circumstances or persons—whichever it may be—have been too strong for me and I have had no alternative but to resign. . . . I own I shall feel rather bitterly when I think of someone else doing the honours of Government House at Calcutta.'

King Edward, with his ready sympathy for personal misfortunes, suggested that it would be fitting if the retiring Viceroy were to receive the Prince and Princess upon their arrival at Bombay. This faced the officials with an intricate predicament, which was resolved

[1] The controversy between Lord Curzon and Lord Kitchener lies outside the scope of this biography. On his arrival in India, Lord Kitchener had insisted that the Military Member of the Viceroy's Council should be subordinate to the Commander-in-Chief. Lord Curzon, backed by the civilian members of the Council, desired to maintain the old system of dual control, being unwilling to place so much power in the sole hands of the Commander-in-Chief. Lord Kitchener, finding himself in a minority of one, threatened to resign. The Cabinet in London, realising that the resignation of Lord Kitchener would have a deplorable effect on public opinion, imposed, in a decision of May 31, 1905, a compromise solution under which the Military Member of the Council was to be relegated to being head of the department of supply. Lord Curzon, in personal consultation with Lord Kitchener, induced the latter to accept some modifications of this compromise. Peace appeared to have been restored, when the India Office appointed the new 'Supply Member' without consulting the Viceroy. Incensed by this affront, Lord Curzon, on August 22, 1905, resigned. To the end of his life he remained convinced that the Cabinet, and especially his old friend Mr St John Brodrick, Secretary of State for India, had treated him shamefully. After seven years as Viceroy he returned to England an angry and embittered man.

without much delicacy of feeling. Mr St John Brodrick, the Secretary of State for India, suggested that, after Lord Minto's arrival, Lord Curzon should hang on for a few days at Bombay and be received by the Prince 'as a private individual'. Sir Walter Lawrence, who had been attached to the Prince as Chief of the Staff,[1] and who had for five years been Lord Curzon's Private Secretary, feared that this arrangement might prove humiliating. He was, he informed Lord Knollys,' 'anxious to avoid, what I rather dread, the public break-down of Lord Curzon. He is ill, and sometimes cannot control his feelings and a scene might be very painful to Their Royal Highnesses and cast a gloom over their arrival.' In the end Lord Minto agreed to postpone his departure from England and it was Lord Curzon who greeted the Prince and Princess on their arrival at Bombay. When Lord and Lady Minto did eventually reach Bombay, they landed after nightfall and were thereafter whisked off to Calcutta without the customary formalities of reception.

The Prince and Princess of Wales left London on October 19, embarked at Genoa in H.M.S. *Renown* and reached Bombay on November 9. It is not intended to recount in any detail the events of that six months' journey[2] or to describe a succession of durbars and reviews, of tiger shoots and elephant hunts, of dusty plains and hot illuminated cities, of emeralds and howdahs, of opulence and squalor. The Prince met many of the more favoured among the Indian Rajahs and had long discussions with the British officials, both military and civilian. At Agra he was pleased to receive the four

---

[1] The Prince was fortunate in obtaining the services of Sir Walter Lawrence. Sir Walter, who was a Balliol man and had had long experience of Indian administration, possessed a wide knowledge of Indian problems and a deep sympathy for the Indian peoples. Apart from the usual members of his household the Prince was accompanied by Sir Pertab Singh as extra A.D.C. Captain Clive Wigram of the Indian Army, who was also attached to the staff, remained on in the Prince's service and eventually succeeded Lord Stamfordham as his Chief Private Secretary. The Prince's former valet, Agar, had retired from ill health and had been succeeded by the devoted Howlett, who remained his personal attendant till the end.

[2] Their itinerary was as follows: Bombay, Indore, Jaipur, Lahore, Peshawar, Jammu, Delhi, Agra, Gwalior, Lucknow, Calcutta, Rangoon, Mandalay, Madras, Bangalore, Mysore, Hyderabad, Benares, Gwalior again, Quetta, Karachi. They left India on March 19, 1906, and after a short visit to Athens for the Olympic games, reached London on May 8, 1906. A full account of the journey is given in Sir Stanley Reed's *The Royal Tour in India*.

former Indian attendants of Queen Victoria who were then living in honourable retirement. He also accepted a visit from 'the Munshi', Abdul Karim, whose influence over Queen Victoria during the last years of her reign had not been approved of by the Royal Family:

'He has', the Prince wrote to his father, 'not grown more beautiful & is getting fat. I must say he was most civil & humble & really pleased to see us. . . . I am told he lives quite quietly (at "Karim Lodge") & gives no trouble at all.'

Towards the end of his tour he had a conversation with Gopal Gokhale, at that time President of the Indian Congress Party:

'I have', the Prince said to him, 'been reading your speech at Benares, in which you said it would be better for India if the Indians had a much larger part in the administration. I have now been travelling for some months in India, seeing vast crowds of Indians in many parts of the continent, and I have never seen a happier-looking people, and I understand the look in the eyes of the Indians. Would the peoples of India be happier if you ran the country?' Mr Gokhale replied: 'No Sir, I do not say they would be happier, but they would have more self-respect.' 'That may be,' the Prince answered, 'but I cannot see how there can be real self-respect while the Indians treat their women as they do now.' 'Yes,' said Mr Gokhale, 'that is a great blot.'*j*

How could the Prince, encompassed as he was by barriers of officials and detectives, hope to penetrate to what Mr Abbott, one of the accompanying journalists, described as 'the shameless abandon, the ineffable filth and sickening misery' which lay below?*k* In the dust before his feet some Maharajah would lay his scimitar encrusted with diamonds and rubies: such gestures were a formal act of homage to the son of the King-Emperor. 'I understand', the Prince had said to Gokhale, 'the look in the eyes of the Indians.' What did that look portend? Were the crowds who thronged to watch him pass animated by no more than an expectation of largesse, a sense of festival, or the awed excitement aroused by so sumptuous a panoply? Or did the myriad masses of India see in him the almost magic symbol of a higher justice, the emissary of a Great Protector, omnipotent but unseen?

The Prince, for all his common sense and realism, was not impervious to the mystery of Monarchy, to the divine responsibilities of kings. He was confirmed during this Indian visit in a belief, which as has already been suggested hung unformulated for ever at the back of his mind, that there existed some almost mystical association between the Sovereign and the common people. When he used the expression 'loyalty' he was not using a word which to him was trite. He was specially satisfied by his visit to Calcutta:

'I must say', he wrote to the King on January 8, 1906, 'that although we had very hard work, our stay in Calcutta was a great success politically. Our visit too was most opportune, as the feeling was very strong against the Government owing to the partition of Bengal & it made them think of something else & the Bengalis certainly showed their loyalty to the Throne in a most unmistakeable manner.'

(4)

It is not surprising that, in this atmosphere of general jubilation, he should have under-estimated the strength of the Congress Party or the immense influence which, under the inspired leadership of Mohandas Gandhi, the movement for non-cooperation and passive resistance would thereafter acquire. Were not the Rajahs who entertained him and the officials by whom he was surrounded convinced that the progress of Indian nationalism could, by wise policy and incidental concessions, be diverted or allayed? Typical of the information and advice which he was given, typical even of the opinion held by many enlightened administrators at the time, is a letter addressed to him after his return by the Viceroy, Lord Minto:[1]

'I cannot but feel', Lord Minto wrote, 'that we are at the commencement of a great change in India. Better means of communication are making it easier for the Indian official to run home for a holiday and he may consequently gradually lose that touch with the native population which used to exist in the old days, whilst, as Your Royal Highness is well aware, the political influence of the "Congress" is making itself more and more felt. At present, if things were left alone here, I do not think the Congress movement is much to be feared; the danger exists at home, when a few Members of Parliament, with a very doubtful Indian connection, manage to keep the pot of disaffection boiling, and to disseminate entirely false views upon the position of affairs in India. A Bengali agitation, in India, carries no weight and little meaning. In England there is the danger that the British public may assume it to be representative of what people at home take to be the people of India, in utter ignorance of the fact that the population of India is a conglomeration of races, the majority of whom would not put up with Bengal supremacy for five minutes. If British influence were withdrawn tomorrow, what would become of Bengali ideas and all the Bengali eloquence which has lately played so large a part? At the same time I am sure it is wise to listen to and be good friends with Bengali leaders. I like Gokhale and believe him to be honest, but I am sure no one knows better than your Royal Highness that it would take countless Gokhales to rule the Punjab and the North West Frontier Province, to say nothing of the East of India.'

These opinions were shared, in the year 1906, not merely by the more old-fashioned civil servants, but also by many, such as Sir Walter Lawrence, who held progressive views. It is evident none the less that the Prince of Wales had come to realise during his few months in India that the climate of opinion was changing and that it would no longer be possible to proceed upon the facile assumptions of Lord Dufferin's days.

There exist in the Royal Archives at Windsor some notes in the Prince's handwriting[m], in which he summarised his impressions. He recognised the increasing influence of the Congress Party and the effect which their gifts of misrepresentation was bound in the end to produce upon the ignorant masses. 'Naturally,' he wrote, 'this is much too big a question for me to go into.' He felt none the less that the attitude adopted by the English towards the Indians ought to be altered and improved:

> 'No doubt', he wrote, 'the Natives are better treated by us than in the past, but I could not help being struck by the way in which all salutations by the Natives were disregarded by the persons to whom they were given. Evidently we are too much inclined to look upon them as a conquered & down-trodden race & the Native, who is becoming more and more educated, realizes this. I could not help noticing that the general bearing of the European towards the Native was to say the least unsympathetic. In fact not the same as that of superiors to inferiors at home.'

He returned convinced that the Indian Civil Servants, from the Viceroy downwards, were demonstrably over-worked and that their numbers and conditions of service should be increased and ameliorated. He deplored the friction between the military and civilian branches of the administration:

> 'The Civilian regards the Soldier as an inferior being & says he governs the country. But where would he be without the soldier? I think this feeling has certainly increased since Lord Curzon's viceroyalty, as his actions never showed sympathy with the Army.'

He was particularly concerned with the attitude adopted by the Government to the native princes. He realised that the word 'native' was an offensive term and one which should be discarded from the vocabulary:

> 'The Ruling Chiefs', he wrote, 'ought to be treated with greater tact & sympathy, more as equals than inferiors. . . . They should no longer be treated as school boys, but even consulted by the Govt. on matters which concern their States individually or as a whole. Why not a Council of all the Chiefs, presided over by the Viceroy, which would

bring them together and enable them to know each other's views? Most important that the Resident or Political Officer should remain as long as possible, so that he can become the personal friend of the Chief & thereby have influence over him.'

Under the guidance of Lord Kitchener (for whom he had a warm personal affection and whom he deeply admired as 'a strong man & a soldier') the Prince had devoted much attention to the Indian Army. In a long private letter which he addressed to the Commander-in Chief before his departure he urged him to pay special attention to the relations between the Indian regiments and their British officers and above all to take steps to improve the conditions of pay and service of the Indian private soldier.

In the speech which on his return to London he made at the Guildhall on May 17, 1906, the Prince endeavoured, as tactfully as possible, to convey some of the impressions he had received and the ideas which he had formulated. He appealed for 'a wider sympathy' on the part of the British administrators. Mr John Morley, who had by then succeeded Mr St John Brodrick as Secretary of State for India, and to whom he submitted the text of his speech in advance, was strongly in favour of this appeal:

'I have thought', he wrote to the Prince on May 14, 'most carefully as to the words "wider sympathy" and I am bound to express my clear opinion that it will be a great pity if they are altered by a single letter. They will have an admirable effect in every quarter and among all classes in India. I regard them as a splendid watchword and I for one shall consider such a watchword a real service to good government.'

Undoubtedly this visit to India and Burma created an effect. The letters which he received on his return have a ring of more than conventional congratulation. The Viceroy assured him that the visit had done 'untold good'. Lord Kitchener could not speak too highly of the impression which the Prince's overt sympathy and solicitude had created in all ranks of the Indian Army, and the Secretary of State expressed the view that 'no piece of national duty was ever more admirably performed'.

The Prince of Wales never forgot the impression made upon him by 'this wonderful and fascinating country'. India thereafter was no mere name to him, but a word alive with many shining associations.

CHAPTER VII

TRANSITION

1906–1910

Mr A. J. Balfour and the problems of the Conservative Party—The 1902 Education Act—Chinese Labour—Ireland and Mr George Wyndham—Tariffs and Free Trade—Mr Balfour resigns and Sir Henry Campbell-Bannerman becomes Prime Minister—Composition of the new Liberal Government—The General Election of 1906—Views of King Edward and the Prince of Wales—The Prince on his return from India resumes his duties—The wedding of King Alfonso and Princess Ena—The Prince of Wales's interest in questions of Home Defence—His relations with King Edward—His visits to Germany and Paris—His mission to Canada—Difficulties of the Liberal Government—The Birrell Education Bill—The Licensing Bill—The Irish Councils Bill—The *Dreadnought* controversy—The situation abroad—Germany's attempts to divide France and England—Mr Lloyd George—His 1909 Budget—The conflict between the two Houses of Parliament—The Parliament Bill—Death of King Edward.

THE Prince of Wales returned from India on May 8, 1906, to find that during his absence the political situation in England had undergone a change. The Conservative, or Unionist, Party, after holding office for eleven years, had been severely defeated in the General Election of January and the control of policy had passed into the hands of the Liberals and their supporters of the left. This change proved deeper and more durable than the customary alternations of power between one party and the other. England was entering upon a period of transition. The age of unrest, which had lasted from 1760 to 1848, had been succeeded by half a century of comparative acquiescence; the General Election of 1906 marks the beginning of a new and prolonged period of national and international disquiet. The revolt of the internal and external proletariat had begun.

Mr Arthur Balfour, who in July 1902, succeeded Lord Salisbury as Conservative Prime Minister, had shown himself a dexterous rather than a compelling leader. His patrician temperament rendered him unsympathetic to the cruder men who were by then ousting the old territorial aristocracy from the control of the Conservative Party. His philosophic aloofness had induced in him the habit of mind, so dangerous in any politician, of being interested in both sides of a

90

case. It was not that he lacked the courage of his convictions: few statesmen have manifested such physical and moral audacity: it was rather that he classed convictions with deliberate forms of belief and much disliked all deliberate forms of belief. Moreover he was unlucky.

The Education Act of 1902 had aroused the Nonconformists to unreasonable but passive resistance and had greatly fortified the unity and the faith of the Liberals. A seemingly incidental ordinance passed by the Transvaal Legislative Council in 1903, providing for the introduction of 'unskilled non-European labourers', had profoundly shocked the conscience of the Liberal Party. The cry of 'Slavery' and 'Chinese Labour' echoed through the land. The resignation of the Irish Secretary, Mr George Wyndham, on the issue of 'devolution' convinced the experts that Mr Balfour had, owing to inattention, missed a unique occasion for a lasting Irish settlement; and suggested to those who did not pretend to understand the Irish problem that he had not displayed unshaken loyalty, consistency, or resolution. Yet these were but minor misfortunes compared with the dissension created within the Conservative Party by Mr Joseph Chamberlain's Tariff Reform League.

Mr Chamberlain had returned from a visit to South Africa in 1902 with the inspired conviction that England could no longer remain a small island isolated off the peninsula of Europe and must in some way federate with her Colonies overseas. He realised that before so difficult a political compact could be achieved it would be necessary (on the analogy of the unification of Germany), to adopt a *Zollverein* or customs union. In a speech which he delivered at Birmingham on May 15, 1903, he advocated a complete abandonment of the traditional policy of Free Trade. Colonial products should henceforward be given preference in the home market and Great Britain should place herself in the position to impose retaliatory duties against all foreign countries who erected tariff barriers against British goods. Mr Balfour, by adopting a detached attitude and by indulging only in the most Delphic utterances on the subject, was, for a few months at least, able to defer a rupture. In September 1903, matters came to a head. Mr Chamberlain resigned from the Cabinet because he was unable to obtain united support for his new policy; three of the Free Trade ministers also resigned because they could not induce Mr Balfour openly and finally to repudiate the heresy of Protection. Mr Chamberlain thereafter founded the Tariff Reform League and conducted a national campaign with vigour and

persistence until stricken down by illness in July 1906. Meanwhile
Mr Balfour was able, with remarkable agility, to keep his party and
his Cabinet together until the autumn of 1905. On November 21 of
that year Mr Chamberlain, who was becoming impatient, insisted
that the electoral platform of the by now rent Unionists should be a
full and unreserved programme of tariff reform. Mr Balfour, although the Conservatives still retained a majority in Parliament of
68,[1] thereupon handed to King Edward the resignation of his
Government without asking for a dissolution. On December 5, 1905,
the King sent for Sir Henry Campbell-Bannerman, the leader of the
Liberal Party, and invited him to form an administration.

The Liberal Cabinet of 1905 contained many of the most gifted,
and some of the most dynamic, personalities that have ever served
the State. Sir Henry Campbell-Bannerman, disregarding the advice
of his doctor, insisted upon assuming the dual function of Prime
Minister and Leader of the House. Mr Asquith became Chancellor
of the Exchequer. The post of Foreign Secretary was at first offered
to Lord Cromer and, on his refusal, given to Sir Edward Grey.
Lord Crewe became Lord President and Mr Herbert Gladstone
Home Secretary. Mr John Morley took the India Office and Mr
Haldane the War Office. Lord Tweedmouth became First Lord of
the Admiralty and Mr Augustine Birrell President of the Board of
Education. The post of Irish Secretary was assumed by Mr James
Bryce. Mr John Burns, who, although of working class origin, had
adhered to the Liberal Party, became President of the Local Govern-
ment Board. Mr Lloyd George (at that date known to the public
mainly as an audacious pro-Boer) received the Board of Trade.
Mr Winston Churchill became Parliamentary Under-Secretary for
the Colonies under Lord Elgin.

The members of this new Cabinet had not, during their long
years in opposition, manifested any subservient regard for the
traditional elements of the British Constitution. 'Certainly,' writes
Sir Sidney Lee[a] with characteristic avoidance of exaggeration, 'no

[1] The figures for the General Election of September 1900, known as
'The Khaki Election', are given by the Constitutional Year Book as
follows:

Conservatives	334	Liberals	185
Liberal Unionists	68	Irish	82
		Labour	1
	402		268

Unionist majority over all parties, 134.

distinctive respect for royalty coloured the creed of the party which now took office.' Mr John Burns, in the past, had been a formidable agitator, a founder of the Social Democratic Federation, a hero of the Trafalgar Square demonstration of February 8, 1886. And Mr Lloyd George was known to hold decided views regarding landlords in general and the House of Lords in particular. King Edward none the less, having a warm personal esteem for Sir Henry Campbell-Bannerman, remained unperturbed:

> 'It is certainly', he wrote to the Prince of Wales on December 15, 1905, 'a strong Government with considerable brain power. Let us only hope that they will work for the good of the country & indeed the Empire. Sir E. Grey will I hope follow in the footsteps of Lord Lansdowne in every respect. Lord Tweedmouth should make a good First Lord & takes the greatest interest in his appointment. Mr Haldane with sound common sense & great powers of organizing ought to make an excellent War Minister, which is much needed as his predecessor was hopeless."

This sensible appraisal of the qualities of the new Government crossed a letter written by the Prince to his father from Amritsar on December 11:

> 'I have just heard the names of the new Cabinet. Fancy John Burns being in it! He may do well, but he will require a lot of looking after. Winston Churchill, I see, is Under Secretary for the Colonies, Lord Elgin will have to look after him! Mr Haldane at the War Office will have his work cut out for him. I wonder whether he will produce some new scheme. Anyhow he is an able man & a great Imperialist & will not allow the Army to be cut down & will be very useful on the Defence Committee.'

On January 8, 1906, Parliament was dissolved. The General Election which followed was the most dramatic in English parliamentary history since the passage of the First Reform Bill. The Liberals and their allies gained a majority of 356 against the Conservatives.[1] As many as 53 Labour members were elected, of whom twenty-nine were sponsored by the Labour Representation Committee and were as such pledged to vote as an independent party.[2]

---

[1] The actual figures were: *Government*, Liberals 377, Irish Nationalists 83, Labour members 53; *Opposition*, Conservatives 132, Liberal Unionists 25. Thus the Liberals, even without the support of the Irish and Labour members, had a clear majority over all parties of 84.

[2] The first two avowed representatives of the working classes to be elected to Parliament were Alexander Macdonald and Thomas Burt who were returned in 1874. They did not constitute an independent group but were attached to the left wing of the Liberal Party. In 1892 two 'Inde-

The news reached the Prince of Wales while he was navigating the Irrawaddy River in the S.S. *Japan*:

'I see', he wrote to the King on January 20, 'that a great number of Labour members have been returned which is rather a dangerous sign, but I hope they are not all Socialists.'

Mr Balfour (who had himself been beaten in East Manchester, a seat he had held for twenty-one years) interpreted the Labour portent with even greater prescience.

'We have here to do with something more important than the swing of the pendulum or all the squabbles about Free Trade and Fiscal Reform. We are face to face (no doubt in a milder form) with the Socialist difficulties which loom so large on the Continent. Unless I am greatly mistaken the election of 1906 inaugurates a new era.'[b]

Mr Balfour was not greatly mistaken.

(2)

Undeterred by these first presages of silent revolution, the Prince of Wales on his return from India resumed his representative duties and the familiar round of public functions. In May of 1906 he represented the King at the wedding of his cousin, Princess Ena of Battenberg, to King Alfonso XIII of Spain. The coach in which, after the ceremony, he and the Princess of Wales drove from the church to the Royal Palace was last but three in the procession. It was followed by that bearing Princess Beatrice and Queen Cristina, mother of King Alfonso. Thereafter came the empty *coche de respeto*, and finally the state coach, surmounted by a golden crown and drawn by six befeathered horses, in which the bride and bridegroom were alone. The procession had reached almost the end of the Calle Mayor when a bomb was thrown from an upper window of No. 88 by the anarchist Mateo Morral. Spectators on the balconies and in the street below were killed or wounded by the explosion and Queen

pendent Labour' candidates (John Burns and Keir Hardie) were returned. Burns thereafter joined the Liberal party and Keir Hardie in 1893 started the 'Independent Labour Party' at Bradford. The Labour Party proper was inaugurated at a meeting held on February 27, 1900, in the Memorial Hall, Farringdon Street, when it was decided to establish 'a distinct Labour Group in Parliament with its own whips'. The Labour Representation Committee was at the same time constituted to organize the group.

Of the 53 Labour members elected in 1906, twenty-nine belonged to the Independent Labour Party and twenty-four were affiliated to the Liberal Party and known as 'Lib-Labs'.

Ena's wedding dress was slashed by flying glass and spattered with blood. The British Ambassador, Sir Maurice de Bunsen, who had paused to watch the procession from an adjoining house, together with members of his staff and officers of King Alfonso's British regiment, the 16th Lancers, were the first to reach the shattered coach and to help King Alfonso and his bride to alight. They then walked beside the *coche de respeto*, into which the King and Queen had been transferred, until it reached the courtyard of the palace. The Prince of Wales, on hearing the explosion, had assured the Princess that it was the first gun of an artillery salute. The King and Queen, on entering the palace, were too dazed to realise what had actually occurred. It was from the Ambassador that the Prince of Wales obtained the first coherent account.[c]

King Alfonso and Queen Ena quickly regained their composure and were able thereafter to take part in the functions which had been arranged. On the night of June 1 there was a gala banquet, followed by a reception which was attended by some five thousand guests:

> 'Very hot affair', the Prince wrote in his diary, '& tiring; much talking, bowing & clicking of spurs. . . . We walked through all the rooms, the heat . . . was awful & every window shut. Had some supper & walked back through the rooms; smell even worse. Got to bed at 12.0 mightily pleased.'

The Prince, although always prepared to perform efficiently any functions demanded of him, did not share his father's taste for ceremony. He preferred fresh air.

In the following month the Prince represented his father at a less inauspicious ceremony. He went to Norway to attend the Coronation at Trondhjem of his brother-in-law, the King of Norway.

During these, the last few years before his accession, the Prince of Wales became increasingly preoccupied with the problems of Imperial and Home defence. In the autumn of 1906 he had been perplexed by the decision of the Government to withdraw certain units from the Mediterranean and Atlantic squadrons for service with the newly created Home Fleet. His anxiety on this subject produced a long and characteristic letter from his former chief, Admiral Sir John Fisher, at that time First Sea Lord, urging the necessity of what he called an *escadre d'élite* to guard our coasts:[d]

> 'Our only possible enemy is Germany. Germany keeps her whole Fleet always concentrated within a few hours of England. We must therefore keep a Fleet twice as powerful within a few hours of Ger-

many. . . . The politicians and the diplomatists will not be the people the public will hang if the British Navy fails to annihilate the whole German Fleet and gobble up every single one of these 842 German merchant steamers now daily on the Ocean! NO!!—it will be the Sea Lords!! Admiral Bridgeman (about the best Admiral we have) is to be Commander in Chief of this new Home Fleet, with his headquarters at the Nore and his cruising ground the North Sea—*where the fight will be!!*—perhaps off Heligoland, which was won by the sword and given up by the pen.'

Although his interests and experience were predominantly naval, the Prince also took an active interest in Lord Roberts' plan for the provision of some territorial force for home defence in the event of invasion. He did not agree with the views of those who held that, so long as we retained the command of the seas, there could be no possible danger of any hostile landing upon our coasts:

'I do not', he wrote to Lord Roberts,*e* 'agree with the opinions expressed by those who belong to the "Blue-Water School" . . . Whether an invasion of England by Germany is possible or not must be greatly a matter of opinion, but in any case I feel as strongly as you do that it is an imperative duty that we should maintain an Army capable of successfully resisting any attack, whether in the form of a raid or a serious invasion.'

He would discuss such problems with the Cabinet Ministers and senior officers with whom he was now in frequent contact. Lord Esher, in a letter to King Edward of March 28, 1907,*f* describes a typical dinner party at the Marlborough Club, at which the Prince was invited to meet Mr Haldane, General Sir William Nicholson, General Douglas Haig, and Colonel Repington:

'What struck Lord Esher . . . was the sober and thoughtful manner in which the Prince expressed evidently carefully considered opinions. That men of that kind should be impressed is important and useful. There was no exaggeration of phrase or idea, but sound common sense, coupled with almost shrewd appreciation of the various problems, both naval and military. H.R.H. not only showed technical knowledge, but a power of clear exposition which astonished Mr Haldane.

'Viscount Esher feels sure that Your Majesty would have been proud and pleased to see the effect produced upon the Prince's hearers and to have heard their observations after H.R.H. had left.'

It was 'in truth an encouragement to King Edward in his declining years to realise that the Prince was taking so serious an interest in public affairs and developing a mature judgement. From time to time, from the wealth of his worldly wisdom, the King would impart, both orally and in writing, incidental items of sound practical advice. He exhorted his son to be regular in his attendance in the House of Lords and frequently to listen to debates in the House of Commons. He warned him, since the Scots were a proud and sensitive race, not to use the word 'English' when he meant 'British'. He advised him, when in Paris, to visit the Musée Carnavalet, but not the Infanta Eulalie.

The closing years of King Edward's reign, which are often represented as gay, opulent and garish, were in fact darkened by the gathering clouds of external menace and internal dissension. In the moods of despondency which would often afflict him the King would find comfort in the thought that his heir and successor possessed such solid virtues and so sound a head:

> Lord Esher, when writing to King George on the day of King Edward's funeral, recalled: 'the many occasions on which the King spoke to me of Your Majesty, and *always* with that peculiar look which he had— half smile, and half pathos—and that softening of the voice, when he spoke of those he loved. He used to say the words "my son" in quite a different tone from any which were familiar to me in the many tones of his voice.'[g]

It must be realised that King Edward, in the final phase, was a perplexed and apprehensive man.

(3)

The German Emperor's insatiable sensitiveness did not allow him to remain satisfied for long with the visit which the Prince of Wales had paid in 1902. He began to complain to the British Military attaché that the Prince seemed reluctant to come again to Berlin and to hint that his failure to visit the German regiment of which he had been appointed Colonel was causing comment and offence. These remarks were passed on to Lord Knollys by Sir Frank Lascelles, the British Ambassador in Berlin. The Prince showed resentment:

> 'What he says', he wrote to Lord Knollys,[h] 'about my reluctance to go to Berlin & that I have not yet paid a visit to my regiment, although I have already been Colonel of it for three years, is *bosh*. It is a pity that the Emperor should always go out of his way to find fault & make complaints. I had no wish whatever to become Col. of a German Regiment; that was forced upon me, & because I have not yet had an opportunity of seeing it, it is continually rammed down one's throat. Although I like Lascelles very much, I fear he has become too German in his ideas for my taste.'

None the less in March 1908 the Prince travelled obediently to Germany and inspected his regiment which was at the time stationed in Cologne. He was obliged to put on a German uniform and to address a few words of rudimentary German to the officers and men. As compensation for this uncongenial duty he allowed himself a few days in Paris on his return journey, staying at the Hotel Bristol. He lunched with President Fallières at the Elysée ('Food moderate & tepid') and had conversations with Monsieur Clemenceau and other French politicians. Mr Reginald Lister, at that time Counsellor of the British Embassy in Paris, and a man of many worlds, succeeded in persuading him to indulge in an uncharacteristic experiment and to sample the night life of Paris:

> 'Went to see "Occupe-toi d'Amélie" the hottest thing I have ever seen on the stage. Then to the Bal Tabarin & the Abbaye at Montmartre & other places. Bed at 3.30.'

In July of 1908 he paid a flying visit to Quebec in order to inaugurate the Plains of Abraham as a National Park. He was on this occasion unaccompanied by the Princess and travelled to Canada and back in H.M.S. *Indomitable*, a new high-powered cruiser, fitted with eight 12″ guns. His obvious enjoyment of the occasion, the immense trouble that he took to treat the French Canadians as estimable fellow-citizens, the sincere and sensible speeches which he delivered both in French and English, combined to create an unexpected effect:

> 'The Prince and people', wrote Lord Grey, the Governor-General, to the King on July 31, 1908,⁴ 'have been delighted with each other and have enthused each other. The Prince of Wales has taught the people of Quebec how to cheer. . . . It seemed to me, as the troops with soldierly smartness and precision marched past the Heir to the Throne that Canada had had suddenly revealed to her, and on the Plains of Abraham, the consciousness of her manhood.' 'I believe', wrote Lord Grey to the Prince himself, 'that the week just passed will be looked back upon in the history of Canada, as an occasion on which a tendency was given to the current of the National life, which will help to widen the outlook, enlarge the horizon and dignify and ennoble the status of every Canadian.'⁵

The Prince's own summary of this undoubted triumph was less rhetorical:

> 'I am indeed thankful', he wrote in his diary, 'that all the functions & ceremonies are over & that they went off so well. It was indeed a strenuous week, but I hope my visit has done good, especially to improve the relations between the English & French Canadians, which have never been so good as they are now.'

During his return journey in H.M.S. *Indomitable*, the pages of the diary do in fact display a certain elation. After all, he was at sea again; at sea in a magnificent cruiser which was seeking to break the speed record; at sea, on the way home to his beloved family; at sea, after a difficult job which, discounting all official adulation, he knew in his heart had been most excellently performed. It was not surprising that his infectious laugh should echo along the quarter-deck or that, black with coal-dust, he should help to stoke the ship. He returned to an England which was becoming increasingly confused.

(4)

The Liberal victory in the General Election of 1906 had to a great extent been due to the solid support of the Nonconformists, who had been outraged beyond reason by the Education Act of 1902. One of the first obligations therefore of the Liberal Government was to introduce a new Education Bill by which these grievances could be allayed. The Bill which Mr Augustine Birrell, laboriously but hurriedly, introduced in 1906 did not soothe the Nonconformists, while arousing passionate opposition on the other side. It was mauled in the House of Commons and amended beyond recognition in the House of Lords. The Government then took the unprecedented and provocative step of proposing that the lower Chamber should reject the Lords' amendments 'as a whole'. The Lords, having thus been challenged, maintained their amendments and the Bill was dropped. The Lords thereafter also rejected the Plural Voting Bill and the Land Valuation Bill. The Liberal majority in the House of Commons, together with their allies of the left, became convinced that the Conservative majority in the House of Lords, with their phalanx of dim and inarticulate backwoodsmen, were determined to obstruct—perhaps even to veto—all Government legislation. Already on June 24, 1907, Sir Henry Campbell-Bannerman had introduced a resolution that 'the power of the other House should be so restricted by law as to secure that within the limits of a single Parliament the final decision of the Commons should prevail'. A conflict between the two Houses had become inevitable: it was realised that this conflict would raise grave constitutional issues and might end by involving the prerogative of the Crown.

The second reward which the Liberal Government felt bound to offer to the Nonconformists was the Licensing Bill. Mr Asquith (who on the retirement and death of Sir Henry Campbell-Bannerman in

April, 1908, had become Prime Minister)[1] brought forward a measure which would have involved the suppression of thirty thousand licensed premises within the next fourteen years. This highly unpopular proposal led to a sensational defeat of the Government candidate at a by-election in Peckham. Encouraged by this manifestation of popular feeling, and still smarting under the rude treatment accorded to their amendments to the Birrell Education Bill, the Lords at this stage committed the first of the many tactical errors which hampered their handling of the controversy which thereafter arose. Instead of debating the Bill seriously in the gilded Chamber the decision to reject it was taken at a private meeting held in Lansdowne House. This Bill was also dropped. The tension between the two Houses became progressively and rapidly acute.

The Nonconformists were not the only group of supporters whom the Government were obliged to placate. They had also to consider the Irish Nationalists. The Irish Councils Bills of 1907—a jejune little sop—was violently rejected by the eighty-three Irish members and was in its turn hastily withdrawn. The impression was conveyed that if and when the Government majority declined (and successive by-elections indicated such a declension) the continued support of the Irish section would have to be purchased at a far heavier price. The menacing spectre of Home Rule began again to shake its troubled locks.

The public in the meanwhile were becoming disturbed by doubts regarding our naval security. The introduction of the *Dreadnought* battleship (a type which rendered all previous designs out of date) suggested the most disquieting thought that the Germans, by concentrating entirely on *Dreadnoughts*, could render obsolete all previous British construction and challenge our former uncontested superiority. Mr Reginald McKenna, who had succeeded Lord Tweedmouth

[1] Mr Asquith, on succeeding Sir Henry Campbell-Bannerman in April 1908, made certain important ministerial changes. Mr Lloyd George became Chancellor of the Exchequer and his place as President of the Board of Trade was taken by Mr Winston Churchill. Lord Crewe succeeded Lord Elgin at the Colonial Office, and Mr McKenna replaced Lord Tweedmouth as First Lord of the Admiralty. Mr John Morley retained the India Office, but in a new guise as Viscount Morley of Blackburn. Sir Edward Grey, Mr Herbert Gladstone, Mr Haldane, and Mr John Burns remained respectively Foreign Secretary, Home Secretary, Secretary of State for War, and President of the Local Government Board. Mr Birrell had already succeeded Mr Bryce in 1907 as Chief Secretary for Ireland.

as First Lord, asked the Cabinet to concede the construction of six *Dreadnoughts*, but the Cabinet agreed to four only. The public clamoured for eight *Dreadnoughts* and once again the Government were forced to give way.[1]

These successive retreats on the part of a Government enjoying so overwhelming a majority created the impression that the Cabinet, however brilliant might be the intellectual equipment of individual members, did not possess the solidarity, the convictions or the determination required to control a world situation of ever increasing menace. The excellent work accomplished by the Liberal Government during its first three years of office (the reorganisation of the Army by Mr Haldane, the introduction of Old Age Pensions and Mr Churchill's schemes for Labour Exchanges and Trade Boards) passed almost unnoticed in the general uneasiness. The British public watched the development of the foreign situation with ever-growing perplexity and alarm.

The German Foreign Office, having always disbelieved in the possibility of an Entente, had reacted to the conclusion of the Anglo-French agreement of April 1904, with provocative clumsiness. Freiherr von Holstein staged a series of *Kraftproben*, or trials of strength, with which to test the strength or weakness of the new combination. In the early spring of 1905 the German Emperor landed suddenly at Tangier and assured the representative of the Sultan of Morocco that he remained the champion of Moorish independence. On June 6 of that year, by methods of intimidation, the Germans secured the resignation of Monsieur Delcassé, one of the main architects of the Entente. On July 23 the German Emperor arranged a private and dramatic meeting with the Tsar of Russia at Björkö and extracted from him an offensive and defensive alliance, which was immediately repudiated by both the Russian and the German Governments. In the late autumn the Germans insisted that the future status of Morocco should be subjected to international agreement. At the Algeciras Conference which followed, Germany failed to dislocate the united front of France and Great Britain and suffered an overt diplomatic defeat. Freiherr von Holstein, as a victim of German mortification, was forced to resign. In 1907 came the Anglo-Russian Convention which created in Germany the panic

[1] Mr Churchill (*The World Crisis, 1911–1914*, p. 37) comments acutely: 'In the end a curious and characteristic solution was reached. The Admiralty had demanded six ships: the economists offered four; and we finally compromised on eight.'

dread of encirclement. In June 1908, the relations between England and Russia were fortified by the visit of King Edward to the Tsar at Reval. On October 6, 1908, Baron von Aehrenthal, the Austrian Foreign Minister, having tricked both his Russian colleague, Monsieur Iswolsky and the German Ambassador in Vienna, suddenly announced the annexation of Bosnia and Herzogovina. It was evident that Russia, weakened though she was by her defeat in the Japanese war and by the internal troubles which had followed, could not and would not again tolerate a similar affront. By the end of 1909 Europe was divided into two hostile and highly sensitive camps; there were many who feared that any further incident would provoke a war such as the world had not witnessed for a hundred years.

Mr Lloyd George, in April 1908, had succeeded Mr Asquith as Chancellor of the Exchequer. Imaginative, resourceful, impetuous, endowed with unusual demagogic powers and compelling personal charm, Mr Lloyd George was not encumbered by the vestigial affections which his colleagues still cherished for the ancient monuments of English tradition. Nor did he possess the tastes, intellectual or other, which British statesmen in the past had striven either to enjoy or to simulate. In their rare hours of relaxation Mr Asquith would study Epictetus or Mr P. G. Wodehouse, Mr Haldane the *Kritik der reinen Vernunft*, Lord Morley *Le neveu de Rameau*; Sir Edward Grey would murmur Wordsworth to himself while observing the habits of the birds and fishes and Mr Birrell would compose another volume of his *Obiter Dicta*. The relaxation of Mr Lloyd George was to sing wild hymns to a harmonium. The very fact that he was closer to the people than were his classic colleagues enabled him to realise more clearly than they that the old Gladstonian formulas were losing their glamour and their potency; and that if Liberalism were not to become outmoded or overwhelmed by the rising tide of socialism, some more stimulating doctrine must be devised. He determined to preach Social Democracy and to lead the attack on privilege—a cause and a battle which were to him supremely congenial.

Before embarking on his later schemes for social betterment, Mr Lloyd George, who required sixteen millions more revenue for the *Dreadnoughts* and the Old Age Pensions, framed what he christened 'The People's Budget'. The provisions of this budget do not today seem confiscatory. Income tax, at the highest level, was raised to one shilling and eightpence in the pound; some extremely complicated, and perhaps vindictive, land taxes were proposed; there were additional duties on spirits and tobacco, a heavy tax on licensed premises, and a simple tax on motor cars and petrol. The Conservatives immediately denounced these proposals as predatory; the Lords, stung to imprudence by the inordinate if amusing insults which Mr Lloyd George hurled at them from the platform, decided that the Constitution was in danger and that they must therefore brace themselves to violate the most cherished of constitutional conventions, namely the unwritten principle that the Upper House must not reject or amend the annual Budget.[1]

The Finance Bill of 1909 was debated in Committee of the House of Commons for forty-two days and was finally passed by 379 to 149 on November 4. On November 30 it was rejected by the House of Lords on the second reading by 350 votes to 75.

The defects or merits of Mr Lloyd George's financial proposals were thereafter overshadowed by the far greater issue of Lords versus Commons. The House of Lords had justified their rejection of Mr Lloyd George's Budget on the grounds, first, that this was no ordinary measure of supply, but a revolutionary change in established financial policy; and, second, that it was doubtful whether the provisions which it embodied really reflected the desires of the electorate. Mr Asquith decided therefore that he must ask for a dissolution and appeal to the country. At the General Election of January 1910, the Liberals lost one hundred and four seats to the Conservatives, and their old overwhelming majority was reduced to two.[2] Placid and even confident, Mr Asquith determined to carry on.

At the opening of the new Parliament on February 21, 1910, King Edward, in his Speech from the Throne, announced that measures would be introduced to 'define the relations between the Houses of Parliament, so as to secure the undivided authority of the House of Commons over finance and its predominance in legislation'. The measures thus announced took the form of three 'Resolutions'. First, that the veto of the House of Lords upon Bills certified

[1] The Conservatives were much embarrassed through the coming battle by the admission which Mr Balfour had made in the course of the debate on Sir Henry Campbell-Bannerman's Resolution of June 24, 1907. 'We all know', he had said, 'that the power of the House of Lords . . . is still further limited by the fact that it cannot touch Money Bills, which if it could deal with, no doubt it could bring the whole executive government of the country to a standstill' (*Hansard* CLXXVI, 929–930).

[2] The actual figures were: Liberals, 275 seats; Conservatives, 273; Irish Nationalists, 82; Labour, 40. Mr Asquith could thus rely, if he could obtain and retain Irish and Labour support, on an overall majority of 124.

by the Speaker to be 'Money Bills' should be abolished. Second, other Bills, if passed by the House of Commons in three successive sessions, should become law, whether the Upper House agreed or not. And third, that the duration of Parliament should be reduced from seven to five years. These three resolutions were passed by the House of Commons on April 14. On the same night, Mr Asquith laid upon the table of the House a Bill by which they should be given legislative effect. This Bill was entitled 'The Parliament Bill'.

In his speech in the House of Commons on April 14, Mr Asquith stated that if the Lords rejected the Parliament Bill 'we shall feel it our duty immediately to tender advice to the Crown as to the steps which will have to be taken if that policy is to receive statutory effect in this Parliament'. He added that 'if we do not find ourselves in a position to ensure that statutory effect will be given to this policy in this Parliament, we shall then either resign our offices or recommend a dissolution of Parliament'.

When pressed for a more precise definition of these cryptic utterances, Mr Asquith resorted to his justifiable, but damaging, formula of 'Wait and See'. The Irish Nationalists, under Mr Redmond, had threatened to vote against the long-deferred Budget unless they were first given a firm assurance that a sufficient number of new peers would be created to swamp any opposition in the Upper Chamber to proposals for Home Rule. Mr Asquith, being unwilling to give any such a guarantee at that stage of the crisis, ignored their menaces. He was justified by the event. Mr Lloyd George's Budget, having now been accorded the somewhat lukewarm approval of the electorate, passed the House of Commons on April 27 by a majority of ninety-three. The next day it was accepted by the House of Lords without a division.

The stage was now cleared for the final conflict between the two Houses over the Parliament Bill. At that moment the course of events was deflected by a wholly unexpected misfortune.

(5)

At 5.50 p.m. on Wednesday, April 27, King Edward, who had been spending a few weeks at Biarritz, reached Victoria Station, where he was greeted by the Prince of Wales. The latter thought him looking well and in good spirits; that evening they went to Covent Garden together to hear Madame Tetrazzini in *Rigoletto*. On Thursday King Edward attended the private view of the Royal Academy and on Friday the Prince of Wales brought his two elder

104

YORK HOUSE

WITH THE GERMAN EMPEROR AT POTSDAM

sons to luncheon at Buckingham Palace. On Saturday the King went down to Sandringham for the week-end, only returning to London on the Monday afternoon. On the morning of Wednesday, May 4, the Prince of Wales went to Kensal Green cemetery to visit the grave of his old tutor, Monsieur Hua. His diary for that day contains the first presage of impending catastrophe:

'Had some very heavy showers. Home at 1.30. Lunched at 1.45. Laking came to see me at 2.15 & gave a bad account of dear Papa, who has another attack of bronchitis. At 3.0 went over to B.P. & saw Papa; his colour was bad & his breathing fast. I didn't stop long as of course talking makes him cough. . . . We are naturally worried & anxious about him. Wrote to Motherdear & Toria to Calais, where they arrive tomorrow. Wish they were here now.'

Queen Alexandra and Princess Victoria had been staying with the King of the Hellenes at Corfu and only reached London on the afternoon of Thursday, May 5. 'It was a great shock to them', the Prince of Wales noted that evening, 'to see Papa in this state.'

His diary for Friday, May 6, is written in a hand which betrays deep agitation:

'I went to B.P. at 10.15, where I regret to say I found darling Papa much worse, having had a fainting fit. It was indeed a terrible day for us all. We hardly left him. He knew us & talked to us between his attacks up to 4.30.

'At 11.45 beloved Papa passed peacefully away & I have lost my best friend & the best of fathers. I never had a word with him in his life. I am heartbroken & overwhelmed with grief, but God will help me in my great responsibilities & darling May will be my comfort as she always has been. May God give me strength & guidance in the heavy task which has fallen on me. I sent telegrams to the Lord Mayor & the Prime Minister. Left Motherdear & Toria and drove back to M.H. with darling May. I am quite stunned by this awful blow. Bed at 1.0.'

CHAPTER VIII

THE MONARCHY

Continuity of the British monarchical tradition—The Royal House of Britain as the oldest of our political institutions—Advantages and disadvantages of hereditary Monarchy—The conflict between Crown and Parliament—The evolution of the conceptions of 'limited Monarchy' and 'responsible government'—Ministers are now responsible for the King's public acts—The Royal Prerogative—Its employment as a convenient instrument of administration—Even in foreign and commonwealth affairs the King can perform no act except on the advice of Ministers—Constitutionally he can dissolve Parliament, dismiss the Government and even refuse the Royal Assent to Bills—In practical politics such powers would not be spontaneously exercised—His only independent function is to choose a Prime Minister from among alternative candidates—The contention that the circumstances with which King George was faced between 1910 and 1914 were abnormal circumstances—Is the King the 'guardian of the constitution'?—Yet if the King possesses limited political *power* he possesses great political *influence*—Definition of this influence—The popularity of the Crown—King George's personal contribution.

(1)

KING GEORGE V succeeded his father on May 6, 1910, and reigned for almost twenty-six years. During that quarter of a century the world witnessed the disappearance of five Emperors, eight Kings and eighteen minor dynasties. The British Monarchy emerged from the convulsion more firmly established than it had been before.

The stability of our monarchical tradition during this period of deep and rapid change was not due solely to King George's straightforwardness and wisdom. It must also be attributed to the elasticity of our constitution, to the capacity possessed by this ill-defined assortment of laws, customs and conventions to adjust itself, without strain or rupture, to fundamentally altered conditions:

> 'A constitution', writes Sir William Anson,[a] 'which began with the rude organization of a group of settlers in a hostile country, has been adapted, first to the wants of a highly civilised race, then to the government of a vast Empire; and this by an insensible process of change, without any attempt to recast it as a whole, or even to state it in written form.'

A written constitution possesses its own codified laws and often provides for some detached tribunal, empowered, if need arises, to give an arbitral decision whether any given Act of State is constitutional or not. An unwritten constitution—although possessing all the merits of elasticity and although hampered by none of the defects of rigidity—inevitably contains some zones of uncertainty.[1] When the ship of state enters these uncharted waters, then the most learned and impartial authorities begin to differ on what the correct constitutional procedure really is. King George, whose constant desire was to abide by his Coronation Oath and to act strictly in accordance with his duties and responsibilities as a constitutional Monarch, was often driven by the winds and tides of events into these zones of uncertainty, and was obliged to determine, with little more than the stars to guide him, which was the true constitutional course to pursue. If any clear conception is to be conveyed of the nature of the problems he encountered, if any understanding is to be acquired of the vocabulary at the time employed, it will be necessary in this chapter to give a short account of the theory of British Constitutional Monarchy as it had developed by the year 1910; and to indicate what were the zones of uncertainty which occasioned such perplexity both to the King and to his Ministers during the first four years of his reign.

(2)

The Royal House of Britain can claim to be the oldest dynasty in Europe and by far the most ancient of our political institutions. King George could trace his descent from Egbert, who ascended the throne of Wessex in 809 and was recognised as Bretwalda in 829. Apart from the interlude of Cromwell's Commonwealth, the direct descendants of Egbert have reigned in England for eleven hundred years. Our Law Courts are only eight hundred years old: our Parliament only seven hundred. It was around the Throne that, in the course of centuries, there accumulated that body of laws, principles, precedents, customs and conventions which we call our Constitution.

In Anglo-Saxon times the 'Kings of the English' had been elected by the Witan from among the more promising males of the Royal line. When the Normans arrived, the elective principle was, in form at least, preserved. The Kings had at first to submit to election, or more accurately 'recognition', by the Commune Concilium. There-

[1] It is helpful to recall the encouragement of Edmund Burke: 'We ought to understand it according to our measure; and to venerate where we are not able presently to understand' (Burke's *Works*, 1872 Edition, III, 114).

107

after the principle of hereditary succession by primogeniture became established.

The advantages of a hereditary Monarchy are self-evident. Without some such method of prescriptive, immediate and automatic succession, an interregnum intervenes, rival claimants arise, continuity is interrupted and the magic lost. Even when Parliament had secured control of taxation and therefore of government; even when the menace of dynastic conflicts had receded into the coloured past; even when kingship had ceased to be transcendental and had become one of many alternative institutional forms; the principle of hereditary Monarchy continued to furnish the State with certain specific and inimitable advantages.

Apart from the imponderable, but deeply important, sentiments and affections which congregate around an ancient and legitimate Royal Family, a hereditary Monarch acquires sovereignty by processes which are wholly different from those by which a dictator seizes, or a President is granted, the headship of the State. The King personifies both the past history and the present identity of the Nation as a whole. Consecrated as he is to the service of his peoples, he possesses a religious sanction and is regarded as someone set apart from ordinary mortals. In an epoch of change, he remains the symbol of continuity; in a phase of disintegration, the element of cohesion; in times of mutability, the emblem of permanence. Governments come and go, politicians rise and fall: the Crown is always there. A legitimate Monarch moreover has no need to justify his existence, since he is there by natural right. He is not impelled, as usurpers and dictators are impelled, either to mesmerise his people by a succession of dramatic triumphs, or to secure their acquiescence by internal terrorism or by the invention of external dangers. The appeal of hereditary Monarchy is to stability rather than to change, to continuity rather than to experiment, to custom rather than to novelty, to safety rather than to adventure.

The Monarch, above all, is neutral. Whatever may be his personal prejudices or affections, he is bound to remain detached from all political parties and to preserve in his own person the equilibrium of the realm. An elected President—whether, as under some constitutions, he be no more than a representative functionary, or whether, as under other constitutions, he be the chief executive—can never inspire the same sense of absolute neutrality. However impartial he may strive to become, he must always remain the prisoner of his own partisan past; he is accompanied by friends and

supporters whom he may seek to reward, or faced by former antagonists who will regard him with distrust. He cannot, to an equal
extent, serve as the fly-wheel of the state.

The disadvantages of hereditary Monarchy are also apparent.
The hazards of heredity render it improbable that any country will
be blessed with a succession of equally wise, dutiful or blameless
Kings. A Monarch moreover, being conscious that he is not physically
of a different mould from other men, may become affected by the
fantasy that his pre-eminence is due to supernatural rather than to
natural agencies:

> 'Kings', announced James I in 1609, 'are justly called gods, because
> they exercise a manner of resemblance to Divine power on earth. . . .
> They have power to exalt low things and abase high things and to
> make of their subjects like men at chess.'

The doctrine of Divine Right, which had already been profoundly shaken by the Reformation, did not survive the execution of
Charles I. Yet the essential political problem remained. Could a system be devised by which the advantages of hereditary Monarchy
could be preserved, without exposing the State to the manifest disadvantages which it might entail? The political aptitudes of the
British people, their congenital dislike of all logical extremes, enabled
them in the course of centuries to work out the required com-
promises. They developed a system which, without any rupture of
continuity, was sufficiently elastic to admit of recurrent change.
They called this system 'limited' or 'constitutional' Monarchy. In
perfecting this instrument they were much assisted by the accidents
of history.

(3)

The struggle between Crown and Parliament centred in
five main questions. Could the King raise taxes without the consent
of Parliament? Could he maintain a private army? Could he institute
special Royal courts of justice? And could he suspend the operation
of laws passed by Parliament or grant his subjects a dispensation
from obeying them?

When in December 1688, King James II escaped to France,
having thrown the Great Seal into the Thames at Vauxhall, he was
deemed to have vacated the throne. The Convention Parliament
thereupon offered the Crown to his daughter Mary and to her
husband, William of Orange, himself a grandson of Charles I. By the
Declaration and Bill of Rights the Convention Parliament formu-

lated the conditions upon which this offer was made and accepted. The King was denied the right of raising taxes, creating special courts of law, or maintaining a standing army without the consent of Parliament. The suspending and dispensing powers of the Crown, namely the power to suspend the operation of a law or to dispense anyone from obeying it, were declared to be 'illegal usurpations'. Parliament was to be convened at regular intervals and freedom of speech and debate was to be guaranteed. The Bill of Rights thus established the firm principle that the King reigned, not by Divine Right, still less under any system of feudal contract, but solely with and by the consent of Parliament.

When the Duke of Gloucester (the only one of Princess Anne's numerous children to survive infancy) died in 1700, Parliament decided that on the death of William III and of his sister-in-law Anne, the succession should pass to Sophia, Dowager Electress of Hanover, and the heirs of her body. The Act of Settlement of 1701, which formulated this decision, contained one all-important addition to the Bill of Rights. It was then laid down that in future Ministers should be 'responsible' for the acts of the Sovereign. It is questionable whether those who drafted the Act of Settlement fully realised the immense future significance of this principle.

The expression 'responsible government' which thereafter became current, includes several different implications. In the first place, it means that Ministers are 'responsible' to Parliament in the sense that they cannot govern without the support of a majority in the House of Commons.[1] In the second place, it means that Ministers are 'responsible' for the 'advice' they tender to the Sovereign and therefore for any action which he may take:

> 'The King', stated Lord Erskine in the House of Lords on April 13, 1807, 'can perform no act of government himself. No act of state or government can be the King's; he cannot act but by advice; and he who holds office sanctions what is done, from whatsoever source it may proceed.'

A subsequent extension of the phrase implies what is known as 'collective responsibility' or 'Cabinet responsibility', namely the joint

---

[1] This essential principle dates from the Grand Remonstrance of the Long Parliament in 1641. King Charles I was informed that he must employ only such Ministers 'as Parliament may have cause to confide in' and was warned that, if he evaded this suggestion, Parliament would find themselves unable 'to give His Majesty such supplies for the support of his own estate nor such assistance to the Protestant party beyond the sea as is desired'.

responsibility of Ministers for each other's actions and misfortunes. The King, under this principle, cannot dismiss an individual Minister without incurring the resignation of the Cabinet as a whole. Apart from these constitutional, or institutional, implications the phrase 'responsible government' contains a metaphysical idea. Not only Ministers, but the official Opposition also, must be guided in their actions and statements by a sense of responsibility; irresponsible acts or utterances should be regarded as obnoxious to the spirit of the constitution.

The historical accident which, during the course of the eighteenth century, firmly established the principle of responsible government and led to the Cabinet system as we know it today, was the advent of the Hanoverians in 1714. King George I was not interested in British politics and was much embarrassed by the fact that he could neither speak nor understand the English language. Even the halting Latin, in which his Ministers sought to convey their desires, was spoken with so strong a public-school accent that it was to him incomprehensible. He therefore ceased to preside (as Charles II had regularly presided) at the meetings of the Cabinet and his place as chairman was assumed by the senior Minister, who gradually became known as the Prime Minister.[1]

In spite of the categorical enactments of the Bill of Rights and the Act of Settlement, in spite of the evolution of 'responsible government' and of the Cabinet system as we know it today, there remained, and still remain, certain discretionary powers in the hands of the Crown. These are known generally as 'The Royal Prerogative', by which is meant those actions which the King and his servants can take (without the authority of an Act of Parliament), by Order in Council, Proclamation, or Sign Manual. Since it was in regard to the exercise of the Prerogative that King George was faced with such recurrent difficulties, its nature and limitations must be examined in further detail.

[1] The term 'Prime Minister' is a nineteenth-century term. In the eighteenth century, when used at all, it was used in a derogatory sense. The office of Prime Minister is unknown to British Law. The term has only thrice been employed in any Act of Parliament, notably in the Chequers Estate Act of 1917. It occurs only in two official documents: namely, the Treaty of Berlin, when Disraeli signed himself 'Prime Minister of England' and when King Edward VII on December 2, 1905, assigned the Prime Minister place and precedence next after the Archbishop of York.

(4)

Walter Bagehot, in his *English Constitution*,[b] gives an entertaining list of some of the many things which Queen Victoria, by exercising her Prerogative, was legally entitled to do without consulting Parliament:

'She could disband the army (by law she cannot engage more than a certain number of men, but she is not obliged to engage any men); she could dismiss all the officers, from the General commanding-in-chief downwards; she could dismiss all the sailors too; she could sell off all our ships of war and all our naval stores; she could make a peace by the sacrifice of Cornwall or begin a war for the conquest of Britanny. She could make every citizen in the United Kingdom, male or female, a peer; she could make every parish in the United Kingdom a "university"; she could dismiss most of the Civil Servants; she could pardon all offenders. In a word, the Queen could, by prerogative, upset all the action of civil government, could disgrace the nation by a bad war or peace, and could, by disbanding our forces, whether land or sea, leave us defenceless against foreign nations.'

That such experiments in the use of the Prerogative could never in fact be attempted is due essentially to the provision that no action can be taken by the Sovereign except on the 'advice' of a Minister accountable to Parliament. Yet some confusion may arise from the fact that many writers, when discussing the Prerogative of the Crown, are apt to employ the word 'Crown' as signifying, at one time the King personally, and at another time the Executive or Government.

The power of the Executive to legislate by Proclamation or Order in Council was during the eighteenth century still regarded with some perturbation. Thus when Lord Chatham in 1766 used the Prerogative to lay an embargo upon all grain ships in British ports, he felt himself obliged thereafter to ask the House of Commons to pass a Bill of Indemnity. 'It was', he explained, 'but a forty days tyranny.' Since that date, we have rid ourselves of these inhibitions: 'delegated legislation' has become a common practice. The Defence of the Realm Act of 1914, for instance, authorised the King in Council to issue regulations affecting, not merely the armed forces, but the rights of private citizens. Among the powers transferred by this Act to the Crown were such unseemly innovations as the right to intern individuals without trial and to prohibit the blowing of cab-whistles at night. Even the forgotten privilege of purveyance was revived by this Act in order to enable the Crown to requisition premises without compensation.[1] By the Emergency Powers Act of

[1] The right of purveyance was denied by the House of Lords in an appeal in the case of the Attorney-General *v.* de Keyser's Hotel in 1920. In spite of D.O.R.A., the principles of Magna Carta were affirmed.

1920, to take another instance, the King in Council was empowered to proclaim a 'state of emergency' and the Government, under such a proclamation, could, without the consent or even knowledge of Parliament, exercise wide discretionary powers to safeguard public order. The powers delegated to the Crown under the Foreign Jurisdiction Act are extensive and of ancient date.

The King also retains, under his Prerogative, the right to issue Sign Manuals or Warrants. Although this right is usually restricted to the authorisation of appointments, the issue of pardons, and similar formal enactments, it can legally be used for far more important executive acts. It was, for instance, under Sign Manual that Queen Victoria abolished the practice of purchasing commissions in the army; an abolition which the House of Lords had refused to sanction as being, in their opinion, a violation of the rights of property.

It must be clearly understood that the use of the Royal Prerogative for delegated legislation is today little more than a governmental or departmental convenience. The expression 'the Crown', when used in such a connection, signifies, not the King personally, but the Government. The device of using the Royal Prerogative, or other forms of delegated legislation, in order to avoid the delays and dangers of Parliamentary discussion is one which offers a recurrent temptation to all Ministers and Departments; it rightly calls for the vigilance of constitutional purists. Yet essentially it is subject to the overriding principle that such uses or abuses of the Prerogative are in no sense the personal responsibility of the King in Council, but exercised by him solely on and with the advice of Ministers, who, in their turn, are strictly accountable to Parliament.

The convention that it is the King, and not Parliament, who declares war and makes peace, who concludes treaties and who alone can cede territory,[1] has encouraged the idea that in external affairs, whether foreign or imperial, he possesses wider constitutional powers both of initiative and action. Foreign policy, it has been argued, is continuous and above party. The King, as representing the nation as a whole, should therefore in international relations be less dependent upon the advice given him by those Ministers who at the moment happen to command the confidence of the House of Commons. It has

[1] The Treaty of Versailles (1783) under which Minorca and Florida were ceded was not the subject of an Act of Parliament. On the other hand the House of Commons was specifically invited to approve the cession of Heligoland (1890) and Jubaland (1927).

similarly been contended that in Commonwealth affairs the King (in that he stands in a unique relation to the several Dominion Governments) possesses a greater latitude of personal action. Each of these theories is fallacious. In Foreign Affairs the King can act only upon the advice of his Foreign Secretary: in Commonwealth affairs he, or his representative, can act only on the advice of a Dominion Government.[1]

It is true that Queen Victoria and the Prince Consort, owing to their family connections with many of the reigning houses of Europe, took a direct interest in, and were on occasions able to influence, the course of foreign policy. Their conflicts with Lord Palmerston are on record.[c] It is also true that King Edward VII, with his intimate knowledge of Continental problems and personalities, was often able, with the approval of the Cabinet but not without some Parliamentary criticism, to engage in personal diplomatic activity and to give audiences to foreign representatives, without any Minister or Official being present.

Such interventions were, however, no more than lubricants to Government policy and did not in any way affect the principle which, in his lapidary manner, Sir William Anson has summarised as follows:[d]

> 'The Sovereign does not, constitutionally, take independent action in foreign affairs; everything which passes between him and foreign princes or ministers should be known to his own ministers, who are responsible to the people for policy, and to the law for acts done.'

(5)

If the King, whether in internal or external affairs, can commit no public act except upon the advice of the Government in office, the question may be asked how his personal responsibility can ever, in any circumstances, become involved. The phrase 'the King can do no wrong' means, not that the Monarch is infallible, but that, since he can do nothing without the advice of Ministers, it is they who are

---

[1] A constitutional problem might occur in regard to matters of common interest to two or more Dominions. If, for instance, a dispute arose between His Majesty's Ministers in the United Kingdom and His Majesty's Ministers in the Union of South Africa in regard to the High Commission Territories, it might well happen that the King was tendered two contradictory sets of advice, each of which he was bound constitutionally to follow.

A further examination of the effect of the Statute of Westminster upon the position of the Crown occurs in Chapter **XXVIII**.

personally responsible if mistakes are made. Can any public issue arise therefore in which the King has to exercise personal initiative or reach an independent decision?

The discussion of this question has sometimes been blurred by the fact that there exist certain functions which, in constitutional theory, the King alone can perform. No one but the King can summon, prorogue or dissolve Parliament. No one but the King can dismiss or appoint a Prime Minister. No one but the King can grant pardons or confer peerages and honours. And no Bill, until it has received the Royal Assent, can become the law of the land. These powers are however limited in practice by the over-riding principle of 'responsible government'. The King is in fact accustomed to follow the advice tendered to him by the Prime Minister of the day, since, if he rejects that advice, the Government will resign, a general election will follow, the Crown may become involved in party controversy and the King may discover (as William IV discovered to his cost) that the opinion of the country is against him. These are dangers which no constitutional Monarch should be expected to incur.

It is thus necessary in every case to draw a distinction between the historical survival of these Prerogative powers and the political expediency of exercising them in practice. Only the most academic jurist would contend that in the twentieth century a constitutional Monarch could, in any important matter, ignore or flout the advice tendered to him by his Cabinet. On the first, perhaps even on the second, occasion that he did so, his intervention might be warmly approved by the electorate. But in the end this personal and independent exercise of the Prerogative would be bound to arouse opposition and to raise doubts regarding the sovereign's neutrality and impartiality which are two of the main components of his influence. What the King certainly can do, in cases when he feels the advice given him is either dangerous or opposed to the wishes of the people as a whole, is to insist that the Cabinet shall furnish him with that advice in written form so that he also may have the opportunity of recording, in writing, that he follows that advice with misgiving and reluctance. Beyond that, in practical politics, he can scarcely go without compromising the influence of the Crown.

In theory, for instance, it would be perfectly constitutional for the King to dissolve Parliament against the advice of the Prime Minister. Such action, in the view of Professor Dicey,[e] might be justifiable 'if there exists fair reason to suppose that the opinion of the

House is not the opinion of the electors. A dissolution in its essence is an appeal from the legal to the political sovereign'. Yet if the King estimates that 'fair reason' exists and the result of the election proves his estimate to have been mistaken, then an awkward, and indeed damaging, conclusion may result. Similarly, the King is perfectly within his constitutional rights in refusing to grant a dissolution when asked to do so by his Ministers. In that event, the Government might resign and, unless the leader of the Opposition were in the position to form and maintain an alternative administration, a general election would follow and the action of the Crown would become a matter of electoral controversy.[1]

The same considerations apply to the undoubted constitutional right possessed by the King to dismiss his Ministers. Unless an alternative Government, able to secure the confidence of the existing House of Commons were immediately available, then again a general election would ensue and the King's action might be exposed to public criticism.

To take a more extreme instance of the distinction between theory and practice, the King could constitutionally refuse the Royal Assent to a Bill which has passed through Parliament. Were he to do so, the clerk at the table of the House of Lords would substitute for the accustomed formula: '*Le Roy le veult*'—the unwonted words: '*Le Roy s'avisera*'. This startling phrase has not been heard in the gilded Chamber for more than two hundred years. Mr Asquith, therefore, had some justification for assuring the House of Commons in 1910 that the Royal Veto, which had not been exercised since 1707, was 'literally as dead as Queen Anne'.

Thus the only 'independent' function which the King can properly be called upon to perform arises upon the death or resigna-

---

[1] Lord Byng, when Governor-General of Canada in 1925, refused Mr Mackenzie King's request for a dissolution, on the ground that the leader of the Opposition was in the position to form and maintain an administration without one. Similarly, Sir Patrick Duncan, when Governor-General of the Union of South Africa, refused to grant a dissolution to General Hertzog in 1939. It has been asserted that King George V temporarily refused a dissolution to Mr Asquith in 1910. This assertion, as will be seen, is incorrect.

Mr Asquith himself on December 18, 1923, enunciated the doctrine that it would be 'subversive of constitutional theory' to contend that the King was bound to grant a dissolution when advised to do so by the Prime Minister in power. An interesting correspondence on this point appeared in *The Times* on April 24, 1950, and succeeding days.

tion of a Prime Minister. The King is then expected to choose, or 'send for', his successor. His choice is of course limited by the fact that the new Prime Minister must command the support of his own party and the confidence of the House of Commons. But it certainly rests with the King, when alternative candidates, each possessing these qualifications, are available, to summon the one whom he regards as best fitted to carry on the Government. King George exercised this discretionary power when in 1923 he chose Mr Stanley Baldwin rather than Lord Curzon. He again exercised it when, in different circumstances, he charged Mr Ramsay MacDonald with the formation of a 'National Government' in 1931.

It would be agreed therefore by most constitutional authorities that the discretionary powers possessed by the King are in normal conditions strictly limited to the choice of a Prime Minister from among two or more equally acceptable candidates. Yet the perplexities which assailed King George during the first four years of his reign arose from the fact that the conditions then created were, in the opinion of many responsible people, not normal but abnormal.

The Parliament Bill, which, after much storm and stress, became law in August 1911, abolished the veto hitherto possessed by the House of Lords on legislation passed by a majority of the House of Commons. In the preamble to that Bill, however, it had been stated that 'it is intended to substitute for the House of Lords as it at present exists a Second Chamber constituted on a popular instead of a hereditary basis'. It was argued by certain purists that until the promise implicit in this preamble had been carried into effect, and a reformed Second Chamber had in fact been created, the Constitution was 'in a state of suspense'. It was contended that pending the re-establishment of the traditional balance between the Three Estates of the Realm, the powers of veto until then exercised by the House of Lords must necessarily devolve upon the King personally.

This most academic theory was seized upon in 1912 by certain politicians who were determined to oppose by any means the passage of the Home Rule Bill. They argued that an abnormal situation had been created to which the accustomed proprieties of constitutional procedure no longer applied. Mr Asquith, having temporarily suspended the powers of veto hitherto possessed by the Upper Chamber, was, they argued, seeking to impose the Home Rule Bill upon the country by using the artificial and unrepresentative majority given him by the Irish vote in the House of Commons. In so doing he was forcing through Parliament a constitutional change of the utmost gravity without having obtained a sufficiently clear mandate from the British electorate. In such wholly abnormal circumstances they contended, the King became 'the guardian of the Constitution' and the ultimate trustee of the rights and liberties of the sovereign people. Under his Coronation Oath he had undertaken to govern according to existing 'statutes and customs'. Now that these customs were being flagrantly violated, it became his duty to assert his Prerogative, even to the extreme point of refusing his Assent to the Home Rule Bill, at least until the electorate had been given a clear opportunity to express their desires. It was even pointed out that, once the powers of the House of Lords had been abolished and until an alternative Second Chamber had been established in its place, there was nothing except the personal intervention of the King which could prevent an unscrupulous Prime Minister, possessing a temporary majority in the House of Commons, from establishing a dictatorship, or at least from prolonging indefinitely the life of the existing Parliament and of his own administration.

King George was not impressed by such fantastic suppositions. But he was sufficiently perturbed by the appeals and warnings which reached him from these constitutional pundits to authorise his Private Secretary to consult the greatest living authority, Sir William Anson, as to whether there was any substance in such a contention. The latter's reply is of interest.' He stated that the King undoubtedly possessed, according to the law of the Constitution, the 'discretionary power' to refuse his Assent to a Bill, but that it was for him to determine whether the advice being tendered to him by the Prime Minister reflected the will of the Nation. If Mr Asquith resigned and his party were returned to power by the electorate, then the King would have been shown to have incorrectly gauged the wishes of the people. The abolition of the powers of the House of Lords did not, in Sir William Anson's opinion, affect the constitutional right of the King to exercise his ultimate veto, 'but it might suggest reasons which did not exist before for the assertion of that right'. Such an opinion, although doubtless incontestable in law, does not appear to be equally sound as a matter of practical politics.[1]

[1] Dr Keith, in his book *The King and the Imperial Crown* (page 183), is somewhat more dogmatic than Sir William Anson. He contends that the King is the final guardian of the Constitution and that his duties and responsibilities in this function were notably increased after the Parliament Bill in 1911.

He seems to base his argument on the contention that any Parliamentary majority in the House of Commons is not necessarily a sure

A further problem of constitutional propriety, a further zone of uncertainty, arises when a Government, on the eve of a general election, advises the King to give pledges, which can become operative only when the election is over. It could be argued that, in certain circumstances, such advance pledges might prove of electoral advantage to the party in power and of disadvantage to their opponents. If the King refuses to give the pledges demanded, he may be accused of rejecting the advice of his responsible Ministers. If he agrees to furnish these advance pledges, he may thereafter be accused of having abandoned his absolute neutrality. It was this predicament which faced King George in November 1910, when Mr Asquith, in anticipation of the impending election, asked him to promise that, in the event of the Government being returned to power, he would exercise his Prerogative to create a number of new peers sufficient to swamp all possible opposition to the Parliament Bill in the Upper Chamber. Constitutional authorities will for long dispute whether Mr Asquith was justified in demanding such a promise and whether it was one which the King should rightly have been expected to accord.[1]

(6)

Although therefore the executive *powers* of the King are strictly limited, both by constitutional theory and by political expediency and practice, the *influence* which he retains, although indefinable,

indication of the real wishes of the electorate. He fortifies his contention, that our present electoral machinery is a most imperfect instrument for recording the real desires of the sovereign people, by giving certain rather disturbing figures. Thus, under a system of Proportional Representation, the Liberal Majority in 1906 would have been, not 354 but 96. He cites other equally distracting statistics to show that the number of seats obtained by any given party in the House of Commons does not necessarily (and in fact very rarely) bear any real relation to the electoral decisions of the sovereign people.

The implication is that the King (being above all lobby statistics) should be guided by the proportions of popular votes recorded, rather than by the numerical list of the seats obtained. His theory is interesting. But it bears little relation to the problems of practical British politics.

[1] A similar 'zone of uncertainty' might be entered if His Majesty's Government in the United Kingdom were to recommend for a peerage or other distinction an individual whose general repute did not seem to qualify him for preferment. If such an individual had been born and bred and had acquired repute in the United Kingdom, the King might feel that he was justified, in such a case, in following the advice tendered to him by his British Ministers. But if (as might well occur) the individual

is very great. It has been excellently described by Sir William Anson:[9]

> 'The real influence of the Sovereign in this country is not to be estimated either by his legal or his actual powers as the executive of the State. The King or Queen for the time being is not a mere piece of mechanism, but a human being carefully trained under circumstances which afford exceptional chances of learning the business of politics. Such a personage cannot be treated or regarded as a mere instrument: it is evident that on all matters of state, especially on matters which concern the relations of our own with other States, he receives full information, and is able to express if not to enforce an opinion. And this opinion may, in the course of a long reign, become a thing of great weight and value. It is impossible to be constantly consulted and concerned for years together in matters of great moment without acquiring experience if not wisdom. Ministers come and go, and the policy of one group of ministers may not be the policy of the next, but all ministers in turn must explain their policy to the Executive Sovereign, must effect it through his instrumentality, must leave upon his mind such a recollection of its method and of its results as may be used to form and influence the action of their successsors.'

The influence which any British King or Queen is able to exercise is derived, not merely from the personal qualities of an individual Sovereign, but also from the respect and affection with which the Monarchy, as an institution, is generally regarded. That these feelings may be largely based on sentiment in no way diminishes their validity or effect. 'The metaphysics', writes Professor Laski[h] 'of limited monarchy do not easily lend themselves to critical discussion.' Yet the fact remains that the Monarchy is today regarded by the people of this island and of the Commonwealth and Empire as the magnet of loyalty, the emblem of union, the symbol of continuity and the embodiment of national, as distinct from class or party, feeling.[1]

---

recommended had been born and bred and had acquired repute in one of the Dominions: and if there were reason to suppose that His Majesty's Ministers in that Dominion would make no similar recommendation: then the King, as fount of honour, would assuredly be justified in withholding his Assent.

In such circumstances His Majesty's Ministers in the United Kingdom would be unlikely to tender their resignations.

[1] The esteem with which the Monarchy is to-day regarded has not a tradition of uninterrupted continuity. It is true that the Chartists of 1838–1848 did not include the establishment of a Republic under their many demands. But the long retirement of Queen Victoria after the death of the Prince Consort did provide an opportunity for a republican movement,

The demonstrations of affection and esteem which marked the Silver Jubilee of King George V came as a revelation to foreign observers and were welcomed by the King himself with modest surprise. They were in fact a tribute to what had been a remarkable achievement. Being a man in whom there was no guile, King George throughout his reign took it for granted that he would receive from successive Cabinets the same natural fidelity as he accorded to them. The candour of his approach, the probity of his nature, the straightness of all his thoughts and actions, did more than create a lasting level of confidence; they shamed the stratagems of more elaborate minds. He was able, with ever-increasing authority, 'to advise, to encourage and to warn'. The advice which he gave his Ministers (and it was persistent and could not be ignored) was invariably in favour of conciliation and accord. He would beg them not to make speeches which might arouse unnecessary antagonisms or commit the Government itself to irretrievable courses. On occasions he would urge them to discuss matters frankly and privately with their political opponents rather than to indulge in parliamentary polemics. He missed no opportunity to encourage such private conferences and his whole influence was exercised towards lowering rather than raising the temperature of party animosities.

The ordinary citizens learnt to regard King George both as the father of his people and as the reflection and magnification of their own collective virtues. Dutifully he subordinated his own preferences

which after the proclamation of the French Republic in 1871 did certainly acquire considerable importance and, under the leadership of Charles Bradlaugh and George Odger, incorporated formidable, if momentary, fellow-travellers, such as Dilke, Joseph Chamberlain, Auberon Herbert, and even John Morley. The movement collapsed after the popular demonstration on the recovery of the Prince of Wales from his serious illness in 1871. The last Republican Conference was held at Birmingham in May 1873 and Dilke in the next year ascribed his former republicanism to 'political infancy'. In 1923 the Labour Conference rejected by 3,694,000 votes to 386,000 the motion: 'Is Republicanism the policy of the Labour Party?'

Professor Laski attributes the collapse of the Republican movement to many causes, among them the immense popularity of Queen Victoria in her later years, the 'immediate' popularity of King Edward VII, and the 'ultimate' popularity of King George V. He also attributes it to the elimination of the aristocratic wedge in the structure of political power and to the fact that, under King George V, the Monarchy became identified with the interests of the ordinary citizen and an 'emollient, rather than an active umpire, between conflicting interests'.[5]

and prejudices, his many unconcealed likes and dislikes, to an excellent perception of his historical function. Under his guidance, ·the British Monarchy emerged from a period of international convulsion, from a period at home of slow silent revolution, with enhanced influence and repute. Throughout those twenty-six years of difficulty and danger King George remained unalterable and unaltered.

CHAPTER IX

THE NOVEMBER PLEDGES

1910

King George's first Council—The Prime Minister hurries back from
Gibraltar—The Accession proclaimed—King Edward's funeral—
The Constitutional crisis—Effect of the General Election of January,
1910—Mr Asquith's position—His statements of December 10,
February 21 and April 14—King Edward's attitude to the problem—
The historical precedents—The Conference between the Government
and the Opposition—Mr Lloyd George's desire for a Coalition
Government—The Conference breaks down—Mr Asquith at York
Cottage—He asks for no guarantees—On his return to London he
changes his mind and demands immediate pledges—Lord Knollys
and the Master of Elibank—The King refuses to give contingent
guarantees—The Cabinet minute of November 15—The King comes
to London—His conversation with Mr Asquith and Lord Crewe on
November 16—He agrees to give the pledges—The King resents the
pledge being kept secret—His feeling that his hand was forced.

(1)

ON SATURDAY, May 7, 1910, the new king drove in a closed carriage
from Marlborough House to St. James's Palace to attend his first
Council. Dressed in admiral's uniform he stood in the Banqueting
Hall with the Privy Councillors grouped around him. 'The most
trying ordeal', he wrote that evening, 'that I ever had to go through.'

> 'My heart is too full', he said to them, 'for me to address you today in
> more than a few words. I have not only lost a father's love, but the
> affectionate and intimate relations of a dear friend and adviser. I am
> deeply sensible of the very heavy responsibilities which have fallen
> upon me. I know that I can rely upon Parliament and the People of
> these islands and of my Dominions beyond the seas for their help in
> the discharge of these arduous duties and for their prayers that God
> will grant me strength and guidance. I am encouraged by the know-
> ledge that I have in my dear wife one who will be a constant help-
> mate in every endeavour for our People's good.'

The Privy Councillors were impressed by the firm tones in which
he said these words and by the simplicity of his bearing.

The Prime Minister at the end of April had embarked in the
Admiralty yacht *Enchantress* for a Mediterranean cruise. The news of

King Edward's death was brought to him at 3.0 a.m. on the morning of May 7 when the yacht was lying in Gibraltar harbour:

'I went up on deck', Mr Asquith recorded subsequently,[a] 'and I remember well that the first sight that met my eyes in the twilight before dawn was Halley's comet blazing in the sky. . . . I felt bewildered and indeed stunned. At a most anxious moment in the fortunes of the State, we had lost, without warning or preparation, the Sovereign whose ripe experience, trained sagacity, equitable judgment and unvarying consideration, counted for so much. . . . Now he had gone. His successor, with all his fine and engaging qualities, was without political experience. We were nearing the verge of a crisis almost without example in our constitutional history. What was the right thing to do?'

An hour later the *Enchantress* was on her way back to Plymouth.

At 9.0 a.m. on Monday, May 9, the Accession of King George V was proclaimed from the balcony of Friary Court, St. James's Palace. The hereditary Earl Marshal, the Duke of Norfolk, was accompanied by Ministers and Privy Councillors in uniform, including Mr Lloyd George and Mr Winston Churchill. The proclamation was read by Sir Alfred Scott-Gatty, Garter King-of-Arms, supported by Norroy King-of-Arms, Windsor Herald, Somerset Herald and the four Pursuivants, Rouge Dragon, Bluemantle, Rouge Croix and Portcullis, dressed in their tabards of scarlet, blue and gold. The voice of Garter King-of-Arms rang out above the silent crowd:

'Whereas it has pleased Almighty God to call to His Mercy our late Sovereign Lord, King Edward the Seventh, of blessed and glorious memory, by whose decease the Imperial Crown of the United Kingdom of Great Britain and Ireland is solely and rightfully come to the High and Mighty Prince George Frederick Ernest Albert:

'We, therefore, the Lords Spiritual and Temporal of this Realm, being here assisted by those of his late Majesty's Privy Council, with numbers of other principal gentlemen of quality, with the Lord Mayor, Aldermen and citizens of London, do now hereby, with one voice and content of tongue and heart, publish and proclaim:

'That the High and Mighty Prince George Frederick Ernest Albert is now, by the death of our late Sovereign of happy memory, become our only lawful right Liege Lord; George the Fifth by the Grace of God, King of the United Kingdom of Great Britain and Ireland, and of the British Dominions beyond the Seas, Defender of the Faith, Emperor of India, to whom we acknowledge all faith and constant obedience, with all hearty and humble affection, beseeching God, by whom Kings and Queens do reign, to bless the Royal Prince George the Fifth with long and happy years to reign over us.'

The silver trumpets sounded and the batteries in the adjoining park began to thunder their salute. A single voice in the hushed crowd started to intone the first bars of 'God save the King'; the hymn was taken up by another voice, and then by a third; in a moment the surge of our national anthem rose massively from the crowds around St. James's Palace, its rhythm punctuated by the crash of guns.

The two elder princes, Prince Edward and Prince Albert, in their uniforms as naval cadets, witnessed the ceremony from the garden wall at Marlborough House. They stood at the salute. The King and Queen had also, from behind a curtain in an upper bedroom, looked down on Friary Court:

'May & I watched from the window of the boys room. Most touching when the crowd sang the National Anthem.'

On May 17 the coffin of King Edward was taken to Westminster Hall, where it was received by the officers of State and the assembled Houses of Parliament. For three days and nights it lay in that dim nave, the crown, the sceptre and the orb flashing in the light of candles as the black and silent crowds filed by. On May 20 the coffin was taken to Windsor and lowered into the vault below the Albert Memorial Chapel. Beside it, at this final ceremony, stood the German Emperor and eight Kings.[1]

(2)

On pages 103 and 104 of Chapter VII a rapid outline was sketched of the initial stages of the constitutional crisis which had cast a shadow over the last weeks of King Edward's life. Some recapitulation will now be necessary if any conception is to be conveyed of the strains and stresses to which Mr. Asquith was thereafter exposed or of the acute personal predicament in which, at the very outset of his reign, the new Monarch became involved. The first phase of the conflict between Lords and Commons culminated on November 16, 1910, on which date the Government, by threatening resignation, extracted a secret pledge from King George that, if need arose, he would create a sufficient number of new peers to swamp all

[1] Apart from the German Emperor, King Edward's funeral was attended by the Kings of Denmark, Portugal, Norway, Spain, Belgium, Greece and Bulgaria. The Dowager Empress of Russia, the Queen Dowager of the Netherlands, the Crown Princes of Rumania, Montenegro, Servia and Greece, and the Archduke Franz Ferdinand of Austria were also present. The United States were represented by ex-President Theodore Roosevelt and France by her Foreign Minister, Monsieur Pichon.

possible opposition to the Parliament Bill in the Upper Chamber. The second phase, which will be dealt with in the following chapter, culminated on August 10, 1911, on which date the House of Lords, by a narrow majority, agreed to a drastic curtailment of their constitutional powers. The Royal Archives at Windsor throw fresh light on each of these transactions.[1]

It will be remembered that in the Parliament elected in 1906 the Liberals had outnumbered the Unionists (which was the name then generally given to the Conservative Opposition and their Liberal-Unionist allies[2]) by 210 and possessed a majority of 84 over all the other parties combined. In the General Election of January 1910, however, the Liberals had lost 104 seats and in the new Parliament they held a majority over the Unionists of only two votes. This meant that thereafter the Government had to depend on the support of the 82 Irish Nationalists under Mr. John Redmond and of the 40 members of the Labour Party. Since each of these groups was in general

[1] It may assist the reader, in following this complicated story, to be reminded of the main dates:

1909. November 30.   House of Lords reject Mr Lloyd George's Budget.
      December 10.   Mr Asquith's Albert Hall speech.
1910. January 14–28.   General Election. Liberals lose 104 seats.
      February 15.   New Parliament meets.
      April 14.   First reading of Parliament Bill. Asquith's speech.
      April 28.   House of Lords passes Budget.
      May 6.   Death of King Edward.
      June 17–
      November 11.   Constitutional Conference.
      November 16.   The King gives pledges to Asquith.
      November 28.   Dissolution. Second General Election. Little change.
1911. February 5.   New Parliament opens.
      February 21.   Parliament Bill again introduced.
      May 15.   Parliament Bill passes House of Commons.
      July 20.   Third reading debate in House of Lords. Asquith informs Balfour of King's November pledges.
      August 7.   Vote of Censure debates in both Houses.
      August 10.   Parliament Bill passed by House of Lords.

[2] In 1886 a body of Liberals had voted against Mr Gladstone's first Home Rule Bill and formed a third party under the name of 'Liberal Unionists'. They consisted of the old Whigs, under Lord Hartington, and the Radical Imperialists, under Mr Joseph Chamberlain. In 1895 the leaders of the Liberal Unionists joined the Conservative Government and this coalition was named 'Unionist'. This name remained the official title of the alliance until January 15, 1922, when the Irish Free State was established.

agreement with the policy of the Government, Mr Asquith could therefore rely upon a working majority of 124 in the House of Commons.

The Unionists had accepted the verdict of the General Election of January 1910 as indicating that the country desired the passage of Mr Lloyd George's Budget. That Budget, which had been rejected by them in the previous November, was accordingly passed by the House of Lords without a division on April 28, 1910. The Unionists did not, however, consider that the January election had given the Government a mandate to alter the balance of the Constitution or to advise the Crown to create a sufficient number of new peers to force the Parliament Bill through the Upper Chamber. By the early spring of 1910 it was thus generally recognised that a second General Election would be necessary before the Government could claim that their intention to restrict the powers of the House of Lords reflected the will of the electorate.

The main body of the Liberal Party, together with their Labour allies, considered it intolerable that a progressive administration, possessing a majority in the House of Commons, should be thwarted by an Upper Chamber composed for the most part of Conservative Peers. Mr Asquith himself fully shared these feelings. It was inevitable also that, after the election of January 1910, Mr Redmond and his party should seek to exploit the tactical advantage given them by the balance of parties in the new House of Commons to secure not merely the introduction of a Home Rule Bill but also legislation such as would prevent the House of Lords from imposing their traditional veto upon any such measure. Mr Redmond had in fact indicated[b] that, if a second General Election were to be held, he would not be prepared to instruct his supporters to vote for Liberal candidates unless the Government undertook to introduce a Home Rule Bill and to obtain advance pledges from the Crown.[1] It is none the less an

---

[1] The implications of the phrase 'advance pledges' (with its many variants, such as 'advance assurances', 'contingent guarantees', 'necessary safeguards', 'hypothetical understandings' and so on) became increasingly controversial. On the one hand it was contended that a Government was justified, when asking for a dissolution, in obtaining promises from the King which would become operative only if, as a result of the election, that Government were again returned to power. On the other hand it was contended that for the King to furnish a Government with such advance pledges would be to anticipate the verdict of the electorate and thus to favour one side as against the other.

It was on this conflict of constitutional theory that the issue turned.

error to suppose that Mr Asquith's policy or actions were dictated to him by Mr Redmond. He would have taken exactly the same line if no Irish party had existed.

The Unionists, for their part, exaggerated the pressure being exercised upon the Prime Minister by the Irish Party and contended, with much bitterness, that Mr Asquith was the prisoner of Mr Redmond, who was exploiting English constitutional difficulties for Irish ends.

During the lifetime of King Edward, Mr Asquith had been able to postpone a collision by mingling procrastination with occasional pronouncements, designed to assuage, or at least to bewilder, his diverse antagonists, supporters and allies. In that it was the disparity of these utterances which accounted for much of the confusion which ensued, it is well to bear them in mind.

On December 10, 1909, when inaugurating the campaign which preceded the General Election of the following January, Mr Asquith had assured an Albert Hall meeting that 'we shall not assume office, and we shall not hold office, unless we can secure the safeguards which experience shows us to be necessary'. If this meant anything at all, it meant that he would not, if returned, agree to form an administration unless he obtained the King's assent to the creation of peers. On February 21, 1910, however, having been returned to office by a reduced majority, he made the following pronouncement in the House of Commons:

> 'To ask in advance for a blank authority for an indefinite exercise of the Royal Prerogative in regard to a measure which has never been submitted to, or approved by, the House of Commons, is a request which, in my judgement, no constitutional statesman can properly make and it is a concession which the Sovereign cannot be expected to grant.'

If that meant anything at all, it meant that the Prime Minister considered it unconstitutional to demand advance pledges from the Sovereign. Yet, as has already been said, in introducing the Parliament Bill on April 14, 1910, only three weeks before King Edward's death, he committed himself to the following utterance, which was not unjustifiably interpreted by his supporters and the Irish as an undertaking that, before again going to the country, he would demand advance guarantees:

> 'Let me add this. In no case shall we recommend Dissolution, except under such conditions as will secure that in the new Parliament the judgement of the People, as expressed in the Election, will be carried into law.'

Mr Asquith's consistent purpose was to keep the name of the King out of party polemics. Interpreted in the light of that honourable and dominant intention his statements were not as contradictory as they seem. At the time, however, they certainly left some confusion in the public mind.

It does not appear that King Edward, before his death, had finally decided upon the attitude which he ought to adopt. He certainly felt that for the Sovereign to confer peerages upon an unspecified number of persons nominated by the Chief Liberal Whip would entail a degradation of the Royal Prerogative and the destruction of the House of Lords. While at Biarritz he seems to have toyed with an ingenious compromise scheme, under which the required majority might be obtained by giving peerages to the eldest sons of those peers who supported the Liberal Government. But what assurance was there that these young men would be either sufficiently numerous or sufficiently obedient to secure the passage of the Parliament Bill?

Mr Asquith assumed that, if the worst came to the worst, the Monarch must necessarily follow the advice tendered to him by the Government in power even at the cost of destroying the House of Lords. But there were several responsible persons, including the Archbishop of Canterbury and Lord Rosebery, who contended that it would be the duty of the King to refuse his assent to so revolutionary a measure. On his return to England, and exactly one week before the day of his death, King Edward was informed by his Private Secretary, Lord Knollys, that, should he refuse his assent to the advice given him by the Government in power, and should Mr Asquith thereupon resign his office, the Leader of the Conservative Opposition, Mr A. J. Balfour, would be ready to form an alternative administration and to go to the country on the constitutional issue. The misfortune was that King Edward did not discuss the problem in any detail with his successor; nor did Lord Knollys inform King George of Mr Balfour's eventual readiness to assume responsibility.[1]

King George, therefore, was faced, immediately on his accession, with an unprecedented constitutional problem of which he had little

[1] On April 29, 1910, Lord Knollys attended a meeting at Lambeth Palace between the Archbishop of Canterbury, Lord Esher and Mr Balfour. A note of the discussion which took place contains the following important passages: 'Mr Balfour made it quite clear that he would be prepared to form a Government to prevent the King being put in the

previous knowledge and in which he was accorded no consistent guidance. His father had left him no clear directives; Lord Knollys and Sir Arthur Bigge, whom he had appointed joint Private Secretaries,[1] did not see eye to eye in the matter; and his friends overwhelmed him with contradictory advice. Unaccustomed as he was to ambiguous phraseology he was totally unable to interpret Mr Asquith's enigmas. Nor were the historical precedents of much avail. Queen Anne it seemed had in 1712 created twelve new peers in order to avert opposition to the Peace of Utrecht; but that had been a very small number and very long ago. William IV in 1832 had, after much wriggling, promised Lord Grey to create eighty new Peers in order to secure the passage of the Reform Bills. That promise (which King William had never actually been called upon to execute) had been justified by the overwhelming public demand that the Reform Bills should be passed. In the present issue, there was no overwhelming popular demand; the British public were comparatively indifferent to the whole controversy. How could the King be certain that, in yielding to Mr Asquith's solicitations, in promising to create as many as 500 new Peers (with the added implication of eventual Home Rule for Ireland), he would be accurately interpreting the considered wishes of the nation? He could not be certain.

(3)

Mr Asquith reached Plymouth in the *Enchantress* on the evening of May 9. On the following morning he was received by the new

---

position contemplated by the demand for the creation of Peers' (R.A. K.2552 (2) 93).

This note was not brought to the notice of King George until after Lord Knollys' retirement three years later. The King then dictated and initialled the following revealing minute:

'It was not until late in the year 1913 that the foregoing letters and memoranda came into my possession. The knowledge of their contents would, undoubtedly, have had an important bearing and influence with regard to Mr Asquith's request for guarantees on November 16, 1910.

'George R.I. January 7, 1914'
(R.A. K.2552 (2) 89).

In spite of Mr. Balfour's assertion of April 29, it is evident from his letter to Lord Lansdowne of December 27, 1910, that he would in fact have hesitated to form a government if he had been invited.

[1] It was at Sir Arthur Bigge's suggestion that Lord Knollys, on the death of King Edward, was appointed joint Private Secretary to King George. This system of dual guidance did not in practice prove satisfactory and Lord Knollys relinquished his appointment on March 17, 1913.

King and the Cabinet was sworn in. He came away from that interview 'deeply moved by the King's modesty and good sense'.[c] On May 18 he had a private audience at Buckingham Palace:

'I gave an audience to the Prime Minister,' King George wrote that evening in his diary. 'We had a long talk. He said he would endeavour to come to some understanding with the Opposition to prevent a general election & he would not pay attention to what Redmond said.'

Mr Asquith immediately got into touch with Mr A. J. Balfour, who agreed to a Conference. This unselfish initiative on the part of the Prime Minister was much resented by the Irish Nationalists and by some of his own more ardent supporters. But at least it gave to the new Sovereign a six months' reprieve.

The first meeting of the Conference was held in the Prime Minister's room at the House of Commons on June 17, 1910. The Government were represented by Mr Asquith, Lord Crewe, Mr Lloyd George and Mr Birrell. The Opposition were represented by Mr A. J. Balfour, Lord Lansdowne, Mr Austen Chamberlain and Lord Cawdor. At first Mr Asquith took an optimistic view of these discussions. 'The Conference', he informed the King, 'has indicated a desire for *rapprochement*.' Twelve meetings were held before Parliament rose for the summer recess at the end of July. But as the weeks passed, the shock caused by King Edward's death, the common desire not to embarrass a new and untried Sovereign, lost something of their early emotional and unifying impetus; party faiths, party loyalties, above all the party machines, intervened to hamper, and finally to disrupt, the unison of these eight men.

Mr Lloyd George, with his quick surgical intuition, realised before long that only a major operation could remove from the body politic the accumulated deposits of party dogmas, prejudices and commitments. In a striking memorandum which he addressed to Mr Asquith on August 17,[d] he advocated the formation of a Coalition Government, by which alone the statesmen, freed from dependence on their party extremists, could deal conjointly with the rapidly increasing dangers of the internal and external situation. Such a Coalition, he intimated, could not only solve the constitutional problem, but could also discover some reasonable federal solution of the Irish question, combine for general social betterment, and even impose upon the country a form of compulsory military training. Mr Asquith showed this memorandum to Mr Balfour as well as to the five members of his own inner Cabinet. Mr Balfour was not in principle opposed to the suggestion, but felt it necessary to consult

Mr Akers Douglas, his former Chief Whip. The latter insisted that any such junction with the Liberals would be regarded by the Unionists as a betrayal of all they stood for. Mr. Balfour (remarking sadly 'I cannot become another Peel in my Party') was forced to refuse.[e]

Mr Lloyd George, to the end of his life, regarded the rejection of his suggested Coalition Government as 'a supreme instance' of the damage done when party politics 'stand seriously in the way of the highest national interests':

> 'In the year 1910', he wrote in his *War Memoirs*,[1] 'we were beset by an accumulation of grave issues—rapidly becoming graver. . . . It was becoming evident to discerning eyes that the Party and Parliamentary system was unequal to coping with them.'

He remained for ever convinced (and there is some substance in his conviction) that, had his 1910 suggestion not been vetoed by the Party machines, there would have been no revolution in Ireland and perhaps no German war.

The Conference, which had opened so auspiciously in June, had by the autumn reached a complete deadlock. The Unionists, in their initial memorandum, had divided legislation into three separate categories: Financial, Ordinary and Constitutional or 'Organic'. As regards Finance, they were prepared to abandon the claim of the House of Lords to reject money Bills, provided that the House of Commons for their part would accept some system under which pure Money Bills could be differentiated from Bills which, 'although technically dealing with little or nothing but Finance, have social or political consequences which go far beyond the mere raising of revenue'. Some progress was made in devising an agreed tribunal which could decide under which definition a particular Money Bill was to be classed.

As regards 'Ordinary' legislation, it was agreed in principle that if, under this heading, an irreconcilable conflict arose between the House of Commons and the House of Lords, the matter should be settled by a Joint Sitting of both Houses. Difficulties then arose as to the composition of the delegation which would represent the House of Lords at these Joint Sittings. The Government contended that such Joint Sittings should be composed of the 670 members of the House of Commons plus a delegation of only 100 members from the House of Lords, chosen upon some system of proportional representation. The Opposition contended that so restricted a delegation of peers was inequitable, but failed to produce any counter-proposal of their own.

As regards Constitutional, or 'Organic', legislation, the Government were willing to offer special safeguards in respect of the Monarchy, the Protestant succession and any Act embodying the conclusions of the Conference itself. It was under this heading that the problem of Home Rule was dealt with and a deadlock reached. The Government insisted that, after the first rejection of a Home Rule Bill by the House of Lords, a General Election should follow and that, if a majority in favour of Home Rule were returned to power, then the resultant Bills would be treated as 'Ordinary' and not as 'Organic' legislation. The Opposition insisted that, after the second rejection of a Home Rule Bill by the House of Lords, the Bill should be referred directly to the electorate as a straight issue for a plebiscite or referendum. Mr Asquith was ill disposed to plebiscites: in fact, the very word 'referendum' would cause his usually tolerant features to writhe into an expression of contemptuous disgust. It was thus mainly on the question of Home Rule that the Conference broke down.*ᵍ*

(4)

By the first week of November 1910, it was recognised that no further compromise was possible between the Government and the Opposition. The period of reprieve had come to an end. The harsh alternatives which had so distressed King Edward during the last weeks of his life now confronted his successor. King George was faced with the necessity of coming to an immediate decision as to what was his constitutional duty in a crisis in regard to which the soundest constitutional experts took completely contradictory views.

On Friday, November 11, Mr Asquith went down to York Cottage, Sandringham:

'At 6.30', the King noted in his diary, 'the Prime Minister arrived. Had two long talks with him. He reported that the Conference had failed & he proposed to dissolve & have a general election & get it over before Xmas. He asked me for *no guarantees*. I suggested that the Veto resolutions should first be sent up to the H. of L. & if they rejected them, then he could dissolve. This he agreed to do.'

This succinct record is confirmed by a minute written on the same evening by Sir A. Bigge.*ʰ* 'He did not', Sir Arthur wrote, 'ask for anything from the King: *no promises, no guarantees during this Parliament.*' A more extended version of the interview was composed by Mr Asquith himself on his return to Downing Street:*ⁱ*

133

'Mr Asquith had the honour of being received by the King at Sandringham on November 11. The object of the interview was, not to tender any definite advice, but to survey the new situation created by the failure of the Conference, as it presents itself at the moment to His Majesty's Ministers. . . .

'Mr Asquith pointed out that this would be the second time in the course of twelve months that the question of the relations between the two Houses had been submitted to the electorate. It was necessary, therefore, that in the event of the Government obtaining an adequate majority in the new House of Commons, the matter should be put in train for final settlement.

'This could only be brought about (if the Lords were not ready to give way) by the willingness of the Crown to exercise its Prerogative to give effect to the will of the nation. The House of Lords cannot be dissolved, and the only legal way in which it can be brought into harmony with the other House is either by curtailing, or adding to, its members. In theory, the Crown might conceivably adopt the former course, by withholding writs of summons. But this has not been done for many centuries: it would be a most invidious practice: and it is at least doubtful whether it can be said to be constitutional. On the other hand, the prerogative of creation is undoubted: it has never been recognised as having any constitutional limit: it was used for this purpose in the eighteenth century, and agreed to be used on a large scale by King William IV in 1832.

'There could in Mr Asquith's opinion be no doubt that the knowledge that the Crown was ready to use the Prerogative would be sufficient to bring about an agreement, without any necessity for its actual exercise.'

It is evident from this careful record that Mr Asquith's intention had been to warn the King of the attitude of the Government before this was crystallised into action by the subsequent meeting of the Cabinet and embodied in an official Cabinet Minute. Sir A. Bigge was optimistic in supposing that no guarantees would be demanded.

On Monday, November 14, Lord Knollys travelled up to London from Sandringham and went straight from Liverpool Street Station to No. 10 Downing Street. He found 'to his surprise' that the Prime Minister's intentions were more definite. 'What he *now* advocates', wrote Lord Knollys that night to the King, 'is that you should give guarantees *at once* for the next Parliament.'*j* Sir Arthur Bigge was instructed the next morning to send the following telegram to Mr Vaughan Nash, the Prime Minister's Private Secretary:*k*

'His Majesty regrets that it would be impossible for him to give contingent guarantees and he reminds Mr Asquith of his promise not to seek for any during the present Parliament.'

Both the King and the Prime Minister were thus involved in a seemingly inextricable predicament.

The King desired only to follow established constitutional practice, and to accept the advice given him by the Government in power. It seemed to him, however, that what Mr Asquith was now asking him to do was to pledge himself to a definite line of action, on the eve of a General Election, and in regard to the very issue upon which that election would be fought. There was no constitutional precedent for such blank and post-dated cheques. If the Liberals were returned with a majority, then it would be his duty thereafter to accept the advice they gave him, however personally reluctant he might be to do so. He much resented the implication that in such an event he might fail to act constitutionally. But supposing that the Unionists and not the Liberals received a majority at the impending election? Might they not contend that he had acted unconstitutionally in giving advance backing to a policy of which both they and the electorate disapproved? If he accepted Mr Asquith's suggestion he might thereafter be accused by the Unionists of having assisted the Liberals. If he rejected Mr Asquith's suggestion. he would be accused of taking the side of the Unionists. The one thing which he wished above all to avoid was being forced into the position of taking sides in a party conflict.

It would have been within his constitutional powers to refuse to follow Mr Asquith's advice, to accept his resignation and to invite Mr Balfour to form a Government. Lord Knollys assured him that Mr Balfour would in any event decline to form an administration. This, as has been seen, was an incorrect assumption. But even if Mr Balfour accepted, his administration would immediately be outvoted in the existing House of Commons and might well fail to obtain a majority in the next. The King would then have found himself in the invidious position into which William IV had been clumsily manoeuvred in 1832.

Mr Asquith also was encompassed by unpleasant alternatives. Being a man of delicate imagination, he fully understood and sympathised with the distracting conflict of duties by which the King was assailed. Yet in the mind of his own party (as his Chief Whip, the Master of Elibank,[1] was incessantly reminding him) he was tied

[1] Alexander Murray, Master of Elibank (1870–1920), was Chief Liberal Whip from 1909 to 1912. In the latter year he went to the House of Lords as Lord Murray of Elibank. Mrs Asquith in her *Autobiography* (II, 145) describes him 'as a rare combination of grit and honey'.

135

by the assurance which he had given on April 14, by which he had, by all reasonable interpretation of his words, pledged himself not to go to the country unless and until he had received previous assurances that, if he returned to power, the Royal Prerogative would be imposed upon the House of Lords. The Chief Whip pointed out to him that if he evaded this pledge, he would be regarded as having betrayed his own Party, to say nothing of the Irish and the Socialists. Yet, if he announced that he had asked for the guarantees and that they had been refused by the King, then the Crown would inevitably be drawn, and to a most damaging extent, into the arena of Party controversy.

The Cabinet, at their meeting on Tuesday, November 15, decided to cut this Gordian knot. They addressed to the King the following somewhat peremptory minute:[1]

'The Cabinet has very carefully considered the situation created by the failure of the Conference, in view of the declaration of policy made on their behalf by the Prime Minister in the House of Commons on the 14th of April, 1910.

'The advice which they feel it their duty to tender to His Majesty is as follows:

'An immediate dissolution of Parliament, as soon as the necessary parts of the Budget, the provision of Old Age Pensions to paupers, and one or two other matters have been disposed of.

'The House of Lords to have the opportunity, if they desired it, at the same time (but not so as to postpone the date of the dissolution), to discuss the Government Resolutions.

'His Majesty's Ministers cannot, however, take the responsibility of advising a dissolution, unless they may understand that, in the event of the policy of the Government being approved by an adequate majority in the new House of Commons, His Majesty will be ready to exercise his constitutional powers (which may involve the Prerogative of creating Peers), if needed, to secure that effect should be given to the decision of the country.

'His Majesty's Ministers are fully alive to the importance of keeping the name of the King out of the sphere of party and electoral controversy. They take upon themselves, as is their duty, the entire and exclusive responsibility for the policy which they will place before the electorate.

'His Majesty will doubtless agree that it would be undesirable, in the interests of the State, that any communication of the intentions of the Crown should be made public, unless and until the actual occasion should arise.'

This Minute was accompanied by a letter from Lord Knollys, who was in close contact and sympathy with Mr Asquith and the Master of Elibank:

'I have just finished', he wrote to the King,[m] 'a conversation with the
P.M. and Crewe and they have shown me the Cabinet Minute, which
I think is couched in studiously moderate terms. I feel certain that you
can safely and constitutionally accept what the Cabinet propose & I
venture to urge you strongly to do so. What is now recommended is
altogether different in every way from any request to be allowed
publicly to announce that you have consented to give guarantees. It
is a great compromise on the part of the Cabinet, made entirely to fall
in as far as possible with your wishes and to enable you to act con-
scientiously.

'Should you not approve of the proposal, it may be that the matter
has not been sufficiently explained to you, and in that case, of course,
I should be quite ready, should you desire it, to go to Sandringham
tomorrow. Or, and what would be better, if you disagree, perhaps you
might think it right to come to London to see the P.M. and Crewe.'

Lord Knollys also enclosed a letter which he had received that
morning from the Master of Elibank urging that it was essential to
'safeguard' the Prime Minister's relations with his own party.

This letter produced an indignant outburst from Sir Arthur
Bigge:[n]

'I have read', Sir Arthur Bigge informed the Master of Elibank, 'your
letter to Knollys. Your arguments are naturally made from the Prime
Minister's position created by his statement of April 14.

'But the King's position must also be considered. His Majesty fully
recognises what must be the ultimate solution of the political situation
if a dissolution takes place and if the Government are returned by an
adequate majority. But why is he to make any promises *now*? Why
should he be asked to deviate by an inch from the strictly constitutional
path? You reply "to safeguard the Prime Minister" and to avoid the
King's name being dragged into the vortex of the political controversies and to prevent a handle being given to the Socialists to attack
the King. But surely, so long as His Majesty adheres to what is constitutional, he can be indifferent to whether the Socialists "so furiously
rage together and imagine a vain thing" or not. His Majesty was
delighted with the Prime Minister on Friday and especially with his
assurance that the King would be *asked for nothing*, no guarantee, no
promises, during this Parliament.

'No! I say. If dissolution there must be—all right. Then "wait and
see" what is the voice of the electorate—and once more, I repeat, the
King will do what is right.'

In summarising this correspondence for the King, Sir Arthur
Bigge added his own commentary:

'The King's position is: he cannot give contingent guarantees. For by
so doing he becomes a Partisan & is placing a powerful weapon in the
hands of the Irish and Socialists who, assured of the abolition of the

veto of the House of Lords, would hold before their electors the certainty of ultimate Home Rule & the carrying out of their Socialist programme. The Unionists would declare His Majesty was favouring the Government and placing them (the Unionists) at a disadvantage before their constituencies. Indeed, it is questionable whether His Majesty would be acting constitutionally. It is not His Majesty's duty to save the Prime Minister from the mistake of his incautious words on the 14th of April.'

In reply to the Cabinet's suggestion that the pledges should be given, but kept secret, Sir Arthur Bigge furnished the King with equally trenchant comments:

'What is the object of the King giving the Cabinet to understand that, in the event of the Government being returned with an adequate majority in the new House of Commons, he will be ready to exercise his constitutional powers, *if his intentions are not to be made public until the occasion arises*? Why should the King not wait until the occasion arises?' 'Is this straight?' asked Sir Arthur Bigge. 'Is it English?' 'Is it not moreover childish?'*o*

On Wednesday, November 16, the King travelled to London and received the Prime Minister and Lord Crewe at Buckingham Palace at 3.30 p.m.:

'After a long talk', he wrote that evening in his diary, 'I agreed most reluctantly to give the Cabinet a secret understanding that in the event of the Government being returned with a majority at the General Election, I should use my Prerogative to make Peers if asked for. I disliked having to do this very much, but agreed that this was the only alternative to the Cabinet resigning, which at this moment would be disastrous.

'Francis (Lord Knollys) strongly urged me to take this course & I think his advice is generally very sound. I only trust & pray he is right this time.'

'I never', recorded Mr Asquith, 'have seen the King to better advantage. He argued well and showed no obstinacy.'*p*

Sir Arthur Bigge was much distressed by this decision. In a memorandum which he wrote on his return to Sandringham on November 18 he expressed his apprehension:*q*

'In less than 48 hours', he wrote, 'Lord Knollys' mind has been entirely changed, as he was adamant as to any assurance being given; today he strongly urges the King to come to a secret understanding & tells me that by advocating resignation rather than agree to any understanding I am exposing the King and the Monarchy to the gravest dangers. He told the King he would have advised King Edward as he had advised King George and that he was convinced his late Majesty would have followed his advice. This quoting what a dead person would do is to me most unfair, if not improper, especially to the King, who has such a high opinion of his father's judgment. But might I not equally have urged that I was perfectly certain Queen Victoria would have done what I advised? . . . I solemnly believe that a great mistake has been made resulting from a dread, which to say the least has been much exaggerated, of danger to the Crown; whereas the real danger is to the position of the P.M. In the conversation of the 16th even the instability of Foreign Thrones was dragged in to intensify this Bogey!

'His Majesty has given way! How could he do otherwise, with the P.M., the leader of the House of Lords and Lord Knollys assuring him he was doing what was right and constitutional? Please God *they* are right and that we may not regret the step taken and find before long that fresh demands will be made entailing, either further concessions, or resistance resulting in more danger to the Throne than that which *might* have been incurred by a bold, fearless and open line of action in the present crisis.'

It is still not apparent why the device of keeping the King's pledge secret should have been regarded as a solution of the difficulty. When, a few weeks later, the King asked Mr Asquith why he had been forced into this secret arrangement, the latter replied that in view of the promises he had made on April 14 'it was necessary to have definite private assurances, otherwise he would have broken his word'.^r The Master of Elibank may have thought that he could, by shadowed hint, allay the suspicions of the Party that the Prime Minister had gone back upon his undertaking of April 14. Lord Knollys may have felt that to keep the pledge a secret might prevent the Crown being, at least by any responsible politician, dragged into the electoral arena. The King's own opinion was voiced, eleven months later, in a conversation with Lord Esher.^s

'What he specially resented was the promise extracted from him in November that he would tell no one. He said: "I have never in my life done anything I was ashamed to confess. And I have never been accustomed to conceal things." '

King George remained convinced thereafter that in this, the first political crisis of his reign, he had not been accorded either the confidence or the consideration to which he was entitled. Against the Prime Minister personally he retained no rancour whatsoever. He realised that Mr Asquith's hand had also been forced. He was fully aware of the qualities of mind and heart possessed by that shy but greatly gifted man.

CHAPTER X

THE PARLIAMENT BILL

1911

King George's interest in Home and Commonwealth affairs—His recreations—His domesticity—The Mylius case—The Coronation—He visits Ireland, Scotland and Wales—The investiture of the Prince of Wales—The renewal of the conflict between Lords and Commons—Mr Balfour's indignation—Lord Lansdowne's proposals for the reform of the House of Lords—The results of the General Election of December 1910—The Parliament Bill again introduced—Lord Lansdowne's amendment—The November pledges are divulged—The Lansdowne House meeting—The Halsbury Club—The Votes of Censure—The final division of August 10—The King's satisfaction with the result.

(1)

ANY monarch, however unambitious he may be, however unaccustomed to self-assertion or self-display, will be conscious that he must inevitably become the symbol, and perhaps the eponym, of a given period of history. He will endeavour therefore to give to his reign the tone and colour best adapted to his temperament; and will prefer, among the varied functions of monarchy, those which are most expressive of his own character and in the closest conformity with his own tastes and aptitudes.

There exists in the Round Tower at Windsor a curious document, dated September 1910, in the handwriting of Lord Rosebery, who as a former Prime Minister possessed the authority of an elder statesman and who could also claim the privileges of a family friend. In this document Lord Rosebery urges the new monarch to adopt a line of his own:

'The King', writes Lord Rosebery, 'has to start without the advantages of his father and with a clear slate; but with this great advantage, that he had served in the Navy, and that he knows the Empire and has expressed his interest in the Empire by memorable words and deeds.

'But it is *now* that he has to give colour and stamp to his reign. *He will be judged by the next two years.*

'If he wishes to make his reign illustrious, he will have to give up the next two years to that task, and give himself up to that and nothing else, just as an ambitious and patriotic Minister would do. He must make himself felt all the time.

'He must make it clear to his subjects that he is earnest and industrious, as indeed he is. That should be the stamp of his reign. He should show that he is willing to deny himself any pleasure to do his duty; more, that he is ready to do anything disagreeable to himself. This is a hard saying, but most truths are hard.

'There is something harder still. He must remember that every word of a King is treasured in this country as if it were God's; that he cannot speak without the chance of his words being noted, and carried, even by servants. To his intimate friends he can no doubt unbosom himself, but even this with precaution. . . .

'Besides devotion to duty and reticence there is something else to be noted, and that is the instinct of striking the imagination.'

Much as he admired the part which his father played in international affairs, King George realised from the outset that it would be impossible for him to repeat, and imprudent for him to imitate, a rôle for which he was so little fitted by predilection or experience. This was a wise decision. Although the initiative taken by King Edward in foreign policy has been much exaggerated (especially by German publicists), it is an undoubted fact that his frequent visits to the Continent and his repeated conversations with foreign potentates and statesmen were regarded as official acts which, although generally beneficial, might, in less adept hands, have become embarrassing. Already, in the House of Commons, some uneasiness had been manifested regarding the diplomatic activity in which King Edward (often unaccompanied by a responsible Minister) delighted to indulge. King George had no inclinations towards diplomacy and, unlike his father, was bored by foreigners. He thus decided to concentrate upon those whom he knew and understood: upon his own people of Great Britain, upon his own people in the Empire and the Dominions:

'A week of intimate talks',[a] recorded Lord Esher from Balmoral in August 1910, 'with the King and Queen. He is brave and frank. He told me very sincerely his aims and ideals. He means to do for the Empire what King Edward did for the peace of Europe. He proposes to attend himself the Indian Durbar in January 1911 and crown himself at Delhi. He means to visit every Dominion. These are bold projects. There will be difficulties with Ministers. Still, he may find a way.'

It was with this in mind that, after his coronation, he went to Ireland, Wales and Scotland; that he undertook the voyage to India; and that from the outset of his reign he sought to identify the monarchy with the needs and the pleasures of ordinary people, paying repeated visits to industrial centres, attending football matches, driving through the poorer districts of London, and visiting miners and workers in their homes.

It is not here intended to deal in any detail with King George's private tastes and occupations; these aspects of his life have been fully described in Mr John Gore's *Personal Memoir*. Yet if we are to form any true estimate of his ability, it must be emphasised that in each of his three favourite recreations he achieved unquestioned supremacy. As a stamp-collector, he was the equal of any of the world's philatelists. As a yachtsman, he knew as much about sailing as the most veteran of the Cowes specialists. And he was recognised as one of the best shots in England, with whom only Lord Ripon and Sir Harry Stonor could compete. It is distinctive to be supreme even in a single hobby; to be a recognised authority in three such different hobbies indicates unusual gifts of concentration, memory and persistence.

King Edward, with his lavish love of pageantry, had done much to restore to the monarchy the splendour which had been shrouded during the widowhood and prolonged retirement of Queen Victoria. King George attached full importance to the ceremonial aspects of monarchy; he was well aware that pomp, if it is to retain its symbolism and its magic, must be, not magnificent merely, but meticulously ordered and planned. He had no tolerance for ceremonial inefficiency. Yet in his private life he preferred more homely ways:

> 'His domesticity and simple life', writes Lord Esher[b] 'are charming. The King allows people to sit after dinner, whether he is sitting or not. There is no pomp. . . . There is not a card in the house.' [1] 'You have no idea',[c] Lord Esher wrote a few months later from Windsor, 'of the change that has come over this place. We are back in Victorian times. Everything so peaceful and domestic. Early rides at 8.30! The King sits mostly in a tent below the East Terrace. He works in his room all the morning.'

Although he would increasingly enjoy his periodic visits to Windsor, although Balmoral provided him with varied opportunities for sport, although early in 1911 he left Marlborough House for Buckingham Palace, it was York Cottage which still remained for him the intimate home, beloved above all others. Queen Alexandra retained the big house at Sandringham until her death in 1925.

[1] This was an over-statement. There was no ban on card-playing in the Royal household. King George himself would occasionally take a hand at bridge. He did not share, however, his father's enjoyment of that pastime and preferred a quiet evening at home, when he could read aloud to the Queen.

King George and Queen Mary continued to live at York Cottage, which they persisted in regarding as convenient, suitable and, in its own little way, impressive:

> 'They showed me', Archbishop Lang had written some years before, 'over their little house with a quite charming and almost naïve keenness. It might have been a curate and his wife in their new home!'[d]

To those who had for years been impelled by social appetites to circle around the fringe of smart society, these modest contentments seemed ridiculously middle-class. The scented and bejewelled paradise, to gain admittance to which they had expended so much wealth and energy, had receded suddenly and melted into the haze of a period piece. They would refer slightingly to the new order as 'this sweeter, simpler, reign'. But the older aristocracy and the great body of public opinion welcomed this return to the more sober English standards of felicity. These were the feelings which King George and Queen Mary reflected, represented and enhanced.

In thus striving to set an example of domestic propriety he was, however, hampered by a strange legend which had for years been clouding his repute. In the first year of his reign he was given the opportunity to exterminate this legend.

A journalist of the name of Edward Mylius had published in the *Liberator* (a seditious publication issued in Paris but circulating in England and overseas) the story that, when in Malta in 1890, King George had contracted a secret marriage with the daughter of an English admiral. The imputation was that his marriage with Queen Mary was therefore bigamous and that the children of that marriage were illegitimate. Mylius was arrested for criminal libel and tried before the Lord Chief Justice and a special jury on February 1, 1911. It was proved at the trial that King George had not been in Malta in 1890 and that the Admiral in question possessed only two daughters, one of whom had never seen the King at all, and the other of whom had met him only twice, first when she was eight years old and on a second occasion, long after both she and he were married. Mylius was convicted and given twelve.months' imprisonment. He was released on December 3 of the same year.

> 'The whole story', the King wrote in his diary for February 1, 1911, 'is a damnable lie and has been in existence now for over twenty years. I trust that this will settle it once and for all.'

Queen Alexandra was even more indignant. She wrote to him from Sandringham on February 4:

'Thank God that vile trial is over and those infamous lies and foul accusations at an end for ever & cleared up before the whole world. To *us* all it was a ridiculous story yr having been married before . . .! Too silly for words—but as the public seems to have believed it, this trial was the only way to let them hear & know the truth, and so have your good name vindicated for ever. My poor Georgie—really it was too bad and must have worried you all the same. It is hard on the best people like you, who really have steered so straight in your life, to be accused of such base things—makes me furious—& many bad people who really are known to lead the worst of lives are never mentioned or attacked ever. . . . It only shows how unfair the world is & how the wicked love to slander the upright and good & try to drag them down to their own level.'

(2)

King George's coronation took place on the morning of Thursday, June 22, 1911. With the Queen beside him he drove in his great coach from Buckingham Palace to Westminster Abbey. From the west door of the Abbey he walked in slow procession to the theatre, or pulpitum, which, as prescribed by the Liber Regalis of 1307, had been set 'between the high altar and the choir, near the four high pillars in the cross of the said church'. This procession, or 'proceeding', was headed by the Chaplains in Ordinary, the Domestic Chaplains, the Prebendaries of Westminster, the Heralds and the officers of the Orders of Knighthood. There followed the standards of South Africa, New Zealand, Australia, Canada and India, each carried by a former Governor-General. The standard of England was borne by Mr Frank Dymoke, hereditary King's champion, that of Wales by Lord Mostyn, that of Scotland by Colonel Scrymgeour-Wedderburn, that of Ireland by O'Conor Don. The standard of the Union was carried by the Duke of Wellington, the Royal standard by Lord Lansdowne. Then came the King's regalia—St. Edward's staff, the sceptre with the cross, the two golden spurs, the sword of temporal justice carried by Lord Kitchener, the sword of spiritual justice carried by Lord Roberts, 'Curtana', or the sword of mercy, carried by the Duke of Beaufort, the orb, the sceptre with the dove, St Edward's crown.[1] Immediately in front of the King, the Bishops of London, Ripon and Winchester, carried the Paten, the Bible and the Chalice. The King in his crimson robe of State was

[1] Most of the ancient regalia were destroyed by Cromwell's orders in 1649. The Ampulla and the Spoon (which is said to date from King John) appear to have survived

flanked by twenty Gentlemen-at-Arms and his train was borne by eight young pages. There followed the high officers of the household and the procession was closed by twenty Yeomen of the Guard.

The Archbishop of Canterbury, advancing successively to the four sides of the theatre, to east and west and south and north, demanded recognition: 'Sirs, I present unto you King George, the undoubted King of this Realm: wherefore, all you who are come this day to do your homage and service. Are you willing to do the same?' At which the trumpets sounded, the boys of Westminster School cried 'Vivat Rex' and the congregation murmured 'God Save the King'.

Then began the ancient ritual, ordained by the practice of a thousand years.[1] The King, kneeling before the altar and laying his hand upon the Bible, took the coronation oath. He swore to 'cause law and justice, in mercy to be executed in all his judgments'; he swore to maintain the Protestant religion and the established church; he swore to 'govern the people of this United Kingdom of Great Britain and Ireland, and the Dominions thereto belonging, according to the statutes in Parliament agreed on and the respective laws and customs of the same'.

The choir began to intone the anthem 'Zadok the priest and Nathan the prophet' and the King, having been divested of his robe and cap of state, advanced to the altar for his anointing. The Archbishop, having poured the consecrated oil from the ampulla, anointed the King upon his head and breast and hands, while four Knights of the Garter held above him a canopy of cloth of gold. The King was then invested with the Colobium Sindonis and the Supertunica, the Lord Great Chamberlain touched his heels with the golden spurs, and he was girt with the sword of state. He then assumed the Armill and the Robe Royal or Pall of Gold and seated himself upon King Edward's chair.[2] The Archbishop put the ruby

[1] The Coronation ceremony falls into four successive phases, each of which possesses historical symbolism, namely: (*a*) The Recognition, which derives from the ancient procedure of recognition by the Witan; (*b*) The Oath, which symbolises a contract between the King and his peoples; (*c*) The Anointing, which represents consecration by the Church; (*d*) The Homage of the Lords Spiritual and Temporal (but not, it will be noted, of the Commons), which is a feudal survival.

[2] The Coronation Throne, known as 'King Edward's Chair', contained the 'stone of destiny' which in 1296 King Edward I removed from the Abbey of Scone in Scotland. According to the legend it was on this stone that the patriarch Jacob rested his head when he dreamt that he saw a

ring on the fourth finger of the King's right hand, the Lord of the Manor of Worksop presented the gloves and the Archbishop delivered into the King's right hand the sceptre with the cross and into his left the sceptre with the dove. The Archbishop, standing before the altar, dedicated St Edward's Crown:

'Then', runs the order of ceremony, 'the Archbishop, with the Archbishop of York and the other Bishops, will come from the Altar; and the Archbishop, having received the Crown from the Dean of Westminster, will reverently place it on His Majesty's Head; when the people with loud and repeated shouts will cry: "God Save the King"; the Peers putting on their Coronets, and the Kings of Arms, their Crowns; the Trumpets sounding, the Drums beating, and, at a signal given, the Great Guns of the Tower, and the Guns in the Park, being shot off.'

Thereafter followed the Homage. Archbishop Davidson first paid homage for himself and the Lords Spiritual. He was succeeded by the young Prince of Wales who, kneeling before his father, recited the words:

'I Edward Prince of Wales do become your liege man of life and limb and of earthly worship; and faith and truth I will bear unto you, to live and die against all manner of folks. So help me God.' The Prince then rose, touched the crown upon his father's head and kissed him on the left cheek. The Peers in their order then did homage, being represented for the purpose by the senior of each degree.

Queen Mary was then anointed, crowned and enthroned. At the moment of her crowning, the peeresses, with a lovely conjoint movement of their arms, assumed their coronets. After a short Communion service and a few further prayers the ritual was concluded. The King and Queen both wearing their crowns returned in procession to the west door of the Abbey where they entered their golden coach. In his left hand the King carried the orb and in his right the sceptre with the cross. The Queen bore in her right hand her sceptre with the cross and in her left hand the sceptre with the dove.

King George was a religious man: for him this ancient ritual was an act of dedication. The blare of trumpets, the salvos of artillery, the archaic ceremony, the swell of anthems, the jewelled emblems, the hierophantic vestments in which he was successively arrayed,

ladder reaching into heaven. Since the thirteenth century all the English Sovereigns have been crowned seated above this stone. Even Oliver Cromwell made use of it at his installation as Lord Protector.

even the thin shafts of sunlight falling upon the fawn and azure hangings, upon the lords and prelates as they passed and repassed across the blue carpet in their robes of scarlet, ermine and gold: all this was no more than an almost unrealised background to the sacred fact that he was being consecrated to the service of his peoples, to whom, kneeling alone before the altar, he had sworn a grave oath.

He was not a man who was able or accustomed to express, at least in writing, the emotions which he felt most deeply, The written word was not his language. His own record of the Coronation is almost disconcertingly restrained:

'*Thursday, June 22nd. Our Coronation Day. Buckingham Palace*. It was over-cast & cloudy with some showers & a strongish cool breeze, but better for the people than great heat. Today was indeed a great & memorable day in our lives & one we can never forget, but it brought back to me many sad memories of 9 years ago, when the beloved Parents were crowned. May & I left B.P. in the Coronation coach at 10.30 with 8 cream-coloured horses. There were over 50,000 troops lining the streets under the command of Lord Kitchener. There were hundreds of thousands of people who gave us a magnificent reception. The Service in the Abbey was most beautiful, but it was a terrible ordeal. It was grand, yet simple & most dignified and went without a hitch. I nearly broke down when dear David came to do homage to me, as it reminded me so much when I did the same thing to beloved Papa, he did it so well. Darling May looked lovely & it was indeed a comfort to me to have her by my side, as she has been ever to me during these last eighteen years. We left Westminster Abbey at 2.15 (having arrived there before 11.0) with our Crowns on and sceptres in our hands. This time we drove by the Mall, St. James' Street & Piccadilly, crowds enormous & decorations very pretty. On reaching B.P. just before 3.0 May & I went out on the balcony to show ourselves to the people. Downey photographed us in our robes with Crowns on. Had some lunch with our guests here. Worked all the afternoon with Bigge & others answering telegrams & letters of which I have had hundreds. Such a large crowd collected in front of the Palace that I went out on the balcony again. Our guests dined with us at 8.30. May & I showed ourselves again to the people. Wrote & read. Rather tired. Bed at 11.45. Beautiful illuminations everywhere.'

On the next day the King and Queen drove in an open carriage through the streets of London. 'A wonderful drive,' he wrote, 'a sight which I am sure could never be seen in any other country in the world.' On June 24 came the naval review at Spithead and on June 29 a Thanksgiving Service at St. Paul's. 'We are deeply touched,' the King wrote in his diary, 'by the great affection and loyalty shown towards us.' On June 30 the King and Queen gave an immense tea-party to 100,000 London children in the Crystal Palace; 'their cheers', he wrote, 'were quite deafening.' After a few days' rest at Windsor he went, on July 7, upon a short state visit to Ireland. As the Royal yacht entered Kingstown, he had a sentimental twinge on recognising, among the ships saluting in the harbour, H.M.S. *Thrush*, his humble little gunboat of twenty years before. The Dublin visit was a triumphant success. King George, as has been said, always cherished the theory (perhaps the illusion) that there existed between the Irish people and the Crown a bond of understanding independent of politics and parties. The Dublin crowds greeted him with vigorous enthusiasm; the warmth of their salutations may have been enhanced by the prospect that some measure of Home Rule would now at last be placed upon the statute book. The King, after so rapturous a welcome, could not have conceived it possible that he would never visit Dublin again.

Mr Lloyd George, with his vivid Celtic imagination, had suggested that the intended visit to Wales should be made the occasion of a local pageant and that the Prince of Wales should formally be invested at Carnarvon Castle in the presence of 10,000 Welsh. The Chancellor of the Exchequer went so far as to coach the young Prince in a few sentences of the Welsh language, including the words '*Mor o gan yw Cymru i gyd*', meaning 'All Wales is a sea of song.'

The investiture of the Prince of Wales took place, as arranged, on July 13. 'The dear boy', his father noted, 'did it all remarkably well and looked so nice.' Mr Lloyd George also was much pleased.

The sunshine of these jubilations did not remain for long unclouded. The King recorded in his diary that on the evening of that very July 13 he had 'an important conversation with the Prime Minister about the political situation'. Four days later we find the following entry dated from Holyrood Palace at Edinburgh:

'Saw Francis (Lord Knollys) who had just come from London & had a long talk with him about the political crisis, which is becoming most disagreeable & giving me a lot of worry & anxiety.'

The battle between Lords and Commons had, after the truce imposed by the Coronation festivities, been resumed. It was entering its final phase. The King returned to Buckingham Palace on July 21.

(3)

It will be recalled that when, on November 16, 1910, the King had given the advance pledges demanded by Mr Asquith, he had done so in the belief that the leader of the Opposition would be unable and unwilling to form an alternative administration. Lord Knollys, as has been shown, had little justification for assuming that this was in truth Mr Balfour's attitude and decision.¹ When, in July 1911, the fact was divulged that the November pledges had been demanded and obtained, Mr Balfour repudiated this assumption with asperity:

> 'I hear', he wrote to Lord Stamfordham¹ on August 1, 1911,ᵍ 'that you and others in confidential relations with the King state that I had intimated that, at the time the Prime Minister obtained the Pledges, I could not and would not take office.
>
> 'I have to remark on this statement (1) that I was not asked; and (2) that I was in complete ignorance of all that was going on between the King and his Ministers: which indeed I never learned till about three weeks ago.
>
> 'If I had been told that the King was being pressed to give a promise to coerce the House of Lords into passing a Parliament Bill, seven or eight months before the Parliament Bill could reach the final stages, and if I had been requested to form a Government, I should have of course complied, though with very grave doubts as to the view which the country would have taken on the subject. Had I been asked, on the other hand, to form a Government in order to protect His Majesty from giving a promise, not merely that a Parliament Bill should be passed over the heads of the Lords, but that it should be passed in a form which by implication carried Home Rule with it, I should not only have formed a Government, but I should have had great hopes of carrying the country with me.'

This letter from the Royal Archives is quoted, not merely because it reveals one of the accidental misunderstandings of history, but because Mr Balfour's evident indignation illustrates the feeling, then widely prevalent in Unionist circles, that the Prime Minister had forced the King to give promises which were to the advantage of the Liberal administration and party. Apart from their partisan emotions, apart from their congenital dread of Home Rule, the Unionists felt, and with some justification, that the Royal Prerogative, and with it the prestige of the Crown, were being exposed to unwarranted humiliation. The King was regarded as the fount of honour. Was it right that he should be forced, under the menace of resignation, to stultify his position and to render himself a puppet in the eyes of foreign potentates by conferring peerages upon some 500 unknown and unnamed gentlemen selected by the Master of Elibank? It was not right.

¹ Sir A. Bigge had been raised to the peerage as Lord Stamfordham in 1911.

Unless these underlying feelings of suspicion and resentment are borne in mind, it is difficult to explain the apparently reckless intemperance thereafter manifested by the more sedulous Unionists. Mr Balfour personally was a vague, and therefore tolerant, man. It was said that he 'forgot everything but forgave nothing'. He certainly never forgave Lord Knollys.

It is now necessary to resume the narrative of the constitutional crisis from the point where it was left on November 16, 1910. The pledges having been obtained under the threat of resignation, the Dissolution of Parliament was announced for November 28. Lord Lansdowne, the leader of the Unionist Party in the House of Lords, proposed that the Parliament Bill should, before the election, be presented to the Upper Chamber and that he should himself, at the same time, introduce his own scheme for House of Lords Reform. Only by this method, Lord Lansdowne argued, could the electors know exactly what were the issues on which they were expected to vote. The Government were at first unwilling to agree to this suggestion but the King persuaded them to do so.[A] The Bill was therefore introduced into the House of Lords on November 16 and a second reading given on November 21. Two days later Lord Lansdowne stated that it would be useless for the Lords to proceed with any further discussion of the Parliament Bill, since there would be now no time before the election to take it in Committee stage. He, on the same afternoon, introduced his own reform proposals.

The preamble to the Parliament Bill had announced the intention of the Government 'to substitute for the House of Lords as it at present exists a Second Chamber constituted on a popular, instead of a hereditary, basis'. The supporters of the Government ceased to be enamoured of this statement once they saw it in cold print. They realised that no Second Chamber, whether elective or selective, could ever be so conveniently vulnerable as a hereditary House of Lords: a more democratically constituted Chamber might command greater prestige and claim greater powers; the horrid spectre of the American Senate began to dance before their eyes. Lord Lansdowne's proposals, as his subsequent 'Reconstitution Bill', died a natural death.[1] The ground was thereby cleared for the election.

[1] Lord Lansdowne's proposals of November 25, 1910, and his 'Reconstitution Bill' of May 8, 1911, embodied the following principles: The reconstituted House of Lords was to consist of 350 'Lords of Parliament' composed as follows: (1) 100 to be chosen by their fellow peers on the ground of merit; (2) 120 to be elected, on proportional representation, by

The General Election of December 1910 produced results little different from those of the previous January.[1] The Liberals and Unionists were now exactly balanced with 272 seats each; Mr Asquith's majority of 126 was thereafter entirely composed of his Labour and Irish allies. The Government had in fact received only 350,000 more votes than their opponents, a majority which, as Lord Hugh Cecil was not slow to remind them, scarcely constituted a sufficient mandate for the introduction of 'revolutionary' legislation.

The new Parliament was opened by the King on February 6, 1911; the Parliament Bill was introduced on February 21 and the Committee stage was reached on March 2. The Bill in its final form passed the House of Commons on May 15 by 362 votes to 241. It reached the House of Lords on May 23 and passed the second reading without a division on May 29. The Coronation festivities then imposed a pause.

On July 4 the battle was resumed. On that date, Lord Lansdowne brought forward his amendment to Clause II. Under this amendment any Bill which affected the Crown or the Protestant succession, which made provision for Home Rule in Ireland, Scotland or Wales, or which raised an issue 'of great gravity on which the judgement of the country has not sufficiently been ascertained' should not become law 'unless and until it has been submitted to, and approved by, the electors in a manner to be hereafter provided by Act of Parliament'.

The Bill, as thus amended, was passed by the House of Lords on July 24. The Cabinet had already decided that the Lords amendments completely altered the whole nature of the Bill and must be rejected as a whole by the House of Commons. They therefore informed the King that a deadlock had been reached and that, as a third dissolution was manifestly impossible, 'it had become their

the House of Commons; (3) 100 to be nominated by the Crown on the recommendation of the Prime Minister; (4) Bishops and ex-officio Lords of Parliament.

Lord Morley made it clear to their Lordships that, whether the Reconstitution Bill was adopted or not, the Parliament Bill would be imposed upon them. This gave 'an air of unreality' to the debate on Lord Lansdowne's scheme. It was given a second reading in the House of Lords and thereafter passed into oblivion.

Lord Lansdowne's reform proposals were referred to at the time as 'this death-bed repentance'. Mr Asquith, speaking at Hull on November 25, 1910, dismissed them as 'to all intents and purposes a ghost'.

[1] The figures were Liberals 272, Unionists 272, Labour 42, Irish 84.

duty to advise the Crown to exercise its Prerogative so as to get rid of the deadlock and to secure the passage of the Bill'.[i] It was this advice which, on his return to London from Edinburgh on July 21, faced the King with a renewal of his predicament. His one hope was that a sufficient number of peers and prelates would be wise enough to follow Lord Lansdowne and abstain from voting, thereby sparing him the humiliation which he feared.

(4)

Early in July, Lord Derby, and subsequently Lord Midleton, had warned the King that a large number of Unionists remained convinced that the Government were bluffing and that the Prime Minister would hesitate, when it came to the moment, to invoke the Royal Prerogative. Accordingly, on July 19, Lord Knollys, with Mr Asquith's consent, informed Mr Balfour of the purport of the November pledges. Mr Balfour asked for a statement in writing. On July 20, therefore, he received the following letter from the Prime Minister:

'I think it only courteous and right, before any public decisions are announced, to let you know how we regard the political situation.

'When the Parliament Bill, in the form which it has now assumed, returns to the House of Commons, we shall be compelled to ask the House to disagree with the Lords amendments.

'In the circumstances, should the necessity arise, the Government will advise the King to exercise his Prerogative to secure the passing into Law of the Bill in substantially the same form in which it left the House of Commons, and His Majesty has been pleased to signify that he will consider it his duty to accept and act on that advice.'

On Friday, July 21, a meeting of 200 Unionist peers was summoned at Lansdowne House. Lord Lansdowne argued that, in view of the King's pledge, it would no longer be possible for the House of Lords 'to offer effectual resistance'. To persist to the point at which some 500 new peers might have to be created would render the Upper House ridiculous and destroy for ever whatever power or prestige it might, even under the Parliament Bill, still retain. He was supported by Lord St Aldwyn and Lord Curzon. Lord Halsbury, Lord Selborne, Lord Milner and others stated that they would prefer 'to die in the last ditch'.

On the same day the Cabinet decided that on the following Monday, July 24, the Lords amendments should be rejected without further reference to the Upper Chamber and that the King should at once be asked to create new peers. This decision was communicated to the King in a Cabinet letter of Saturday, July 22, and provoked the following reply, written by Lord Knollys under the King's instructions:[1]

'The King did not receive your Cabinet letter yesterday until after he had seen you.

'He now desires me to say that he has never understood that you proposed to recommend that a creation of peers should take place *previous* to the Parliament Bill being referred to the House of Lords after the rejection of their amendments by the House of Commons, so as to give the former House the opportunity of considering the reasons of the House of Commons objecting to them, the amendments.

'This, H.M. believes, would be in accordance with the procedure usually followed in the case of a "difference" between the two Houses, and he is confident that on the present occasion especially, it would be a mistake, from a tactical point of view alone, to depart from it.

'He has been fully under the impression that the peers would as far as possible be conciliated by every reasonable attention and civility being shown to them; and it is repugnant to his feelings that they should be treated with a want of consideration, or harshly, or cavalierly. To do so, moreover, will probably have the effect of increasing the number of those who intend to vote.

'He is afraid therefore that, unless you are able to give him some good reasons in support of your proposal, he will be unable to agree to it. The King believes also that to reject the amendments en bloc by the House of Commons will likewise help to increase the irritation among the Unionist peers.'

The Prime Minister deferred immediately to the King's wishes.

The situation was daily becoming more tense and political passions more inflamed. The King confided to his diary that he was feeling 'greatly depressed and worried'. Lord Halsbury was hourly gaining new recruits to his 'last-ditcher' revolt against Lord Lansdowne's leadership and guidance. In the House of Commons he had by then secured an ardent band of followers, including Lord Hugh Cecil, Mr George Wyndham, Sir Edward Carson and Mr F. E. Smith. On Monday, July 24, when the Prime Minister rose in the House of Commons to make his statement, he was howled down amid scenes of such disorder that the Speaker, in pursuance of Standing Order 21, felt obliged to adjourn the House.

'The ugliest feature', Mr Winston Churchill wrote to the King, 'was the absence of any real passion or spontaneous feeling. It was a squalid, frigid, organised attempt to insult the Prime Minister.'

On Tuesday, July 25, the supporters of Lord Halsbury gave a dinner to their veteran leader at the Hotel Cecil. A telegram from

Mr Joseph Chamberlain was read to the assembled Unionists urging no surrender. Mr Austen Chamberlain, in replying to the toast of 'The House of Commons', referred to 'this revolution, nurtured in lies, promoted by fraud, and only to be achieved by violence'. The Prime Minister, he contended, had 'tricked the Opposition, entrapped the Crown and deceived the people'. Such was the enthusiasm aroused by this dinner-party that the younger Unionists proposed then and there to drag Lord Halsbury in triumph from the Strand to No. 4 Ennismore Gardens. They only desisted from this project when it was pointed out to them that such a journey might prove tiring for a man of eighty-seven.

On August 7 Mr Balfour, in the House of Commons, moved a vote of censure on the Government, on the ground that the advice which they had given to the King was 'a gross violation of Constitutional Liberty'. That vote was lost by 246–365. On the same day a similar vote of censure in the House of Lords was carried by 281–68. Speaking in that debate, Lord Crewe, for the Government, stated that the King had given the November pledges with 'natural and legitimate reluctance'. This chivalrous statement confirmed the last-ditchers in their obsession that the Government were bluffing and that at the last moment the King would refuse. Lord Stamfordham was alarmed by this new danger. On the morning of August 10, the day on which the final vote would have to be taken in the House of Lords, he wrote to Lord Morley, referring to the 'fixed and obstinate belief' of the last-ditchers and stating that it was imperative 'to dispel this false idea':

> 'For this reason, the King authorised me to suggest that some statement might be made by you—to the effect that in the event of the Bill being defeated the King would agree to a creation sufficient to guard against any possible combination of the Opposition by which the measure could again be defeated.' *k*

The night of August 10, 1911, was one of the hottest on record; the thermometer during the day had registered 100°. In a packed and stifling Chamber the long controversy between Lords and Commons drew to its end. Up to the last moment, in spite of powerful speeches by Lord Curzon and the Archbishop of Canterbury, the issue remained in doubt. Lord Morley rose and, drawing from his pocket the statement which he had agreed to with Lord Stamfordham, read it slowly aloud. There was a moment of intense silence and then a peer asked him to read it again. He did so, adding the words: 'Every vote given against my motion will be a vote for a large and prompt creation of peers.'[1] [1]

The Division was taken in an atmosphere of strained excitement. At 10.40 p.m. the tellers announced the final figures. The Government had won by a majority of seventeen votes. Apart from their own eighty supporters, they had received the votes of 13 prelates and 37 Unionist peers. Lord Lansdowne and his supporters had abstained. 'We were beaten', exclaimed Mr George Wyndham, 'by the Bishops and the Rats.' The *Observer*, on the following Sunday, denounced 'the ignoble band, clerical and lay, of Unionist traitors, who had made themselves Redmond's helots'.

The King at Buckingham Palace had been awaiting the verdict with impatient anxiety:

'At 11.0,' he wrote in his diary, 'Bigge returned from the House of Lords with the good news that the Parliament Bill had passed with a majority of 17. So the Halsburyites were thank God beaten! It is indeed a great relief to me & I am spared any further humiliation by a creation of peers. . . . Bigge and Francis have indeed worked hard for this result.'

The next day he left for Yorkshire:

'I am afraid', he wrote to Lord Stamfordham on August 16,[m] 'it is impossible to pat the Opposition on the back, but I am indeed grateful for what they have done & saved me from a humiliation which I should never have survived. If the creation had taken place, I should never have been the same person again.'

[1] Sir Almeric Fitzroy in his *Memoirs* (II, pp. 457–458) records a conversation with Lord Morley which well illustrates the King's perplexity at this time. Lord Morley told him on August 8, 1911, 'that the King was much exercised in his mind by the criticism he had incurred by consenting to the creation of peers. He shrinks, it appears, from the language probably held in the Carlton Club, but, as Lord Morley told him, it was better to run the risk of that than to be denounced from every platform as the enemy of the people. His natural sensitiveness has been aggravated by the receipt of a large number of anonymous letters which he insists on reading for the "amusement" they afford; but it is an indulgence that rankles. The charge too of having betrayed the Irish "loyalists" touches him closely. . . . The King's extreme conscientiousness was, in Lord Morley's opinion, one source of his susceptibility, and lack of experience reflected itself in some hesitation and self-distrust. But a strong sense of obligation, coupled with a desire to shape his conduct according to the most correct standard of constitutional propriety, fortified resolution when it had been translated into action'.

CHAPTER XI

UNREST

1911–1912

The King's desire for conciliation—The growth of industrial disaffection—Riots in South Wales—Sidney Street—The Railway Strike—The Coal Strike—The menace of syndicalism—The reversal of the Taff Vale and Osborne judgements—The National Insurance Act—The King and the working classes—The Protestant Declaration—The beginning of the female suffrage movement—Other indications of coming change—The retirement of Mr A. J. Balfour from the leadership of the Unionist Party—Mr Bonar Law—The King proposes to visit India—Lord Morley suggests difficulties—The Cabinet give their grudging consent—The question of the regalia—The problem of the boons—The King and Queen leave for India on November 11, 1911—The entry into Delhi—The Durbar—The reception at Calcutta—Effect of the visit—The King returns to England on February 5, 1912.

(1)

THE PASSAGE of the Parliament Bill on that torrid night of August 10, 1911, spared the King the necessity of exercising his Prerogative in circumstances which would have done damage to the dignity of the Crown. It did not mark the end of constitutional tension. There were those, as has been said, who contended that until the preamble of the Parliament Act had been brought into effect and a reformed Second Chamber established with newly defined powers, the laws and customs of the Constitution must be regarded as 'in suspense'. It was asserted that during this transitional period the rights of veto until then possessed by the House of Lords devolved upon the King personally. This argument might well have been dismissed as academic; but it was used and exploited for partisan purposes in the Home Rule controversy which thereafter ensued.

It must be repeated that during the first four years of his reign King George, while still inexperienced and untried, was confronted with internal and external problems which, in their significance, intensity and scope, were incomparably more intricate and alarming than any which had faced his immediate predecessors. The reign of Queen Victoria can be regarded as a period of ever-widening stability: the reign of King Edward VII as an interlude of lavish prosperity and power; in the reign of King George, the foundations of stability were shaken, our power and prosperity diminished, and new forces were brought into operation which, within a quarter of a century, changed the structure of the world.

King George was a man of peace: he hated strife even as he distrusted innovation. Determined as he was to safeguard his position of neutrality, unaffected as he remained by any extreme formulas either of the right or of the left, he followed the middle path of continuity and thus came to personify the ordinary British citizen's dislike of passionate doctrines and preference for compromise and toleration. King George was not an imaginative man; he possessed no histrionic faculties and was utterly incapable of courting popularity by demagogic means. It was but gradually that his impartiality and common sense came to be recognised and appreciated by the nation as a whole. Only those who were closest to him realised that he also possessed, and continuously exercised, a remarkable gift for conciliation. This was something more than a negative distaste for controversy and disunion; it was a positive and incessant activity which led him on every suitable occasion to deprecate provocation and to encourage concord. The pages of his diary, the letters and memoranda preserved in the Royal Archives, reveal the persistence, the vigilance, often the ingenuity, with which he pursued his aim of mitigating strife: unfalteringly and assiduously he strove to create good blood.

This important aspect of his character and office was, in the last year of his reign, well summarised by Mr J. A. Spender, who was a most competent witness, having been in the closest touch with the politics and politicians of the age:[a]

> 'Plunge into the record of any critical occasion, domestic or foreign, and the King will be found wise, cool and self-effacing, with a remarkable faculty for rejecting bad advice and a keen eye for the points of unity and conciliation. Now and again in the German and Austrian documents we come across the confidential reports by Ambassadors of their talks with him, in which if anywhere he might be caught off his guard. The King has nothing to fear from these disclosures. They show him to be shrewd and observant, and more aware than some of his Ministers of the general drift of events.'

During the opening years of King George's reign, Great Britain was riven by new and incalculable dissensions and Europe by old but equally incalculable animosities. It required great imperturbability of spirit to preach concord to so chaotic a world.

(2)

The first half of King Edward's reign had been soothed by a welcome interlude of industrial peace: from 1906 onwards the waters of acquiescence began to seethe and hiss with discontent. In 1907 Mr J. H. Thomas had welded the main body of railwaymen into one gigantic union and a serious strike was averted only by the creation of Conciliation Boards. In the autumn of 1910 strikes, accompanied by violence, broke out in the Rhondda and Aberdare valleys. Mr Winston Churchill, at that time President of the Board of Trade, was able to prevent bloodshed by sending strong reinforcements of Metropolitan Police into the area and by placing the military under the tactful command of Sir Nevil Macready.[b] On January 7, 1911, the citizens of London were startled to learn that a battle was in progress in Sidney Street between the Scots Guards and a group of anarchists who had barricaded themselves into a house and were firing from the windows upon the police and fire brigade. By that time Mr Churchill had become Home Secretary and was observed, clad in a large fur coat and a small top hat, peeping coyly round the corner of Sidney Street while the bullets whistled around. The King intimated that it was no part of the functions of a Cabinet Minister, however adventurous he might be, to take a personal share in a battle in the East End. In the spring of 1911 an unauthorised strike took place on the North Eastern Railway; in June the Sailors and Firemen's Union refused to work and in July the dockers struck and were joined by the carters and vanmen. The situation at one moment appeared so menacing that troops were moved from York to Manchester. In all, during that summer of 1911, there were as many as 864 strikes and lock-outs, involving nearly a million workers, and resulting in the loss of ten and a quarter million working days.

Of all these strikes the two most important were the railway strike of August 17–19, 1911, and the coal strike of February 26 to April 11, 1912. The former, which was due to the refusal of Mr Thomas and his union to accept the decisions of the Conciliation Board, was not universally responded to and lasted only three days. Yet at the time it aroused much apprehension. The whole of the Aldershot garrison was transferred to London. Parliament was summoned and special constables were enrolled. The gun-makers of St James's Street and Pall Mall sold out their stock of revolvers within forty-eight hours. The King, who was at Bolton Abbey, telegraphed to Mr Churchill enquiring whether he was satisfied that order could be preserved. 'The difficulty is', replied Mr

Churchill, 'not to maintain order but to maintain order without loss of life.'[c] Mr Lloyd George, although Chancellor of the Exchequer, then intervened with all his personal magnetism and ingenuity. He persuaded Mr Thomas to call off the strike within three days. The King was profoundly relieved:

> 'Very glad', he telegraphed to Mr Lloyd George on August 20, 'to hear that it was largely due to your energy and skill that a settlement with regard to this very serious strike has been brought about. I heartily congratulate you and feel that the whole country will be most grateful to you for averting a most disastrous calamity. It has caused me the greatest possible anxiety.' [d]

Even more alarming was the great coal strike which broke out in the spring of 1912, lasted for five weeks and cost the country the loss of thirty million working days. The miners were demanding a minimum wage of 5s. a day for men and 2s. a day for boys. The Prime Minister summoned a conference of owners and workers and, when these negotiations broke down on March 15, resorted to the unprecedented step of forcing acceptance by Act of Parliament. The Minimum Wages Bill was introduced on March 19 and received the Royal Assent on March 29. It was not generally realised at the time that this direct intervention of the State in an industrial dispute marked the first of many moves away from the traditional liberal doctrine of *laissez-faire*.

It is not easy for the modern generation (accustomed as they are to organised Trade Unionism, to the machinery of mediation and arbitration in industrial disputes) to understand the perplexity and alarm with which the statesmen and citizens of the 1910–1914 period regarded these successive upheavals. They saw in them (and it would be an error to say that they were wholly mistaken) the presage of a rising of the proletariat and the injection into our political life of the dangerous Continental theory of syndicalism, with its battle cry of 'they who rule industrially will rule politically' and its firm belief in the efficacy of direct action. Mr Tom Mann, with his compelling personality, had won many adherents in our industrial centres to the theories which he had derived from his association with French syndicalists and the I.W.W. in the United States. Fortunately, our congenital trust in representative government, our long habituation to the electoral system, proved sufficiently healthy to withstand this foreign virus. The community's powers of resistance were fortified by governmental wisdom and forbearance.

The statesmen of the time had the imagination to detect the

causes as well as the symptoms of this fever. They realised that, whereas the Franchise Acts of 1865 and 1884 had accorded political equality to the wage-earners, the younger generation were becoming impatient of the dragging steps with which social justice and economic security lagged behind. It should be remembered that, of the eight million regularly employed workers in 1911, as many as two and a half million were earning at full-time rates not more than 15s. to 25s. a week. In 1911 63% of the railway workers were being paid less than one pound a week. Since 1900 the average weekly wage had not risen by more than twopence farthing, whereas the purchasing value of the pound had dropped to seventeen shillings and sixpence. The Government realised in time that if the doctrine of direct action were not to obtain a hold on the Labour movement, the workers must be afforded fuller opportunity to express their sense of frustrated power through legally recognised organisations; and that the economic insecurity which oppressed them must, by legislative measures, be alleviated.

Their first action, therefore, was to release the Trade Unions from the disabilities from which they had suffered as a result of the Taff Vale judgement and the Osborne case.[1] Their second step was to create within the Board of Trade a department of mediation in industrial disputes and to place that department in the able and conciliatory hands of Sir George Askwith.[2] Their third and most

[1] In 1900 a strike occurred in the Taff Vale Railway in South Wales. The Company claimed damages against the Amalgamated Society of Railway Servants who had intervened in the dispute. On appeal, the Company were accorded £23,000 damages with costs. Much indignation was expressed in Trade Union circles against this judgment. A Royal Commission was appointed to enquire into the law governing such issues, with the result that in 1906 the Government passed the Trades Disputes Act which protected Trade Unions against similar actions in future.

In 1908 Mr W. V. Osborne, a foreman porter at Clapham Junction and an ardent Liberal, won an action against the same Society of Railway Servants, restraining them from using any portion of their funds for the purpose of promoting the candidature of Labour members. The Trade Union Act of 1913 provided that Trade Unions could use their funds for political purposes but that these funds must be specially earmarked and their members could, if they so desired, 'contract out'.

It should be remembered also that, on August 20, 1911, the Government passed a Bill providing that Members of Parliament should be paid a salary of £400 a year. This, to some extent, relieved Labour members from the irksome necessity of being dependent upon Trade Union funds.

[2] Sir George Askwith was born in 1861, became Assistant Secretary to the Board of Trade in 1907, Comptroller General of their Labour Depart-

important step was the National Insurance Act of 1911.[1] This Act met with bitter opposition on the part of employers and the British Medical Association but under the wise administration of that supreme Civil Servant, Sir Robert Morant,[2] it became the corner stone of the great edifice of social security which has since been erected. In the end it was to justify the romantic boast of its originator:

> 'I can see', said Mr Lloyd George, 'the Old Age Pensions Act and the National Insurance Act, and many another Act in their trail, descending like breezes from the hills of my native land, sweeping into the mist-laden valleys, and clearing the gloom away, until the rays of God's sun have pierced the narrowest window.'

By such measures did the Government dilute and thereby mitigate the revolutionary spirit which, between 1910 and 1914, had created such alarm. The King took an intense personal interest in these disputes: his papers contain numerous notes and memoranda addressed to him by Mr Lloyd George or Sir George Askwith in reply to his repeated enquiries. He was sensitive to the personal suffering occasioned to working families by these incessant strikes and lock-outs; depressed by the animosity they engendered; and deeply perturbed by the gulf which seemed to be widening between the classes. He determined to do all within his power to bridge that gulf. In the years that followed he devoted time and energy to bringing

ment in 1911 and Chairman of the Fair Wages Advisory Committee. In 1919 he was created a peer under the title of Lord Askwith of St. Ives. He died in 1942.

[1] Mr Lloyd George's Insurance Act of 1911 fell into two parts, covering (1) Sickness, and (2) Unemployment. Section I affected 15 million workers and was based upon a contributory and compulsory basis. The employer contributed 3d a week, the State 2d and the male worker 4d and the female worker 3d. Sickness benefit was to be at the rate of 10s. a week for men and 7s. 6d. a week for women. Medical attendance and drugs were to be free, and the doctors were to be paid 4s. per patient per annum, a figure which, under pressure from the B.M.A., was raised to 9s. 6d.

The unemployment section applied to certain trades only and covered only 2,250,000 workers. Unemployed persons were to receive a benefit of 7s. a week with a maximum of fifteen weeks in any one year. Unemployment insurance, as originally planned, was to be on a strictly actuarial basis. This sound foundation could not for long be maintained.

[2] Sir Robert Morant was born in 1868 and devoted most of his life to educational work. He was responsible for Mr Balfour's Education Act of 1902 and was Permanent Secretary to the Board of Education from 1903 to 1911 and Chairman of the Insurance Commission from 1912 to 1919. He died in 1920.

the Crown into direct relations with the proletariat and, by constant visits to industrial centres, by personal relations with the workers themselves, to create and animate a sense of solidarity. No British Monarch before his time had manifested so constant, or so obviously sincere, a liking for his poorer subjects. The astonishing popular manifestation which marked his Jubilee in 1935 showed him that they, for their part, had understood.

(3)

Typical of the King's avoidance of anything which might provoke unnecessary controversy or needlessly wound the susceptibilities of any section of his subjects, was the firm, and even obstinate, attitude which he adopted to what was known as 'The Protestant Declaration'. Under this survival from the panic created by the Popish Plot of 1678, the Sovereign was obliged, 'on the day of the first meeting of the first Parliament' to read out a declaration in which he asserted his own orthodoxy, condemned the doctrine of transubstantiation, and proclaimed from the throne that 'the Invocation or Adoration of the Virgin Mary or any other Saint, and the Sacrifice of the Mass, as they are now used in the Church of Rome, are superstitious and idolatrous'.

Even before his accession, King George had objected to this formula, considering that it was calculated to cause deep offence to British Roman Catholics. He had long discussions on the subject with Canon Dalton and the Archbishop of Canterbury and when he ascended the throne he informed the Prime Minister that he would not consent to open Parliament unless a more tolerant formula were substituted for the outrageous declaration which, under the Bill of Rights, he was by law obliged to make. Mr Asquith was delighted by the King's refusal and immediately set about drafting a form of words which, he imagined, would meet with universal assent. The mere rumour that the old formula was to be altered provoked opposition in more extreme protestant quarters and pamphlets were circulated bearing such ominous and ancient titles as 'Papal Despotism' and 'Let the Protestant people reply'. Mr Asquith continued, undeterred by any fear of popish infiltration, to draft his formula. On June 28, 1910, he submitted to the House of Commons a revised Declaration, under which the King should merely affirm that he was a faithful member of 'the Protestant Reformed Church by law established in England'. Both the nonconformists and the

Anglican bishops raised objections to this wording, and the Archbishop of Canterbury then proposed the simpler phrase 'I declare that I am a faithful Protestant and will uphold the Protestant succession'.* This final formula, as passed by both Houses, received the Royal Assent on August 3, 1910. It was thus an innocuous Declaration which, when opening his first Parliament on February 6, 1911, the King read from the throne.

Apart from the incessant labour unrest, apart from the increasing anxiety occasioned by our relations with Germany and by the menace of German naval construction, apart from the acute perplexities and dissensions aroused by the Parliament Bill, there were other indications that the old crust of habit was disintegrating and that new and perplexing movements or ideas were bubbling up from underneath. Now that the veto of the House of Lords had been abolished, it was evident that Mr Redmond and the Irish Nationalists would oblige Mr Asquith to force a Home Rule Bill through both Houses of Parliament. Although in 1911 it was not foreseen that this measure would bring the country to the brink of civil war, it was certainly realised that it would provoke a political controversy of extreme bitterness. Some of the advocates of female suffrage were already abandoning the legal methods which they had hitherto pursued and were planning direct action and those varied and ingenious forms of militancy which proved of such embarrassment in the three years that followed. These grave issues, and the endeavours made by the King to mitigate the acerbity and passion they engendered, will be described in later chapters.

Even in the world of art and literature the old conventions were being questioned and new and perplexing heresies being substituted. Mr H. G. Wells and Mr Bernard Shaw were already exercising a disturbing influence on the younger generation and forming many restless minds. In November 1910, at the Grafton Galleries, was held an exhibition of post-impressionist art, including such unsettling pictures as Van Gogh's 'Postman' and Manet's 'Bar'. It was small comfort to those who were outraged by these innovations to reflect that in the same year the Royal Academy exhibited Mr Cope's portrait of Lord Clarendon and Mr Harold Speed's portrait of Miss Lilian Braithwaite. A year later the Russian ballet first descended upon London. On November 7, 1911, the King witnessed a performance of *Les Sylphides* at Covent Garden. 'Madame Pavlova and M. Nijinsky', he wrote in his diary, 'certainly dance beautifully.' The landmarks of the past were being obliterated one by one: the future loomed uncertain, unfamiliar, imponderable, dark.

It was a misfortune for the King that at this juncture he should have been deprived of the counsels of an elder statesman whom he much esteemed. Mr A. J. Balfour had been saddened by the lack of prudence which, during the Parliament Bill crisis, had led so many of his followers to support the last-ditchers under Lord Halsbury. He left England for Bad Gastein in a mood of philosophic contempt. On his return in September 1911, he found that a campaign had been organised against him under the slogan of 'B.M.G.' or 'Balfour Must Go'. On October 7, the Halsbury Club was inaugurated by his critics within the Party, and at the same time he received from Mr Walter Long a letter intimating, in blustering terms, that the moment had come for him to relinquish the leadership of the Unionists. On November 7 he wrote a private letter to the King stating that he intended to announce his resignation within the next two days. It was the custom that the Home Secretary should, when Parliament is sitting, send a daily report to the King on the proceedings of the House of Commons. On Mr Winston Churchill's appointment as First Lord of the Admiralty in October 1911, his place at the Home Office had been taken by Mr Reginald McKenna. The latter's report to the King for November 9 is significant as coming from so confirmed a Liberal:

> 'The news of Mr Balfour's retirement arrived early in the afternoon and was received with equal astonishment and regret. It is not too much to say that admiration for his courage and incomparable parliamentary abilities and personal affectionate regard for him are universal through the House.'

The King was not informed of, and would certainly not have admired or understood, the hurried stratagems by which thereafter both Mr Walter Long and Mr Austen Chamberlain were induced to withdraw their candidatures and themselves to propose the name of Mr Bonar Law[1] as Mr Balfour's successor. The proceedings which

[1] Andrew Bonar Law was born on September 16, 1858, in the manse of Kingston (later Rexton), New Brunswick, which was not at that date part of the Dominion of Canada. His father, a Presbyterian Minister, had been born near Portrush in Co. Antrim, Northern Ireland. At the age of twelve he was sent to live with his mother's family in Glasgow and at the age of sixteen entered his uncle's office; he remained a junior clerk for twelve years but at the age of twenty-eight became a partner in the firm of William Jacks, iron merchants. In December 1900, at the age of forty-

took place at the Carlton Club on November 13, 1911, remain, in spite of all that has been written about them, essentially obscure. The King was puzzled by the fact that this almost unknown iron merchant from Glasgow should have unanimously been acclaimed as the leader of the Conservative Party. He was at that date unacquainted with Mr Bonar Law's melancholy, austere and combative nature, or with the slow precisions of his mind:

> 'He is', Lord Derby wrote to the King on November 16,¹ 'a curious mixture. Never very gay, he has become even less so since the death of his wife, to whom he was devoted. But still he has a great sense of humour—a first-class debater—and a good, though not a rousing, platform speaker—a great master of figures, which he can use to great advantage. He has all the qualities of a great leader except one—and that is he has no personal magnetism and can inspire no man to real enthusiasm.'

Lord Derby added the opinion that when the time came to fight the Home Rule Bill the Unionist Party would regret having dispensed with the leadership of Mr A. J. Balfour. 'And I hope', he added, 'that they will be ashamed of themselves.'

By the time he received this letter, the King was already on his way to Delhi.

(4)

Ever since his visit to India in the winter of 1905–1906 King George had remained under the spell of that multitudinous country and had followed with intense personal interest the agitations, movements and reforms of the intervening five years. He was well aware that the defeat of a European by an Asiatic Power in the Russo-Japanese war had given a new impetus to Indian nationalism and that even moderate leaders, such as Gopal Ghokale, were being forced by their younger followers to adopt a more intransigeant attitude. The Morley-Minto reforms of 1909, under which repre-

two, he entered the House of Commons as Conservative member, first for Gorbals, and eventually for the Bootle division of Lancashire. In May 1915, he joined the Coalition Government as Minister for the Colonies. On December 7, 1916, he became Chancellor of the Exchequer in Mr Lloyd George's Government. After the coupon election of November 1918, he became Lord Privy Seal and leader of the House of Commons. On October 23, 1922, he succeeded Lloyd George as Prime Minister, an office which he held for only 209 days. He resigned for reasons of health on May 20, 1923, and died on October 30 of that year.

sentative institutions were introduced upon a small and somewhat artificial scale, and as a result of which S. P. Sinha became a member of the Viceroy's Council, were intended to bring educated Indian opinion into closer touch with the administration; they were not intended, as Lord Morley assured him, to lead directly or indirectly to parliamentary government in India. Their aim was to enhance the self-respect of the Indians rather than to increase the power of the nationalists. King George remained under the impression which he had derived from his first visit, and in which he was confirmed by the views of so experienced an administrator as Sir Walter Lawrence,[1] that it was unfortunate that the ruling chiefs were not accorded a more representative share in the Government. He felt that the Indian rulers were being gradually ousted by the politicians and the legislative councils, and that Lord Lytton's original conception of a Council of Princes (a conception by which Lord Curzon had himself at one moment been attracted) would do much to counterbalance the influence of the nationalists. Much as he admired the impartial efficiency of our bureaucratic system, he felt that the personal and paternal methods adopted in the Native States were often more closely in accord with the feelings and traditions of the people themselves. He believed that his own presence in India as King-Emperor would do much to revive and consolidate the loyalty of the Indian masses. From the first moment of his accession he decided that, after his coronation in London, he would travel to India and crown himself as Emperor at Delhi. He foresaw that so unprecedented a suggestion would not immediately commend itself to his Ministers. But for all his self-effacement and modesty, there was in him a strain of obstinacy, which the Cabinet had already come to recognise and respect.

When, in the early autumn of 1910, the Prime Minister came on a visit to Balmoral, the King broached this proposition in a tentative form. Mr Asquith was somewhat taken aback by the novelty of the suggestion and intimated that it would be fitting, before any decisions were come to or any announcements made, that the opinion of the Secretary of State for India should be obtained in writing. On

---

[1] Sir Walter Lawrence was born in 1857, educated at Cheltenham and Balliol, and passed first into the Indian Civil Service in 1877. He was Private Secretary to Lord Curzon as Viceroy between 1898 and 1903 and accompanied King George on his first visit to India in 1905. He died in 1940. His book *The India We Served* is a monument to his culture and intelligence.

September 8, 1910, therefore, the King wrote to Lord Morley the following letter:[9]

'When the Prime Minister was here last week, I spoke to him on a subject which has for some time been on my mind, and, having done so, I am anxious that you also, as Secretary of State for India (and it is only right that you should be the first after him to be informed by myself of what I mentioned to Mr Asquith) should know.

'Ever since I visited India five years ago I have been impressed by the great advantage which would result from a visit by the Sovereign to that great Empire. The events which have unfortunately occurred since 1906 have only strengthened that opinion. I am convinced that were it possible for me, accompanied by the Queen, to go to India and hold a Coronation Durbar at Delhi, where we should meet all the Princes, officials and vast numbers of the People, the greatest benefits would accrue to the Country at large. I also trust and I believe, that if the proposed visit could be made known some time before, it would tend to allay unrest and, I am sorry to say, seditious spirit, which unfortunately exist in some parts of India.

'Of course I am aware that this proposal of mine is an entirely new departure, but knowing your broad and liberal views and great experience, I feel sure that you will appreciate the wisdom of such a step and recognize the necessity of creating new precedents when circumstances justify them.

'I feel confident that my Ministers, after giving the question careful consideration, will appreciate my motives, which are actuated by a deep sense of duty and my sympathetic interest in the peoples of India, and will approve of an undertaking, the fulfilment of which I have so much at heart.'

Lord Morley, on September 12, replied to this letter in terms which were agile, tactful and not discouraging:[h]

'Viscount Morley, with the tender of his humble duty, begs leave to thank Your Majesty for writing to him so fully on a subject of such supreme importance. Your Majesty does no more than justice to Lord Morley in believing that he would not be afraid of making a new precedent in the present difficult circumstances in India. That such a step as Your Majesty proposes would be well calculated to strike the imagination of people in India, and to give fresh life to English interest and feeling about Indian subjects, is quite certain, and could not in itself be other than extraordinarily advantageous. Some difficulties, however, as was to be expected in a case of this novelty, present themselves.

'The cost of such a proceeding, with all the grandeur of it, would be great, and would presumably have to be borne by India. Apart from the general body of Indian tax-payers, the Princes and ruling chiefs would no doubt be eager to demonstrate their loyalty on the scale of splendour natural for such an occasion, and this splendour would be very costly, as the last Durbar only too abundantly proved. Again stress may be laid on embarrassments that might arise to public business at home, from the absence of the Sovereign from home for so long a time and at such immense distance. Points of this kind are sure to be present to Your Majesty, as may be also the best answers to them.

'Your Majesty is assuredly right in assuming that, in considering the question, Ministers will recognize and warmly appreciate the strong sense of Imperial duty, and the sympathetic, almost passionate, interest taken in the people of India that inspire the present proposal in Your Majesty's mind. Nobody has better reason to know, and to be grateful for, this commanding interest than Lord Morley. If he remains Indian Secretary he will count it a high honour indeed to take part in such discussion as, upon returning to London, Your Majesty intends.'

The proposal was submitted to the Cabinet two months later, and on November 8, 1910, Mr Asquith's Private Secretary informed Lord Knollys of their somewhat hesitant approval:

'The King's visit to India was agreed to by the Cabinet this afternoon, though not without a certain amount of criticism, and with a strong expression of opinion that the decision was not to be taken as precluding the discussion at a later stage of how the expenses were to be borne.'

The visit having been approved in principle, a long correspondence then ensued between the Viceroy and the Palace in regard to the detailed arrangements. Lord Hardinge, who warmly welcomed the proposal, appointed a Durbar Committee under the chairmanship of Sir John Hewett, who was assisted by an active secretary, Mr E. V. Gabriel. From the outset the King laid it down that 'all classes should have a chance of seeing him close at hand'. This decision caused distress to those who were responsible for security measures and there were many who felt that, in thus exposing himself to the terrorists, the King would be taking risks. He refused to be influenced by their arguments.

Two serious problems then arose. The King's original idea had been that he should 'crown himself at Delhi'. The officials pointed out that this would create an awkward precedent in that it would oblige all his successors to undergo a similar installation. The Archbishop of Canterbury objected that such an action would amount to a second Coronation, that a religious service of Consecration would be indispensable, and that this would be unfitting for a ceremony attended by so many Moslems and Hindus. It was therefore

168

IN INDIA

CORONATION COACH LEAVING THE COURTYARD OF
BUCKINGHAM PALACE

decided that the King should appear wearing his crown and receive the homage of the Princes and rulers seated upon his throne. A further difficulty then arose. It was discovered that no man was entitled in law to remove the crown from out of the kingdom; an entirely new crown had therefore to be manufactured. At one time it was suggested that this Imperial crown should after the Durbar be preserved in the fort at Delhi. It was then objected that this again would establish a precedent which might prove inconvenient to King George's successors and even that the existence, in the very centre of India, of this august emblem of Imperial sovereignty might prove an irresistible temptation to potential usurpers. In the end it was decided that the Imperial crown should, after the Durbar, be brought back to England and housed, with the other regalia, in the Tower of London.

The second problem was more serious. It was the problem of boons. It was foreseen that Indian opinion would interpret the visit of the King-Emperor as an almost miraculous event; and that the boons which, according to immemorial custom, would have to be accorded, must in their magnitude be proportionate to the occasion. The Viceroy had at first suggested that, apart from the usual remission of taxes and penal sentences, the British Government should make a gift to India of a crore of rupees (£666,666) to be devoted to technical education. This proposal was firmly rejected by the Cabinet. The Viceroy then proposed as an alternative that two separate major boons should be proclaimed at the Durbar. The first was the reversal of Lord Curzon's 'unintentional but grievous mistake' in partitioning Bengal. The second was the transference of the capital from Calcutta to Delhi. The Cabinet, when they came to consider these proposals, accepted them with some reluctance. On the one hand they doubted whether such boons would in fact arouse the enthusiasm which it was desired to create: on the other hand they were not at all certain that it was wise to identify the King-Emperor personally with changes of so important a nature which were bound to lead to much controversy in India.

These sad prognostications were not in every respect confirmed. But the criticisms which had been raised, the doubts and hesitations which had been expressed, did not encourage the officials who accompanied the King to India to view the prospect with any exuberant optimism. The success of the Durbar took them by surprise.

At a Privy Council held on November 10, 1911, a Council of State (consisting of the Archbishop of Canterbury, the Lord Chancellor, the Lord President of the Council, and Prince Arthur of Connaught) was set up to act in the King's name in all matters 'affecting the safety and good Government of Our Realm'. The Council of State were not however empowered to dissolve Parliament or to grant 'any rank, title or dignity of the peerage', or to 'act in any manner of things on which it is signified to Us, or appears to them, that Our special approval should be previously obtained'.

(5)

The King and Queen left England on November 11, 1911, and landed at the Apollo Bandar, Bombay, on December 2.[1] Five days later they made their state entry into Delhi. 'There were large crowds all the way,' the King noted that evening, 'but they were not particularly demonstrative.' Mr John Fortescue[i] attributes the chill of this reception to the fact that the people had expected the King to enter on an elephant and did not recognise him as he rode past in Field-Marshal's uniform, flanked by the Governor-General and the Secretary of State for India. The procession passed onwards to the King-Emperor's camp, which had been laid out with great elaboration and consisted of 40,000 tents giving shelter to some 300,000 people.

The Durbar itself took place on Tuesday, December 12, in an enormous amphitheatre, on the southern rim of which had been erected a tented canopy, or Shamiana, and in the exact centre of which stood a slim pavilion, raised upon a double platform, and surmounted by a bulbous golden dome. The King and Queen, wearing their crowns, drove from their camp to the Durbar amphitheatre, escorted by the Tenth Hussars and the Imperial Cadet Corps: their arrival was heralded by a salute of one hundred and one guns.

---

[1] The King and Queen travelled to India in the *Medina*, the latest addition to the P. & O. fleet and a fine vessel of 13,000 tons. They were accompanied by Lord Crewe, who had succeeded Lord Morley at the India Office, Lord Stamfordham, Sir Edward Henry, chief of the Metropolitan police, Sir James Dunlop Smith as political officer, Lord and Lady Shaftesbury, the Duke of Teck, Lord Durham, Lord Annaly, Sir Derek Keppel, Captain Godfrey Faussett, Sir Charles Cust, Lord Charles Fitzmaurice, Major Clive Wigram and Sir Havelock Charles. Mr John Fortescue was attached as historian of the visit and Mr Jacomb Hood was appointed the official artist. The *Medina* was escorted by four cruisers and the whole flotilla was under the command of Admiral Sir Colin Keppel, with Captain Chatfield as his flag captain. The *Medina* carried 32 officers and 360 petty officers and ratings, plus 210 Royal Marines. There were in all 733 people on board.

Descending in front of the Shamiana, the King and Queen, preceded by Indian attendants carrying peacock fans, yak-tails and golden maces, and flanked by heralds, Gentlemen-at-Arms, Scottish Archers[1] and officers of State, took their places under the canopy. They wore their coronation robes and their heavy purple trains were carried by ten Indian pages chosen from the families of the Princes and the ruling chiefs. The King read a short speech of welcome and the ceremony of homage then began. Led by the Governor-General, the long and glittering file of Rajahs passed before the King-Emperor and did obeisance. One of their number, the Gaekwar of Baroda, advanced towards the dais swinging a walking stick in his hand. 'One chief', wrote Mr John Fortescue with excellent restraint, 'marred the proceedings for a moment by a laboured ungainliness of bearing which lent itself to misrepresentation.'[ⁱ] This ceremony of homage lasted for a whole hour and when it was finished the guns fired a salute, the trumpets rang out, and the King and Queen descended from the canopied dais and walked slowly across to the pavilion. The two thrones had been set upon a platform reached by a series of steps; thus elevated above the troops and dignitaries who thronged the arena, the King and Queen were visible even to the most distant observer upon the Spectators' Mound. The Governor-General then advanced and read aloud a list of minor boons, such as increased expenditure on education, a grant of extra pay to all soldiers and civil servants and the release of certain criminals and debtors. When Lord Hardinge had finished, the King, to the surprise of all, himself rose and in a clear voice proclaimed the two major boons, the revision of the partition of Bengal and the transference of the capital to Delhi. The Durbar was then closed and the King and Queen departed. When they had left, the crowd rushed across to the pavilion and prostrated themselves, pressing their foreheads against the marble steps.

On the following day a national festival was held on the plain between the eastern wall of the fort of Delhi and the river Jumna. The King and Queen again put on their robes and crowns and showed themselves from Shah Jehan's balcony to a crowd of some half million people. On December 15 the King laid the foundation

---

[1] This was the first time that the Royal Company of Archers had served as a Scottish Bodyguard out of Scotland. They were represented in India by Lord Mar and Kellie, the Hon. Norman Macleod and the Hon. William Graham. For this exotic occasion they wore with their court uniforms white solar helmets adorned by a green plume.

stones of the new capital[1] and on the next day he departed on a most successful shooting expedition to Nepal. The Queen did not accompany him, preferring an arduous round of sightseeing in Rajputana.

Some doubts had been expressed as to whether it would be prudent for the King, before leaving India, to pay a visit to Calcutta, which was regarded as a hot-bed of sedition. He insisted on adhering to the original programme, and the reception accorded to him fully justified his decision. He was greeted enthusiastically by the people of Calcutta: 'it was a forest of waving arms.'

'The King', wrote Mr Stanley Reed, editor of the *Times of India*, to Lord Northcliffe, 'has been wiser than all of us. We were all filled with doubts. The depressing chilliness of the state entry into Delhi seemed to confirm them. But from that point there was no interruption in the crescendo wave of popular enthusiasm. It reached an unparalleled pitch in Calcutta and has left a deep and ineffaceable impression behind it.' Mr Reed was too experienced a man to suppose that this impression would check the flow of Indian nationalism; in fact he believed that it would enforce those aspirations. 'But', he added with rare prescience, 'Indians will now work for the realisation of those aspirations within the Empire.'[k]

On January 10 the King and Queen bade farewell to India:

'It is', he said in his final speech, 'a matter of intense satisfaction to me to realize how all classes and creeds have joined together in true-hearted welcome. Is it not possible that the same unity and concord may for the future govern the daily relations of their public and private lives? . . . To you, the representatives of Bombay I deliver this our loving message of farewell to the Indian Empire. . . .' (At this point the King paused for a few seconds in obvious emotion) . . . 'May the Almighty ever assist me and my successors to promote its welfare and to secure to it the blessing of prosperity and peace.'[l]

'I know', he wrote to Queen Alexandra while on his return journey, 'that many people in England, for various reasons, were against our going to India, but I am sure that if they could have been present with us & seen all we saw, they would have changed their minds & said they were wrong. From first to last during the

[1] These foundation stones caused future trouble. The King in laying them had referred to them as 'the first stones of the Imperial capital which will arise from where we now stand'. It was later decided that the site first chosen for the new Delhi was unsuitable and another site was selected. The stones were then, with the King's consent, moved to a different locality. In the House of Commons on June 10, 1912, Lord Ronaldshay repeated the malicious rumour that 'in the hurry of the moment an old tombstone was made use of for a foundation stone'. This was untrue. The stones had been carefully chosen from a mason's yard in the Chandni Chauk at Delhi.

five weeks we spent in that wonderful country everything we did was a splendid success: even my most sanguine expectations were surpassed. May & I were indeed deeply touched at the genuine love & affection shown us by the millions of people who saw us at the different places we went to. At Calcutta, where we spent ten days, the people became more & more enthusiastic each day & were quite as demonstrative as they are in England, which is most unusual in the Indian people. I actually broke down in reading my farewell speech in Bombay; I simply couldn't help it.' 'What joy', he wrote later from Malta, 'that there are only 9 more days before we meet! I shall then feel proud that our historical visit to India has been accomplished, successfully I hope, & that I have done my duty before God & this great Empire & last, but not least, that I have gained the approval of my beloved Motherdear.'

The King and Queen landed at Portsmouth on February 5, 1912. They found England threatened by a coal strike and hushed under snow.

CHAPTER XII

AGADIR

1911

The year 1911 also important as marking a new phase in the relations between the Triple Alliance and the Triple Entente—King George's approach to foreign affairs—His contact with the Foreign Office and the Ambassadors in London—The Revolution in Portugal—The expansion of the German Navy—Admiral von Tirpitz—King George and the German Emperor—The latter comes to London for the unveiling of the Queen Victoria Memorial—He raises the Morocco question—Conflicting versions of the conversation which then took place—The Franco-German negotiations—The French expedition to Fez—The despatch of the *Panther* to Agadir—Sir Edward Grey's warning—The Germans maintain an ominous silence for seventeen days—Mr Lloyd George's speech at the Mansion House—The danger of war—The Cambon–Kiderlen negotiations satisfactorily concluded on November 4—Effect in Germany of this diplomatic defeat—The Agadir crisis as a prelude to the 1914 war.

(1)

AT midnight on December 31, while still at Government House, Calcutta, King George said farewell to the old year. 'Goodbye!' he wrote in his diary. 'Dear old 1911! The most eventful year of my life!'

It had been the year of his Coronation: the year in which the Parliament Bill had faced him with a galling conflict of duties: a year of threats and portents: a year of social and industrial commotion: a year in which the thunder of Irish strife already grumbled in the west; while in the east, the German enigma assumed once more its fearful sphinx-like shape. At home, the old order was disintegrating and no man could foretell the pattern of the new. Abroad, the Concert of Europe, which had averted a major catastrophe for more than a hundred years, was being replaced by an uncertain balance of power and the great nations definitely ranged themselves—unwillingly, apprehensively, suspiciously—into two armed coalitions.

In the last three chapters an account has been given of the national problems with which, during this period, King George was confronted. It is now necessary, before passing on to 1912, to consider the international tension which, in that same year 1911, culminated in the first of many grave conjunctures.

174

It has already been remarked that King George, until his accession, had taken little interest in, and acquired but a superficial knowledge of, the intricate network of our foreign relations. He did not share his father's taste for the patterns of diplomacy and possessed in such matters an almost open mind. The Austrian Ambassador, Count Mensdorff,[1] reported to his Government in May 1910[a] that the new King had no special affection for, or prejudice against, any foreign country, although his personal sympathies appeared to incline to the side of his mother's relations rather than to that of his father's. Count Mensdorff was tempted to attribute exaggerated importance to dynastic affiliations. It was true that King George was much attached to the Danish Royal Family, that he had a warm affection for his cousin, the Tsar of Russia, and that throughout his life he was constantly concerned with the fortunes of successive Kings of Greece. But his relations with the German Emperor were equally correct, even amicable, and displayed a shrewder understanding of that Monarch's nervous and impulsive temperament than any sympathy that King Edward had been able to acquire. In any case, King George would never have allowed his family inclinations or aversions to colour the conduct which his position as a Constitutional Sovereign prescribed.[2]

With his usual diligence, and with the advantage of a most retentive memory, he would study the telegram sections and the printed despatches which reached him every morning from the Foreign Office. He was in constant communication with Sir Edward Grey, and, when in London, would grant repeated audiences to the Permanent Under Secretary. The British Ambassadors and Ministers accredited to foreign countries would, by almost every bag, write private letters to Lord Stamfordham explaining, or enlarging upon,

---

[1] Count Albert Victor von Mensdorff-Pouilly-Dietrichstein was Austrian Ambassador in London from 1904 to 1914. He was distantly related to the Royal Family, since his grandmother, Princess Sophia of Saxe-Coburg-Saalfeld, had been Queen Victoria's aunt. He was thus first cousin, once removed, to both Queen Victoria and the Prince Consort.

[2] King George, on his accession, was related to many of the ruling families of Europe. On his mother's side, he was the nephew of King Frederick VIII of Denmark (1843–1912), the nephew of King George of the Hellenes (1845–1913), the first cousin and brother-in-law of King Haakon VII of Norway (1872–   ) and the first cousin of Nicholas II, Tsar of Russia (1868–1918). On his father's side he was the first cousin of William II, German Emperor (1859–1941) and a first cousin by marriage of Alfonso XIII, King of Spain (1886–1941).

the official reports which they sent home. The King rapidly acquired a detailed familiarity with the international problems confronting his Government, and, thus equipped, was able to exercise in his intercourse with foreign representatives that discretion which only expert knowledge can provide.

In those distant days, there were only nine ambassadors accredited to the Court of St James's. All of them were men of peace; some of them were men of outstanding ability.[1] During the prolonged crisis created by the two Balkan Wars (which lasted from the autumn of 1912 to the spring of 1914) these great Ambassadors, under the modest but inspired leadership of Sir Edward Grey, succeeded, for a while, in reconstituting what was in fact a Concert of Europe. They represented all that was most wise, honourable and pacific in the Old Diplomacy; they formed a distinguished group.

King George was on intimate terms with each of them. They would spend repeated week-ends at Windsor and from time to time one or other of their number would stay for a week at Balmoral. The despatches in which they informed their Governments of the King's

[1] Monsieur Paul Cambon, the French Ambassador, had been appointed to London in 1898, at a time when French feeling was still smarting under the humiliations of Fashoda. His patient persistence, his acquired understanding of our national character, his perception that no British Government could be harried into foreign commitments, the influence which he continued to exercise on successive French Cabinets, rendered him both the architect and the custodian of the Entente.

Count Paul Wolff-Metternich, the German Ambassador, was indolent, well-intentioned and wise. The excellent advice which he furnished to his Government was negatived by the insidious reports simultaneously sent to them by the Military and Naval Attachés in London and by the Counsellor, Baron von Kühlmann. Count Metternich was recalled in 1912 on the unfair grounds that he had not warned his Government of the line which Great Britain would take in the Agadir crisis. He was succeeded by the formidable Marschall von Bieberstein, who died within five months and was himself succeeded by Prince Lichnowsky.

Count Benckendorff, the Russian Ambassador, was a loyal champion of Anglo-Russian co-operation, but his influence in St. Petersburg suffered from the fact that he was suspected in nationalist circles of possessing but a faint Pan-Slav heart.

Marquis Merry del Val, the Spanish Ambassador, was a competent diplomatist, hampered by a deficient sense of proportion. Count Mensdorff, the Austro-Hungarian Ambassador, was much esteemed in English society and exerted throughout a calming influence upon the hotheads at Vienna. The Italian Ambassador, Marchese Imperiali, was on the whole an equable man. The United States, Japanese and Turkish Ambassadors played subsidiary roles.

opinions and attitude have now been published. They reveal that the King was in the closest harmony with the policy of his Government; that he possessed a surprising knowledge of the details of the questions at issue; and that his attitude throughout was conciliatory, outspoken, robust and sensible. His reputation, unlike that of many other European statesmen of the time, was enhanced by these disclosures.

(2)

King George's first experience of the necessity of subordinating personal affections to the requirements of State policy occurred when a revolution broke out in Portugal in the autumn of 1910. On the night of October 4 the young King Manuel was entertaining the President of Brazil at the castle of Belem. News was brought to him that certain regiments in the capital had mutinied, had murdered their officers, and were advancing towards the centre of the city. Instead of joining his mother, Queen Amélie, at Cintra, King Manuel, with commendable courage, drove direct to Lisbon and established himself in the Necessidades Palace. By midnight the Republican forces had secured complete control of Lisbon and the warships in the Tagus started to bombard the palace. King Manuel was persuaded to escape by the garden gate and drove to Mafra, where he was rejoined by his mother, Queen Amélie, and his grandmother, Queen Maria Pia. On October 6, by which date it was evident that the revolution had triumphed, the Portuguese Royal Family embarked on their yacht at Ereceire and sailed for Gibraltar. From there the yacht was sent back to Oporto. King Manuel and his family accepted the proffered hospitality of Sir Archibald Hunter, the Governor of Gibraltar; they possessed nothing but the clothes in which they stood; King Manuel was obliged to borrow the dinner jacket of His Excellency's aide-de-camp, Captain Darby. Meanwhile, in London, the Marquis de Soveral, who remained until his death the devoted servitor of his Royal master, suggested to King George that a British warship should be sent to Gibraltar to transport the Portuguese Royal Family to England. Sir Edward Grey felt that such a gesture was excessive. King George, not wishing to leave in the lurch an unfortunate family, with whom he and his father had for so many years been on terms of cordial friendship, insisted upon sending the Royal yacht, the *Victoria and Albert*. Sir Edward Grey, with some misgivings, agreed to this suggestion. The Foreign Secretary was anxious, none the less, to forestall any criticism which such action might arouse by immediately according official recognition to the Republican Government at Lisbon. King George was unwilling that Great Britain should thus be the first of the Great Powers to accept and thereby fortify the revolution. Sir Edward Grey insisted, and the King, with his accustomed good sense, withdrew his objections. Thus King Manuel and his mother were transferred from Gibraltar to Southampton in the Royal yacht and proceeded to Woodnorton. For many months, for many years, thereafter King George, through the British Minister at Lisbon, sought to persuade the Portuguese Government to restore their personal belongings to King Manuel and Queen Amélie. In the end his intervention was not unsuccessful; nor were our relations with our oldest ally in any way troubled by the episode.

The essential factor in our foreign policy during this pre-war period was the rapid and alarming increase in the power of the German Navy. While it determined our own naval construction and dispositions, it also obliged us to abandon for ever the system of splendid isolation, to conclude and renew our alliance with Japan, and to enter into ever closer co-operation with France and Russia. To the naval problem, even when he was Prince of Wales, King George had given expert attention. Although he was bombarded with pleas and counter-pleas from his former commanders and colleagues in the Navy, he managed to maintain an attitude of neutrality. He deeply regretted, and remained aloof from, the internecine quarrel which arose between Admiral Lord Charles Beresford and Sir John Fisher. He strove to approach the problem, with all the technical controversies which it aroused, in an impartial spirit.

The German Navy, in 1870, had consisted of only four armoured ships, which had played but an inconspicuous part in the Franco-Prussian war. Even in 1888, when William II became Emperor, the German Navy was manned by no more than seventeen thousand men and cost the Exchequer less than two and a half million pounds a year. The young Emperor was convinced that, if Germany were really to become a World Power, 'the trident must be in our hands'. 'When I began my reign,' he wrote in after years,[b] 'I at once energetically took in hand the development and reform—in fact, one may say the foundation anew—of the Imperial German Navy.' The Reichstag did not share these ambitions and refused to grant the necessary credits. 'Twelve precious years,' the Emperor wrote,[c] 'never to be retrieved, were lost by the failure of the Reichstag.' In 1897 Admiral von Tirpitz succeeded Admiral Hollman; the German

Flottenverein, or Navy League, was created as an instrument of propaganda. In the following April, Admiral von Tirpitz persuaded the Reichstag to pass a Navy Bill which, while it provided Germany with a powerful fleet of battleships and cruisers, was not excessive. The outbreak of the South African War and the arrest by British cruisers of two German merchantmen, created a new atmosphere and a new opportunity. Admiral von Tirpitz informed the Emperor that what was needed was a battle-fleet 'which can be stationed between Heligoland and the Thames'. The Reichstag in 1900 were therefore induced to consent to a further Bill providing for such a battle-fleet, the whole programme to be completed within seventeen years.[1] Admiral von Tirpitz professed to fear that, pending this completion, Germany must pass through 'a danger zone', since there was a risk of England 'trying to force a preventive war' in order 'to nip our fleet in the bud'.[d] This apprehension was not rendered less fantastic by the fact that Sir John Fisher, in one of his moments of ebullience, did actually suggest to King Edward that it might be a good thing to 'Copenhagen' the growing German fleet before it became too strong. 'Fisher', King Edward replied, 'you must be mad!'[e]

Admiral von Tirpitz may have possessed outstanding naval genius; but he was also, to quote Mr Winston Churchill, 'a sincere, wrong-headed, purblind old Prussian.' 'It is almost pathetic', adds Mr Churchill, 'to read the foolish sentences in which, on page after page of his memoirs,' the Admiral asserts that Anglo-German relations would be improved by naval rivalry.[f] The Emperor, for his part, contended that a large German fleet would 'bring the British to their senses by sheer fright'. The Germans had every right, if they so desired, to challenge our command of the seas. The mistakes they made were, firstly to under-estimate the effect which such a menace would produce in this country and overseas: secondly, to ignore the possibility that world opinion might consider it inordinate ambition on the part of a country, already possessing the strongest army in the world, to compete also for naval supremacy: and thirdly, not to foresee that to antagonise Great Britain and Russia simultaneously (the first on the high seas, the second in the Near and Middle East)

---

[1] The 1900 Navy Bill provided for:
   A Battle Fleet, consisting of: 2 first flagships, 32 battleships, 8 large cruisers, 24 small cruisers.
   A Foreign Fleet, consisting of: 3 large cruisers and 10 small cruisers.
   In reserve, 4 battleships, 3 large cruisers and 4 small cruisers.

would end by drawing these two Powers together and thereby creating the very encirclement which they so dreaded.

Our endeavours to secure some mitigation of this ascending scale of naval construction met with small response. The German Emperor dismissed as 'groundless impertinence' *g* the tentative suggestions that we made from time to time for some general disarmament agreement: when Sir Charles Hardinge raised the matter at Kronberg in August 1908, he was severely snubbed. There were some Germans, however, who realised that Great Britain would never, however economical or pacific her Government might be, allow her maritime security to be seriously imperilled. Herr von Bethmann-Hollweg, who succeeded Prince Bülow as Chancellor in 1909, was fully conscious that this insane competition could only bring Germany to the abyss; he was unable to exorcise the spell which von Tirpitz had cast upon the Emperor and the German public. Baron von Kühlmann also was well aware that the propaganda of the *Flottenverein* had in the course of years created in the German mind a feeling of excited grandeur, which could only be diluted or diverted by the provision of some equally glamorous vision. Only by dangling before their expectant eyes the prospects of a vast colonial Empire in Africa and Asia could these elated aspirations be assuaged. *h*

The British Admiralty, as was inevitable, took steps to counter this increasing menace. Sir John Fisher strengthened our Home Fleet by withdrawing capital ships from the Mediterranean. On February 10, 1906, the first Dreadnought was launched and the race for naval power entered a new and even more competitive phase.[1]

(3)

King George preferred concord to tension: he regretted the acerbity which had entered into Anglo-German relations and he

[1] The Germans contended that by creating the Dreadnought type, and thereby rendering obsolete all previous battleships, we sacrificed the advantage of numbers which until then we had possessed. Admiral von Tirpitz goes so far as to claim that by introducing the Dreadnought we enabled Germany to start level with ourselves and 'automatically doubled' the fighting force of the German Navy (*Memoirs*, I, p. 263). We certainly took a risk, but it must be remembered that the Kiel Canal had to be widened and deepened before it could pass Dreadnoughts from the Baltic to the North Sea. This work could not be, and was not, completed until the late summer of 1914, and at the cost to the Reich of twelve million pounds. By then, our superiority in Dreadnoughts was assured.

sought to introduce a less irritable, less touchy, tone into the manners both of London and Berlin. Baron von Kühlmann, who was a close and clever observer, expressed the opinion that it was from the year of King George's accession that he would date the first deliberate efforts of British statesmen and publicists to understand the German problem.¹ The early Victorian conception of 'dear little Germany' scarcely survived the blood and iron of the Bismarck epoch. The Edwardians were almost equally at fault in identifying the German Empire with the caricature of a braggart youth, claiming with vulgar, vaunting voice to share, perhaps even to acquire, the privileges of his elders and betters. By 1910 a less ignorant diagnosis of the German malady had qualified our earlier assumptions. People began to realise that here was a newly welded nation of some sixty million gifted, industrious but neurotic people; a nation which had arrived so late at the imperialist banquet that she had only been accorded a few grudging scraps; a nation elated by her seething intelligence and energy and naturally claiming her own place in the sun. It was unfortunate that the psychological misunderstanding which persisted during the first ten years of the century should, for so many Germans and Englishmen, have been set, formulated and crystallised by distorted preconceptions of the personalities of King Edward and William II. For the Germans, King Edward seemed the personification of the leisured self-assurance, the indolent condescension, which they assumed to be the general attitude of England towards Germany and which filled them with envy, mortification and rage. To the English, the Emperor William II seemed the personification of the flamboyant self-assertiveness of the new Germany, a type of energy which they pretended to find amusing, but which in fact created a vague and increasing apprehension. It is a misfortune when two great fraternal nations come to misconceive each other in terms of their respective caricatures: we failed to appreciate their sensitiveness and they failed to realise our pride; and when, between 1910 and 1914, less impetuous, less superficial, more serious impressions began to percolate, the gulf had already widened; the damage had been done.

The difficult nephew-uncle relationship which had so galled the German Emperor during King Edward's lifetime, was now replaced by the happier, easier, association of elder and younger cousin. King George had always been grateful for the sympathy manifested by the Emperor during the difficult years of the South African War and he was touched by the deep and perfectly sincere veneration with which

William II honoured the memory of their common grandmother, Queen Victoria. In May 1910, they had stood alone together beside the catafalque of King Edward in Westminster Hall and had silently clasped hands in token of confidence and friendship. Anxious as he was to mitigate the bitterness which had arisen between the two countries, King George felt that it would be useful to renew this amicable association. The unveiling of the memorial to Queen Victoria had been fixed for the second week in May 1911. King George wrote to the German Emperor inviting him, as the eldest of Queen Victoria's grandchildren, to be present at this inauguration. He received a warm and affectionate reply:

'Let me thank you most cordially', the German Emperor wrote on February 15, 1911, 'for the very kind letter in which you invite Dona and me to be present at dear Grandmama's unveiling. You cannot imagine how overjoyed I am at the prospect of seeing you again so soon & making a nice stay with you. You are perfectly right in alluding to my devotion & reverence for my beloved Grandmother, with whom I was on such excellent terms. I shall never forget how kindly this great lady always was to me & the relations she kept up with me, though I was so far her junior, she having carried me about in her arms! Never in my life shall I forget the solemn hours in Osborne at her deathbed when she breathed her last in my arms! These sacred hours have riveted my heart firmly to your house & family, of which I am proud to feel myself a member. And the fact that for the last hours I held the sacred burden of her—the creator of the greatness of Britain—in my arms, in my mind created an invincible special link between her country & its People & me and one which I fondly nurse in my heart. This your invitation so to say sanctions these ideas of mine. You kindly refer to the fact of my being her eldest grandson: a fact I was always immensely proud of and never forgot.'

This letter was a sincere expression of the better side of the German Emperor's strangely ambivalent feelings towards his mother's country. He believed that the occasion might serve to improve the relations between England and Germany and was disappointed when both Herr von Bethmann-Hollweg and Sir Edward Grey insisted that the visit should be regarded as a purely family gathering and that no political conversations should take place.[k] The three days which the Emperor spent in London were none the less auspicious; the crowds in the streets greeted him with marked enthusiasm; he returned to Berlin with 'the best impressions'; never, as he informed his Chancellor, had he felt the atmosphere at Buckingham Palace to be 'so free, so open, or so friendly'.

The ceremony of the unveiling took place on the morning of

May 16. Preceded by Beefeaters, the King and the Empress, the Emperor and Queen Mary, walked in slow procession from Buckingham Palace along a wide blue carpet, flanked by Gentlemen-at-Arms. The large monument which Sir Thomas Brock had erected was of dazzling whiteness, unrelieved by the bronze figures of Peace and Progress, of Industry and Agriculture, which today flaunt the hammer and the sickle at the Palace gates. The façade behind them was still the dingy frontage which Edward Blore had designed in 1846; Sir Aston Webb's engaged and tidy columns were still to come. The King pulled the cord and the white canvas which draped the statue fell in a soft heap. The sun shone, the guns saluted, the bands played national anthems, the distant crowds cheered in rapture, and the choir of Westminster Abbey sang 'Oh God, our help in ages past'. Those who were present at this ceremony never forgot the sunshine, the colour and the high auguries of that May morning.

The German Emperor was deeply moved. This did not prevent him, at the very hour of his departure, when King George had come to his apartments to bid him a last few words of farewell, from raising a political question which was again causing international concern. He raised the question of Morocco.

(4)

It will be recalled that under the Franco-German Agreement concluded on February 8, 1909, Germany had recognised France's special responsibility for preserving peace and order in Morocco, while France had promised that Germany should be given equality of economic opportunity. The latter undertaking was interpreted in Berlin as securing a Franco-German 'economic condominium'.[1]

For a while the 1909 Agreement worked smoothly enough, but disputes and difficulties soon arose. Sultan Abdul Aziz (an intelligent but lax young man) had in 1908 been deposed by his brother, Mulai Hafid. The short civil war which this occasioned had left Morocco in a state of internal chaos. The tribes refused to recognise the Sultan's authority and eminent foreign residents were kidnapped and held to ransom by local brigand bands. Divergent interpretations were moreover given in Berlin and Paris to the implications of the 'economic condominium'. The new Sultan had accorded conflicting concessions to French and German firms and a bitter argument arose as to the degree to which German capital and technicians could participate in the construction and management of the projected

183

railway system. By the end of 1910 the German Government were accusing the French of wishing to evade their economic promises.

By January 1911, insurgent tribes had invested the Moorish capital and the Sultan appealed for French assistance. His appeal was warmly supported by the European residents in Fez, who were in fact in danger of their lives. The French Government thereupon landed troops at Rabat and despatched a relief column under General Moinier, who was instructed to rescue the Sultan and the Christian community. On March 5, 1911, M. Jules Cambon, the French Ambassador at Berlin, officially notified Herr von Kiderlen-Waechter, the new German Foreign Secretary, of this relief expedition. He received a sullen and disturbing reply. Herr von Kiderlen informed him that if French troops were to occupy Fez, it would mean that the Sultan would cease to be an independent Sovereign. This would imply that both the Act of Algeciras and the Franco-German Agreement of 1909 had lost all validity and Germany must therefore resume her 'complete liberty of action'. An ominous silence ensued.

It is now clear from published German documents that Herr von Kiderlen-Waechter had already decided that the 'economic con-dominium' would in practice prove unworkable and that Morocco was not worth a war. What he hoped to do was to inveigle France into direct negotiations, to isolate her from Great Britain and Russia, and to force her to pay a vast sum, in terms of colonial territory, for Germany's assent to her Moroccan enterprise. In order to exert the required pressure it would first be necessary (since such are the sad operations of the German mind) to obtain a pawn or lever. On May 3, 1911, Herr von Kiderlen composed a memorandum[m] in which he stated that Germany 'must secure an object which will make the French ready to give us compensation'. The lever, or '*Faustpfand*', which he contemplated was the simple expedient of sending a German warship to some southern Moorish port.

Such was the position when the German Emperor came to London for the unveiling of the Queen Victoria memorial. The Emperor, being a pacific man, had not been much attracted by Herr von Kiderlen's suggested stratagem. Ever since his own unfortunate visit to Tangier in 1905 he had loathed the Moorish question; he feared that so intemperate an act might unnecessarily disturb Germany's relations, not with France only, but also with the latter's friends. It was this subject therefore that, in an off-hand manner, he raised with King George a few minutes only before they were both leaving for the railway station.

Accounts differ as to what actually transpired in the course of that conversation. There exists no mention or record of it in the Royal Archives. The version which, many years later, the Emperor gave in his *Memoirs* is probably correct:

'I asked him if he considered that the French methods were still in accordance with the Algeciras Agreement. The King remarked that the Agreement, to tell the truth, was no longer in force, that the best thing to do was to forget it; that the French, fundamentally, were doing nothing different in Morocco from what the English had previously done in Egypt; that, therefore, England would place no obstacles in the path of the French, and would follow their own course; that the only thing to do was to recognize the *fait accompli* of the occupation of Morocco and make arrangements for commercial protection with France.'[n]

In a note made by Herr von Bethmann-Hollweg on the Emperor's return to Berlin[o] it is added that William II had assured his cousin that he would 'never wage a war for the sake of Morocco' but that Germany might claim compensations in Africa. To this suggestion, notes Herr von Bethmann-Hollweg, His Majesty made no reply. This may well be true. But at a subsequent date, when the despatch of the German cruiser *Panther* to Agadir had created a major European crisis, the Emperor spread the story that, when at Buckingham Palace, he had warned King George of his intention to take this action and that His Majesty had agreed. The Emperor could not understand therefore why the British Government thereafter had adopted an attitude of outraged surprise.[1]

King George, when he heard this story, was much perplexed:

'What really happened', he said to Count Mensdorff,[p] 'was that, just before the Emperor was leaving, he raised the Morocco question. . . .

---

[1] Sir Cecil Spring Rice, at that time British Minister at Stockholm, informed King George in a private letter of September 24, 1911 (R.A. M.229.5) that the German Emperor on the occasion of a naval review at Stettin, had told the King of Sweden that he had warned King George of his intention to send a warship to southern Morocco and that the latter had raised no objection. The Germans, Sir Cecil added, interpreted this as a deliberate manoeuvre on our part to embroil Germany and France. First we 'encouraged' Germany to send a cruiser to Agadir and then we urged France to resist the ensuing pressure. If such were in fact their suspicions, their distortion of King George's motives was typical of their distressing habit of seeing in chance incidents some elaborate stratagem, conspiracy or 'system'.

I will not deny that he perhaps could have said something about a ship, although I do not recall it. If he did, I thought of Mogador: in any case, he did not mention Agadir. And I absolutely did not express to him my own, or my Government's consent to any such action.'

The King added that it was his personal conviction that the German Emperor was a man of peace. The difficulty was that he might not for ever be strong enough to control his own militarists, since he was sensitive to their criticisms of his unwarlike hesitations. 'No man,' remarked King George, 'likes to be called a coward.'

The Emperor William, in common with other members of the Hohenzollern family, and indeed with most of his compatriots, was inclined to note and to remember only what he desired to hear. He would disregard, or dismiss as 'arrant hypocrisy' the conciliatory speeches of statesmen or the leading articles of the more responsible newspapers; he would base deductions upon some chance article contributed to a regimental magazine. It is evident none the less that he returned from that May visit to London, deeply affected by the friendliness of his reception, and convinced that the British Government and people were in a mood of amicable acquiescence. The doubts which had at first assailed him regarding the wisdom of sending a warship to southern Morocco, melted in the sun of that delightful experience. He now agreed with Herr von Kiderlen-Waechter that the moment had arrived to seize a *Faustpfand*, on the assumption that Great Britain would stand aside. He was mistaken in this assumption.

(5)

On July 1, 1911, the German Ambassador, Count Wolff-Metternich, walked across to the Foreign Office and, in the absence of Sir Edward Grey, handed to the Permanent Under-Secretary, a Note stating that his Government had despatched a gunboat to Agadir for the purpose of protecting the lives and properties of certain 'Hamburg merchants' established in that area. Sir Arthur Nicolson said he would immediately inform Sir Edward Grey of this grave communication but pointed out that Agadir was not a trading port and that, to the best of his knowledge, there were no German merchants, whether from Hamburg or elsewhere, south of the Atlas mountains.[1] On his return to London on July 4, Sir Edward Grey

[1] According to Herr Friedrich Rosen (who had been German Minister in Morocco from 1905–1910) a young employee of the Hamburg-Morocco Company of the name of Wilberg had been hurriedly despatched

had an interview with the German Ambassador, in which he informed him that the despatch of a German gunboat to Agadir had created 'a new, highly important and delicate situation', that Great Britain (whose commercial interests in Morocco were far more important than any German interests) must insist on taking part in any discussions which might ensue, and that we should not recognise any arrangement made without our knowledge and consent.^q To this formidable intimation the German Government vouchsafed no answer for seventeen days.

The reason for this 'oppressive silence' was that the German Government hoped, by using the lever they had secured at Agadir, and by isolating France from Great Britain, to force the French to pay enormous compensation in return for a free hand in Morocco. They were encouraged in this expectation by the fact that M. Caillaux, who had recently succeeded Monsieur Monis as head of the French Government, was known to be an advocate of a new deal with Germany and a hostile critic of the Entente with Great Britain. In the negotiations which continued between M. Jules Cambon and Herr von Kiderlen-Waechter, the latter had started by demanding as his price the whole of the French Congo. He warned M. Cambon that, if her demands were disregarded, Germany might be forced to adopt 'extreme measures'. News of this menace reached the British Government, who became seriously concerned. On July 21 Sir Edward Grey invited Count Metternich to visit him, commented upon the seventeen days' silence which the German Government had observed, and insisted that Great Britain must be admitted to the discussions.

That evening the Lord Mayor gave his annual dinner to the Bankers of the City of London. The principal speaker on that occasion was the Chancellor of the Exchequer who, after paying the accustomed compliments to our great merchant community and lauding the financial stability of the realm, added this fulminating passage, which he had previously submitted to the Prime Minister and Sir Edward Grey:

'If', said Mr Lloyd George, 'a situation were to be forced upon us in which peace could only be preserved by the surrender of the great and beneficent position Britain has won by centuries of heroism and

---

to the Agadir area in order to impersonate the 'Hamburg merchants'. He experienced difficulty in penetrating the passes of the Atlas mountains and only reached Agadir after the *Panther* had arrived (Rosen, pp. 338–350).

achievement, by allowing Britain to be treated, where her interests were vitally affected, as if she were of no account in the Cabinet of Nations, ... then I say emphatically that peace at that price would be a humiliation, intolerable for a great country like ours to endure.'

It must be remembered that at the time Mr Lloyd George was regarded abroad as the leader of the pacifist wing of the Cabinet and as an ardent champion of agreement with Germany. That such a man, at such a moment, should use language so forceful and incisive filled the Germans with consternation and the French with revived courage. The immediate German reaction was to retort with violence; on July 24 the unfortunate Count Metternich was instructed to deliver to the British Government an intimation of so stiff a character that Sir Edward Grey feared that it meant war. Precautionary orders were issued to the fleet, extra guards were placed upon our naval depots and magazines, and the military manoeuvres which were then taking place were cancelled 'owing to the scarcity of water in Wiltshire and the neighbouring counties'. These movements, unprovocative though they were, did not escape the notice of the German Government. Herr von Kiderlen-Waechte adopted a less minatory tone in his negotiations with that great diplomatist, Monsieur Jules Cambon. In the end, on November 4, 1911, an agreement was concluded between France and Germany by which the former obtained a free hand to establish a Protectorate in Morocco and at the price, not of the whole Congo, but of an area of only 100,000 square miles. The Agadir crisis was over: the efficacy of the Entente had been reaffirmed.

(6)

It may seem strange that the presence in an unknown Atlantic harbour of one little ship, carrying a complement of only 125 men, should have brought Europe to the very lip of catastrophe. The German object had been to secure great accretions to the colonial territory she already held in Africa; and at the same time to manifest to the world, and above all to France and Russia, that British democracy was too indolent and peace-loving to provide, in times of menace, a stable buttress for the Triple Entente. Had not the rulers of Germany been blinded by the fallacy that you can persuade great nations by force; had the methods of the German Foreign Office been less blustering and more consistent; the France of M. Caillaux might well have been induced to surrender much of her own Colonial territory and Great Britain might well have hesitated, until it was too late, to intervene.

The Agadir crisis proved, as Sir Edward Grey judged, 'a fiasco for Germany'.[r] 'There is no doubt,' wrote Mr Winston Churchill, 'that deep and violent passions of humiliation and resentment were coursing beneath the glittering uniforms which thronged the palaces through which the Kaiser moved.'[s] Admiral von Tirpitz, loudly proclaiming that Germany had suffered the severest diplomatic humiliation in her history, insisted that the only way to salve these wounds was immediately to introduce a tremendous Supplementary Naval Estimate.[t] Lord Haldane, on looking back in after life to the years before the war, expressed the view that it was Germany's diplomatic discomfiture at the time of Agadir which drove the Emperor finally away from Herr von Bethmann-Hollweg and into the camp of Admiral von Tirpitz and his even more violent associates. 'The Agadir incident', concluded Herr von Rosen,[u] 'brought the danger of war substantially nearer.' 'The consequences', wrote Sir Edward Grey, in his melancholy wisdom, 'of such a foreign crisis ' not end with it. They *seem* to end: but they go underneath and reappear later on.'

The threat of sudden war, with which the country had so unexpectedly been faced between the months of July and November 1911, obliged Mr Asquith's Government immediately to review the co-ordination of our defences, the nature of our commitments and our general relations with all Foreign Powers. The Dominion Prime Ministers who were present in London for the Coronation festivities had already, on May 26, 1911, attended a full meeting of the Committee of Imperial Defence. Certain arrangements had been agreed to for naval and military co-operation in time of war and consent was given to the renewal of the Anglo-Japanese alliance for a further period of ten years.[1] On August 23, 1911, at the height of the Agadir crisis, a special meeting of the Committee of Imperial Defence was summoned to examine the state of our preparedness; the meeting was addressed for one and three-quarter hours by General Sir Henry Wilson, Director of Military Operations.[v] It was discovered that the plans prepared by the War Office conflicted

---

[1] This alliance, which had first been concluded in 1902, was therefore, on July 13, 1911, renewed until 1921. It enabled Japan to occupy Korea and it helped us to strengthen our naval position in home waters. In 1901, for instance, we kept 5 battleships and 33 cruisers in the Pacific: in 1910 we had no battleships there and only 19 cruisers.

with those which the Admiralty had in mind. The Prime Minister decided therefore that it was essential to create a Naval War Staff in the Admiralty and he invited Mr Winston Churchill to undertake this delicate task. Mr Churchill succeeded Mr Reginald McKenna as First Lord on October 23, 1911. On relinquishing his post as Home Secretary for this fresh and congenial activity Mr Churchill addressed to the King a letter, the conventional tone of which fails to conceal a natural buoyancy.

'In delivering my seals to Your Majesty this morning I should be sensible of many regrets at ceasing to be Your Majesty's Principal Secretary of State, were it not for the fact that the great service of the sea, upon which the life and honour of the realm depends, is one with which Your Majesty is so intimately associated by a life-time of practical experience, and that I know I may recur to Your Majesty for aid and support in the duties entrusted to me by Your Majesty's gracious favour.'

Meanwhile, the unofficial exchange of views, which since 1906 had been proceeding, without the knowledge of the Cabinet as a whole, between members of the French and British General Staffs, were allowed to continue, on the strict, and oft repeated, understanding that these conversations should not be interpreted as committing either Government in the event of war.[1]

By the late autumn of 1911, with the signature of the final Cambon-Kiderlen Agreements of November 4, the crisis appeared, for the moment at least, to have receded. The King was able to leave for India with an easier mind.

[1] During the first Morocco crisis of 1905–1906 the French Government had enquired whether, in the event of war, we should be able to send an Expeditionary Force of 100,000 men to protect the French left flank. Mr Haldane, after consultation with Sir Henry Campbell-Bannerman, Mr Asquith and Sir Edward Grey, thereupon authorised General Grierson, at that time Director of Military Operations at the War Office, to enter into unofficial conversations with Major Huguet, the French Military Attaché in London. It was largely as a result of these conversations that Mr Haldane realised it would be necessary 'to attempt a complete revolution in the organisation of the British Army at home'. These discussions continued in a somewhat desultory form for years and were given more detailed application after 1912 under the energetic impulse of Sir Henry Wilson. They will again be mentioned at a later stage. (See Haldane, *Before the War*, pp. 30–33, and Repington, *The First World War*, volume I, chapter I.)

CHAPTER XIII

TENSION

1912

The Italian seizure of Tripoli—Discussions with Germany on naval armaments—Sir Ernest Cassel—The Haldane mission—The German Navy Law of 1912—Our counter-measures—The King resumes his accustomed routine—His visit to the Fleet—And to Aldershot—His tours in South Wales and the West Riding—The autumn manoeuvres —First signs of the Irish Controversy—The Home Rule Bill introduced into the House of Commons, April 11, 1912—Mr Asquith in Dublin—The Blenheim rally—The Ulster Covenant—Suggestions that the King should refuse the Royal Assent—Mr Bonar Law's proposals—Disorder in the House of Commons—The King complains to Mr Asquith that he is not kept sufficiently informed—Sir Edward Grey and M. Sazonov at Balmoral—The First Balkan War— Prince Henry of Prussia at York Cottage.

(1)

THE GRAVE commotion occasioned by the Agadir crisis and the prospect that France would now obtain, with the tacit consent of the Great Powers, a protectorate over Morocco, induced Italy to declare war on Turkey with the object of securing for herself the Libyan provinces of Tripoli and Cyrenaica. Sultan Mehmed V, on September 28, 1911, addressed to King George a despairing telegram begging him 'in his quality of August Defender of the Sanctity of Treaties and as Protector of peace' to bring about a pacific settlement of the conflict. The King replied that he must 'in accordance with invariable practice, reserve the questions at issue for discussion through my Ministers'.[a] He was well aware of the serious implications of the Italian action and of the repercussions which it was bound to have upon Moslem feeling in India and elsewhere. He was warned by Sir Arthur Nicolson that this flagrant attack by a Great Power upon the integrity of the Ottoman Empire would be certain to excite the appetites of smaller countries and that 'the Balkans will begin to move'.[b] It was evident that the Concert of Europe was in process of dislocation. A determined, and for a while not unsuccessful effort, was made to recreate it.

The first essential was to reach with Germany some form of understanding which, by removing points of friction, might (on the analogy of our Agreement with France in 1904, and with Russia in 1907) alleviate the present tense atmosphere of rancour and distrust. The occasion was not inauspicious. The British Government had been seriously alarmed by the sudden danger which had faced them in July 1911: the German Government had realised that their successive *Kraftproben*, or trials of force, had served to integrate rather than to disintegrate the Triple Entente. Moreover they had been perturbed by the financial panic which their bellicose attitude during the Morocco crisis had aroused among the bankers of Berlin and Hamburg. The German Chancellor, Herr von Bethmann-Hollweg, was overtly anxious to reach some settlement: it was hoped that, if compensations were offered to Germany in other fields, she might be willing to abate, or at least to postpone, the formidable increase in naval construction which she was then known to be contemplating.

Unofficial discussions first took place between Herr Albert Ballin of the Hamburg-America Line and Sir Ernest Cassel. On January 29, 1912, the latter arrived in Berlin bringing with him a memorandum which had been approved by the British Cabinet and in which it was indicated that, if Germany were willing to reduce or retard her new naval programme, Great Britain would be prepared to discuss colonial compensations and even to consider some formula debarring either party from entering into aggressive designs or combinations against the other. The German Emperor interpreted this last suggestion as implying an unconditional offer of British neutrality in the event of Germany becoming involved in a war.[c] Herr von Bethmann-Hollweg, while welcoming the overture, stated that unfortunately the Supplementary Navy Estimates, or 'Novelle', had already been approved.[d] Sir Ernest Cassel returned to London with the distressing information that the Novelle would provide for the construction of three new German Dreadnoughts. He added that both the Emperor and the Chancellor had intimated that they would be glad notwithstanding to welcome a visit from a British Minister. The Cabinet immediately decided that Lord Haldane should go to Berlin in order to explore the ground. He reached the German capital on February 8, 1912.

Lord Haldane's conversations were not facilitated by the fact that, on the day after his arrival in Berlin, Mr Winston Churchill delivered in Glasgow a speech in which he referred to the German navy as 'a luxury'. The German word '*Luxus*' possesses associations less inoffensive than its English equivalent; the Emperor and

Admiral von Tirpitz were indignant. 'Nobody', King George remarked to Count Mensdorff, 'regretted Winston's slip more than Winston.' But offence had been caused.

The King followed the course of these short and fruitless negotiations with intense interest. 'His Majesty could not', remarked Lord Haldane afterwards, 'have displayed a warmer desire for my success.'*e* Herr von Bethmann-Hollweg took the unusual step of sending a personal message to King George, thanking him for 'the confidence he had shown in his policy'.*f* It was true that the King believed in the sincerity of the Chancellor's desire for peace; all he feared was that the Emperor in the last resort would listen only to Admiral von Tirpitz: 'a formidable man, a sort of Fisher'. These apprehensions were not unjustified.

In his successive conversations with the Emperor and Herr von Bethmann-Hollweg, Lord Haldane endeavoured to obtain some assurance that the new Navy Law would be modified or retarded in return for colonial compensations and some neutrality formula. Such places as Zanzibar, Angola and the Belgian Congo were mentioned as possible areas of German expansion. It was the neutrality formula which caused the main difficulty. Herr von Bethmann-Hollweg suggested that Great Britain and Germany should bind themselves not to make or join any combination directed against the other and to maintain a 'benevolent neutrality' should either of them become involved in war. Lord Haldane pointed out that such an engagement would prevent us from coming to the assistance of France if she were attacked by Germany and was, in any case, inconsistent with our treaty obligations to Japan, Portugal and Belgium. He put forward an alternative formula, by which we should undertake not to join 'any combination for purposes of aggression' and should remain neutral in a war in which Germany 'could not be said to be the aggressor'. The Germans, with some justice, pointed out that the word 'aggressor' was a purely relative term and not one which could figure with any precision in a contractual obligation.

Lord Haldane then returned to London, bringing with him the draft of the German Novelle, or Supplementary Navy Law. It was in truth a formidable document.[1] 'The maintenance', wrote Mr

[1] The Novelle of 1912 provided for:
    1 Fleet flagship.
    5 Squadrons of 8 battleships each.
   12 Large cruisers.
   30 Small cruisers.

Churchill to Sir Edward Grey after the Admiralty experts had examined these estimates, 'of twenty-five battleships (which, after the next four or five years will all be Dreadnoughts) exposes us to constant danger, only to be warded off by vigilance, approximating to war conditions.'*g* In face of such a menace, the Cabinet did not feel justified in pursuing the colonial proposals which Lord Haldane had adumbrated; nor were they prepared to accept the neutrality formula which he had advanced. The Haldane mission failed, therefore, in its main purpose, which was to secure a reduction in German naval armaments. Admiral von Tirpitz was overjoyed. 'After Haldane's visit', he writes with glee, '—when our extravagant desire for an understanding led the English to believe for a time that they could treat us like Portugal—the Government in London refused an agreement on neutrality.'*h* It was from that moment that the military party began to acquire increasing control over the Emperor and the destinies of Germany.

Mr Churchill's reaction to the Novelle was immediate. On March 18, 1912, in presenting the Naval Estimates to the House of Commons, he laid down the principle that our naval construction during the next five years must remain at 60% in Dreadnoughts over Germany and at a ratio of two keels to one for every additional ship that she laid down. He at the same time decided that it was desirable, as a temporary measure, to withdraw our battleships from the Mediterranean, in order to have in home waters a Third Battle Squadron in full commission.[1] Supplementary Naval Estimates had again to be presented on July 22. Meanwhile the German Novelle was laid before the Reichstag on April 14 and passed a month later.

(2)

On his return from India, the King resumed his routine of functions and visits, of audiences and reviews. Day after day, week

8 Large cruisers for foreign service.

10 Small cruisers for foreign service.

6 Submarines to be constructed annually up to a total of 72.

The most significant feature of this law was the creation and maintenance of a Third Battle Squadron of eight battleships.

[1] There were some experts who regarded as dangerous this weakening of our naval power in the Mediterranean. They argued that it would render us too dependent upon the French navy at Toulon and might lead to a combination of the Italian and Austrian fleets against us. Lord Esher warned the King that it would mean the loss of India and Egypt, the disruption of the Entente, the weakening of the Commonwealth, and the eventual subservience to Germany of both Italy and Spain (R.A. G.393.5)

after week, year after year, his diary records the recurrent similitude of these incessant public duties. However worried he might be by the dangers of the internal or external situation, however perplexed by the enigma of his own constitutional obligations, the forefront of his life was always filled by the ceaseless durance of ceremony, by the need, on every occasion, to confront, with apparent pleasure, the staring of a million eyes. It is necessary, when relating the efforts and energies of this lifetime of devoted service, when examining the vast events which stride across that quarter of a century, to bear in mind the appointed burdens which marred his privacy and made such heavy claims upon his vigour. Some conception of this unremitting activity can be conveyed by recording a few only of the varied duties which occupied him during the early months of 1912. They are no more than typical of those which, in every year of his reign, he was constrained to fulfill.

On February 6, the day after they had landed at Portsmouth, the King and Queen drove in state to the City and attended a Thanksgiving Service in St Paul's Cathedral. Lord Curzon, in an interview which lasted for more than an hour, criticised with his accustomed trenchancy the transference of the Indian capital to Delhi and the reversion of the partition of Bengal. On February 14 the King and Queen drove to Westminster for the opening of Parliament. February 22 offered a sudden vacuum: 'Went for a solitary walk in the garden with my umbrella as a companion.' Within a week there followed the grave anxiety of the coal strike. In the early spring the King was deprived for a few weeks of the services of Lord Stamfordham. During the latter's illness, his place was taken by the Assistant Private Secretary, Major Clive Wigram:

> 'Wigram', the King wrote to Lord Stamfordham on April 29, 'has done quite splendidly: never made a mistake: is simply a glutton for work, besides being a charming fellow. I am indeed lucky in having found a man like him.' [i]

In May, the King paid a visit to the Fleet at Portland. Accompanied by his second son, as well as by Mr Churchill and Captain Roger Keyes, he boarded the submarine D4, under the command of Lieutenant Nasmith, and enjoyed the experience of travelling submerged for a distance of three miles. A week later he spent five days at the Royal Pavilion, Aldershot, inspecting the troops under General Sir Douglas Haig's command. On his return to London, he entertained at Buckingham Palace the Archduke Franz Ferdinand of Austria and his wife, the Duchess of Hohenberg: 'They are both charming & made themselves very pleasant.' On June 24 the new German Ambassador, Baron Marschall von Bieberstein, presented his letters of credence.[1] During these same weeks, the King attended a jamboree of the Boy Scouts, laid the foundation stone of the new City Hall and was rowed in the state barge along the course at Henley. On the next day the King and Queen left for South Wales and Yorkshire.

King George, as has been said, always considered it essential that the Sovereign should travel throughout the country and should show himself to those of his subjects who could but rarely witness the great pageants of London. These recurrent tours of the industrial and mining areas (during which the King and Queen would drive through the surrounding villages, visit factories, mills and mines, and speak to the workers in their homes) became a marked feature of his reign. He was delighted, on this occasion, by the reception accorded to him in South Wales: 'They gave me an extraordinary welcome. It was all Keir Hardie's constituency.' A few days later he and the Queen were in the West Riding of Yorkshire, establishing their headquarters at Wentworth Woodhouse and motoring through the surrounding district. On July 9 they visited the Cadeby colliery and thereafter went down the Elsecar mine, remaining for more than half an hour at a thousand feet below the earth. On their return that evening to Wentworth Woodhouse the news was brought to them that a serious accident involving the death of 78 miners, had occurred in the Cadeby colliery after their departure. Late though it was, the King decided to drive back to Cadeby. 'We went', he wrote, 'to enquire & express our sympathy with those who had lost their dear ones. There was a large crowd of miners outside the offices & they appreciated our coming.' During their last evening at Wentworth Woodhouse the Sheffield Choir came out to serenade them, accompanied by a torchlight procession which the miners had organised. The King stepped out on to the portico and expressed his thanks:

[1] Baron Marschall von Bieberstein was born in Baden in 1842. In 1890 he succeeded Count Herbert Bismarck as Secretary of State. In 1897 he was appointed German Ambassador in Constantinople, where he remained for almost fifteen years. In May 1912, after the dismissal of Count Metternich, he was appointed Ambassador in London, but died in September of that year. He was a man of forceful personality and might, had he lived, have countered the influence of Admiral von Tirpitz and done much to improve Anglo-German relations (see Kühlmann, p. 374).

'My friends', he said to them, 'It has been a great pleasure to us to visit your homes and see you at your daily work. We are deeply touched by the reception given to us wherever we have been during the last four days; a reception which we shall never forget and which made us feel we were among true friends. Again we thank you for your hearty welcome. We wish you Good night! Good luck!'

On July 12 the King and Queen returned to Buckingham Palace. 'We must have seen', he wrote in his diary that night, 'at least 3,000,000 people since Monday.' A week later a State Ball was given at the Palace to some two thousand guests. 'Thank goodness!' the King commented, 'The last Court function this year!' After a week at Cowes, and a few days' visit to the Duke of Devonshire at Bolton Abbey, the King and Queen went to Balmoral. Within a fortnight he was on duty again, attending the autumn manoeuvres at Cambridge. He stayed in the Master's Lodge at Trinity College and was much entertained by the vivacity of Dr Butler's conversation. It was on this occasion that he first met General Foch of the French General Staff: 'I had', he recorded, 'several long talks with him.' The King returned to Balmoral on September 20.[1]

These routine and ceremonial activities provide a contrast to the political troubles with which he was at the time assailed. It was during the spring and summer of 1912 that the Irish problem first faced him with an issue, more disturbing even than the battle between the Commons and the Lords.

(3)

The General Elections of 1910 and the abolition of the veto of the House of Lords had rendered it inevitable that Mr Asquith would introduce, and force through Parliament, a Bill providing for some measure of Home Rule in Ireland. The Irish Nationalists under Mr Redmond were resolved to use the determinant vote which they possessed in the House of Commons in order to compel the Government to fulfil the somewhat hesitant promises which they had made.[2]

---

[1] An amusing account of these manoeuvres is given in General Seely's *Fear and be Slain* (pp. 79 ff).

[2] It should be realised that at this date Mr Redmond and his followers in the House of Commons were assumed to be fully representative of Irish opinion and wishes. The United Irish League, the Ancient Order of Hibernians and the Irish Republican Brotherhood were at the time believed to represent only an eccentric minority. The Labour movement under James Larkin and Connolly, with headquarters at Liberty Hall, Dublin, was regarded as a syndicalist organisation. The Gaelic

The Protestants of Ulster, warmly supported by the Unionist Party in England, had determined that they would never allow themselves to be subjected to the rule of a Roman Catholic Parliament sitting in Dublin. On February 21, 1910, Sir Edward Carson had accepted the leadership of the Irish Unionist Party. In September 1911 he addressed a meeting at Craigavon and assured the assembled Ulstermen that if a Home Rule Bill were forced through the English Parliament he would refuse to submit to it and would establish a separate Government in Belfast.

On April 11, 1912, Mr Asquith introduced his Home Rule Bill into the House of Commons.[1] Sir Edward Carson warned him that Home Rule for Southern Ireland would also entail Home Rule for Ulster. The Prime Minister replied that 'it was impossible to concede the demand of a small minority to veto the verdict of the Irish Nation'. The Bill passed its second reading in May 9 by a majority of 101, and reached the Committee stage on June 11. It was then that Mr Agar Robartes, the Liberal member for the St Austell Division of Cornwall, first suggested that the four Protestant counties of Antrim, Armagh, Londonderry and Down should be excluded from the operation of the Bill. The Government refused to accept this suggestion. Mr Redmond stated that the Irish nation must not be subjected to partition. Sir Edward Carson warned the House that he would only consider exclusion if to the four counties mentioned were also added Fermanagh and Tyrone. The House dispersed for the summer recess in a mood of confused bitterness.[2]

League was dismissed as merely antiquarian. Sinn Fein at the time was assumed to be composed mainly of intellectuals who, while preaching independence, were unlikely to resort to anything more dangerous than passive resistance.

[1] The Home Rule Bill of 1912 strikes us today as a half-hearted proposal. It envisaged the establishment in Dublin of an Irish Parliament, consisting of two Chambers, and having control of all Irish matters not specifically reserved for the Imperial Parliament at Westminster. These reserved items were so numerous and important that they 'virtually reduced' the Irish National Parliament to the status of a glorified County Council (*Alison Phillips*, p. 63).

[2] A further measure which created acute controversy at the time, and which only became law by the operation of the Parliament Act, was the Welsh Disestablishment Bill. This had originally been brought forward by Mr Asquith in 1909 but was deferred and reintroduced in April 1912. It was rejected by the House of Lords in February 1913, again passed by the House of Commons, again rejected by the House of Lords in July 1913, and passed for the third time by the House of Commons in May 1914. It

On July 20 Mr Asquith crossed to Dublin and addressed an enthusiastic meeting at the Theatre Royal. He dismissed as 'a mere strategic manoeuvre', the suggestion that any portion of Ulster could be excluded from the operation of the Home Rule Bill. On July 27 a vast Unionist demonstration was held at Blenheim Palace. Sir Edward Carson on that occasion was presented by the Duke of Norfolk with a golden sword. It was then also that Mr Bonar Law, as leader of the Unionist Party, flung down the gauntlet of defiance:

> 'I can imagine', he said, 'no length of resistance to which Ulster will go, which I shall not be ready to support and in which they will not be supported by an overwhelming majority of the British people.'

It is not surprising that Mr Asquith should have described this speech as 'the reckless rodomontade of Blenheim', saying that it provided for the future 'a complete grammar of anarchy'. Neither Mr Bonar Law nor Sir Edward Carson was likely to be deterred by such reproofs. On September 28, 1912, in the City Hall at Belfast, on a small round table draped with the Union Jack, Sir Edward Carson was the first of many hundred thousands to sign the solemn Ulster Covenant. He and his followers 'being convinced in our consciences that Home Rule would be . . . subversive of our civil and religious freedom, destructive of our citizenship, and perilous to the Unity of the Empire', pledged themselves 'as loyal subjects of His Gracious Majesty King George V', to use 'all means which may be found necessary to defeat the present conspiracy to set up a Home Rule Parliament in Ireland . . . and to refuse to recognise its authority'. By November 22 it was announced that this Covenant had been signed by half a million of the men and women of Ulster. It was no longer possible for Mr Asquith to contend that the Ulster protest was 'a mere strategic manoeuvre'. Even in 1912 it was clear to many observers that the Home Rule controversy might threaten the realm with the abhorrent prospect of civil war: and even at that early date there were some who sought to persuade the King that, should such a danger materialise, it was his right, and indeed his duty, to exercise his Prerogative and, when the Bill had finally been forced through both Houses of Parliament, to refuse the Royal Assent.

received the Royal Assent in September 1914, but, since it was regarded as controversial, was accompanied by a Suspensory Bill postponing its operation for the duration of the war. The Act finally came into operation on March 21, 1920, and in the following month Dr A. G. Edwards was enthroned as Archbishop of Wales. It is not easy to understand why a measure so just and logical in itself should have aroused such violent opposition.

In Lord Esher's journal there occurs the following significant entry for January 26, 1912:[j]

'The King is properly disturbed by a speech of Bonar Law's in which he throws the onus on H.M. of "deciding" whether the Royal Assent is to be given to the Home Rule Bill, on H.M's own initiative—whatever the advice of his Ministers may be. This is new departure in doctrine, the result of the Parliament Act.'

Lord Esher at the time expressed the opinion that the King was not a free agent in such matters and that he would, in the last resort, be constitutionally obliged to follow the advice of the Ministers in power. Yet the King did certainly possess, Lord Esher contended, the power of 'remonstrance'; he was at liberty to frame his objections in writing, to communicate them to the Cabinet, and to insist upon obtaining a written reply.

Lord Halsbury was also among those who considered that, since the Constitution had been 'suspended' by the abolition of the House of Lords veto, the King, as guardian of that Constitution, was bound to bring the Royal Prerogative into operation. 'It is said', Lord Halsbury was quoted as asserting, 'that the King must do what he is bid. If so, he is not much of a King. I say that it is for His Majesty alone to decide whether the thing proposed to be done is good or the reverse for his country'.

The King, as Mr J. A. Spender noted, possessed an excellent gift for ignoring bad advice. He would have paid but little attention to Lord Halsbury, had not the same distressing doctrine, in a somewhat different form, been urged upon him by the Leader of the Opposition. Sir Austen Chamberlain, in his *Politics from Inside*[k] gives a startling account of a conversation which took place between the King and Mr Bonar Law after a dinner party at Buckingham Palace on May 3, 1912. The King, it seems, had expressed the hope that no scenes of violence would take place in the House of Commons during the coming session. Mr Bonar Law, according to Sir Austen Chamberlain's account, then addressed the King in the following disturbing language:

' "Our desire", (replied Mr Law) "has been to keep the Crown out of our struggles, but the Government have brought it in. Your only chance is that they should resign within two years. If they don't, you must either accept the Home Rule Bill, or dismiss your Ministers and choose others who will support you in vetoing it: and in either case, half your subjects will think you have acted against them."

'The King turned red; and Law asked "Have you ever considered

THE ENTRY INTO DELHI
(Lord Hardinge, the King, Lord Crewe)

THE UNVEILING OF THE VICTORIA MEMORIAL
(The King and the German Emperor)

that, Sir?" "No," said the King, "it is the first time it has been suggested to me."

'Law added: "They may say that your Assent is a purely formal act and the prerogative of veto is dead. That was true, as long as there was a buffer between you and the House of Commons, but they have destroyed this buffer and it is true no longer." '

In repeating this conversation to Sir Austen Chamberlain, Mr Bonar Law commented: 'I think I have given the King the worst five minutes he has had for a long time.'

On subsequent consideration Mr Bonar Law modified his original opinion. When staying at Balmoral in the following September he had frequent discussions with the King upon the constitutional issues involved and, before leaving, embodied his views in a written memorandum:[1]

'If the Home Rule Bill passes through all its stages under the Parliament Act & requires only the Royal Assent, the position will be a very serious & almost impossible one for the Crown. . . . In such circumstances, Unionists would certainly believe that the King not only had the constitutional right, but that it was his duty, before acting on the advice of his Ministers, to ascertain whether it would not be possible to appoint other Ministers who would advise him differently & allow the question to be decided by the Country at a General Election. . . . In any case, whatever course was taken by His Majesty, half of his people would think that he had failed in his duty & in view of the very bitter feeling which would by that time have been aroused, the Crown would, Mr Bonar Law fears, be openly attacked by the people of Ulster & their sympathisers if he gave his assent to the Bill, & by a large section of the Radical Party if he took any other course.

'Such a position is one in which the King ought not to be placed & Mr Bonar Law is of opinion that if H.M. put the case clearly to the Prime Minister, he would feel that it was his duty to extricate the King from so terrible a dilemma.

'Mr Bonar Law also ventured to suggest to His Majesty that, when any crisis arises, it might be well to consult informally Mr Balfour, Lord Lansdowne or himself & he assured His Majesty that any advice given under such circumstances would not be influenced by Party considerations.'

On the reassembly of Parliament, and after he had had time to take further stock of the situation and presumably to consult his colleagues, Mr Bonar Law made the surprising suggestion that the Opposition might, as an alternative, resort to methods which would render impossible all further debate in the House of Commons:

'The fact remains', he wrote to Lord Stamfordham on November 16, 1912, 'that if the Government succeed in carrying out their programme two results will follow. They will be bound to coerce Ulster, and that will mean civil war; and, as I pointed out to His Majesty, there will then be the other result, which I think is not less important; they will make the position of the Crown impossible. I do not elaborate this, for you understand exactly what I mean.

'Well, if it is in our power to prevent it, we shall not permit this; and sooner or later, if the tension does not come to an end in some other way, we shall have to decide between breaking the Parliamentary machine and allowing these terrible results to happen. When faced with the choice of such evils as these, we shall not, I think, hesitate in considering that the injury to the House of Commons is not so great an evil as the other.

'I may say, also, that I think what has happened in the House of Commons is an indication of what may happen in the larger field. The Speaker felt that he had to intervene and there is always the risk that the time will come when the nation will expect His Majesty to take, in regard to the whole nation, the same attitude which has been taken by the Speaker in regard to the House of Commons. I dread this, but the necessity may come.'

The incidents in the House of Commons to which Mr Bonar Law alluded in the last paragraph of this letter bear some relation to his suggestion that the Opposition might be forced to resort to violent obstruction. On November 11 the Government were defeated by twenty-two votes on an amendment moved by Sir F. Banbury to the financial resolutions of the Home Rule Bill. On the following day Mr Asquith announced his intention of moving that this vote be rescinded. The Speaker ruled that such a motion, although without precedent, was not out of order. When, however, on November 13, the Prime Minister rose to put his motion, the Opposition created such a turmoil that the Speaker was twice obliged, under Standing Order 21, to adjourn the House. It was in the disturbance which ensued that Mr Ronald McNeill seized a book from the table and hurled it at Mr Winston Churchill across the floor. The Speaker was so outraged by this scene of uproar that he threatened to resign.[m]

In the anxiety of the moment Mr Asquith omitted to inform the King of these occurrences nor did the report of the Home Secretary make more than passing reference to the conflict that had taken place:

'My dear Prime Minister,' the King wrote in his own hand from York Cottage on November 16, 'I know how busy you are during what must be a most anxious time for you and your Government, but I cannot help feeling that it is only due to me that I should be kept informed on all important events which arise in Parliament and as to decisions come to in regard to them by the Cabinet. I must remind you that I was never informed by you of the defeat of the Government on Monday and of your consequent action, though the usual report from the Home Secretary was sent me. Equally, I was left uninformed by you of the serious and deplorable occurrences in the House of Commons on Wednesday, necessitating two adjournments. . . . I quite appreciate all your difficulties and sympathize with you accordingly, but I do look to my Prime Minister for that confidence which will ensure his keeping me fully informed on all matters, especially those which affect questions of such grave importance to the State, and indeed to the Constitution. For my part it has been, and always will be, my earnest endeavour to show you that confidence which a Prime Minister has a right to expect from his Sovereign.

'The Queen and I are very glad that you and Mrs Asquith are coming to Windsor at the end of next week.'[n]

The Prime Minister replied, apologising for the oversight and promising that it would not occur again. But as the year 1912 drew to its end, the King was saddened by the new bitterness of party conflict and by the presage of further strife to come.

(4)

In the autumn of 1912 the King seized a welcome opportunity to ease and improve the relations between Great Britain and Russia, which had become increasingly tense owing to a conflict of policy in regard to Persia.[1] The Russian Foreign Minister, Monsieur Sazonov,[2] had left St Petersburg on a tour of the European capitals

[1] The Anglo-Russian Convention of 1907 had provided that Persia should be divided into three zones: A Russian zone in the north, a British zone in the south, and a neutral zone in the middle. The Russians, under the stimulus of their active Minister in Tehran, M. Hartwig, had for long been violating the spirit of the agreement. In 1908 the Cossack Brigade, under a Russian commander, Colonel Liakoff, had bombarded the Persian Parliament and the Deputies had sought sanctuary in the compound of the British Legation. In 1909 Mohammed Ali Shah had been deposed in favour of his son Ahmed (then twelve years of age) and had in his turn taken sanctuary in the Russian Legation before being sent into exile. In 1911 the ex-Shah had returned to Persia in a Russian steamer but had been again forced to leave. An ex-Balliol man, Nasr-ul-Mulk was appointed Regent.

[2] Sazonov (Serghei Dmitrievich, 1866–1927) had served for six years as Counsellor of the Russian Embassy in London. In 1906 he was appointed Minister to the Vatican and in 1909 he became assistant to the then Foreign Minister in St Petersburg, M. Iswolsky. In 1910 he succeeded M. Iswolsky as Foreign Minister. As brother-in-law to the Prime Minister, M. Stolypin, he was able to exercise great influence. He was dismissed from his post shortly before the Revolution of 1917 and died in France in 1927.

and the King invited him and Sir Edward Grey to come up to
Balmoral together in order to discuss in calm and quiet the circumstances which had caused this tension. M. Sazonov's arrival was
heralded by a warm letter of recommendation which the Tsar of
Russia addressed to the King from Beloviesk on September 14:[o]

> 'Dearest Georgie,
>   'I cannot let M. Sazonov go to England without writing a few lines
> to you. I am glad you will see him. He is a straight-forward and honest
> man & I appreciate him highly. . . . I always read the *Daily Graphic*
> and therefore follow closely all your movements and all you have to
> do. It astonishes me often how enduring you and dear May are both!'

Sir Edward Grey and M. Sazonov arrived at Balmoral on September 23 and during the next two days they discussed the difficulties which had arisen in Persia as well as the general European
situation. The Russian Foreign Minister said he did not wish to keep
Russian troops in Northern Persia indefinitely, but that internal
conditions were so chaotic that Russia must be allowed to preserve
some sort of 'stability'. What Persia needed, he said, was a strong
man. Sir Edward Grey agreed that the Regent, Nasr-ul-Mulk, was
perhaps too weak for his position, but insisted that Great Britain
would never agree to the return of the ex-Shah; he added that the
continued presence of Russian troops in Northern Persia was exposing him to invidious criticism in the House of Commons and was
much resented by Moslem opinion within the Empire. In regard to
the European situation, he evaded M. Sazonov's hint that he would
welcome staff conversations between British and Russian military
and naval experts, and confined himself to saying, that if Germany
ever sought to crush France, Great Britain would be obliged to come
to the latter's assistance.[p]

Inevitably this visit of the Russian and British Foreign Secretaries
to Balmoral aroused much speculation in the foreign, and even in
the British, Press.

> 'Of course.' the King wrote to Queen Alexandra on September 21 and
> 30, 'the newspapers are already writing all sorts of nonsense about the
> meeting. I thought it would be much easier & pleasanter if they came
> up here & talked matters over quietly. . . . The conversations were
> most satisfactory in every way & most friendly; they are both honest,
> straightforward men & at once said what they could do, & what
> they could not do. This visit will I am sure have done much to prevent
> misunderstandings.'

In a letter which, after M. Sazonov's departure, the King wrote to the Tsar of Russia, he expressed himself as much relieved by the success of the Balmoral conversations:[q]

'I cannot say how charmed May & I were with M. Sazonov & how pleased we were that he was able to spend a few days with us in our Highland Home, & that during this time he had opportunities for several long & friendly conversations with Sir Edward Grey.

'I cordially agree with you that M. Sazonov is straight-forward & honest, & I am sure that he found Sir Edward Grey the same. It was only possible between two statesmen of such similar natures that any misunderstandings between our two countries could have been frankly discussed & cleared up. I am glad to say the results of these conversations have been most satisfactory.

'You know what importance I attach to the maintenance of most friendly & intimate relations between our two countries & I feel sure that you will be satisfied with the report which M. Sazonov will be able to make to you—& that you will agree that his visit to England will do much to strengthen those relations, to maintain & strengthen which I know you are as keen about as I am.

'You will like to hear that M. Sazonov made a most excellent impression upon everyone who met him. Amongst others who happened to be here, was Mr Bonar Law, the leader of the Opposition, which I think was a happy coincidence; for I am glad to tell you that in regard to our Foreign Policy the Opposition are in full agreement with the Government, whose only opponents are a small & insignificant body belonging to their own extreme left.'

M. Sazonov, for all his frankness, did not inform Sir Edward Grey of the secret pact which, with Russian approval, had been concluded in the previous March, between Serbia, Bulgaria and Greece. On October 17, 1912, the three Balkan allies declared war upon Turkey and within three weeks the Turkish armies, severely defeated at Kirk Kilissé and Lulé Bourgas, were falling back, demoralised and stricken with cholera, upon the inner defences of Constantinople. It seemed as if the Near Eastern rivalry between Austria and Russia (which had been much envenomed by the former's annexation of Bosnia-Herzogovina) must now lead to a general conflagration. Sir Edward Grey, with the assistance of the five Ambassadors in London, succeeded in averting this catastrophe. King George, in repeated conversations with the Austrian Ambassador, urged him to persuade his Government to do nothing which might lead to an explosion of feeling among the Russian Pan-Slavs.[r] Ships of the five Powers were sent to the Golden Horn to protect their nationals, and by December a peace conference between Turkey and her enemies was assembled, under the auspices of the Great Powers, in St James's Palace.

In the first week of December, Prince Henry of Prussia, the German Emperor's brother, paid a visit to York Cottage. The King informed Sir Edward Grey of the conversation that then took place:[s]

'York Cottage,
'Sandringham,
'December 8, 1912

'My dear Grey,
'Prince Henry of Prussia paid me a short visit here two days ago. In the course of a long conversation, he asked me point blank, whether, in the event of Germany and Austria going to war with Russia and France, England would come to the assistance of the two latter Powers. I answered "undoubtedly, Yes—under certain circumstances". He expressed surprise and regret, but did not ask what the certain circumstances were. He said he would tell the Emperor what I had told him. Of course Germany must know that we would not allow either of our friends to be crippled. I think it is only right that you should know what passed between me and the Emperor's brother on this point. I hope to see you when I come to London at the end of this week.

'Believe me,
'Very sincerely yours,
'George R.I.'

In repeating this conversation to Count Mensdorff, the King added a few further particulars. He said that Prince Henry had been 'horrified' by the statement that we should not allow France or Russia to be crushed. The King had then said to his German cousin: 'Do you believe that we have less sense of honour than you? You possess signed Alliances: we unsigned Ententes. We cannot allow either France or Russia to be overthrown.' Count Mensdorff duly reported this conversation to Vienna.[t]

On December 9, Sir Edward Grey replied to the King's letter:[u]

'Sir Edward Grey presents his humble duty and begs to thank Your Majesty for the information respecting what has passed with Prince Henry of Prussia.

'Sir Edward Grey thinks it would be dangerous & misleading to let the German Government be under the impression that under no circumstances would England come to the assistance of France and Russia, if Germany and Austria went to war with them, and he thinks it very fortunate that Your Majesty was able to give an answer to Prince Henry that will prevent him from giving that impression at Berlin.

'Your Majesty's Government is not committed in the event of war, and the public opinion of this country is, so far as Sir Edward Grey can judge, very adverse to a war arising out of a quarrel about Servia. But if Austria attacked Servia aggressively, and Germany attacked

Russia if she came to the assistance of Servia, and France were then involved, it might become necessary for England to fight (as the German Chancellor said that Germany would fight) for the defence of her position in Europe, and for the protection of her own future and security.'

Sir Edward Grey was optimistic in supposing that Prince Henry would convey, or the Emperor derive, a correct impression of the conversation at York Cottage. What Prince Henry in fact reported to his brother was that Great Britain was peace-loving, and that if war broke out Germany would have to reckon, 'perhaps on English neutrality, certainly not on her taking the part of Germany, and probably on her throwing her weight on the weaker side.' The Emperor as usual noticed only the words that he wanted to see: he concluded that he could count on our 'neutrality' if trouble arose. 'Well that settles it,' he scribbled in the margin of Prince Henry's letter, 'we can now go ahead with France.'*v*

Prince Henry's own account of what he had reported to the Emperor is embarrassed and tangled: after his return to Germany, he wrote to King George as follows:

'Kiel, December 14, 1912

'My dear Georgie,

'The day after my return to Kiel I wrote a letter to William in which I carried out your instructions to the letter, carefully hereby omitting the one sore point, which I put down, as my personal impressions, gathered from conversations with friends, during my recent stay in England, to the effect that I thought, if Germany were drawn into a war with Russia & may be, as a result of this, with France, England *might* be neutral, but that I feared she *might* also, *under circumstances*, side with our foes; William sent me a reply in which he said, that my impressions were, he was sorry to say, correct, in as much as Haldane had, in a conversation with our Ambassador, on the 6th of December, the day I was kindly received by you at Sandringham, stated the fact point blanc [*sic*] officially from the part of Sir E. Grey. W. further mentioned, that though this was felt as rather a blow, he would have to take the consequences.

'We all feel, that England is hereby adhering to her old principle, not allowing any nation to predominate on the continent. You will I hope be aware of the fact, that the responsibility which England herewith takes, as regards the worlds peace is very great.

'Germany has not, believe me, the least intention of going to war with any one and never had, this she has proved in more than one case, during 43 years! We always were—& I am still—in hopes that England & Germany might go together, for the sake of the world's peace! Mind you Georgie, we are not afraid, but we mean no harm to any one! Please consider the situation once more, before it is too late! If England & Germany were united, even mutually, who on earth would dare stir? Haldane's statement of the 6th however leaves, alas, no doubt & you will not be astonished if we, in future, do all we can to be prepared against any blow, which may, or may not be dealt, with an object to ruin our existence.

'England, I take it, has got it in her hands, to keep, or to maintain the world's peace!

'You will I hope understand, that my "impressions" have not created any bitter feelings, but that it was Haldane's statements of the 6th which have.

'You know me well enough by now & you know that my feelings on the subject are absolutely sincere. I always have & always shall consider it my duty to avoid misunderstandings & try & smooth difficulties between both our countries. Your dear Father trusted me & I hope you will do the same! You also know, that I am a loyal German subject & that my duty lies first with my sovereign, who, I am thankful to say, believes in me. Might I once more suggest that under the circumstances you should consider the question of your visiting Germany i.e. William first, next year?

'Please think about it seriously—it might do a world of good!

'With many fond messages to dear Mary, please believe me always, dear Georgie.

'Yr. most devoted cousin

'Henry P.'

The above letter is not either intelligent or important. It is quoted textually, since it illustrates the amazing capacity for incomprehension with which the Hohenzollern family, with all their gifts and virtues, were as a clan afflicted. Prince Henry's failure accurately to report the words used by King George at York Cottage, and the Emperor's impetuous selection of the one word he wanted, enable us to understand why, in far graver circumstances, a similar case of misreporting and misinterpretation occurred in July 1914.

CHAPTER XIV

IRELAND

1913

Internal affairs during 1913—The Marconi enquiry—Women's Suffrage —External affairs—The Balkan Wars and the Ambassadors' Conference—Improvement of our relations with Germany—The Portuguese Colonies and the Baghdad Railway—The King's visit to Berlin—The German Emperor and Lord Stamfordham—The French President visits London—Mr Walter Hines Page—The Government discourage the King from visiting the Dominions—The Home Rule controversy—The arming of Ulster—The Irish National Volunteers —Mr Birrell's early optimism—The King is advised by some Unionists that he ought to intervene—Mr Asquith's reticence—The audience of August 11—The King's memorandum—Mr Asquith's reply—The King's letter to Mr Asquith of September 22 reviewing the whole situation.

(1)

THE year 1913 was almost completely overshadowed by the Irish question. King George was fully prepared, if such were the desire of the two nations, that Home Rule should be accorded to the Irish. He believed that, if the problem were handled with tact and generosity, Ireland would become a friendly and contented Dominion, co-operating with other Dominions in joint allegiance to the Crown. What he dreaded was that the tension between the Roman Catholics and the Protestants in Ireland (reflected as it was in the increasing party strife between Unionists and Liberals in the House of Commons) might cause lasting damage to our Parliamentary tradition, involve the Crown in an odious constitutional dilemma and, at a time of serious international disorder, weaken the country by internal dissension and even expose it to the disaster of civil war.

Before considering the stages through which the Irish controversy passed during the year 1913, and the distracting constitutional riddle which it created, it will be convenient to deal with the internal and external events which occurred during the interlude between the Agadir crisis and the First World War. At home, we had what was somewhat unfairly described as the 'Marconi Scandal', and the grave administrative perplexities caused by the methods adopted by the more extreme agitators for Women's Suffrage. Abroad, the year was marked by Sir Edward Grey's calm handling of the Balkan agitation and by a definite improvement in our relations with Germany. Whereas our domestic politics, during the year 1913, were riven by excited animosity, in foreign affairs the Great Powers temporarily recreated the Concert of Europe and enjoyed a delusive lull before the storm.

The Imperial Conference which had met in 1911 had recommended the construction of a chain of wireless stations within the Empire. In 1912 Mr Herbert Samuel, then Postmaster-General, accepted the tender put forward by the Marconi Company, subject to ratification by Parliament. The shares of the Marconi Company, which in July 1911, were at 46s. had risen by April 1912, to eight pounds. The Managing Director of the Marconi Company was Mr Godfrey Isaacs, brother of the Attorney-General, Sir Rufus Isaacs. During the summer recess of 1912 rumours began to circulate that certain members of the Government had speculated in Marconi Shares. On October 11, 1912, Mr George Lansbury, in the House of Commons, hinted that certain Ministers had used their previous knowledge of the Government's intentions to indulge in 'disgraceful, scandalous, gambling in these shares'. Sir Rufus Isaacs, speaking from the front bench, denied having 'had one single transaction with the shares of that Company'. The Government then appointed a Select Committee to enquire into the tender in its technical aspects and at the same time to investigate the allegations that had been made.

On April 4, 1913, Mr Asquith had an audience with the King and informed him that, in the previous January, Lord Murray of Elibank, Sir Rufus Isaacs and Mr Lloyd George had confessed to him that, although they had had no dealings in the shares of the British Marconi Company, they had in fact bought some shares in its American counterpart. Realising that these facts would now be disclosed, they feared that they might be placed in 'a terribly awkward position' and offered their resignations. Mr Asquith loyally refused to accept their resignations but stated that he considered their conduct 'lamentable' in itself and 'so difficult to defend'.[a]

The truth came out when Sir Rufus Isaacs, together with Mr Herbert Samuel (who was wholly ignorant of the transactions of his colleagues) brought a libel action against the *Matin* newspaper. Sir Rufus Isaacs on that occasion admitted that he and two of his friends had dealt in the shares of the American Marconi Company. The

Select Committee, in their report of June 13, exonerated the Ministers from all charges of corruption. In a minority report, however, Lord Robert Cecil accused them of having committed a 'grave impropriety' and of having 'been wanting in frankness and respect for the House of Commons'. In the debate that followed Mr Asquith contended that his colleagues had not departed from 'rules of obligation', although they had certainly departed from 'rules of prudence'. The House then passed a resolution clearing the Ministers of the charge of corruption and accepting their expressions of regret. Mr Lloyd George, for one, recovered rapidly from this unpleasant episode. Within a few weeks he was representing himself as a St Sebastian, plucking the arrows from his quivering flesh and hurling them back at his persecutors. A month later he was contending that the whole Marconi scandal had been nothing more than an attempt on the part of the Conservatives to 'upset democratic Government'. He entirely failed thereafter to recall that it was the magnanimity of Mr Asquith which had saved him from disgrace.

The methods of violence which, under the leadership of Mrs Pankhurst (and much to the distress of the more constitutional advocates of the extended franchise), had since 1906 been pursued by the Women's Social and Political Union were less amenable either to Parliamentary equivocation or to administrative routine. On January 23, 1913, the Franchise and Registration Bill was introduced into the House of Commons. Mr Asquith had made it known that the Government would accept amendments extending the suffrage, at least to women householders of over twenty-five years of age. Before, however, these amendments could be put, it was necessary to introduce a covering amendment, deleting the word 'male' wherever it occurred in the text of the Bill. This preliminary amendment was moved by Sir Edward Grey himself, but was ruled out of order by the Speaker as altering the whole nature of the Bill. Mrs Pankhurst and her followers were impatient of these points of Parliamentary procedure; they concluded that Mr Asquith had escaped, whether from cunning or stupidity, from his own assurances; the ardour of their militancy was much inflamed. The King was apprehensive regarding the fate of our national works of art and enquired of the Home Secretary whether he was satisfied that the public galleries and museums could safely remain open: Mr. McKenna replied, optimistically perhaps, that there was no cause for alarm.[b] Meanwhile, many of the women who had been cast into prison on various charges of assault and damage had resorted to a hunger strike. The Home Secretary, in desperation, drafted his 'Prisoners (Temporary Discharge for Health) Bill 1913', subsequently known as the 'Cat and Mouse Act'. The King had been disgusted by the accounts he had read of the methods of forcible feeding which were applied to these devoted captives by the prison authorities. On March 27 Lord Stamfordham was instructed to approach the Home Secretary:

> 'The King desires me to write to you upon the question of "forcible feeding". His Majesty cannot help feeling that there is something shocking, if not almost cruel, in the operation to which these insensate women are subjected through their refusal to take necessary nourishment. His Majesty concludes that Miss Pankhurst's description of what she endured when forcibly fed is more or less true. If so, her story will horrify people otherwise not in sympathy with the Militant Suffragettes. The King asks whether, in your "Temporary Discharge of Prisons Bill" it would not be possible to abolish forcible feeding.'c

Mr McKenna replied that the system was as repugnant to the prison authorities as it was to the King himself and that he hoped that, under the new Act, it would be possible to restrict forcible feeding to a few exceptional cases.

The King's sympathy for Mrs Pankhurst and her followers was not increased by the constant demonstrations, scenes and even outrages to which, when he appeared on public occasions, he was constantly exposed.

(2)

The Balkan Wars[1] confronted Europe with a situation of great peril. Within a few violent weeks the Turkish armies had been driven

[1] There were two Balkan Wars:

(1) The first was fought between Bulgaria, Greece, Serbia and Montenegro on the one side, and Turkey on the other. It lasted from October 17, 1912, to May 30, 1913. The Greeks captured Salonika on November 9, 1912, Adrianople surrendered after a long siege on March 26, 1913, and the Montenegrins entered Scutari on April 22. Peace between Turkey and the four Balkan allies was signed in London on May 30, 1913.

(2) The second Balkan War was provoked by King Ferdinand of Bulgaria, who felt that he had been accorded an insufficient share of the spoils. On June 30 he suddenly attacked the Greek and Serbian armies. Profiting by the confusion, Turkey again entered the fray and recaptured Adrianople. When it was quite certain that the Bulgarians would be beaten the Rumanians also joined in the battle. By July 31 King Ferdinand was obliged to sue for peace and a final treaty was signed at Bucharest on August 10, 1913.

back to the inner defences of Constantinople and the Sultan had lost Macedonia, Albania, Epirus and Western Thrace. On November 9, 1912, when the Bulgarian batteries at Chatalja were already rattling the windows of the Turkish capital, the King addressed to Mr Asquith a telegram of sympathetic counsel:

'I feel for you having to speak on Foreign Affairs at the Guildhall this evening, but know that in this critical situation you will be careful not to commit England in any way. I am sure that the less said the better. If we can induce Russia and Austria to continue to work together, the demands of the Balkan States, which naturally perhaps are somewhat exaggerated, may be kept within reasonable bounds. I hope Russia and France realize that in these delicate negotiations we wish to preserve our present cordial relations with them, the maintenance of which seems to me of supreme importance.' *d*

In the months that followed, two separate conferences took place in London. The first was a direct discussion between Turkey and the four victorious Balkan States. After a temporary interruption, occasioned by a revolution in Turkey, articles of peace were signed at St James's Palace on May 30, 1913. The second conference, which was known as the 'Ambassadors' Conference', took place in Sir Edward Grey's room at the Foreign Office and was composed, under the chairmanship of the British Foreign Secretary, of the Ambassadors in London of France, Italy, Germany, Austria and Russia. These meetings, which were informal and intermittent, lasted from December 1912, until August 1913. 'The details', Sir Edward Grey wrote in after years,*e* 'with which we dealt were insignificant—in themselves mere sparks: but we were sitting on a powder magazine.' The Ambassadors' Conference did in fact represent, during those dangerous nine months, the wisdom and the authority of the Concert of Europe. It was a lasting regret to Sir Edward Grey that the same Conference could not be revived in July 1914, to deal with an even graver predicament. He had come to set great store by the 'good faith, the good will, the singlemindedness, the freedom from all egotism and personal rivalries, which had during those months been manifested by those five elderly and moderate men'.*f*

The main point of friction was not, as some had feared, the future of Constantinople and the Straits, nor even the Bulgarian access to the Aegean, but the northern and southern frontiers of the new State of Albania. In the south, Italy wished to prevent Greece from obtaining the territory in Epirus which would have given her command of the Corfu Channel. This frontier remains, essentially, undetermined to this day. In the north, the Austrians refused to allow Serbia and Montenegro to retain the areas they had conquered; it was feared that, if Russia backed their claims, a serious clash of interests and prestige might result. The Albanian problem was further complicated by the occupation of Scutari by Montenegro in April 1913. The Powers summoned King Nikita to evacuate the city and the Austrian Government threatened that, if the Conference of Ambassadors failed to secure his consent, they would be obliged to settle the matter on their own. King George spoke strongly to Count Mensdorff, urging him to warn his Government that if they took isolated action it might lead to an explosion of Pan-Slav feeling in Russia and create a danger of war.[g] It was then suggested that the Powers should themselves send troops to Scutari and turn King Nikita out. King George remarked that he was not going to allow the lives of British soldiers to be risked for so trivial a venture. The German Emperor, on being informed of this objection, scribbled the marginal comment: '*Seine Majestät is kein Militär*'—'The King does not possess a military mind'—a remark which was more accurate than many of his impulsive apophthegms.[h] In the end King Nikita was forced to evacuate Scutari under the threat of an international naval blockade.

Such were the difficulties and dangers which during those months of 1913 Sir Edward Grey, with the assistance of the five Ambassadors, managed to solve and avert. The King was warmly appreciative of his success. 'My dear Grey,' he wrote to him on August 18, 1913:[i]

'Now that the Conference of Ambassadors is adjourned and its Members have separated for their well-earned holiday, I wish to offer you my sincere congratulations upon the satisfactory results achieved, and to express my high appreciation of the able manner in which you have presided over the Conference, and steered its course through the many rocks and shoals among which it might have been at any time wrecked. You have by your patience, tact and statesmanship, secured Peace, and gained the confidence of all the European Powers while inspiring a similar confidence in the Parliamentary Opposition in this Country.

'I heartily share these feelings of absolute reliance in your management of our Foreign Policy, and join in the sentiments of gratitude so generally expressed towards you by your fellow-countrymen.'

It is doubtful whether this distribution of the European provinces of the Ottoman Empire would have been completed without major disturbance had not the relations between Germany and England then entered upon a calmer and more reasonable phase. Although the German Government failed to respond to Mr Churchill's repeated suggestions for a 'naval holiday', they had come to realise that no British Government could afford to allow German naval construction seriously to challenge our island security and that a succession of sharp lunges against the fabric of the Triple Entente only served to solidify its structure. The two Governments therefore, during the course of 1913, settled down to a realistic business deal. The British Cabinet, with vicarious generosity, offered the Germans a share in the reversion of the Portuguese colonies. A Treaty to that effect was initialled by Sir Edward Grey and Prince Lichnowsky in August 1913, but its conclusion was postponed, owing to the fact that Sir Edward Grey insisted that both the Treaty itself and its secret predecessors should be laid before Parliament. This seemed to the Germans a fantastic qualm.[1]

The British Government at the same time opened direct negotiations with Germany and Turkey in regard to the Baghdad Railway.[2] We agreed to the railway being carried as far as Basrah (which implied that the whole of Mesopotamia would become a German sphere of influence) but insisted that we should preserve our existing rights and privileges in the Persian Gulf and on the Shatt-el-Arab. A Convention embodying the results of this negotiation was initialled on June 15, 1914. The King viewed these railway schemes with some

[1] Under this Treaty Germany was to obtain Angola, the northern part of Mozambique and the islands of St. Thomé and Principe. In 1898 Mr Balfour had entered into a Secret Treaty with Count Hatzfeldt, providing for British and German 'spheres of economic influence' in Portugal's African colonies. The Marquis de Soveral got wind of this deal and secured, in 1899, what was known as 'The Treaty of Windsor', by which Great Britain reaffirmed her obligations under the alliance with Portugal which had existed since the fifteenth century. Sir Edward Grey, with a certain ingenuousness, suggested that all three Treaties should be published at the same time.

[2] In 1902 the German Government had obtained from the Sultan of Turkey a concession for constructing a railway to Baghdad. This was opposed by Russia, France and Great Britain who insisted that the matter was one which affected the interests of all four Powers. In 1911, under the Potsdam Agreement, the Russians made a direct deal with Germany, approving of the railway being continued to Baghdad and even agreeing that a branch line could be constructed from Baghdad to the Persian frontier at Khanikin, where it could eventually link up with the lines which Russia intended to construct in northern Persia. We were much disturbed by this agreement.

apprehension. What most alarmed him was the promise made by Russia, under the Potsdam Agreement, that the German-controlled Baghdad Railway might one day link up at Khanikin with the Russian-controlled trans-Persian line. He feared that the Germans, with their greater efficiency, might eventually dominate the whole enormous network and provide themselves with a through line from Berlin (via Constantinople, Baghdad, Khanikin and Persia) to the Indian frontier. He urged the Russians to retain the Persian section of the railway entirely in their own hands. 'The control of Russia', he said to Count Benckendorff,[j] 'would be a security for England: that of Germany, a danger.' These huge railway schemes, with all the benefits and the dangers they implied were whirled into dust by the hurricane of the 1914 war.

The improvement in the relations between Great Britain and Germany was emphasised by the visit which the King and Queen paid to Berlin in May 1913. The occasion was the marriage of the Emperor's only daughter, Princess Luise of Prussia, to Duke Ernst August of Brunswick-Lüneburg: an event which put an end to the long-standing enmity between the Houses of Hohenzollern and Brunswick. The Tsar of Russia was also invited to be present. Sir Edward Grey insisted that the meeting should be regarded 'as a purely family affair', and the King went to Berlin unaccompanied by any Minister.[k] He was glad indeed to have this private occasion to renew his old affectionate relations with his Russian cousin: 'Had a long & satisfactory talk with dear Nicky; he was just the same as always.' The German Emperor could not refrain from discussing high politics with his fellow potentates; he claimed thereafter that he had obtained from the Tsar of Russia and the King of England an assurance that their Governments would respect the integrity of what remained of the Ottoman Empire and that Constantinople should rest in the possession of the Sultan. To Lord Stamfordham he delivered a long lecture upon the folly of the British Government in siding with the Latins against the Teutons; in imagining that he, the grandson of Queen Victoria, would ever allow England to be threatened at sea; and in obstinately ignoring the Yellow Peril which remained the only real menace to Western civilization:

'Look at this Morocco business!' the Emperor exclaimed. 'I know that Sir John French was over in France, or your staff officers were, and you promised to send 100,000 troops and *that's what made us sore.*[1]

[1] The German Government were of course aware that ever since 1904–1905 Staff Conversations had been proceeding between British and French

I am a man of peace, but now I have to arm my Country, so that whoever falls on me I can crush. And crush them I will. If Austria is attacked by Russia I am bound to help her; the aged Emperor, with his past defeats, sorrows etc., could *not* be left to stand alone. There is no ill feeling between Russia and Germany. You talk a good deal about the balance of power and that to maintain it you joined the Entente. But Germany holds the balance of power.'*m*

When accepting the German Emperor's invitation to his daughter's wedding, the King had been careful, in order that no uneasiness might be caused, to intimate to M. Cambon that he would welcome a visit from the President of the French Republic in the following month. Monsieur Poincaré arrived in London on June 24. It was the first time that he had seen King George:

'I was immediately struck', he wrote,*n* 'by his resemblance to his cousin, the Tsar of Russia. Yet his colour was not so pale, his expression less dreamy, his smile less melancholy & his gestures less timid.'

The State visit of the French President, although it led to no new political transactions, did much to alleviate the suspicions which had been aroused in France by our negotiations with Germany over the Baghdad Railway and the Portuguese colonies and by the recent meeting of the King and the two Emperors in Berlin.

On May 30, two days after the King's return from Germany, the new United States Ambassador, Mr Walter Hines Page, presented his letters.[1] From the first moment of their acquaintance, feelings

experts. In fact, Mr Haldane had so informed the German Military Attaché at the time. The more pacific members of the British Cabinet, when they were eventually informed of these conversations, expressed alarm that they might commit the Government in the event of war. Accordingly, in October 1912, Sir Edward Grey and M. Cambon exchanged letters affirming that these conversations did not in any way commit their respective Governments, who would, if any danger arose of an unprovoked attack, discuss together whether they should take joint action to preserve peace. In these discussions the plans agreed to by the two General Staffs would 'at once be taken into consideration'. The Grey-Cambon letters became known to the German Government in March 1913.

[1] Mr Walter Hines Page (1855–1919) was a native of North Carolina, a good classical scholar, a man of firm republican convictions, fine human sympathies, and acute if unconventional intelligence. He had been editor of the *Atlantic Monthly* and in 1899 had founded with his great friend Frank N. Doubleday the famous publishing firm of Doubleday, Page Inc. He was a strong supporter of President Wilson and also possessed the confidence of Colonel House.

of warm regard and confidence were established between these two
men, who possessed many qualities in common. Relations between
Great Britain and the United States were at the time somewhat
strained owing to differences of policy in regard to Mexico and the
Panama Canal tolls.[1] Profiting from the personal influence which
he possessed with the President and Colonel House, and using the
great authority which he immediately acquired with Sir Edward
Grey and the Cabinet, Mr Page was able to remove these causes of
friction. He was, as events proved, a firm believer in co-operation
between the two English-speaking peoples, who between them could
maintain the peace of the world. 'What I want,' he said, 'is to have
the President of the United States and the King of England stand
up side by side and let the world take a good look at them.'⁰ Mr Page
did not live to witness the consummation of this desire.

The King meanwhile had not abandoned his original intention
of paying a personal visit to each one of the Dominions. He had
been anxious, at the end of 1912, to accept General Botha's invitation that he should come out to South Africa and open the new
Parliament buildings. The Cabinet firmly discouraged such a proposal. His acceptance, they said, would lead to similar invitations
from other Dominions and would thus 'entail the prolonged absence
of the Head of the State from the United Kingdom'. His presence
in England during those last two years before the war was in truth
an inescapable necessity.

(3)

The Irish conflict of 1913 opened with rapid and almost per-
functory moves, as in a game of draughts. On January 1 Sir Edward
Carson proposed an amendment excluding the province of Ulster
from the operation of the Home Rule Bill. Mr Redmond denounced
this proposal with the phrase: 'Ireland is for us one entity. It is one
land.' Sir Edward Carson's amendment was defeated by ninety-

[1] In February 1913 Victoriano Huerta proclaimed himself President
of Mexico. He was supported by local British Oil interests but President
Wilson denounced him as a usurper and refused to accord recognition.
In the end, after the Americans had been obliged to occupy Veracruz, he
resigned (July 14, 1914) and was eventually succeeded by Carranza.
Under the Hay-Pauncefote Treaty of 1901 the United States had
agreed that there should be no discrimination against foreign vessels using
the Panama Canal. Thereafter preferential charges were accorded to
American coastal shipping. The British Government protested and, on
March 5, 1914, President Wilson informed Congress that these preferences

seven votes. On January 16 the third reading of the Bill was passed by the House of Commons by a majority of one hundred and ten. On January 30, the Bill, as had been foreseen, was rejected by the House of Lords. This meant that the Bill would return to the House of Commons, pass through all its stages again, and eventually be forced through both Houses by the operation of the Parliament Act. It was thus bound to become law by the summer of 1914. On March 12, in the debate on the Address, the Opposition brought forward an amendment to the effect that it would be improper to proceed with the Home Rule Bill 'while the constitution of Parliament is still incomplete and without reference to the electors'. Mr Asquith replied with bland optimism that 'the reform of the Second Chamber will not now be long delayed'.[1] Mr Bonar Law contended that a law passed under such conditions 'could not, and ought not to, command respect and obedience'. The problem remained in a condition of suspended acrimony.

In the apparent interlude that followed, both sides mustered their forces, chose their positions, and prepared for the coming battle. The bitterness engendered was such that, for the first time since the Reform Bills, members of the opposing parties refused to meet each other socially. 'Somehow', remarked the United States Ambassador, 'it reminds me of the tense days of the slavery controversy, just before the Civil War.'[p]

The Ulster Protestants began immediately to enrol and drill. On the recommendation of Lord Roberts, they appointed a retired army officer, General Sir George Richardson, as their Commander-in-Chief. By September 1913 as many as 56,000 men had been enrolled: in the following March the total strength of the Ulster Volunteer Force was estimated at 84,000.[q] By the end of 1913, the Irish were a 'dishonourable' breach of the Hay-Pauncefote Treaty and must be rescinded. This courageous action on the part of the President made a profound impression abroad.

[1] In 1917 a Committee was appointed under Lord Bryce to consider the constitution of a revised Second Chamber. It recommended that 246 members of the new Chamber should be elected by the House of Commons and that a quarter of the new Chamber should be chosen by a Joint Committee of the two Houses from existing hereditary peers. This new Chamber was to be accorded no powers beyond a minimum delaying power and full rights of discussion. These recommendations were not carried out, since it was felt that no Second Chamber, however carefully devised, would prove either as vulnerable and therefore as unassertive as a hereditary Chamber, or more honourable, experienced and intelligent than the existing House of Lords.

Catholics decided to create a force of their own. At a meeting held in the Rotunda at Dublin on November 25, the National Volunteers were inaugurated and 4,000 men at once enrolled. The Labour leader, Mr James Larkin, at the same time started to organise his 'Irish Citizen Army'; for the purpose of training these irregulars he secured the more expert assistance of an Ulster Protestant, Captain J. R. White.[1]

For a while Mr Asquith and his colleagues strove to persuade themselves and others that the menace of armed conflict was a gigantic bluff on the part of the Unionist Opposition. On July 24, Mr Augustine Birrell, the Irish Secretary, had an audience with the King at Buckingham Palace. The substance of their conversation was recorded by Lord Stamfordham:[r]

'The King saw Mr Birrell and the position of affairs in Ireland was discussed for an hour. The latter declared the situation to be artificial and discounted the seriousness of the state of things in Ulster as being due to Carson, who had lost his head—not an Orangeman, a Dublin man. As to fighting, there would be no one to fight. A "Provisional Government" would not last a week, as the whole country so governed would be cut off from the outside world. . . . If only the Opposition would come to Parliament and table a scheme for Ulster "contracting out" of the Bill,—say for ten years, at the expiration of which a referendum might be taken as to whether they should come under Home Rule or not—he would accept it. . . . The King replied "But Mr Redmond would never agree to this plan". Mr Birrell answered "He would have to agree!"—"But he would turn you out"—"Let him—a d—d good thing if he did!"

' "But", Mr Birrell continued, "the Opposition won't do this, because they are hoping something will turn up—that either Heaven, the King, or some other agency, will bring about a General Election and the Government will be beaten and Home Rule shelved."

'The King pointed out that apparently the Government were "drifting" and that with this "drift" his own position was becoming more and more difficult. This Mr Birrell admitted, but said that it was for the Opposition to move.'[2]

---

[1] James Larkin was a Liverpool boy with a long pale face and great powers of mass excitation. On October 27, 1913, he was sentenced to seven months' imprisonment for sedition but was released on November 13. He was secretary of the Irish Transport Workers Union and disguised his revolutionary campaign under the title 'The fiery Cross'. Captain White was the son of Field-Marshal Sir George White, the defender of Ladysmith (see his autobiography *Misfit*).

[2] It is only fair to Mr Birrell to record that within a few weeks of this conversation he modified his view that the Ulster situation was 'artificial'. In the first week of September he wrote to Lord Stamfordham: 'That there

Mr Birrell was not mistaken in believing that some of the more ardent members of the Opposition hoped to secure the King's intervention. They contended that, since the Constitution was in suspense, the Government had no right, without a specific mandate from the people, to introduce organic changes into the structure of the realm. They hoped that the King would insist upon a dissolution, that Mr Asquith would resign his office and that Mr Bonar Law would then be able to form an alternative Government and go to the country on the issue of Home Rule versus the rights and liberties of Protestant Ulster. They were convinced that, in that event, the electors would return them to power with a substantial majority.

The elder statesmen were not either unanimous or convincing. Lord Lansdowne and Mr Bonar Law were of opinion that the King would do right in insisting that the people should first be given an opportunity to express their own views on the Home Rule policy of the Government.[s] Lord Loreburn, Lord Cromer and Lord Rosebery considered that it would be unwise for the King to refuse to follow the advice of the Government in power, but that he should inform them in writing that he assented against his personal judgment, since he feared that their policy would lead to civil war. Meanwhile, the King's peace of mind was disturbed by the flood of private, and often anonymous, letters which poured into Buckingham Palace. Correspondents from Ulster assured him that the workers and peasants in the four counties looked upon him as their sole guardian and protector. 'Surely,' the cry went up, 'the King is not going to hand us over to the Pope?' Lord Stamfordham was frequently troubled by the effect which these passionate letters produced upon the King's sentiments and sympathies. 'Pray, Sir!' he had written to him when momentarily absent, 'do not give a thought to the irresponsible, and as a rule anonymous, letterwriters who dare to address their cowardly and insulting words to you.'[t] But the King was troubled none the less.

The strange thing was that, although so many Peers, Privy Councillors and commoners thought it right to obtrude upon the King their advice, their exhortations and their reproaches, the one man who, during those spring and summer months of 1913, had never even alluded to the subject was the Prime Minister himself.

is great *perturbation* is certain; and the notion that it is all *bluff* may be dismissed. Personally, I cannot bring myself to believe in civil war, even in its mildest terms' (R.A. K.2553. II. 5).

Mr Asquith believed in the strict avoidance of all evitable pain: he allowed sleeping scorpions to lie. By the end of July, however, the King had come to the conclusion that the Prime Minister's reticence might, if prolonged indefinitely, end by landing everybody concerned in false positions. He therefore summoned Mr Asquith to an audience in London on August 11. During the week preceding this interview, the King was down at Cowes and, while his beloved *Britannia* seethed past the familiar buoys and landmarks of the Solent, he considered carefully what he should say to Mr Asquith and what his own attitude ought, in duty, to be. In principle, he agreed with the argument that there ought to be a General Election before the Home Rule Bill, with its attendant menace of civil strife, became the law of the land. In practice, he foresaw that Mr Asquith would not agree to a dissolution, that he would tender the resignation of his Government and that at the ensuing Election many Liberal candidates would seek to divert attention from the threatened coercion of Ulster by accusing the Crown of interference in party issues. Moreover, he had no personal desire at all to see Mr Bonar Law succeed Mr Asquith, for whom he had acquired (and for ever retained) feelings of warm affection. The only possible solution, he felt, was an agreed settlement between the leaders of the two parties; that settlement might be furthered by taking up the idea of general 'devolution' (as sponsored by Lord Dunraven and others) under which some form of local autonomy would be granted, not to Southern Ireland only, not only to Ulster, but also to Scotland and Wales."[1]

With this in mind he drafted a memorandum in his own handwriting which, at the audience of August 11, he handed to the Prime Minister. This memorandum must be quoted in its entirety:[v]

[1] The Devolution idea expanded into a scheme for a federal solution of the whole problem. The proposal was that there should be one Imperial Parliament at Westminster and one Imperial Executive. Subject to them would be (*a*) an English Parliament and Executive, (*b*) a Scottish Parliament and Executive, (*c*) an Irish Parliament and Executive, (*d*) a Welsh Parliament and Executive, and, if necessary, (*e*) an Ulster Parliament and Executive. 'Four or five Parliaments', wrote Austen Chamberlain to Lord Lansdowne on November 2, 1913, 'may be a nuisance but can hardly be a serious danger to Westminster sovereignty. One Parliament might claim equality: five could not' (*Politics from Inside*, p. 571).

The ingenious device for hamstringing the Dublin Parliament came to nothing, since Mr Asquith rightly insisted that Irish Home Rule was an urgent matter, whereas the other autonomies could wait.

'August 11, 1913.

'Although I have not spoken to you before on the subject, I have been for some time very anxious about the Irish Home Rule Bill, and especially with regard to Ulster.

'The speeches not only of people like Sir Edward Carson, but of the Unionist Leaders, and of ex-Cabinet Ministers; the stated intention of setting up a provisional Government in Ulster directly the Home Rule Bill is passed; the reports of Military preparations, Army drilling etc.; of assistance from England, Scotland and the Colonies; of the intended resignation of their Commissions by Army Officers; all point toward rebellion if not Civil War; and, if so, to certain bloodshed.

'Meanwhile, there are rumours of probable agitation in the country; of monster petitions; Addresses from the House of Lords; from Privy Councillors; urging me to use my influence to avert the catastrophe which threatens Ireland.

'Such vigorous action taken, or likely to be taken, will place me in a very embarrassing position in the centre of the conflicting parties backed by their respective Press.

'Whatever I do I shall offend half the population.

'One alternative would certainly result in alienating the Ulster Protestants from me, and whatever happens the result must be detrimental to me personally and to the Crown in general.

'No Sovereign has ever been in such a position, and this pressure is sure to increase during the next few months.

'In this period I shall have a right to expect the greatest confidence and support from my Ministers, and, above all, from my Prime Minister.

'I cannot help feeling that the Government is drifting and taking me with it.

'Before the gravity of the situation increases I should like to know how you view the present state of affairs, and what you imagine will be the outcome of it.

'On the 24th July I saw Mr Birrell, who admitted the seriousness of the outlook.

'He seemed to think that perhaps an arrangement could be made for Ulster to "contract out" of the Home Rule scheme, say for 10 years, with the right to come under the Irish Parliament, if so desired, after a referendum by her people, at the end of that period. But it was for the Opposition to come forward with some practical proposal to this effect.

'Is there any chance of a settlement by consent as suggested by Lord Loreburn, Lord Macdonnell, Lord Dunraven, Mr W. O'Brien, Mr Birrell, Lord Lansdowne, Mr Bonar Law and others?

'Would it be possible to have a Conference in which all parties should take part, to consider the whole policy of devolution, of which you, in introducing the Home Rule Bill in April 1912, said "Irish Home Rule is only the first step"?

'Would it not be better to try to settle measures involving great changes in the Constitution, such as Home Rule all round, Reform of the House of Lords etc., not on Party lines, but by agreement?'

On being handed this paper on August 11, Mr Asquith asked if he might take it away with him and furnish a considered reply. He did not agree that the Crown need be placed in a difficult position; so long as the King acted constitutionally, his position was unassailable. If he considered that the action which his Ministers advised would prove detrimental to the Country, it was his duty to '*warn*' them, if necessary in writing, and thereafter the sole responsibility would rest with them. Meanwhile he signified that he was perfectly willing to consider any practical scheme which would enable Ulster to 'contract out' of the Home Rule Bill; and that, although he was not in favour of an actual conference between the several leaders, he was prepared to encourage a settlement by consent.[w]

Mr Asquith's 'considered reply' to the King's memorandum took the form of two separate documents, the first dealing with the constitutional issues involved and the second with the Irish problem itself.

In the first paper the Prime Minister recalled that the veto of the Crown had not been exercised for two hundred years and that the principle had since become firmly established that the occupant of the Throne must, in the last resort, act upon the advice of his Ministers. This admirable principle had secured that the Sovereign was removed 'from the storms and vicissitudes of party politics' and that the impersonal status of the Crown rendered it 'an invaluable safeguard for the continuity of our national life'. Whatever the Unionists and a few constitutional lawyers might assert, the Parliament Act 'was not intended in any way to affect and, it is submitted, has not affected, the Constitutional position of the Sovereign'. Undoubtedly the King possessed the right to dismiss his Ministers, even when they held a majority in the House of Commons, but that right had not been exercised since the days of William IV, whose action at the time of the Reform Bills did not constitute an auspicious precedent. If the King were, in present conditions, to dismiss a Government which retained the confidence of the House of Commons he might render the Crown 'the football of contending factions'. 'This', concluded Mr Asquith, 'is a constitutional catastrophe which it is the duty of every wise statesman to do the utmost in his power to avert.'[x]

In his second paper, which dealt specifically with the Irish problem, the Prime Minister stated that, although there was serious danger of 'organised disorder' in Ulster, he did not believe that it would attain the dimensions of civil war. To hold a General Election *before* the Home Rule Bill became law would, not only stultify the whole purpose of the Parliament Act, but would also, supposing that the electors decided against Home Rule, face the new Government with the equal problem of armed risings among the Catholics of Southern Ireland. An Election held *after* the Bill became law would be an entirely different matter: it would then be open to the new Parliament to consider whether to approve, repeal, or amend the Home Rule Act. He was not in principle opposed to a conference between the leaders of the several parties, including Sir Edward Carson and Mr Redmond, but he feared that there existed an 'unbridgeable chasm of principle' between the two sides which would render it difficult, except in so far as minor adjustments were concerned, to find a basis 'upon and from which the deliberations of any conference could proceed'.*y*

The King replied to the Prime Minister's two papers in a private letter, dated from Balmoral on September 22, 1913.*z* This letter is so important as an illustration of King George's conception of the duty of a Sovereign to 'advise, to encourage, and to warn', that, in spite of its length, it must be reproduced:

Balmoral Castle,
22nd September, 1913.

My dear Prime Minister,

I am most grateful to you for your very clear and well reasoned Memorandum which you have been good enough to draw up for me on the Government of Ireland Bill.

Acting upon your own suggestions that I should freely and unreservedly offer my criticisms, I do so upon quotations taken from it.

Referring to the Constitutional position of the Sovereign, you say 'in the end the Sovereign always acts upon the advice which Ministers feel it their duty to offer . . . and his subjects cannot hold him in any way accountable'.

Fully accepting this proposition, I nevertheless cannot shut my eyes to the fact that in this particular instance the people will, rightly or wrongly, associate me with whatever policy is adopted by my advisers, dispensing praise or blame according as that policy is in agreement or antagonistic to their own opinions.

While you admit the Sovereign's undoubted power to change his advisers, I infer that you regard the exercise of that power as inexpedient and indeed dangerous.

Should the Sovereign *never* exercise that right, not even, to quote Sir Erskine May, 'in the interests of the State and on grounds which could be justified to Parliament'? Bagehot wrote, 'The Sovereign too possesses a power according to theory for extreme use on a critical occasion, but which in law he can use on any occasion. He can *dissolve . . .*'.

The Parliament Act 'was not intended in any way to affect, and it is submitted has not affected the Constitutional position of the Sovereign'.

But the Preamble of the Bill stated an intention to create a new Second Chamber; that this could not be done immediately; meanwhile provision by the Bill would be made for restricting the powers of the House of Lords.

Does not such an organic change in the Constitutional position of one of the Estates of the Realm also affect the relations of all three to one another; and the failure to replace it on an effective footing deprive the Sovereign of the assistance of the Second Chamber?

Should the Home Rule Bill become law I gather you consider that there is a 'certainty of tumult and riot and more than a possibility of serious bloodshed', but you do not anticipate 'anything which could rightly be described as Civil War'.

If, however, the union which you contemplate of the 'considerable and militant minority' of Roman Catholics in North-East Ulster with the forces of the executive is carried into effect, will not the armed struggle between these sections of the people constitute Civil War, more especially if the forces of Ulster are reinforced from England, Scotland and even the Colonies, which contingency I am assured is highly probable?

Do you propose to employ the Army to suppress such disorders?

This is, to my mind, one of the most serious questions which the Government will have to decide.

In doing so you will, I am sure, bear in mind that ours is a voluntary Army; our Soldiers are none the less Citizens; by birth, religion and environment they may have strong feelings on the Irish question; outside influence may be brought to bear upon them; they see distinguished retired Officers already organising local forces in Ulster; they hear rumours of Officers on the Active List throwing up their Commissions to join this force.

Will it be wise, will it be fair to the Sovereign as head of the Army, to subject the discipline, and indeed the loyalty of his troops, to such a strain?

Have you considered the effect upon the Protestant sentiments in these Islands and the Colonies of the coercion of Ulster?

I quite admit the grave prospects resulting from a rejection of the Bill.

But is the demand for Home Rule in Ireland as earnest and as National to-day as it was, for instance, in the days of Parnell?

Has not the Land Purchase Policy settled the agrarian trouble, which was the chief motive of the Home Rule agitation?

I am assured by resident Landowners in the South and West of Ireland that their tenants, while ostensibly favourable to Home Rule, are no longer enthusiastic about it, and are, comparatively speaking, content and well-to-do.

The hierarchy of the Church of Rome is indifferent and probably at heart would be glad not to come under the power of an Irish Parliament.

The application of forcible methods to govern Ireland, were the Bill rejected, would in your opinion 'offend the conscience of Great Britain'.

But surely not more so than their application against Ulster?

With regard to your objections to a General Election between now and the beginning of next Session.

It is the case, unfortunately, that Sir Edward Carson and his friends declare that they would not be influenced by a verdict at the Polls in favour of Home Rule. And here let me assure you that I view with the gravest concern the advocacy of what Sir Edward Carson openly admits to be illegal measures in the resistance of North-East Ulster to the constituted law and authority of the land. Still we have the assurance of the Unionist leaders that in the event of the Country declaring in favour of Home Rule, they will support the Government instead of supporting Ulster, as they intend to do if an appeal to the Country is refused.

Is due consideration given to the fact that although Home Rule has been before the Country for 30 years, the present Bill differs materially from any previous Home Rule Bill; that it has never been before the Country; that it is opposed by practically the whole of the House of Lords; by one third of the House of Commons; by half the population of England, and that it was forced through the House of Commons, pages of it never having been discussed?

I recognise your argument that the proposed General Election would not be fought on Home Rule, but on a 'score of other issues', so that you would not obtain a mandate *pur et simple* upon Home Rule.

But I suppose this argument might be equally urged to show that the General Election of December 1910 gave no verdict in favour of Home Rule.

Would it not be right in order to ensure a lasting settlement, to make certain that it is the wish of my people that the Union of Ireland shall be repealed by a measure which was not put before them at the last Election?

Is there any other Country in the world which could carry out such a fundamental change in its Constitution upon the authority of a single chamber?

Is there any precedent in our own Country for such a change to be made without submitting it to the Electorate?

To the suggestion that a General Election should take place after Assent has been given to the Bill, I see the most serious objections.

Granted that this policy is adopted, I assume that once the Bill is

227

passed, outbreaks will occur in Ulster if they have not done so at an earlier date.

Meanwhile Great Britain and Ireland will be plunged into the throes of a General Election.

If the Government are returned to power, Ulster will probably resist more vigorously than ever.

On the other hand, if the Government are defeated, a new Ministry will be formed, Parliament reassembled, the Home Rule Bill perhaps repealed, followed by revolt in the South and West of Ireland, and finally the Sovereign's Assent asked for to repeal the Act to which only a few months before he had affixed his signature.

I can hardly think that Ministers contemplate placing the Country and the Sovereign in such a position. . . .

Recollecting my conversations with you on August 11th, and with Mr Birrell a fortnight earlier, I trust that some agreement may be found on the lines then suggested, such as leaving out North-East Ulster from the Scheme for a certain period, say five or ten years, with the power to come under the Irish Parliament, if so desired, after the question is put to the test of a Referendum in the reserved Counties.

The objection urged that this arrangement would involve the desertion of the Protestants in other parts of Ireland, is met by the fact that the Nationalist minority in Ulster would be placed at a similar disadvantage.

It seems inconceivable to me that British commonsense will not ultimately find a solution to this terrible prospect of rebellion and bloodshed in so rich and flourishing a part of my Dominions.

Assuming that the aim of both political Parties is to secure good Government, prosperity and loyal contentment for the Irish people, it must be admitted that these objects cannot be attained by the policy so far advocated by either Liberal or Conservative Governments.

Therefore, we can only hope for the attainment of these objects by common agreement upon some alternative course.

Nevertheless, I entirely recognise all the grave difficulties which must confront anyone who endeavours to secure by consent the settlement of a question which has divided Ireland for many generations.

I rejoice to know that you are ready and anxious to enter into a Conference if a definite basis can be found upon which to confer.

For my part, I will gladly do everything in my power to induce the Opposition to meet you in a reasonable and conciliatory spirit.

For it behooves us all to withhold no efforts to avert those threatening events which would inevitably outrage humanity and lower the British name in the mind of the whole civilised world.

I have endeavoured to comment frankly upon your Memorandum, and I trust that in your next letter you will give your views upon the various points referred to before I have the pleasure of seeing you here on the 6th October.

The Memorandum has been seen by no one except my Private

Secretary, nor have I mentioned the fact that I have received it to anyone.

>Believe me,
>>My dear Prime Minister,
>>>Very sincerely yours,
>>>>GEORGE R.I.

Mr Asquith replied to this formidable letter on October 1. He knew that he would be seeing the King within a few days and he therefore confined himself to reaffirming what he had written before. For the King to dismiss the Government might entail consequences 'very injurious to the authority of the Crown'; repellent as it might be to have to take measures of coercion against Ulster, it was the duty of a Government to see that the law was enforced; even if this entailed the use of the military. Mr Asquith did not anticipate that the troops would fail to do their duty. The Prime Minister concluded with a significant sentence:

'I am still as anxious as anyone can be that the dangers to social order incident, either in the passing or the rejection of the Bill (and the latter is in my opinion by far the more formidable contingency) should be averted by some special arrangement in regard to the North East, which is not inconsistent with the fundamental principle and purpose of the Bill.'[2a]

From that point onward the controversy was concentrated on the conditions which Mr Asquith and Mr Bonar Law, Mr Redmond and Sir Edward Carson, would accept for the exclusion of Ulster from the operation of the Home Rule Bill. The discussions which ensued, in which the King played an important mediatory part, culminated in the Buckingham Palace Conference of July 1914. They will therefore be examined in the next chapter.

CHAPTER XV

BUCKINGHAM PALACE CONFERENCE

1914

Mr Balfour's view of the Irish situation—The King's conversations at Balmoral—His interview with the Prime Minister—Mr Asquith holds two secret meetings with Mr Bonar Law—A deadlock is reached—The King tries to break the deadlock—He raises with Mr Asquith the question of the Royal Assent—His speech from the Throne—Further efforts to secure a compromise—The Prime Minister, in moving the second reading of the Home Rule Bill, offers the exclusion of Ulster—The Curragh incident—The Larne gunrunning—The Prime Minister considers the moment has arrived for the leaders of the parties to meet in Conference—They are summoned to Buckingham Palace—The Conference fails—The Austrian ultimatum to Serbia—The King and Prince Henry of Prussia—The Declaration of War.

(1)

MR ARTHUR BALFOUR, from his ivory tower at Whittingehame, watched the clash of personalities and parties with a detached but observant eye. On September 23, 1913, he sent to Lord Stamfordham, for communication to the King, a copy of a letter which he had that day written to Mr Bonar Law. 'I look', he wrote, 'with much misgiving upon the general loosening of the ordinary ties of social obligation.' He foresaw with apprehension that the Irish of the south would be bound sooner or later to imitate the armed Covenanters of the northern counties; that if British troops were ordered to coerce Ulster, many officers would send in their resignations; and that in the House of Commons the Opposition might be provoked to scenes of violence such as 'would strip that Assembly of even those few rags of consideration which have been left it by seven years of Radical Government'. He agreed that the ideal solution would be to hold a General Election before the Home Rule Bill was forced through both Chambers. But as Mr Asquith was unwilling to demand a dissolution, and as the King was equally unwilling to dismiss a Government still commanding a majority in Parliament, then the only possible solution was to agree to a compromise by which the Ulster counties would be excluded from the operation of the Bill.*

This letter and the simple doctrine it embodied crystallised the successive ideas which, during the past few months, had been passing through the King's mind. On October 1 Lord Stamfordham wrote to Mr Bonar Law,[b] saying that the King was most anxious to bring about a conference between the leaders of the several parties, but that the Cabinet felt that they could not themselves initiate such a proposal. Would he, Mr Bonar Law, put down a motion or an amendment to that effect? Mr Bonar Law replied that his Party would not consent to his taking such an initiative, since it would imply that he accepted the principle of Home Rule, an implication which would wound the feelings of all Irish loyalists. Mr Bonar Law felt that any such invitation should come from the King himself. 'If', he wrote, 'it originated with him, it would be easier for the leaders of my Party to agree to it.'[c]

While at Balmoral that September, the King had taken the opportunity to discuss the situation with the many Ministers and statesmen who came there in attendance or as his guests. The comments which he made in his diary upon their respective attitudes were synthetic rather than analytical. He had found Lord Crewe 'fairly sympathetic', Sir Edward Grey 'nice and sensible', Lord Lansdowne 'not very satisfactory', Mr Winston Churchill 'sensible and fairly reasonable', Mr Balfour himself 'serious and very sympathetic'. Mr Lewis Harcourt (who like many timid men was inclined to become strident when he wished to appear courageous) struck him as 'most unsatisfactory': he stated afterwards that Mr Harcourt had employed 'bludgeoning words'.[1] On October 6 the Prime Minister himself arrived: 'Had a conversation with him before dinner on political situation. He owned it was serious, but was optimistic as usual.'

Mr Asquith remained three days at Balmoral and Lord Stamfordham summarised in a memorandum the main points which emerged from the repeated discussions which took place.[d] The Prime

---

[1] Lord Esher, who had originally been of opinion that in no circumstances should the King go counter to the advice of his Ministers, changed his mind and contended that, in view of the danger of civil war, it was now the King's duty to dismiss Mr Asquith and to entrust the Government to some 'neutral' statesman, such as Lord Rosebery, in order that a General Election could be held. The King replied that he did not in the least want to be deprived of the services of his present Ministers, partly because he trusted Mr Asquith personally, and partly because the departure of Sir Edward Grey would be a European misfortune. Lord Esher told the King that 'he ought not to worry himself to death, but put the matter aside. The King turned abruptly away with some emotion' (Esher, vol. III, p. 155).

Minister did not think that, in view of Sir Edward Carson's attitude and speeches, a conference between party leaders could serve any useful purpose: it would prove, he said, either 'a tea party or a bear garden'. The Government did not intend to arrest Sir Edward Carson for sedition, since that would be 'to throw a lighted match into a powder barrel'. The King asked the Prime Minister whether he did not consider the threat to coerce Ulster as 'un-English and contrary to all Liberal and democratic principles'. Mr Asquith did not deny this imputation. What he did do was to promise immediately to enter into secret conversations with Mr Bonar Law, in order to find whether any possible basis of settlement could be devised. He was not sanguine as to the result.

The King was relieved that the Prime Minister had, to this extent, agreed to the course which His Majesty had for long been urging upon him. He felt confident that once Mr Asquith and Mr Bonar Law got down to discussing the position face to face, and independently of their own extremists, some compromise would be found which would avert rebellion or civil war, and relieve him of the odious alternatives of having either to condone bloodshed or resort to a controversial exercise of his Prerogative:

> 'The King seems', reported Count Mensdorff four days later,[e] 'firmly resolved to maintain a strictly constitutional attitude and to resist all suggestions (which are constantly being made to him, especially from Opposition quarters) that he should intervene personally.'

The Prime Minister, on his return from Balmoral, held two secret meetings with Mr Bonar Law. The first took place on October 14, when a tentative agreement was reached for the exclusion of the Ulster counties. The second took place on November 6, by which time, as Mr Asquith reported to the King,[f] 'opinion was stiffening among the rank and file on both sides, and the idea of a compromise, and even a Conference, was regarded with growing disfavour and suspicion.' Mr Bonar Law showed no ardent desire to continue these conversations: he allowed six weeks of silence to elapse.[g] [1]

[1] It is clear that some misunderstanding arose between Mr Asquith and Mr Bonar Law at the second interview. The latter was left under the impression that the Prime Minister had promised to submit to the Cabinet the proposal to exclude Ulster, and had undertaken that they would agree. Mr Asquith, however, had merely said that he would 'report the substance of the conversation' and would then, if his colleagues approved, ask Mr Birrell to approach Mr Redmond. Mr Bonar Law remained convinced thereafter that the Prime Minister had failed to keep his word (R.A. K.2553, VI, 103).

(2)

By the beginning of 1914 a deadlock appeared to have been reached. On January 2, 1914, the King wrote to Lord Stamfordham from Sandringham repeating his determination to continue working for a settlement by consent:[h]

'I must confess that I am greatly concerned & I begin to feel that these private conversations between the P.M. & B.L. & Carson are going to fail for the reasons I put on paper some weeks ago. . . . I am perfectly prepared to take the proper responsibility which belongs to the Sovereign of this Country, but I shall continue so long as I can to persuade the parties concerned to come to an agreement & I shall certainly do all in my power to prevent civil war & bloodshed in Ireland. If I was to say to the P.M. "You must either settle this question by consent, or else go to the Country"—he would say at once: "That is what the Unionists say! They want an election and won't accept our proposals, which we think fair!" . . . No—the more I think of it all, the more worried I get. But I am not discouraged, and, with your kind help, common sense, good judgement & advice, I think I shall come out on top; at least I mean to try to! . . . If you think it necessary later, I shall certainly ask the P.M. to come here to see me for one night; he can stay at Park House. I shall keep on bothering him as much as possible.'

On February 5 the King gave an audience to the Prime Minister at Windsor. He warned Mr Asquith that, if the negotiations failed and civil war resulted, many army officers would resign their commissions rather than fight. 'But whom', Mr Asquith enquired, 'are they going to fight?' The King went on to say that Ulster would never, no matter what guarantees were given, consent to be placed under a Dublin Parliament. A General Election would 'clear the air', would show whether the Government really possessed a mandate for Home Rule, and in any case relieve the King and the Prime Minister of responsibility for what followed. Mr Asquith replied that a General Election would settle nothing and that, whatever might be the consequences, the responsibility would rest, not with the King, but with his Ministers:

'The King replied', Lord Stamfordham recorded,[i] 'that, although constitutionally he might not be responsible, still he could not allow bloodshed among his loyal subjects in any part of his Dominions without exerting every means in his power to avert it. Although at the present stage of the proceedings he could not rightly intervene he should feel it his duty to do what in his own judgement was best for his people generally.

'The Prime Minister expressed no little surprise at this declaration and said he never thought that anything of this kind was contemplated

233

and, "if he might speak frankly", he earnestly trusted His Majesty did not think of refusing Assent. Such a thing had not been done since the reign of Queen Anne and would inevitably prove disastrous to the Monarchy. His Majesty could, however, if he chose dismiss his Ministers. But in that case, it would be most unfair to do so once this new Session had begun; otherwise, the whole work of the past two years would, through the action of the Parliament Act, be sacrificed. It ought to be *done at once*, before Parliament meets on the 10th instant; though he would respectfully deprecate such a course & would offer his strong advice against it, not for his own sake so much as for that of the Crown. He hoped he had not so far forfeited the King's confidence as to justify such a step.

'His Majesty said that the Prime Minister had *not* forfeited his confidence & that he had no intention of dismissing his Ministers, although his future action must be guided by circumstances. The King said he was ready to do anything in his power to bring about a settlement by consent. He would see the P.M. at any time, and if the latter would only give him a hint, he would send for Mr Bonar Law, or even Sir E. Carson, and endeavour to induce them to come to an agreement; and he would not mind were his efforts rebuffed.'[1]

[1] The King's considered opinion upon the right of the Sovereign to withold Assent to a Bill passed by Parliament was expressed in a letter which, on July 31, 1914, he drafted in consultation with Lord Loreburn. This letter was never despatched to the Prime Minister in view of the imminence of war. The draft contained the following initial paragraph (R.A. K.2553, VI, 56):

'The bill for the better Government of Ireland having now passed through the necessary stages, the King concludes that, by the terms of the Parliament Act, it will come on, automatically, for his Assent, unless the House of Commons direct to the contrary.

'Much has been said and written in favour of the proposition that the Assent of the Crown should be withheld from the measure. On the other hand, the King feels strongly that that extreme course should not be adopted in this case unless there is convincing evidence that it would avert a national disaster, or at least have a tranquillizing effect on the distracting conditions of the time. There is no such evidence.'

The King then pointed out that the Bill reached him under a novel procedure, 'the result of a drastic, though as yet incomplete, change in the British Constitution,' and without its 'being reinforced by the verdict of the Electorate, upon which the ultimate responsibility should properly be placed in a self-governing State'. He therefore felt entitled to ask his Ministers to provide him with 'a statement of the full and considered reasons' which impelled them to advise him to give his Assent and asked that this statement should be laid before him 'in a form which can be put on record for the use of his successors and referred to if any necessity should hereafter arise'.

Since this letter was never despatched, it is not quoted in the text, but relegated, as a *pièce justificative*, to a note.

On February 10 the King opened Parliament in state:

'My speech was rather long, & unfortunately the Lord Chancellor gave me the paper in small print, instead of the one in large type, which put me out. I laid great stress on the paragraph about Home Rule for Ireland, in which I appeal for a peaceful settlement.'

The paragraph in question, which had of course been drafted in Cabinet, ran as follows:

'In a matter in which the hopes and fears of so many of My subjects are keenly concerned, and which—unless handled now with foresight, judgement and in the spirit of mutual concession—threatens grave future difficulties, it is My most earnest wish that the goodwill and co-operation of men of all parties and creeds may heal disunion and lay the foundations of a lasting settlement.'

The King felt that this appeal had 'created a very good impression on all sides', and he took the occasion again to urge the Prime Minister publicly to state what he was prepared to offer as a settlement. 'May not harm be done', he wrote to him,[j] 'by raising false hopes & by delaying the announcement of what is the limit of your concessions?' At the same time he instructed Lord Stamfordham to urge Mr Bonar Law to be moderate in his own speeches and to curb those of his supporters:

'No Britisher', Lord Stamdfordham wrote to Mr Bonar Law,[k] 'likes being told that he is a coward or that he has got the "funks". And if the Government are held up to contempt because they are running away from their Bill in terror of Civil War, they will stiffen up and make an agreement still more difficult.'

The King also authorised his Private Secretary to visit Sir Edward Carson at his private house in the hope of persuading him not to make a violent speech when the Home Rule Bill was again introduced into Parliament. Sir Edward Carson informed Lord Stamfordham that he certainly intended to press the Prime Minister to say whether or no his Government were in favour of the exclusion of Ulster. All this delay, he said, was becoming intolerable and he did not know for how much longer he would be able to control his followers who were becoming more and more indifferent to personal risk, and who were confident, to a man, that 'the King would not desert them'. At the same time Sir Edward Carson expressed his personal regard for Mr Asquith and his trust in his sincerity; all that he himself desired was a settlement which would satisfy the people of Ulster.[l]

Meanwhile, Mr Birrell and Mr Lloyd George had been exercising their dazzling gifts of persuasion upon Mr Redmond. Unwillingly he had agreed to the exclusion of Ulster for a period of years; the Unionists intimated that, if this meant that Ulster would automatically come under Dublin when the period of years had expired, they would be wholly unable to consider any such compromise.

On March 9, 1914, the Prime Minister in the House of Commons moved the second reading of the Home Rule Bill. He then made a courageous gesture of conciliation. He offered Ulster exclusion for a period of six years. Sir Edward Carson asked what would happen at the expiration of that period, and Mr Asquith replied by pointing out that the period would only expire in July 1921, by which date two General Elections would have been held in England and other Parliaments might have been chosen who would reverse the whole procedure. Both Mr Bonar Law and Sir Edward Carson stated that exclusion must be absolute and without a time limit. 'We do not want', the latter exclaimed, 'a sentence of death with a stay of execution for six years.' Mr Redmond replied that it had meant a cruel sacrifice for him to accept even a limited and conditional exclusion and that his Party could not consider going beyond the proposal which the Prime Minister had made.[1]

On March 19 the King had a long and intimate conversation with Mr Asquith in which he urged upon him the increasing gravity of the situation and the dreadful predicament which would face the Crown if civil war broke out. On the one hand he was being appealed to to exert his Prerogative; on the other hand the left-wing papers were accusing him and 'Court hangers-on' of bringing undue pressure to bear:[m]

> 'The King said he had always been frank with Mr Asquith and told him all he heard. As to "Court hangers-on", he only discussed political affairs with his Private Secretary, who was also in the Prime Minister's confidence. His one object had been to help the Prime Minister, who had, he knew, done all in his power to secure a peaceful settlement.

[1] The Government proposal was that each of the Ulster counties (including the cities of Londonderry and Belfast) should ballot separately as to whether they desired inclusion within the Home Rule area. Any county in which there was a clear majority for exclusion might contract out for six years. After that period, it would automatically come under the jurisdiction of the Dublin Parliament. It was generally assumed that Donegal, Monaghan and Cavan would vote for inclusion; that in Fermanagh and Tyrone the vote would be almost equally divided, with a possible Catholic majority; and that the city of Londonderry would also vote for inclusion.

Mr Asquith said he too had been accused, even by some of his friends, of weakness in giving in to Court influence which of course was absurd. At the same time it was only out of his great consideration for the King that he had gone on trying during these weary months to effect a settlement. He was deeply grateful to the King, without whose help he could not have achieved as much as had been done. Throughout, the King had, he considered, behaved in exactly the manner a Constitutional Sovereign should act.'

That same afternoon, in the House of Commons, Mr Bonar Law moved a vote of censure on the Government. In referring to the impending coercion of Ulster, he said that the attitude of the Army was for the Army to decide. The debate was still proceeding when Sir Edward Carson strode starkly out of the House with a look of destiny upon his haggard covenanter face. A whisper flew round the benches that he was taking the night mail for Belfast: there were few who doubted that on the next morning the Provisional Government of Ulster would be proclaimed.

(3)

On March 18, 1914, Sir Arthur Paget, the General Officer Commanding the troops in Ireland, was summoned to London. He had interviews with Colonel Seely, the Secretary of State for War, with Sir John French, the Chief of the Imperial General Staff, and with Sir Spencer Ewart, the Adjutant-General. He also saw the members of the Cabinet Committee which had been specially constituted to follow the hourly developments of the Irish situation.[1] The instructions which Sir Arthur Paget then received were verbal only and were not, unfortunately, recorded in writing. The Government contended later that all Sir Arthur Paget had been asked to do was to secure that the military and naval depots and magazines in northern Ireland were adequately protected against any sudden raid by mischievous persons. Sir Arthur Paget seems to have derived a different impression of their intentions. He returned to Dublin on March 19 and in the early morning of Friday, March 20, he summoned his Generals and Brigadiers and informed them that they must immediately present to the officers under their commands an ultimatum with a two hours' limit. Either these officers must agree to take part in 'active operations' in Ulster, or they must send in their resignations, be dismissed from the service and forfeit their

[1] This Committee was composed of Mr Birrell, Mr Churchill, Colonel Seely and the Attorney-General.

pensions. General Hubert Gough, commanding the Third Cavalry Brigade, returned with this ultimatum to the Curragh Camp. He informed his officers that he himself had decided to resign his commission rather than take part in 'active operations' against the Ulster Volunteers. As many as fifty-seven senior and junior officers resolved to follow his example and to send in their papers.

On learning of this startling strike, Sir Arthur Paget drove quickly to the Curragh and sought to persuade the officers to reconsider their decision. According to General Gough's account,[n] he then told them that all Ireland, within the next twenty-four hours, would 'be in a blaze', that it would be necessary to 'hold the line of the Boyne' and that as many as 25,000 troops were being sent from England as reinforcements. He said that his instructions were 'the direct orders of the Sovereign' and not merely the commands of 'those dirty swine, the politicians'. It is of course possible that, in subsequently recording these remarks, General Gough's recollection of the actual words used may have been at fault; but General Paget, even in his less excited moments, was not a man of measured language or meek tact.

The King first heard of this deplorable episode when he opened his newspaper on the morning of Saturday, March 21:

> 'Had a most harrassing day', he wrote in his diary, 'on account of General Gough & most of the officers of the Cavalry Brigade resigning at the Curragh, as it appears they were asked if they would fight against Ulster. . . . Saw Colonel Seely & I spoke very strongly to him. Lord Roberts came to see me & was in despair about it all & said it would ruin the Army. . . . I had an interview with Sir John French & impressed upon him the gravity of the situation & that if great tact were not shown there would be no Army left. Worked with Bigge. Wrote to the Prime Minister. We dined alone, read in the evening. Bed at 11.0 very tired.'

The King wrote to Mr Asquith complaining that he had never been informed of the instructions given to Sir Arthur Paget, or of the proposed movement of military detachments into Ulster, or of the naval dispositions which, it was rumoured, were also contemplated. What rendered him particularly indignant was that his own name should have been mentioned in the address given by Sir Arthur Paget to the officers at the Curragh. When he tackled the General on this subject, the latter lamely replied that 'all orders to the Army were the King's orders'.[1]

[1] The extent to which irresponsible people were apt to drag the King's name into the Ulster controversy is illustrated by what may be called the

238

The Government took quick steps to mitigate the damage which the Curragh incident had caused. On March 22 they issued a statement that it had not been their intention to move troops into Ulster for any purpose other than the protection of the ammunition depots. General Gough was summoned to the War Office, informed that Sir Arthur Paget's ultimatum had been the result of 'a misunderstanding' and instructed to resume his command. General Gough refused to return to Ireland unless he were first given a written assurance which he could show to his officers. A minute was therefore composed—and initialled by Colonel Seely, Sir John French and Sir Spencer Ewart—stating that His Majesty's Government 'have no intention whatever of taking advantage of their right to use the forces of the Crown to maintain law and order to crush political opposition to the policy or principles of the Home Rule Bill'. General Gough returned in triumph to the Curragh. 'All is the same as before,' the King wrote in his diary, 'so the danger for the moment is over.'

The Curragh incident none the less left behind it a sequence of unpleasant consequences. Abroad, it was taken as a sign that Great Britain would for some time be paralysed by mutiny and dissension. At home, it created the double suspicion that the Cabinet would always surrender to a determined minority and that, whatever assurances they might give in public, the Government had in fact planned to coerce Ulster by a rigorous blockade.[1] The Cabinet repudiated

'Repington incident'. Colonel Repington, on page 69 of volume I of his published diary, stated that Sir Edward Carson had informed him that the Government had decided to arrest the Ulster leaders and were only deterred by the King's personal intervention. When Lord Stamfordham made enquiries, Sir Edward Carson replied that he had never said anything of the sort. 'Repington', he wrote, 'is the limit!' (R.A. O.1631, 3). Colonel Repington thereupon agreed to delete the offending passage from subsequent editions. In 1921, at the time of the King's visit to Belfast, the *Daily Herald* revived the story that the King had intervened to prevent his Ministers from carrying out their intentions. An official denial was issued to the Press on July 15, 1921, above the signature of the Lord Chancellor as Keeper of the King's Conscience.

[1] In a two-page article entitled 'The Plot that Failed' *The Times* newspaper on April 27 contended that what the Government had really contemplated was 'a calculated scheme for the investment of Ulster by land and sea'. As evidence for this they cited the order issued to the 3rd Battle Squadron of eight battleships to concentrate at Lamlash in the Isle of Arran: the appointment of General Nevil Macready as C.-in-C. in Belfast with powers to establish martial law; and a speech by Mr Churchill

the specific assurances which had been given to General Gough by Colonel Seely and the latter, together with Sir John French and Sir Spencer Ewart, resigned. With commendable fortitude, Mr Asquith himself assumed the post of Secretary of State for War.

The Curragh incident was followed a month later by an exploit which convinced the public, the Government, and the Irish nationalists, that any attempt to coerce Ulster would entail a major operation of war. On the night of April 24–25 Sir Edward Carson's Volunteers were secretly mobilised and succeeded without interference in landing at Larne a consignment of 25,000 rifles and three million rounds of ammunition. The Cabinet decided that this audacious outrage must be punished by instant and effective action. They considered prosecuting Sir Edward Carson and his lieutenants for felony and treason and proclaiming the whole Ulster movement to be a treasonable conspiracy. Mr Redmond advised them against any such provocative reprisals. In the end they referred the matter to the Attorney-General for Ireland and no more was heard.

The King, as a result of these incidents, intensified his efforts to secure a settlement by consent. Already on April 7 he had written to the Prime Minister warning him that 'time was slipping away' and that prompt steps must be taken if a national calamity were to be averted. 'I have', he wrote, 'absolute confidence in your ability to bring about a peaceful solution whenever you put into force the great powers you possess.'⁰ On June 11 he again sought to encourage Mr Asquith to take a firmer and less dilatory line. He contended that the Prime Minister underrated his own powers and that 'if he put his foot down, both Mr Redmond and the Liberal Party would accept his terms'. Mr Asquith replied that His Majesty had formed too high an estimate of a Prime Minister's authority. 'But', he added, 'in the last moment I shall run any risk of self-sacrifice.'ᵖ

Meanwhile Mr Asquith resumed his private discussions with Mr Bonar Law and Sir Edward Carson, while concurrent and unofficial negotiations were held between Lord Rothermere, Lord Murray,

at Bradford on March 14 in which he said 'Let us go forward together and put these grave matters to the proof'.

It might be argued on the other hand that the Government were bound to take precautions to meet the possibility that Sir Edward Carson would proclaim a Provisional Government and that the ammunition depots would be raided. And that these precautions were cancelled, not because of the Curragh incident, but because the dangers they were planned to meet did not in fact materialise.

and Mr Redmond. By the end of June it seemed not impossible that an understanding could be reached for the exclusion of Ulster without a time limit or conditions, provided only that the two parties could agree as to the geographical boundaries of the new autonomous province. The issue was thus narrowed down to the question whether the counties of Fermanagh and Tyrone should or should not be incorporated in Ulster. It was agreed that the Home Rule Bill should become law, but that at the same time an Amending Bill should be introduced, by which the four or six Ulster counties should be excluded from its operation.

As early as May 1 the King had approached the Speaker and enquired whether, if the opportunity arose, he would be willing to preside at a conference between the several parties to the dispute. Mr Lowther assured His Majesty that he would be only too glad to be of assistance. On May 17 and again on June 19 the King urged the Prime Minister to take advantage of the Speaker's readiness. Mr Asquith on both occasions replied that the moment was not yet ripe. On July 17 the King received from the Prime Minister a letter stating that in his opinion the occasion for a conference had at last arrived:[q]

'An arrangement is not only possible, but practicable, in regard to Fermanagh, on the basis of the Nationalists giving up the city of Londonderry and the Unionists conceding South Armagh and the Catholic parts of South Down. But under present conditions, neither party is prepared to give way, in the sense of partition, in regard to the County of Tyrone.

'If the Amending Bill is brought up for debate on Monday in the House of Commons, neither the Government nor the Opposition, in view of the dominating opinion of their respective followers, can at the moment publicly offer any acceptable form of compromise.

'The probable, and indeed inevitable, course of the debate will be to accentuate and to emphasize differences; to elicit on both sides irreconcilable statements of policy and purpose; to bar the road to settlement; and to open the way to violent and regrettable action.

'It appears to Mr Asquith, after consultation with his colleagues, that it is his duty to advise Your Majesty, before the crisis becomes acute, to intervene with the object of securing a pacific accommodation.

'He has, therefore, the honour to propose that, before the debate opens, he should be authorised to answer that Your Majesty will invite the representatives of all parties concerned—both British and Irish—to a Conference to be held, under Your Majesty's auspices, at Buckingham Palace for a free and full discussion of the outstanding issues.

'It may be that such a Conference will be unable at the moment to attain a definitive settlement, but it will certainly postpone and may avert dangerous and possibly irreparable action, and in Mr Asquith's opinion it is not only within the competence, but at such a time part of the duty, of a Constitutional Sovereign to exert his authority in the best interests both of the United Kingdom and of the Empire.'

The King replied, cordially welcoming the Prime Minister's advice. 'It is', he wrote,ʳ 'a pleasure to me that the Conference will take place in my house, where I shall gladly welcome its members.' 'The Irish of both sections', Mr Asquith warned Lord Stamfordham,ˢ 'attach the greatest importance to their being summoned to the Conference by the King. Only so can they save their faces with their more extreme supporters.'

The conference was thus convened in the Forty-Four room at Buckingham Palace on July 21.[1] The King had prepared a speech of welcome, which he took the precaution of first submitting to the Prime Minister for his approval.[2] Having delivered his address, the King withdrew, leaving the Conference to its deliberations.

[1] The Government were represented by the Prime Minister and Mr Lloyd George, the Opposition by Mr Bonar Law and Lord Lansdowne, Ulster by Sir Edward Carson and Captain J. Craig, and the Irish Nationalists by Mr Redmond and Mr Dillon. The chair was taken by Mr James Lowther, Speaker of the House of Commons.

[2] The text of the King's speech was as follows:
'Gentlemen,

'It gives me infinite satisfaction to receive you here today, and I thank you for the manner in which you have responded to my summons. It is also a matter of congratulation that the Speaker has consented to preside over your deliberations.

'My intervention at this moment may be regarded as a new departure. But the exceptional circumstances under which you are brought together justify my action.

'For months we have watched with deep misgivings the course of events in Ireland. The trend has been surely and steadily towards an appeal to force, and today the cry of Civil War is on the lips of the most responsible and sober-minded of my people.

'We have in the past endeavoured to act as a civilising example to the world, and to me it is unthinkable, as it must be to you, that we should be brought to the brink of a fratricidal war upon issues apparently so capable of adjustment as those you are now asked to consider, if handled in a spirit of generous compromise.

'My apprehension in contemplating such a dire calamity is intensified by my feelings of attachment to Ireland and of sympathy for her people who have always welcomed me with warm-hearted affection.

'Gentlemen, you represent in one form or another the vast majority of

The conference held four meetings between July 21 and 24, but in spite of the desire of the leaders of the two English parties to reach some basis of agreement, neither Mr Redmond nor Sir Edward Carson could agree upon the geographical limits to be given to the term 'Ulster'. The conference broke down, essentially, upon the question of Fermanagh and Tyrone. On July 24 the Speaker addressed a short note to the King, informing him that the conference, 'being unable to agree, either in principle or in detail' upon the area to be excluded from the operation of the Home Rule Bill, had 'brought its meetings to a conclusion'. Before their departure from Buckingham Palace, the King received each of the representatives in private audience. Mr Redmond assured him that, once the Home Rule Bill was on the Statute Book, 'the Nationalist Party would be able to do many things to meet the views of Ulster which at present were impossible'.[1] The King was satisfied that the conference, in spite of its failure, had created 'a more friendly understanding'.[1]

While waiting in the anteroom at Buckingham Palace to say goodbye to the King, the Speaker picked up a copy of the evening paper. He read with astonishment and horror the terms of the Austrian ultimatum to Serbia.[u]

my subjects at home. You also have a deep interest in my Dominions over seas, who are scarcely less concerned in a prompt and friendly settlement of this question.

'I regard you then in this matter as trustees for the honour and peace of all.

'Your responsibilities are indeed great. The time is short. You will, I know, employ it to the fullest advantage and be patient, earnest, and conciliatory in view of the magnitude of the issues at stake. I pray that God in his infinite wisdom may guide your deliberations so that they may result in the joy of peace and settlement.'

[1] The Amending Bill, under which Ulster was to be excluded from the operation of the Home Rule Bill, was due for debate on July 31. In view of the European situation it was (with the consent of Mr Bonar Law, Mr Redmond and Sir Edward Carson) indefinitely postponed. On August 3, after Sir Edward Grey's speech, Mr Redmond assured the Government that they could safely withdraw all their troops from Ireland and that the Nationalist and Ulster volunteers would join forces to defend the island against any foreign invasion. The Home Rule Bill then passed through both Houses accompanied by a simultaneous Act providing that it should not come into force until after the war, the Government promising before then to bring in a Bill to regulate the position of Ulster. The King signed the Commission giving the Royal Assent to the 'Government of Ireland Bill' on the evening of September 17, 1914.

(4)

Mr Winston Churchill in a famous passage of his *World Crisis* has described how, on that evening of July 24, the Cabinet, having 'toiled for hours around the muddy byways of Fermanagh and Tyrone', were startled from their weariness by the quiet voice of Sir Edward Grey reading to them the text of this fatal ultimatum. The King, in common with the majority of his subjects, had been so deeply concerned with the menace of civil war in Ireland that his attention had been diverted from the even graver events which, since the assassination of the Archduke Franz Ferdinand at Sarajevo on June 28, had been accumulating on the continent of Europe. His first mention of the impending disaster occurs in his diary for Saturday, July 25:

> 'Had a long talk with Sir Edward Grey about Foreign Affairs. It looks as if we were on the verge of a general European war. Very serious state of affairs.'

This is not the place to chronicle the frantic efforts made during those last eleven days of peace to avert the avalanche which, shifting silently at first, acquired hour by hour an ever more thunderous and inescapable momentum. The occasions of a war are less instructive than its remoter causes. Enough has already been said to indicate that the relations between Great Britain and Germany, having settled down to an agreed if unformulated naval ratio, having survived the dangers of the Agadir crisis and the two Balkan wars, had since 1912 entered upon a more realistic and co-operative phase. It may be true, as Lord Haldane averred,[v] that had British statesmen since 1878 been less 'illiterate' about the spirit and traditions of the German people, they might have prevented Europe from being sundered into two armed camps. It may be true, as Professor Sidney Fay has commented, that war might have been averted had Sir Edward Grey been in the position (which he was not) either to tell Germany that Great Britain would certainly come in, or to tell France and Russia that she would certainly stand out. It may be true that, had William II been less emotionally shattered by this fresh blow dealt to the aged Austrian Emperor, he might, with his pacific instincts and with the aid of Herr von Bethmann-Hollweg, have succeeded before it was too late in curbing the recklessness of the Austrian Foreign Office and General Staff. But this is not the place to assess the comparative war-guilt of the four Great Powers. We are concerned only with the part played by King George during those relentless eleven days.

The King, as has been said, had striven with success to establish with the German Emperor relations of personal amity and trust. He had also been careful to cement, by every means in his power, the friendship between Great Britain and her two Entente partners. In April, accompanied by Sir Edward Grey, he had paid a state visit to Paris, when the warmth of his reception had impressed all observers. As recently as June 16 he had written a private letter to the Tsar of Russia, exhorting him to dissuade his Government from actions in Persia which could only put a strain upon Anglo-Russian co-operation.[w] His relations with Sir Edward Grey were of unclouded mutual confidence; the Cabinet knew that the King would support and further their policy in every word and deed. It was by a foolish mischance that certain words attributed to the King at the very height of the crisis should have been misreported to, or misinterpreted by, the German Emperor.

In the early morning of July 26 Prince Henry of Prussia, who had been yachting at Cowes, dashed in to Buckingham Palace to say goodbye on his return to Germany. On reaching Kiel on July 28 he wrote to his brother the Emperor a letter in which he quoted King George as saying 'We shall try all we can to keep out of this and shall remain neutral.' The Emperor interpreted this as an official assurance of England's neutrality and when Admiral von Tirpitz questioned the validity of such chance remarks, his Sovereign answered 'I have the word of a King and that is enough for me'.[x] On August 10, the Emperor, in a telegram to President Wilson, again asserted that he had received from King George an assurance of England's neutrality. The United States Ambassador in Berlin, Mr James Watson Gerard, repeated this assertion in his book *My Four Years in Germany*, which was serialised in the *Daily Telegraph* in 1917. Lord Stamfordham immediately issued a statement that the whole story was 'absolutely without foundation'.

Lord Stamfordham added that he had been unable to find among the King's papers, or in his diary, any detailed record of this conversation. The diary merely contains the sentence 'Henry of Prussia came to see me early: he returns at once to Germany'. But there does exist in the Royal Archives[y] a half sheet of notepaper on which the King recorded (possibly some time after the event) his own version of the interview:

'Prince Henry of Prussia came to see me on Sunday July 26 at 9.30 a.m. and asked me if there was any news. I said the news was very bad & it looked like a European war & that he better go back to Germany at once. He said he would go down to Eastbourne to see his sister (Queen of Greece) & he would return to Germany that evening. He then asked what England would do if there was a European war. I said 'I don't know what we shall do, we have no quarrel with anyone & I hope we shall remain neutral. But if Germany declared war on Russia, & France joins Russia, then I am afraid we shall be dragged into it. But you can be sure that I & my Government will do all we can to prevent a European war!' He then said—'Well, if our two countries shall be fighting on opposite sides, I trust that it will not affect our own personal friendship'. He then shook hands & left the room, having been with me about eight minutes.'

Prince Henry, in after years, himself admitted that, in the excitement of the moment, he may well have interpreted as a definite assurance what was no more than an incidental expression of an anxious hope.[1] The German Emperor's impulsive distortion of King George's words did not, however, affect the situation either one way or the other. The armies were already moving towards the frontiers: already the die had been cast.

From July 31 onwards the telegrams poured in upon Buckingham Palace. That evening a letter was brought from Paris by the hand of

[1] The story was revived in 1938 when Captain Erich von Müller (who had been a German Naval Attaché in London in 1914) wrote a letter to the *Deutsche Allgemeine Zeitung* to the effect that King George had unquestionably assured Prince Henry that England would remain neutral. Lord Wigram, thereupon, sent a letter to *The Times* newspaper refuting this statement. This evoked a letter to Lord Wigram from Dr Kurt Jagow, Archivist to the Hohenzollern family, expressing full agreement with Lord Wigram's denial. 'I know', wrote Dr Jagow, 'from personal knowledge of the statements made by the late Prince Henry that there can be no question of any promise on the part of His Majesty the King' (R.A. Q.251.5. 18). Dr Jagow then wrote for the *Berliner Monatshefte* of July 1938, an article disposing for ever of this legend. In this article he quoted a letter written by Prince Henry himself to the *Süddeutsche Zeitung* of December 11, 1921, in which he confessed that too much emphasis had been laid on the words 'remain neutral'. 'I later discovered', wrote Prince Henry, 'that it had been represented as a promise by the King to remain neutral—an interpretation which in no way corresponded to the facts and which I have myself contradicted.'

It should be noted also that Prince Lichnowsky, in his official report of the conversation of July 26, merely stated that King George had expressed to Prince Henry a desire that the crisis might be settled peaceably. It was the Naval Attaché in London, who in a telegram to the German Admiralty, mentioned the alleged promise of neutrality. Here again is an instance of the Emperor's regrettable tendency to ignore the reports of his Ambassadors and to attach undue credit to the supplementary reports of the Attachés. (See the Kautsky documents, vol. I, nos. 201 and 207.)

Monsieur William Martin in which the President of the French Republic urged the King that peace could only be preserved if Great Britain announced immediately that she was ready to enter the war on the side of the Entente. On August 1 came a telegram from the German Emperor, stating that he had just received 'the communication from your Government offering French neutrality under the guarantee of Great Britain'. He assured the King that he would refrain from attacking France if she offered her neutrality and if that neutrality were 'guaranteed by the British Fleet and Army'.[z] The reply to this fantastic proposal was drafted in pencil on a scrap of notepaper by the Foreign Secretary. 'I think', the King answered, 'there must be some misunderstanding of a suggestion that passed in friendly conversation between Prince Lichnowsky and Sir Edward Grey.'[za] In those harried days there were many such misunderstandings and cross-purposes. On August 3 came a telegram from the King of the Belgians making a 'supreme appeal' for the intervention of the British Government to safeguard Belgium's neutrality.[zb] The King—'paralysed', as Monsieur Poincaré observed,[zc] 'by constitutional rules'—could only reply to these appeals in terms of the most conventional sympathy. On the afternoon of August 3 Sir Edward Grey made his decisive speech in the House of Commons. From that hour, the whirlwind of clashing doubts subsided: England, after a moment of hushed awe, faced with excitement the certainty of battle:

> 'Tuesday August 4th. I held a Council at 10.45. to declare war with Germany. It is a terrible catastrophe, but it is not our fault. An enormous crowd collected outside the Palace; we went on the balcony both before & after dinner. When they heard that war had been declared, the excitement increased & May & I with David went on to the balcony; the cheering was terrific. Please God it may soon be over & that he will protect dear Bertie's life. Bed at 12.0.'

Two days later, the United States Ambassador was received in audience. The King raised his hands in anguished despair: 'My God, Mr Page, what else could we do?'

CHAPTER XVI

THE KING AND THE WAR

1914-1915

With the outbreak of war, the King is relieved of central responsibility—
The condition of public opinion in 1914—The King's equable
attitude—The agitation regarding Garter banners and enemy
Princes—Prince Louis of Battenberg—The King objects to the
appointment of Lord Fisher as First Sea Lord—Reviews and inspec-
tions—Prince Albert and the Prince of Wales—The King's concern
with conscientious objectors and enemy prisoners—The Royal
Assent given to the Home Rule Bill—The King and the Navy—
The retreat from Mons—Lord Kitchener—The Munitions shortage
—'The King's Pledge'—The 'Shell Scandal'—The Dardanelles—
Resignation of Lord Fisher—The First Coalition Government—
Lord Haldane.

(1)

IN dealing with the first four years of King George's reign it has been
possible, without falsification of perspective, to describe from the
Sovereign's own point of view the conflict between Lords and Commons and the long-drawn struggle for Home Rule. These two controversies, in that they directly affected the Royal Prerogative and
the duties of a Constitutional Monarch, placed the King in a central
position. With the outbreak of war he was relieved of central
responsibility. The biographer is thus at this stage faced with a problem of composition. If he seeks to describe the war, then his principal
figure will immediately fade away into the clouds of battle. If, on the
other hand, he attempts to depict the King as a symbolic leader,
raising his baton against a background of fleets and armies, then the
focus of the picture will be incorrect. The contrast, moreover, between the most arduous activities of even the most eminent non-
combatant, and the endurance of those who fought on land, at sea
and in the air, in itself raises problems of proportion and taste. It
has been thought preferable, therefore, in the chapters covering the
war, to· avoid military narrative and to endeavour, by a series of
disconnected illustrations, to suggest answers to the simple question:
'How, during those four dark years, was the King's influence
brought to bear?'

The position of a Constitutional Monarch, in times of national

248

strain and indignation, may become invidious. Although possessing no executive powers, he is credited by his people with supreme responsibility. Being the sole representative of the Nation as a whole, he may be expected, and even tempted, to voice, not merely the will and virtue of his subjects, but also their momentary moods and passions. Public opinion, it must be recalled, was less stable in the first than in the second war. The civilian population, faced as they were with the unprecedented horror of a major catastrophe, did not in 1914 display the same patience, charity, confidence or sense of proportion as were so stolidly manifested by their successors of 1939. In all wars rumours ramp and individuals are unjustly maligned; but the suspiciousness, credulity and inequity of the civilians during the first war were in excess of any similar emotions provoked by the even greater and more immediate perils of 1940.

In private conversation King George was not wont to hide or understate his views; the language that he employed had about it the tang and exuberance of the salt sea waves. Yet in his public utterances he was scrupulous in avoiding anything discordant with the dignity of his office or out of harmony with what he believed to be the essential equity of the British character. His popularity grew from the fact that he never courted it; that he never allowed himself to be deflected by the transient gusts of public agitation from what, in his unsophisticated fashion, he felt to be just or unjust, right or wrong. His subjects recognised, when the skies had cleared, that throughout the storm he had represented and enhanced those equable qualities which they had assumed to be so indigenous; and had lost awhile.

King George was not either pro-French, pro-Russian, or pro-German: he was undeviatingly pro-British. But it did not occur to him that the Germans, having become our enemies overnight, had suddenly ceased to be human; nor did he share the hysteria which, from August 1914 onwards, induced so many of his subjects to abandon their reason, their dignity, and their sense of fair play.

Five days after the outbreak of hostilities, the King was surprised to receive from the War Office a proposal that the German Emperor and his son should publicly be deprived of their honorary commands of British regiments. He answered that their names should remain in the Army List until they themselves resigned. Lord Roberts was then brought in to persuade him to reconsider this decision. He finally agreed that the names should quietly be dropped from the next edition of the Army List, but he refused to issue any public notice to that effect.[a] A delirious agitation then arose in regard to the presence

249

in St. George's Chapel at Windsor of the Garter banners of enemy Emperors, Kings and Princes. The King held the view that these banners, which were symbols of past history, should remain above the stalls 'at all events until after the war, when there may be other developments'. The matter was ventilated in the public prints and it was even suggested that the Chapel should be raided by patriots and the banners torn down by force. On the advice of the Prime Minister a notice was issued on May 13, 1915, to the effect that the names of the eight enemy Knights of the Garter had been struck off the roll of the Order. On the same day the banners were quietly removed. The King insisted, however, that the brass plates bearing the names and titles of these foreign potentates should remain affixed to their stalls. 'They are', Lord Stamfordham wrote to the Dean of Windsor, 'historical records and His Majesty does not intend to have any of them removed.' *b* 'The King', he explained, 'was not inspired by a desire for any dramatic action and, had it not been for a somewhat hysterical clamour headed by Mr Bottomley in the columns of *John Bull* and by the *Daily Mail* for the instant removal of the banners, they would probably by the King's orders have been in due course unostentatiously taken down.'

An agitation then arose regarding the position of those foreign Princes who were still technically members of the British Royal House. Questions were asked in the House of Commons. The King held the view that such matters were 'too petty and undignified' to occupy the attention of Parliament at the outset of a dangerous war. Mr Asquith felt however that the clamour thus artificially instigated must in some manner be allayed. He appointed a committee of the House of Lords, under the chairmanship of Lord Bryce, to investigate the position of these foreign Princes. The agitation then subsided: but it had occasioned harm.[1]

More important in their consequences, and much more painful to the King, were the attacks made in the *Globe* and other newspapers upon Prince Louis of Battenberg, the First Sea Lord. It was with deep regret that Mr Winston Churchill, First Lord of the

[1] The report of the Bryce Committee led to the introduction of the Titles Deprivation Act of 1917. This Act provided that a Committee of the Privy Council should make recommendations which should become law after lying on the tables of both Houses for forty days. The Committee did not table its recommendations until August 1918 when they recorded that the Duke of Cumberland, the Duke of Brunswick and Viscount Taaffe (Baron of Ballymote) had adhered to the King's enemies. They were deprived of their titles by Order in Council dated March 1919.

Admiralty, was obliged to accept the resignation of this gifted sailor. The mortification felt by Mr Churchill at having thus to surrender to popular clamour, was in later years mitigated by the fact that he was able, during the second war, to provide Prince Louis' son, Lord Mountbatten, with opportunities for high achievement. At the time, the necessity was insuperable and harsh; it also raised in urgent form the problem of Prince Louis' successor. The King was obliged to condone what amounted to the dismissal of a man whose capacity and character he much admired. He was at the same time constrained to assent to the appointment as Prince Louis' successor of a veteran admiral in whose judgement he placed little reliance. The anxiety caused to him by this episode is reflected in his diary:

'*October 29, 1914*. Spent a most worrying and trying day. . . . At 11.30 saw Winston Churchill who informed me that Louis of Battenberg had resigned his appt. as 1st Sea Lord. The Press & Public have said so many things against him being born a German, & that he ought not to be at the head of the Navy, that it was best for him to go. I feel deeply for him: there is no more loyal man in the Country.

Churchill then proposed that Lord Fisher shd. succeed him as 1st Sea Lord. I did all I could to prevent it & told him he was not trusted by the Navy & they had no confidence in him personally. I think it is a great mistake & he is 74. At the end I had to give in with great reluctance. . . .

At 3.15. I saw the Prime Minister. I used the same arguments as I had to Churchill with regard to Fisher, but had to approve. At 4.0 I saw poor Louis, very painful interview, he quite broke down. I told him I would make him a Privy Councillor to show the confidence I had in him, which pleased him.

October 30. Received Lord Fisher (whom I had not met for six years) on his appt. as 1st Sea Lord. He is now 74. He seems as young as ever. I only trust he will do well at Admiralty.'

A more extended account of this episode is contained in a Memorandum by Lord Stamfordham.*c* The King appealed to the Prime Minister to prevent the appointment of Lord Fisher:

'His Majesty knew the Navy and considered that the Service distrusts Lord Fisher & that the announcement of the proposed appointment would give a shock to the Navy which no one could wish to cause in the middle of this great war. It was also stated that Lord Fisher had aged. He talked & wrote much, but his opinions changed from day to day. Mr. Asquith said that he had never heard this before.

The Prime Minister replied that he gathered from the First Lord that there was no one else suitable for the post. The Board was weak and incapable of initiative; the Navy had not fulfilled the hopes & expectations of the Country; anything that *had* been done was due to

Mr. Churchill. Mr. Asquith believed that Lord Fisher's appointment would be welcomed by public opinion. . . .

The King declared . . . that he could not oppose his Ministers in this selection, but felt it his duty to record his protest. The Prime Minister rejoined: "Perhaps a less severe term,—'misgivings',—might be used by Your Majesty".'

Later in the day the King signed the appointment and at the same time wrote as follows to Mr Asquith:

Buckingham Palace,
October 29, 1914.

'Dear Prime Minister,

Following our conversation this afternoon, I should like to note that, while approving the proposed appointment of Lord Fisher as First Sea Lord, I do so with some reluctance and misgivings. I readily acknowledge his great ability and administrative powers, but at the same time I cannot help feeling that his presence at the Admiralty will not inspire the Navy with that confidence which ought to exist, especially when we are engaged in so momentous a war. I hope that my fears may prove groundless.'

(2)

The King's tasks and duties as leader of an Empire at war were manifold and incessant. The general public were not informed of the ceaseless routine of labour that he underwent, since the censor rightly prohibited any undue references to his inspections and journeys. But the soldiers in training, the soldiers at the front, the sailors at Scapa Flow, Rosyth, Invergordon, Harwich and Dover, above all perhaps the workers in the munition factories, were aware of his constant presence among them, and came to welcome his animating confidence and the cheerful vigour of his discourse. It would be wearisome to catalogue in detail all the routine duties which during the war absorbed so much of the King's energies. A summary will suffice. During the fifty-one months that the war lasted he paid seven visits to the Grand Fleet or to the subsidiary naval bases; on five separate occasions he spent several days with the armies in France; he held 450 inspections, visited 300 hospitals and personally conferred some 50,000 decorations. He undertook repeated tours of the industrial areas and scarcely a month passed in which he failed to visit some munition factory. When the bombing started he would drive down to the damaged areas and talk to the injured in the wards. No previous Monarch had entered into such close personal relations with so many of his subjects.

We realise today that the First German War was divided into

three periods of most unequal length. There were the first forty days of dangerous and rapid movement: these were succeeded by four sanguinary years of deadlock; and then in August 1918 came the final rush of unimagined victory. At the time it all seemed an unbroken monotone of strain and apprehension, lightened at moments by a few fleeting rays of success, but more often darkened by recurrent disappointment and misfortune. King George did not possess a sanguine disposition; he was not the type of man who derives elation from the glamour or excitement of war; he was acutely sensitive to the squalor and wastage of battle and to the atrocious human suffering that it involves. 'He feels profoundly', wrote Lord Esher,[d] 'every pang that war can inflict.' Within the first few weeks three members of his personal household (Lord Crichton, Lord John Hamilton and Lord Charles Fitzmaurice) were killed; at a later date Lord Stamfordham lost his only son; the casualty lists as they lengthened were scanned with anguish and left a weight of sadness in his mind.

His two elder sons were already old enough to serve in the armed forces. Prince Albert was a midshipman (later a sub-lieutenant) in H.M.S. *Collingwood* of the First Battle Squadron. Although for some months he was absent on sick leave, owing to complications arising from an operation for appendicitis, he recovered in time to take part in the Battle of Jutland, an experience which he much enjoyed. The Prince of Wales presented a more complex problem. He served successively as A.D.C. on the personal staff of the Commander in Chief in France, as Staff Captain to the General Officer Commanding the Mediterranean Expeditionary Force, and as General Staff Officer to Lord Cavan in Italy. Lord Kitchener, with his accustomed bluntness, intimated to the Prince that, although it would not matter very much if he were killed or wounded, it would be extremely embarrassing if he were taken prisoner. The officers responsible for the Prince's safety were distressed by the ingenuity with which he would evade their vigilance. 'The risks', one of them reported to Lord Stamfordham, 'will be accentuated by H.R.H.'s enthusiasm.' Their anxieties were not unfounded. In September 1915 Lord Cavan, then commanding the Guards Division, reported to the King[e] that the Prince had accompanied him on an inspection of the battle front at Vermelles. They had left their cars under cover and walked to the trenches. The Germans had taken the occasion to plaster that sector with shrapnel. On their return to the cars they found them riddled with holes and the Prince's driver dead.

The King sympathised with his eldest son's desire to visit the trenches, but he also understood the added anxiety which his presence might give to those responsible:

> 'The King', wrote Lord Stamfordham to Lord Cavan⸍ 'entirely agrees to the understanding that when the Prince goes up to the front under instruction neither you nor Gathorne Hardy will be held responsible for his personal safety. His Majesty realizes that Gathorne Hardy[1] himself, acting in the spirit of the C. in C's orders, will run no unnecessary risks, but of course risks there must be. We can only hope and pray that all will be well and His Majesty feels that this change will be good for the Prince and also that his occasional presence forward will be appreciated by the men.'

During the whole course of the war the King was kept very fully informed of events and problems on the home and battle fronts. Not only did he receive the regular minutes of the Cabinet and War Councils, not only was he in constant touch with Ministers, but the Commanders and their subordinates in the field would provide him with frequent personal information, and in addition there were the confidential reports addressed to him by the Viceroy, the Governors General overseas and the Ambassadors and Ministers at foreign capitals. His naval friends would write him long private letters, in which they described their experiences and not infrequently voiced their anxieties or complaints. He would read these voluminous documents with scrupulous care. 'The King's knowledge', recorded Lord Esher⸢ 'of all the details of what goes on is remarkable, and he never seems to forget anything that he is told.' It was a relief for the military and naval commanders to be able, without incurring the reproach of professional disloyalty or political intrigue, thus to confide in the Head of their own Services, whose experience was akin to their own, whose judgement dependable, whose discretion absolute, and whose influence great.

Apart from the official and semi-official papers which would reach him almost hourly in their neat red boxes, the King was deluged by a flood of private correspondence. His loyal subjects appear to have regarded him both as the arbiter of justice and the vehicle of bright ideas. He would receive letters, from responsible as well as irresponsible quarters, discoursing upon such varied themes as the administration of the National Relief Fund, the bad relations

---

[1] The Hon. Frank Gathorne-Hardy, Grenadier Guards, was a General Staff Officer at G.H.Q. He was promoted Brigadier, General Staff, on January 3, 1916.

existing between the Red Cross and the Royal Army Medical Corps, the alleged pro-German utterances of the Head Master of Eton, the conduct of the Australian troops in Cairo, the visits of society ladies and other tourists to Head Quarters in France, the efficiency of gas masks, the prices charged to our troops by French civilians, the iniquity of the blockade, the cowardice of the Foreign Office, the bombing of Belgian towns, or the preferential exchange of individual prisoners.

The King would in general instruct his secretaries to pass these letters on without comment to the Department concerned. Yet he took personal pains to investigate cases of alleged unfairness. 'One feels now,' wrote Lord Stamfordham to Lord Esher,[h] 'more than ever, that if an injustice is done, or likely to be done, to an Officer in the Army, His Majesty is the proper person to look into the subject.' He was constantly concerned with the treatment of prisoners of war, whether in England or Germany.

> 'His Majesty', wrote Lord Stamfordham to Lord Kitchener on November 14, 1914[i] 'feels certain that you will agree that we should endeavour to extend such treatment to the German officers who are our prisoners of war as will compare favourably with that received by our officers now interned in Germany. Indeed, the King would like to think that when this war is over it would be truly said that we had shown the example in generous and magnanimous consideration of our prisoners of war.'

Sometimes, on his own initiative, the King would make suggestions to Ministers. He would write to the Home Secretary about the treatment of enemy aliens and conscientious objectors. When he heard that the latter were being interned at Dartmoor he commanded Lord Stamfordham to state that 'His Majesty feels that their new condition of life will not be very different from that of imprisonment'.[j] He suggested at an early stage of the munitions shortage that a larger number of women might be employed in the manufacture of shells and that Mrs Pankhurst might be found useful as a recruiting agent. He suggested that in winter the men at the front might be provided with white coats when no man's land was deep in snow. He would write to the Commander in Chief enquiring whether religious services were adequately provided for the Indian troops or suggesting that he should have a few Dominions Officers attached to his staff. He addressed frequent enquiries to the War Office and the Ministry of Munitions as to the progress of the Stokes Gun or the Tanks. His most useful function, he felt, was not to inflict upon Ministers or commanders his own views of policy or strategy, but, with constant vigilance, to 'advise, to encourage and to warn'.

(3)

The declaration of war imposed a temporary lull in party strife. The expected split in the Liberal Government did not occur; Lord Morley, John Burns and Charles Trevelyan were the only three Ministers to resign. On August 5 Mr John Redmond had assured the House of Commons that England could withdraw every man and gun from Ireland, since the Irish in cooperation with the Ulster volunteers, would themselves defend their coasts against the enemy. Mr Asquith was so encouraged by Mr Redmond's gesture that he believed that the gap left by the Buckingham Palace Conference might now be bridged. The Unionists insisted however that the Home Rule Bill must be postponed until the end of the war. 'The King', record Mr Asquith's biographers,[k] 'again offered his services to procure accommodation and commented with some severity upon the obstinacy of politicians who prolonged these recriminations in a time of national crisis.' The Prime Minister felt obliged to place the Home Rule Bill upon the statute book, accompanying it with assurances to Ulster and a pledge that Home Rule would not come into operation while the war lasted. The Unionists represented this action as a breach of his pledge not to introduce controversial legislation in war-time. In spite of their indignation, the Royal Assent was given to the Home Rule Bill on September 17, 1914.

Meanwhile the King had been much encouraged by the instantaneous offers of help received from the Dominions and India. The Viceroy had assured him that there was 'no cause for anxiety anywhere'. 'In fact,' wrote Lord Hardinge[l] 'a wave of loyalty has been spread throughout the land and everybody is vying with each other to help England in this emergency.'

The Fleet, after the test mobilisation of July, had, thanks to Mr Churchill's audacious initiative, been kept in being. On the night of July 29–30 the whole Navy passed silently and with darkened lights through the Straits of Dover and by the next day had reached their battle stations facing Germany. The Grand Fleet, under the command of Sir John Jellicoe,[1] was stationed in the northern

---

[1] The Board of Admiralty, on August 2, had appointed Sir John Jellicoe to succeed Sir George Callaghan, whose health was deemed

approaches, the battleships at Scapa Flow and Cromarty, the battle cruisers at Rosyth. On August 5 the King addressed the following signal to Sir John Jellicoe:

'At this grave moment of our national history I send to you, and through you to the officers and men of the Fleets of which you have assumed command, the assurance of my confidence that, under your direction, they will revive and renew the old glories of the Royal Navy and prove once again the sure shield of Britain and of her Empire in the hour of trial.'

A series of misfortunes followed. On August 10 the German battle cruiser *Goeben*, accompanied by the light cruiser *Breslau*, having evaded the vigilance of our admirals, steamed almost unmolested into the Dardanelles and thereby determined Turkey's entry into the war against us. On September 21 the three cruisers *Hogue, Cressy* and *Aboukir*, were sunk by U-boat 49 and on October 27 it was learnt that the super-dreadnought *Audacious* had struck a mine and foundered off Lough Swilly. On November 1 Rear Admiral Sir Christopher Craddock (who but a few weeks before had written to the King: 'I know, Sir, you will grant us latitude. In time we *must* succeed' *m*) encountered off Coronel a superior German squadron under Vice-Admiral Graf von Spee and the *Monmouth* and the *Good Hope* were sunk with all hands. It was not until December 8 that this defeat was avenged by Vice Admiral Sir Doveton Sturdee's victory of the Falkland Islands. Yet the effect on British opinion of that decisive action, which in fact cleared the seven seas of all German detached squadrons, was damped by the German raid on the Yorkshire coast on December 16:

'Yesterday morning,' the King wrote indignantly in his diary, 'four large German cruisers, it being foggy, appeared off the east coast of Yorkshire about 8.0 o'clock, & shelled Hartlepool & Scarborough for 40 minutes, doing considerable damage, killing about 40 women, children & civilians and maiming & wounding about 400. This is German *kultur*.'

The British public, who had assumed that our Fleets would be immediately victorious everywhere, were disconcerted by these misfortunes. They did not understand the nature of modern sea-power

---

unequal to the impending task. The King and Mr. Churchill both felt extremely sorry for Admiral Callaghan, 'Received Sir George Callaghan,' the King wrote in his diary for August 10, 'a painful interview, as he has just been superseded by Jellicoe in command of the Home Fleet, as he is considered too old (62) & not equal to the strain. I think he has been very badly treated.'

or realise that it was the slow stranglehold which the Navy obtained over Germany that more than any other factor won the war. The King, whose devotion to his old profession was passionate and even blind, was distressed by these misconceptions. Yet by the end of 1914 the war at sea had become comparatively stabilised. The German High Seas Fleet remained behind the protection of their minefields; their excursions thereafter were short and rare.

Between August 12 and August 17 the British Expeditionary Force of five divisions had been safely transported to France. On August 24 at Mons our armies encountered the first full impact of the enemy. 'It was', writes Sir Duff Cooper,[n] 'nothing less than the clenched fist of the huge German Army that struck the five divisions of the Expeditionary Force full in the face.' The retreat began. Within the space of thirteen days, our troops, fighting continual rearguard actions, retired a distance of one hundred and sixty miles.

Lord Kitchener, when on the point of returning to Egypt, had been hastily recalled to London and appointed Secretary of State for War. He was much perturbed by the reports received from Sir John French, the Commander in Chief.[1] 'I do not', he wrote to Lord Stamfordham on August 25,[o] 'like these retirements. Unless Joffre can take the offensive, the left flank may be badly turned before we can act effectively.' On August 30 Sir John French, writing from Compiègne, informed Lord Kitchener that he proposed to withdraw the British armies behind the Seine, leaving Paris on his right flank. The Cabinet, realising that this further retreat would create a perilous gap between the British and French armies, sent Lord Kitchener to France with instructions to persuade the Commander in Chief to remain in the battle line. The interview between the two soldiers took place in the British Embassy in Paris. Lord Kitchener succeeded in convincing Sir John French that it was essential for him to maintain contact with his allies. This interview, although it contributed substantially to the victory of the Marne, did not improve the personal relations between the Commander in Chief (who was of

[1] Sir John French (1852–1925) had commanded the Cavalry Division in the South African War and acquired fame owing to his relief of Kimberley and capture of Bloemfontein. He was Chief of the Imperial General Staff 1912–1914 and appointed Commander in Chief of the Expeditionary Force in August 1914. On his resignation in December 1915 he was raised to the peerage as Viscount French of Ypres. Until May 1918 he was C. in C. Home Forces and then became Lord Lieutenant of Ireland. He resigned in 1921 and was given an earldom.

a sensitive disposition)[1] and the Secretary of State for War. The King, whose confidence in Lord Kitchener was greater than that which he reposed in Sir John French, was, in the months that followed, much concerned with this divergence.

Meanwhile Russian armies under Rennenkampf and Samsonov had invaded East Prussia. Although by August 30 these armies had been annihilated by Hindenburg and Ludendorff at the battle of Tannenberg, the German High Command had been so alarmed by the invasion that they had withdrawn two army corps from the Western front. General von Kluck, commanding the First German Army, hoping by a rapid lunge to separate and destroy the French and British, wheeled prematurely inwards and exposed his flank. General Joffre, much assisted by the intuition of General Galliéni, was quick to detect this error. On the morning of September 5 he decided that the retreat should go no further and that the French and British armies should assume the offensive on the following day. 'The terrible period of retirement is ended,' wrote Sir John French to the King on September 5,[p] 'and an advance, in which we must in a day or two battle with the enemy on a very large scale, begins at day-break tomorrow.'

The victory of the Marne was 'not a miracle, but a brilliant advantage snatched from the enemy's errors'.[q] It destroyed all German hopes of reaching a quick decision in the west. Thereafter came the Aisne, the first Battle of Ypres and what is known as 'the rush to the sea'. 'The Battle of the Aisne', Sir John French wrote to the King on October 2,[r] 'is very typical of what battles in the future are most likely to resemble. Siege operations will enter largely into tactical problems and the spade will be as great a necessity as the rifle.' This was an understatement. Already by September 14, 1914, the four years of trench deadlock had begun.

(4)

During his first visit to the front in December 1914 the King held long conversations with President Poincaré, 'who made himself most agreeable & is very optimistic about the war, as are Generals Joffre & French'. King George did not share this optimism. He had been

---

[1] 'He is', wrote Lord Esher to Lord Stamfordham in December 1916 (*Journals and Letters of Lord Esher*, Vol. IV, page 79), 'not an intriguer, but just a passionate little man with, as you say, hot temper and uncontrolled feelings. Anyone can work him up into a sort of mad suspicion, so that he falls an easy prey to the people around him.'

warned by Lord Kitchener, whose word he trusted, that the war was bound to last for several years. The Secretary of State for War had realised from the outset that the plan devised by the Committee of Imperial Defence and elaborated in exact detail by Lord Haldane would prove inadequate for the necessities of a prolonged continental campaign. He immediately set himself to the task of creating a British Army of seventy divisions, the maximum strength of which, he calculated, would be reached in the third year of war. Three million men responded to his appeal for volunteers:

> 'No one but Lord Kitchener', wrote Sir Edward Grey in retrospect,[s] 'measured the dimensions of the war with such prescience. . . . Without that contribution, the war might have been lost, or victory rendered impossible.'

The efficacy of Lord Kitchener's genius was diminished by certain defects of experience and temperament. He had been so used to reserve for himself the sole decision in administrative matters that he did not understand the division of departmental responsibility or even the delegation of business. When expounding in Cabinet his plans or policy he adopted so stilted a posture that he conveyed the impression (and it was not always a false impression) that he distrusted the discretion of his colleagues and was withholding essential facts. Nor was he receptive of new ideas. 'Move his mind', wrote Lord Haldane,[t] 'on to modern lines I could not.' His colleagues in Cabinet were at first overawed by the magnificence of Lord Kitchener's appearance and by the glamour of his public prestige. He was in truth a formidable figure. His vast stature, the slow congested movements of his body, face and mind, suggested an enormous and resplendent monolith. Even the least impressionable of Ministers could be cowed by the stare of affronted anger, or incomprehension, in those blue but disparate eyes. 'The members of the Cabinet', Mr Lloyd George has admitted, 'were frankly intimidated by his presence.' [u]

It was only gradually that Lord Kitchener's dominance declined. His colleagues became increasingly irritated by his refusals to explain his departmental brief. He possessed no gift for exposition or argument. 'Neither his words nor his pen', writes his official biographer,[v] 'were a rapid or wholly effective vehicle for his thoughts.'

Only with the King and the Prime Minister did Lord Kitchener feel wholly at his ease. Mr Asquith, who did not place garrulity among the highest of human endowments, welcomed his inarticulate stolidity. The King, who had known Lord Kitchener for thirty years, regarded him with affection and esteem. He created him a Knight of the Garter and placed York House at his disposal as a private residence. 'The King', Lord Esher recorded,*ʷ* 'said that whatever happened he meant to support Lord K. . . . He complained only of one fault in the Secretary of State for War. It was that Lord K. was so voluble that he, the King, could never get a word in edgeways.' A more intimate tribute to the relations of mutual trust existing between them is contained in a letter written to the King by Sir George Arthur a few days only after Lord Kitchener's death:*ˣ*

> 'How often Sir George Arthur has heard Lord Kitchener say that the King's unstinted and unswerving support enabled him (and perhaps alone enabled him) to carry into being the vast military scheme of which the fulfilment was accomplished the very day on which the wise and faithful servant of the King was called home.'

On March 13, 1915, after the battle of Neuve Chapelle, Sir John French reported that his armies were short of shells, especially of high explosives.[1] The Prime Minister decided, in spite of Lord Kitchener's objections, to constitute a Munitions of War Committee under the chairmanship of Mr Lloyd George. Into this new channel the Chancellor of the Exchequer diverted the cataract of his stupendous energy. For the moment he was unable to do much more than place advance orders and plan for future expansion; the full effect of his vitality and vision was not felt until the following May, when he was appointed Minister of Munitions in the Coalition Government.

One of Mr Lloyd George's first preoccupations was the condition of Labour. He was particularly distressed by the suggestion that full employment and high wages were leading to increased drinking among the working classes. The French and Russians had prohibited the sale of absinthe and vodka. Why should not we make an even more glorious gesture by imposing total prohibition? What was needed was a dramatic example. Who more fit to set this example than the King himself?

Mr Lloyd George, when in crusading mood, was irresistible. On March 29, 1915, he bustled into the King's audience room, his little arms swinging with excitement, his eyes flashing flame, his lower lip protruding with scorn of those who drank. The King was affected by

[1] In the whole of the South African War 273,000 rounds had been fired. One million rounds were expended in the first six months of the 1914–1918 war. By November 1916 the consumption rose to 1,120,000 a week.

his enthusiasm. The next morning he instructed Lord Stamfordham to write to Mr Lloyd George:[y]

> 'His Majesty feels that nothing but the most vigorous measures will successfully cope with the grave situation now existing in our Armament factories. . . . If it be deemed advisable, the King will be prepared to set an example by giving up all alcoholic liquor himself and issuing orders against its consumption in the Royal Household, so that no difference shall be made, so far as His Majesty is concerned, between the treatment of rich and poor in this question.'

Mr Lloyd George replied the same day, stating that the Cabinet had been much gratified by the King's offer and adding that if His Majesty's resolve could be made public he was certain that 'all classes would hasten to follow the lead thus given by the Sovereign'.[z] A notice was therefore published that as from April 6 no alcohol would be absorbed by the Royal Family or Household:

> 'This morning,' the King wrote in his diary, 'we have all become teetotallers until the end of the war. I have done it as an example, as there is a lot of drinking going on in the country. I hate doing it, but hope it will do good.'

The 'King's Pledge', as it came to be called, did not arouse the response which Mr Lloyd George anticipated. Very few of his subjects followed his example; the House of Commons rejected with sturdy indignation any suggestion of teetotalism. Mr Lloyd George's crusade left His Majesty and his Household high and dry.[1]

(5)

On May 9, 1915 Sir John French had watched the abortive battle of Festubert from the top of a ruined church tower and had decided then and there to launch a 'shell shortage' campaign.[z,a] He invited the assistance of Colonel Repington, the military correspondent of *The Times*, and despatched to London a secretary and an aide de camp with instructions to inform and incite Lord Northcliffe and certain members of the Opposition. On May 21, in the *Daily Mail*, there appeared a leading article under the headlines 'The Tragedy of the Shells. Lord Kitchener's Grave Error'. The Prime

---

[1] After the King's serious accident at the front in October 1915, his doctors insisted that the pledge should at least temporarily be suspended. A bulletin was issued above the signatures of Sir Frederick Treves and Sir Bertrand Dawson informing the public that it was 'necessary on medical grounds that the King should take a little stimulant daily during his convalescence. As soon as the King's health is quite restored, His Majesty will resume the total abstinence which he has imposed upon himself for public reasons'.

Minister could not remain indifferent to this campaign against Lord Kitchener, since he was well aware that the shortage of munitions would be exploited by the Unionist Party with devastating effect. His administration had moreover been shaken by other misadventures.

The naval attack on the Dardanelles had been broken off on the evening of March 18, 1915. The Turks, as is now known, had by then almost run out of ammunition; had the attack been resumed on March 19, it might well have succeeded. "Not to persevere,' commented Mr Churchill, 'that was the crime.' *z,b* Meanwhile Lord Kitchener had reluctantly agreed to send troops under Sir Ian Hamilton to occupy the Gallipoli peninsula. The Turks, under the able direction of Liman von Sanders, exploited the pause that followed. Thus when the troops eventually landed on April 25 they were faced with what Sir Ian Hamilton described as 'a regular Gibraltar'. They failed to reach their objectives and here again a long period of trench deadlock settled in.

Lord Fisher, in the War Council, had adopted a sphinx-like attitude towards the Dardanelles operations. He contended later that he had considered it improper to contradict the First Lord in the presence of his colleagues. So soon as the landings had proved abortive, he decided to disengage his responsibility. On May 15, on a minor issue, he sent in his resignation and informed Mr Churchill that he was leaving at once for Scotland. The Prime Minister then conveyed to him a letter, summoning him 'in the King's name' to return to his post. Lord Fisher replied by tabulating the conditions on which he would consent to withdraw his resignation. He demanded, among other things, 'complete professional charge of the war at sea, together with absolute sole disposition of the Fleet and the appointment of all Officers of all ranks whatsoever and absolutely untrammelled command of all the sea forces whatsoever'. In communicating this paper to the King, Mr Asquith remarked that it 'indicated signs of mental aberration'.*z,c* Lord Fisher's resignation was accepted on May 22.

The King was shocked by Lord Fisher's attitude and by the abrupt abandonment of his post at a moment when it was believed that the German Fleet was about to put to sea. He was in no sense mollified by the excited explanations which Lord Fisher thereafter addressed to him from his retreat in Scotland. Meanwhile Mr Asquith had been informed by Mr Bonar Law that the Opposition intended to raise the question of Lord Fisher's resignation in the

House of Commons. The Liberal Government might have resisted the 'shell scandal' and the crisis at the Admiralty if these strains had occurred separately; coming together, they were more than any administration could withstand. On May 17 Mr Asquith informed Lord Stamfordham that he had come to the conclusion that the Government must be 'reconstructed on a broad and non-party basis'. On May 22 the King saw the Prime Minister and urged him, when forming his new Cabinet, to create a separate Ministry of Munitions under Mr Lloyd George and thus relieve Lord Kitchener 'of all work and responsibility in regard to ammunition'.[z.d] On the evening of May 24 Mr Asquith was able to submit to the King the names of the First Coalition Government.[1]

> 'There were', wrote Mr Asquith in after years,[z.e] 'two concessions of a personal kind which were insisted on by Mr Bonar Law and his friends and which I made with the greatest reluctance. One was the substitution of another Lord Chancellor for Lord Haldane, against whom, on the strength of his having once referred to Germany as "his spiritual home", there had been started one of those fanatical and malignant outcries which from time to time disgrace our national character. The other was the transfer of Mr Churchill from the Admiralty, where he was to be succeeded by Mr Balfour, to an inferior office in the Cabinet.'

Sir Edward Grey also was outraged by Lord Haldane's dismissal. He regretted ever after that he had not at the time himself resigned in protest. 'The thing', he wrote, 'left a scar.'

The King received Lord Haldane on May 26 and personally conferred upon him the Order of Merit.[2]

[1] The main posts in the First Coalition Government were distributed as follow: Prime Minister, Mr Asquith: Lord Chancellor, Sir S. Buckmaster: Lord President, Lord Crewe: Lord Privy Seal, Lord Curzon: Chancellor of the Exchequer, Mr McKenna: Secretaries of State—Home, Sir J. Simon: Foreign, Sir Edward Grey: War, Lord Kitchener: Colonies, Mr Bonar Law: India, Mr Austen Chamberlain: Minister of Munitions, Mr Lloyd George: First Lord of the Admiralty, Mr Balfour: President of the Board of Trade, Mr Runciman: President of the Local Government Board, Mr Long: Chief Secretary for Ireland, Mr Birrell: Attorney-General, Sir E. Carson: Board of Education, Mr Henderson: Chancellor of the Duchy, Mr Churchill.

[2] It was characteristic of the King that he never forgot, when opportunity offered, to redress an injustice which the political necessity of the moment had obliged him to condone. In November 1918, when victory had at last been achieved, Lord Stamfordham wrote to Lord Haldane: 'The King directs me to tell you how deeply he appreciates all you have done to make our victory possible and how silly he thought the outcry against you.'

SIR ARTHUR BIGGE, LORD STAMFORDHAM

THE KING AND KING ALBERT OF BELGIUM

CHAPTER XVII

THE KING AND THE SERVICES

1915-1916

The misfortunes of 1915—Sir John French—The King's accident in France—Sir Douglas Haig becomes Commander in Chief—The King's visits to munition factories—The Military Service Bill—The misfortunes of 1916—Air-raids—The King's attitude towards reprisals—Conscription becomes inevitable—Lloyd George and Bonar Law threaten to resign—The King's influence is invoked—Parliament accepts compulsory service—The Easter rising in Dublin—The King's relations with Sir Douglas Haig—The King and the Navy—The Battle of Jutland—Sir David Beatty succeeds Sir John Jellicoe—Foreign Affairs—The struggle between King Constantine and M. Venizelos.

(1)

'THE year 1915', comments Mr Churchill,[a] 'was disastrous to the cause of the Allies and the whole world. . . . Thereafter the fire roared until it had burnt itself out.' In the West, successive allied attacks were repulsed with heavy losses.[1] In the East, General Falkenhayn's break-through at Gorlice cost the Russians vast quantities of much needed munitions and two million men. General Cadorna's offensive on the Isonzo also failed. Our minor campaigns were equally unfruitful. The landing at Suvla Bay on August 8 petered out in sullen stagnation; in December all our forces were withdrawn from the Dardanelles. In the Balkans, an allied attempt to rescue Serbia from the German onslaught came too late to affect the issue; by the winter the Serbian armies were straggling miserably through the Albanian mountains while the French and British forces were locked up at Salonika, where they remained for two and a half years. In Mesopotamia, General Townshend, having advanced almost to within sight of Baghdad, was on December 8 surrounded by the Turks at Kut-el-Amara, and was forced to surrender in the following April. The year 1915 was thus a year of almost unrelieved misfortune.

[1] The autumn offensives in Champagne and Artois cost the French and British armies 242,000 casualties; on the British sector alone, the Battle of Loos, which gained us 8,000 yards of the German trench system, lost us 2,407 officers and 57,985 men.

Ever since the retreat from Mons the King had entertained doubts as to the suitability of Sir John French for the post of Commander in Chief. These doubts were not diminished by the part played by Sir John French in the campaign launched by Lord Northcliffe against Lord Kitchener:

> 'Of course,' the King wrote to the Duke of Connaught on May 23, 1915, 'French may be a good soldier, but I don't think he is particularly clever & he has an awful temper. Whether he is now suffering from the strain of the campaign or from swollen head I don't know, but he is behaving in a very odd way, which adds to my many anxieties I know you never had a very high opinion of him. He is also trying to intrigue against Kitchener with the politicians and the Press.'

These anxieties were increased by reports the King received indicating that the Commander in Chief was not making any real effort to compose his differences with Lord Kitchener or with his allies:

> 'He has', wrote Sir William Robertson[1] to Lord Stamfordham on June 23, 1915, 'never really, sincerely and honestly concerted with the French; while they regard him as by no means a man of ability or a faithful friend, and therefore they do not confide in him. Joffre and he have never yet been a mile within the heart of each other. Further he has never fully laid his opinions before the Government. He has too much taken the stand of doing as he wishes and telling the Government nothing. I have been very concerned about this for a long time past.' [b]

Sir Douglas Haig, commanding the First British Army, although reticent on the subject, had been offended by the Commander in Chief's failure to accord him due credit for the Battle of Neuve Chapelle, and was even more indignant when, at Loos, Sir John delayed until too late to send up the reserves.

On October 21 the King left for his second visit to the armies in

[1] Sir William Robertson (1860–1933) had enlisted as a private in the 16th Lancers in 1877. He was granted a commission in 1888. He passed through the Staff College in 1898. He fought with Lord Roberts in South Africa. He became a colonel in 1903 and a major-general in 1913. In August 1914 he was appointed quarter-master general of the Expeditionary Force and in January 1915 Chief of the Staff to Sir John French. In December 1915 he was made C.I.G.S. In February 1918, owing to differences with Mr Lloyd George, he was transferred to the Eastern Command. In May of that year he succeeded Sir John French as Commander in Chief of the Home Forces. From April 1919 to March 1920 he commanded the British Army of Occupation in Germany. On his retirement he was promoted Field Marshal. He wrote two autobiographical books, *From Private to Field Marshal* and *Soldiers and Statesmen*.

France. He stayed at the Chateau de la Jumelle at Aire. His conversations with the Army Commanders convinced him that there must be an immediate change in the high command:

> 'The troops here are all right,' the King wrote to Lord Stamfordham on October 25,° 'but I find that several of the most important Generals have entirely lost confidence in the C. in C. and they assured me that it was universal & that he must go, otherwise we shall never win this war. This has been my opinion for some time.'

On October 27 these fears were confirmed by a conversation with Sir William Robertson.

> 'Had a long serious talk', the King wrote that evening in his diary, 'with General Robertson & he is strongly of opinion that a change should be made here as soon as possible. He thinks D.H. [Sir Douglas Haig] would be an excellent C. in C. & that he would work well with Joffre. Now they pay no attention to the present C. in C. & he says that Wilson[1] should go at once as he is not loyal.'

On the next day, Thursday, October 28, the King drove to inspect the First Army at Labuissière. From there he went to Hesdigneul and rode down the lines of the 1st Wing, Royal Flying Corps. He was mounted on a chestnut mare which had been lent him by Sir Douglas Haig. The men raised a sudden cheer as he passed them, the mare reared in fright, slipped on the wet ground and fell backwards with the King partially under her:

> 'They picked me up', the King dictated subsequently for his diary, '& took me back to Aire in the motor as quickly as possible; I suffered great agonies all the way. . . . During October 29, 30 and 31 I suffered great pain and hardly slept at all as I was so terribly bruised all over and also suffered very much from shock.'

[1] Sir Henry Wilson (1864–1922) entered the Rifle Brigade in 1884 and after rapid promotion was appointed Commandant of the Staff College in 1906. In 1910 he became Director of Military Operations at the War Office and was one of the main champions of close coordination with the French General Staff. To a large extent he organised and perfected the Expeditionary Force. In 1914 he became deputy Chief of the Staff to Sir John French and chief liaison officer with the French armies. In the autumn of 1915 he received the command of the IVth Army Corps and in November 1917 was appointed British Military Representative on the Versailles War Council. In February 1918 he succeeded Sir William Robertson as C.I.G.S. He was made a Field Marshal after the armistice. In February 1922 he retired and offered his services to the Government of Northern Ireland. He was murdered by Irish gunmen in London in June 1922. His *Life and Letters* were published by Major-General Sir C. E. Callwell in 1927. This publication was welcomed by his enemies and deplored by his friends.

On November 1 the King was carried on a stretcher to the ambulance train for Boulogne, where he was placed on board the hospital ship *Anglia*. He reached Buckingham Palace in a state of exhaustion:

'The injuries', wrote his physician, Sir Bertrand Dawson,[d] 'were more serious than could then be disclosed. Besides the widespread and severe bruising, the pelvis was fractured in at least two places and the pain was bad, the subsequent shock considerable, and convalescence tedious. . . . How well I remember that insistant urging of G.H.Q. that we should get the King to England before the Germans had time to bomb the house, indifferently sheltered in a small wood, and how we insisted we must wait until there had been some recovery from the shock and time enough to know there were no internal injuries. And then the Channel crossing when he did go—the worst possible. The sea-sickness with that injured and bruised frame meant bad pain for him and anxiety for us.'

It was four weeks before the King was able to hobble with two sticks along the balcony outside his bedroom. Those closest to him realised thereafter that he was never quite the same man again.

On November 12, 1915 Lord Kitchener left England to report on the evacuation of Gallipoli and the general situation in the Near East and Egypt. His colleagues cherished the 'mute hope' that he would remain abroad. Mr Asquith, who had discussed the matter fully with the King, decided that the moment had come to secure Sir John French's retirement. He therefore despatched Lord Esher to General Headquarters, hoping that this tactful emissary might induce the Commander in Chief to resign spontaneously. Lord Esher found on his arrival that Sir John French was inclined to 'show fight'. The King was opposed to any further delay:

'As to Sir John French' Lord Stamfordham wrote to the Prime Minister on December 2, 'the King thinks that you have shown him every consideration, both in the manner by which you endeavoured to arrange his resignation and also respecting the conditions you offered with a view to making the suggested course as easy and acceptable as possible to him. But, in His Majesty's opinion, Sir John is not treating you with similar regard. He therefore hopes that you will now ask Sir John to give effect to the suggestion conveyed to him nearly a week ago through a mutual friend, in which His Majesty understood he expressed his willingness to acquiesce. Moreover the King feels that General Headquarters should not be left much longer without a C. in C.'[e]

Four days later Mr Asquith wrote to the King saying that he had received from Sir John French a letter tendering his resignation and

that he proposed to accept the offer. Sir John French was created a
Viscount and given command of the Home Forces. Sir Douglas Haig
was appointed Commander in Chief in his place.

(2)

With the active encouragement of Mr Lloyd George, the King,
on recovering from his accident, devoted much of his time to proving
to the munition workers that their services were regarded by the
country as of an importance equal to those of the men in the armies
and fleets:

'The story', writes Mr Lloyd George,' 'of the steps taken to organize
labour for the munition factories, and to induce them to put forward
their best efforts and submit to control and the suspension of cherished
trade union regulations and practices, would not be complete without
a tribute to the vitally important help rendered by the King to the
nation by heartening and encouraging the munition workers and those
who were creating the district organizations. It would be hard to overestimate the value of the national service rendered by the Sovereign's
visits to munition areas and the personal relations he established with
the workers there. . . . Nothing could be happier than the spontaneous
resolve of the King to go about among them, to shake them by the
hand, talk with them, and make a direct appeal to their patriotism
and citizenship. . . .

From the Clyde the King went to the Tyne, where he also spent
two days, and spoke personally with a number of foremen and workers
in the armament works and shipyards. . . . He thanked the workmen
in a speech for what had been done, but urged that more was still
required. He voiced the hope that "all restrictive rules and regulations
would be removed, and that all would work to one common end and
purpose". This was a courageous gesture on the King's part to help
forward the solution of the very difficult problem of suspending the
trade union restrictions which at the time were seriously hampering
output. He moved among the workers, chatting freely with them. He
picked out one worker, at Sheffield, whom he recognised as having
served with him when he was a midshipman in H.M.S. *Bacchante*. He
watched another making shells and remarked to him: "I am glad you
realize the importance of the work in hand. Without an adequate
supply of shells we cannot hope to win". Words like these, uttered
"man to man" by the Head of the State to the artisan, naturally ran
like wildfire through the works. It was this directness of personal contact, free from pomp or any trace of arrogance or aloofness, which
made the King's visit to the munition areas such a valuable aid in the
task of raising the worker's enthusiasm and breaking through the
reluctance to accept new methods and regulations.'

Meanwhile the ever-increasing demand for the imposition of

compulsory military service was creating a conflict within the Cabinet. Up till July 1915 Lord Kitchener had been able to secure by voluntary enlistment as many men as, at that date, he could equip or train. He foresaw that future requirements would necessitate more drastic measures. On July 5, 1915, was passed the National Registration Act, by which a precise inventory was taken of the manpower resources of the country. On August 24 an informal conference was held at Buckingham Palace to consider whether, and if so when and how, compulsion should be introduced:

> 'I went to see the King,' recorded Mr Asquith,[g] 'and was joined at the Palace by Kitchener. Balfour and Edward Grey. We four sat in conclave with the Sovereign on the subject of compulsion for nearly two hours: a very unusual proceeding. What, of course, affects him most is, not the abstract merits of the question, but the growing division of opinion and the prospect of a possible political row.'

As a temporary palliative, and with the unavowed purpose of convincing the dissident Liberals and the Labour leaders that conscription was now inevitable, the 'Derby scheme' was promulgated on October 23 together with a Proclamation issued in the King's name. Under this scheme men were asked to 'attest' their willingness to serve when wanted and were classified in twenty-three groups according to age, status and occupation. When launching the Derby scheme, the Prime Minister undertook that married men would not be called up until all the unmarried had been taken; and he promised that, if sufficient unmarried men failed to volunteer, a Compulsion Bill would be introduced. By the end of 1915 there were still more than a million bachelors who had failed to attest. Mr Asquith judged that he must now redeem his promise and apply compulsion to these recalcitrants. A Military Service Bill was therefore drafted, under which all single men between the ages of 18 and 41 would be compelled to attest. This Bill provoked what the King had most dreaded, a serious split within the ranks of the Liberal Government.

Sir John Simon, being in principle opposed to any form of compulsion, resigned his post as Home Secretary, Mr McKenna, the Chancellor of the Exchequer, also threatened resignation, on the ground that the finances of the country could not afford so large an increase of the armed forces. Mr Runciman took a similar line, contending that our export trade would suffer if so many young men were withdrawn from industry. To the Prime Minister's dismay, Sir Edward Grey unexpectedly ranged himself with Mr McKenna and Mr Runciman.

The King, who had gone to Sandringham for Christmas, immediately returned to London and received the Prime Minister at Buckingham Palace on the morning of December 30. He assured Mr Asquith that 'he would stand by him and support him, even if all his colleagues were to leave'.[h] Thus fortified, Mr Asquith was able to induce Sir Edward Grey, Mr McKenna and Mr Runciman to remain in the Cabinet. Only Sir John Simon insisted on resigning.

The Military Service Bill was then accepted by the Cabinet and became law on January 27, 1916. But this, as will be seen, was not the final settlement.

(3)

The year 1916 was one of ever-increasing strain, danger and disappointment. On February 21 the Germans opened their attack upon the fortress of Verdun; on April 24 occurred the Easter rising in Dublin; on June 1 came the terrible communiqué announcing our losses in the Battle of Jutland; on June 5 Lord Kitchener was drowned; on July 1 opened the long ordeal of the Somme; the dismissal of M. Sazonov on July 23 and his replacement by the pro-German Stürmer raised the spectre of a separate Russian peace; in August Rumania entered the war, only to be crushed within four months by Mackensen and Falkenhayn; the repulse with terrible losses of General Brusilov's offensive in September brought the gloomy conviction that the Russian armies would be incapable of any major operations in future; and the Franco-British forces at Salonika remained impotent spectators of the ever-increasing exploitation by Germany of Turkey and the Balkans as of the internal battle between King Constantine and M. Venizelos. The ordinary citizen—alarmed by the mounting casualty lists, apprehensive of the U-boat menace, inconvenienced by air-raids and food shortages unable to understand the hesitation of the Foreign Office either to grasp the Greek nettle or to risk antagonising the United States by an unrestricted application of the blockade—came to suspect that some secret influence was paralysing all our energies; rumours began to circulate as to the presence of 'a hidden hand'. It is to the credit of the public that they should have spurned with such unanimity the peace offers which in December 1916 were dangled before their exhausted eyes. But it is not surprising that, in the same month, they should have insisted, with almost equal unanimity, on a change in the supreme direction of the war.

Ever since, in September 1914, he had been warned by the Prime

Minister that there was some danger of 'bomb-throwing by Zeppelin airships', the King had regarded the indiscriminate slaughter of civilians as an unseemly act of war. Although, much to Queen Mary's distress, he refused to take personal precautions, and would gaze fascinated from the balcony of Buckingham Palace as these silver German fish slid past above the searchlights and the shells, he was deeply angered by the deaths and mutilations that were caused. 'It is simple murder,' he wrote in his diary after a visit to Charing Cross Hospital, 'and the Germans are proud of it.' He did not feel, however, that reprisals offered the best response, or agree with Lord Fisher's suggestion that batches of German prisoners would be shot for every raid that occurred.ᶦ Even less did he approve of the sinking of unarmed vessels at sight. 'It is simply disgusting,' he wrote to his younger son on March 31, 1915, 'that Naval Officers could do such things.' Yet when, a fortnight later, he learnt that the Cabinet intended to impose 'differential treatment' upon the crews of captured German submarines, he instructed Lord Stamfordham to address to the Prime Minister an immediate warning:ʲ

'The King wishes you to see the enclosed correspondence with reference to the German submarine prisoners. His Majesty is sorry that their treatment differs from ordinary prisoners of war. By some people they are regarded, and spoken of, as "Pirates". In the King's opinion, they have but obeyed orders,—brutal and inhuman though these orders may be. In any case, either they are criminals and should be tried and punished as such; or they are prisoners of war and ought to be treated accordingly. But apparently the nature of their punishment is decided according to what, in the circumstances, the Admiralty may consider right.

His Majesty cannot agree with this principle, and, further, the treatment laid down in the Admiralty memorandum seems to him unduly severe, even admitting—which he does not—that a difference should be made in dealing with these prisoners. A separate room in a Detention Quarter may, I suppose, be freely translated as a "cell in prison", the food allowance differing but little from prison diet.

The King feels that a refusal to allow a representative of the American Embassy to report on the condition of the prisoners will still further aggravate the situation, and he trusts you will be able to arrange with the First Lord and the Foreign Office for the request to be granted.

The King yields to no one in abominating the general conduct of the Germans throughout this war; but none the less he deprecates the idea of reprisals and retaliation; he has always hoped that at the end of the war we shall as a Nation stand before the world as having conducted it as far as possible with humanity and like gentlemen.'

The King's warning on this occasion was amply justified by the events that followed. On hearing of the treatment accorded to their submarine prisoners, the Germans immediately selected thirty-nine British officers and placed them in solitary confinement. The King at this caused a strong letter to be written to Mr Balfour, who had by then become First Lord of the Admiralty:[k]

'The King knows how difficult it is to give in, but we are dealing with people who have no regard for justice, mercy or righteousness, and for the sake of humanity and pity upon our gallant soldiers, His Majesty hopes that the German conditions—unfair, unjust and unreasonable though they be—may be complied with.'

The Government thereupon retreated from the position which they had unwisely adopted and thenceforward German submarine crews when captured received the same treatment as other prisoners of war.

(4)

By April 1916 it became apparent to the Army Council that the Military Service Act passed in the previous January was insufficient to provide the reinforcements which would be required. On the evening of April 15 Lord Reading, the Lord Chief Justice, paid a private visit to Lord Stamfordham and warned him that another and more serious Cabinet crisis was impending. The Prime Minister had only secured the passage of the Military Service Act by promising that it would not be extended to apply to unattested married men. Mr Lloyd George was now threatening to resign unless the Act were amended to include every available man of military age. If Mr Lloyd George persisted in his resignation, Mr Bonar Law would probably follow suit. The Coalition Government would dissolve and the country be faced with all the dangers and perplexities of a General Election. Lord Reading suggested that, although it might be unwise for the King to exert 'personal pressure' on Mr Lloyd George, it might be possible for His Majesty to exercise his influence to 'find some means of accommodation'.[l]

On the following morning Lord Stamfordham went to see Mr Bonar Law at Pembroke Lodge. He found him wrestling gloomily with a personal dilemma. If he sided with Mr Lloyd George, he might be exposing the country to serious internal unrest and disturbance. If he sided with Mr Asquith, he would be betraying his own Party, for whom conscription had always been 'one of the cardinal points of policy'. Might not a possible course be for Mr

Asquith to resign and for the King then to send for him, Mr Bonar Law? In that event he could reply that he was unable to form a Government without a majority in the House of Commons. The King would then again send for Mr Asquith who could reconstruct his administration on an even broader basis. By such a device the face of everybody would be saved. Mr Bonar Law was not, however, much enamoured of his own proposal; he hung his head sideways in saddened doubt.[m]

Lord Stamfordham then visited Mr Lloyd George, whom he found in a mood of exuberant pugnacity. The Prime Minister was not conducting the war with sufficient 'energy and determination'. Why was he so frightened of the Trades Unions? The Prime Minister was being bullied by Mr J. H. Thomas, who was 'the greatest blatherer living'. Why was he so terrified of what would happen in the two storm-centres, the Clyde and South Wales? The trouble to be expected from the Clyde was much exaggerated. As for South Wales, 'they are my own flesh and blood and I can answer for them.' Was a General Election really such a horrible prospect? What did it matter if the Government did fall? 'We politicians always imagine that no one can govern the country except ourselves.' To talk of the effect that a split would have upon our Allies was little short of 'rubbish'. 'Tell the King', said Mr Lloyd George, 'that I should be breaking my Privy Councillor's oath were I to act differently to what I am now doing.'

> 'During this interesting interview,' Lord Stamfordham recorded, 'I was struck by Mr L.G's energy, keenness, & earnest determination. But he contemptuously brushed aside any difficulty which was suggested.' [n]

In the end Mr Lloyd George triumphed and his confidence in the spirit of the country was shown to have been well-founded. On April 20 a compromise was agreed to in Cabinet and on April 25 and 26 took place two Secret Sessions of the House of Commons. Mr Asquith was so encouraged by the spirit of the House that he withdrew his compromise arrangement and on May 3 introduced a Bill to impose immediate and general conscription. This Bill was passed with only 37 votes of dissent and received the Royal Assent on May 25. The prophets of strikes and revolution were discredited.

The King was delighted by this happy conclusion of the controversy. He addressed to the Prime Minister a letter of warm congratulation written in his own hand:[o]

'It is with the greatest satisfaction that I learn of the happy agreement arrived at by the Cabinet today. I do most heartily congratulate you on having by your patience and skill extricated the Country from a position, the dangers of which it was impossible to overestimate. I do indeed trust that this solution will prove final and that your Coalition Government, once more united, will gain renewed strength & greater confidence of the Country to enable you to prosecute with the fullest energy the continuance of the war to a victorious end.

During the last six years you & I have passed through some strenuous & critical times & once again, thank God, we have weathered the storm. . . . In expressing my relief at the termination of the crisis, I wish again to assure you of my complete confidence in my Prime Minister.

Believe me, v. sincerely yours,

George R.I.'

Mr Asquith replied by assuring the King that 'the happy agreement arrived at was a triumph of patriotism & British good sense over every kind of sinister influence'.[p]

Mr Lloyd George's abandonment of his threat to appeal to the country, Mr Asquith's surrender on the issue of conscription, were hastened, if not caused, by the very serious events which occurred that week in Dublin. On April 22 the German ship *Aud*, carrying a large consignment of rifles and other munitions, was intercepted off the coast of Ireland. On the same day Sir Roger Casement,[1] who had been landed in Kerry from a German submarine, was recognised by a coastguard at Banna and taken into custody. In spite of these mishaps, the Irish Volunteers, assisted by James Connolly's 'Citizen's Army' decided to proceed with the 'parade' which had been announced to take place in Dublin on April 24. On that Easter Monday they suddenly seized and occupied the Post Office, St Stephen's Green, the Four Courts and Jacob's biscuit factory. Looting broke out in the city, British soldiers were murdered in the streets, and a great part of Sackville Street went up in flames. Reinforcements were sent across from England and Sir John Maxwell placed in command. By April 30 the insurrection had been suppressed and the leaders arrested. Fifteen of these were tried by Court Martial and summarily executed: nearly two thousand of their followers were

[1] Sir Roger Casement (1864–1916) was born in Co. Dublin, entered the British Consular Service and acquired fame by his remarkable report on Belgian atrocities in the Congo. He retired in 1912 and devoted the rest of his life to the cause of Irish Independence. After his arrest on April 24, 1916, he was brought to London, tried for treason, and executed on August 3.

transported to England and interned. Mr Birrell, the Irish Secretary, resigned.

On May 11 Mr Asquith crossed to Dublin to examine the situation on the spot. On his return, he informed the House of Commons that he had asked Mr Lloyd George to negotiate a settlement with the Irish Parliamentary Party. On June 10 Mr Redmond announced that Mr Lloyd George had offered immediate Home Rule to Ireland, subject to the exclusion of Ulster for the period of the war. On July 11, Lord Lansdowne in the House of Lords made the contradictory statement that the exclusion of Ulster would be 'permanent and enduring' and that meanwhile order would be maintained in Ireland under the Defence of the Realm Act. Mr Redmond described this statement as 'an insult' and a breach of faith. Mr Lloyd George's negotiations came to nothing, since the Unionists in the Coalition would not agree to any sacrifices such as Mr Redmond or his supporters could accept. On July 31 it was announced that Mr Duke, a Unionist, was to succeed Mr Birrell as Chief Secretary for Ireland. Mr Redmond denounced this appointment as indicating 'the restoration of the Castle régime, with a Unionist executive'. The hesitation of the Government left Ireland bewildered and resentful. The Easter rising, which had been condemned as a bloodstained failure, came to be regarded as a signal success. The British, it was whispered, yielded only to violence; and violence thereafter became the watchword of Sinn Fein.

(5)

In the new Commander in Chief, Sir Douglas Haig, the King possessed an old and valued friend:[1]

'I know', he wrote to him on his appointment, 'you will have the confidence of the troops serving under you & it is almost needless to assure you with what implicit trust I look forward to the successful conduct of the War on the Western front under your able direction. Remember that it will always be a pleasure to me to help you in any way I can to carry out your heavy task & important responsibilities. I hope you will from time to time write to me quite freely & tell me how matters are progressing.' *q*

---

[1] While still a young officer, Sir Douglas Haig had been much favoured by King Edward VII. He had been invited to stay at Sandringham as early as 1898. In May 1905, when at Windsor for Ascot week, he met Miss Dorothy Vivian, a Maid of Honour to Queen Alexandra. They were married in the Private Chapel at Buckingham Palace on July 11 following.

Sir Douglas did not hesitate to avail himself of this invitation. The letters of Sir John French had been few and stilted: Sir Douglas Haig wrote to the King frequently and without reserve. He would discuss such matters as his relations with the French Generals, the dictatorial attitude adopted by M. Poincaré, the friction between the Canadian divisional commanders and the Canadian depot at Shorncliffe, the excellent influence exercised by the army chaplains, the advantage of General Nivelle possessing an English mother, or even the manners of Lord Curzon:

'He made himself most agreeable during his stay here. I thought him much changed since his Oxford days and also since I saw him in India as Viceroy. He is now much more natural and not at all pompous. I do wish the Country could have the advantage of his great talents in some capacity. He strikes me always as a great statesman.' *r*

With Mr Asquith, Sir Douglas Haig's relations were confident and friendly·

'I felt', he wrote after Mr Asquith had been in France, 'that the old gentleman was head and shoulders above any other politician who had visited my headquarters in brains and all-round knowledge. It was quite a pleasure to have the old man in the house—so amusing and kindly in his ways.' *s*

The mutual distrust which existed and developed between Mr Lloyd George and the Commander in Chief caused the King re-current concern. 'The inability of these two men' comments Sir Duff Cooper, 'to understand one another or to work harmoniously together is a melancholy fact which has to be recorded.' *t* Mr Lloyd George did not vouchsafe to the opinions of Generals, Admirals and senior officials the same rapturous welcome that he often gave to the bright ideas of their subordinates. He was irritated by Sir Douglas Haig's exquisite, if slightly formal, manners, by the obduracy of his arguments, by his refusal to agree that the war could only be won by a major campaign in the Balkans. The King sought by every means in his power to alleviate this personal friction. In August 1916, in the hope of fortifying the Commander in Chief's position, he suggested to the Prime Minister that the time had come to make Sir Douglas Haig a Field Marshal.*u* Mr Asquith replied that such an honour seemed premature. In the following September the King raised the matter with Mr Lloyd George himself who replied that it would be better to wait until the battle of the Somme had been fought to a successful conclusion. Sir Douglas Haig was not gazetted a Field Marshal until January 1917.

The King's relations with Sir John Jellicoe, Commander in Chief of the Grand Fleet, although frank and continuous, were less intimate. It was through his former friends or shipmates—through Admirals Wemyss, Colville and Beatty—that he maintained the closest touch with his old profession:

'I often look back', Sir Rosslyn Wemyss wrote to him on August 11, 1914, 'at the happy days of long ago, and there forms itself before my mind a picture of gun-rooms, of old mess-mates, and of youths without care or anxieties. Then my mind turns to the present, and I see Your Majesty transformed from the cheery midshipman into the Sovereign, with all the load of anxiety, trouble and responsibility, and I cannot but help feeling much moved.' *v*

'We are haunted', wrote Sir David Beatty, 'by the fear that possibly "the day" may never come.'*w* That much desired day arrived on May 31, 1916, and proved a disappointment. The King had been warned that the German High Seas Fleet had put to sea and that a great battle was impending off the coast of Jutland. In anxious excitement he waited for the first report. It reached him in the form of a signal scribbled without punctuation by an Admiralty clerk.

'Our losses Queen Mary Indefatigable Invincible Defence Black Prince Sparrow Hawk Ardent Fortune Tipperary Turbulent also missing at present Shark Nestor Nomad.'

The shock occasioned by this message was increased by personal anxiety regarding Prince Albert. The *Collingwood*, in which he was serving, had been heavily attacked by torpedo craft; of the main German battleships they had seen no more than the distant orange stabs of their guns, flashing in the twilight mist; they had watched the *Defence* explode and sink; they had passed the wreck of the *Invincible*, her two halves 500 yards apart:

'Prince Albert', reported Captain J. C. Ley of the *Collingwood*, 'was in bed on sick list when we prepared for action, but got up and went to his turret, where he remained until we finally secured guns next day. Though his food that evening and night was of an unusual description, I am glad to tell your Majesty that he has been quite well since and looks quite well again.' *x*

In a letter to his parents Prince Albert gave his own description of the Battle of Jutland:*y*

'I was in A turret and watched most of the action through one of the trainers telescopes, as we were firing by director, when the turret is trained in the working chamber and not in the gun house. At the commencement I was sitting on the top of A turret and had a very good view of the proceedings. I was up there during a lull, when a German ship started firing at us, and one salvo "straddled" us. We at once returned the fire. I was distinctly startled and jumped down the hole in the top of the turret like a shot rabbit!! I didn't try the experience again. The ship was in a fine state on the main deck. Inches of water sluicing about to prevent fires getting a hold on the deck. Most of the cabins were also flooded.

The hands behaved splendidly and all of them in the best of spirits as their heart's desire had at last been granted, which was to be in action with the Germans. Some of the turret's crew actually took on bets with one another that we should not fire a single shot. A good deal of money must have changed hands I should think by now.

It was certainly a great experience to have been through and it shows that we are at war and that the Germans can fight if they like.'

A fortnight after the battle, the King paid a visit of inspection to Rosyth, Invergordon and Scapa Flow. He stayed with Sir John Jellicoe in the *Iron Duke*. By then the shock occasioned by the first report of our losses had been mitigated by further information; the Germans also had suffered heavily and did not again venture upon a major action in the high seas.[1] The King, who knew so much about the chances and perils of naval warfare, was not the man to criticise the tactics or strategy of the Commander in Chief. He would have agreed with Mr Churchill that Sir John Jellicoe was the only commander on either side, whose orders 'in the space of *two or three hours* might nakedly decide who won the war'.[2]

In December 1916 Sir John Jellicoe was appointed First Sea Lord and the command of the Grand Fleet devolved upon Sir David Beatty:

'I have known you', the King wrote to the latter on December 3,[2.a] 'for upwards of thirty years, ever since we were shipmates together in the Mediterranean; I have watched your career with interest and admiration & I feel that the splendid fleet which you now command could not be in better hands, that you enjoy the full confidence of your

---

[1] In the Battle of Jutland the British lost three battle cruisers, three cruisers and eight torpedo craft. The Germans lost one battleship, one battle cruiser, four light cruisers and five torpedo craft. Our casualties were 6,945 officers and men, those of the Germans 3,058. Our tonnage loss 115,025 compared with the German loss of 61,180. Our heavy armour-piercing shells were of inferior quality to those used by the Germans. (See Lord Chatfield's *The Navy and Defence*, Vol. I, Chapter XVI, and Mr. Churchill's *World Crisis*, Vol. III, page 167 ff.)

officers & men, whose loyal & devoted services you can count on as surely as did your distinguished predecessor. You have my hearty good wishes & those of the whole Empire. May God bless you & my fleet & grant you victory.'

'I pray God grant me', Sir David Beatty replied,[z,b] 'a right judgement in all things, to enable me at all times to prove worthy of the Trust that Your Majesty has honoured me with.'

(6)

From time to time during the war the King would receive communications from the Heads of Foreign States. M. Poincaré would write him ceremonial letters in his own hand, congratulating him upon some British victory; the Queen of Holland, the Kings of Denmark and Sweden, would write politely protesting against the rigours of our blockade; the King of the Belgians would beg him to restrain our aviators from bombing Belgian towns; the King of Spain would make useful and intelligent suggestions for the mitigation of some of the horrors of war; the Queen of Rumania's letters were intimate, patriotic, gallant and unconventional.[1] The King's replies to these communications were generally drafted for him in the chill but excellent style of the Foreign Office. What is strange, and to the biographer disappointing, is that the few letters which he exchanged with the Tsar of Russia, with whom he was on terms of such affectionate intimacy, were (with the solitary exception noted below) written in an equally conventional and stilted style. They contribute nothing to the history of the period.

In so far as Foreign Affairs were concerned, the King's main preoccupation was with the problem of Greek neutrality and the conflict between King Constantine and M. Venizelos. The former, who may well have regarded a German victory as inevitable, wished to keep his country neutral; the latter desired to enter the war on the side of the Allies.[2] The situation was complicated by two personal factors. King Constantine, who was the one man whom M. Veni-

---

[1] King Carol of Rumania died on October 10, 1914. He was succeeded by his nephew, the Crown Prince Ferdinand, who had married King George's first cousin, Princess Marie of Edinburgh.

[2] M. Venizelos had already on two occasions (August 1914 and March 1915) offered to place the Greek armies at the disposal of the Allies. The first offer was rejected, since Sir Edward Grey did not wish to prejudice his scheme for a Balkan block; the second, because Russia was unwilling that Greek troops should share in the anticipated capture of Constantinople.

zelos had been unable to charm, suspected his Prime Minister of wishing to foment an internal revolution and to establish a Republic. And General Sarrail, the French Commander in Chief of the allied forces at Salonika (who was a 'political' soldier of the left and who had evidence to show that the Greek General Staff were in communication with Berlin) was determined by intervening forcibly and constantly in Greek internal affairs, to protect himself against any menace to his left flank.

The attack launched by Bulgaria against Serbia in September 1915 rendered operative the Graeco-Serbian Treaty of Alliance. M. Venizelos immediately mobilised the Greek Army, but was at once dismissed by King Constantine. The Chamber, in which the Venizelists held a majority, was dissolved; from the ensuing General Election the Liberal Party of M. Venizelos abstained in protest; M. Zaimis became Prime Minister in M. Venizelos' place. On the advice of General Sarrail, France, Great Britain and Russia, claiming their rights as the 'Protecting Powers' under the Convention of 1832, thereupon insisted that the Greek Army should be demobilised and asked for further 'guarantees'. In August 1916, on the entry of Rumania into the war, M. Venizelos with his party leaders seceded to Salonika, where he established a Provisional Government of his own.

Sir Edward Grey had most unwillingly been dragged into this position. It seemed to him that, having entered the war in defence of the neutrality of Belgium, it was wrong for us to impose our will upon another small neutral, and one whom, if matters went badly, we should be unable to protect.[z.c] The King, who had been visited in London by Prince George and Prince Andrew of Greece, and who had begged them to induce their brother, King Constantine, to 'see reason',[z.d] was so perturbed by the development of the situation that he addressed to the Prime Minister a letter of unaccustomed emphasis:[z.e]

Windsor Castle.
4th Sept., 1916.

My dear Prime Minister,

    I am anxious at the way matters appear to be drifting in Greece, where, at the instigation of France, the Allies have agreed upon certain action which seems to me harsh and even open to question whether it is in accordance with International law. We have not only taken over control of the Posts and Telegraphs, demanded dismissal of enemy agents, but ordered proceedings to be taken against Greek subjects, who are supposed to have been accomplices in acts of corruption and espionage. Are we justified in interfering to this extent in the internal Government of a neutral and friendly country, even though we be one of the guarantors of its Constitution? Are we acting up to our boasted position as the protector of smaller Powers?

I cannot help feeling that in this Greek question we have allowed France too much to dictate a policy, and that as a Republic she may be somewhat intolerant of, if not anxious to abolish, the monarchy in Greece. But this I am sure is *not* the policy of my Government. Nor is it that of the Emperor of Russia, who, writing to me a few days ago said:

"I feel rather anxious about the internal affairs in Greece. It seems to me the protecting Powers, in trying to safeguard our interests concerning Greece's neutrality, are gradually immersing themselves too much in her internal home affairs to the detriment of the King."

I cannot refrain from expressing my astonishment and regret at General Sarrail's arbitrary conduct towards those troops who, loyal to their King and Government, refused to join the Revolutionary movement at Salonika. Could not a protest of some kind be sent to the French Government against General Sarrail's proceedings which are so strongly deprecated by Monsieur Zaimis?

While of course acknowledging the necessity for our working in concert with our Allies, I consider that *we* are the partner in the Alliance who, if we choose to do so, could take the lead and decide the policy. For our Sea Power alone, to say nothing of our financial superiority, make us the predominant Power and indispensable to our Allies in determining the War.

Public opinion in Greece, as well as the opinion of the King, is evidently changing and if the Allies would treat her kindly and not, if I may say so, in a bullying spirit, she will in all probability join them.

I do not wish to interfere in the action of my Government, but I regard it as my duty to place on record my views on this question at the present moment.

(signed) George R.I.

The King's apprehensions were not unjustified. At the end of November 1916 Admiral Dartiges de Fournet appeared with a Franco-British squadron at the Piraeus and presented to King Constantine an ultimatum, demanding compliance with certain drastic conditions, including the surrender by the Greek Army of much of their equipment and material. He returned to his flagship under the impression that King Constantine would consent, provided that it were made clear that he had only surrendered to a demonstration of force. On December 1 therefore the Admiral disembarked detachments of French and British marines, who advanced on Athens. Much to their surprise, they were met with armed resistance; several casualties were caused and the main force, including the French

Admiral, were surrounded in the Zappeion gardens, from where they had to be withdrawn in circumstances of extreme humiliation.

King Constantine, in some alarm, then addressed to the King a telegram in which he sought to justify his action.[2.8] The Allied landing, he contended, had been resisted, only because it was known to be part of a Venizelist conspiracy and the prelude to a Venizelist rising. On December 11, King George returned to this appeal a reply which can have left no doubts whatever in his cousin's mind:[2.9]

December 11th, 1916.

'I have received Your Majesty's telegram of December 6th. The recent events that have occurred in Greece have caused me deep pain and concern. I am unaware of the conspiracy to which you refer, but I know that no agents of the Allied Powers were connected with anything of the kind. The Allied Powers have, from the outset, confined their demands upon Greece to the observance of a benevolent neutrality. Unfortunately this condition has not been observed. Not only have the proceedings of Your Majesty's Government been open to grave objection, but the Allied Powers have received indubitable proof of action on the part of the Greek Government, both damaging to their naval and military interests and of direct assistance to the enemy's forces.

This made it necessary for them, in the interests of their own safety, to ask for certain material guarantees, in the justifiability of which, it is only fair to observe, Your Majesty had given reason to believe that you were disposed to agree. When, however, difficulties arose with Your Majesty's Government in regard to the execution of those guarantees, the Allied Powers saw themselves obliged to order certain formal measures at Athens in the nature of a military demonstration, in order that the Greek Government should realize that the demand of the Allies was serious. Your Majesty was fully informed beforehand of the nature and scope of those measures, and gave to the Allied Commander, two days before the demonstration was to take place, a written assurance of the maintenance of public order. Relying on this assurance, small detachments of Allied troops were landed, only to be met by an unsuspected and unprovoked attack by Greek troops, posted for this purpose by the Greek Government.

I take note of Your Majesty's assurance that you deplore the useless bloodshed and I note with satisfaction your declaration that you harbour no designs against the Allied Powers and will never attack them. But my Government can only take a very serious view of the events resulting in the death of my gallant troops. These events have aroused a feeling of deep and widespread indignation among my people; a feeling intensified by accounts received from many including neutral sources of the treatment to which Venizelists in Greece are now being subjected. Your Majesty will understand that the demands, which, in

283

conjunction with the Allied Powers, my Government must now make, will include reparation for the unprovoked attack made by your troops and guarantees for the future.

There followed an uneasy pause. Greece hovered thereafter on the brink of revolution; and the British public, who rightly recognised that M. Venizelos was our friend, and who with less justice assumed that King Constantine was our enemy, remained for long suspicious and perplexed.

CHAPTER XVIII

THE LLOYD GEORGE COALITION

1916-1917

Mr Lloyd George dissatisfied with the conduct of the war—Sir Edward Carson forms the nucleus of a Unionist opposition—Embarrassment caused thereby to Mr. Bonar Law—Sir Max Aitken brings Mr Lloyd George, Sir Edward Carson and Mr Bonar Law together—Mr Asquith unable to accept Mr Lloyd George's plan for a War Council under the latter's chairmanship—Mr. Asquith resigns—The King refuses Mr. Bonar Law's request for a Dissolution—Buckingham Palace Conference—Mr Lloyd George forms his Cabinet—The German Peace Note—The King's advice to Mr Lloyd George—President Wilson's Note—The King and Colonel House—The United States at war with Germany—The Russian Revolution—The Tsar and his family are invited to England—Disagreements between Mr Lloyd George and the Generals—The Calais Conference—Sir Douglas Haig's letter to the King and his reply—The collapse of the Nivelle plan.

(1)

THE year 1916, as has been said, imposed upon the British people a succession of strains and disappointments: Verdun, the Easter rising in Dublin, Kut, Jutland, the exhaustion of Russian military power, the Somme, the Rumanian catastrophe, and the inexplicable tangle of Greek affairs. These ordeals did not produce a mood of defeatism; in fact, the disquiet which spread in the late autumn of 1916 was increased by rumours that certain members of the Cabinet were in favour of a negotiated peace. The public temper was one rather of baffled pugnacity; the impression widened that Mr Asquith and his Cabinet were not conducting the war with sufficient zest.

Mr Lloyd George, who had succeeded Lord Kitchener as Minister of War, shared this impression. For long he had been urging a change of political machinery. What he now demanded was the creation of a small War Council composed of three or four Ministers with himself as chairman. Mr Asquith, while admitting the need for more concentrated and expeditious political direction, insisted that his own authority as Prime Minister must remain supreme. He estimated that, even if Mr Lloyd George resigned from the Cabinet, he would himself retain the loyalty of the Liberal Party. Nor did he expect that many of the Unionist members of the Coalition would contemplate allying themselves with, still less serving under, Mr Lloyd George. This estimate was optimistic.

The Unionist Party had never viewed the Coalition with any massive enthusiasm. On October 1915, Sir Edward Carson, whom Mr Asquith had been obliged to admit into his Government as Attorney General, resigned in protest against what he regarded as the betrayal of Serbia. It was around him that, in the months that followed, the nucleus of a Unionist Opposition began to form. Matters did not come to a head until November 8, 1916, when Sir Edward Carson raised in the House of Commons the minor issue of enemy property in Nigeria. In the division that followed only 73 of the 286 Unionists voted with the Government. This placed Mr Bonar Law, their official leader, in an awkward position. On the one hand, he did not wish to abandon Mr Asquith, to associate himself with Mr Lloyd George, or to plunge the country into a political crisis; on the other hand, he was unwilling to see the leadership of the Unionists slide slowly into other hands. Sir Edward Carson also had his apprehensions. He foresaw that if he pushed his opposition too far, the Coalition might appeal to the country, all dissidents might be eliminated, and Mr Asquith returned to unchallengeable power. It was largely owing to the persistence and ingenuity of Sir Max Aitken[1] that Mr Bonar Law was able to master his scruples and Sir Edward Carson his apprehensions. At a series of meetings held in Sir Max Aitken's apartment in the Hyde Park Hotel a triple alliance was concluded between Mr Bonar Law, Sir Edward Carson and Mr Lloyd George. Neither Mr Asquith, nor the Liberal or Unionist Parties, were fully aware at the time of the nature and purport of this alliance. Lord Northcliffe and the editors of the *Daily News* and *Daily Express* were more accurately informed.

Meanwhile Mr Asquith had been discussing direct with Mr Lloyd George the functions and status of the new War Council. By the evening of Sunday, December 3, he was under the impression that agreement in principle had been reached between them and that no more would now be required than a slight redistribution of Cabinet posts. He informed the King accordingly.

[1] Sir Max Aitken, subsequently Lord Beaverbrook, was the compatriot as well as the devoted friend of Mr Bonar Law. He entered Parliament in 1910 as Conservative member for Ashton-under-Lyne. He was knighted in 1911, received a baronetcy in 1916 and a peerage in 1917. In his book, *Politicians and the War*, he has given a full and frank account of these negotiations.

On the morning of Monday, December 4, there appeared in *The Times* a leading article attacking Mr Asquith personally and showing that the writer had been informed in detail of the course of these confidential negotiations. The Prime Minister assumed, rightly or wrongly, that this article had been inspired by Mr Lloyd George himself.[1] His attitude stiffened accordingly. He informed Mr Lloyd George that the proposed War Council would prove unworkable unless the Prime Minister retained 'supreme and effective control of War Policy'. He added that he could not agree to Sir Edward Carson replacing Mr Balfour as First Lord of the Admiralty and as a member of the new War Council. Mr Lloyd George replied on the morning of Tuesday, December 5, that he could not accept this version of the agreement which he had reached with Mr Asquith on Sunday, and would feel it his 'duty to leave the Government in order to inform the people of the real condition of affairs'. At 1.0 p.m. on that day the Liberal members of Mr Asquith's Cabinet, with the exception of Mr Lloyd George, met in Downing Street and while pledging unflinching loyalty to their leader, unanimously decided that Mr Lloyd George's conditions could not be accepted.

Shortly afterwards Mr Asquith was visited by three important Unionists, Lord Curzon, Lord Robert Cecil and Mr Austen Chamberlain. They informed him 'to his great surprise' *a* that they would now be forced to deprive him of their support. They had discovered 'that Mr Bonar Law and Sir Edward Carson were now solid with Mr Lloyd George, and they saw no prospect of holding their party if this formidable trio went into Opposition, and were backed, as they would be, by the chief part of the Conservative Press'. They added that they had been informed that Mr Lloyd George could command the support of the Labour section and of a considerable number, if not of the majority, of the Liberals. Being thus abandoned, Mr Asquith realised that he had no alternative but to resign.

'At 7.0 p.m.', the King wrote in his diary for Tuesday, December 5, 'the Prime Minister came to see me & placed his resignation in my hands, which I accepted with great regret. He said that he had tried to arrange matters with Lloyd George about the War Committee all day,

[1] The article was written by Mr Geoffrey Robinson, Editor of *The Times*, who was spending the week-end at Cliveden. Mr Lloyd George, who had had an interview with Lord Northcliffe on that Sunday evening (see Tom Clarke, *My Northcliffe Diary*, page 106) vehemently denied that he had had cognisance of the article. It is possible that Mr Geoffrey Robinson obtained his information from Sir Edward Carson.

but was unable to. All his colleagues, both Liberal and Unionist, urged him to resign as it was the only solution of the difficulty. I fear that it will cause a panic in the City & in America & do harm to the Allies. It is a great blow to me & will I fear buck up the Germans.

After dinner I sent for Mr Bonar Law, who came at 9.30 & I asked him to form a Government; he said he would consult his friends & let me know tomorrow morning, but he did not think he would be able to do so.'

In sending for the leader of the Unionists the King was acting in strict accordance with constitutional precedent. From a memorandum[b] written late that night by Lord Stamfordham it seems that this interview was unsatisfactory. Mr Bonar Law began by saying that he had always striven to make good blood between the Prime Minister and the Secretary of State for War; that he had urged the former, long before the Press campaign started, himself to reform the War Committee; but that in the end he had come to the conclusion 'that he must decide between Mr Asquith or Mr Lloyd George, and, as he believed the latter would win the war before the former could do so, he had decided to follow Mr Lloyd George'. Mr Bonar Law added that both he and Mr Lloyd George had for long been convinced that the war was being mismanaged:

'To this', writes Lord Stamfordham, 'the King demurred and said that the politicians should leave the conduct of the war to experts. Mr Bonar Law said that Robertson and the soldiers were all wrong, with the result that we have lost Serbia, Rumania and very likely Greece. The King expressed his entire disagreement with these views. . . .'

A more important divergence arose between the King and Mr Bonar Law on the question of a Dissolution. The King was opposed to a General Election in war time, fearing that it might have a disintegrating effect. He had foreseen that Mr Bonar Law, if invited to form a Government, might make it a condition of acceptance that the existing Parliament should be dissolved. He had thus, during the course of that evening, asked Lord Haldane, as a former Lord Chancellor, whether the Sovereign would be constitutionally justified in refusing to accept such a condition:

'Will you', wrote Lord Stamfordham,[c] 'be very kind and tell me, if the King were asked to dissolve Parliament as a condition of anyone undertaking to form a Government, could His Majesty constitutionally refuse to do so?'

Lord Haldane furnished his opinion in writing:[d]

'1. The Sovereign ought at no time to act without the advice of a responsible Minister, excepting when contemplating the exercise of his prerogative right to dismiss Ministers. The only Minister who can properly give advice as to a Dissolution of Parliament is the Prime Minister.

2. The Sovereign, before acting on advice to dissolve, ought to weigh that advice. His Majesty may, instead of accepting it, dismiss the Minister who gives it, or receive his resignation. This is the only alternative to taking his advice.

3. It follows that the Sovereign cannot entertain any bargain for a Dissolution merely with a possible Prime Minister before the latter is fully installed. The Sovereign cannot, before that event, properly weigh the general situation and the Parliamentary position of the Ministry as formed.

Haldane. 5 Dec. 1916'

Fortified by such expert judgement, the King informed Mr Bonar Law that he would refuse, if asked, to accord him a Dissolution:

'Mr Bonar Law', Lord Stamfordham records,* 'questioned the advisability of His Majesty refusing and hoped that the King would consider before adopting that attitude. Indeed he himself might succeed in forming a Government if he appealed to the Country.'

Mr Bonar Law left Buckingham Palace to consult his friends.

(2)

By the next morning, Wednesday, December 6, Mr Bonar Law had come to the conclusion that he might succeed in forming a Government, if only he could persuade Mr Asquith to join it in a subordinate capacity. Mr Asquith, although he had held the office of Prime Minister for a longer period than any statesman since Lord Liverpool, was incapable of permitting feelings of personal dignity to affect his judgement; he merely doubted whether such a combination would prove workable in practice. Mr Balfour, when consulted, made the suggestion that the King should be asked immediately to summon a Conference to discuss the formation of a National Government. Such a Conference, for all he knew, might succeed in persuading Mr Asquith to serve under Mr Bonar Law. The King readily assented to this proposal and the Conference met at Buckingham Palace at 3.0 that afternoon. It was attended by Mr Asquith, Mr Lloyd George, Mr Bonar Law, Mr Balfour and Mr Arthur Henderson. The King presided. Lord Stamfordham's record of the proceedings must be quoted in its entirety:'

'*Report of a Conference held at Buckingham Palace on Wednesday,*
December 6th at 3 p.m.

Previous to the Meeting, the King had seen Mr Balfour alone, who had explained to His Majesty his views of the situation and what seemed a possible solution.

The proceedings were opened by the King who explained that, having accepted the resignation of Mr Asquith, he had called upon Mr Bonar Law to form a Government last night, and the latter had asked for time to consider, and had given his reply this morning to the effect that he asked His Majesty to summon this Meeting, and the King thanked the Members for having acceded to His Majesty's request.

The King called upon Mr Balfour, who, speaking as an ex-Prime Minister and old Parliamentary hand, pointed out that the War Committee as hitherto constituted, had proved an ineffective and unworkable body, and reform was necessary if the War was to be carried out successfully. At the same time he was of opinion that no Government would be strong enough to carry on the War without Mr Asquith, and he urged him to join an Administration with Mr Bonar Law as Prime Minister.

Mr Bonar Law then followed by an appeal to Mr Asquith to join the new Government on patriotic grounds. The Unionist Members of the late Government would not work under Mr Asquith as Prime Minister.

Mr Henderson, as leader of the Labour Party, frankly confessed he did not believe he could get the consent of his party to support any Government of which Mr Asquith was not a member, and he earnestly appealed to Mr Asquith to join and serve under Mr Bonar Law.

Mr Lloyd George repudiated any personal feeling whatever against the Prime Minister, and nothing which had occurred should interfere with his feelings of friendship towards him. There had been a misunderstanding between him and Mr Asquith, and the latter had himself proposed methods by which the War Committee could be reformed, and its work carried out with him (Mr Lloyd George) as Chairman, but under the personal control of the Prime Minister. On Tuesday morning, however, he received a letter practically withdrawing these proposals and consequently he had felt it his duty to resign. He believed that unless a real War Committee, with full and independent powers, was constituted, we should go to ruin and lose the War, which up till now had been mismanaged. He had no ambition to be Prime Minister, and was ready to see Mr Asquith form another Government, and stand out, at the same time giving it his full support. Failing that, he appealed to Mr Asquith to join the Government under Mr Bonar Law.

Mr Asquith maintained that the Prime Minister and nobody else could preside over the War Committee, otherwise decisions might be arrived at which he could not agree to, which would result in friction and delay. In his opinion the War Committee had done admirable work. As to strictures upon the conduct of the War, he was unable to remember any case in which a decision had been arrived at without the concurrence of Mr Lloyd George. Mr Asquith continued by denouncing in serious terms the action of the Press. The Prime Minister's work was sufficiently heavy and responsible without his being subjected to daily vindictive, merciless attacks in the columns of the newspapers, and he urged that whatever Government might come into Office, measures should be taken to prevent the continuance of this Press tyranny. He had been accused of clinging to Office, but he appealed to all those present as to whether such a charge was justifiable. He could honestly say that on waking this morning he was thankful to feel he was a free man. Mr Asquith referred in touching terms to the unquestioning confidence the King had invariably placed in him, of which he had received His Majesty's assurance only two days ago. He deeply valued it, and only hoped that his successor might enjoy the same generous trust and support which His Majesty had graciously reposed in him.

The King now called the attention of the Meeting to the fact that although the matter had been fully discussed, no decision had been come to.

Mr Balfour, in reply, said that he considered it was impossible for Mr Asquith to form a Government after what Mr Bonar Law had said about his party. A Government without Mr Lloyd George was impossible. Apparently Mr Bonar Law was ready to form a Government if Mr Asquith would agree to accept a subordinate place, but, failing this, he would propose that Mr Lloyd George should form an Administration.

The result of the Meeting was an agreement that Mr Asquith should consider the proposals made to him, and let Mr Bonar Law know as soon as possible whether he would join the Government under him. If the answer was in the negative, Mr Bonar Law would not form a Government, but Mr Lloyd George would endeavour to do so.'

The King dismissed the Conference at 4.30 p.m. Mr Asquith returned to Downing Street and called the Liberal ex-Ministers into consultation. Mr Arthur Henderson also attended the meeting. Mr Asquith asked his former colleagues whether, in their opinion, he ought to join a Government formed by either Mr Bonar Law or Mr Lloyd George. With the exception of Mr Edwin Montagu[1] and Mr

---

[1] Mr Edwin Montagu (1879–1924) entered Parliament in 1906 and from 1910–1914 held the post of Parliamentary Under Secretary at the India Office. In 1917 he became Secretary of State for India and the originator of the Montagu-Chelmsford reforms. In December 1919 he induced Parliament to accept his Government of India Bill under which dyarchy was established. In March 1922 he was forced to resign owing to a disagreement with Mr Lloyd George and he lost his seat at the ensuing election. The premature death of this imaginative, gifted and melancholy man was a severe loss to British politics.

Henderson they expressed the decided view that such an arrangement would be impracticable. Mr Asquith was himself convinced
that if he remained in the Government, even in a subordinate
capacity, the Press attacks would continue and that any subsequent
failure would be attributed to his presence. He foresaw moreover
that friction was bound sooner or later to develop between himself
and Mr Lloyd George in regard to the relations between the Cabinet
and their military advisers and that an even more damaging political
crisis would then inevitably arise. The Liberal Ministers decided
therefore that it was preferable in the national interest that they and
their leader should form a 'sober and responsible Opposition,
steadily supporting the Government in the conduct of the war'.*
Mr Bonar Law was so informed.

> 'At seven,' the King's diary continued, 'I received Bonar Law, who
> told me that he could not form a Government, as Asquith refused to
> serve under him. So I sent for Lloyd George & asked him to form a
> Government, which he said he would endeavour to do.'

During the morning and afternoon of the next day, Thursday,
December 7, Mr Lloyd George applied his remarkable powers of
solicitation and persuasion to obtaining recruits. He was aware that
the more prominent Liberal Ministers in Mr Asquith's Cabinet had
pledged themselves not to take office under his leadership; his
endeavour to include Mr Winston Churchill was vetoed by Mr
Bonar Law; he failed, at least for a time, to secure the help of Mr
Edwin Montagu. The Unionists proved more amenable. Lord
Curzon and Lord Milner hastily agreed to become members of the
proposed 'War Cabinet'. Mr Balfour, when asked to succeed Sir
Edward Grey as Foreign Secretary, accepted with the words 'You
put a pistol at my head'. In the end, as Mr Asquith's biographers
remark with some acidity, 'there were not enough pistols to go
round'.* After a meeting with the leaders of the Labour Party, Mr
Lloyd George was confident that they also would furnish their support. By the evening of the same day he was able to drive to Buckingham Palace in triumph:

> 'December 7 Thursday,' the King wrote in his diary, 'Mr Lloyd
> George came at 7.30 & informed me that he is able to form an ad-
> ministration & told me the proposed names of his colleagues. He will
> have a strong Government. I then appointed him Prime Minister &
> First Lord of the Treasury.'

On Monday, December 11, the retiring Ministers delivered up

their seals and their successors were sworn in.[1] The King, in affectionate sympathy for Mr Asquith, offered him the Garter: it was politely and gratefully refused.

(3)

Mr Lloyd George had not been in office for twenty-four hours when it was learnt that Germany was about to make proposals for peace. Apart from their desire to sow dissension among the allies and to confuse public opinion in the United States, the German Government had three motives for selecting that particular moment. Although their armies appeared to be victorious everywhere, the civilian population, with hard winter months before them, were already feeling the strain of our blockade. President Wilson was known to be preparing a Note to all the belligerents asking them to state their peace terms; the Germans feared that this might imply some form of mediation and were anxious to take the wind out of the President's sails. And in the third place the military party had already

[1] The following Ministers resigned with Mr Asquith: Sir Edward Grey (Lord Grey of Fallodon), Lord Crewe, Lord Buckmaster, Mr McKenna, Mr H. Samuel, Mr Runciman, and Mr Montagu. The following Unionists agreed to serve under Mr Lloyd George: Lord Curzon, Lord Finlay (Lord Chancellor), Mr Bonar Law (Chancellor of the Exchequer), Sir George Cave (Home Office), Mr Balfour (Foreign Office), Mr Walter Long (Colonies), Mr Austen Chamberlain (India), Lord Derby (War Office), Sir A. Stanley (Board of Trade), Sir Edward Carson (Admiralty), Sir F. E. Smith (Attorney General), and Mr H. E. Duke (Ireland). Dr Addison became Minister of Munitions and Mr H. A. L. Fisher took the Board of Education.

Mr Lloyd George introduced three innovations, (I) A War Cabinet consisting of himself as chairman assisted by Lord Curzon, Lord Milner, Mr. Arthur Henderson and Mr Bonar Law. (II) Several specialised new Ministries, namely: Shipping under Sir J. Maclay, Food under Lord Devonport and later under Lord Rhondda, Pensions under Mr George Barnes, Labour under Mr John Hodge, an Air Board under Lord Cowdray, and a Ministry of National Service under Mr Neville Chamberlain. (III) A Cabinet Secretariat was established under Sir Maurice Hankey. Henceforward the handwritten reports furnished daily to the King by the Prime Minister were replaced by detailed minutes circulated to the King and the Cabinet.

Mr Asquith's Coalition Government of 25 members had been composed of 14 Liberals, 10 Unionists and 1 Labour. Mr Lloyd George's Coalition Government, including Under Secretaries, comprised 33 members, of whom 15 were Unionists, 12 Liberals, 3 Labour, and 3 not members of either House of Parliament.

decided on unrestricted submarine warfare and hoped by a prior peace gesture to muffle the shock which this decision would cause.

The King, who was constantly receiving from his Danish friend, Mr H. N. Andersen,[1] first-hand information regarding internal conditions in Germany, was afraid that Mr Lloyd George, with his impulsive vehemence, might reject the German overture in terms of such violence as to strengthen the militarists in Berlin and alienate moderate opinion in the United States. He, therefore, in his own hand, addressed to him a tactful warning:[1]

> Buckingham Palace, December 13
> 1916.
> 'Dear Prime Minister,
> The Press announcement that Germany is about to approach the Allies of the Entente with a Note embodying Peace Negotiations brings us to a critical stage, demanding the utmost care and delicate handling. In these circumstances I am sure you will agree that it is most desirable that no public utterances on this subject should be made in responsible quarters until the Note has been received, considered by the Government, and their decision arrived at after consultation with the Allies.
> Meanwhile I trust it will be possible to prevent any question being put forward in Parliament until you can make your pronouncement. One misplaced word might do irreparable harm and I am sure you will be the first to recognize the supreme importance of safeguarding our position at this juncture. We must be most careful with regard to the United States.'

The German Peace Note, when delivered through the American Embassy in London, proved to be a gesture rather than a concrete proposal. While affirming the 'indestructible strength' of Germany and her allies, the German Government vaguely suggested that the time had come to enter into peace negotiations. They did not, however, give the slightest indication of the terms which they were pre-

---

[1] Mr Hans Niels Andersen (1852–1937) was a man of influence and wisdom. Born of working-class parents in the Danish island of Loland, he had served as a cabin boy in a brig trading to the Far East. When in Siam he had founded a shipping and timber business which eventually expanded into the East Asiatic Company. He was the first man to introduce Diesel engines into ships. He became an intimate friend of the Danish Royal Family and by them was introduced to King George, the German Emperor and the Tsar of Russia. During the war he conducted negotiations with the belligerent Governments on behalf of Danish trading interests and was constantly travelling between London, St Petersburg and Berlin. King George, as well as the British Foreign Office, held him in high esteem.

pared either to offer or accept. The King still felt that our reply should be carefully considered and undramatic. On December 16 he wrote again to Mr Lloyd George:[1]

> 'At this critical time I am impressed with the feeling how urgently important it is that the Speech which you deliver in Parliament on the German Note should be couched in terms of the utmost dignity and statesmanship. The whole world will anxiously await and scrupulously weigh every word that falls from your lips. . . . We must not, even inadvertently, put ourselves in the wrong and we should endeavour to avoid alienating the sympathy of the moderate party in America.
> I am sure you will appreciate my anxiety in this matter.'

Less than a week after the receipt of the German overture, President Wilson's formal Peace Note of December 18 was handed to each of the belligerent Powers. Some recapitulation will here be necessary if the circumstances of the President's intervention, which were widely misunderstood at the time, are rightly to be understood.

(4)

On May 7, 1915, the *Lusitania* was torpedoed without warning by a German submarine. Colonel House,[1] the President's friend and emissary, who was then in London, agreed with the Ambassador, Mr Page, that America's only reply to such an outrage must be a declaration of war:

> 'Mr House', the King wrote in his diary for May 8, 'came to see me after luncheon & told me that he thinks America will most likely go to war with Germany on account of the drowning of so many Americans on bd. the Lusitania.'

President Wilson was not of this opinion. In a speech which he delivered at Philadelphia on May 10 he declared that 'there is such a thing as being too proud to fight'. The President, although a master of English prose, although inspired by imaginative and exalted ideas, was sometimes too self-centred to estimate the effect on others of his esoteric choice of words. The British public, anguished by an unsuccessful war, saw only that American citizens had been ruthlessly murdered; they failed to comprehend the President's humane hesitations; nor did they understand that he was

---

[1] Edward Mandell House (1858–1938) was born at Houston, Texas, and played an important part in the nomination of Woodrow Wilson in 1912. He thereafter became the President's Ambassador at large, and owing to his discretion and sagacity exercised a great and beneficent influence in world affairs. For reasons which still remain somewhat mysterious he became estranged from the President in 1918.

faced in his own country by potent advocates of the 'Freedom of the Seas', who regarded it as an equal outrage that the British Admiralty should, in their ever-increasing exercise of the blockade, violate what had hitherto been regarded as fundamental principles of international law.

Instead, therefore, of treating the sinking of the *Lusitania* as a case for war, the President embarked upon an exchange of Notes with the German Government, who showed great ingenuity in confusing the issue by subsidiary arguments and thereby prolonging the controversy for several months.

Early in 1916 Colonel House came to Europe on a second mission. He was received by the King on the morning of January 14:

> 'I called at Buckingham Palace', he wrote,[k] 'at eleven o'clock and had a pleasant hour with the King. He was not at all pessimistic as to the attitude of the United States, but, on the contrary, as soon as I explained some doubts in his mind, he cordially agreed with our position.'

The purpose of Colonel House's journey went beyond that of an ordinary visit of investigation. The complete victory of Germany would, he felt, be a disaster for world democracy: the complete victory of the Allies might mean that France, Russia and Italy would insist upon annexations and indemnities such as 'would not be in the interest of permanent peace'.[l] His aim was to elicit from the Allies a statement of their peace-terms such as would appeal to American and neutral opinion as reasonable and just. If the Germans rejected these terms then 'America would enter the war against Germany'.

The President accepted this formula but inserted the word 'probably' between the words 'would' and 'enter' in the operative phrase. Colonel House had derived from a short visit to Berlin the impression that the German Government were determined to secure what he called 'a victory peace'. He placed all his hopes upon the British Government. Although Sir Edward Grey was personally in favour of his plan, the Cabinet did not feel that any peace negotiations could be entered into at a moment when our military fortunes were at so low an ebb. To the end of his life Colonel House maintained that, by our hesitation in those early months of 1916, we destroyed all hope of a reasonable peace.[m]

Shortly after Colonel House's return to the United States the Germans sank the unarmed passenger ship, the *Sussex*, without warning. President Wilson threatened the rupture of diplomatic

THE KING AND A YOUNG WORKER, SUNDERLAND

THE KING AND THE TSAR WITH THEIR RESPECTIVE
HEIRS

relations unless the German Government 'should immediately declare and effect the abandonment of their present methods of submarine warfare'. The German Government gave the required assurances. An expectant pause followed.

In November 1916 President Wilson was elected for a second term. Having won his election mainly on the slogan 'He kept us out of the War', he felt unable to resume the original plan and formula of Colonel House. The Note which he began to draft on November 21 was, in so far as Germany was addressed, far less minatory. He was still drafting his Note when the Asquith Government fell and were succeeded by that of Mr Lloyd George. The latter was known to be opposed to all negotiation and President Wilson therefore hesitated to despatch his Note until he could ascertain the attitude of the new British Government. He was still hesitating when the Germans launched their own Peace Note of December 12. The President then modified his original draft and despatched it on December 18.

It was not a happy document. Instead of offering mediation, it merely invited the belligerent Powers to state their peace terms and suggested an 'interchange of views'. It contained one phrase which was resented by the Allied peoples. In his first draft the President had inserted the sentence 'The cause and objects of the war are obscure'. Colonel House pointed out that such words would cause deep offence. The President therefore altered them in his final draft to read 'the objects which the belligerents on both sides have in mind are virtually the same'. The British public were outraged by this assertion, since it seemed to place them on the same footing as the German aggressors. The King, according to Mr Page, was so angered by this sentence that he 'wept while expressing his surprise and depression'.[n] Nor did President Wilson improve matters by sending a message to the Senate on January 22, 1917, pleading for 'peace without victory', and on the basis of self-determination. But in any case the Allied terms, when communicated to Washington, proved so drastic that any 'interchange of views' became, given the existing military situation, utterly impossible.[1]

---

[1] The Allied terms were: The restoration of Belgium, Serbia and Montenegro: the evacuation of invaded territory in France, Russia and Rumania with just reparation: the cession of Alsace-Lorraine; self-determination for subject nationalities in Austria, Hungary and Turkey: the exclusion of the latter from Europe: and an international convention to provide security against further aggression. No mention was made of colonial distribution.

The German terms, which were privately communicated to President

On January 31, 1917, the dispute between Germany and the United States entered a quick and final phase. The Germans had for long believed that their only hope of winning the war was to starve Great Britain into submission. They fully realised that a resort to unrestricted submarine warfare would result in the United States entering the war against them. But they calculated that Great Britain could be brought to her knees before a sufficient number of American troops could be trained, equipped, or transported to Europe. Their estimate, as will be seen, was not quite so fantastic as has sometimes been asserted.

On February 1, 1917, the Germans announced that thenceforward their submarines would impose an unrestricted blockade on Great Britain. On February 3, President Wilson broke off diplomatic relations. He was still waiting, however, for an 'overt act'. On February 26 the British Intelligence Service intercepted, and immediately communicated to Washington, a message to the German Minister in Mexico City, instructing him to offer the Mexican Government, in return for an alliance against the United States, the sundered provinces of New Mexico, Texas and Arizona. On the same day the steamer *Laconia* was torpedoed with the loss of American lives. On April 2 President Wilson came to Congress and invited them to declare the existence of a State of War between the United States and Germany. 'It is a fearful thing', he said, 'to lead this great peaceful people into war.'

On Saturday, April 7, the King made a laconic entry in his diary:

'Windsor Castle. Six degrees of frost in the night. The United States of America declared war against Germany yesterday by a large majority in the Congress: 373 to 50.'

(5)

To the historian, with his knowledge of subsequent developments, the acquisition of so potent an associate as the United States appears as a miraculous solace for the simultaneous elimination of Russia. The peoples and statesmen of the time did not estimate this dual

Wilson by the German Ambassador, included: the restoration of Belgium 'under special guarantees for the safety of Germany': restitution of French territory, in return for frontier rectifications and compensation to be paid to Germany by France: Germany and Poland to receive in the east a frontier which would protect them strategically and economically against Russia: the return of the German colonies: and the Freedom of the Seas.

event in terms either of such gigantic profit or such disastrous loss. Relieved though they were that the United States had at last rallied to the cause of democracy, they did not foresee the speed or weight of American assistance. To them the Russian Revolution portended,[1] not the quick disintegration of mighty armies, but the abolition of an autocratic system, the incompetence and corruption of which had hitherto prevented Russia from fully exercising her enormous power. The general feeling was reflected in a telegram addressed on March 21 by Mr Lloyd George to the head of the Provisional Government in Petrograd. In this message the British Prime Minister expressed the 'sentiments of the most profound satisfaction' with which the peoples of Great Britain and the British Dominions had welcomed the adoption by Russia of 'responsible government'. He described the Revolution as 'the greatest service that the Russian people have yet made to the cause for which the Allies are fighting'. The King intimated to Mr Lloyd George that he regarded the wording of this message as 'a little strong'. The Prime Minister explained that his telegram had, 'to a considerable extent', been drafted by the Russian Chargé d'Affaires, M. Constantine Nabokov.⁰.[2]

On hearing that the Tsar had abdicated, the King sent him the following telegram of personal sympathy:

'Buckingham Palace, March 19, 1917. Events of last week have deeply distressed me. My thoughts are constantly with you and I shall always remain your true and devoted friend, as you know I have been in the past.'

[1] The main dates of the Russian Revolution are as follows: December 29, *1916*, Rasputin murdered. *1917*: January, the Duma is adjourned and the Congress of Zemstvos at Moscow is prohibited; March 8, the Tsar leaves for his headquarters; March 9–11, bread riots in Petrograd; March 12, Guards regiment mutiny and Winter Palace and fortress of St Peter and Paul are stormed; March 15, the Tsar abdicates in favour of his brother; Provisional Government established under Prince Lvov; March 22, the Emperor taken to Tsarskoe where he and his family are placed under arrest; April 4, Lenin arrives at the Finland Station; July, Bolshevik rising in Petrograd crushed by Kerensky; Kornilov attempts counter-revolution; August, the Tsar and his family transferred to Tobolsk; November 7, Bolshevik Revolution. *1918*: March 3, Bolsheviks sign Treaty of Brest Litovsk with the Germans; July 16, Tsar and his family murdered at Ekaterinburg.

[2] Count Benckendorff, the highly esteemed Russian Ambassador, had died of influenza in London in January 1917. No successor was appointed either by the Tsarist or the Provisional Government and the Russian Embassy remained for long in the hands of a Chargé d'Affaires.

This message was telegraphed by the War Office to Major-General Sir John Hanbury Williams, British Military Representative at Russian Headquarters. It arrived after the Tsar had been removed from Mohilev under arrest. Sir John therefore repeated the King's telegram to Sir George Buchanan, British Ambassador at Petrograd, who handed it to M. Miliukov, Foreign Minister in the Provisional Government, with the request that it might be forwarded to the Tsar. The next day M. Miliukov sent for Sir George Buchanan and informed him that he thought it better not to send on the telegram as it 'might be misinterpreted and used as an argument in favour of (the Tsar's) detention'.[p] The Ambassador reported this statement to the Foreign Office in an official telegram which was circulated to the Cabinet. The Prime Minister's secretary then telephoned to the Palace asking to be furnished with the original text of the King's message. The King replied that, since his telegram to the Tsar was a private and unofficial communication, he did not feel disposed to communicate its text to the Cabinet, although he would be pleased to let the Prime Minister see the telegram if he so desired. In any case, since the message had never been delivered to the Tsar, he felt that it should now be cancelled. A telegram was sent to Sir George Buchanan to that effect.[q]

This comparatively trivial incident rendered it evident that any efforts the King could make to comfort and assist his unfortunate cousin might, unless cautiously handled, embarrass the moderate elements in the Russian Provisional Government and even be misinterpreted at home. On March 19 Sir George Buchanan had been officially instructed to inform M. Miliukov that 'any violence done to the Emperor or his family would have a most deplorable effect and would deeply shock public opinion in this country'. M. Miliukov, who was desperately anxious for the Imperial family to leave Russia, fearing that their lives might be endangered in the event of a counter-revolution, enquired whether the British Government would be willing to grant them an asylum in England. At a meeting which took place at Downing Street on March 22 between the Prime Minister, Mr Bonar Law, Lord Stamfordham and Lord Hardinge,[1] it was agreed that, since the proposal had been initiated by the Russian Government, it could not possibly be refused. Sir George Buchanan was therefore instructed to inform M. Miliukov

[1] On his return from India Lord Hardinge, in June 1916, had succeeded Sir Arthur Nicolson as Permanent Under Secretary for Foreign Affairs.

that asylum would be granted to the Imperial family in England for the duration of the war.[r]

The King, who would have preferred the Tsar and his wife to find refuge in Switzerland or Denmark, doubted the wisdom of this arrangement. On March 30 he instructed Lord Stamfordham to write to the Foreign Secretary:[s]

'The King has been thinking much about the Government's proposal that the Emperor Nicholas and his family should come to England. As you are doubtless aware, the King has a strong personal friendship for the Emperor and therefore would be glad to do anything to help him in this crisis. But His Majesty cannot help doubting not only on account of the dangers of the voyage, but on general grounds of expediency, whether it is advisable that the Imperial Family should take up their residence in this country. The King would be glad if you would consult the Prime Minister, as His Majesty understands that no definite decision has yet been come to on the subject by the Russian Government.'

Mr Balfour replied on April 2:[t]

'His Majesty's Ministers quite realize the difficulties to which you refer in your letter, but they do not think, unless the position changes, that it is now possible to withdraw the invitation which has been sent, and they therefore trust that the King will consent to adhere to the original invitation, which was sent on the advice of His Majesty's Ministers.'

By this time the suggestion that the Tsar and his family should be given asylum in this country had become publicly known. Much indignation was expressed in left-wing circles and the King, who was unjustly supposed to be the originator of the proposal, received many abusive letters. Sir George Buchanan, moreover, pointed out that the presence of the Imperial family in England would assuredly be exploited to our detriment by the extremists as well as by the German agents in Russia. The King felt that these disadvantages had not been sufficiently considered by the Government. On April 10, he instructed Lord Stamfordham again to suggest to the Prime Minister that, since public opinion was evidently opposed to the proposal, the Russian Government might be informed that His Majesty's Government felt obliged to withdraw the consent which they had previously given:

'I reminded the Prime Minister', Lord Stamfordham recorded,[u] 'about what had been said as to the King's attitude regarding the King of Greece, and the exception taken to His Majesty having received the brothers of King Constantine when they were in London. And I said that no doubt we should have similar complaints respecting the Emperor and Empress, who, of course, the King would see if they came to England: as not only are they His Majesty's relations but the Emperor has been a staunch friend and Ally of this Country ever since he ascended the Throne twenty-three years ago. I added that even if the Government publicly stated that they took the responsibility for Their Imperial Majesties coming, the People would reply that this was done to screen the King.'

Mr Lloyd George now realised that the question of asylum was more difficult than he had first supposed. Since M. Painlevé, the French Minister of War, happened at that moment to be in Downing Street he was called in to consultation and asked whether the French Government would give the Russian Royal Family asylum in France. He replied in the affirmative and a telegram was thus sent to Sir George Buchanan instructing him to place this alternative suggestion before M. Miliukov. But by then the influence of the moderate elements in Russia had been already undermined.

It is doubtful whether, even if immediate action had been taken, the escape of the Imperial Family could have been contrived. The Tsar, who was fatalistically blind to the coming danger, would probably have refused to leave Russian soil; and in any case his children were ill at the time and unable to travel. After the first few weeks M. Miliukov and his friends were without real power and the soldiers and workers would have prevented the Tsar's departure by force. In August 1917 the Imperial family were removed to Tobolsk. On April 15, 1918, they were taken under harsher custody to Ekaterinburg. It was there, on the night of July 16–17, 1918, that they were murdered by the Bolsheviks in the house of the engineer Ipatiev.

(6)

The King, although he much admired Mr Lloyd George's energy, resourcefulness and moral courage, although he was charmed by the Prime Minister's humour and vivacity, was apprehensive of his unorthodox methods and distressed by his failure to establish relations of confidence with Sir Douglas Haig or Sir William Robertson.

The tension between the soldiers and the politicians reached a climax in February 1917. General Nivelle,[1] who had succeeded

---

[1] General Nivelle (1856–1924) had acquired renown by repulsing the initial German attack on Verdun and by later recapturing the fort of Douaumont. He succeeded General Joffre in December 1916.

General Joffre as Commander in Chief of the French armies, had planned for that year a synchronised offensive upon all fronts. Mr Lloyd George desired that, for the purpose of this offensive, the British Army should be placed under General Nivelle's orders. A conference between British and French ministers and generals was due to take place at Calais on February 26, for the ostensible purpose of discussing transport arrangements. At a Cabinet meeting held on February 24, to which neither the Secretary of State for War nor the C.I.G.S. were invited, the Prime Minister was authorised to take the occasion of the Calais Conference to secure unity of command. The King, the Generals and the Secretary of State for War were not, at the time, informed of this decision. Accompanied by Sir William Robertson, the Prime Minister on February 26 left for Calais, where he was joined by Sir Douglas Haig, M. Briand, General Nivelle and General Lyautey.[1] The Conference assembled that afternoon in a sitting-room at the Hotel Terminus. In a letter which he wrote to the King on February 28° Sir Douglas Haig furnished a detailed account of what transpired.

After the transport problems had been rapidly disposed of,[2] Mr Lloyd George invited General Nivelle to disclose his plans for the forthcoming campaign. Sir Douglas Haig's letter continues:

'When Nivelle had finished, L.G. insisted that he (Nivelle) had something further to put before the meeting. Eventually the question of "Command on the Western Front" was discussed, but evidently not in the manner which L.G. had hoped, for finally he said that he would like the French to formulate their proposals in writing and requested them to give him a copy by dinner time. It was then within an hour of dinner, so I presumed the paper had already been prepared. Indeed, this must have been the case, because later in the evening L.G. told Robertson and myself that the British Cabinet had discussed the French proposal a few days previously. . . . That same evening I saw Mr Lloyd George with General Robertson and I told the former that I could be no party to placing the British Army in France under a French Commander in Chief and that it would be madness to attempt

[1] General Lyautey (1854–1934) remained Minister of War for only three months. His real work was the pacification of Morocco and the establishment of the French Protectorate on a sound basis. He was made a Marshal of France in 1921.

[2] Mr Lloyd George in his *War Memoirs* does not devote to the Calais Conference the same detailed examination that he accords to other transactions. 'Transport', he says, 'occupied much of our time' (Vol. III, page 1502).

such a thing and hope to win the war. I gave a few reasons and spoke plainly. Mr Lloyd George agreed that the French proposals went too far, but informed us that the British Cabinet had decided that for the forthcoming operations the British Army should be directly under General Nivelle to take his orders. He asked General Robertson and myself to help him to comply with this decision by drawing up a scheme.'

The next morning a compromise arrangement was accepted, under which, during the preparatory stages, Sir Douglas Haig was not bound to accept General Nivelle's directives, although, once the battle was engaged, he must conform to the orders of the French Commander in Chief, while reserving for himself 'a free hand to choose the means and methods of utilising the British troops in that sector of operations allotted by the French Commander in Chief'. Since this compromise did not go much beyond the arrangements which had always existed between the French and the British commanders, Sir Douglas Haig and Sir William Robertson felt justified in signing the document. But they were left with the disturbing impression that, with French connivance, the Prime Minister had intended to present them with an accomplished fact:

'I think', Sir Douglas Haig's letter continued, 'that, as the actual document stands, no great difficulty should occur in carrying on just as I have been doing, provided there is not something *behind* it. It is for this reason that I have written so fully, in order that Your Majesty may be watchful and prevent any steps being taken which will result in our Army being broken up and incorporated in a French corps. . . .

Your Majesty will observe that in my dealings with Mr Lloyd George over this question I have never suggested that I should like to resign my Command, but on the contrary I have done my utmost to meet the views of the Government, as any change of Command at this time might be a disadvantage to the Army in the Field. It is possible however that the present War Cabinet may think otherwise and deem it best to replace me with someone more in their confidence. If this is so, I recommend that the change be made as soon as possible because of the proximity of the date fixed for the commencement of operations.

At this great crisis in our History, my sole object is to serve my King and Country wherever I can be of most use, and with full confidence I leave myself in Your Majesty's hands to decide what is best for me to do at this juncture.'

This assuredly was a difficult letter for any Constitutional Monarch to answer. The reply which, by His Majesty's command, Lord Stamfordham returned was a masterly combination of tact and propriety: *w*

Buckingham Palace,
'My dear Haig,   March 5 1917.

The King desires me to thank you for your Secret letter of the 28th February. You can well understand it was anything but agreeable reading to His Majesty. The King was unaware either that the question of the Command on the Western Front had been discussed at the War Cabinet Meeting on Saturday 24th February, or that it was to be the principal matter for consideration at the Calais Conference. It was not until the 28th February that His Majesty received the Minutes of the Meeting of the 24th, and later in the afternoon a copy of the Calais Agreement was sent to His Majesty within half an hour of his receiving the Prime Minister. Had the ordinary procedure been followed and the King informed of this momentous change in the conduct of the Campaign His Majesty would have unquestionably demanded further explanation before giving his consent to the proposal.

On my remarking to the Prime Minister that the Agreement conferred very extended powers to General Nivelle, he replied that these were concurred in by Sir William Robertson, and that both you and he had signed the Agreement.

The King recognises the paramount necessity of guarding against any possibility of the French—in the event of the attack failing—being able to lay the blame upon us. But at the same time His Majesty considers that it would have been possible to entrust the general direction and carrying out of the scheme to General Nivelle, while you gave effect to the instructions which you received from Lord Kitchener on taking over Command of the British Forces.

His Majesty appreciates the reasons which led you, at the request of the Prime Minister, to sign the Calais Agreement, but feels that your having done so it would be prudent now not to discuss these terms, but to take advantage of the period before the "move" begins to clear up with General Nivelle all points upon which you are doubtful or not satisfied. Apparently this would not be difficult as the King understands that General Nivelle more than once during the Conference disclaimed any dissatisfaction on his part or any desire for the holding of the Conference.

The King begs you to dismiss from your mind any idea of resignation. Such a course would be in His Majesty's opinion disastrous to his Army and to the hopes of success in the coming supreme struggle. You have the absolute confidence of that Army from the highest to the lowest rank: a confidence which is shared to the full by the King. Such a step would never have His Majesty's consent, nor does he believe that it is one entertained for a moment by his Government.

The King is sorry to think that in the few weeks which yet remain for the completion of your arrangements for the Attack your mind should be occupied and disturbed by a matter which everyone naturally presumed would have been settled as a primary factor in the initiation of this important and far reaching undertaking.

In conclusion I am to say from His Majesty you are not to worry:

you may be certain that he will do his utmost to protect your interests, and he begs you to continue to work on the most amicable and open terms with General Nivelle, and he feels all will come right.'

The great concerted offensives which General Nivelle had planned for 1917 proved a failure. In the East, the Russian armies were in process of disintegration; the Italians, who remained quiescent during the spring and summer, were in the late autumn badly shaken by the defeat of Caporetto; in the West, the Germans anticipated the allied offensive by cutting off their salient and withdrawing to the Siegfried line. Many French units mutinied and as a result General Nivelle was replaced by General Pétain. The brunt of the campaign fell upon the British armies, whose fine successes,— the Battle of Arras, the capture of the Messines Ridge, and the tank surprise at Cambrai—were clouded by the mud and misery of Passchendaele.

CHAPTER XIX

DEFEAT AND VICTORY

1917-1918

The effect of the Russian Revolution—Attacks upon the Monarchy in Great Britain—Lord Stamfordham's equable attitude—The Royal House becomes the 'House of Windsor'—The Irish Convention—The attempts to induce Austria to make a separate peace—Prince Sixte of Bourbon-Parma—The Reichstag Resolution and the Pope's Peace Note—Lord Lansdowne's letter—The King's solicitude for our prisoners of war and his dislike of reprisals—General Pershing arrives—Mr Lloyd George's appreciation of the war situation—The Mesopotamia Report—The King's defence of Lord Hardinge—Renewed differences between Mr Lloyd George and Sir William Robertson—The King tries in vain to persuade the latter not to resign—The Ludendorff offensive—The King's last visit to the Front—The beginning of the end—The surrender of Bulgaria—The collapse of Germany—The armistice.

(1)

THE collapse of the Tsarist system spread tremors of alarm or expectation throughout the world. Those who, until then, had hoped that the advent of socialism would be so gradual as to be almost painless were startled by the spectre of imminent and ruthless change. The proletariate, shaken out of acquiescence by sudden visions of world solidarity and power, were roused to a sense of exciting and urgent opportunity. Even in Great Britain where Republicanism was assumed to have died in 1872, there were some who exploited the occasion to deride the monarchical tradition and to advocate an English Revolution upon Russian lines.

On March 31, 1917, a mass meeting was held in the Albert Hall, under the chairmanship of Mr George Lansbury, to celebrate the fall of Tsardom. Although the speeches delivered were comparatively innocuous, the Censor prohibited any detailed reports of the meeting, an error that permitted all manner of rumours and suspicions to creep around. On April 21 Mr H. G. Wells addressed to *The Times* a letter asserting that the moment had come to rid ourselves of 'the ancient trappings of throne and sceptre' and urging that Republican societies should immediately be formed. In another connection Mr Wells referred to the sad spectacle of England struggling through adversity under 'an alien and uninspiring Court'. The King was incensed by this imputation. 'I may be uninspiring,' he remarked to a visitor,[a] 'but I'll be d——d if I'm alien.' On May 23 a letter, above the signatures of Mr Ramsay MacDonald and other left-wing socialists, was circulated to Trades Unions and Labour organisations, inviting them to send delegates to a Convention to be held at Leeds on June 3. This letter announced, not only that the Convention would 'do for this country what the Russian Revolution had accomplished in Russia', but that it would call for the establishment of 'Councils of Workmen's and Soldiers' delegates' throughout the land.[b]

Lord Stamfordham, with his accustomed sense of balance, did not exaggerate these symptoms of ferment. He had his own clear views as to the proper function of a Constitutional Monarchy in a changing world:[c]

> 'We must endeavour to induce the thinking working classes, Socialist and others, to regard the Crown, not as a mere figure-head and as an institution which, as they put it, "don't count", but as a living power for good, with receptive faculties welcoming information affecting the interests and social well-being of all classes, and ready, not only to sympathise with those questions, but anxious to further their solution. Regarding Labour troubles and industrial disputes, I know, of course, that the role of arbitrator is not one which the Sovereign can adopt, but if opportunities are seized, during His Majesty's visits to industrial centres, in conversation with the workmen, to show his interest in such problems as employers and employed will have to solve, these men will recognise in the Crown those characteristics—may I say "virtues"?— which I have ventured to enumerate above.'

Mr Lloyd George in his *War Memoirs*[d] pays a further tribute to the King's initiative in visiting industrial areas at a moment of disaffection and unrest:

> 'There can be no question that one outstanding reason for the high level of loyalty and patriotic effort which the people of this country maintained was the attitude and conduct of King George. . . . In estimating the value of the different factors which conduced to the maintenance of our home front in 1917, a very high place must be given to the affection inspired by the King and the unremitting diligence with which he set himself in those dark days to discharge the function of his high office.'

Lord Stamfordham warmly encouraged the King's desire to move freely and frequently among his people. He was fully cognisant of the criticisms which, in the confused and restless state of public opinion, were then being made. Not only did he read the newspapers of every shade and colour but he was in constant communication with such people as Mr St. Loe Strachey, Colonel Unsworth of the Salvation Army, Mr Hagberg Wright, the Bishop of Chelmsford or Canon Woodward, Rector of Southwark, whose activities brought them into touch with different sections of the community. The only rumour which seems to have disturbed his equanimity was the suggestion that the King was surrounded by a complacent phalanx of courtiers, who carefully concealed from him all unpleasant facts:

'Even at the risk', he wrote to Lord Revelstoke in June 1917,[e] 'of being egotistical, I unhesitatingly can say that I do not believe that there is any Sovereign in the world to whom the truth is more fearlessly told and who receives it with such good will—and even gratitude—as King George. There is no Socialist newspaper, no libellous rag, that is not read and marked and shown to the King if they contain any criticism friendly or unfriendly to His Majesty and the Royal Family. As to "counteracting insidious propaganda", I venture to think that no better course can be followed than that the King should adhere to those lines of duty to the State and of strict observance of his Constitutional position which have been His Majesty's guiding principles during the exceptionally stormy and arduous seven years of his reign.'

The King, as his tutors had observed when he was a boy, was sensitive to criticism, essentially diffident and prone to discouragement. The phrase of some impatient intellectual, the gibes of some weary commentator, rankled unduly. When in May 1917 he was told that it was whispered that he must be pro-German since he and his family had German names, 'he started and grew pale'.[f] Lord Stamfordham, when appealed to, was forced to admit that many members of the Royal Family did in fact bear names of Teutonic origin. Mr Farnham Burke of the Royal College of Heralds was then consulted and asked what was in fact the King's own name. He was not quite positive. He was certain it was not 'Stewart'; he doubted whether it was 'Guelph'; he surmised that it must be either 'Wipper' or 'Wettin'. The King decided that some new name must be adopted. Several alternatives were considered. The Duke of Connaught suggested 'Tudor-Stewart'; both Lord Rosebery and Mr Asquith felt that such a name might have inauspicious associations. The names 'Plantagenet', 'York', 'England', 'Lancaster', 'D'Este' and 'Fitzroy' were all in their turn considered and rejected. Finally Lord Stamfordham, having discovered that at one time Edward III had been called 'Edward of Windsor', suggested this natural English name. It was immediately welcomed.[1] On July 17 the following announcement was approved by the Privy Council and published in the Press on the morning of July 18:

'We, of Our Royal Will and Authority, do hereby declare and announce that as from the date of this Our Royal Proclamation Our House and Family shall be styled and known as the House and Family of Windsor, and that all the descendants in the male line of Our said Grandmother Queen Victoria who are subjects of these Realms, other than female descendants who may marry or may have married, shall bear the said Name of Windsor:

And do hereby further declare and announce that We for Ourselves and for and on behalf of Our descendants and all other descendants of Our said Grandmother Queen Victoria who are subjects of these Realms, relinquish and enjoin the discontinuance of the use of the degrees, styles, dignities, titles and honours of Dukes and Duchesses of Saxony and Princes and Princesses of Saxe-Coburg and Gotha, and all other German degrees, styles, dignitaries, titles, honours and appellations to Us or to them heretofore belonging or appertaining.[2]

[1] 'Do you realize' wrote Lord Rosebery to Lord Stamfordham on June 26, 'that you have christened a dynasty? There are few people in the world who have done this, none I think. It is really something to be historically proud of. I admire and envy you' (R.A. O.1153, XVI, 354).

[2] The members of the Royal Family who were residing in England and who bore German titles were at the same time invited to relinquish these titles and to adopt British surnames. Thus the King's two brothers-in-law, the Duke of Teck and Prince Alexander of Teck, became respectively Marquis of Cambridge and Earl of Athlone with the family name of Cambridge. The King's two cousins, Prince Louis of Battenberg and Prince Alexander of Battenberg, became respectively Marquis of Milford Haven and Marquis of Carisbrooke, with the family name of Mountbatten.

The King took the opportunity to define and restrict the use of the titles 'Royal Highness', 'Prince' and 'Princess'. Letters Patent gazetted on December 11, 1917, declared that:

'The children of any Sovereign of the United Kingdom, and the children of the sons of any such Sovereign, and the eldest living son of the eldest son of the Prince of Wales, shall have and at all times hold and enjoy the style, title or attribute of Royal Highness, with their titular dignity of Prince or Princess prefixed to their respective Christian names, or with their other titles of honour. That, save as aforesaid, the titles of Royal Highness, Highness, or Serene Highness and the titular dignity of Prince or Princess shall cease, except these titles already granted and remaining unrevoked.'

It was 'tacitly understood' that in accepting peerages of the United Kingdom and thereby entering the House of Lords these members of the Royal Family 'would not identify themselves with any political Party'. (Lord Stamfordham to Mr George Barnes, June 19, 1917. R.A. O.1153, IV, 109.)

(2)

On March 7, 1917, the Prime Minister wrote to the King, stating that he had received information that Mr Redmond and his followers, being alarmed by the increasing influence of Sinn Fein, intended to stage a demonstration in the House of Commons and to issue some sort of appeal to the Dominions, the United States and neutral countries. In order to anticipate such action the Cabinet had decided that it would be wise 'to put ourselves right with the civilised world'. He proposed therefore to make an immediate statement in Parliament, offering Home Rule 'to that part of Ireland that wants it', while adding that no British Government could 'now or at any time hand over Ulster to the rest of Ireland against its will'.*g* The King replied that he considered this 'an excellent idea'. Mr Lloyd George made his statement that very afternoon. Mr Redmond and his Party, protesting that they would never accept the partition of Ireland, walked out of the House.

On May 1 Mr Lloyd George offered Mr Redmond two alternatives, either immediate Home Rule with the exclusion of Ulster, or the summoning of an Irish Convention, representing all parties and shades of opinion and empowered to discuss, and to submit to the Imperial Parliament, a scheme for the future self-government of Ireland within the Empire. Mr Redmond rejected the first alternative but accepted the second. The Sinn Fein leaders immediately announced that they would boycott the Convention.

On June 11 the Prime Minister announced the composition of the Convention. It was to consist of 101 representative Irishmen, including the Irish Nationalists, the Ulster Protestants, the Southern Unionists, the Roman Catholic Bishops and the Church of Ireland Archbishops of Armagh and Dublin. The Government reserved for themselves the right of nominating the Chairman as well as fifteen prominent non-party Irishmen. Among those thus nominated were Dr Mahaffy, the Provost of Trinity College, and Mr George Russell. As a gesture of amity and good faith the Irish deportees interned after the Easter rising were immediately to be released:

'Very glad', the King wrote to Lord Stamfordham,*h* 'that the Government are going to grant an amnesty to the Irish prisoners as it ought to help the Convention. I see it is to be announced in the House today & I have never been asked for my approval. Usual way things are done in present day. I better join the King of Greece in exile!' [1]

[1] After the events of December 1, 1916, the Protecting Powers insisted that the Greek Army should be withdrawn to the Peloponnesus. In June

On July 25 the Convention assembled in Trinity College, Dublin. Sir Horace Plunkett[1] was elected Chairman and Sir Francis Hopwood[2] secretary. The deliberations of the Convention continued over the ensuing seven months. Several Committees were established and investigations were conducted, and evidence taken, both in Cork and Belfast. On November 21, 1917, the Grand Committee of the Convention issued a report suggesting that there should be one Parliament for the whole of Ireland, the Protestants both in the North and South being guaranteed 40% representation in the Lower House. This solution was rejected by the representatives of Ulster and the Southern Unionists. On April 5, 1918, the majority of the Convention recommended a scheme under which there should be one Parliament for the whole of Ireland with an executive to be responsible to it. Foreign Affairs and Defence were to be reserved for the Imperial Parliament, but the Irish Parliament were to have control over Finance. The Protestants of the North were resolute in their determination not to surrender the control of Finance to a Dublin Parliament. It was on this rock, essentially, that the Convention was wrecked.

During the whole period that the Convention lasted the King received from its Chairman, Sir Horace Plunkett, regular, volumin-

1917 M. Jonnart, as High Commissioner, appeared at Athens with a powerful naval squadron and demanded the deposition of King Constantine. He suggested that the latter with his wife and family should find asylum in the Isle of Wight. This proposal aroused King George's 'strong disapproval' (R.A. Q.838, 177). On June 12, 1917, King Constantine, with his wife and eldest son, retired to Switzerland, leaving the second son Alexander upon the throne. The latter died of blood poisoning after a short and lonely reign and in December 1920 King Constantine was recalled to Athens by plebiscite. After the disaster in Asia Minor he was a second time deposed, being succeeded by the Crown Prince George. He died at Palermo on January 11, 1923.

[1] Sir Horace Plunkett (1854–1932) devoted his life to the Irish agricultural cooperative movement. His political ambition was to keep Ireland united within the British Commonwealth. In 1922 he accepted membership of the Irish Senate, but resigned a year later after his house in Co. Dublin had been burned down by the rebels. He then retired to Weybridge, where he died.

[2] Sir Francis Hopwood had been Permanent Secretary at the Board of Trade and the Colonial Office. From 1912–1917 he served as a Civil Lord of the Admiralty. He accompanied King George on his visit to Canada as Prince of Wales in 1908. He was an intimate friend of Lord Stamfordham who frequently benefited by his wide knowledge and sagacious advice. In 1917 he was raised to the Peerage as Lord Southborough.

ous and optimistic reports. Sir Francis Hopwood did not share this optimism. He repeatedly warned Lord Stamfordham against all sanguine expectations. Mr Redmond had, he said, lost all influence in Ireland and Sinn Fein would never accept anything that the Convention, even if it proved unanimous, might recommend:

> 'There must', he wrote on October 27, 1917,[1] 'be another episode of blood & tears & sorrow & shame before we can settle this difficult business.'

(3)

The King was kept fully informed of the tentatives made throughout the year 1917 and the early months of 1918, to detach Austria from the German alliance. The old Emperor Francis Joseph died on November 21, 1916, after a reign of sixty-eight years. He was succeeded by his great-nephew Charles, who had married Princess Zita of Bourbon-Parma and who was known to be anxious to extract Austria from the war before the Hapsburg Empire dissolved into its component parts. The difficulty was, not only that Germany had by then acquired practical control over Austrian policy, but that Italy, who had been promised large slices of Austrian territory as payment for her entry into the war, was determined to veto any terms such as Austria could accept.

In February 1917 Sir Francis Hopwood was sent on a secret mission to Copenhagen, where it was hoped that, with Mr Andersen's assistance, he could establish contact with Count Mensdorff. The Germans got wind of this manoeuvre and Count Mensdorff felt it more prudent to remain aloof. In the same month Prince Sixte of Bourbon-Parma, the Austrian Emperor's brother-in-law, visited M. Poincaré and enquired on what terms France would be prepared to make peace. M. Poincaré demanded the cession to France of Alsace Lorraine and the Saar basin, the restoration of Belgium and Serbia, and the acquisition by Russia of Constantinople. On March 20 the Emperor Charles wrote to his brother-in-law in his own handwriting, accepting these proposals, but stating that the future of Constantinople must depend upon the establishment of settled Government in Russia.[1] At the Conference of St. Jean de Maurienne in April Baron Sonnino, the Italian Foreign Minister, was informed

[1] This letter from the Emperor of Austria was published by M. Clemenceau in April 1918. The Emperor strenuously, but fruitlessly, denied its authenticity.

of these overtures: he became scarlet with indignation and denounced any negotiations with Austria which did not include the full acceptance of Italy's territorial demands. The idea of detaching Austria continued none the less to exercise a fascination over Mr Lloyd George and President Wilson. Mr Lloyd George invited Prince Sixte to London and on May 23 took him to see the King:

'At 3.0 the Prime Minister brought Prince Sixte of Bourbon (brother of Empress of Austria) who is serving in the Belgian Army. He came to inform me that the Emperor of Austria had written to him to try & arrange for a separate peace with the Entente. The difficulty will be Italy. It is of course very secret: only M. Poincaré and M. Ribot know. It would be a great thing if it could be brought about.'

The dream of direct negotiation with Austria was not finally dispelled until, in December 1917, General Smuts met Count Mensdorff in Geneva and was informed that the Austrian Government were not in the position to make a separate peace but would gladly lend their good offices for general peace negotiations. This statement was confirmed in a message conveyed a few weeks later to Lord Stamfordham from Slatin Pasha,[1] who, while asserting that he regarded himself both as a 'faithful subject of the Austrian Emperor' and 'a British General and a loyal servant to King George',[*] added that any idea that Austria was physically in the position to detach herself from Germany was an utter illusion. President Wilson thereafter remained the only man who still believed in the feasibility of a separate peace with the Austro-Hungarian Empire.

These were not the only peace proposals which, during those dark months, came to cause confusion or to raise fallacious hopes in the minds of the belligerent peoples. On two occasions the King of Denmark wrote to King George suggesting that the moment had come

---

[1] Sir Rudolf Slatin Pasha, G.C.V.O., K.C.M.G. (1857–1932) resigned from the Austrian Army as a young man and took service under Gordon in the Sudan. He was captured by the Dervishes and kept a prisoner by the Khalifa for eleven years. In 1895 he escaped to Egypt and served with distinction in the Omdurman campaign. From 1900 to the outbreak of War he was Inspector General of the Sudan. In 1907 he was made an honorary Major General in the British Army. He happened to be on leave in Austria when war broke out. Refusing to take any action whatsoever against his former employers, he devoted himself to Red Cross work and was able to be of assistance to many British prisoners of war. At one time he was accused of having adhered to the King's enemies; this accusation was later found to be unjustified; he was invited to England, received by the King, and his British honours were restored to him.

for neutral mediation. The King replied that he feared that 'the end of this appalling war seems still a long way off' and that Great Britain would not be satisfied by anything short of 'an honourable and lasting peace'.[k] On July 19, 1917, Herr Erzberger[1] induced the Reichstag to pass a resolution demanding peace without annexations and indemnities. The German Emperor informed the Party leaders that within a month all British ships would be driven from the seas and that then 'all Europe, under my leadership, will begin the real war against England—the Second Punic War'. On August 1, 1917, the King received from the Cardinal Secretary of State, Cardinal Gasparri, a letter asking him to forward to the French Government, the Italian Government and the Government of the United States 'the concrete proposals of peace' sponsored by the Pope 'in his anxiety to do all that he can do to secure an end to the conflict which has for more than three years devastated the civilised world'.[l] The King replied that he had forwarded the Pope's Note to those with whom the Holy See was not in diplomatic relations:

> 'His Majesty the King', the reply continued,[m] 'has received these proposals with the most sincere appreciation of the lofty and bene-volent intentions which animated His Holiness and His Majesty's Government will study them with the closest and most serious atten-tion.'

In the end the Pope's Peace Note was, by agreement between the Allies, politely answered by referring His Holiness to the statement of peace terms sent to President Wilson in January 1917.

More disturbing in its effect upon British public opinion was the letter addressed by Lord Lansdowne to the *Daily Telegraph* on November 29, 1917. The outburst of indignation occasioned by this letter was, as it now seems, largely artificial. Lord Lansdowne had done no more than suggest that the prolongation of the war would 'spell ruin to the civilised world', and urge that there should be some coordination of allied war aims. Moreover, before sending the letter to the *Daily Telegraph*, he had, as Lord Burnham told the King, taken the precaution to consult Colonel House and Lord Hardinge,

---

[1] Herr Matthias Erzberger (1875–1921), leader of the Centre Party, was quick to sense the failure of the submarine campaign and the inevit-able collapse of Austria. In September 1918 he joined the coalition formed by Prince Max of Baden and in November accepted the invidious post of head of the German Armistice Commission. He was largely instrumental in inducing the Weimar Government to accept and sign the Treaty of Versailles. He was murdered on August 26, 1921.

who had both approved its terms.[n] Mr Bonar Law voiced the common opinion when he denounced the letter as 'nothing less than a national misfortune'. It was certainly ill-timed. Since in that autumn of 1917 Russia was no longer a military factor, Italy was shattered by the disaster of Caporetto, a stalemate had been reached on the Western Front, the massive strength of America was still undeveloped, and Great Britain was as yet uncertain whether she had mastered the lethal menace of the submarine campaign.[1]

(4)

The King meanwhile continued as before his ceaseless round of visits and inspections, nor did he abate his efforts to inculcate more humane standards or to ease the friction between the politicians and the soldiers. The strain was great. Already in August 1916 the United States Ambassador had found him looking 'ten years older'.[o] To Queen Alexandra, who had suggested that he was undertaking too many engagements he replied:[p]

> 'I am not too tired. In these days I must go about & see as many people as possible & so encourage them in their work. They appreciate it, I believe, & I am quite ready to sacrifice myself if necessary, as long as we win this war. . . .'

He was constantly urging the Government to take more active steps to relieve the condition of our prisoners of war in Germany. He wrote to Lord Robert Cecil, drawing his attention to the plight of our civilian prisoners interned in Ruhleben Camp, and urging him to reach some arrangement with the Germans whereby civilian prisoners could be exchanged.[q] He wrote to the Prime Minister expressing his fear that the men who had been prisoners since 1914 would either die in captivity or else return in an embittered and vindictive mood, 'full of hatred of our governing classes for having

---

[1] The Germans, on adopting unrestricted submarine warfare on February 1, 1917, calculated that they would sink 600,000 tons a month and bring us to our knees in five months. In April 1917, their peak month, they did in fact sink 423,000 tons and the position appeared to be one of extreme and imminent danger. It was largely owing to Mr Lloyd George's insistence that the convoy system was adopted. The first experimental convoy left Gibraltar on May 10; by the end of July it was applied to all homecoming vessels; by August it was extended to out-going vessels also. All manner of anti-submarine measures were also devised and the average monthly losses declined immediately. By the time of the Armistice 88,000 ships had been convoyed with the loss of only 436. By the second quarter of 1918 new construction exceeded sinkings.

316

left them to their fate, while the Officers have been rescued, and either repatriated or interned in neutral countries':

'The King earnestly entreats you', wrote Lord Stamfordham,' 'to do all in your power to at least obtain the release of as many as possible of the 1914 prisoners, otherwise he fears that few of them will return at the end of the war.'

The King remained none the less strongly opposed to any form of reprisals, feeling that they would be 'contrary to the British character' and that 'in any case we should inevitably be beaten by our enemies if we attempted to play their game'.' When, after our defeats in the spring and early summer of 1918, an outcry arose demanding the internment of all aliens indiscriminately, the King treated this clamour with scorn. Mrs Asquith, who saw him during this period, was so entranced by his attitude that she wrote to Lord Stamfordham one of her most breathless letters:'

'Dearest Lord Stamfordham,
     I can't tell you *how* much H. and I enjoyed our lunch with the King and Queen. As you know, I've loved him since he was a little middy & I'm alas! incapable of telling the smallest lie—*such* a draw-back in life!—I never heard King Edward talk more sensibly & with greater insight and wisdom, and such "vrai dire"—never as well as K.G. the other day. He has come on immensely—*au fond* has always had goodwill, simplicity and fine courage. I had tears in my eyes—and have still—when he spoke of the vindictive and unnecessary murder of the poor Czar and I was moved to deepest admiration by his revolt against this alien stunt. "Intern me first" he said—and showed fairness and Christianity and real moral indignation over the whole low business.'

In June 1917 General Pershing with the advance guard of the United States Army arrived in London and was received with his staff at Buckingham Palace. The General was struck by the 'charm and simplicity' of his reception, but somewhat embarrassed when the King, explaining that he was 'not a politician and did not see things from their point of view', expressed the hope that as many as possible of the American troops would serve with the British Army. General Pershing replied that America was determined to create an army of her own. The King then addressed General Pershing's staff:"

'It has always', he said, 'been my dream that the two English-speaking nations should some day be united in a great cause, and today my dream is realised. Together we are fighting for the greatest cause that peoples can fight. The Anglo-Saxon race must save civilisation.'

(5)

Fully as he recognised and appreciated the momentum given to our war effort by the dynamic genius of Mr Lloyd George, the King as has been said, was often disconcerted by the flash and sparkle of the Prime Minister's ideas and impulses and by his impatient, and sometimes ruthless, intolerance of the professional mind.

On October 18, 1917, Mr Lloyd George had a long conversation with the King, and divulged with his accustomed wealth of imagery, his own conception of the future of the war.° The Russians and the Italians were out of the battle; it was evident that the French did not intend to 'do much more fighting'; and we could not expect great assistance from the United States during the course of 1918. It was obvious therefore that the brunt of the fighting during the next year would fall upon the British. We should be expected 'to sacrifice the flower of our Army in a single-handed offensive'. What then could be the condition of the Allies when victory was achieved? France would be left with her new armies almost intact; Russia, 'possibly resuscitated', would once more be a great military Power; and America would by then have landed a powerful force and would claim the credit for the Allied victory. Great Britain, with her ranks thinned through sustained fighting, would be so weak as to be unable to assert herself 'or to make her voice heard and her will prevail in the momentous decisions to be come to in the Council of Peace':

> 'This, the Prime Minister said, shall never be. It was his duty to ensure that whenever the climax is reached England is at the zenith of her military strength and in a position more than to hold her own among the Nations of the World.'

He proposed therefore that we should insist on obtaining from our Allies a precise statement whether or no they were ready, during the course of 1918, to resume a serious offensive. If not, then we should content ourselves with remaining on the defence in Flanders, curtail our subsidiary campaigns, and liberate as many men as possible for employment at home, especially for shipbuilding and agriculture. In this way we 'could hold the enemy on the Western front until such time as our Allies consented to cooperate in a general offensive'. It was for the politicians to lay down the general plan and to estimate the moment when the climax would be reached; the details could then be left to the professional soldiers and sailors to work out.

318

The King, who remained obstinately convinced that high strategy was a matter for experts, was not encouraged by this imaginative forecast; its validity depended, all too obviously, upon whether the enemy would also, during the next twelve months, consent to remain quiescent.

Mr Lloyd George, moreover, with his quick sense of drama, had a tendency, when public feeling was aroused, to search for eminent scapegoats. The King had a warm feeling for scapegoats and disliked seeing public servants thrown to the wolves. A difference of opinion thus arose between them as a result of the report of the Mesopotamia Committee which was published in June 1917. The report censured the Viceroy, Lord Hardinge, the Commander in Chief India, Sir Beauchamp Duff, the Commander of the Expeditionary Force in Mesopotamia, Sir John Nixon, and the chiefs of the Medical Services. Nor did it accord 'complete immunity' to Mr Austen Chamberlain, the Secretary of State for India. The latter, having in the House of Commons made a spirited defence of the Viceroy on the ground that he had not been directly responsible and that it 'would be an evil day for this House and for this country if a great public servant were to be hounded out of public life in response to the clamours of an ill-informed and passionate mob'.*w* decided that he had no course but to resign:

> 'When a Minister', he wrote to the King, 'can no longer protect those who have served or are serving under him, when his own actions are made the subject of review by a Judicial Tribunal. . . . Mr Chamberlain submits that it is not consonant with the honour of public men or of Your Majesty's Government that that Minister should continue in his employment.' *x*

Mr Chamberlain's action was typical of his chivalrous integrity; but the problem of Lord Hardinge, who on his return from India had, with considerable public spirit accepted the onerous post of Permanent Under Secretary at the Foreign Office, was not so easily solved. On July 9 the Prime Minister asked Lord Curzon to suggest to Lord Hardinge that it would be fitting for him to send in his resignation before the Mesopotamia report came up for debate in the House of Commons. The King happened at the moment to be absent on a visit to the front, but Lord Stamfordham, knowing the King's attitude on the subject, went to the Prime Minister and informed him that His Majesty would regret it if Lord Hardinge were forced to resign, 'not only for personal reasons, but from a sense of loyalty to public servants, who should not be thrown over by the

Government'. Mr Lloyd George was annoyed by this intervention. He informed Lord Stamfordham that:

'He would strongly deprecate any action on the part of the King which might be interpreted as showing partiality or favour to Lord Hardinge; already the public are disposed to attribute to pressure from "influential quarters" any hesitation to adopt prompt and drastic measures in dealing with inefficiency. As Prime Minister he would point out the unwisdom of the King's championing, as it were, Lord Hardinge's case.' [v]

The King, on hearing of this, telegraphed to Lord Stamfordham saying that he considered Lord Hardinge would be well advised to place his resignation in the hands of the Foreign Secretary pending the debate in the House of Commons.[z] Lord Hardinge acted accordingly, but Mr Balfour refused to accept his resignation and urged him to defend himself in the House of Lords.[z.a]

The Mesopotamia Report was debated in the House of Commons on July 12 and 13. Mr Bonar Law, on behalf of the Government, suggested that a Judicial Court of Enquiry should be established to examine further into the responsibility of individuals. Mr Asquith protested against any such proposal, arguing that the House of Commons was the only tribunal that could properly judge the errors of statesmen. The House accepted this view and the Court of Enquiry was abandoned. Lord Hardinge remained at his post.

An even more serious controversy arose over the dismissal of the Chief of the Imperial General Staff, Sir William Robertson. On January 22, 1918, Mr Lloyd George had a long conversation with Lord Stamfordham, and 'opened his heart' in regard to the conduct of the war. His attitude was one of 'profound dissatisfaction with and distrust of the Army'. He considered the present administration of the War Office 'rotten and extravagant in men, money and material'. He did not believe that it would ever be possible to break through on the Western Front. Only the day before he had seen 'a very able officer, a colonel', who had confirmed his worst suspicions. The time had come for drastic change.[z.b]

'The Prime Minister', writes Mr Churchill,[z.c] 'was moving cautiously but tirelessly towards the conception of a unified command.' To achieve this objective Mr Lloyd George resorted to a series of 'extremely laborious and mystifying manoeuvres'. Already on September 25, 1917, he had given the French Minister of War a private assurance that he would assist in securing that all the armies on the Western Front should be placed under a French Commander in Chief.[z.d] At the Rapallo Conference, held in November 1917, after the disaster of Caporetto, he advanced a stage further. He proposed the creation of a Supreme War Council 'to watch over the general conduct of the war on the Western Front'. This Council was established at Versailles under the chairmanship of General Foch. Sir Henry Wilson was appointed to it as permanent British military representative:

> 'It was his undoubted intention', writes Mr Churchill[z.e] 'to arm the Cabinet with an alternative set of military advisers, whose opinions should be used to curb and correct the "Robertson-Haig" point of view.'

On February 2, 1918, at a meeting of the Supreme War Council, Mr Lloyd George obtained a decision to create a General Reserve of thirty divisions and to entrust this force to an 'Executive Committee' composed of the military representatives on the Versailles Council under the chairmanship of General Foch. It was this new Committee that would instruct the Commanders in Chief as to when, where and how the General Reserve could be used. Sir William Robertson, as Chief of the Imperial General Staff, objected strongly to this dual control. He was supported, although not with unwavering consistency, by Lord Derby, the Secretary of State for War. Mr Lloyd George endeavoured to solve the difficulty by suggesting that Sir William Robertson should himself go as British military representative to Versailles and should be succeeded as C.I.G.S. by Sir Henry Wilson. The powers exercised by the C.I.G.S. under the Kitchener-Robertson agreement were at the same time to be curtailed. Sir William Robertson refused to assent to this arrangement and tendered his resignation. Lord Derby then invoked the assistance of Lord Stamfordham, asking him to persuade Sir William Robertson to remain on as C.I.G.S. and to try to work the dual arrangement. Sir William Robertson replied that 'even for the King' he must refuse to assist in carrying out what he regarded as a wholly unworkable duplication of responsibility.

Lord Stamfordham then had an interview with the Prime Minister, and represented to him that the King 'strongly deprecated the idea of Robertson being removed from the office of C.I.G.S.'. Mr Lloyd George replied that 'he did not share His Majesty's extremely favourable opinion of Sir William Robertson' and added that if the King insisted on retaining the services of the latter 'the Government could not carry on and His Majesty must find other Ministers'. He added that 'the Government must *govern*, and this was practically military dictation'. Lord Stamfordham replied that the King 'had no idea of making any such insistence'.²·¹

Sir William Robertson therefore resigned his position as C.I.G.S. and was appointed to the Eastern Command.¹ Sir Henry Wilson became C.I.G.S. in his place and was succeeded on the Versailles Council by Sir Henry Rawlinson.

(6)

At 4.30 a.m. on March 21, 1918, General Ludendorff began his fearful final offensive; it continued for four months and took the form of five successive waves. The first wave struck the British Vth Army under Sir Hubert Gough. By the night of March 22 General Gough was obliged to order a general retirement to the line of the Somme.² It seemed that the enemy might at last succeed in separating the French and British and driving the latter back upon the Channel ports. 'We are', wrote Sir Henry Wilson on March 24, 'very near a crash'.²·⁹ General Pétain, fearing for the safety of Paris, hesitated to come to our assistance. It was at this moment of dire peril, and largely at the instigation of Sir Douglas Haig himself, that, at Doullens on March 26, the principle of unity of command was at last adopted. Henceforward the responsibility for meeting the German onslaught was concentrated in the hands of General Foch.³

On March 28 the King crossed to France, since it was felt that

---

¹ In May 1918 Sir William Robertson was made Commander in Chief of the Home Forces upon Lord French's acceptance of the post of Lord Lieutenant of Ireland. In 1920 he received his baton. 'By command of the King,' Lord Stamfordham wrote to him on March 30, 1920, 'I write to tell you with what great pleasure His Majesty has this morning signed a submission from the Secretary of State promoting you to the rank of Field Marshal' (R.A. F.1493, 6).

² This first stage of General Ludendorff's offensive, known as the 'Battle of St Quentin', lasted from March 21 till April 4. The Germans penetrated our positions on a base of 74 miles to a depth of no less than 38 miles. They captured 90,000 prisoners, 1,200 guns and immense quantities of stores. As a result of this defeat General Gough was deprived of his command. 'I trust', he wrote to Colonel Wigram (R.A. Q.1377) 'that the King realises how stoutly, calmly and well my Army fought through that ordeal.' It has often been stated that General Gough was treated as a scapegoat for this tremendous reverse. 'No episode' writes Mr Churchill (*World Crisis*, IV, page 426) 'in his career was more honourable than the disaster which entailed his fall.'

³ General Foch was not made a Marshal of France until August 7, 1918. In November 1918 he was appointed a British Field Marshal also.

his presence with the troops would assist in restoring confidence. He visited as many units as possible, motoring 315 miles in three days. He returned to England in a mood of sombre anxiety.

On April 9 came the second German attack. General Plumer was driven from Messines and the Germans advanced to within striking distance of the junction of Hazebrouck. On April 12 Sir Douglas Haig issued his Order of the Day: 'With our backs to the wall, and believing in the justice of our cause, each one of us must fight to the end.'

The anxiety aroused in England by these two reverses found expression in the complaint that Mr Lloyd George had refused to grant Sir Douglas Haig the reinforcements he had asked for and had insisted upon his extending an already weakened front. The Prime Minister replied by asserting that our armies in France were stronger on January 1, 1918, than they had been on January 1 of the previous year. This statement was contradicted in a letter written to *The Times* on May 7 by General Sir Frederick Maurice, until quite recently Director of Military Operations. In a debate in the House of Commons on May 9 Mr Asquith pressed to a division a motion that these discrepancies should be investigated by a Select Committee. Mr Lloyd George insisted on treating the motion as a vote of censure and succeeded, after much discomfiture, in weathering the storm.[1]

On May 27 General Ludendorff delivered a surprise attack upon the French in the sector of the Chemin des Dames and penetrated their lines to a depth of thirteen miles. 'There is a possibility', wrote Sir Henry Wilson on June 1, 'perhaps a probability, of the French Army being beaten.' [z.h]

'Yes,' the King wrote to Queen Alexandra on June 2, 'I am grateful for your prayers; they are a comfort to me & will help me to get through all these anxious days & I fear more lie ahead of us. But we must be courageous & go on to the end, however long it may take, as I shall never submit to those brutal Germans & I am sure the British Nation is of the same opinion.'

During those four months of repeated anxiety the King's resolution was fortified by the indomitable confidence of his Prime

---

[1] In this debate 106 members of the Liberal Party voted with Mr Asquith against Mr Lloyd George. Their names were noted and, when it came to the 'Coupon Election' of 1918, they were punished accordingly. The 'Maurice Debate' is important in political history as marking the first stage in the disintegration of the Liberal Party.

Minister. Only those who served with or under Mr Lloyd George throughout that dire ordeal can rightly appreciate and remember how much the State then owed to his vitality, resource and unflinching moral courage. Others flagged or wavered: Mr Lloyd George, at the very moment of defeat, remained exuberantly sure.

On June 9 came the fourth German lunge at Compiègne; it was checked by General Mangin. On July 15 began the ultimate offensive in Champagne, the *Kaiserschlacht*, attended by the German Emperor in person. From the summit of a specially constructed gazebo he watched the distant drifting smoke of battle, waiting hour after hour in the warm summer rain for the news of final victory. It never came. On July 18 General Foch struck suddenly upon the Marne salient. The Battle of Champagne was broken off. The Emperor climbed down from his gazebo and returned to the Imperial train; through the night it rumbled towards Spa and exile. While in the presence of his staff the Emperor still maintained his pose of triumphant hilarity; but an observer noticed that, when he returned to his own coach, he walked dejectedly; pausing in the thin corridor to gaze intently at the photographs upon the wall: photographs taken in the old days at Ischl or Konopischt, at Björkö or Corfu; photographs of stags spread upon the gravel at Balmoral or of tea under the tent at Osborne House.[2,1]

It was not realised at the time that General Foch's counterstroke of July 18 marked the beginning of the end. On August 7, 1918 the King paid his fifth and final visit to the Front. It was an auspicious date.[1] At dawn on August 8 the British Fourth Army, led by 450 tanks, broke through the German lines and advanced nine miles. It was on that day that General Ludendorff realised that the spirit of his men, after all those years of superb endurance, had at last been broken.[2] Marshal Foch at once decided to deliver a series of hammer blows, so rapidly successive as to prevent the German High Com-

[1] 'Your Majesty's visits to the Army in France' wrote Sir Douglas Haig on August 15 (R.A. Q.832, 140) 'have always been most heartily appreciated, but I venture to think that during the last two visits it has been demonstrated more than on any other occasion during this war, how heart and soul the Army is behind you, Sir. In March things looked black indeed; and on the last occasion our anxiety was beginning to pass away. Your Majesty's presence and kindly words brought home to one and all how very much our King is Head of the Army.'

[2] 'Der 8 August', he wrote in his *Memoirs*, 'ist der schwarze Tag des deutschen Heeres in der Geschichte dieses Krieges.' (Errinerungen, page 547. See also Hindenburg's *Aus Meinem Leben*, pp. 358 ff.)

mand from switching its reserves. On August 10 the French Third
Army went into the attack; on August 17 the French Tenth Army
followed further to the south; on August 21 the British Third Army
launched a local offensive, to be followed by the British First Army
on August 26. By the beginning of September the Germans found
themselves back in the Siegfried line. On September 12 the American
Army under General Pershing heavily defeated the enemy at St
Mihiel. On September 29 Sir Douglas Haig began his assault upon
the Siegfried line and on the same day came the news that Bulgaria
had surrendered. Something like panic seized German Headquarters. On October 3 a new German Government under Prince
Max of Baden addressed to President Wilson an appeal for an
immediate armistice. On October 5 the British crashed through the
Siegfried line and out into the open country beyond. By then
Generals Ludendorff and Hindenburg had recovered from their
sudden panic of September 29 and were determined to resist the
great pincer movement which Marshal Foch was known to have
planned. It was then too late. The wind of defeat had already spread
through the armies and reached the home front behind. On October
30 Turkey capitulated and on November 4 Austria signed an
armistice which placed all Austrian communications in Allied hands.
On November 9 Prince Max of Baden handed over the Government
to the Socialist leader, Herr Friedrich Ebert; the abdication of the
Emperor and the establishment of the German Republic were proclaimed from the steps of the Reichstag. On November 10 the Emperor crossed the Belgian frontier into Holland. At dawn on Monday,
November 11, the armistice was signed in Marshal Foch's train in
the Forest of Compiègne. At 11.0 a.m. that morning the First World
War came to an end.

CHAPTER XX

RECONSTRUCTION

1918-1921

Armistice celebrations—The King's address to Parliament—He visits the battlefields—President Wilson in London—Mr Lloyd George asks for a dissolution—The King agrees with reluctance—The 'coupon election'—The King asks Mr Lloyd George to take Mr Asquith to the Peace Conference—The Unionist majority—The King and the Peace Conference—Austria—Rumania—The signature of the Treaty of Versailles—The German Princes petition the King against the trial of the German ex-Emperor—The King resumes his old routine—Demobilisation—Industrial unrest—The end of the post-war boom—The Coal Strike—The Railwaymen and Transport Workers—The King's concern for the unemployed—His desire to promote concord—His disapproval of controversial war memoirs—The Two Minutes Silence—The burial of the unknown warrior.

(1)

INSTANTLY the sober spaces of the streets of London were striped with people running differently: within fifteen minutes the roads and squares were blocked by shouts and colour and gesticulation. Men and women rushed out from shops and offices, clambering upon the stranded omnibuses and lorries, or surging together in a boisterous tide towards the Palace. The royal pages draped the centre balcony with its valance of red and gold. The King and Queen appeared.

Far into the night the crowds stood massed around the Victoria Memorial or clustered upon the captured German cannon that lined the Mall. The King tried to speak to them, but his voice was drowned in one continuous roar of ecstasy, relief and triumph. He looked down upon a myriad upturned faces, uniform as the stones upon a shingle beach, upon ten thousand staring eyes, upon mouths opened in a universal paean. He looked beyond them to the summit of the Nelson column, flickering curiously in the light of unseen bonfires; or to where in the darker distance Big Ben hung suspended as a silent moon. The agony was over: Britain had conquered; she was safe.

During that jubilant week the King became for his people the hierophant of victory. On five successive days, accompanied by the Queen, he drove in an open carriage through the poorer quarters of London:

'Nine miles', he wrote in his diary, 'through waves of cheering crowds. The demonstrations of the people are indeed touching.'

In St Paul's Cathedral was held a service of thanksgiving. In the Royal Gallery of the Palace of Westminster the King received an address of congratulation from the assembled Lords and Commons in the presence of the representatives of the Dominions and India. In reply he spoke to them of the achievements of the fighting services, of the patience of the civilian population and the self-sacrifice of the workers, of the courage of the Mercantile Marine and fishing fleets, of the help rendered by the Commonwealth and Empire, of the endurance of our Allies:

> 'May good-will and concord at home', he concluded, 'strengthen our influence for concord abroad. May the morning star of peace, which is now rising over a war-worn world, be here and everywhere the herald of a better day, in which the storms of strife shall have died down and the rays of an enduring peace be shed upon all nations.'

That night he left for Edinburgh to review the Fleet assembled— on the very eve of the surrender of the German navy—in the Firth of Forth. On his return to London he inspected disabled soldiers and sailors in Hyde Park:

> 'There were between 30,000 and 35,000 present: they were most enthusiastic & in riding down the lines they broke through & came round me to shake hands. I was nearly pulled off my horse.'

On November 27 he crossed to France, As he drove with M. Poincaré from the Bois de Boulogne station in Paris he was greeted with fervour by the crowds that packed the Champs Elysées. He described his reception as 'a great demonstration of gratitude to England for what she has done for France'. Thereafter he visited the battlefields, the war cemeteries and the devastated areas: Arras and St. Quentin, Le Cateau and Mons, Ypres and Passchendaele, Cambrai and Zeebrugge:

> 'At each place I got out & walked through the troops who cheered me. It was not stiff, the men often following me through the town. A fine drizzle which was pretty wetting and plenty of mud.'

On December 11 he returned to England to prepare for the reception of the President of the United States. Mr and Mrs Woodrow Wilson reached London from France on the afternoon of Boxing Day. Through decorated streets the King, with the President beside him, drove from the station to Buckingham Palace: the Queen and Mrs Wilson followed in the second carriage. The men and women who thronged the pavements and the windows welcomed the President with awe and hope: to them he seemed a theocratic figure, the prophet of a finer revelation. Mr Wilson responded to their respectful plaudits by raising his top hat and smiling a wide but arid smile. There was no presage, on that December afternoon, of the tragedy to come.

There followed a state banquet at Buckingham Palace and a luncheon at the Guildhall. After a short visit to Manchester the President returned to France, confirmed in his sad fallacy that, however much the politicians in his own and other countries might threaten or manoeuvre, he alone understood and could enforce the wishes of the common man. The King, during their short converse, derived no impression of the shadows of vanity and suspicion that marred the splendour of Woodrow Wilson's mind and heart. 'He is quite easy to get on with,' the King commented in his diary, 'He made a nice speech.'

On December 31, after bidding farewell to the President at Victoria Station, the King and Queen left for Norfolk. It was not a happy homecoming. Their youngest son, Prince John, who had for long been an invalid, died on January 18: he was buried at Sandringham.

(2)

Mr Lloyd George, from the moment that victory seemed assured, had turned his mind to the need of holding an immediate General Election. On November 2, 1918, he had discussed the matter with Mr Bonar Law and on November 5 he asked the King to grant him an early dissolution. The King endeavoured to persuade the Prime Minister to abandon, or at least to postpone, this project. The arguments on both sides are well recorded by Lord Stamfordham in a memorandum dated November 5, 1918:[a]

'The King saw the Prime Minister this evening, who asked His Majesty to grant a dissolution of Parliament, although he was aware from previous conversations with the King that he did not favourably view such a step.

His Majesty began by giving the Prime Minister his reasons for deprecating a General Election at the present time, pointing out that the Government had already the support of the House of Commons for the continuance of the War and settlement of Peace, and Mr Asquith, as Leader of the Opposition, had recently stated that his Party would continue their support.

There was considerable risk from the unknown factors of the soldiers' and women's votes, and the King understood that a large percentage of the soldiers would be practically disenfranchised through lack of time in circulating their voting papers, which would be unpopular in the Army.

He reminded the Prime Minister of the precedent of the Khaki Election in 1900, which brought back the Unionists with a large majority and kept them in power on what was really a fictitious vote, and ended in ruining them and keeping them out of Office ever since.

Having the election in the winter, at a time of shortage of coal and food, would not be conducive to a contented frame of mind on the part of the electors with the Government.

The Prime Minister admitted the force of His Majesty's objections, but urged that they were more than outbalanced by the arguments which, after three months of careful consideration, appealed to his judgment.

He seemed inclined to discount the danger of disenfranchising the the soldiers, and thought the women were more likely to vote "sanely" now, than later on when there might be discontent.

The suggested General Election would not be at all on all fours with the Khaki Election of 1900, for in the latter case Parliament had only been in session for five years out of eight years existence, whereas the present Parliament not only has no further years to run, but has already exceeded its statutory term of life by a considerable period.

For every reason it seems to be the unique moment to appeal to the electorate, now that a great load is, as it were, removed from the mind of the people by the early prospect of a termination of the War; and it is important that the Election should take place now, rather than at a later period when demobilization may be in progress and thousands of both the military and civil population thrown out of employment, thereby causing considerable unrest in the country.

The present House of Commons is dead and does not represent the voice of the people, and it is impossible for any Ministry to carry on the Government of the country during what must be a most difficult period—namely that of reconstruction—unless it has behind it a Parliament genuinely representative of the electorate.

By this arrangement the election could be over before any unrest is likely to occur. The Government watchword to the country would be "Unity". This can only be secured by a Coalition Government, and an appeal to that end will be made to the electors by the leaders of the three Parties—Mr Lloyd George, Mr Bonar Law and Mr Barnes.

After hearing the Prime Minister's views, the King granted his permission for the dissolution of Parliament at an early date.'

It has since been suggested that the King ought to have maintained his initial objections to this dissolution, on the ground that the electorate were in too excited a mood to express a balanced judgement; and that in any case he should not have permitted Mr Lloyd George to 'cash in' on victory. Such criticisms are based upon a faulty interpretation of the functions of Constitutional Monarchy. The King did in fact exercise his right to 'warn' Mr Lloyd George against the course he proposed to adopt; yet once the Prime Minister rejected that warning, the only alternatives open to the King were either to accept Mr Lloyd George's resignation, which was politically impossible, or to follow his advice. Mr Lloyd George can scarcely be blamed for insisting upon a dissolution in that winter of 1918; it is not the election itself that is open to criticism but the methods by which, and the manner in which, it was conducted. 'The will of the people', comments Mr Berriedale Keith,[b] 'is not necessarily wise, but the duty of the King is, not to override its will, but to assume that it shall be duly ascertained and then fairly acted upon.' It was in no sense the fault of the King if thereafter the will of the people was unduly ascertained or acted upon in a manner that some subsequent historians have condemned as inequitable.

The moment the dissolution was announced the Labour Party decided to resume their independence and not to stand at the election as supporters of the existing Government. Mr Lloyd George —ignoring the appeal of the Manchester Liberals that he should make his peace with Mr Asquith and thus recreate a united Liberal Party—entered into a compact with Mr Bonar Law. Under this arrangement all candidates who were classed as loyal to the Coalition were to receive a badge or certificate in the form of a letter of recommendation jointly signed by Mr Lloyd George and Mr Bonar Law. It was this certificate that was denounced by Mr Asquith as a 'coupon' and thereby gave to the General Election of December 1918 the damaging title of 'the coupon election'. Sir George Younger, the chairman of the Unionist party organisation, was quick to seize the occasion and to earmark for the candidates of his own party a large proportion of the prospective seats.[1] Mr Lloyd George busied himself with dividing the Liberal candidates into sheep and goats; the sheep were those who had supported him at the time of the Maurice debate; the 106 Liberals who had voted against him on that occasion were labelled goats and denounced as 'conspirators who had plotted against their country at a moment of grave danger'. Nor can it be

[1] Sir George Younger (1851–1929) had been Unionist member for Ayr Burghs since 1906. Since the age of seventeen he had been chairman of the family brewery, a post that he retained until his death. He became head of the Unionist party organization in 1917 and at the Carlton Club meeting of October 19, 1922, was largely instrumental in persuading his party to abandon Mr Lloyd George. In February 1923 he was raised to the peerage as Viscount Younger of Leckie.

said that the tone of the electoral speeches was either elevated or prudent. Although two days after the Armistice Mr Lloyd George had urged his followers to 'put away all base, sordid, squalid ideas of vengeance or avarice', he had within the three ensuing weeks pledged himself to prosecute the Kaiser, to punish the German generals and officers, to expel and exclude all Germans from Great Britain, and 'to exact the last penny we can get out of Germany up to the limit of her capacity'. The pledges given and the speeches made by other Coalition candidates were even more immoderate.

Polling took place on December 14, but owing to the time required to collect the ballot papers of those serving abroad, the results were not announced until December 28.[1] The Coalition, although they had polled no more than 52% of the total votes, acquired as many as 526 seats in the new Parliament. Labour increased its representation to 63. The Independent Liberals were reduced to 33. Mr Asquith himself was defeated in East Fife, a seat that he had held for thirty-two years.

The King had always retained for his first Prime Minister feelings of affectionate esteem. One of his first acts, on hearing of the Armistice, had been to send to Mr Asquith a personal message of congratulation. 'I look back with gratitude', he had telegraphed on that morning of November 11, 'to your wise counsel and firm resolve in the days when great issues had to be decided, resulting in our entry into the War.' On November 19 he wrote to Mr Lloyd George urging him to 'consider the advisability' of including Mr Asquith among the United Kingdom delegates to the impending Peace Conference:

'You served', the King wrote, 'for many years in Mr Asquith's Government and know his worth as a lawyer, a statesman, and a man of clear dispassionate judgement. The fact of his having been Prime Minister at the outbreak of War invests him with a special authority valuable to you in Council. I feel that your selection of him as a member of the Conference would be applauded both at home, in the Dominions and abroad.' *c*

Mr Lloyd George returned no reply to this letter. When he saw the King on November 25 he merely stated that nothing could be

---

[1] It will be recalled that the Representation of the People Act 1918 had more than doubled the number of the Electorate. It gave the vote to women over thirty years of age, abolished the property qualification for men and extended the franchise to naval and military voters. (See Anson, *Law and Custom of the Constitution*, Vol. I, fifth edition, pp. 121 ff.)

331

decided until after the Election, adding that the situation would be eased if Mr Asquith would consent to enter the Government.[d] When, a few days later, Mr Asquith himself told the Prime Minister that, although unwilling to accept a post in the Government, he would be glad to serve as a member of the Peace Delegation, Mr Lloyd George mumbled something about 'considering the proposal', glanced at his watch and stooped down to pick up some books that had fallen to the floor.[e]

It was thus with special distress that the King heard that Mr. Asquith had been defeated in East Fife. He at once addressed to him a warm letter of sympathy and comfort. 'I regret very much', he wrote to Prince Albert on December 31, 'that Mr Asquith has been defeated. It is very ungrateful, after all he has done for his country.' 'One always took it for granted,' commented Lord Stamfordham,[f] 'that no Peace Conference would be possible without Asquith and Grey. But such ideas seem now to be quite out of date.'[1]

The coupon election certainly accorded Mr Lloyd George and his Government an overwhelming mandate to direct with full authority their policy of peace and reconstruction. But at the Peace Conference that followed, Mr Lloyd George found himself hampered, both by the electoral pledges he had rashly indulged in, and by the low intellectual level of the House of Commons which he and Mr Bonar Law had jointly secured. On entering Parliament a few months later, Mr J. C. Davidson[2] communicated to Lord Stamfordham some trenchant observations on the quality of his Unionist colleagues:[g]

---

[1] There exists in the Royal Archives a significant minute addressed by Lord Stamfordham to Sir Clive Wigram on March 11, 1929: 'The King's memory is really wonderful. When on Saturday I told H.M. that LL.G. was now saying he *wanted* Asquith to go to the Peace Conference & that I remembered how H.M. had urged LL.G. to take Asquith, the King said, "Oh, but surely there was a letter?"

Here it is and you will see that LL.G. *never* returned to the subject after the Coupon Election.'

[2] Mr J. C. Davidson had been Private Secretary to Mr Bonar Law from 1915–1920. He entered the House of Commons in 1920 as Unionist Member for Hemel Hempstead, and immediately became Mr Bonar Law's Parliamentary Private Secretary. In 1923 he was made Chancellor of the Duchy of Lancaster and served as Chairman of the Unionist Party from 1927–1930. Thereafter he again became Chancellor of the Duchy until raised to the peerage in 1937 as Viscount Davidson of Little Gaddesden.

'Now a word about individual members. The first thing that struck me on entering the House of Commons was the high percentage of hard-headed men, mostly on the make, who fill up the ranks of the Unionist Party. The old fashioned country-gentleman, and even the higher ranks of the learned professions, are scarcely represented at all. I cannot bring myself to believe that this is a good thing and I cannot help hoping that the next Parliament will be less full of the modern, and to my mind unscrupulous, characters which are to be found in the present House. . . .'

His Majesty minuted this letter with the words 'A great pity. G.R.I.'.

(3)

With the proceedings of the Peace Conference the King was not directly concerned. He would receive the regular minutes of the Conference and its Committees, as well as those of the discussions that took place within the British Empire Delegation. From time to time the Prime Minister would furnish him with a personal report on some aspect of special interest or significance; and on his occasional visits to London Mr Lloyd George would verbally expound to the King the problems that had arisen, the nature of his relations with President Wilson, M. Clemenceau or Signor Orlando, and what prospects there existed of securing an early and enduring peace.

Typical of such communications was a letter addressed to the King by the Prime Minister and dated from the Villa Majestic, Rue La Pérouse, Paris, on February 5, 1919. It concerned the delicate and indeed provocative question of British Empire representation:[*]

'The greatest difficulty', wrote Mr Lloyd George, 'during the week arose over the question of representation. The Dominions claimed representation at the Peace Conference commensurate with their great sacrifices for the common cause. They claimed with great justice that they should all be treated on exactly the same basis as the lesser Allies such as Belgium and Serbia. The other Great Powers, however, who met them in the most friendly and generous spirit pointed out that if the full claim of the Dominions was conceded the British Empire would have so great a delegation at the Peace Conference as inevitably to arouse criticism and resentment among other nations, none of whom would have more than five delegates. They further pointed out that the Dominions were in a different position from Belgium and Serbia inasmuch as their interests were supported not merely by their own delegates but by the five members of the British Empire delegation who would be present at all discussions and would sit in the innermost councils of the Allies. After a very amicable discussion it was finally decided that Canada, Australia, South Africa and

333

India should have two representatives apiece and New Zealand one representative. This decision was regarded by the Dominions with great satisfaction though the representatives of New Zealand, which had only one representative, and Newfoundland which was excluded from direct representation altogether, felt a little disappointed. It was found possible, however, to mitigate this feeling by including one and sometimes two Dominion representatives in the British Empire delegation on formal occasions. The spectacle of the representatives of the British Empire occupying no less than 14 seats in the most prominent position at the Conference table was an eloquent testimony to the sacrifices which the British Empire had made in the war and to its commanding influence in the world today. . . .'

As the Peace Conference waxed in fury, these personal reports from Mr Lloyd George became less frequent and voluminous.

Only rarely, in so far as Foreign Affairs were concerned, did the King consider it incumbent upon him to furnish warnings or to tender advice. As early as November 1918 he had drawn the Foreign Secretary's attention to the danger of a union between Germany and Austria. He suggested that it might be well to retain for Austria some port upon the Adriatic, in order to prevent her becoming entirely dependent for her export trade on German transport and outlets.[i] Mr Balfour's reply, although sagacious, displayed an optimistic disregard of the passions which the very idea of an Anschluss between Germany and Austria would be bound to arouse:[j]

Foreign Office, November 11 1918.

My dear Stamfordham,

The problem raised by the King is by no means new, and I have given it considerable thought.

I do not see that we can really oppose the union of the Germans of Austria with the rest of the Germanic peoples—provided it is clearly desired by the inhabitants themselves. To do so would violate one of the cardinal principles for which the Allies have been fighting—the right of self-determination. Nor am I clear that such a union would be politically disadvantageous. It would greatly increase the strength of South Germany as opposed to the North and the leadership might pass from the hands of Prussia. I know that many people in France do not share this view, but it seems to me to have much force. The Austro-Hungarian Empire as it existed before, a great reservoir of non-German man-power yet completely subservient to Germany, was I think much more dangerous to the peace of the world than would be a Germany enlarged by the addition of the German Austrian provinces.

Things are however at present in such chaos that it is really impossible to predict the future of those parts of Europe.

I have always had in view the necessity of securing some economic outlet for Austria on the Adriatic. This should not be difficult to arrange at the Peace Conference.

Yours ever, Arthur James Balfour.

(p.s. If Germany got the German Austrian Provinces and *lost* what she ought to lose to the Poles, the French, and the Danes, her net gain would (I believe) be insignificant.)'

The withdrawal of the enemy forces of occupation from Rumania enabled the King again to resume correspondence with his cousin, Queen Marie, who throughout the period of defeat and humiliation had done so much by her example to maintain and fortify the spirit of her subjects. The first letter that he received from her after the liberation of Rumania is illustrative of her buoyant grandeur:*

Jassy 12/25th Nov. 1918.

My dear George,

You will never know what it meant for us the first communication with you all again. We were like buried alive, smothered, cut off from the living and suddenly light broke in upon us with such a rush that we were nearly blinded.

Your dear letter was brought to me by Lieut. Griffith Evans, who has such a big soul in such a frail body, and you cannot imagine the pleasure it gave me. I never doubted but that you would be a faithful friend and uphold our country and its interests, but to hear it again from you yourself after the awful silence that had fallen upon us for about 9 months was a wonderful moment of happiness.

I can only tell you dear George that I held firm as only a born Englishwoman can. Nothing shook me, neither threats, nor misery, nor humiliation nor isolation. At the darkest hours when no news reached us I clung firmly to my belief in your strength and fidelity. I knew you would win and I kept my people from giving way even at a moment when many had become doubters, luck having been from the beginning so dead set against us. And even if you had not been victorious, I would have stuck to you, for me there are no two forms of fidelity. Forgive me for talking so much of myself, but I have been so insulted and flouted since we were given over into the enemy's hands that really it is my hour now! . . .'

Slowly the Peace Conference drew to its exhausted end. There came the March crisis and the May crisis and then the final signature of peace in the Galérie des Glaces of the Palace of Versailles:

'Buckingham Palace. June 28 (1919). We got the news about 4.30 that peace had been signed at Versailles at 4.0 o'clock. A large number of people collected in front of the Palace & at 6.0 a salute was fired of 101 guns. May & I & the children went out on the centre balcony & there was a great demonstration of loyalty. One of the Guards bands

335

played in the forecourt. We stopped on the balcony for 40 minutes. After dinner I received a letter from the Prime Minister telling me peace was signed, brought by Mr Davidson in an aeroplane. At 9.15 we again went on the balcony, a larger crowd than ever, probably 100,000. David & I each made a short speech. At 11.0 they turned searchlights on and we again went out. Today is a great one in history. Please God the dear old Country will now settle down & work in unity.'

The letter which Mr Davidson brought by air from Paris that evening ran as follows:

> Galérie des Glaces du Château de Versailles.
>
> 'Mr Lloyd George with his humble duty to Your Majesty has the honour to announce that the long & terrible war in which the British Empire has been engaged with the German Empire for more than four years & which has caused such suffering to mankind has been brought to an end this afternoon by the Treaty of Peace just signed in this hall.
>
> He desires on behalf of all the Plenipotentiaries of Your Majesty's Empire to tender their heartfelt congratulations to Your Majesty on the signature of a Treaty which marks the victorious end of the terrible struggle which has lasted so long & in which Your Majesty's subjects from all parts of the Empire have played so glorious a part.
>
> D. Lloyd George. June 28, 1919. 4.0 p.m.

The King did not in fact regard the Treaty of Versailles and its attendant instruments with any marked confidence or satisfaction. We find him writing to the Foreign Office in November 1919, drawing their attention to the misery still imposed upon the Austrian people.[m]

> 'The King is shocked at the condition of things in Vienna as described in Lindley's despatch of Nov. 4. His Majesty asks whether Lord Curzon[1] could not communicate its contents to the Conference in Paris with a view to the prompt adoption of some measures for the provision of those necessaries of life which, owing to the conditions of the Peace Treaty, seem to be withheld from the people, especially at a time when the rigours of an early winter have to be faced.'

An embarrassing situation was created by Article 27 of the Treaty of Versailles, under which the German Emperor was arraigned 'for a supreme offence against international morality and the sanctity of treaties'. On June 4, 1919, the Supreme Council of the Conference had agreed that the ex-Emperor should be brought to trial. The King regarded this indictment as ill-judged. Even before

[1] Lord Curzon succeeded Mr Balfour as Foreign Secretary on October 24, 1919.

the coupon election took place he had agreed with Lord Stamfordham's commentary on the issue:[n]

'The majority of people', the latter had written to him on December 5, 1918, 'appear to have lost their balance about the Kaiser. But
there are *some* thoughtful minds who think we shall land ourselves in
hopeless difficulties if a so-called International Tribunal is embarked
on. It certainly will not be "international" if only the allied countries
find the Judges who will themselves be the accusers. . . . The cooler
heads advocate the Falkland Islands and no trial. But sending Na-
poleon to St Helena did not prevent his nephew becoming Emperor
and the Kaiser's sons cannot all be hanged!'

After the Supreme Council had invited the Netherlands Government to extradite the ex-Emperor, the King received a petition
signed by the King of Saxony, the Duke of Würtemberg and the
Grand-Duke of Baden.[o] It was not in every respect a tactful document; but it was one to which a convincing or logical reply could
not, with great facility, be framed:

'At this late hour' it ran, 'the German Princes turn to Your Majesty
with an earnest and urgent appeal. If the monstrous suggestion is
carried out demanding that His Majesty, the German Emperor, should
be delivered up by Neutral Countries in order to vindicate his conduct,
then the world will witness the spectacle of an independent Monarch,
overcome in honourable warfare by his enemies' superiority, being
brought, contrary to the laws of warfare and of nations and to the
traditions of Christian lands, before a Court of Justice composed of his
enemies who are in every way incompetent to judge him. In the name,
and on behalf of, all unanimously thinking German Princes, we
approach Your Majesty, whose family originated among us, and beg
you to listen to our warning. We know that our Emperor acted to the
best of his knowledge and with the highest intentions, in full con-
sciousness of his kingly responsibility.
    If Your Majesty, by tolerating his trial, lays hands on the Royal
Dignity of a great and at one time friendly and related Ruler, then
every official authority, every throne (including the English throne)
will be threatened. We trust to the wisdom of Your Majesty to prevent
a crime, the responsibility for which would weigh heavily on Your
Majesty's shoulders.'

The King referred this letter to the Foreign Secretary and the
Prime Minister. Lord Curzon considered that the letter was 'im-
pertinent' in tone and substance and that no reply should be returned. The King felt however that it would be a mistake to leave
such an appeal unanswered and in the end a reply was drafted by
the Foreign Office pointing out that the indictment of the ex-

Emperor figured in the text of the Treaty and as such became the joint responsibility of all the Signatory Powers.

An analogous difficulty occurred some months later when the Allies insisted upon the delivery to them of a number of German generals and officers who had been catalogued as 'war criminals'. On February 9, 1920, the German Crown Prince wrote to the King offering his own person as a scapegoat for his compatriots. 'If', he wrote, 'the Allied and Associated Governments require a sacrifice let them take me instead of the nine hundred Germans, whose only fault was that they served their Fatherland in War.' No reply, it seems, was returned to this foolish, but not ignoble, gesture. In the end, the Netherlands Government stoutly and most conveniently refused to deliver up the ex-Emperor; he was permitted to remain in Holland until his death.

(4)

On June 29, 1919, the King went in person to welcome Mr Lloyd George on his triumphal return from the Peace Conference:

> 'He drove with me to Buckingham Palace & got a splendid reception from large crowds.'

On July 19 the Victory Parade was held in London. The King took the salute from a pavilion erected at the base of the Victoria Memorial. Foch and Pershing, Beatty and Haig passed before him at the head of their detachments. 'The most impressive sight', he wrote, 'I ever saw.'

Slowly the old peace-time routine was re-established. In August 1919 the King and Queen returned to Balmoral: 'delighted to be in this dear place again after six years & to see all our nice people again'. On February 10, 1920, he opened Parliament in full state, wearing his crown. On March 22 was held the first levée since the war: 'It was refreshing to see the old fulldress uniform again.' On June 10 took place the first Court for six years. On July 10 he was again at Portsmouth in the *Victoria and Albert* which he had not seen since the dramatic Spithead review of July 1914. On February 15, 1921, on the occasion of the opening of Parliament, the Guards appeared again in their scarlet tunics and bearskins. This surface resumption of pre-war pageantry and customs did not conceal the fact that fundamentally the structure and spirit of society had changed.

In the early weeks of 1919 the public were startled from complacency by the disorders that attended the demobilisation of the armies. The Cabinet had adopted an imprudent scheme of demobilisation, under which the first men to be released were the key men, required for industry, who were in fact the very men who had been the last to be called up. Riots occurred in Glasgow and Belfast and at Luton the town hall was burnt down by an angry mob. At Calais a serious military mutiny occurred. Mr Churchill was hurriedly transferred to the War Office and succeeded within a few weeks in restoring order by scrapping the original scheme and introducing a fairer method under which priority of release was based on length of service and number of wounds. When once the Churchill plan had been established men were demobilised at the rate of 50,000 a day and discontent subsided.

It had been expected that the period of reconstruction would be marked by heavy unemployment. The unemployment insurance scheme attached to the 1911 Health Act applied only to a limited number of trades and provided relief at the rate of only 7/- a week. The Government now promised a system of complete contributory assurance and in the meantime they agreed to provide ex-soldiers and ex-munition workers unable to find employment with a non-contributory dole of 25/- a week. Owing, however, to the post-war boom, which lasted until the end of 1920, industry was able to absorb all the labour available. Although some four million men were rapidly demobilised, the number of unemployed for November 1919 was no more than 300,000.

In spite of the ease with which industry absorbed this sudden flood of released labour, the workers themselves were restless and suspicious. The strikes that were declared during the course of 1919 surpassed all previous records and during the year thirty million working days were lost. The ferment of unrest which, during the early period of reconstruction, infected the proletariat can be ascribed to various causes. Apart from the psychological dislocation caused by the war there was a feeling that if the Government could spend seven millions a day in destroying their enemies they could well afford to redeem their promise to render Britain a land fit for heroes to live in. With the rise in the cost of living the workers were at a loss to tell what their wages really represented nor could either they or their employers accurately assess, in terms of current supply and demand, the strength of their respective forces. Moreover, during the war the Trades Unions had accepted an industrial truce and the Shop Stewards, who until then had been little more than local officials appointed by their district committees, had begun to

339

assume functions of leadership in the several factories. These stewards, many of them affected by the example of the Russian soviets, began to regard themselves as no longer subordinate to the Trades Unions but as directly elected by, and representative of, the workers themselves. They lent themselves readily to syndicalist theories and to conceptions of direct action. Today we can appreciate that all this restlessness was an inevitable result of dislocation and in some ways a valuable process of re-growth: at the time, it appeared to the authorities as a presage of turmoil.

The King, although deeply distressed by the prevailing discord, did not exaggerate the menace either of the Council of Action or of the Triple Alliance between the railwaymen, the transport workers and the miners. On February 9, 1919, he had had a conversation with Mr J. H. Thomas, leader of the N.U.R. 'He is', he wrote in his diary, 'a good and loyal man':

> 'Last year', he wrote to Lord Stamfordham on January 3, 1920,[*]
> 'has been a difficult one for us all, but I think we can congratulate
> ourselves that we have come through it better than any other country
> & please God 1920 will see things settle down & that the present
> unrest will gradually decrease as trade improves & unemployment
> becomes less. Labour is certainly gaining strength politically & will do
> so more in the future, but surely as their power increases so will their
> responsibility, therefore they will be less inclined to listen to the
> extremists. I feel that each year my responsibilities increase. I shall
> ever do my best to meet them & I know that so long as I can count on
> your kind help & advice they will be lightened.'

Trade did not improve and the post-war boom that lasted until December 1920 began rapidly to decline. In that month the unemployment figures rose to 700,000; by March 1921 they were over 1,300,000; by June they had passed the two million mark. The export price of coal fell in the early months of 1921 from 55/- to 24/-. The Government announced that on March 31 they intended to decontrol the mines and to suspend the subsidy of five million pounds a month that had sufficed hitherto to stabilise prices and wages. During the war, moreover, the Government had negotiated national agreements with the Miners Federation. The miners desired this system to continue since it enabled the more prosperous mines to create a pool for the support of those that were working at a loss. The owners, however, insisted upon a return to the area system. On April 1 the miners declared a strike. On April 8 the railwaymen and transport workers announced that, unless the miners and owners

340

came to an agreement, 'the full strike power of the Triple Alliance' would be brought to bear by midnight on April 12.

The King, who was at Windsor, returned hurriedly to London. The apprehension caused by this threat of a triple strike is well reflected in the weekly letters that he addressed to Queen Alexandra:

'On Friday', he wrote on April 10, 'the Railway men & Transport workers informed us that they also were going to strike on Tuesday next, so I at once decided to return to London. There is no doubt that we are passing through as grave a crisis as this country has ever had. All the troops have been called out; Kensington Gardens is full of them. The public are entirely on the side of the Government.'

'As you can imagine,' he wrote on April 17, 'we have been through a very serious week. Up to 3.0 o'clock on Friday afternoon it looked as if the Railwaymen and Transport Workers would strike for a certainty at 10.0 o'clock at night. The leaders of the two unions suddenly settled that they would not strike; whether they found out that their people were very half-hearted about it (which was true) or whether they thought the miners' case not good enough to support, I do not know. It was indeed a great relief to us all that we were spared the chaos and misery which would have been caused by the dislocation of the life of the people. The Government had made the most elaborate preparations for feeding the people of London and all over the country, and this might also have deterred them from striking at the eleventh hour Alas! The miners' strike continues.'

'I went to a football match', he wrote on April 24, 'at which there were 73,000 people; at the end they sang the National Anthem and cheered tremendously. There were no bolsheviks there! At least I never saw any. The country is all right: just a few extremists are doing all the harm.'

When the unemployment figures increased during the autumn of 1921 the King repeatedly conveyed to the Prime Minister his growing concern:

'The King', Lord Stamfordham wrote to Mr Lloyd George on September 1, 'is daily growing more anxious about the question of unemployment during the coming winter. . . . The people grow discontented and agitators seize their opportunities; marches are organised; the police interfere; resistance ensues; troops are called out and riot begets riot and possibly revolution. His Majesty knows that this matter is engaging the serious attention of his Government and feels sure that, even among the many absorbing questions which confront you, you are not losing sight of what seems to be not only a serious but almost insoluble problem.'[q]

Three weeks later the King instructed Lord Stamfordham to write an even more trenchant letter to Sir Maurice Hankey, the Secretary of the Cabinet:[r]

341

'I do not know whether you have returned from leave, but I am writing to you because the King does not want to bother the Prime Minister with any letters which are not absolutely necessary for him to receive. At the same time His Majesty is very much troubled about the unemployment question. . . . As the King hopes that the question will come before the Cabinet at an early date, he would ask you to lay before them, either this letter, or its general contents.

His Majesty does not know what the Cabinet Unemployment Committee are likely to recommend; but he does most earnestly trust that the Government will agree to some scheme by which work, and not doles, will be supplied to the unemployed, the great majority of whom, His Majesty understands, honestly want to work. Emergency works, such as road-making, land reclamation, light railways, forestation although unremunerative, will nevertheless be doing some good and meet the claim of those who demand work and not charity.

It is impossible to expect people to subsist upon the unemployment benefit of 15/- for men and 12/- for women.

The King appeals to the Government to meet this grave, but he believes temporary, difficulty, with the same liberality as they displayed in dealing with the enormous daily cost of the war.'

(5)

The King's unceasing endeavours to promote concord and to allay dissension were not confined to the areas of politics and industry. He strongly disapproved of the publication of contemporary memoirs calculated to perpetuate personal bitterness or to revive forgotten controversies. When he read in a Sunday newspaper that Mrs Asquith was about to serialise her autobiography and to include therein important letters from Lord Stamfordham, he wrote to the latter in some perturbation:[s]

'What on earth does this mean? People who write books ought to be shut up. Can you find out what this refers to?'

More serious was the distress occasioned to him by the publication of Lord French's book entitled '1914'. He instructed Lord Stamfordham to address to the Field Marshal a letter of grave rebuke:[t]

Windsor Castle, May 8 1919.
'My dear French,
    The King desires me to say how much concerned he is by the publication of your book upon the War, which inevitably will give rise to controversy and personal recriminations among officers in our own and the French Army now living and the representatives of those who are dead. Your high rank in the Army and your position as His Majesty's representative in Ireland invest your utterances with special

importance, and for this reason the King regards as very serious the fact of your having "entered the lists" and given to the world, when the War is theoretically not ended, your account of that part of its history during which the British forces were under your Command.

You know how difficult it is to write history, even when events are fresh in men's minds, and the King would deprecate it if, in the hoped-for days of rejoicing and happiness, a discordant note were sounded by angry disputes and personal wrangling with regard to either the conduct of operations or the leadership of troops, crucial features and important turning-points as they were in the history of the campaign.'

There is no record in the Royal Archives of what reply Lord French returned to this reprimand.

In October 1919 Lord Milner wrote to Lord Stamfordham suggesting that the first anniversary of Armistice day might be marked by a solemn moment of national silence. The proposal originated from a South African, Sir Percy Fitzpatrick, who had been impressed by the effect of the 'two minutes pause' which during the war had been observed daily in Cape Town as a 'salute to the dead'. The King was in favour of the proposal but felt that it was a matter for the Cabinet to decide. The Cabinet, in spite of Lord Curzon's objections, agreed that at the stroke of 11.0 on November 11 a two minutes silence should be observed.

When the second anniversary of the Armistice was approaching, the Dean of Westminster, the Very Rev. Herbert Ryle, suggested that when the permanent cenotaph was unveiled on November 11, 1920, the body of an unknown warrior should be buried in Westminster Abbey in the presence of the King and the heads of the fighting services:

'His Majesty' Lord Stamfordham replied on October 7, 1920,[u] 'is inclined to think that nearly two years after the last shot fired on the battlefields of France and Flanders is so long ago that a funeral now might be regarded as belated, and almost, as it were, reopen the war wound which time is gradually healing.'

The suggestion, which had in fact been first made by the Rev. David Railton, at one time Chaplain at the Front and subsequently Vicar of Margate, was warmly sponsored by Mr Lloyd George and Sir Henry Wilson. The King withdrew his original objections and, after unveiling the Cenotaph on November 11, walked behind the gun carriage bearing the coffin of the unknown warrior to its place in the Abbey. He was relieved to admit that his original apprehensions were unjustified: he found the ceremony appropriate and impressive.

CHAPTER XXI

THE IRISH TREATY

1921

The advance of Sinn Fein—Conscription extended to Ireland—Measures of repression—Sinn Fein win the General Election and proclaim an Irish Republic—The Black and Tans—The King protests against reprisals—The Northcliffe interview—The Home Rule Act of December 1920—The King opens the Parliament of Northern Ireland—Effect of the King's speech—The King urges the Prime Minister to enter into immediate negotiations—Mr Lloyd George's first approach to Mr De Valera—General Smuts' visit to Dublin—Mr De Valera comes to London—The Government offer Ireland Dominion Status—The offer rejected—The King persuades the Prime Minister to send a conciliatory reply—The invitation of September 7—Mr. De Valera accepts the invitation—The London Conference—Heads of Agreement signed on December 6, 1921—The Irish Treaty ratified—The King's satisfaction at this result.

(1)

THE Convention of 1917 had been summoned in the expectation that a reunion of notable Irishmen would succeed in framing a system of Home Rule acceptable to the country as a whole. It was not at the time realised that the decision of Sinn Fein to boycott the Convention would rob it of effective reality. The English, with their tendency to approach Irish problems in a mood of complacency, failed until it was too late to recognise that Sinn Fein, under the guidance of Eamon De Valera,[1] was becoming the determinant force in Irish

[1] Eamon De Valera was born in New York on October 14, 1882, the son of a Spanish father and an Irish mother. His father died when he was two years of age and he was thereafter entrusted to the care of his grandmother in Co. Limerick and bred and educated in Ireland. In 1913 he became a member of the Irish Volunteers, was captured at the time of the Easter rebellion in 1916, and was condemned to life imprisonment at Dartmoor. Released under the general amnesty of June 1917, he was in January 1918 chosen as 'President of the Irish Republic'. Arrested again in May 1918, he escaped from Lincoln jail in February 1919. On the establishment of the Free State in December 1921 he headed the republican rebellion and was imprisoned by the Free State Government in August 1923, being released in the following July. As leader of the Fianna Fail party he entered the Dail in 1927 and after the election of 1932 became President of the Irish executive council. His subsequent career is outside the scope of this biography.

politics: a force combining the mysticism of ancient yearnings with a practical efficiency that was new and fierce.

Mr John Redmond, the leader of the Irish Parliamentary Party in the House of Commons, died on March 8, 1918. He was succeeded by Mr John Dillon. On April 9, under the impact of the German offensive, Mr Lloyd George rushed through Parliament a Man-power Bill extending conscription to Ireland. Mr Dillon and his followers immediately withdrew from Westminster and joined with Sinn Fein in issuing a manifesto denying the right of the Imperial Parliament to impose compulsory military service on the Irish people. The Irish Roman Catholic bishops, who had hitherto remained ostensibly neutral, denounced the Act as 'an oppressive and inhuman law, which the Irish have the right to resist by all means consonant with the laws of God'.

The British Government felt that so overt a defiance of Parliament could not be submissively ignored. Although, as the German menace waned, they did not in practice enforce conscription upon Ireland, they decided to reassert what, with some euphemism, were called 'the principles of orderly government'.

On May 6 Field Marshal Lord French was appointed to succeed Lord Wimborne as Lord Lieutenant. On May 17 Mr De Valera was arrested and transported to Lincoln Jail. On May 20 Mr Arthur Griffith and other Sinn Fein leaders were deported to England; on July 3 Sinn Fein and its affiliated bodies were declared 'dangerous associations'; and on the same date the whole western seaboard of Ireland was pronounced a military area. Mr Dillon, who by then had returned to the House of Commons, denounced these measures as placing Ireland 'under the unfettered tyranny of military government'.

At the General Election of December 1918 Sinn Fein captured as many as 73 of the 105 Irish seats. The old Irish Parliamentary Party was reduced to six members; Mr Dillon himself was defeated. Sinn Fein celebrated this victory by assuming the title of the 'Irish Republican Party'. On January 21, 1919, those of them who were not under arrest in England met as the Dail Eireann in the Mansion House at Dublin, signed a Declaration of Independence, and elected Mr De Valera as 'President of the Irish Republic'. The British Ministers and public did not, at the time, attach sufficient importance to these events. The Dail also chose Count Plunkett and Mr Arthur Griffith as the delegates of the Republic accredited to the Peace Conference in Paris. Mr Lloyd George succeeded in persuading President Wilson that the Irish problem was a purely domestic issue and that the self-styled representatives of the Irish Republic had no right to be heard.

Having been denied the opportunity to plead their claim to self-determination before an international tribunal, the Irish leaders decided to resort to direct action. Already a social and economic boycott had been proclaimed against the Irish Constabulary. In the autumn of 1919 the policy of assassination was applied; throughout 1920 it continued with increasing ferocity. No juries could be found to convict the assailants; the British forces of 60,000 regulars and 15,000 armed police proved unable to cope with the 3,000 Irish guerillas; anarchy, accompanied on each side by many atrocities, spread throughout the land.

On April 4, 1920, Sir Hamar Greenwood[1] was appointed Chief Secretary for Ireland. On July 10 it was announced that the by then depleted ranks of the Irish Constabulary were to be reinforced by specially recruited ex-service men. These new recruits were dressed in khaki uniforms with black hats and armlets. They became known as the 'Black and Tans'.

(2)

As early as September 1919 the King had expressed to the Government his anxiety lest, without any clear conception of policy, they might be drifting into an impossible position:

'His Majesty asks', wrote Lord Stamfordham to Mr Bonar Law on September 11, 1919, 'what does his Government intend to do towards further protecting the lives of unoffending people in Ireland—and in order to introduce into Parliament measures for the Government of the country?' *a*

'For the present', Mr Bonar Law replied, 'the policy of His Majesty's Government must be what it has been throughout—of supporting the Irish Government in taking whatever measures they think necessary to secure orderly Government in Ireland.' *b*

Throughout the course of 1920 and the early months of 1921 the reports that the King received from his ministerial and other ad-

---

[1] Sir Hamar Greenwood was born at Whitby, Ontario, in 1870 and had served for eight years in the Canadian militia. He entered the British House of Commons in 1906 and became Under Secretary at the Home Office in 1919. He was raised to the peerage in 1929 as Baron Greenwood of Llanbister.

visers were contradictory but disquieting. Lord French, on his occasional visits to London, would confess that the whole situation was 'shocking and lamentable'. Sir Hamar Greenwood, after his appointment as Chief Secretary, adopted a more optimistic tone. In November 1920 he was assuring Lord Stamfordham that 'everywhere the move is upward towards improvement'.[c] In the following April he expressed the view that 'now that the Republican movement is crumbling, owing to the gallant police and military, the Republic exists no longer.'[d]

Sir Nevil Macready, commanding the British military forces in Ireland, was less satisfied. He deprecated the expression 'murder gang' so readily applied by English politicians to the Sinn Fein leaders; the term 'fanatical patriots' would, he suggested, be more appropriate. He realised that the discipline and morale of his troops were being exposed to a strain that was almost intolerable. Although it was evident that the Sinn Fein movement could, if desired, be suppressed by force, he intimated that this would entail an operation of war more extensive and bitter than would be acceptable to the judgement or conscience of the British people. His implication that conciliation was preferable to violence was in accordance with the King's own natural tendencies.[e]

His Majesty regarded himself—and it was an honourable illusion—as the protector of his Irish, as well as of his British, subjects. He complained repeatedly of the scant courtesy shown by British officers to perfectly harmless individuals, such as Mrs Annan Bryce, who were detained or examined on suspicion.[f] He was outraged by the reprisals carried out by men wearing the British uniform:

'The King', Lord Stamfordham wrote to Sir Hamar Greenwood in May 1921, 'does ask himself, and he asks you, if this policy of reprisals is to be continued and, if so, to where will it lead Ireland and us all? It seems to His Majesty that in punishing the guilty we are inflicting punishment no less severe upon the innocent.'[g]

In July 1921 a newspaper in the United States published what purported to be an interview with Lord Northcliffe, in which the latter had stated that the King was opposed to the Irish policy of the Government and had protested to them against the activities of the Black and Tans. 'I cannot', the King was represented as saying, 'have my people killed in this manner.' The interview was repudiated by Lord Northcliffe and described by Mr Lloyd George in the House of Commons as 'a complete fabrication'. Yet, however unauthorised,

347

it was not in fact a fanciful presentation of the King's feelings at the time. He certainly expressed the view that the Black and Tans should be disbanded and that the constabulary should be subjected to military discipline under the command of Sir Nevil Macready.[h]

The British Cabinet meanwhile had not failed to mitigate the exercise of force by movements of conciliation. A new Government of Ireland Bill was passed under which two Irish Parliaments were to be established, the one in Dublin and the other in Belfast. The principle of unity was to be maintained by the creation of a 'Council of Ireland' composed of members of each of the two legislatures 'with a view to the eventual establishment of a Parliament for the whole of Ireland'. Questions of Foreign Policy and Defence were to be reserved for the Imperial Parliament in London. Once the two Irish legislatures had merged into a single Irish Parliament, questions of finance and excise were to be settled by direct negotiation with the British Government. This Bill received the Royal Assent on December 23, 1920. At the same time Lord Edmund Talbot, a leading English Catholic, was appointed Lord Lieutenant in the place of Lord French. He assumed the title of Lord FitzAlan.

Attempts were at the same time made to enter into surreptitious contact with the leaders of the Sinn Fein movement. In April 1921 Lord Derby, disguised in coloured glasses and under the name of 'Mr Edwards', crossed to Dublin and had an interview with Mr De Valera. In May, Sir James Craig, Prime Minister of Northern Ireland, agreed, with commendable courage, to place his head within the lion's mouth: he drove by devious ways to the place where Mr De Valera was concealed and spent nearly two hours in conversation with his formidable antagonist. Throughout the period confidential exchanges took place between the British Government and the Sinn Fein leaders through the agency of Mr Alfred Cope, Assistant Under Secretary at Dublin Castle. None of these interviews or communications availed to bring agreement nearer or to abate the reign of terror that was distracting the land and filling the minds and hearts of British citizens with the mixed anguish of perplexity, resentment and shame.

(3)

It had been decided that on June 22, 1921, the King should cross to Belfast and open in person the first session of the new Ulster Parliament established under the Government of Ireland Act of 1920. The speech that he made on that occasion exercised so strong an influence upon the future course of Anglo-Irish relations that the circumstances in which it was composed must be examined in some detail.

The story that the King rejected the first draft prepared by the Irish Office on the ground that it was lacking in 'effective humanity', and that thereafter he substituted for it a speech written by himself with the assistance of General Smuts, is not exact in every particular and incidentally implies a departure from established constitutional procedure.[i] Neither the King nor General Smuts ever saw the original draft and had thus no means of knowing whether it was or not a 'blood-thirsty document'. The origins of the Belfast speech, although unusual, were not quite so abnormal as the legend avers.

On June 13, 1921, General Smuts, who had arrived in England for the Imperial Conference, was invited to luncheon at Windsor. He found the King 'anxiously preoccupied' by his forthcoming visit to Belfast. The King feared that the advice given him by his Ministers that he should in person open the new Ulster Parliament might be regarded by the Southern Irish as a deliberate affront. Lord Stamfordham and other members of the Royal household expressed the indignant opinion that it was inconsiderate of Sir James Craig and the British Cabinet thus to expose the King to grave personal danger. General Smuts held the view that His Majesty could not but follow the advice tendered to him by his Ministers; but he suggested that this 'small dangerous affair' might be turned into something great and beneficent. Why should not the King seize the opportunity to address a message of peace to the whole of Ireland? The King was impressed by this suggestion. He asked General Smuts, with Lord Stamfordham's assistance, to put his ideas into writing. Thus encouraged, General Smuts withdrew and returned later with what was the first draft of the Belfast speech.[j]

Lord Stamfordham, with his ever-cautious regard for correct constitutional procedure, did not consider it fitting for the King himself to put before the Cabinet the draft of so important and unusual a pronouncement. He therefore asked General Smuts to convey the draft to the Prime Minister in the form of a personal suggestion. On his return to London, therefore, General Smuts addressed to Mr Lloyd George a long private letter enclosing, merely as an illustration, a sketch of the sort of speech that in his opinion the King ought to deliver. His letter is dated June 14, 1921, and is of considerable interest:[k]

'My dear Prime Minister.

I am very sorry to hear that indisposition is keeping you away from London at this moment. The great urgency and importance of the following matter must be my excuse for writing you this note.

I need not enlarge to you on the importance of the Irish question for the Empire as a whole. The present situation is an unmeasured calamity; it is a negation of all the principles of government which we have professed as the basis of Empire, and it must more and more tend to poison both our Empire relations and our foreign relations. Besides, the present methods are frightfully expensive in a financial no less than a moral sense; and what is worse they have failed. What is to be the next move, for the present situation may not last? I believe there are certain hopeful elements in the present position, of which full use should immediately be made—with perhaps far-reaching results. In the first place the establishment of the Ulster Parliament definitely eliminates the coercion of Ulster, and the road is clear now to deal on the most statesmanlike lines with the rest of Ireland.

In the second place, the King (as he tells me) is going to Belfast next week to open the Ulster Parliament. Now it is questionable whether the King should go at all. But his going would be fully justified if the occasion were made use of by him to make a really important declaration on the whole question. I believe that in the present universal mistrust and estrangement the King could be made use of to give a most important lead, which would help you out of a situation that is well-nigh desperate. The Irish might accept it as coming from the King, and in that way the opening might be given you for a final settlement. I would suggest that in his speech to the Ulster Parliament the King should foreshadow the grant of Dominion status to Ireland, and point out that the removal of all possibility of coercing Ulster now renders such a solution possible. The promise of Dominion status *by the King* would create a new and definite situation which would crystallise opinion favourably both in Ireland and elsewhere. Informal negotiations could then be set going with responsible Irish leaders and the details—financial and strategic—might be discussed with the Dominion Prime Ministers, if you like to do so.

I enclose a suggested declaration to be inserted in the King's speech. Such a declaration would not be a mere kite, but would have to be adopted by you as your policy, and the King could of course only make it on your advice. I am not acquainted with the details of the Irish situation, but I should consider the attempt well worth the making and think you would in doing so be supported by all the Dominion Prime Ministers.'

The 'Declaration' enclosed in General Smuts' letter to Mr Lloyd George was much shorter than the speech as eventually delivered. It began by affirming the King's 'love and sympathy' with Ireland as a whole. It went on to say that the opening of the Belfast Parliament, implying as it did the impossibility of any coercion of

Ulster, would remove what had been an insurmountable obstacle to agreement. And it intimated that this agreement might be based upon the grant to Ireland of Dominion status and of those 'principles and ideals of freedom and cooperation' which would lead Ireland 'out of the miseries of the present to the happiness and contentment which characterises all my other self-governing Dominions'.

On the morning of June 17 Lord Stamfordham called at Downing Street and pointed out that the King had 'been kept in the dark' with regard to the speech that he was to make at the opening session of the Belfast Parliament. The King, Lord Stamfordham added 'especially after his recent conversation with General Smuts' felt that 'he should be made acquainted with the views of the Cabinet' in view of 'the critical condition of affairs in Ireland and the intense anxiety throughout the whole of the Dominions for some solution other than that of the Government's present policy regarding Ireland'.[1]

The Prime Minister at once agreed that the drafts which had been prepared by the Irish Office were 'inappropriate' and that a completely new speech should be composed, wider in scope and more personal in tone. The writing of this revised version was entrusted to Sir Edward Grigg,[1] at the time one of Mr Lloyd George's secretaries. On June 18 the Prime Minister took this draft to Windsor and submitted it to the King, who expressed his warm approval.

On June 21 the King, with a magnificent naval escort, crossed in his yacht from Holyhead to Belfast. On the morning of Wednesday, June 22, he landed at Donegal quay and drove in an open carriage to the new Parliament:

> 'I think', he wrote in his diary, 'my speech was appreciated. In it I made an appeal to the whole of Ireland for peace. . . . Our visit has been a great success & everything has gone off beautifully. We really got a wonderful welcome & I never heard anything like the cheering. . . .'

[1] Sir Edward Grigg (b. 1879) after leaving Winchester and New College joined the editorial staff of *The Times* and became Assistant Editor of the *Outlook*. He served in the Grenadier Guards during the war, becoming G.S.O.I. and a lieutenant colonel. He accompanied the Prince of Wales to Canada, Australia and New Zealand in 1919 and became Private Secretary to Mr Lloyd George in 1921. In 1922 he entered the House of Commons as Liberal National member for Oldham. In 1925 he became Governor of Kenya Colony and in 1933 he again entered Parliament as M.P. for Altrincham. In 1945 he was raised to the peerage as Baron Altrincham. He is the author of many important books on Imperial and political questions.

351

On June 23 the King returned to London and was welcomed at the station by the Prime Minister and members of the Cabinet. The citizens of London, as he drove to Buckingham Palace accorded him a triumphant greeting. His visit had in truth been auspicious:

'Certainly', wrote Mr Churchill, 'every loyal subject must feel a special debt of gratitude to Your Majesty for the unswerving sense of public devotion which led to the undertaking of so momentous a journey.' [m]

The Prime Minister was overjoyed:

'I am confident', he wrote, 'that I can speak not only for the Government of the United Kingdom but for the whole Empire in offering to Your Majesty and the Queen the hearty congratulations of all Your loyal subjects on the success of Your visit to Belfast. We have been deeply moved by the devotion and enthusiasm with which You were greeted and our faith in the future is strengthened by the reception given to Your Majesty's words in inaugurating the Parliament of Northern Ireland.

None but the King could have made that personal appeal; none but the King could have evoked so instantaneous a response. No effort shall be lacking on the part of Your Ministers to bring Northern and Southern Ireland together in recognition of common Irish responsibility, and I trust that from now onwards a new spirit of forbearance and accommodation may breathe upon the troubled waters of the Irish question.

Your Majesty may rest assured of the deep gratitude of Your peoples for this new act of royal service to their ideals and interests.' [n]

The speech as finally delivered may have borne but little relation to General Smuts' original 'declaration'; but its inception was undoubtedly due to the vision of that statesman and to the influence he possessed with the King and Government. The Cabinet and the public were grateful to the King for having ventured, at so troubled a time, to drive with the Queen beside him through the streets of Belfast. Those who actually heard the speech never forgot the intense conviction with which it was delivered or the emotion it aroused. It in fact inaugurated a new and wiser stage in the whole disordered story and, if for that reason alone, it must be textually reproduced:

'Members of the Senate and of the House of Commons

For all who love Ireland, as I do with all my heart, this is a profoundly moving occasion in Irish history. My memories of the Irish people date back to the time when I spent many happy days in Ireland as a midshipman. My affection for the Irish people has been deepened by successive visits since that time, and I have watched with constant sympathy the course of their affairs.

I could not have allowed myself to give Ireland, by deputy alone, my earnest prayers and good wishes in the new era which opens with this ceremony, and I have, therefore, come in person, as Head of the Empire, to inaugurate this Parliament on Irish soil. I inaugurate it with deep-felt hope, and I feel assured that you will do your utmost to make it an instrument of happiness and good government for all parts of the community which you represent.

This is a great and critical occasion in the history of the six counties, but not for the six counties alone; for everything which interests them touches Ireland, and everything which touches Ireland finds an echo in the remotest parts of the Empire.

Few things are more earnestly desired throughout the English-speaking world than a satisfactory solution of the age-long Irish problems, which for generations embarrassed our forefathers, as they now weigh heavily upon us.

Most certainly there is no wish nearer my own heart than that every man of Irish birth, whatever be his creed, and wherever be his home, should work in co-operation with the free communities on which the British Empire is based. I am confident that the important matters entrusted to the control and guidance of the Northern Parliament will be managed with wisdom and moderation; with fairness and due regard to every faith and interest, and with no abatement of that patriotic devotion to the Empire which you proved so gallantly in the Great War.

Full partnership in the United Kingdom and religious freedom Ireland has long enjoyed. She now has conferred upon her the duty of dealing with all the essential tasks of domestic legislation and government, and I feel no misgiving as to the spirit in which you who stand here today will carry out the all-important functions entrusted to your care.

My hope is broader still. The eyes of the whole Empire are on Ireland today—that Empire in which so many nations and races have come together in spite of the ancient feuds, and in which new nations have come to birth within the lifetime of the youngest in this hall. I am emboldened by that thought to look beyond the sorrow and anxiety which have clouded of late my vision of Irish affairs. I speak from a full heart when I pray that my coming to Ireland today may prove to be the first step towards the end of strife amongst her people, whatever their race or creed.

In that hope I appeal to all Irishmen to pause, to stretch out the hand of forbearance and conciliation, to forgive and forget, and to join in making for the land they love a new era of peace, contentment and goodwill.

It is my earnest desire that in Southern Ireland, too, there may ere long, take place a parallel to what is now passing in this hall; that there a similar occasion may present itself, and a similar ceremony be performed. For this the Parliament of the United Kingdom has in the fullest measure provided the powers. For this the Parliament of Ulster is pointing the way.

The future lies in the hands of my Irish people themselves. May this historic gathering be the prelude of the day in which the Irish people, north and south, under one Parliament or two, as those Parliaments may themselves decide, shall work together in common love for Ireland upon the sure foundation of mutual justice and respect.'

(4)

The King was anxious that the atmosphere created by his speech in Belfast should not be allowed to evaporate. On the morning of July 24 Lord Stamfordham visited the Prime Minister, bringing with him a memorandum in which the King strongly advised his Government that no time should be lost:[o]

'His Majesty', Lord Stamfordham recorded, 'pressed the Government not to miss the psychological moment for taking advantage of the King's utterances, which His Majesty really believed, judging from the Press and other sources, were generally well received in Ireland. But the moment was a very fleeting one, especially when dealing with a quick-witted, volatile and sentimental people, and the opportunity must not be let go by.'

The Prime Minister assured Lord Stamfordham that he and the Cabinet entirely shared the King's opinion. In fact, a letter was already being drafted, inviting Mr De Valera and Sir James Craig to meet British Ministers in conference in London.

This letter of invitation was taken to Dublin that evening by Mr Cope and handed to Mr De Valera. An identical letter was also sent to Sir James Craig. It stated that the British Government were deeply anxious that 'the King's appeal for reconciliation in Ireland should not have been made in vain'. 'We wish', the letter continued, 'that no endeavour should be lacking on our part to realise the King's prayer and we ask you to meet us, as we will meet you, in the spirit of conciliation for which His Majesty appealed.'

Mr De Valera replied on June 28 to the effect that he also was desirous of securing a lasting peace between the Irish and the English, but that he could see 'no avenue by which it can be reached if you deny Ireland's essential unity and set aside the principle of national self-determination'. On the same day Sir James Craig accepted the invitation.

Mr De Valera's answer had not however been a blank refusal. He had indicated that he would reply more fully when he had discussed the matter with 'certain representatives of the political minority in this country'. He accordingly invited Sir James Craig,

354

Lord Midleton and three others to confer with him in the Mansion House in Dublin. Sir James Craig refused, on the ground that he had already accepted Mr Lloyd George's invitation to a meeting in London. Lord Midleton accepted. He immediately ascertained that Mr De Valera would only consider coming to London if the British Government would agree that, pending the results of any discussion, both sides should sign a truce. Lord Midleton hurried over to London and with some difficulty induced the Prime Minister to give his written consent to this concession.

Meanwhile General Smuts had also been invited by Mr De Valera to come to Dublin. He arrived there on July 5 under the name of 'Mr Smith', and had two long discussions with Mr De Valera, who was supported by Mr Griffith, Mr Barton and Mr Duggan. On his return to London he saw the King at Buckingham Palace and furnished him with a detailed account of what had passed:[p]

'General Smuts explained to Mr De Valera that he did not come as an emissary of the British Government, nor did he bring any offer from them. In fact he had nothing to do with the British Government. He came as a friend who had passed through very similar circumstances and he could assure them that in England there was an intense desire for peace: that the King himself was most anxious for a settlement, and General Smuts could assure them that the words uttered in the King's speech at Belfast were a true interpretation of His Majesty's feelings. Mr De Valera expressed distrust of the British Government or of a Conference at the invitation of the British Prime Minister. . . . General Smuts pointed out to Mr De Valera in the strongest possible terms that in refusing the invitation he would be making the greatest mistake of his life. The invitation from the Prime Minister was unconditional, and a refusal on his (De Valera's) part would have the worst possible effect and would turn public opinion against him in America, indeed all over the world, and even in Ireland. . . .'

Mr De Valera, as General Smuts had expected, laid great stress on the 'partition of Ireland' as implied in the Home Rule Bill. General Smuts argued that it was not partition, but that Ulster, which had always blocked previous settlements, was now out of the way. Mr De Valera then turned to the question of the Republic; the Irish people wanted a Republic, expected a Republic, and had in fact elected him as 'President' of the Republic. General Smuts replied by saying that he had himself had experience of a Republic and could assure him that free membership of the British Commonwealth was a far more comfortable status. 'As a friend,' he said, 'I cannot advise too strongly against a Republic. Ask what you want, but not a

355

Republic.' Mr De Valera admitted, according to General Smuts' account, that 'If the status of a Dominion is offered me, I will use all our machinery to get the Irish people to accept it.'

General Smuts returned from Ireland under the impression that Mr De Valera would agree to come to London. He was not mistaken in this forecast. Mr De Valera accepted the invitation on July 8. On July 10 a formal truce was signed in Dublin between Sir Nevil Macready and Mr Richard Mulcahy, Chief of Staff of the Irish Republican Army. On July 12 Mr De Valera, accompanied by Mr Arthur Griffith and Mr Erskine Childers, arrived in London. Their first conversation with the Prime Minister took place on July 14 and lasted from 4.30 to 7.15 that evening. Two further discussions took place on July 15 and 17. Mr Lloyd George, in reporting to the King, expressed the view that these interviews had passed off 'reasonably well'. 'On the whole,' he wrote, 'I think he saw the force of what I said, but he constantly seemed to draw back while I was speaking to him.' ^q These recurrent withdrawals on the part of Mr De Valera were not always, as the Prime Minister supposed, gestures of diplomatic caution. In the face of such voluble and dexterous vivacity, they represented a retreat natural in a man accustomed to melancholy brooding; a retreat into the long caverns of race-memory, hallowed by the blood of saints and martyrs; a retreat into his own solitary reticence, into an inner darkness lit by rare smiles of compassion; smiles too faint to stir the muscles of the lips, but flickering suddenly and shortly, as the reflection of distant lightning in a sombre summer night.

On July 20 the Prime Minister, after consulting the Cabinet, presented to Mr De Valera a long document enumerating the final British proposals. They constituted an offer of Irish freedom such as no former nationalist would, in his wildest dreams, have conceived to be possible. Ireland was to be granted Dominion status with complete autonomy in taxation and finance, her own law courts, police, and defence forces. All that Great Britain demanded in return was that the Irish army should be kept 'within reasonable limits', that the Royal Air Force should be granted facilities in Irish airports, that the British Navy should be accorded essential 'rights and liberties' in Irish harbours, and that no protective duties should be imposed by the Irish State against British imports. Any settlement, moreover, must allow 'for full recognition of the existing powers and privileges of the Government of Northern Ireland, which cannot be abrogated except by their own consent'.

On the next morning Mr De Valera came to Downing Street and informed the Prime Minister that this offer was unacceptable. Mr Lloyd George informed the King immediately:[r]

> 10 Downing Street.
> July 21, 1921.
>
> Sir,
> Your Majesty will, I know, be deeply disappointed to hear that Mr De Valera, who came to see me this morning, had declared himself unable to accept the proposals which I sent him, after submitting them to you, last night—and given as a basis for discussion.
>
> He demanded that Ireland should have Dominion status *sans phrase*, any condition such as that regarding the Royal Navy, which we consider vital to the safety of these islands, to be left for arrangement at a subsequent date between the British and Irish Governments. He also demanded that Ulster should become a part o the Irish Dominion. Failing this, he demanded, as his only alternative, complete independence for Southern Ireland.
>
> I told him that the British Government could not consider his alternatives, and added that if they represented his last word, the only question remaining to be discussed between us was the date and hour at which the truce should terminate. This made a deep impression on him, and he turned quite livid. I pressed it in order that there might be no charges of breach of faith on either side. I also said that I would publish our proposals immediately.
>
> He asked me not to publish them immediately, as this would increase his difficulties. He proposed to return to Ireland and to send me counter-proposals. He also said he would try to confer with Sir James Craig.
>
> I accepted this, and I understood that he returns to Ireland tomorrow. The truce continues pending the communications which he has promised.
>
> There is, I fear, little chance of his counter-proposals being satisfactory, but I am absolutely confident that we shall have public opinion overwhelmingly upon our side throughout the Empire and even in the United States when our proposals are published.'

Lord Stamfordham replied to this letter saying that the King had learnt with 'deep disappointment' that Mr De Valera had rejected an offer that appeared to His Majesty to be most wise and generous. He was glad that the door was still open for further discussion, but he doubted whether Mr De Valera's counter-proposals would be acceptable.[s] These counter-proposals were received on August 11. They confirmed Mr De Valera's initial rejection of the British offer, insisted that no basis of agreement could be found other than that of 'amicable but absolute separation', and suggested that the question of Ulster, as well as that of the Irish share of the National debt, might, if all else failed, be submitted to 'external arbitration'.

On reading this communication, the King, who was staying at Bolton Abbey on his way to Balmoral, wrote at once to Lord Stamfordham:[1]

'I received de Valera's answer in Cabinet box yesterday. It is a hopeless document, written by a dreamer & visionary with nothing practical about it. . . . I hope you will see the P.M. & hear what he proposes to do. I suppose the Cabinet came to some decision yesterday. I trust they will do nothing in a hurry. The great thing is to prolong the negotiations & keep the truce as long as possible. I should publish both the offer of the Government & de Valera's answer as soon as possible; it might help the P.M. & make the moderates force de Valera to be reasonable. . . .'

The Prime Minister, on August 13, replied to Mr De Valera's letter stating that the Government were unable to go beyond the proposals made on July 20 which 'presented to the Irish people an opportunity such as never dawned in their history before.' The British had no desire to derogate from Ireland's full status as a Dominion, but they could not accept either secession or arbitration. No mention was made in this communication of any intention to terminate the truce.

On August 16 the Dail assembled in the Mansion House in Dublin and the members took the oath to the Irish Republic. On August 25 the Dail unanimously rejected the British offer. It seemed that a complete deadlock had been reached.

(5)

Communications were not however sundered. Mr De Valera continued to exchange Notes with the Prime Minister, in which historical precedents were enlivened by quotations from O'Connell, Thomas Davis, and Abraham Lincoln. On August 26 Mr Lloyd George wrote to Mr De Valera stating that the truce could not indefinitely be prolonged; that its termination would be 'deplorable'; and that it had become the duty of each of them to cease exchanging academic arguments and consider whether some basis could not be found 'upon which further negotiations can usefully proceed'. Mr De Valera on August 30 replied to this suggestion by insisting on the full application of the principle of self-determination and by asserting that no further negotiations would be possible unless the respective plenipotentiaries met 'untrammelled by any conditions save the facts themselves'.

The Prime Minister by that time was on holiday at Gairloch

in Ross-shire; the King was staying at Moy Hall. On the morning of September 7 Mr Lloyd George came to Moy Hall bringing with him a draft of the reply to be sent to Mr De Valera's letter of August 30. The leading members of the Cabinet had meanwhile been asked to assemble in the Town Hall at Inverness:

> 'The Prime Minister', recorded the King's Assistant Private Secretary, Major Hardinge,[1] 'told His Majesty that various members of the Government, including the Viceroy and the Secretary for Ireland, had advised the despatch of a sharp Note, amounting almost to an ultimatum, in reply to Mr De Valera's communication. It had been suggested that a time-limit should be fixed.
>
> The King very strongly deprecated any action on these lines, which would be interpreted as an attempt by a large country to bully a small one into submission, and would undo at once all the good that had been done.
>
> The Prime Minister laid before the King the draft of the proposed reply. His Majesty suggested numerous alterations in the text—the elimination of all threats and contentious phrases (e.g. "Dominion Status")—and the invitation to Sinn Fein representatives to meet the Prime Minister at once for further negotiations.
>
> The Prime Minister then withdrew, and in company with Sir Edward Grigg, drew up a new draft to conform to His Majesty's wishes, the conciliatory wording of which was in marked contrast to the aggressive tone of the original one. The P.M. then left. He submitted the amended draft to the Cabinet, and it was accepted almost verbatim and handed to Mr Barton in the afternoon.' *u*

Major Hardinge at the same time provided Lord Stamfordham, who had not accompanied the King to Moy Hall, with a succinct summary of what had taken place:

> 'The P.M. came this morning and the King had a very satisfactory interview with him. The draft of the reply which the P.M. brought with him was most aggressive, and it was entirely due to H.M. that the whole tone of it was changed.' *v*

The amended reply to Mr De Valera, which was handed to Mr Barton at the Town Hall of Inverness on the afternoon of September 7, was in fact the prelude to the final negotiations. It invited Mr De Valera to discuss the British proposals 'on their merits' and to enter a conference in order to 'ascertain how the association of Ireland with the community of nations known as the British Empire can best be reconciled with Irish national aspirations'. On September 12 Mr De Valera agreed to enter a Conference on these terms.

[1] Major Hardinge had succeeded Lord Cromer as Assistant Private Secretary on April 1, 1920.

An argument then developed as to whether or not the Irish plenipotentiaries should come to the conference as recognised representatives of an independent state. Mr De Valera, in a telegram of September 17, pointed out that he had already been in conference with Mr Lloyd George and that 'in these conferences and in my written communications I have never ceased to recognise myself for what I was and what I am. If this involves recognition on your part, then you have already recognised us'. The King was afraid that all this haggling over terminology might provoke a rupture. On September 18 he telegraphed to the Prime Minister:*w*

'Just received Mr De Valera's telegram of the 17th. I cannot help thinking that it is intended to be conciliatory and to show his anxiety for immediate conference. Has he not made rather a good point that your previous conversations were unconditional and that hence you recognised him as what he considered himself to be and have been? I only send this being anxious to avoid any chance of the extremists attributing to you responsibility for abandonment of the Conference. My one wish is to help you in this most difficult situation.'

On September 30 Mr De Valera finally agreed to send delegates to a conference in London on the basis of the British invitation of September 7. The King, having by his advice, his warnings and his encouragement, contributed so materially to this fortunate conclusion left the future conduct of the negotiations entirely in the hands of the Prime Minister. During the two months that the conference lasted he refrained from all comment or intervention. His attitude throughout furnishes a classic example of correct constitutional behaviour and of the proper functioning of Monarchy in a parliamentary State.

The Conference opened at Downing Street on October 11. The British plenipotentiaries were Mr Lloyd George, Lord Birkenhead, Mr Winston Churchill, Sir Hamar Greenwood, Sir L. Worthington Evans, Mr Austen Chamberlain and Sir Gordon Hewart. The Irish were represented by Mr Arthur Griffith, Mr Michael Collins, Mr Duggan and Mr Gavan Duffy. Mr De Valera decided to remain in Dublin. The discussions, which were tense and often protracted, lasted until December 5. At 2.30 on the morning of December 6 an agreement was signed granting to 'The Irish Free State' the position of a Dominion within the Commonwealth.[1]

[1] These Articles of Agreement provided for the establishment of an Irish Free State possessing within the Commonwealth exactly the same status as any other Dominion; the office of Lord Lieutenant was abolished

360

'I got the joyful news', the King wrote in his diary for December 6, 'the first thing this morning from the P.M. that at 2.30 this morning articles of agreement were signed between the British representatives & the Irish delegates, involving complete acceptance of the British Government's proposals. . . .

It is mostly due to the P.M.'s patience & conciliatory spirit & is a great feather in his cap. I trust that now after seven centuries there may be peace in Ireland.'

'The happiest and greatest event', the King wrote to Prince George, 'that has happened for many years is the signing of the agreement with regard to the settlement of the question of Ireland which took place in the early hours of the 6th. It means peace in Ireland. For 700 years the Statesmen have all failed to find a solution & therefore the Prime Minister & his colleagues are indeed to be congratulated on this great achievement.'

The Irish agreement was ratified without delay by the British Parliament. After a fierce debate, in which Mr De Valera pleaded

and the representative of the Crown in the Free State was to be appointed in the same manner as the Governor-General in Canada; the Free State accepted in principle a share of the National Debt; the armed forces of the Free State were not to be proportionately greater than those of the United Kingdom; certain harbour facilities were to be granted to Great Britain who might maintain detachments at Queenstown, Berehaven, and Lough Swilly; the Treaty was not to apply to Northern Ireland and a Boundary Commission was to be appointed to fix the boundaries between Eire and Ulster according to the wishes of the inhabitants. It should be remembered that the promise of a Boundary Commission was an important concession and one that materially influenced the Irish delegation to sign the Heads of Agreement. It was a provision however that was never executed. In 1925 such a Commission was constituted under the chairmanship of Mr Justice Feetham, a judge of the South African High Court. The Government of Northern Ireland refused to be represented on the Commission and the representative of the Free State resigned. The Commission was in the end disbanded and as a consolation the Free State was released from the obligation under the Treaty to assume a share of the National Debt.

Considerable controversy developed later in regard to the form of oath provided for in Article IV: 'I do solemnly swear true faith and allegiance to the Constitution of the Irish Free State as by law established, and that I will be faithful to H.M. King George V his heirs and successors by law, in virtue of the common citizenship of Ireland with Great Britain and her adherence to membership of the group of nations forming the British Commonwealth of Nations.' This formula was abolished by the Irish in 1932.

A lucid and unbiassed account of the negotiations and the proceedings of the London Conference will be found in Lord Pakenham's *Peace by Ordeal*. The fifth volume of Mr Churchill's *World Crisis* is also illuminating and valuable.

passionately for the rejection of the Treaty, it was accepted by the Dail by a narrow majority of 64 to 57. Mr De Valera resigned and was succeeded by Arthur Griffith.

The civil war which thereafter ravaged the Free State and led to the death of many valiant men was in no sense the responsibility of His Majesty's Government.

CHAPTER XXII

THE END OF COALITION

1922-1923

The Prince of Wales' visits to the Dominions and India—The King's relations with his children—The decline in the prestige of Mr Lloyd George—The Cannes Conference—The Genoa Conference—The Chanak crisis—The Carlton Club Meeting—Mr Bonar Law succeeds Mr Lloyd George as Prime Minister—The King and the Greek Royal Family—Our relations with France and Italy—The King's visit to Rome—The Lausanne Conference—The King on the Sudan —Mr Bonar Law's illness and resignation—The King sends for Mr Baldwin—Lord Curzon's disappointment—Mr Baldwin's first administration—He asks for a dissolution—The King seeks to dissuade him—The resultant Election.

(1)

IT is with a shock of sad surprise that a busy man of later middle-age realises that his sons and daughters are no longer children. The King, at the time of the armistice, was fifty-three. The Prince of Wales was twenty-four; Prince Albert on the verge of twenty-three; Princess Mary twenty-one; Prince Henry eighteen and Prince George sixteen:[1]

> 'Yes,' the King wrote to Lord Stamfordham on January 3, 1920, 'my sons have begun well, especially the eldest, who has become most popular & has already made a name for himself. They will be of great assistance to me in the future.' [a]

The Prince of Wales, during the war, had served in France, Egypt and Italy. With the coming of peace he was despatched on three wide tours. In August 1919 he left on a four months journey to Newfoundland, Canada and the United States. In March 1920 he visited

---

[1] Prince Albert was created Duke of York on June 5, 1920. On April 26, 1923, he married Lady Elizabeth Bowes-Lyon, daughter of the fourteenth Earl of Strathmore. Prince Henry was created Duke of Gloucester in 1928 and in November 1935 married Lady Alice Montagu-Douglas-Scott, daughter of the seventh Duke of Buccleuch. Prince George was created Duke of Kent in October 1934 and in November of that year married Princess Marina, daughter of Prince Nicolas of Greece. Princess Mary married Viscount Lascelles, eldest son of the fifth Earl of Harewood on February 28, 1922.

Australia and New Zealand, calling at Barbadoes, Honolulu, Fiji and Bermuda. He returned to England in October. He was accorded a separate establishment at York House, St. James's Palace, and remained in England for twelve months.

In the autumn of 1921 the Government decided, after prolonged hesitation, that a royal visit to India might avail to mitigate dissension and to salve discontent. This was a hazardous experiment. The calamity of Amritsar was still, two years after the event, infecting the Indian peoples with bitter violence; Mahatma Gandhi had only recently concluded with the Moslem leaders an alliance for the overthrow of British rule. The Indian visit was not an unqualified success. Serious riots occurred in Bombay; at Benares and Allahabad the Prince was subjected to an organised boycott. Yet again and again the sullen crowds were moved by the gaiety and pathos of his personality; they forgot their resentment and responded with enthusiastic acclaim to the shy courage with which he moved among them. The officials may have doubted whether the political effects of this tour justified the risks entailed; but there was nothing but unstinted admiration for the personal part the Prince had played. After visiting the North-West Frontier Province, the Prince sailed by way of Colombo, Singapore and Hong Kong for Japan, where he remained four weeks. He returned to England on June 20, 1922, after an absence of eight months.

It was with ardent and often anxious interest that the King followed the imperial progresses of his eldest son. He was all too regularly supplied with cuttings from the Dominion and American newspapers and would scrutinise these extracts with scrupulous if bewildered care. Accustomed as he was to the traditional reticence of the British press, the King did not fully appreciate the more vivid temper of overseas journalism, or realise that these intrusive reporters were less interested in official functions, which the Prince performed with due solemnity, than in those interludes of relaxation, when he behaved with the unconventionality of a most vivacious young man. The King was perturbed to learn that at a rodeo at Saskatoon the Prince had entranced the assembled crowds by jumping on the back of a bronco and riding round the ring. He was rendered anxious by paragraphs intimating that at receptions or dances the Prince, when confronted with the wives of officials, was apt to take evasive action and to prefer the company of people of his own age. In vain did the Governors of the several Colonies or Dominions assure His Majesty of the correctitude of the Prince's conduct and of the 'blazing popularity' that he had acquired. The King was less assuaged by these official assurances than he was irritated by the flippant or imaginative press cuttings that he conned.

Mr John Gore, in his *Personal Memoir*,[b] has devoted several penetrating pages to an analysis of King George's unwillingness or inability to appreciate the changing habits of the younger generation. Even in this political biography it is necessary—if only to assure the reader that no single shadow has been shirked—to make some allusion to the fact that the King failed to establish with his children, at least until they married, those relations of equable and equal companionship that are the solace of old age. How came it that a man, who was by temperament so intensely domestic, who was so considerate to his dependents and the members of his household, who was so unalarming to small children and humble people, should have inspired his sons with feelings of awe, amounting at times to nervous trepidation? He may have felt that, bred as they had been in the artificial atmosphere of a Court, they needed a discipline, the rigours of which he alone was in the position to apply. He may have exaggerated the contrast between the remembered ordeals of his own youthful training and what seemed to him the softer slackness of a degenerate age. He may have sought—sometimes by irritated disapproval, more often by vociferous chaff—to check in them what he vaguely recognised as the revolt of post-war youth against the standards and conventions in which he had himself been nurtured. He may even have regarded his immediate family as a ship's company of whom he was the master and the martinet, and have adopted towards them a boisterous manner which, however suited to the quarter-deck, appeared intimidating when resounding amid the chandeliers and tapestries of palatial saloons. Although sensitive, he did not always exercise imaginative insight into the sensibility of others. In seeking to instil into his children his own ideals of duty and obedience, he was frequently pragmatic and sometimes harsh.

This attitude of restless and sometimes querulous disapproval melted away so soon as his children married; thereafter he ceased to complain of their conduct, their apparel or their friends. Immediately they found again the genial affection that had endeared him to them in their childhood.

On February 28, 1922, Princess Mary was married to Lord Lascelles:

'I went up', the King wrote that evening, 'to Mary's room & took leave of her & quite broke down. . . . Felt very down & depressed now that darling Mary has gone.'

On April 26, 1923, his second son, the Duke of York, married Lady Elizabeth Bowes-Lyon in Westminster Abbey:

'You are indeed a lucky man,' the King wrote to him three days later, 'to have such a charming & delightful wife as Elizabeth. I am sure you will both be very happy together. I trust you both will have many many years of happiness before you & that you will be as happy as Mama & I am after you have been married for 30 years. I can't wish you more. . . . You have always been so sensible & easy to work with & you have always been ready to listen to any advice & to agree with my opinions about people & things that I feel we have always got on very well together. Very different to dear David.'

For his daughter-in-law, the Duchess of York, the King acquired and for ever retained, the deepest affection:

'The better I know,' he wrote to her husband from Balmoral on September 20, 1923, 'and the more I see of your dear little wife, the more charming I think she is & everyone falls in love with her here.'

Even in his later years, when illness had come to cloud his old high spirits, she at least was able to revive his gaiety:

'I miss him dreadfully', she wrote to Lord Dawson of Penn after his death. 'Unlike his own children, I was never afraid of him, and in all the twelve years of having me as a daughter-in-law he never spoke one unkind or abrupt word to me, and was always ready to listen and give advice on one's own silly little affairs. He was so kind and so *dependable*. And when he was in the mood, he could be deliciously funny too! Don't you think so?' *c*

The Prince of Wales did not marry during his father's life time.

(2)

It might have been expected that, with the conclusion of the Irish Agreement of December 6, 1921, Mr Lloyd George would have maintained and fortified the predominance that he had enjoyed since the fall of Mr Asquith. From that moment, however, his position weakened. Many of his Unionist allies regarded the Irish settlement, not as a triumph of patient negotiation, but as a surrender, even as a betrayal. A difference of opinion arose between him and the Unionist Chief Whip in regard to the timing of the next General Election: nor did Sir George Younger appreciate the Prime Minister's distribution of honours or the accumulation, under his personal control, of large election funds. The King himself questioned the suitability of some of those whom the Prime Minister recommended for high distinction. Mr Lloyd George insisted, and the King, with explicit reluctance, was obliged to give his assent.

It was not, however, on domestic issues, but as a result of errors or misfortunes in foreign policy, that, during the course of 1922, the fissure within the Lloyd George coalition widened into a final breach. The Prime Minister had become increasingly enamoured of international negotiation. Finding that his dexterity was hampered by the phlegmatic caution of the Foreign Office, he had surrounded himself with a small, gifted and obedient cohort of extraneous advisers. Lord Curzon, the Foreign Secretary, was obliged to accept these intrusions upon the responsibility of his office: but he did not do so light-heartedly, or without many a groan of warning, without many deep sighs of discontent. His friends in the Conservative Party were well aware that the Foreign Secretary viewed with grave misgiving some of the more imaginative of the Prime Minister's excursions. The blame for the checks, the disappointments and the calamities that followed was thus increasingly, but not always quite fairly, attributed to Mr Lloyd George alone.

The tale of misfortune began with the Cannes Conference on January 1922. The French, fearing that their own Prime Minister, M. Briand, was succumbing to the Celtic wizardry of Mr Lloyd George, summoned him back to Paris, and dismissed him from office. M. Briand was succeeded by M. Poincaré, who was obstinate in his belief that he had a mission to defend and promote the interests of France. The Cannes Conference came to an abrupt and disagreeable end. All hopes were then fixed upon the World Reconstruction Conference to be held at Genoa in April. To this Conference Mr Lloyd George had invited, not the enemy Powers only, but also the United States and Soviet Russia. The United States declined the invitation: Germany and Russia accepted with alacrity. Six days after the Conference opened, the German delegate Dr Rathenau and the Russian delegate M. Chicherin signed a separate and secret treaty at Rapallo, agreeing immediately to re-establish full diplomatic relations and to renounce all reparations as between themselves. It was felt in England that Mr Lloyd George's endeavour to reintroduce Soviet Russia into the comity of nations had resulted only in a split between the Allies and a mysterious and disturbing alliance between Berlin and Moscow. Mr Lloyd George returned from Genoa with damaged prestige.

The final rupture of the Lloyd George coalition was occasioned by the Chanak crisis of September.[1] The armies of Mustapha Kemal, having driven the Greeks into the sea, advanced in jubilation to the boundary of the neutral zone, which, under the conditions of the armistice, was occupied by allied forces on both sides of the Dardanelles. The French and Italians recalled their own detachments to the safety of the European shore. The slender British forces stood their ground in Asia, while the Turkish soldiers spat and gibbered at them across the barbed wire at Chanak. On the afternoon of September 17, Mr Churchill, in the temporary absence of Lord Curzon, issued a communiqué, inviting the Dominions and our allies to assist us in resisting the Kemalist aggression by force of arms. The British public realised, with sudden dismay, that they were on the verge of a new and totally unwanted war.

The King, who was at Balmoral, followed these developments with disquiet. He ordered his special train to remain in readiness at Ballater in case his immediate presence in London might be required:

> 'The King is sure', Lord Stamfordham wrote to the Prime Minister on September 20, 'that you all are as averse as he is to a renewal of war and that everything will be done to avoid such a calamity, consistently with what we hold to be British justice and good faith.' *d*

On September 20, Lord Curzon crossed to Paris. The interview with M. Poincaré was conducted on both sides in a tone of violent acerbity.

[1] On May 15, 1919, the Greek armies, with the consent of President Wilson and M. Clemenceau, and with the ardent encouragement of Mr Lloyd George, landed at Smyrna and pushed on into the interior of Asia Minor. On April 23, 1920, the Turkish National Assembly met at Ankara and elected Mustapha Kemal as President. On August 10, 1920, the Allies imposed upon the Sultan's Government the Treaty of Sèvres, under which Turkey was dismembered. This gave a new impetus to the Kemalist movement. In October 1920 the young King Alexander of Greece, who had ascended the throne on the deposition of his father, King Constantine, died unexpectedly of blood poisoning. At the ensuing elections in November M. Venizelos was heavily defeated and King Constantine was recalled. The Allies seized this occasion to repudiate their obligations towards Greece. Deprived of support, the Greek armies maintained their precarious position in Anatolia, while the strength and confidence of Mustapha Kemal's movement correspondingly increased. On October 20, 1921, a French emissary, M. Franklin-Bouillon, concluded a separate and secret agreement with Mustapha Kemal. On August 18, 1922, the Kemalist armies launched an offensive against the Greeks in Asia Minor. The Greeks were routed, The Turks entered Smyrna in triumph on September 9.

'He behaved', Lord Curzon recorded,[e] 'like a demented school-master screaming at a guilty school boy. I have never seen so deplor-able or undignified a scene. After enduring this for some time, I could stand it no longer and rising broke up the sitting and left the room.'[1]

Owing to the tactful intervention of the Italian representative, Count Sforza, calm was restored and the afternoon sitting proceeded on more constructive lines. M. Poincaré agreed that a French General should co-operate with Sir Charles Harington, the General Officer Commanding the British forces of occupation, in inducing Mustapha Kemal to accept an agreed line of demarcation. The King was much relieved by this relaxation of tension:

> 'His Majesty', Lord Stamfordham wrote to Lord Curzon on Septem-ber 26, 'naturally followed with the utmost interest your doings in Paris. You will not be surprised that the reading of your reports astounded His Majesty, arousing his fullest sympathy with you, sub-jected to such an exhibition of temper and ill manners as Poincaré presumed to display. The King all the more appreciates the patience and control with which you met this violent outburst, and trusts that the arrangements which you were able to secure may happily avert the dangers of war.'[f]

Fortunately Great Britain possessed in Sir Charles Harington and in Sir Horace Rumbold, the High Commissioner, intermediaries of exceptional sagacity and moderation. In spite of further incidents, including a revolution in Greece and a second deposition of King Constantine, a Convention was concluded with Mustapha Kemal at Mudania on October 11. This Convention provided for a standstill pending formal negotiations of peace:

> 'His Majesty', wrote Lord Stamfordham to Sir Charles Harington on October 13, 'feels that you have earned the gratitude of your fellow-countrymen for the wisdom, tact, patience and firmness displayed by you both in council and in the carrying out of the Government's instructions.'[g]

[1] Lord Curzon had always entertained a special antipathy for M. Poincaré. When the latter, on ceasing to be President of the Republic, and before becoming Prime Minister, was on a private visit to London the King invited him to luncheon. Lord Curzon was enraged by what seemed to him a gratuitous act of courtesy. 'We in the F.O.', he wrote to Lord Stamford-ham on October 2, 1921, 'entertain very strong views about that gentleman, who has not ceased since he left office to show the most marked hostility to this country and the Prime Minister in particular and who has on more than one occasion grossly violated political etiquette and the normal stan-dards of honour by publishing confidential documents in the French Press.' M. Poincaré was none the less invited to luncheon at Buckingham Palace and accorded the Victorian Chain with a badge in brilliants.

The Conservative Party had never adopted an affectionate attitude towards the Prime Minister's Greek policy. Although in no sense a Hellenist, Mr Lloyd George regarded Greece as a small and mountainous country striving to liberate her co-religionists in Anatolia from the infidel Turk. The Conservatives, sensitive as they were to Moslem feeling in India, wished to put an early end to what they considered the unnatural antagonism between Turkey and Great Britain. The Chanak crisis came as a climax to these doubts and apprehensions.

On October 13 Mr Lloyd George warned the King that he might have to ask for an immediate dissolution. On October 16 he wrote saying that the Conservative Ministers intended to summon a meeting of their adherents on the 19th and that 'upon the decision taken at that important gathering will depend the continued existence of the Coalition'.[h]

'It is my hope', the King replied,[i] 'that the result will not cause the break-down of my Government, for many reasons, especially when questions like Ireland and the Near East are still unsettled. I trust you will be able to remain my Prime Minister.'

On the morning of Thursday, October 19, the Conservative Party met at the Carlton Club. The decisive speech was, much to the surprise of those present, made by Mr Stanley Baldwin, President of the Board of Trade. He described Mr Lloyd George as a dynamic force. 'A dynamic force' he added, 'is a very terrible thing'. Mr Bonar Law then moved that the Conservative Party should stand at the ensuing election as 'an independent Party with its own Leader and its own programme'. This motion was carried by 187 votes to 87.

At 5.0 p.m. that afternoon Mr Lloyd George went to Buckingham Palace and tendered his resignation. Lord Stamfordham was at once despatched to 24 Onslow Square to consult with Mr Bonar Law. The latter replied that he was not now the official leader of the Conservative Party[1] and that in any case that Party 'for the moment had broken up'. Lord Stamfordham pointed out that unless a new Government were constituted immediately and elections held, it would be impossible to ratify the Irish Treaty by December 6 and

[1] Mr Bonar Law had resigned the leadership of the Conservative Party in March 1921 for reasons of health. His place had been taken by Mr Austen Chamberlain. The latter, in opposing the motion passed at the Carlton Club meeting sacrificed the sure prospect of becoming Prime Minister. He was accustomed, to his worldly detriment, to place loyalty above ambition.

that the Treaty would therefore lapse. Mr Bonar Law was with no unnecessary delay re-elected leader of the Conservative Party and kissed hands as the new Prime Minister at 5.30 p.m. on Monday, October 23. At the ensuing election the Conservatives were returned with 344 seats. The Labour Party won in 138 constituencies, thereby doubling their former representation. The Asquithian Liberals secured 60 seats and the Lloyd George Liberals 57.[1] Mr Austen Chamberlain, Lord Balfour, Lord Birkenhead and Sir Robert Horne remained loyal to Mr Lloyd George.[2] The new Parliament was opened in state on November 23.

'I am sorry he is going,' the King wrote in his diary on taking leave of Mr Lloyd George, 'but some day he will be Prime Minister again.'

This was not a correct forecast.

(3)

It was rarely, as has been said, that the King tendered advice to his Ministers on questions of Foreign Policy: he was far more concerned with domestic and imperial affairs and with the maintenance in public life of standards consonant with the character of the British people. His close relationship with the Greek Royal Family, and the reliance that they placed in his judgement and influence, might, however, have exposed him to embarrassment, had he been less scrupulous in subordinating personal affections to his responsibilities as a constitutional Sovereign. His Greek cousins did not always appreciate the nature of these limitations or display the tact

---

[1] These figures are those given by the Annual Register, the compilers of which may be assumed to be unbiased.

[2] The main appointments made by Mr Bonar Law were as follows: Lord Salisbury succeeded Lord Balfour as Lord President; Lord Cave succeeded Lord Birkenhead as Lord Chancellor; Mr Baldwin succeeded Sir Robert Horne as Chancellor of the Exchequer; the Duke of Devonshire succeeded Mr Winston Churchill as Colonial Secretary; Lord Derby succeeded Sir Laming Worthington-Evans as Minister of War; Mr Amery succeeded Lord Lee of Fareham as First Lord of the Admiralty; Mr Edward Wood succeeded Mr H. A. L. Fisher as President of the Board of Education: Mr Neville Chamberlain succeeded Mr Kellaway as Postmaster General; Sir Samuel Hoare succeeded Mr F. E. Guest as Secretary for Air; and Lord Curzon remained Secretary of State for Foreign Affairs. Mr Churchill, who was in hospital at the time, recovered from a severe operation to discover that 'I had lost not only my appendix but my Office as Secretary of State for the Dominions and Colonies'. He did not re-enter the Cabinet until 1924.

and the discretion that the circumstances required. Thus, in May 1920, ex-King Constantine, from his exile in Lucerne, wrote to King George thanking him for the support given to Greece by the British delegation to the Paris Peace Conference.*j* The King replied expressing the hope that 'the traditional warm feeling between Greece and England will ever continue' and adding that, 'in spite of all that has happened' his personal feelings towards King Constantine remained unchanged.*k* A false version of this letter was communicated to the royalist press in Athens, asserting that King George had expressed the hope that 'a solution of the present situation may shortly be found satisfactory both to the ex-King and the Greek people'. It was considered necessary to issue an official denial of this assertion.

King George felt much sympathy with King Alexander of the Hellenes in his lonely and unwanted eminence. He intimated to M. Venizelos that he hoped the young King would be allowed to marry the charming Mlle Manos, an intimation welcomed by the Greek Prime Minister, who himself was only too anxious to bless this romance. When King Constantine was recalled to Athens the Admiralty issued instructions that the *Averoff*, in which he was travelling from Italy, should not be saluted on her passage by any ships of the Royal Navy. The King regarded this departure from accustomed naval courtesy as unduly vindictive: on his advice our ships were withdrawn discreetly out of sight.

With the collapse of the Greek armies in Anatolia a revolution broke out in Athens and King Constantine was for a second time deposed. On November 28, 1922, the revolutionary Government, in spite of the warnings addressed to them by Lord Curzon, executed the Ministers and Generals held responsible for the disaster. Diplomatic relations between Great Britain and Greece were immediately severed and our Minister left Athens that very night. Meanwhile the revolutionary Government had also arrested King Constantine's brother, Prince Andrew, and his life was in immediate danger. Mr Gerald Talbot who in the past had rendered some service to Colonel Plastiras, the Greek revolutionary leader, was secretly despatched to Athens and succeeded in rescuing Prince Andrew and bringing him in safety to Paris. Neither the King nor Lord Curzon had any previous knowledge of Mr Talbot's mission; they were none the less delighted by its success. On his return to London Mr. Talbot was received by the King and given the K.C.V.O.

His Majesty felt and expressed some anxiety at the delay in

summoning the Lausanne Conference which, as provided in the Mudania Convention, was to negotiate a new treaty between Turkey and the Allies. He feared that if too long a pause were to intervene, some incident might occur that could lead to an outbreak of hostilities. Lord Curzon replied to his representations in a characteristic letter:[1]

> 'Poincaré wants to get me to Lausanne—without any previous conversations or understanding with the Allies—in order (1) to save himself from being forced into a quarrel with the Turks, owing to their impossible behaviour, and (2) to put me in a position where—deserted as usual by France and Italy—I shall be beaten on every point and forced either to conclude a humiliating Peace or to break up the Conference.
>
> I will not fall into this trap. I do not mean to go until I have some clear idea whether Allied unity means something or absolutely nothing. Whether in fact we are going to stand out on any point, or whether I am to get on to my stomach and crawl. If this latter, I had sooner crawl in Downing St. than before the eyes of the world at Lausanne.'

The proceedings of the Lausanne Conference were followed by the King with anxious interest:

> 'Lord Curzon', Sir Horace Rumbold wrote to him on December 18, 1922, 'is the life and soul of the Conference and supplies all the driving power. I shudder to think what would have happened if he had not been there.' [m]

The first Lausanne Conference was broken off by Lord Curzon on February 4, 1923. In the following April discussions were resumed, the British delegation being on this occasion headed by Sir Horace Rumbold. On July 24 the negotiations, so powerfully initiated by Lord Curzon and so ably continued by Sir Horace Rumbold, resulted in a Treaty of Peace. Upon this Treaty were founded the relations of mutual respect and amity thereafter persisting between Great Britain and the new Turkey.

In foreign as in domestic affairs King George consistently exercised his influence to promote concord and allay dissension. He much regretted our quarrels with France over the Near Eastern and German questions, even as he deplored he alienation of Italy. Although he did not share Lord Curzon's personal antipathy towards M. Poincaré, he admitted that the latter's Ruhr and Rhineland experiments were a mistake:

> 'I consider', he wrote to Lord Stamfordham in January 1923, 'the French will make a grave error if they go into the Ruhr. By doing so

they will make Germany bankrupt & turn her bolshevik & throw her into the arms of Russia.' [n]

He was correct in foreseeing that the occupation of the Ruhr would lead to inflation and the consequent ruin of the German middle class. But it was not into the arms of Russia that Germany was thereafter driven: it was into the arms of Adolf Hitler.

It had been arranged that in May 1923 the King and Queen should pay a state visit to Rome. The King was anxious that the occasion should be taken to repair our relations with Italy and suggested that some colonial adjustments, notably in the Jubaland area, should be made. He asked that he might be accompanied by a Minister. The Cabinet were afraid that the presence of a Minister might tempt Signor Mussolini to demand political concessions and that the resultant disappointment would detract from any good impression that the visit might create. The King did not agree with this view:

'We might', he minuted, 'be more generous to Italy especially after all we have got out of the war.' [o]

Lord Curzon remained adamant. The visit was deprived of all political significance:

'I regret it,' the King wrote on his return, 'as I am sure the Italian people wish to be our friends, as shown by the wonderful reception they gave us in Rome and elsewhere for eight days.' [p]

It would be an error to suppose that His Majesty, in his desire to restore good relations with our war-time allies, was inclined to placate foreign potentates by the sacrifice of important British interests. When, for instance, the King of Egypt[1] desired to assume

[1] On December 18, 1914, with the entry of Turkey into the war, Egypt was declared a British Protectorate. The Khedive Abbas Hilmi was deposed in favour of his uncle Prince Hussein who assumed the title of Sultan of Egypt. On his death in October 1917 King Hussein was succeeded by King Fuad.

On November 13, 1917, Zaghlul Pasha, the leader of the Egyptian Nationalists, demanded independence. He was arrested in March 1919 and deported to Malta. Lord Allenby was appointed British High Commissioner in Egypt. Zaghlul Pasha was released and a mission under Lord Milner sent to Egypt to examine the situation. This resulted in the Milner-Zaghlul agreement of 1920, under which we recognised the independence of Egypt and the latter agreed not to enter into any treaties with foreign

the supplementary title of 'King of the Sudan' Lord Stamfordham was commanded to write to Lord Curzon in forceful terms:

'The King finds it unnecessary to express his earnest hope that you will not listen to any suggestions for giving the King of Egypt the further title of "King of the Sudan", for His Majesty considers that we have pledged our word to the people of the Sudan that they shall always be under British rule.'

Lord Stamfordham reminded the Foreign Secretary that the King, on his return from India in 1912, had called at Port Sudan and had assured the assembled chiefs and notables of the continuance of British protection. 'So that on this question', Lord Stamfordham added, 'the King regards himself as a personal guarantor of British good faith.' *q* Lord Curzon replied that he was in entire agreement with His Majesty. The King was not wholly satisfied. 'I fear', he minuted, 'Allenby is inclined to be weak about the Sudan; but he must not be allowed to be.' *r*

No final settlement of the problem of Egypt or the Sudan was reached during the King's lifetime.

(4)

On April 27, 1923, Mr Bonar Law visited the King at Buckingham Palace and informed him that he had been ordered a sea voyage on account of his health. It was arranged that during his absence Lord Curzon should act as deputy Prime Minister, while Mr Stanley Baldwin should become leader of the House of Commons. On Mr Bonar Law's return to England it was found that he was suffering from cancer of the throat.[1] On May 20 he wrote to the King tendering his resignation.*s*

When the head of a Government resigns, or is defeated in Parliament, the choice of his successor devolves upon the King alone. He is obliged to exercise the Prerogative on his own responsibility, since there no longer exists a Prime Minister by whom he can be advised.

Powers prejudicial to British interests and to permit the presence of British troops in Egypt. No mention of the Sudan was included in this agreement.

The Milner-Zaghlul agreement was never ratified and subsequent negotiations with Adly Pasha broke down on the military question.

On February 28, 1922, the British Government issued a 'Declaration' recognising the independence of Egypt subject to certain 'reserved questions'. These reserved questions included the defence of Egypt and the future of the Sudan. It was in the Constitution, promulgated in 1923, that King Fuad assumed the additional title of 'King of the Sudan'.

[1] Mr Bonar Law died on October 30, 1923.

In ordinary circumstances little uncertainty arises as to the successor whom the King should designate. If a Prime Minister resigns owing to defeat in Parliament, the King will send for the leader of the Opposition. If a Prime Minister, whose supporters still command a majority in the House of Commons, resigns for reasons of ill-health, there is seldom any doubt who among possible successors has the confidence of the Party in power. Moreover, the retiring Prime Minister will usually himself indicate to the King the name of his successor.[1]

On this occasion no such certainty existed. Mr Bonar Law was himself too ill to make any precise recommendation. Opinions within the Conservative Party were divided. There were those who contended that Lord Curzon, owing to his high abilities and distinguished service, as well as to the fact that during Mr Bonar Law's absence he had acted as head of the Government, possessed a prior claim. Others held the view that, in a Parliament in which Labour constituted the largest Opposition Party, the Prime Minister must be a Member of the House of Commons. The King, although he personally held the latter opinion, felt it more proper to consult some of his Privy Councillors before coming to a final decision.

Lord Salisbury, the Lord President of the Council, held the view that the claims of Lord Curzon should not lightly be ignored. Mr Bridgeman, the Home Secretary, and Mr Amery, the First Lord, were in favour of Mr Baldwin. Lord Balfour, who had hastily been summoned from his sick-bed at Sheringham, while admitting the unquestionable claims of Lord Curzon, expressed the view that, in the present state of politics, the Prime Minister ought to be in the House of Commons:

> 'Lord Balfour', wrote Lord Stamfordham,[*] 'said he was speaking regardless of the individuals in question, for whereas, on one side, his opinion of Lord Curzon is based upon an intimate, life-long friendship, and the recognition of his exceptional qualifications; on the other, his knowledge of Mr Baldwin is slight and, so far, his public career has been more or less uneventful and without any signs of special gifts or exceptional ability.'

The King decided, on the strength of this advice, and in con-

[1] No doubts, for instance, arose when Mr Balfour succeeded Lord Salisbury in 1902 or Mr Asquith Sir Henry Campbell Bannerman in 1908. The closest analogy is the situation that arose in 1894. On the resignation of Mr Gladstone, Queen Victoria had herself to decide between the rival claims of Lord Rosebery and Sir William Harcourt.

formity with his personal judgement, to send for Mr Baldwin. He felt, however, that in view of the deep mortification that this decision would inevitably cause to Lord Curzon, it would be kinder if he were warned in advance. Lord Stamfordham therefore addressed to Lord Curzon, who was at Montacute, a telegram inviting him to come to London. 'Would it be possible', he telegraphed, 'for me to see you in London tomorrow?' 'I will', Lord Curzon replied, 'be at Carlton House Terrace at 1.20.' " Unfortunately Lord Curzon interpreted Lord Stamfordham's telegram as an intimation that he had been sent for by the King. When therefore Lord Stamfordham visited him at Carlton House Terrace at 2.30 p.m. on Tuesday, May 22, his announcement that within less than an hour Mr Baldwin would receive his appointment came as a bewildering shock. The incident has not always been accurately recorded by contemporary historians:[1] Lord Stamfordham's memorandum on the conversation furnishes an authentic account:"

'At 2.30 p.m. I saw Lord Curzon at his home.

I began by recounting the incidents between Saturday evening, when the King learnt from the Evening Papers of the sudden return to London of the Prime Minister, up to Sunday afternoon, when Mr Bonar Law's resignation was placed in the King's hands: and the consequent exceptionally difficult position in which His Majesty was placed, particularly as, owing to the condition of Mr Bonar Law's health, His Majesty was deprived of consultation with him: and I endeavoured gradually to break to Lord Curzon that, while estimating at its highest value the predominant position occupied by Lord Curzon in the Government, and indeed in the political life of the country, His Majesty, after due consideration, felt compelled, though with great regret, to ignore the personal element, and to base his choice upon what he conceived to be the requirements of the present times: viz. the continuance of the Prime Minister in the House of Commons. That His Majesty recognised that this matter was one of the few in which the Sovereign and no one else is personally responsible, and that he believed he would not be fulfilling his trust were he now to make his selection of Prime Minister from the House of Lords.

Lord Curzon listened quietly to all I endeavoured to say, and then proceeded to reply with considerable feeling but with restraint and without bitterness. He said that the message which I had conveyed to him was the greatest blow and slur upon him and his public career, now at its summit, that he could have ever conceived. He recapitulated his position in and his services to his country, the continuous years that he had been a Cabinet Minister: the difficulties and almost persecutions which he had endured under Lloyd George's administration: his two visits to Paris last year, the results of which, he honestly believed,

---

[1] See, for instance, Harold Nicolson's *Curzon: The Last Phase*, pp. 353 ff.

had saved this country from war: his achievements at Lausanne, where he had raised the prestige and position of England to above that of all the other countries there represented: that he had been Leader of the House of Lords for some years and, since Mr Bonar Law's absence, had been acting as Prime Minister—and now to be turned out because he was a Peer and the Labour Party in Opposition were unrepresented in the Upper House. He most strongly protested against what he concluded was the principle implied by the King's decision—that no Member of the House of Lords could be Prime Minister: and with that protest he should retire from public life, making it clear to the country his reason for doing so, but retiring with no animosity or feelings of opposition against his Party: but only with the deep wound which had been inflicted upon his pride, ambition and loyalty to His King, his country and his Party. . . .

While Lord Curzon naturally felt his supersession by a comparatively inexperienced and unknown man, he spoke in the warmest and most friendly terms of Mr Baldwin.

On taking leave, he asked when the King would make the appointment—I replied "At once".

I returned at once to Buckingham Palace and reported to the King what had passed at my interview with Lord Curzon. His Majesty immediately afterwards saw Mr Baldwin and offered him the post of Prime Minister.'

Lord Curzon did not permit his mortification to cloud for long his compelling sense of public service. To him it fell a few days later to propose Mr Baldwin as leader of the Conservative Party and to welcome him as Prime Minister to the Cabinet room. He agreed to continue as Foreign Secretary under the new leadership. The King appreciated such magnanimity. On May 29 he sent for Lord Curzon and thanked him personally:[w]

'Today,' recorded Lord Stamfordham, 'the King saw Lord Curzon and expressed his feelings of admiration and gratitude for the very generous and patriotic manner in which Lord Curzon had accepted the decision come to by His Majesty to appoint Mr Baldwin as Prime Minister, which the King more than realised must have been a terrible disappointment: and at the same time His Majesty wished to express his appreciation of the admirable and chivalrous speeches which Lord Curzon had made at the first Cabinet, when he welcomed Mr Baldwin as Prime Minister, and also at the Meeting of the Conservative Party on Monday, 28th May.

The King told him that he was sure the whole country shared His Majesty's views and also admired the wholehearted manner in which he had given his support to Mr Baldwin, to whom Lord Curzon's continuance in the Office of Foreign Minister was of the utmost importance and support.

His Majesty further dwelt upon the very deep regret which he had experienced in coming to a decision which, while he believed it to be the right one, nevertheless he knew would be hurting to Lord Curzon, whom he had known for some 35 years and regarded as an old friend, while his personal acquaintance with Mr Baldwin was that of having met and spoken to him on a few recent occasions.

Lord Curzon thanked the King and gratefully acknowledged the consideration which His Majesty had shown to him in informing him of the decision come to before he had actually seen Mr Baldwin. . . .'

(5)

The administration thus established under the leadership of Mr Stanley Baldwin enjoyed a short but not untroubled life. The unemployment figures remained obstinately at 1,300,000. The French continued in occupation of the Ruhr and the Germans in desperation adopted an attitude of passive resistance. The mark had fallen in August to 19,800,000 to the pound sterling; by the end of 1923 it had depreciated to the fantastic figure of 22,300,000,000. Our relations with Italy, and incidentally the prestige of the League of Nations, were deeply shaken by what is known as 'the Corfu incident' and by the settlement thereafter imposed on Greece by the Ambassadors' Conference.[1]

Mr Baldwin, who had always been a protectionist, decided that tariff reform offered the only solution of our internal difficulties. His hands were tied, however, by a pledge given by Mr Bonar Law in the previous year, to the effect that no fundamental changes in the fiscal arrangements of the country would be introduced during the life of the present Parliament. The Prime Minister was resolved, against the advice of many of his colleagues, that a new election must be held.

On November 12, 1923, Mr Baldwin came to York Cottage, Sandringham, and informed the King that he must ask for a dis-

[1] On August 27, 1923, General Tellini, Italian representative on the Graeco-Albanian frontier commission, was murdered by bandits. Signor Mussolini held the Greek Government responsible for this assassination, despatched the Italian navy to Corfu and bombarded the citadel, killing many Greek and Armenian refugees who were its only occupants. The Greek Government appealed to the League of Nations, who, in spite of the fact that the Assembly was then in session, transferred their responsibility to the Ambassadors' Conference in Paris. The latter fined the Greek Government half a million pounds and (although it was never proved that they were in any sense responsible) imposed other humiliating penalties. This was the first, and perhaps the most lamentable, of many subsequent gestures of appeasement.

solution. His Majesty exercised all his influence to dissuade him from such a course. Mr Baldwin remained convinced that an Election on the tariff issue offered the only way out of his difficulties:

> 'This afternoon,' the King wrote,ˣ 'the Prime Minister came to see me and asked for an immediate dissolution: he said that probably after a speech he was making on Tuesday he would dissolve Parliament.
>
> He assured me that it was absolutely necessary for him to appeal to the Country as he had gone so far that it was not possible for him to change his mind. I then pointed out to him that I strongly deprecated a dissolution at this moment as I had implicit confidence in him and in the Conservative Party now in power, and I considered that as most countries in Europe, if not in the world, were in a chaotic and indeed dangerous state, it would be a pity if this Country were to be plunged into the turmoil of a General Election on a question of domestic policy which will arouse all the old traditional bitterness of the hard fought battles between Protection and Free Trade: also that it was quite possible that his majority might be reduced, or that he might not get a majority at all.
>
> I was therefore prepared to take the responsibility of advising him to change his mind, and I was also prepared for him to tell his friends that I had done so.
>
> He answered that he had gone too far now and that the Country expected a dissolution; he would appeal to the Country at once, and he hoped to get the General Election over by about the 6th December, and he was ready to stand or fall by the result.
>
> I asked him whether all the Peers who were his colleagues were in favour of tariff reform, and he said that several of them were, perhaps, too Conservative and did not want a change.
>
> He also said he had seen Mr Austen Chamberlain and Lord Birkenhead today, and they had both assured him that they would give him their whole and entire support in this election; and he asked me whether he might make these two additional Cabinet Ministers without salaries, and I gave my approval.
>
> I also asked him if he did not think that this would unite the Liberal Party and he said yes, probably it would, and it would be a very good thing if it did.
>
> G.R.I.'

The results of the Election were declared on December 8. The Conservatives lost 88 seats, their membership of the House of Commons being reduced from 346 to 258. Labour rose from 144 to 191 and the Liberals, momentarily reunited under the banner of Free Trade, rose from 117 to 158.

An unprecedented Parliamentary situation was thereby created. In place of the familiar two-party balance of Government versus Opposition, the electorate had sent to Westminster 258 Conservatives, 191 Labour members, and 158 Liberals. None of these three Parties possessed an absolute majority; yet each of them—provided they could command the acquiescence, if not the support, of one of the other two—could form a Government. The key position was held by the Liberals. If they pledged their support to the right, then a Conservative Administration could remain in power. If they agreed to tolerate the left, then Mr Ramsay MacDonald could hope, under sufferance, to form the first Labour Government.

How, in such circumstances, was the King to exercise his prerogative?

CHAPTER XXIII

THE FIRST LABOUR GOVERNMENT

1924

Mr Baldwin's desire to resign immediately—The King urges him first to meet the new House of Commons—Various suggestions for new groupings—The King makes it clear that if Mr Baldwin is defeated he will send for Mr Ramsay MacDonald and offer him the post of Prime Minister unconditionally—Mr Baldwin is defeated and Mr Ramsay MacDonald is sent for on January 22, 1924—The King's attitude towards his first Labour Government—The Prime Minister also becomes Foreign Secretary—The King interviews all the Labour Ministers—The problem of the Royal Household—The problem of Court Dress—The internal policy of the new Government—Their relations with their National Executive—Foreign Policy—Mr Mac-Donald re-establishes co-operation with France and Italy—M. Herriot succeeds M. Poincaré—The London Conference and Agreement—The Geneva Protocol—The recognition of the Soviet Government and the ensuing negotiations—The summer recess—The Campbell case—Defeat of the Labour Government—Mr MacDonald asks for a dissolution—The Zinoviev letter—The General Election—Resignation of Mr MacDonald—Mr Baldwin forms a new administration.

(1)

MR BALDWIN, after the poll had been declared, withdrew to the graceful solitudes of Chequers. He was aware that many of his colleagues blamed him for having insisted, against their advice, upon so calamitous an election. His first instinct was to resign immediately rather than face inevitable defeat in Parliament.[a] The King regarded this procedure as incorrect. He pointed out to Mr Baldwin that the Conservatives would still be the largest single party in the new House of Commons and that it was his duty as Prime Minister to confront that assembly and thus enable the elected representatives of the people to decide whether they wished to support him or not. 'The Sovereign', he asserted,[b] 'ought not to accept the verdict of the Polls, except as expressed by the representatives of the Electorate across the floor of the House of Commons.' Mr Baldwin accepted this constitutional precept.[1] He at the same time indicated his unwillingness to conclude

[1] Five years later, in June 1929, both the King and Mr Baldwin took the opposite view. They then held that, with the vastly extended franchise, the decision of the Polls represented the verdict of the people and must be acted upon immediately (see page 434).

382

an alliance with the Liberals for the sole purpose of keeping Labour
out. He had, he explained, 'killed one coalition and would never join
another'. Moreover, it seemed to him unfair that the two bourgeois
parties should league together in order to deny to Labour the opportunities that they had won.[c]

Other leading Conservatives did not view the problem with equal
detachment; it seemed horrible to them that their leader should with
such equanimity hand over the destinies of the country and Empire
to a socialist minority. Lord Birkenhead had much alarmed them by
suggesting that, if Mr Ramsay MacDonald were given office, he
would immediately introduce confiscatory legislation and, when
defeated, go to the country with an enticing revolutionary programme. As usual at such moments of perturbation, Lord Stamfordham was deluged with all manner of bright ideas. Various combinations and permutations were suggested. Lord Balfour advanced a
very tentative opinion that a Conservative Government might still
survive under his own leadership or that of Mr Neville Chamberlain;
Lord Younger suggested that Mr Baldwin might agree to serve in a
coalition under Mr Asquith; Lord Derby felt that Mr Austen
Chamberlain ought to succeed Mr Baldwin and might then be able
to secure Liberal support; Mr St. Loe Strachey, editor of the *Spec-
tator*, made the startling proposal that Mr McKenna (who was not
then even a Member of Parliament) should be asked by the King to
form a.'Government of National Trustees' who should hold office for
a period of two years. Mr Asquith, when consulted, was quite positive that once Mr Baldwin was defeated in Parliament, the King
ought to summon the leader of the Labour Party. There were some
who feared that if Mr Ramsay MacDonald were sent for, he would
insist upon obtaining a dissolution and thus expose the country to yet
another General Election. The King, they urged, ought in such circumstances to refuse this request. There were others who indicated
that, even if the King did offer Mr MacDonald the opportunity of
forming a Government, he should only do so under certain conditions.

In all this confusion of counsel, in all this welter of ingenuity, the
King maintained without deviation the ordinary point of view.
'There are', he wrote,[d] 'really no precedents for the present situation.
I must use my own judgment as each case arises.'

That judgment was sound. The King made it perfectly clear from
the outset that Mr Baldwin must face Parliament and only resign
after a defeat in the House of Commons. He made it equally clear

that, when that event occurred, it was his constitutional duty to send for Mr Ramsay MacDonald as leader of the next largest party in the State. And he also made it clear that it would not be right for him, in sending for the leader of the Labour Party, to attach any conditions to his offer, or to 'permit any attempt to prevent Mr MacDonald having the same facilities which would be accorded to any Minister entrusted by the Sovereign with the formation of a Government'.*

'I must confess', wrote Lord Stamfordham to Mr St Loe Strachey on December 14, 'that at the present moment I feel that His Majesty should do his utmost not to hamper in any way Mr Ramsay Mac-Donald in what we must all admit will be a task of almost incalculable magnitude. And I expect that the King will be interpreting the general feeling of the people of the country, that, true to British ideas, the Government, whoever they should be, should have a fair chance.'*

On January 15, 1924, the King opened the new Parliament. On January 21 the Conservatives were defeated in the House of Commons by seventy-two votes. The next day Mr Baldwin came to Buckingham Palace and handed in his resignation. The King did not consult the retiring Prime Minister as to who should be his successor. 'I never', His Majesty recorded subsequently,* 'consulted Mr Baldwin in any way when he came to resign, nor asked his advice as to whom to send for.'

'At 12.15', the King wrote in his diary for January 22, 1924, 'I held a Council, at which Mr Ramsay MacDonald was sworn in a member. I then asked him to form a Government, which he accepted to do. I had an hour's talk with him, he impressed me very much; he wishes to do the right thing.

Today 23 years ago dear Grandmama died. I wonder what she would have thought of a Labour Government!'

A more detailed version of this historic audience is contained in the memorandum written by Lord Stamfordham, at the time:*

Tuesday, 22nd January 1924.
Today the King saw Mr Ramsay MacDonald and entrusted to him the formation of a new Government, which he undertook.

He assured the King that, though he and his friends were inexperienced in governing and fully realised the great responsibilities which they would now assume, nevertheless they were honest and sincere and his earnest desire was to serve his King and Country. They may fail in their endeavours: but it will not be for want of trying to do their best.

The King told Mr Ramsay MacDonald that he might count upon his assistance in every way. His Majesty only asked for frankness between them. The King referred to recent utterances of Mr Lansbury, in which he went out of his way to express a threat and a reminder of the fate which had befallen King Charles I.[1] His Majesty was not affected by these personal attacks but did take exception to Mr Lansbury's basing his remarks upon the idea of intrigues at Court. The King said Mr Ramsay MacDonald might be certain that—with the exception of his Private Secretary, part of whose duty was to keep His Majesty informed as to the views of the men in the various schools of political opinion, and of the Assistant Secretaries—he did not discuss these matters with anyone else but formed his own judgment.

His Majesty went on to say that, little expecting to occupy his present position, he served in the Navy for 14 years—and thus had opportunities of seeing more of the world and mixing with his fellow creatures than would otherwise have been the case: while during the past 14 years he had naturally gained much political knowledge and experience of the working of the machinery of Government under 4 different Prime Ministers. He always follows Foreign Affairs with especial interest and is inclined to wonder whether Mr Ramsay MacDonald had fully considered the heavy responsibilities and duties incurred by undertaking the office of Secretary of State for Foreign Affairs in addition to that of Prime Minister. The King referred to the case of Lord Salisbury who, in spite of his great knowledge of Foreign Affairs, found it difficult to carry on the duties of both offices: indeed he did very little of the work of the Prime Minister, whereas now-a-days the latter position in itself and its heavy responsibilities must be a serious tax upon anyone holding that office. Mr Ramsay MacDonald explained that for the moment he had no one to appoint to the Foreign Office, but perhaps later on he might be able to hand it over to someone else.

The King spoke of the recognition of Russia. Mr Ramsay MacDonald said that he had heard from Monsieur Benes himself that Monsieur Poincaré had asked him to go to Russia and arrange for the recognition of the Government by France. Signor Mussolini was on the point of recognising Russia and if we were left out we should find that other countries had forestalled us in all business enterprises. The King said he was sure that Mr Ramsay MacDonald would understand how abhorrent it would be to His Majesty to receive any representative of Russia who, directly or indirectly, had been connected with the abominable murder of the Emperor, Empress and their family, the King's own first cousin, and His Majesty hoped that the representative might be a Minister and not an Ambassador.[2]

---

[1] At a meeting held at the Shoreditch Town Hall on January 5 Mr George Lansbury had suggested that certain circles, and even the leaders of the two main parties, were bringing pressure to bear on the King in order to deny Labour the fruits of victory. 'Some centuries ago', he said, 'a King stood against the common people and he lost his head.'

[2] In those days the theory was that a Minister was accredited by a Government to a Government, whereas an Ambassador was accredited

The King referred to the unfortunate incident at the recent Meeting at the Albert Hall, presided over by Mr Ramsay MacDonald, at which the *Marseillaise* and the *Red Flag* were sung. Mr Ramsay MacDonald spoke very openly and said he was sure the King would be generous to him and understand the very difficult position he was in *vis-à-vis* to his own extremists; and he could assure His Majesty that, had he attempted to prevent the *Red Flag* being sung on that occasion, a riot would inevitably have ensued. Moreover there was a very serious possibility on Monday night of the *Red Flag* being sung in the House of Commons and it had required all his influence and that of his moderate and immediate friends to prevent this taking place: they had got into the way of singing this song and it will be by degrees that he hopes to break down this habit.

Later in the afternoon, after the House of Commons had sat and adjourned, the King saw Mr Ramsay MacDonald who kissed hands on appointment and gave His Majesty a list of his Government and discussed the qualifications of the respective Members.

Mr J. R. Clynes in his *Memoirs*[1] has given a vivid account of the King's reception of his first Labour Ministers. The passage deserves to be quoted:

'King George sent for Mr MacDonald. Arthur Henderson, J. H. Thomas and myself accompanied our leader to Buckingham Palace, to that fateful interview of which we had dreamed, when a British Sovereign should entrust the affairs of the Empire to the hands of the people's own representatives.

As we stood waiting for His Majesty, amid the gold and crimson magnificence of the Palace, I could not help marvelling at the strange turn of Fortune's wheel, which had brought MacDonald the starvelling clerk, Thomas the engine-driver, Henderson the foundry labourer and Clynes the mill-hand, to this pinnacle beside the man whose forebears had been Kings for so many splendid generations. We were making history.

We were, perhaps, somewhat embarrassed, but the little, quiet man whom we addressed as "Your Majesty" swiftly put us at our ease. He was himself rather anxious; his was a great responsibility, and I have no doubt that he had read the wild statements of some of our extremists, and I think he wondered to what he was committing his people.

The King first created MacDonald a Privy Councillor, and then spoke to us for some time. He gave us invaluable guidance from his deep experience, to help us in the difficult time before us, when we should become his principal Ministers. I had expected to find him

by the head of the State to the Sovereign. Thus if a Soviet Minister were appointed instead of an Ambassador, the King's relations with him could have been confined to pure formality. The distinction between Ambassadors and Ministers has, since then, been almost entirely obliterated.

unbending; instead he was kindness and sympathy itself. Before he gave us leave to go, he made an appeal to us that I have never forgotten:

"The immediate future of my people, and their whole happiness, is in your hands, gentlemen. They depend upon your prudence and sagacity." '

(2)

In forming his Cabinet Mr MacDonald struck a carefully considered balance between the Fabian and the Trades Union elements in the Labour Party.[1] The only extreme socialist included in the government was Mr Wheatley, who became Minister of Health. It had been expected that Mr MacDonald, on accepting office, would abstain from creating any peers. Some representation of the Government in the House of Lords was, however, essential. The Prime Minister solved the problem by including three existing peers (Lords Haldane, Chelmsford and Parmoor) within his Cabinet and by only creating three new peers (Sir Sydney Olivier, Mr Arnold and General C. B. Thomson) who possessed the advantage of having no male heirs. These arrangements were very generally approved.

[1] The main posts in the first Labour Cabinet were distributed as follows:

Prime Minister and Foreign Secretary: Mr Ramsay MacDonald.
Lord Privy Seal and Deputy Leader of the House: Mr J. R. Clynes.
Lord President of the Council: Lord Parmoor.
Lord Chancellor: Lord Haldane.
Chancellor of the Exchequer: Mr Philip Snowden.
Home Secretary: Mr Arthur Henderson.
Colonies: Mr J. H. Thomas.
War: Mr Stephen Walsh.
India: Sir Sydney Olivier (Lord Olivier).
Air: Brigadier General C. B. Thomson (Lord Thomson).
First Lord of the Admiralty: Lord Chelmsford.
President of the Board of Trade: Mr Sidney Webb.
Minister of Health: Mr John Wheatley.
Education: Mr C. P. Trevelyan.
Labour: Mr Thomas Shaw.
Chancellor of the Duchy: Colonel Josiah Wedgwood.
Financial Secretary, Treasury: Mr William Graham.
Chief Whip: Mr B. C. Spoor.
U.S.S. for War: Major C. R. Attlee.

The Prime Minister appointed as his private secretaries Sir Ronald Waterhouse, Mr R. P. Gower and Mr C. P. Duff. Mr Snowden's private secretary was Mr P. J. Grigg and Mr Edward Marsh ministered to Mr J. H. Thomas.

The only serious criticism was that Mr MacDonald, in assuming the dual responsibilities of Prime Minister and Foreign Secretary, was undertaking a super-human task. In the very first month of his premiership, for instance, he was obliged to answer, in his dual capacity, as many as sixty parliamentary questions in a single afternoon. Mr MacDonald's achievements as Foreign Secretary were quick, startling and beneficial. It is improbable that any other man could so rapidly have altered the whole tone of international relations. But for these achievements he paid a formidable price. The effort of those nine months was so gigantic that it damaged his health; his powers of assimilation, memory and concentration were seriously overstrained. The pressure of external affairs prevented him, moreover, from devoting to internal politics the close attention that they merited; mistakes were made. Above all, the cloud of overwork that hid the Prime Minister from his colleagues and supporters produced an impression of misty and even conceited aloofness—an impression which, as it hardened into a grievance, created an ever-widening rift between Mr MacDonald and the rank and file of his own party.

The relations between the King and his new Prime Minister were from the outset those of unhesitating mutual confidence. The King was attracted by Mr MacDonald's quiet moderation, by his unfailing considerateness, by the deliberate blend in his manner and voice of silk and tweed, of cosmopolitan distinction and Scottish sense. Mr MacDonald, for his part, was flattered and even dazzled by His Majesty's forthright friendliness; grateful for the King's evident eagerness to do everything within his power to help the new Government; impressed, as all were impressed, by the Sovereign's candour.[1]

---

[1] As an example of the King's desire that the new Prime Minister should not be embarrassed through ignorance of customary usage, the following Memorandum may be quoted, summarising, for Mr MacDonald's information, the procedure to be followed in matters requiring the Sovereign's approval. (R.A., K. 1917):

House of Commons.

A letter is written to the King every day during the Session by the Leader of the House of Commons, describing the proceedings of the House. A telegram briefly reporting any outstanding particulars in the proceedings is sent every evening by one of the Whips.

Cabinet.

1. No change is made in the constitution of the Ministry until the King's approval has been obtained.

2. No mention should be made publicly or privately of any matters

The King took special trouble to get to know each of his new Ministers personally:

'I have', he wrote to Queen Alexandra on February 17, 'been making the acquaintance of all the Ministers in turn & I must say they all seem to be very intelligent & they take things very seriously. They have different ideas to ours as they are all socialists, but they ought to be given a chance & ought to be treated fairly.'

No exceptions were made. 'Received Mr Wheatley', the King noted in his diary for February 22, 'the Minister of Health. He is an extreme socialist & comes from Glasgow. I had a very interesting conversation with him.' The King and Queen were also anxious that the wives of the new Labour Ministers should not be embarrassed by

which have transpired in Cabinet, without the approval of His Majesty being first obtained.

3. Before a Minister goes abroad he should acquaint the King of his intention to do so.

Foreign Office.

All important Foreign Office Despatches are submitted to His Majesty before being sent abroad.

Ecclesiastical Preferment.

A very important responsibility. The Archbishop of Canterbury will be found very fair and liberal-minded with a wide knowledge of the personnel of the Church and always ready to advise. It is important that the letters which convey the offer of important preferment should be written by the Prime Minister himself.

Honours and Appointments.

It is hoped that a firm hand will be kept on the distribution of Honours. With the exception of the last Government, the bestowal has been extravagant. Especial care should be taken with regard to appointments to the Privy Council. Mr Gladstone said that a Privy Councillorship used to be regarded as a greater honour than a Peerage.

Before any person is offered an Appointment under the Crown, or an Honour, the King's approval should be obtained, until which time the individual in question should not be approached on the subject.

All recommendations for Honours are submitted in conjunction with the Prime Minister with the exception of the Order of Merit and the Royal Victorian Order (which are made on the King's initiative).

Except in very special cases, Submissions for Honours are only made twice a year, i.e. New Year's Day and the King's Birthday.

The number of names submitted on each occasion for Baronetcies and Knighthoods, other than those for the Dominions, should not respectively exceed 8 and 24.

The King deprecates the bestowal of Honours on Ministers while in Office.

being invited, or offended by not being invited, to Court functions. Mrs Sidney Webb, with Fabian austerity, held the view that socialist womanhood should be indifferent to such matters. Mrs Philip Snowden was more realistic: it was on her advice that the wives of Ministers were invited to afternoon receptions.

A less amenable problem arose in connection with nominations to the Royal Household. Hitherto the senior offices of the Court had been regarded as political appointments, made on the advice of the Prime Minister in power. Mr Ramsay MacDonald, not having at his disposal a sufficient number of candidates anxious to assume such functions, proposed that this practice be abandoned and that in future the King should appoint or retain such Court officials as he thought fit. The King, while welcoming the idea that some of the senior members of his Household should become, so to speak, permanent officials, felt that it would be improper were he to surround himself exclusively with his personal friends, and that at least some members of the Labour Party should receive Court appointments. Lord Stamfordham recalling, with his accustomed caution, the fierce Bedchamber Question of 1839,[1] suggested that if the political character of these Household appointments were to be abolished, it might be well if the King were first to consult the leaders of the two other parties, so that 'they could have no grievance on finding that this particular patronage had disappeared'.[j] Lord Balfour, when informed, was opposed to the abolition of these political appointments since it was of assistance to a Prime Minister, when forming a Government, to possess some sops wherewith to reward those supporters who were not qualified for ministerial office. Mr Asquith, on the other hand, was entirely in favour of these offices becoming permanent and independent of political or party fluctuations. In the end a sensible compromise was agreed to. The posts of Lord Chamberlain and Lord Steward were to be filled at the Sovereign's discretion. Six other Household appointments were to be political only in the sense that they would terminate with a change of Government. Peers accepting such posts were to take no part in Parliamentary votes or

[1] After Lord Melbourne's resignation in 1839 Sir Robert Peel, on being invited to form an administration, insisted that the Queen should dismiss the Whig ladies of her Household and replace them by his own nominees. The Queen refused to do so, with the result that Sir Robert Peel declined office and Lord Melbourne carried on till 1841. The conflict, which at one time threatened to raise serious constitutional issues, was in the end settled by the Prince Consort tactfully inducing the Whig ladies to resign.

proceedings. The three political Lords-in-Waiting and the three officers of the House of Commons (the Treasurer of the Household, the Controller and the Vice-Chamberlain) were to be chosen by the Prime Minister and appointed on his advice.

The three latter appointments were then offered by Mr Mac-Donald to Mr T. Griffiths, Mr Parkinson and Mr Davison, and accepted by them. A difficulty then arose as to the wearing of uniform. The King attached to correctness of vesture an importance that to some people seemed exaggerated. As his father before him, he possessed in such matters the eyes of a falcon and could from a great distance detect the tiniest misplacement of a ribbon or a badge. In regard to the niceties of civilian apparel he was almost equally observant and exacting. He himself favoured the fashion before the last and was inclined to regard any deviation from the norm of the previous decade as indicating affectation, effeminacy, or potential decadence. His meticulousness in such matters can partly be ascribed to a sailor's passion for minute tidiness: but it was also due to a reasonable realisation that slovenliness or incongruity are as destructive of the magic of ceremony as two saucepans tied to the howdah of a state elephant. In permitting exceptions to what until then had been the rigid protocol for court functions, the King was making a real effort to understand the special difficulties and embarrassments of his new Labour Ministers.

The latter were perfectly prepared to wear some sort of uniform, provided they were not expected to wear knee-breeches (which they feared might expose them to the ridicule of their comrades) or to purchase full dress at a cost beyond their means. Considerable discussion on the subject then took place between Lord Stamfordham and Mr Benjamin Spoor, the Chief Government Whip:

'This question of uniform', the King minuted,[k] 'is becoming very intricate & confused. Whatever decision the Cabinet Ministers come to, I will agree to, but they must all do the same. It would look very odd if some were in uniform and some in evening clothes at a Levée. . . . In no case do I expect anyone to get more than the Levée coat; full dress is not necessary on account of the expense.'

Lord Stamfordham, with his accustomed kindliness, ascertained from the principal Court Tailor that the full cost of Levée dress would amount to £73. 2s. 6d. Realising that this was a sum that few Labour Members would be willing to expend, Lord Stamfordham made further enquiries. On January 10, 1924, he wrote to Mr Benjamin Spoor the following attractive letter:[l]

'Dear Mr Spoor,

I have ascertained from Messrs Moss Bros., 20 King Street, W.C. 2. (Telephone No. Gerard 3750), which is I believe a well known and dependable Firm, that they have in stock a few suits of Household, Second Class, Levée Dress from £30 complete. This comprises trousers, coat, cock-hat, and sword and is the regulation dress.'

(3)

On February 12, 1924, Mr Ramsay MacDonald and his colleagues first took their seats upon the Government bench:

'Beyond the fact', Mr MacDonald wrote to the King on February 13, 'that the Galleries and the House itself were unusually crowded, there was little in yesterday's proceedings to indicate that the occasion was unique in the annals of the British Parliament. . . . There can be few precedents for the spectacle of four ex-Chancellors of the Exchequer sitting in a row on the front Opposition bench, and two ex-Prime Ministers sitting beside each other on the benches below the gangway.'

Mr MacDonald, in that his supporters numbered less than a third of the House of Commons, was obliged to advance with caution. He announced at the outset that he would not resign if outvoted on a minor issue and would only relinquish office if defeated on a major question of policy or on a motion of confidence. During the course of the next eight months his Government were in fact defeated as many as twelve times. In domestic matters, such legislation as he felt able to introduce was carefully modulated in order that no harsh note should shock the ears of his Liberal patrons. Mr Snowden's budget was a model of free trade finance; he reduced or abolished the duties on tea, coffee, cocoa and sugar; the McKenna duties were swept away; a gentle hint was given that pensions for widows might, in the following year, be accorded. The wages of agricultural workers and the unemployment benefit were slightly increased. But the only legislative measure introduced by the first Labour Government that bore any intimate relation to their principles and desires was the Housing Bill, sponsored with cogency by Mr Wheatley. Under this Bill grants were accorded to Local Authorities enabling them to construct houses which could be rented to poorer families. Apart from this, the domestic policy of Mr MacDonald's first Government was diffident, conciliatory, undramatic and very mild.

The National Executive of the Labour Party, convinced that they had been democratically elected in order both to stimulate and control the activity of the Cabinet, did not approve of this moderation. Mr George Lansbury, who at that date exercised much influence on

La Galerie des Glaces
du château de Versailles

Mr Lloyd George with his humble duty to Your Majesty has the honour to announce that the ~~great~~ long & terrible war in which the British Empire has been engaged with the German Empire for more than four years & which has caused such suffering to mankind has been brought to an end this afternoon by the Treaty of Peace just signed in this hall.

He desires on behalf of all the Plenipotentiaries of Your Majesty's Empire to tender their heartfelt ~~best~~ congratulations to Your Majesty on the signature of a Treaty which marks the victorious end of the terrible struggle which has lasted so long & in which your Majesty's subjects from all parts of the Empire have played so glorious a part

D Lloyd George

June 28th 1919 4 p.m. ————

THE TREATY IS SIGNED

ROME VISIT

the Executive, was a man of quick emotions and a slow sense of reality: in a voice throbbing with tortured idealism he would reprove Ministers for their deviations from strict Socialist doctrine or for their failure to give legislative effect to many of the main items of the Party programme. The Prime Minister was irritated by these interruptions: it seemed incredible to him that any man could be so unrealistic as not to recognise that in domestic matters the Labour Government were not their own masters; and that it was only in the field of foreign policy that they could act courageously and thereby acquire prestige. His impatience with Mr Lansbury increased the sad gap between himself and the true believers. The latter did not appreciate that he was urgently anxious, in the inevitably short term accorded to him, to loosen the tight tangle in which world diplomacy had become enmeshed. Mr MacDonald wished to re-establish relations of confidence and co-operation with France and Italy: to break the deadlock over reparations; to secure a French evacuation of the Ruhr; and to reintroduce Germany into the comity of Nations. He wished to further the cause of general disarmament by strengthening the machinery of international arbitration; and to bridge the gulf that, both politically and commercially, sundered Great Britain from Soviet Russia. Within the space of eight months he was able either to attain or promote all these seven objects. The Labour Party, in their blind hatred, have never accorded to his memory due recognition of this astonishing achievement.

On February 25 the Prime Minister, abandoning the rigid convention of a diplomatic Note, addressed to M. Poincaré a long personal letter, deploring the impression that had been created that France wished 'to ruin Germany and dominate the Continent' and appealing to him to come to some understanding with his former allies in regard to 'fundamental aims'. His initiative was favoured by the events that followed. In January a Committee of experts had been appointed, under the chairmanship of General Dawes, to advise the Reparation Commission on the financial position of Germany and on the problem of transferring reparation payments into foreign currencies. The Dawes Committee produced their report in April. While making technical recommendations as to the establishment of a 'Transfer Committee', they laid down the principle that Germany could never achieve financial stability until she regained possession of all her economic resources. By that time the French public (alarmed by a sudden weakening of the franc) had come to realise that the Ruhr and Rhineland experiments were unlikely to prove

393

remunerative; while the Germans had come to realise that passive resistance could never, in the long run, have proved a possible policy. In May, elections were held both in France and Germany. M. Poincaré was defeated and succeeded by M. Herriot; Dr Stresemann received support for his policy of conciliation. Having conducted a satisfactory discussion with M. Herriot at Chequers, the Prime Minister felt justified in summoning to London a Conference of all the Powers interested in reparation. After three weeks of patient and dexterous negotiation Mr MacDonald reached a point when it seemed safe to invite the Germans also to attend. On August 30, 1924, the 'London Agreement' was signed at St. James's Palace. All the Powers accepted the recommendations of the Dawes report and the French pledged themselves to the evacuation of the Ruhr.[1] The King addressed to the Prime Minister his warmest congratulations on this signal triumph.

At the same time Mr MacDonald sought to remove a grievance that had long rankled in the breast of Signor Mussolini. On July 15, 1924, an agreement was signed in London, whereby the Juba valley and the Port of Kismayu were transferred from Kenya Colony to Italian Somaliland.[2]

The most ambitious of all Mr MacDonald's schemes of pacification was the 'Protocol for the pacific settlement of International Disputes' which, in September of that year, he propounded to the fifth Assembly of the League of Nations at Geneva. After agreement with M. Herriot, and with the assistance of his colleagues Mr Arthur Henderson and Lord Parmoor, the Prime Minister laid before the

[1] Evacuation began immediately, but was not completed until July 31, 1925.

[2] Under Article 13 of the Treaty of London of April 26, 1915, it had been provided that, in the event of France or Great Britain increasing their possessions in Africa, Italy could claim 'some equitable compensation', particularly upon the frontiers of Somaliland and Libya. At the Paris Peace Conference it was agreed between Lord Milner and Signor Scialoja that these concessions should 'form part of the general settlement of all the issues raised at the Conference'. Lord Curzon claimed that an important item in this 'general settlement' was the agreement reached between M. Venizelos and Signor Tittoni, under which the Dodecanese Islands should be ceded by Italy to Greece. On the fall of M. Venizelos the Italians repudiated this agreement and Lord Curzon's contention was that they should not be given Jubaland until the Greeks got Rhodes and her eleven sisters. Mr MacDonald was quick to realise that, in view of Articles 13 and 8 of the Treaty of London, we were not on firm ground in connecting these two questions.

Assembly a proposal, whereby each country pledged itself to submit any dispute to arbitration and all other members of the League undertook to go to war with any country refusing to abide by an arbitral decision. The collective security thus established was to be the prelude to a general Disarmament Conference to be held later. The proposal was in principle accepted unanimously; the protocol was actually signed by France and nine other countries before the Assembly dispersed. The Prime Minister had by then realised that the days of his own Government were numbered. The Conservatives were opposed to the Protocol, fearing that it would mean subordinating our essential safety to the decisions of a few international lawyers. Mr MacDonald did not survive long enough to submit his scheme to Parliament: the Geneva Protocol was formally rejected by Mr Austen Chamberlain in March 1925.

(4)

The Labour Party, in their election manifesto, had proclaimed as one of the main objectives of their foreign policy 'the resumption of free economic and diplomatic relations with Russia'. Mr Mac-Donald's first action, on becoming Prime Minister and Foreign Secretary, had therefore been to recognise the Soviet Government as the legal Government of Russia and to invite them to enter into negotiations with a view to the conclusion of a trade agreement. The Russians despatched M. Rakowsky to London, with the rank of Chargé d'Affaires. The negotiations on the British side were entrusted to Mr Arthur Ponsonby, Mr MacDonald's versatile Parliamentary Under-Secretary.[1] On August 5 it was announced that the negotiations had broken down: on the very next day Mr Ponsonby startled the House of Commons by stating that, not only had negotiations been resumed, but that two Treaties were now ready for signa-

[1] Mr Arthur Ponsonby was the third son of Queen Victoria's Private Secretary, Sir Henry Ponsonby, and a brother of Sir F. Ponsonby, Treasurer to King George. After eight years as a member of the Diplomatic Service, he entered Parliament as a Liberal in 1906. He was much criticised for his outspoken opposition to King Edward's visit to the Tsar in 1908. He thereafter joined the Labour Party and sat in Parliament as member for the Brightside division of Sheffield until raised to the peerage in 1930. He held the position of Parliamentary Under-Secretary at the Foreign Office (1924), the Dominions Office (1929) and Ministry of Transport (1929–1931). In the latter year he became for a few months Chancellor of the Duchy of Lancaster. He was the author and editor of many entertaining books.

ture. The first Treaty, a Commercial Treaty, provided that Great Britain should receive from Russia most favoured nation treatment, in return for which she would extend to the Soviet Government the benefits of the Exports Credits Scheme. Under the second Treaty, called a 'general' Treaty, Russia acknowledged the claims of British bondholders for compensation for their holdings of Russian Imperial bonds and for property confiscated. Neither of these two treaties caused the Opposition any profound perturbation. What alarmed them was a provision that, once British claims against Russia had been met, a third Treaty would be negotiated enabling the Soviet Government to negotiate a loan, with the approval of the British Treasury, upon the London market.

Both the Conservative and the Liberal Oppositions were angered by this provision. They suspected, and not without reason, that the sudden resumption and conclusion of the negotiations on August 6 had been due to pressure exercised upon the Prime Minister from outside. They were incensed that Mr MacDonald, who in June had promised that there was no intention of granting a loan to Russia, should in August have agreed to, and even signed, treaties that envisaged just such a loan. Nor were they pleased that these sudden agreements should have been sprung upon the House of Commons on the very eve of the summer recess. It is curious that Mr Mac-Donald did not himself fully realise the resentment aroused in both sections of the Opposition by these Russian negotiations and the manner of their presentation. It was in a mood of satisfaction that he wrote to the King on August 8, 1924:

'So the first stage of the Session comes to an end. From more than one point of view the Session has been historical. The Prime Minister may perhaps justly claim that he has shown the Country that the Labour Party is fit to govern, and that the system of minority government, although accompanied by inconveniences, is a feasible proposition.

Looking back on the Session, the Prime Minister has every reason to be satisfied. The Budget was undoubtedly a remarkable success; there is a better atmosphere in foreign affairs; lastly the Government, in spite of not having a majority in the House of Commons, has succeeded in carrying through the House measures relating to domestic affairs to which it attached great importance, such as the Housing Bill and the Agricultural Wages Bill. The work of the Session has at any rate removed in the minds of the people the ignorant prejudices and fears which existed before it took office. . . .

The path in front of the Government is by no means smooth. It is faced with a very critical position in Ireland[1] and a very critical position in the House on the question of the Anglo-Russian Treaty, but in each case there is an interval for calm reflection by all Parties in the House, which may possibly prevent the crisis from coming to a head. . . .'

This interval for calm reflection did not produce the effects that the Prime Minister had hoped. The more they thought about it, the more certain did the Conservatives become that the hidden and irresponsible influence of the National Executive and the T.U.C. was exercising pressure upon the Cabinet of a nature that could not be reconciled with the sacred principle of Parliamentary supremacy. The Liberals were beginning to fear that the success and moderation of the Government were attracting more and more votes to Labour and damaging the coherence and future of their own Party. They were correct in their apprehension. When therefore the House of Commons met in September, for the purpose of giving the Government powers to nominate an Ulster representative on the Irish Boundary Commission, they gathered in a mood of suspicion and resentment. The experiment, it was felt, of keeping Labour in office had continued long enough; perhaps it had been a dangerous experiment. What became known as 'The Campbell Case' became the occasion, although not the cause, of the destruction of the first Labour Government.

[1] The Government of Northern Ireland refused to appoint a representative to the Boundary Commission provided for under article 12 of the Irish Treaty. They stated that they would defend themselves by force if it was proposed to take from them one inch of territory. On September 17, 1924, the King instructed Lord Stamfordham to write directly to Sir James Craig expressing his anxiety. 'The King feels', wrote Lord Stamfordham, 'that the solution of the problem is only to be found by agreement between you and Cosgrave. He earnestly trusts that you will continue to work to this end, for he knows that as a great Irishman you believe, as he does, that such a consummation would be for the lasting peace, happiness and prosperity of Ulster itself, Ireland as a whole, and of the British Empire generally.' (R.A., K. 1953. 1.)

In the end the House of Commons had to pass a special Bill empowering the Government to appoint directly a representative of Northern Ireland. The Boundary Commission eventually broke asunder and the matter had to be settled by a new agreement concluded on December 3, 1925, under which Eire recognised the existing boundary and in return was released from the obligations of Article 5 of the 1921 Treaty under which she had agreed to assume an 'equitable' share of the British National Debt.

(5)

The Attorney General, Sir Patrick Hastings, upon the suggestion of the Public Prosecutor, but without the knowledge of the Home Secretary, had instituted proceedings against a Mr J. R. Campbell, acting Editor of a communist publication entitled *The Workers Weekly*. Mr Campbell was accused of sedition under the Mutiny Act of 1795 for having published an article inciting the military not to obey orders when instructed to take action against strikers. Certain members of the Labour Party and its affiliated organisations were incensed by this indictment, since they had themselves, some years before, and in company with Mr Ramsay MacDonald himself, protested against the prosecution of Mr Tom Mann for an exactly similar offence. The Attorney General thereupon abandoned all proceedings, alleging that he had since discovered that Mr Campbell was only the acting editor of the paper and possessed an excellent war record. Mr Campbell himself insisted upon making the inconvenient revelation that the Government had called off the proceedings as a result of pressure brought upon them by their own left wing.

On first hearing of the incident the King had expressed some doubts regarding the expediency of first threatening and then withdrawing the action. The Prime Minister sought to allay His Majesty's anxiety:[m]

> 'I understand', he wrote to Lord Stamfordham from Lossiemouth on August 22, 'that the King is rather disturbed about that Communist prosecution. Pray assure him that I am equally disturbed. There was a muddle somewhere, and I am making enquiries. . . . I was furious when I heard that the prosecution was started. I know these people far too well to pay the least attention to anything they do. They are a miserable lot of creatures, out for notoriety and mischief, and the mere fact that we prosecuted them played into their hands. Of course what they did was criminal, but it was of a nature where commonsense and not merely red tape and the letter of the law came into play. I knew nothing about it until I saw it in the newspapers. Then I sent for the Attorney General and the Public Prosecutor and gave them a bit of my mind. . . . They replied that the whole matter could be dropped. I told them that, as they had begun, they had to go through with it. Later on I was informed that the editor was prepared to write a letter which would amount to an apology for what he had done. I agreed that, if he did that, the matter might be dropped. From that time, until I saw the report of the further appearance at Bow Street, no information reached me and I was never consulted. By the report, I found that no such letter had been written but that, nevertheless, the Government had not pressed the prosecution. It was further explained

that it was owing to the fact that I had been summoned as a witness and that certain awkward questions were to be put to me. Nothing would have pleased me better than to have appeared in the witness box, when I might have said some things that might have added a month or two to the sentence which the Judge would have given them. As a matter of fact no attempt was ever made to summon me and the first I heard of it was when I read the story in the newspapers. That motive, therefore, never entered into the minds of anyone responsible for the proceedings. It is all one of those malicious newspaper stunts which are becoming so common nowadays.'

Mr MacDonald was before long to learn that there was something more in the agitation than a mere August search for sensation on the part of the Press. On October 1 he was asked in the House of Commons whether he had himself given any instructions that the charge against Mr Campbell should be withdrawn. He replied that he had not been consulted. He then realised, from the temper of the House, that the issue was one that would be pushed to a vote of confidence:

'I regret all this', he wrote to Lord Stamfordham on October 2, 'as I hope I have given His Majesty abundant evidence that national interest was the first concern of my Government and that I was willing, given fair play in Parliament, to carry on the work for some time yet, so as to allow the Nation to feel some confidence and security and to face its commercial, and international problems in particular, without being distracted by Party or partisan squabbles. I have now to confess to you that I am beaten and that it looks as though I can go no further. . . . Coalitions stink so much in the nostrils of our people that to try one now would be a colossal blunder. I see nothing for it but another appeal to the country as quickly as possible.'[n]

Events now moved to a rapid conclusion. The King, who was up at Balmoral, despatched Lord Stamfordham to London with instructions to obtain the opinion of the leaders of the two Opposition parties. Neither Mr Asquith nor Mr Baldwin showed any desire either to assume office or to enter a coalition. On October 8 in the House of Commons Sir Robert Horne moved a vote of censure on the ground that the Government, under pressure from their extremists, had 'interfered with the course of justice'. He was supported, on behalf of the Liberals, by Sir John Simon, who moved that a select committee be appointed to examine the circumstances in which the Campbell prosecution had been withdrawn. The Prime Minister replied that if either of these two motions were carried the Government would resign. Mr Asquith, in the last speech that he made in the House of Commons, endeavoured with gay urbanity to preach conciliation. The debate was pressed to a division and the Government were defeated by 364 votes to 198.

That night the King travelled down to London from Scotland. Mr. MacDonald came to see him at 10.0 a.m. on Thursday, October 9, and asked for an immediate dissolution:

'The Prime Minister', Lord Stamfordham recorded, 'spoke in no complaining terms of the manner in which Sir Robert Horne moved the vote of censure on behalf of the Conservatives—it was a statesmanlike, legal-minded and fair speech: but he thought Sir John Simon's was a poor performance, with the result that the outcome of the division roused little enthusiasm even among the victors. °

It was with reluctance that the King felt himself obliged to grant Mr MacDonald's request for an immediate dissolution. In one of his infrequent personal minutes he recorded the reasons for this disinclination: *p*

'In granting the Prime Minister's request to dissolve Parliament, I could not help regretting the necessity for doing so, being aware how strongly the country at large deprecates another General Election within less than a year and all its attendant dislocation of trade, of the daily business-life of the community and the consequent adverse effect upon the employment of labour, as well as the great expense thereby incurred. I am sorry also that the appeal to the electorate cannot be made upon a more vital issue than that raised last evening in the House of Commons. Further, there is the possible contingency that the General Election may return to Parliament the three political Parties in numbers similar to those of the present House of Commons: a result that would tend to increase the objections now prevailing against any such appeal.   G.R.I.'[1]

---

[1] The King's action in granting Mr MacDonald a dissolution in 1924 has often been criticised. It is pointed out that, as Mr Asquith stated publicly in December 1923, the King was under no constitutional obligation to grant a dissolution to a Prime Minister not possessing a majority in Parliament. It was frequently stated, and notably by Professor Keith in his *Responsible Government in the Dominions* (Vol. I, p. 147), that the King agreed with Mr MacDonald 'immediately' and 'without even considering whether the Government could be carried on without a dissolution'. These assumptions are incorrect. The King did not agree 'immediately': he agreed with the utmost reluctance and only after he had ascertained from the leaders of the Conservative and Liberal Parties that they themselves were unable or unwilling to form an Administration.

Moreover, as Professor Keith rightly asserts in his *The King and the Imperial Crown* (p. 172), a refusal of Mr MacDonald's request might have been regarded by the Labour Party as a departure from the 'absolutely fair and impartial attitude' which the King had invariably striven to maintain.

On October 9 the House of Commons, having passed the Irish Boundary Bill, was formally prorogued:

'No sensational incident', Mr MacDonald wrote to the King on October 10, 'marked the final stage of this Parliament. . . . The curtain was rung down upon the Labour Government's first experiment in parliamentary government. . . . The Prime Minister himself does not think that he will offend against the canons of modesty if he puts forward certain claims in regard to the work of the Government. They have shown the country that they have the capacity to govern in an equal degree with the other Parties in the House. . . . They have also shown the country that patriotism is not the monopoly of any class or party. Finally they can justly claim that they have left the international situation in a more favourable position than that which they inherited.'

On that same day, October 10, there came into the hands of the Foreign Office a copy of a letter (dated Moscow, September 15), purporting to be addressed to the Central Committee of the British Communist Party by Zinoviev, Chairman of the E.K.K.I. the Presidium of the Third International. The letter stated that it was essential to bring into the movement 'the army of the unemployed', to create communist cells among the soldiers, sailors and munition workers, and to organise risings in Ireland and the Colonies. 'Only then', the letter added, 'will it be possible to count upon the complete success of an armed insurrection' or to turn 'an imperialist war into a class war'. Mr MacDonald had for long been anxious to obtain positive evidence of Soviet interference in our domestic affairs: he had already instructed the Foreign Office that, if and when reliable evidence were discovered, a Note of protest should be addressed to Mr Rakowsky, the Russian Chargé d'Affaires, drawing his attention to this flagrant violation of the Anglo-Russian agreement. He added that the correspondence should then be published in the Press, since he regarded publicity as the only sure method of countering Russian propaganda. When, therefore, the Zinoviev letter was received in London, the Foreign Office, after taking what steps they could to verify its authenticity, sent it to Mr MacDonald, who was conducting a flying election campaign from Scotland to Wales, together with a draft of the proposed Note to Mr Rakowsky. The papers reached the Prime Minister at Aberavon. He made several alterations to the draft in his own handwriting and returned it to the Foreign Office. He neither initialled the draft, nor suggested that he would like to see a fair copy. By the time the amended draft had reached the Foreign Office it had been learnt that the *Daily Mail* had also obtained a copy of the Zinoviev letter and intended to publish it in their morning edition. On hearing of this Sir Eyre Crowe, Permanent Under-Secretary at the Foreign Office, authorised the immediate despatch of the Note to Mr Rakowsky and the communication of the whole correspondence to the Press:

> 'What would have been the impression', wrote Sir Eyre Crowe to the Prime Minister on October 25, 'if—as would inevitably happen—it was discovered that the Foreign Office had been in possession of the incriminating document for some time, but had concealed this fact and had refrained from all action? Would it not have been said that information vitally concerning the security of the Empire had been deliberately suppressed during the elections, which were meanwhile to be affected by Bolshevik propaganda? I thought it would be wrong to allow my Government, and my Prime Minister personally, to be exposed to such a calumnious charge if it could be avoided. This was one of my motives in so strongly urging a public and instant protest.'

A copy of Sir Eyre Crowe's letter of explanation was sent to the King at Sandringham:

> 'Under the circumstances', he minuted on October 26, 'Crowe was quite right to publish the letter, although it has certainly put the P.M. & his Party in a hole & their opponents will make great capital out of it. But it would have been much worse if the *Daily Mail* had published it & the F.O. had remained silent.
>
> I suppose there is *no doubt* that Z's letter is *genuine*? I see the Communists say it is a forgery. (Sgd.) G.R.I.'[q]

The Zinoviev letter, and the covering Note of protest to Mr Rakowsky were published together in all the newspapers on Saturday, October 25, four days before polling day. On that day and the next Mr MacDonald remained silent on the subject, thereby increasing the bewilderment of his followers and the suspicions of his opponents. On Monday afternoon at Cardiff the Prime Minister made a jumbled reference to the matter in a speech which merely added to the confusion. Polling took place on Wednesday, October 29. The Conservative Party won 413 seats, thereby obtaining a majority over the other two Parties combined. Labour lost forty-two seats and the Liberals over a hundred, their numbers in Parliament being reduced to forty. Inevitably there were those who ascribed these results to the shock occasioned to the public by the issue, four days before the poll, of the Zinoviev letter. Assuredly these sensational revelations induced many who would normally have abstained to record their votes: but it must be emphasised that, although the Labour Party lost a number of seats, they actually gained a million more votes than they had been accorded in 1923. Such damage as was done to them by the publication of this letter of dubious authenticity was certainly neither deep nor durable.

At 5.30 p.m. on November 4 Mr Ramsay MacDonald was received by the King, who accepted his resignation. The King assured the retiring Prime Minister 'that he would always regard him as a friend and that, whether in office or out of office, His Majesty trusted that he could always look to him to do his best for the country and for the Throne'.[r] 'I like him', the King noted in his diary more curtly, 'and have always found him quite straight.'

At 7.0 the same evening the King sent for Mr Baldwin and entrusted him with the formation of a new Government. He urged him to come 'to really close and powerful grips with such questions as housing, unemployment, and cost of food and education' and to select for this purpose 'able, efficient and energetic administrators'. He suggested that it would be very welcome to himself if Mr Austen Chamberlain were chosen for the post of Foreign Secretary:[s]

> 'The King', Lord Stamfordham recorded, 'dwelt upon the importance of combating the idea of anything like class war, which the extremists in the Labour Party were inclined to make a sort of war-cry. The Opposition would come back to Westminster disappointed and embittered: and the King expressed an earnest hope that the Prime Minister would restrain his followers from doing anything in the House of Commons to irritate their opponents, and even to refrain from replying to, or in any way taking notice of, attacks and recriminations which may be initiated by the Opposition. Otherwise it is to be feared that there may be disagreeable incidents and unruly disorder in the House.'[t]

The Conservative Government was sworn in on November 7.[1] On December 9 the King opened the new Parliament in state:

> 'My speech was, I think, the longest on record & took 20 minutes to read. The crown gave me an awful headache. I could not have borne it much longer.'

---

[1] The main appointments in Mr Baldwin's second Government were as follows:

Foreign Office, Mr Austen Chamberlain: Lord President of the Council, Lord Curzon: Lord Chancellor, Lord Cave: Lord Privy Seal, Lord Salisbury: Chancellor of the Exchequer, Mr Winston Churchill: Home Office, Sir William Joynson-Hicks: Colonies, Mr Leo Amery: S. of S. for War, Sir Laming Worthington Evans: S. of S. for India, Lord Birkenhead: S. of S. for Air, Sir Samuel Hoare: First Lord of the Admiralty, Mr Bridgeman: Board of Trade, Sir Philip Lloyd-Graeme: Minister of Health, Mr Neville Chamberlain: Agriculture, Mr Edward Wood: Education, Lord Eustace Percy: Chancellor of the Duchy, Lord Robert Cecil.

CHAPTER XXIV

THE STORM BEFORE THE CALM

1925–1926

Mr Baldwin leaves the conduct of Foreign Policy to the Foreign Office—
Mr Austen Chamberlain's ideas and policy—Fate of the Geneva
Protocol—The idea of a Security Pact—Lord D'Abernon's letters to
the King—Herr von Schubert's memorandum—Negotiations and
signature of the Locarno Treaties—Death of Queen Alexandra—
Germany's membership of the League Council—Spain's objections—
The King writes to King Alfonso—Mr Baldwin's moderation in home
politics—Mr Churchill returns to the gold standard—The King's
Mediterranean cruise—The Coal crisis—Mr A. J. Cook—Mr Bald-
win surrenders and promises a subsidy—Sir Herbert Samuel as chair-
man of the Royal Commission—The subsidy is to be discontinued—
Mr Cook forces the T.U.C. to support the miners—The General
Strike of May 4–May 12, 1926—The King's anxiety—He preaches
moderation—He is opposed to any provocative legislation—Sir
Herbert Samuel intervenes—The T.U.C. abandon the miners and
call off the General Strike—The King's Message to his people—The
Coal Strike continues—The King sees no objection to the Russian
Trades Unions providing relief—Mr Churchill's action—The Coal
strike ends on November 11, 1926.

(1)

MR BALDWIN was an indolent and therefore unassuming man. Sharing
as he did the solid, sentimental virtues of the English bourgeoisie, he
also possessed an intuitive understanding of the thoughts and feelings
of the proletariat. In that he never strove to be clever, he conveyed
the impression that he never sought to outwit. It was this impression,
fortified by decency of heart and mind, that enabled him to sur-
mount during the course of his unexpected career three crises of great
delicacy. He was not a man addicted to intellectual analysis: he
regarded logical processes as un-English: he preferred to rely upon
instinct, and would sniff and snuff at problems like an elderly
spaniel. Even when sitting at question time in the House of Commons, he would sniff frequently at the order-paper in his hand. Unlike most Prime Ministers, he had no desire at all to display or vaunt
his prowess, charm and power upon the European scene. He was only
too glad to entrust the direction of Foreign Policy to the Foreign
Minister and his staff.

Mr Austen Chamberlain was well prepared to profit by this free
opportunity. In him the administrative capacity of the Chamberlain

404

family was lightened by imaginative sentiment. He envisaged international problems as floating shapes: coloured pink, or blue, or mauve: whereas his brother, Mr Neville Chamberlain, was inclined to interpret affairs in terms of typewritten maxims, absorbed during his early Birmingham manhood and thus only rarely applicable to continental temperaments or an altering age.

One of Mr Austen Chamberlain's first actions on assuming charge of the Foreign Office was to summon to his room a conference of all the senior, and some of the junior, members of his staff. As a result of this conference a comprehensive memorandum was prepared, indicating the number and complexity of our foreign commitments and suggesting that economies must now be made. Finality was impossible: it would be difficult indeed to achieve stability: but some suggestion of safety, some sense of security, could with skill and persistence be conveyed. It might take many years before the old Concert of Europe, with its admirable balance of power, could be recreated: meanwhile it was essential, while not damaging our close connection with France, to do something to salve the septic inflammation between that country and Germany and to reintroduce the latter into the comity of nations. This was all the more necessary, the memorandum contended, in view of the disappearance of Russia as a factor accountable in the European balance of power. For the moment, 'impending and imponderable', Russia was detached from European affairs; the day might come when she constituted the most menacing of all European uncertainties. It was thus 'in spite of Russia, even because of Russia', that a policy of security must be framed.

Mr Austen Chamberlain was in full accord with such conceptions and anxious to further a policy of general appeasement. He had never approved of Lord Curzon's combative attitude, or of what he regarded as Lord Robert Cecil's impracticable fanaticism. 'It seems to me', he had written, 'that we are becoming the scold of Europe. We run about shaking our fists in people's faces.'[a] He determined therefore to grasp hands.

The Geneva Protocol which Mr MacDonald had accepted subject to the approval of Parliament, and which M. Herriot had actually signed, and the French Chamber ratified, was unpopular with the Conservative Party and disliked in the Dominions. With the fall of Mr MacDonald and the advent of Mr Baldwin, it was evident that there was no prospect at all of the new House of Commons accepting the Protocol. Before, however, finally denouncing it, Mr

Chamberlain realised that it would be necessary to offer something in its place. An Anglo-French regional alliance under the League of Nations would only emphasise our commitments without relieving our anxieties. What he desired was to reach some tripartite pact between France, Great Britain and Germany, whereby Germany should enter voluntarily and as an equal partner into joint pledges of non-aggression. In this idea he was warmly supported by Lord D'Abernon, His Majesty's gifted and most influential Ambassador in Berlin.[1]

The Germans themselves had for some time been fiddling and fumbling with the idea that some such 'safety curtain' might offer a way out of their difficulties.[2] It was not, however, until January 20, 1925, that Herr von Schubert, Secretary of State at the German Foreign Office, handed to Lord D'Abernon a specific proposal for a pact under which the Western European Powers would pledge themselves not to resort to war and would enter jointly into a new agreement providing for the perpetual demilitarisation of the Rhineland as a substitute for Articles 42 and 43 of the Treaty of Versailles.

The King was much impressed by this offer. 'Very interesting', he minuted.[b] 'Surely this would give France every security she would possibly wish for & for as many years as she likes?'

'If', Lord D'Abernon wrote to His Majesty on February 9,[c] 'the Allies can be persuaded to negotiate rapidly and to treat the present German

---

[1] Sir Edgar Vincent, who was created Lord D'Abernon in 1914, had spent most of his early youth in the Near East and as Governor of the Imperial Ottoman Bank from 1889–1897 had made a considerable private fortune. After seven years in Parliament as Conservative Member for Exeter, and after serving on several Royal Commissions, he was in 1920 chosen by Mr Lloyd George as our first post-war Ambassador at Berlin. His knowledge of finance and his compelling personality gave him immense influence with successive German Governments. He had been the first to see the need of establishing what he called 'a safety curtain' between France and Germany. He was a man of energy and culture. He married Lady Helen Duncombe, the most beautiful woman of her time. He died in 1941.

[2] Chancellor Cuno on December 31, 1922, and again on January 2, 1923, had made some such suggestion. In the German Reparation Note of May 2, 1923, a non-aggression pact on a reciprocal basis had been tentatively proposed. On September 2, 1923, in a speech at Stuttgart, Dr Stresemann had himself offered France and Belgium voluntary 'guarantees of security'. On February 11, 1924, the German Embassy in London addressed a clumsy memorandum to the Foreign Office suggesting security guarantees, providing that their 'sovereignty' over the Rhineland remained intact. None of these overtures met with any real response.

Government with a certain degree of confidence, I believe that a Pact of Non-Aggression which would give the French real security and which would, at the same time, give Europe a much enhanced prospect of peace, can be arranged.'

The King immediately addressed to Mr Chamberlain a letter urging that 'now is a unique, but perhaps only a passing, moment, and one not to be lost to expedite the work of peace.'ᵈ Mr Chamberlain's reply of February 9, 1925, does credit to his statesmanship:ᵉ

'My dear Stamfordham
    I am working entirely in the spirit of His Majesty's wishes. It is not an easy task, for the French are very fearful and therefore often unwise and aggravating, and the Germans seem to be singularly obtuse to their own interests and the effect of what they say and do upon French opinion.
    I regard it as the first task of statesmanship to set to work to make the new position of Germany tolerable to the German people in the hope that, as they regain prosperity under it, they may in time become reconciled to it and be unwilling to put their fortunes again to the desperate hazard of war. I am working not for today or tomorrow but for some date like 1950 or 1960 when German strength will have returned and when the prospect of war will again cloud the horizon, unless the risks of war are still too great to be rashly incurred and the actual conditions too tolerable to be jeopardised on a gambler's throw. It is on the realisation of this double factor that the hope of permanent peace depends. I believe the key to the solution is to be found in allaying French fears, and that unless we find means to do this we may be confronted with a complete breakdown of our friendly relations with France and an exacerbation of her attitude towards Germany.
    It is not an easy task that confronts His Majesty's Government and His Foreign Secretary, but His Majesty will see how strong have been the representations that I have recently made to Monsieur Herriot and how carefully I watch and welcome any advance in the attitude of the German Government.'

(4)

The discussion that followed upon Herr von Schubert's memorandum of January 20, 1925, might well have drained away into the sands of inertia had it not been for Mr Chamberlain's unremitting vigilance and pliancy. Varied difficulties arose. The British made it perfectly clear that, although they would gladly enter into a Pact of Non-Aggression covering Germany's Western frontier, they were not equally prepared to guarantee the Polish corridor. Security on the eastern frontier must, in so far as Great Britain was concerned, be based upon the Covenant of the League of Nations: it would therefore be essential to secure Germany's immediate entry into the League as a permanent Council Member. In France, the fall of M. Herriot and the succession of M. Briand caused only a momentary interruption. More serious was the election, on the death of Herr Ebert on February 28, of Field Marshal Hindenburg as President of the German Republic. It was feared in Paris that the hero of Tannenberg and the idol of the Junkers might seek to counter Dr Stresemann's policy of conciliation. It was, moreover, evident that the artificers of the policy—Lord D'Abernon, Mr Chamberlain, M. Briand and Dr Stresemann—were in advance of their own public opinions, and that caution and tact would be required if the scheme were not to provoke opposition in the French Chamber, the Reichstag, and even the House of Commons.

The four artificers of Locarno, although temporarily blended for a common purpose, were of contrasting type. Lord D'Abernon possessed all the impulse, virtuosity, glamour and impatience of a Renaissance patrician. Mr Chamberlain combined the starched appearance of a city magnate with boyish emotionalism and adult force. M. Briand, with his heavy Breton face stuck neckless and awry upon heavy Breton shoulders, would suddenly allow his imagination to lash his shrewdness into an idealistic escapade. Dr Stresemann's physical appearance reflected the composite nature of his character and mind. The thick neck reminded observers that he was the son of a Berlin publican; the bald bullet head suggested Prussian obstinacy and rage; the pallid face and delicate white hands denoted sensitiveness and refinement; the small, watchful, restless, pink-lidded eyes flashed suspicion; the way his tongue would at moments dart between red lips indicated almost reptilian quickness and resource; his ears were huge. A Berliner, it would be supposed, with all the wit and pugnacity of a Berliner; a patriot who suffered horribly from his country's collapse; a man of power forced by bitter circumstances to become excessively adroit. Between these four different men Dr Benes (who had not at that date adopted the slow movements of an elder statesman) scuttled rapidly: proposing, soothing, stimulating, mediating, with infinite good intention, persistence and ingenuity.

The almost hysterical jubilation that greeted the Locarno treaties, the reaction that set in thereafter, have obscured the fact that they constituted a remarkable diplomatic achievement. Germany of her own free will had accepted some of the most vital provisions imposed upon her by the Treaty of Versailles. Had it not been for the economic crisis of 1930 to 1931 and the advent of Hitler,

Locarno might well have justified the hopes that were formed at the time:

> 'The principal part', wrote Lord D'Abernon to the King,[f] 'of the honour which attaches to the Locarno achievement should accrue to England and to Your Majesty's Government. As far back as January 1921 it was constantly urged by me that German Ministers should consider the necessity of affording proof of their pacific orientation, and throughout subsequent years I have contended that there was no satisfactory solution to the problem of the pacification of Europe except on the basis of mutual security. Unless France were reassured as to the safety of her frontiers, there would always be anxiety and unrest. Unless, on the other hand, security was reciprocal and Germany was guaranteed against the recurrence of episodes such as the Ruhr invasion, it would be impossible for the German people to settle down and pursue the policy of conciliation. . . .'

On October 16, 1925, which happened to be Mr Chamberlain's birthday, the treaties were initialled at Locarno amid scenes of almost orgiac gush. 'I felt myself', wrote Mr Chamberlain to Sir William Tyrrell, 'a little child again in spirit.'[g] On December 1 the final signature took place in London in circumstances of greater dignity. 'This morning', the King recorded in his diary, 'the Locarno Pact was signed at the Foreign Office. I pray this may mean peace for many years. Why not for ever?'[1]

The relief experienced by the King at this first important step towards the pacification of Europe was clouded by a personal calamity. On December 1, 1924, Queen Alexandra had celebrated her eightieth birthday at Sandringham, surrounded by her children

---

[1] There were seven Locarno Treaties, namely: (1) The Treaty of Mutual Guarantee between Germany, Belgium, France, Great Britain and Italy. Under this the signatories guaranteed the inviolability of the German-Belgian and the German-French frontiers as fixed by the Treaty of Versailles. Great Britain and Italy were committed to go to war if France attacked Germany or Germany attacked France. (2) Four arbitration treaties between Germany, France, Belgium and Germany, Poland and Czechoslovakia. (3) Two treaties of guarantee between France and Poland and Czechoslovakia.

In addition there was a collective Note addressed to Germany by the allies and explaining the implications of Article XVI of the Covenant of the League of Nations.

The logical consequences of the Treaties of Locarno were the evacuation of occupied Rhine territories and the entry of Germany into the League of Nations.

The Locarno Pact was broken when Hitler invaded the Rhineland in March 1936.

and grandchildren. The death of her devoted comptroller, Sir Dighton Probyn, at the age of ninety-one; the realisation that her beloved friend and companion Miss Charlotte Knollys, had also reached the mature age of ninety;[1] her own failing memory and utter deafness; all these combined early in 1925 to quench even her un-flinching vitality. 'My poor old head', she had written to the King in October 1923, 'is coming to a break-down soon.' 'I shall soon', she wrote to him on March 9, 1925, 'be going.' It was not, however, until the following autumn that this gay, loving, generous life reached its end. She died at Sandringham on November 20 within eleven days of her eighty-first birthday:

> 'Darling Motherdear', the King wrote on November 22, 'was this morning taken to our little church where she has worshipped for 62 years.'

On November 23 the funeral took place in Westminster Abbey. On November 27 Queen Alexandra was buried beside King Edward VII in St George's Chapel at Windsor. All the memories of childhood dependence and adult devotion flowed back in solemn gratitude: the King experienced that stark moment of abandonment when a man realises suddenly that he is no longer a son.

(3)

The heavenly alchemy of the Locarno spirit, the triumphant splendour of those autumn days, did not prove of long endurance. Almost immediately the vanity of nations came to mar that glorious dawn.

The implication of the treaties had been that Germany would immediately be admitted to the League of Nations on the basis of equality with the Great Powers and therefore with a permanent seat on the Council.[2] A special session of the Assembly was announced for March 1926 in order to give effect to these arrangements. Difficulties

---

[1] Miss Charlotte Knollys actually survived until April 1930, dying at the age of ninety-five.

[2] Under Article 4 of the Covenant, the Council of the League was to be composed of the representatives of the Principal Allied and Associated Powers (i.e. France, Great Britain, Italy, Japan and the United States) sitting as Permanent Members, with four non-permanent members from other States. These four seats were originally filled by the representatives of Belgium, Greece, Spain and Brazil, who came to regard themselves as semi-permanent members. When, therefore, it was proposed to admit Germany as a Permanent Member both Spain and Brazil (as well as

410

immediately arose. M. Briand suggested that, in order to balance the grant of a permanent seat to Germany, a similar seat should simultaneously be granted to Poland. Spain and Brazil demanded, under threats of vetoing the admission of Germany, and even of themselves withdrawing from the League, that the Covenant should be amended so as to admit as many as nine permanent members. Dr Stresemann was already having difficulty with the German nationalists, who regarded the League as a mere engine of the Versailles *Diktat*; he pointed out that if the permanent membership were thus to become inflated, it might be difficult for him to induce the Reichstag to support Germany's application for admission. The King entirely agreed with the view that no revision of the Covenant should be attempted until after Germany had been admitted as a permanent member:

'His Majesty', wrote Lord Stamfordham to Sir Austen Chamberlain[1] on February 18, 1926,[*h*] 'wishes me to express his earnest hope that the Government will not agree to any proposal to admit either Poland or Spain into the Council until Germany's entry is a *fait accompli*, when she will then have a voice in considering any such additions of membership—otherwise His Majesty foresees a dangerous possibility of the arrangements with Germany proving abortive.'

Owing to these disturbances it proved impossible to elect Germany at the special Assembly held in March, and all that could be done was to appoint a committee to consider and report on the future composition of the Council. It became evident from the discussions in this Committee that the claim of Spain and others to be accorded permanent seats would not be successful:

'This', wrote Sir Austen Chamberlain to the King on May 28[*i*], 'will be a cruel blow to one of Spain's most cherished aspirations and there is reason to fear that she may now decide to withdraw from the League. The retention of Spain at the cost of the exclusion of Germany would be too high a price to pay. At the same time, the power and prestige of the League depend largely on its universality and the withdrawal of Spain would be a serious blow to its prestige.'

China and Poland) claimed also to become Permanent Members. In June 1926 a compromise was effected under which an intermediate class of semi-permanent members would be created. Spain and Brazil then notified their withdrawal from the League. Spain was later induced to reconsider her decision. Brazil remained obstinate and ceased to be a member of the League.

[1] On the signature of the Treaties of Locarno Mr Chamberlain had been created a Knight of the Garter.

Sir Austen was so anxious to prevent this damaging withdrawal that he took the most exceptional step of asking the King to write a personal letter to King Alfonso urging moderation:

'Sir Austen has', he wrote, 'no need to remind Your Majesty of the potent influence exercised at critical moments by a personal appeal from the Sovereign of this country and Empire. Sir Austen thinks that King Alfonso might be peculiarly sensitive to any sympathy shown by Your Majesty, for the Spaniards are a very proud race and in this matter their pride is touched.'

The King immediately adopted Sir Austen's advice. In a letter dated the 31st of May 1926,[j] he begged King Alfonso to use his influence with the Spanish Government to persuade them to accept the sub-committee's report. So far from losing prestige by such a surrender, Spain would, if possible, enhance it by action 'in such true accord with the spirit of the League':

'My confidence', the King concluded, 'in the inborn generosity of the Spanish character emboldens me to hope for a favourable response to my appeal: and to find in it another striking proof of the devotion of Spain to the League of Nations and to the cause of Peace for which it stands.'

King Alfonso replied to this on June 9. Although his letter[k] began with an affectionate '*Querido Gorge*' [*sic*] and ended 'I remain your affectionate brother and cousin', its style was less characteristic of King Alfonso's directness than of the decorative evasions of a Spanish Government Department:

'As is natural', he wrote, 'we respect any criticism which in this connexion may not quite coincide with our own: but to sever ourselves from the ideal to which we cling of our historic and present position, could only be done at the expense of that intimate satisfaction, and of that appreciation which is exclusively subjective, which are so necessary as stimulants to any endeavour. It is evident that Spain could not continue to interest herself in the work which the League of Nations is so loyally endeavouring to accomplish, so long as her own position in the League is to be of a precarious, or still less of an intermittent, character. . . . I repeat to you once more how happy I should have been if national circumstances had permitted me to agree with your amiable initiative. You will however from your own experience understand how much importance you and I must attach to public opinion.'

In the end Spain yielded to the wishes of the majority and Germany was, somewhat belatedly, admitted to the League in September 1926. By then the Locarno spirit had lost many of its healing properties. In the hope of further easing the wounds that Spain had suffered, the Foreign Secretary had urged Lord Stamfordham to persuade the King to pay a State Visit to Madrid. His efforts were not successful:

> 'I failed', Lord Stamfordham wrote on July 11, 1926,[1] 'to get His Majesty to smile at all upon the idea of a State Visit to Madrid, though I adduced those reasons that appealed to you in favour of such a step. In fact the King's view is that State Visits have ceased to be of any political importance; and he looks forward to the time, say in another year, when he will be in the position to invite King Alfonso to Sandringham on a private visit during the shooting season, when the latter would much enjoy the sport that would be provided for him.'

(4)

At home also the year 1925 appeared at first to presage the end of war conditions and the beginning of what, in disregard of the decencies of the English language, was called 'a return to normalcy'. After the disquiet of minority rule and a three party system, the country welcomed the stability of a Government possessing a majority over all parties combined. It was comforting also to realise that Mr Baldwin was determined to temper authority with moderation. In the first session of the new Parliament the Prime Minister, encouraged by the King's appeal for tact and conciliation, profited by the opportunity afforded him by Mr MacQuisten's motion[1] to deliver a homily upon the organic nature of the State, coupled with a plea for 'industrial peace and spiritual co-partnership'. His speech impressed the House of Commons and convinced the public that Mr Baldwin was a man immune to partisan prejudice or rancour, whose central purpose was to serve the Nation as a whole. Mr Churchill also, in his first budget, created an impression of confidence and courage. The pound sterling had for some time been approaching its pre-war parity and the Chancellor of the Exchequer decided that the moment had come to 'look the dollar in the face'. The return to the gold standard, although criticised by Mr J. M. Keynes and some of the industrialists, was welcomed with general pride: there were many

---

[1] A Scottish Conservative, Mr MacQuisten, introduced a Bill to amend the law relating to the political levy imposed upon their members by the Trade Unions. This threatened to revive the old controversy about the Osborne judgment and to call in question the conciliatory legislation of 1913. Mr Baldwin rejected the proposal on the ground that it would only cause extreme bitterness in Labour ranks. In so doing he was in full accord with the excellent advice the King had given him.

financiers who rejoiced that henceforward London would retain unchallenged its position as the banking centre of the world.

On February 15 the King, who since his childhood had been subject to bad colds, developed a bronchial attack. For thirteen days he was unable to write his diary in his own hand: a breach of habit that indicated serious illness. On his recovery, the doctors insisted upon a Mediterranean cruise. The older the King grew, the more deep-seated became his repugnance to foreign travel. He surrendered most unwillingly. On March 19, accompanied by the Queen he joined the *Victoria and Albert* at Genoa for a cruise in the Sicilian sun. He avoided all official functions; he was hospitable to the British residents in the ports he visited; and he spent much of his time reading Sir Sidney Lee's biography of King Edward VII. 'Very interesting & well written', he commented, 'but not always quite accurate.' He returned to London on April 25.

It seemed thereafter that the placid routine of pre-war days was to be resumed. On June 3 there took place the Trooping of the Colour, to which ceremony the King had personally invited Marshal Foch. On June 5 he paid an official visit to Stoke-on-Trent and Newcastle. On June 9 he was present at the inauguration of Bristol University. The following week he was at Windsor for the Ascot meeting. On June 29 he opened Canada House, proceeding thereafter on visits to Newmarket and Knowsley. Yet already the bright sunshine of expected prosperity was being dimmed by gathering clouds:

'The King feels', Lord Stamfordham wrote to the Prime Minister on June 21, 'you will not be surprised to hear with how much concern he regards the continued depression in our trade and industries and the marked increase in unemployment. From all sides—(and the King meets people of different classes and occupations)—His Majesty hears of the gravity of the situation and the attitude almost of despair of coping with it. Apparently there are many and adverse opinions as to the cause of, and remedy for, these unhappy conditions: but the King earnestly hopes that before Parliament adjourns for the autumn recess, if not sooner, the Government may be able to put before the country some definite policy to deal with, and if possible to avert, the dangerous state of things with which we shall otherwise be confronted in the coming winter.'*m*

The mining industry, which during 1923 and 1924 had enjoyed a temporary boom, found itself exposed after the evacuation of the Ruhr to the full force of foreign competition. In the spring of 1925 abortive discussions took place between the owners and the miners and on the last day of June the former gave a month's notice of their intention to terminate the existing agreements and to replace them by others more severe. The miners, under the dynamic leadership of Mr A. J. Cook,[1] who was satisfied in his own mind that the Trades Union Council would support his action by declaring sympathetic strikes, rejected these proposals. The dispute reached a climax in the last days of July.

The King, who was at Goodwood, followed the quick developments of those three days with acute anxiety:

'July 29. I am very anxious & worried about the coal strike. I fear a strike now is inevitable at the end of the week. It will play the devil in the country. I never seem to get any peace in this world. Feel very low and depressed.

July 30. I fear a coal strike is inevitable & I shall have to return to London tomorrow. Just my luck!

July 31. Last night the Cabinet agreed to offer the owners & miners financial assistance for nine months, pending a Royal Commission on the working of the Coal Mines, which they accepted. So, thank God! there will be no strike now. I am much relieved.'

This last-minute surrender on the part of the Government did not, however, meet with universal approval. Lord Stamfordham was of opinion that Mr Baldwin had been forced, much against his will, to give way to a syndicalist agitation.[n] There were others who felt that it was a disgraceful act on the part of the Government thus to bribe the owners not to serve their lock-out notices.[o] Mr Ramsay MacDonald, after attending the Trades Union Congress at Scarborough in September, feared that the triumph of the left wing elements in the Council would have unfortunate consequences:

'The whole Congress', he wrote to Lord Stamfordham,[p] 'was dominated by the belief that in the Coal dispute non-political industrial action brought the Government to its knees & the present state of feverish uncertainty and of widespread ill-will was never absent from the minds of the delegates. . . . The situation is not good. There is a

---

[1] Mr Cook had started life as a Baptist lay preacher and after the publication of his bellicose pamphlet *The Miners' Next Step* became Secretary of the Miners' Federation and a member of the T.U.C. He believed in using the strike weapon for political purposes and described himself as 'a humble follower of Lenin'. After the failure of the General Strike he paid a visit to Russia, where he suffered much disillusion. Thereafter he used his influence to promote compromise and conciliation. He was a man of honesty and intelligence. His death in 1931 was a serious loss to the Trades Union movement.

widespread feeling that strong language and brave resolutions should be adopted; and loyalty to the poor devils who have to bear the burdens of action is not very strong.'

Mr MacDonald was only partially comforted by the firm anti-communist line taken in the following week at the Labour Party Conference in Liverpool. He feared that the poison of syndicalism had corroded the rank and file of the Trades Union movement. His pessimism was not unfounded.

The Royal Commission promised by Mr Baldwin was constituted under the chairmanship of Sir Herbert Samuel, and issued a report on March 11, 1926. This report advocated a thorough reorganisation of the entire industry. The royalty owners should be bought out; many of the smaller companies should be amalgamated; and wide technical improvements should be introduced. The Commission was not in favour of repealing the 1919 legislation limiting underground working to seven hours; they suggested a small reduction of wages, less drastic than that demanded by the owners; and above all they urged that the subsidy should not be continued. The report was, after a fortnight's delay, accepted by the Government. Mr Cook, while agreeing to the recommendations regarding reorganisation, stubbornly refused to accept or consider any reduction in wages. As the month of April came to its close, and the expiration of the subsidy was impending, the pressure exercised by Mr Cook on the unfortunate Mr Pugh, Chairman of the T.U.C., became intense. The country awoke to the fact that they were faced with the imminent calamity of a General Strike.

(5)

On the afternoon of Saturday, May 1, the T.U.C. decided to call a sympathetic strike in certain vital industries, such as the transport services and the printing trade, to begin at midnight on Monday, May 3. At 9.0 p.m. that Saturday evening an informal discussion took place between the Prime Minister, Lord Birkenhead, Sir Arthur Steel-Maitland and the representatives of the T.U.C. The impression was derived that, if the Government were prepared to continue the subsidy for a fortnight, negotiations could be opened. At noon on Sunday, May 2, the Cabinet insisted that the complete withdrawal of all strike notices must be a condition preliminary to any negotiations or to the continuance of a subsidy. This decision was conveyed to Mr Arthur Pugh and Mr J. H. Thomas, and by nine that evening it seemed that the T.U.C. were prepared to urge the miners to accept these conditions.

At 11.0 p.m. on that Sunday evening the Cabinet were still in session when news was received that some compositors and printers had refused to set up the leading article intended for the morrow's *Daily Mail*. The Cabinet attached importance to this seemingly trivial incident. A document was drafted then and there stating that, since the conversations of that afternoon, it had come to the knowledge of the Government that instructions had been issued by the T.U.C. calling for a General Strike to begin on the following Tuesday, and that overt acts had already taken place, including gross interference with the freedom of the Press. The Government therefore demanded that the T.U.C. should publicly repudiate the action taken in regard to the *Daily Mail* article and should issue an immediate and unconditional withdrawal of the instructions for a general strike. This document was handed to Mr Pugh and Mr Thomas by the Prime Minister at 12.45 a.m. on the morning of Monday, May 3. The T.U.C. were unable to contemplate so abject a surrender. The strike was therefore declared on the morning of Tuesday, May 4.

It has since been suggested that the Government deliberately broke off negotiations since they desired to precipitate a trial of strength while conditions were comparatively favourable to themselves. Such an imputation is exaggerated. It is true, however, that whereas the Government had for months been perfecting arrangements to meet just such an emergency, the T.U.C. were hesitant, bewildered, disunited and wholly unprepared. It was known that Mr Pugh was frightened and that Mr Thomas had told the T.U.C. on April 30 that the Transport workers would be mad to bring the country to the verge of disaster merely out of sympathy for Mr Cook. The Cabinet may thus have been influenced in their decision by a knowledge of divided counsels among their antagonists as compared to their own unity and resolution. They were encouraged also by the support of the House of Commons and by the helpful attitude of the leaders of the official Labour Party:

'The House of Commons', wrote Mr Baldwin to the King on May 4, 'rose to its greatest heights yesterday. . . . So far from there being any disturbance, the atmosphere throughout the debate was grave, solemn and impressive. . . . The leaders of the Labour Party were sincerely anxious of finding an honourable way out of the position into which they have been led by their own folly.'

The Government were also much comforted during those days by the brilliantly constructive speeches made from the Liberal benches by Sir John Simon, speeches which contrasted with what Mr Baldwin described to the King as Mr Lloyd George's 'vague and indeterminate vacillations, his niggling criticisms of the Government, and his insincere fraternisation with the Labour Party'. The events of those nine anxious days served to increase the prestige of Sir John Simon almost as much as they increased that of the Prime Minister himself.

On the morning of Monday, May 3, the King had left Windsor for Buckingham Palace. During the period that the strike lasted he remained in London, receiving almost hourly reports on the situation and giving audiences to Ministers every morning and afternoon. As always in moments of real danger his tendency towards discouragement was replaced by buoyant obstinacy: 'I have', he wrote in his diary on May 7, 'passed through many anxious times during the last 16 years.' When Mr St Loe Strachey intruded with the suggestion that the King should summon another Buckingham Palace Conference to establish a 'Committee of Reconciliation' the King replied that he 'absolutely declines to entertain the idea of intervention on his part, except, of course, at the request of the Prime Minister.'*q* While urging the Government to take all possible steps to protect from violence or intimidation all those who volunteered to assist in the maintenance of essential services, the King was opposed to anything that might drive the strikers to desperation. When on May 8 the *British Gazette* (an emergency bulletin edited by Mr Winston Churchill) published an announcement that the Armed Forces of the Crown would receive the full support of the Government 'in any action that they may find it necessary to take in an honest endeavour to aid the Civil Power', the King caused an immediate protest to be addressed to the War Office. 'His Majesty', wrote Lord Stamfordham,*r* 'cannot help thinking that this is an unfortunate announcement and already it has received a good deal of adverse criticism.'

A more difficult problem was that raised by the proposal to place an embargo on Trades Union funds and to prevent the payment to strikers of monies received from foreign sources. The Cabinet decided that on May 11 they would introduce a Bill 'to amend the law with respect to illegal strikes' under which it would be an indictable offence to devote Trades Union funds to a strike 'which is intended to intimidate or coerce the Government or the community'. Pending the passage of such legislation, an Order in Council was issued under the Emergency Proclamation prohibiting banks from paying out monies to any person acting in opposition to the National interest. The King warned the Government of the undesirability, at a moment when the strikers were behaving with moderation, of passing such provocative Orders and Bills. He informed the Home Secretary and Attorney General that 'anything done to touch the pockets of those who are now only existing on strike pay might cause exasperation and serious reprisals on the part of the sufferers'. He also impressed upon the Prime Minister that, in his judgment, it would be 'a grave mistake to do anything which might be interpreted as confiscation, or to provoke the strikers, who until now had been remarkably quiet'.[8] The King's warnings had their effect: the Cabinet decided to introduce no provocative legislation unless it became essential to do so; milder counsels prevailed.

After the strike had continued for eight days, it became evident that the strikers would not succeed in intimidating the ordinary citizen or coercing the Government. Sir Herbert Samuel, profiting by the authority he had acquired as Chairman of the Royal Commission, considered the moment had come to intervene. He issued a memorandum on his own responsibility advocating measures 'suitable for adoption and likely to promote a settlement in the coal industry'. He recommended that the Government should grant a final subsidy of three million pounds in order to restart the industry and that the recommendations of the Commission's report should immediately be put into effect. The T.U.C., who by that time were all too anxious to grasp at any means of escaping from their predicament, sought to persuade the miners to accept Sir Herbert's mediatory proposals. Mr Cook was still adamant in rejecting any basis of negotiation that implied a reduction of wages. The T.U.C. thereupon refused 'to follow the Miners Executive in a policy of mere negation'.

At noon on May 12 Mr Arthur Pugh came to Downing Street and informed the Prime Minister of the unconditional withdrawal of the General Strike. In writing to the King, Mr Baldwin described Mr Pugh's statement as 'short, simple, dignified and courageous'. On entering the House of Commons that afternoon Mr Baldwin received an ovation; it was noticed that Mr Ramsay MacDonald's appearance was not greeted by his own adherents. The Mother of Parliaments then turned her attention to the second reading of the Merchandise Marks Bill.

'At 1.0. p.m.', the King wrote in his diary for Wednesday, May 12, 'I got the good news that the T.U.C. had been to the Prime Minister & informed him that the General Strike was forthwith called off unconditionally. It is indeed a great relief to me as I have been very anxious about the situation. Our old country can well be proud of itself, as during the last nine days there has been a strike in which 4 million men have been affected; not a shot has been fired & no one killed; it shows what a wonderful people we are. . . The Government have remained firm & backed up by the people have won a great victory for law & order. . . . Saw Sir W. Horwood (Head of the Police) & congratulated him on the splendid way in which the Police carried out their arduous duties during the strike. Hardly any of them were seriously injured even.'

It was customary at the time to congratulate ourselves on the wonderful temper manifested by all concerned and to laud this manifestation of British sense and good-humour. There was some justification for such complacency. The King issued the following message from Buckingham Palace on the evening of 12th May:

'To My People,
    The Nation has just passed through a period of extreme anxiety. It was today announced that the general strike had been brought to an end. At such a moment it is supremely important to bring together all my people to confront the difficult situation which still remains. This task requires the cooperation of all able and well-disposed men in the country. Even with such help it will be difficult, but it will not be impossible. Let us forget whatever elements of bitterness the events of the past few days may have created, only remembering how steady and how orderly the country has remained, though severely tested, and forthwith address ourselves to the task of bringing into being a peace which will be lasting because, forgetting the past, it looks only to the future with the hopefulness of a united people.

(Signed) George R.I.'

In cold fact, however, there had during the strike been as many as 1760 prosecutions for incitement and 1389 for violence. Nor was any great confidence felt by those who were cognisant of the situation that, had the strike continued for many days longer, tranquillity and order could have been maintained. As it was, the miners, feeling that they had been betrayed by the traitor Thomas and the pusillanimous Pugh, determined to continue the strike upon their own. In vain did the Government pass through Parliament legislation giving effect to the recommendations of the Royal Commission. The miners remained obdurate. Certain Conservatives, on discovering that with the approval of the Soviet Government monies were being sent to the strikers by the Russian Council of Trades Unions, demanded that the Trade Agreement with Russia should be denounced and all diplomatic relations severed. The Government confined themselves to addressing to Moscow a mildly-worded protest. The King disapproved of this action:

> 'The King', wrote Lord Stamfordham to the Home Secretary on June 14, 1926, 'is a little anxious with regard to our remonstrances made to the Soviet Government about the money coming from Russia in aid of the families of the miners who are on strike. His Majesty is sure you and the Government will differentiate between money sent in aid of the General Strike (to which we could unquestionably take exception) and that contributed on behalf of those suffering from the Coal Strike. It would be disastrous if the Government's action could in any way justify a cry from the Socialist Party that the former were attempting to stop financial aid from Russia or from any other country to save the miners' women and children from starvation.'[1]

Slowly as the year proceeded the miners began, one by one, to drift back to work. In August Mr Churchill, in the absence of the Prime Minister, made a further approach to the Miners' Executive. In order to save the latter's face, regional agreements were negotiated, district by district, on a basis of a reduction of wages and an eight-hour day. On November 11, 1926, the coal strike came to an end. It had cost the country one hundred and fifty millions in loss of exports alone; the unemployment figure had risen to over two million. Yet the tragedy was felt to be a common tragedy and not a purely class tragedy; there was little heresy hunting and no victimisation. Every section of the community felt sorry for the other sections, as well as for themselves.

CHAPTER XXV

A QUIET INTERLUDE

1927–1930

A period of calm follows on the Locarno Treaties and the General Strike
—Domestic Legislation—The Trades Disputes Act—The Prayer
Book controversy—The King resumes the regularity of his life—The
visits of foreign potentates—The King's indignation at criticism in
the House of Commons of the visit of the Duke and Duchess of York
to Australia—Is the King entitled to comment on what passes in
Parliament?—The King's constant desire to maintain the standards
of public life—First symptoms of the King's illness—An operation
performed on December 12—The move to Bognor—The King leaves
Bognor for Windsor—His relapse—Return to London—The Thanksgiving Service followed by a second operation—Slow convalescence—
The General Election of May 1929—Mr Baldwin resigns—Mr
Ramsay MacDonald forms the Second Labour Government.

(1)

THE period between 1926 and 1931, the period that is between the
General Strike and the formation of the National Government, was
both abroad and at home the least politically eventful of King
George's reign. It is true that during those five years important
changes were made in the structure of the British Commonwealth;
that India by successive stages progressed towards independence;
and that many ancient imperial maxims were modified or discarded.
These developments, in that they can best be treated separately,
will be given later consideration. In the present chapter, now that
the ground has become less encumbered, it is hoped to advance with
quicker strides.

In Europe, the Locarno treaties and the entry of Germany into
the League of Nations had undoubtedly relieved tension and created
a momentary sense of safety. The Weimar Republic, under the venerable and unifying aegis of President Hindenburg, and in the confident expectation of an early evacuation of the Rhineland, had begun
to forget about the Treaty of Versailles, to settle down to the comfort
of a stabilised currency, and to exploit the delights of intellectual
adventure and sensual relaxation. The spectre of reparations, as the
spectre of Allied Debts, came to be regarded as bogies, terrifying only
to the uninitiated. An epoch of peace, even of progress, appeared to
be impending.

At home, the position of sedative authority that Mr Baldwin had acquired and the hopes of a trade revival induced at least an expectation of stability. The unemployment figures declined.[1] It was believed that the General Strike and the long-drawn anguish of the coal crisis had discredited the advocates of direct action and suggested to the ordinary worker that a stoppage in one industry was apt to create unemployment in another. In the House of Commons, the Labour Party were, as the Prime Minister reported to the King, 'not so much embittered as dispirited'. 'They do not', he wrote, 'as do other Parties, seem to appreciate to the full the joys and functions of opposition.' At the same time Mr Baldwin was delighted at the progressive elimination of the more unintelligent members of his own Party:

> 'The most noticeable feature', he wrote to the King, 'is the youth and activity of the back-benchers. During the Coalition Government there was an excessive element consisting of men who obviously bore recent traces of newly won and easily acquired prosperity. It is a source of satisfaction to all that this element has been largely diminished and that in its place has appeared a band of keen and ardent young Conservatives, with a genuine desire to serve the public interest, rather than that of any particular class or faction or their own particular selfish interests.'

The domestic legislation introduced during those years by Mr Baldwin's Government was, on the whole, conciliatory. Nobody was surprised when the Prime Minister gently dropped Lord Cave's scheme for the reform of the Second Chamber. The extension of the franchise to women of twenty-one, although denounced by the Harmsworth Press as 'the flapper vote', scarcely raised a ripple of attention. The Derating Bill, and the English Local Government Bill (introduced by Mr Neville Chamberlain with masterly persuasiveness), won general approval. The Trades Disputes Act was more controversial: the Labour Party observed its passage with sullen resentment and a lively expectation that the position would eventually be reversed.[2] Even the raid on the premises of Arcos, the

---

[1] The average monthly figures of unemployment during the seven years following on the General Strike can be summarised as follows:

1926.	1,401,891.	1930.	1,915,237.
1927.	1,111,771.	1931.	2,650,461.
1928.	1,231,109.	1932.	2,745,000.
1929.	1,230,164.		

[2] The 'Trades Disputes and Trades Unions Act 1927' was an inevitable corollary to a General Strike. It declared any strike illegal if designed to

Russian Trade Delegation, which might easily have been exploited as a most farcical and unwarranted solecism, was accepted meekly by the Opposition as little more than an unfortunate episode. Labour, it seemed, was becoming tired of syndicalism and bored by Russia.

It struck foreign observers as strange that the only controversy capable during those years of arousing the fiercer passions was that which, somewhat unexpectedly, arose over the reformed prayer book. Some clergymen of the Church of England had come to adopt practices which were not in strict accord with the instructions laid down in 1662, especially in regard to the reservation of the Sacrament. The Royal Commission of 1906 had pronounced that 'the law of public worship is too narrow for the religious life of the present generation', and had advocated that the 1662 prayer book should be brought up to date, or at least supplemented. This new prayer book was completed in 1927. On March 23 of that year the Archbishop of Canterbury, Dr Randall Davidson, wrote to the King in premature jubilation:[a]

Lambeth Palace, S.E.

'Sir,

An incident has taken place today in English life and in the story of Your Majesty's reign which seems to call for a dutiful communication to Your Majesty from myself. I have only this afternoon left my bed, after a week of influenza & this is the first letter that I write.

I refer of course to the publication today of the *New Prayer Book*, or the *Composite Book*, which will, if it obtains the sanctions which are still required, give new life to the public services of the Church of England while retaining all that we have learned to reverence & love in the Prayer Book of the past. *That* Prayer Book retains its place in the new Book, & may still be used unchanged wherever it is desired. But, as Your Majesty will see from the copy which I herewith enclose there is abundant enrichment with Prayers for the Empire, for Industry, for Commerce, for the Parliaments Overseas, and for much that belongs to the life of what people call a Democratic Age.

Should Your Majesty find that there are any points calling in Your Majesty's view for further enquiry or explanation prior to the Measure going before the Church Assembly and then before Parliament I need

---

coerce the Government by imposing hardship on the community and that to take part in such a strike was an offence in law. No person refusing to take part in an illegal strike could be victimised. Trades Union funds must not be devoted to such a strike. The political levy to be confined to those workers who 'contracted in'. And Civil Servants were not to join unions connected with the T.U.C.

424

THE KING AND MARSHAL FOCH

PRINCESS ELIZABETH AT BOGNOR

not say how ready I am to place myself, at a moment's notice, at Your Majesty's service, for any help that I can render.

I have the honour to be

Sir

Your Majesty's obedient humble servant

(Signed) Randall Cantuar.'

The additions to, or departures from, the 1662 prayer book were not obligatory; they merely furnished a 'permissive alternative': clergymen could either stick to the old practice or take legal advantage of the new. This composite prayer book was passed by the Church Assembly in July and shortly afterwards by a large majority in the House of Lords. On December 15 the House of Commons, mainly owing to the powerful objections cherished by Sir William Joynson-Hicks to the reservation of the sacrament, rejected it by 238 votes to 205. The Bishops, startled by the virulent interest suddenly taken by the House of Commons in ecclesiastical matters, withdrew their composite prayer book quietly, deciding again to submit the book to Parliament once the 'avoidable misunderstandings' that had arisen could be explained away. In March 1928 the book, slightly amended to forestall possible criticism, and accompanied by explanatory statements, was for the second time submitted to Parliament. It was again thrown out by the House of Commons by 266 votes to 220. The situation thereafter remained exactly the same as it had been before.[1] To Dr Randall Davidson the blow was as heavy as it had been unexpected:

> 'No one', wrote the Archbishop of York to Lord Stamfordham,[b] 'can realise better than you how greatly distressed our very dear friend of Canterbury has been by the happenings in the House of Commons. . . . But, though the blow seems rather to have stunned him, and to have taken out the zest of life, Cantuar is bearing up with his usual courage.'

Dr Randall Davidson resigned on November 12, 1928, and was succeeded as Archbishop of Canterbury by the Archbishop of York, Dr Cosmo Gordon Lang.

Had this controversy arisen in 1918 instead of in 1927, the King might have been exposed to a predicament of the kind that he most dreaded and been faced with the odious alternative of deciding

[1] The position is summarised with his accustomed concision by D. C. Somervell on p. 408 of *The Reign of King George V*. 'What', writes Mr Somervell, 'was the result of the rejection of this measure? It was that things remained as they had been before the measure was introduced. Reservation of the sacrament remained in the same category as driving a motor car at more than twenty miles an hour. It continued to be illegal, and it continued to be allowed.'

between two sections of his subjects in a matter of grave emotional significance to each. Until the passage of the Church of England Assembly Act of 1919, it rested with the Sovereign, independently of Parliament, to approve or disapprove canons passed by the Convocations of Canterbury or York. With the passage of that Act the Royal responsibility was assumed by Parliament. The King was therefore able detachedly to observe the dispute arising out of the reformed prayer book from the unassailable fortress of his constitutional position.^c He was glad of this security. Typical of the many protests addressed to him as Defender of the Faith was a petition from a group of Ulster covenanters:

'To our Gracious Sovereign, King George V.

We, some of your most loyal subjects, have for some time past been watching with some alarm and with sore hearts the infamous designs of the Bishops of Canterbury and York, and other Bishops, in their endeavour to bring the Church of England over to the Church of Rome. . . .'

Assuredly the King was fortunate in being relieved by the Act of 1919 of any responsibility in doctrinal matters.[1]

(2)

During the whole of 1927, and for the first ten months of 1928, the King was able, undisturbed by any major foreign or domestic crisis, to enjoy the regularity of life. He was, as has been said, a man who preferred continuity to variation, the familiar to the surprising, the accustomed to the unexpected. His love of orderliness expressed itself in the extreme neatness of his personal habits as in his insistence on punctuality and exactitude on the part of his Ministers and the members of his household. He believed that, with a little forethought, time itself could be made to conform to a pattern; he loved the symmetry of anniversaries, statistics, repetitions, coincidences, and

[1] The above passage was based upon the opinion of Berriedale Keith (*The King and the Imperial Crown*. Chapter XIV, pp. 370–371). The Archbishop of Canterbury has since pointed out that the Act of 1919 in no manner affected the exercise of the prerogative. In giving the Royal Assent to measures passed by the Church Assembly and approved by Parliament, or to canons passed by the two Convocations, the Sovereign, even before the passage of the 1919 Act, possessed no responsibility different from that for ordinary legislation: he acted in ecclesiastical as in lay matters wholly on the 'advice' of Ministers.

426

recurrences; it was a satisfaction to him to arrange his journeys and displacements so that they occurred tidily within the same week of every year. The idea of going abroad, and thereby breaking the rhythm, filled him with distaste.

Although he was averse from paying State visits to foreign potentates, he was perfectly prepared, if the Government so desired, to incur the expense and trouble of entertaining Kings and Presidents in his own home at Buckingham Palace. There is no doubt that these eminent visitors were affected by the splendour of the British Court and impressed by the calm efficiency of the ceremonial, which, following in his father's footsteps, King George had brought to such a degree of perfection that it seemed effortless. Thus in May 1927 M. Doumergue, President of the French Republic ('A nice man & easy to get on with'), paid an official visit to London. In the following July, King Fuad of Egypt spent three days at Buckingham Palace before establishing himself at Claridge's Hotel. 'He speaks French', the King noted, 'and seems quite easy to get on with.' In March 1928 came a State Visit from the King and Queen of Afghanistan. There were other less official visits and many private audiences. In September 1927 King Boris of Bulgaria, a gifted and ill-used monarch, came to Buckingham Palace. The King took an immediate liking to him: 'a very nice boy & talks English quite well.' On November 5 he received King Feisal of Iraq, 'a charming personality'. On May 31 he had given an audience to Mr Charles Lindbergh, who had come to London after his dramatic flight to Le Bourget. The King found him 'A very nice boy & quite modest'. Mr Lindbergh himself, being the staunchest of Republicans and much embarrassed by thrones, was immediately comforted by the breezy questions that the King put to him about the details of his solitary flight. The King could always be relied upon to put unpretentious people at their ease.

It would be an error to suppose that King George, in his unfailing desire to observe the strict proprieties of constitutional theory, was ever subservient to Ministers, or that he hesitated to defend his own rights, privileges and dignities whenever he considered that they were assailed.

On January 26, 1927, the Duke and Duchess of York had left for Australia in order to open the first Parliament to meet at the new Federal capital of Canberra. On February 17 a debate took place in the House of Commons in which Mr Ammon and Mr David Kirkwood suggested that a 'pleasure trip of this kind' should not be undertaken at a moment of industrial depression. In reporting this debate to the King, Mr Baldwin sought to make light of the incident, suggesting that the two Labour members had not seriously meant the vivacious expressions that they had used:

> 'His Majesty', wrote Lord Stamfordham to the Prime Minister on February 21, 'read your report with the interest with which he always follows the graphic, and often amusing, accounts of the debates. But of that on February 17 you take a less serious and, I suppose, more "House of Commons" view than does the King. . . . Though Parliament may discount these utterances as the irresponsible babble of the extremists of the Labour Party for the consumption of their constituents, His Majesty takes a graver view of these flippant, discourteous, if not insulting allusions to his Family; and the King objects to his Family being made a target to be shot at by Members of the Labour Opposition, unrebuked by their Leader (though one of their Party, Mr Shiels, had the courage to express disagreement with the speeches of his colleagues), and undefended by any Members of the Government.
>
> So long as the Monarchy and the Empire exist, it is but natural that the Dominions should look for periodical visits from Members of the Royal Family. But for the reasons I have endeavoured to explain the King has decided in future to refuse permission for any Member of the Royal Family to pay such official visits, unless the expenses incurred are defrayed by the respective Dominions: and His Majesty desires that this decision may be duly recorded.'[d]

This was not the first occasion when the King had conveyed to Mr Baldwin his disapproval of the light-heartedness with which he appeared to dismiss breaches of parliamentary decorum. An analogous protest, made in the summer of 1925, almost created a constitutional incident. Mr Baldwin, in his daily report to the King, had stated that during an all-night sitting the House had come to resemble 'St. James' Park at midday—Members lying about the benches in recumbent positions'. The King instructed Lord Stamfordham to write to the Prime Minister stating that such unseemly behaviour ought not to be treated with levity. 'Members of Parliament', Lord Stamfordham wrote, 'now include ladies, and such a state of things as you describe seems to His Majesty hardly *decorous*, or worthy of the tradition of the Mother of Parliaments.'[e] Mr Baldwin would have taken this reproof with affectionate placidity, had it not been that Lord Stamfordham had suggested that his letter might be shown to the Speaker. This surely was a sudden challenge to the sacred principles established by the Declaration of Rights. The Prime Minister immediately despatched his Private Secretary, Sir

428

Ronald Waterhouse, to Buckingham Palace with a demand that Lord Stamfordham's letter be withdrawn. Sir Ronald brought with him the draft of a communication, which, in the event of Lord Stamfordham's letter not being withdrawn, the Prime Minister would feel obliged to sign. This communication reminded the King 'that one of the earliest historical objects of the House of Commons was to exclude the Crown from interfering in its proceedings', and concluded by quoting Erskine May as laying down that 'the King cannot take notice of anything said or done in the House, but by the report of the House itself'.*

Lord Stamfordham pointed out to Sir Ronald Waterhouse that the custom of the Leader of the House addressing to the King a daily record of the debates in Parliament had been established since the reign of George III. Was he now to regard these reports as unconstitutional? Sir Ronald replied that although from long usage they might be assumed to fall 'within the ambit of the unwritten constitution', and although the King in private conversation might allude to the contents of the reports, yet any written representations based upon them might well be regarded as a trespass upon the privileges of the house.* After consulting the King, Lord Stamfordham wrote to Sir Ronald Waterhouse* stating that the offending letter would be withdrawn, but adding that the King could not help 'thinking that his subjects generally would not be surprised were they to know that the information conveyed to him, be it official or not, had been commented on in such terms as those of my letter.'

This absurd episode did not arise from any wish on the part of King George to undo the work accomplished by the Glorious Revolution of 1688, but was an instance of his constant preoccupation with the levels of public life and conduct. The archives at Windsor contain numerous intimations addressed to Ministers by the King's Private Secretaries calling attention to some breach of custom or some lapse into vulgarity. Many of these reminders would today appear old-fashioned; others were justifiable comments on bad practices. Thus in June 1925 the King wrote to the Prime Minister expressing grave doubts whether it was a good thing that Cabinet Ministers should 'write articles for the newspapers, receiving payment for the same'.* He was constantly distressed by the space given in the public prints to the reports of divorce cases. 'It is abominable', he wrote, 'that the Press should publish all this filth, but I suppose it is liked in this age.' He consulted the Lord Chancellor as to whether it would not be possible to try *in camera* such divorce cases as 'led to the exposure of intimate relations between man and woman which the unwritten code of decency, indeed of civilization, has hitherto recognised as sacred and beyond the range of public eye or ear.'*

Lord Birkenhead replied that he did not think it would be possible.

Thus by the autumn of 1928 the calm rhythm that the King found so congenial had almost been established. It was interrupted by an illness, so serious that it threw him out of action for ten months.

(3)

The King was at Sandringham between November 10 and November 19 and then came up to London. He conducted his usual business and gave his accustomed audiences until the late afternoon of Wednesday, November 21.

'I was taken ill this evening', he wrote in his diary for that day, 'Feverish cold they call it & I retired to bed.'[1]

Sir Stanley Hewett, who was at once summoned, sent for Lord Dawson of Penn to hold a consultation. They realised immediately that a serious illness was impending. A blood test taken at midnight indicated acute septicaemia: the centre of infection was then identified as at the base of the right lung. A week later the King's condition became grave; a telegram was sent to the Prince of Wales, who was in East Africa, warning him that there 'was cause for anxiety': he decided to return to England immediately. The news of the Prince having left for home was published in the newspapers on December 1, and the bulletin issued from Buckingham Palace on the day following referred to 'a decline in the strength of the heart'. It was obvious by then that the King would for long be incapable of dealing with public business and that a Council of State must be appointed. A warrant was therefore prepared nominating six Councillors (The Queen, the Prince of Wales, the Duke of York, the Archbishop of Canterbury, the Lord Chancellor and the Prime Minister) to act in place of the King during His Majesty's illness. The preamble to this warrant ran as follows:

---

[1] There occurs a gap in King George's diary from November 21, 1928, to April 27, 1929. The gap is filled by a few entries in the Queen's handwriting, noting the crucial dates. Even when the King resumed writing his diary it was some months before his handwriting recovered its former stability. It is only on September 19, 1929, that the entry 'I rode my white pony this morning for the first time since November 17' is written with his accustomed firmness.

'George the Fifth, by the Grace of God, of Great Britain, Ireland and the British Dominions beyond the Seas, King, Defender of the Faith, Emperor of India. To All Archbishops, Dukes, Marquesses, Earls, Viscounts, Bishops, Barons, Baronets, Knights, Citizens and Burgesses, and all other Our faithful Subjects whatsoever to whom these Presents shall come, Greeting!

Whereas We have been stricken by illness and are unable for the time being to give due attention to the affairs of Our Realm, Know Ye that for divers causes and considerations concerning Us and the tranquillity of Our Realm, Us hereunto especially moving, We of Our most especial grace, certain knowledge and mere motion, do nominate and appoint . . .'

The problem then arose as to the means by which the King, in the hearing of his Privy Council, could give his assent to this transference of power into other hands. On December 4 Lord Dawson informed Lord Stamfordham, who in his turn informed Sir Maurice Hankey, that the King would be capable that morning of holding a Council. It was arranged that the necessary quorum of Privy Councillors should assemble in the Audience Chamber adjoining the King's bedroom.

'The procedure agreed to', Lord Stamfordham recorded afterwards,[k] 'was that the Home Secretary, acting as Lord President, should stand in the doorway and read the Order, to which the King afterwards affixed his signature. The rest of the Councillors, namely the Duke of York, Prime Minister and Lord Stamfordham, were in the Council Chamber, at the fire-side end of the room. The acting Lord President was standing within a few yards of the King's bed. He read the order, and the King quite clearly said, as is the custom, "Approved". The document was then handed to Lord Dawson (who was in the King's bedroom and not in the room with the Privy Councillors) and he held it while the King signed.

His Majesty expressed a wish to see the Privy Councillors, but Lord Dawson felt that this was inadvisable.'

The first crisis in the King's illness was reached on December 11, the very day on which the Prince of Wales reached London: he found his father barely conscious:

'The King's will to live', records Lord Dawson's biographer,[l] 'was brave and strong: yet his very determination, side by side with the profound distress and sense of illness produced by the irritative state of the nervous system under infection, added also, as Dawson noted, to the wear and tear of the fever. The whole body and mind was one battle-ground. It was not a typical pleuro-pneumonia but a case of severe general blood infection and toxaemia, and neither pleural puncture nor the study of a new and excellent set of X-rays disclosed what the doctors were looking for. The original pleural abscess was just behind the diaphragm and impossible to drain.'

On the afternoon of December 12, the twenty-second day of the illness, Lord Dawson, gazing at the unconscious figure on the bed, determined to make one more attempt to find the fatal fluid. Within a few seconds he had located the exact place. That evening an operation was performed. Three daily bulletins were issued to the public on that day and on the four days following As Christmas approached, and the King maintained the desperate struggle, hopes began to revive. The churches in England were kept open day and night for prayers of intercession. On December 29 the *Lancet* ventured the statement that 'convalescence is now in sight'. On February 9 the King was taken in an ambulance from Buckingham Palace to Craigweil House at Aldwick near Bognor. On February 12 he was allowed his first cigarette for two and a half months. On March 27 he was well enough to give an audience to the Prime Minister.

On that same day the Archbishop of Canterbury, Dr Lang, came down to Craigweil to do homage. He suggested that the moment had come when the King should address a message to his people giving thanks for his recovery. Lord Dawson, when consulted, expressed the opinion that such a message would be premature. The King, for several further months, remained in a precarious state of health. On May 15, 1929, he was at last strong enough to leave Bognor for Windsor:

'Reception at Windsor', he wrote in his diary, 'from the children and the Eton boys. Very glad to be home again after 13½ weeks at Bognor.'

On May 20 the King suffered a relapse and Lord Dawson was again summoned. It was found that a local abscess had formed at the site of the operation. The King responded well to renewed treatment and by the middle of June it was decided that a public Thanksgiving Service could be held on July 7. The King was determined that, having left London in an ambulance, he would return to it in state. On July 1 he motored from Windsor as far as the Albert Hall, where he and the Queen changed into state landaus and drove the remaining distance to Buckingham Palace:

'We had indeed a wonderful welcome home after these long tedious months of illness.'

On July 7 the King and Queen attended a Thanksgiving Service in Westminster Abbey. Very few of those who were present at that magnificent ceremony or who lined the streets knew that the King's wound was still unhealed. A few days later the King received Mr J. H. Thomas, who was always apt to regale His Majesty with ribald jokes. The King laughed so hilariously at one of Mr Thomas's stories that he had a further relapse. On July 15 another operation had to be performed and a second rib removed. His wound did not heal completely until September 25. Lord Stamfordham, in deep affection, begged his master to consent to spend at least a few weeks of autumn in a warmer climate. 'I was told', he wrote to Lord Athlone, 'in rather strong language that nothing of the sort would take place.'ᵐ

The King was not by temperament an equable man. Even before his illness, there had come moments when Lord Stamfordham had been startled to recognise in those blue eyes a fixity of expression that recalled for him Queen Victoria's sharp indignation. The King was a bad patient and an even worse convalescent. Like all men who possess few internal resources and whose greatest pleasures are associated with outdoor life, the King became restless and irritable when his physical liberties were circumscribed. The chaff in which he indulged so gaily sometimes assumed during those weary months an irascible tone. He was often querulous; he frequently indulged in moods of self-pity; and he was terribly difficult to persuade. Lord Dawson found, during those weary months of convalescence, that one of the most dangerous of enemies was the demon boredom. Fortunately, the King had a liking for the cinema and much of his tedium could thereby be relieved. He was fond, moreover, of young children, and the constant presence of Princess Elizabeth (who figures conspicuously in the diary as 'sweet little Lilibet') acted as a useful emollient to jaded nerves.

The King's recovery from so prolonged and terrible an illness was widely recognised as due to the skill of his doctors and the efficiency of his nurses.[1] It left him delicate and older than his sixty-four years.

Those months of suffering, strain and impatience should not, however, be computed in terms of wastage. The people of Great Britain, faced with the possibility of the King's death, were startled

[1] During the successive phases of his illness the King was attended by eleven doctors and five nurses, under the general direction of Lord Dawson and Sir Stanley Hewett. Sister Catherine Black, of London Hospital, proved so adept at managing the King that she was persuaded by Lord Dawson to remain on after his recovery. She therefore stayed with the King until the day of his death.

by the realisation of how much each one of them really cared. Men and women were surprised, not only by the intensity of their own feeling, but also by the reflection of that intensity in others. It came as a revelation to many that here was no transitory wave of mass sentiment, but a personal anxiety shared by all. Rarely has an emotion been both so intimate and so diffused. For all his diffidence, the King could not fail to be encouraged by this national tribute to his personality: ailing though he was, he became fortified thereafter in facing the final political crisis of his declining years.

(4)

The Parliament elected in October 1924 was by then approaching its natural term of life, and Mr Baldwin decided to ask for a dissolution in the spring of 1929. The Conservatives appealed to the country under an enormous photograph of Mr Baldwin looking his most sedative and with the slogan 'Safety First'. Labour offered a more dynamic programme, and there were many leading Socialists who boasted that they and they alone possessed the secret of how to cure unemployment. Polling took place on May 31. It was the largest General Election ever held in Great Britain: each of the three parties put up some 500 candidates, and the electorate, owing to Mr Baldwin's extension of the female franchise, had been increased by five million. The Conservative and the Labour Parties each polled in the neighbourhood of eight million votes, while the Liberals gained as many as five million. The proportion of seats held by the three parties in the new House of Commons did not, owing to our eccentric electoral system, bear any close relation to the number of votes cast. Labour was returned with 287 seats, the Conservatives with 261, and the Liberals with 59.

It will be recalled that in December 1923, when a similar situation had arisen in which none of the three parties possessed a majority over the other two, the King had held the view that the duty of the Prime Minister was to remain in office until defeated in the House of Commons. In 1929 Mr Baldwin, after careful thought, decided that it would be more honest to resign immediately. There were some experts who felt that his right course would be to face the new House of Commons and thereby oblige Mr Lloyd George and the Liberals to declare their hand. Lord Stamfordham did not, on this occasion, agree with this view:

'No!' he wrote to Sir George Murray on June 3,[n] 'If I were Prime Minister I should not give a moment's consideration to what Lloyd George would or would not do; nor to any other of what might be called the "expert parliamentarian" points of view. The fact is that you and I, who naturally are inclined to look back to precedents, must remember that they are almost as little applicable to England today as they would be to China. Democracy is no longer a meaningless sort of shibboleth; and, with the enormous increase of voters by the women's franchise it is the actual voice, and for better or worse the *political* voice, of the State.'

Mr Baldwin entirely shared this opinion. He informed the King that the public might regard it as 'unsporting' of him if he did not resign immediately, and might suspect that he was contemplating some deal with the Liberals to keep Labour out. He thus came to Windsor on Tuesday, June 4, and handed to the King the resignation of his Government. That same afternoon Lord Stamfordham saw Mr Ramsay MacDonald:[o]

'After enquiries about the King, he told me that his one wish was to go to sleep; he had not slept for more than a fortnight. . . . I gathered that he had settled very little with his colleagues. Evidently things are not going quite easily; indeed he said that he was by no means certain yet that he would tell the King that he was prepared to form a Government. Without his saying anything definite, it was evident that the Foreign Office.was his difficulty; indeed he said that he had offered to give up the Prime Ministership and go to the Foreign Office himself, but this was not agreeable to the Party. . . .

I told Mr MacDonald that I expected that the King would speak to him about the Executive Committee, which was popularly supposed to have much control upon the Labour Government when they were in office. He assured me that this was not the case: that there were two of the Cabinet appointed to act as sort of liaison officers between the Party and the Government and he emphasised that the Government were never influenced by, and certainly never followed, the dictates of the Committee, unless their views coincided with those of the Government.'

On the morning of Wednesday, June 5, Mr MacDonald motored down to Windsor. The King, who had not yet recovered from his relapse of May 20, received him in his bedroom. They discussed several of the proposed appointments and the King suggested that Mr J. H. Thomas, owing to his close intimacy with Mr MacDonald, might prove an excellent Foreign Secretary. Mr MacDonald replied that, whoever was appointed to that post, he would retain in his own hands the conduct of Anglo-American relations, to which he attached supreme importance. The King asked Mr MacDonald whether he

435

was satisfied in his own conscience that his Party were justified in assuming the title 'Labour'. How many of the gentlemen whose names they had been discussing had ever undertaken hard manual work? Mr MacDonald replied that he himself at least had actually gained that qualification. He then kissed hands and agreed to form an administration.[p]

On Saturday, June 8, the members of the new Government came down to Windsor to receive their seals of office and to take their oaths. Miss Margaret Bondfield on that occasion was sworn in as the first woman Privy Councillor. The King expressed his regret that, owing to his relapse, he had been unable as he had hoped to receive his new Ministers at Buckingham Palace and had been obliged to impose upon them the inconvenience of coming down to Windsor. Before returning to London, Mr MacDonald requested Lord Stamfordham to convey to the King the thanks of himself and his colleagues for the kind manner in which His Majesty had received them.[q] The second Labour Government was thus inaugurated with becoming courtesy and esteem.[1]

[1] The main posts in Mr MacDonald's second administration were distributed as follows: Chancellor of the Exchequer, Mr Philip Snowden: Secretary of State for Foreign Affairs, Mr Arthur Henderson: Lord Privy Seal, Mr J. H. Thomas: Lord President, Lord Parmoor: Lord Chancellor, Lord Justice Sankey: Dominions, Mr Sidney Webb: Home, Mr J. R. Clynes: India, Mr Wedgwood Benn: War, Mr Tom Shaw: Air, Lord Thomson: Health, Mr Arthur Greenwood: Labour, Miss Margaret Bondfield: Agriculture, Mr Noel Buxton: Board of Trade, Mr William Graham: Admiralty, Mr A. V. Alexander: First Commissioner for Works, Mr George Lansbury: Scotland, Mr W. Adamson: Transport, Mr Herbert Morrison: Chancellor of the Duchy, Sir Oswald Mosley.

CHAPTER XXVI

FINANCIAL CRISIS

1929–1931

Mr MacDonald hampered by his minority position—He passes a Coal Bill but fails with his Trades Union Bill, Education Bill and Electoral Reform Bill—His visits to the United States—The Rapidan conversations—Anglo-American naval parity—The London Naval Conference—Mr Snowden at the Hague—Mr Henderson resumes diplomatic relations with Russia—The King receives a Russian Ambassador—Anglo-Egyptian negotiations—The resignation of Lord Lloyd The problem of unemployment—Mr J. H. Thomas and Sir Oswald Mosley—The Llandudno Conference—Committee Room 14—Economic condition of Europe—Sir Arthur Balfour's grim paper—The Credit Anstalt collapses—Financial panic in Vienna and Berlin—The Seven Power Conference—The crisis shifts to London—The problem becomes political—The King's health—His personal bereavements and troubles during 1931—The death of Lord Stamfordham.

(1)

IN forming his second Administration Mr Ramsay MacDonald again found himself hampered by the fact that, although he possessed the strongest single Party in the House of Commons, he could at any moment be defeated if the 59 Liberals combined with the 261 Conservatives. His domestic legislation therefore was tentative and vague. He was able, it is true, to secure the passage of a Coal Mines Bill, providing for the division of the fields into district areas and for the reduction of working hours from eight to seven and a half. His other projects were either blocked or amended out of recognition. The first measure that the Labour Party had undertaken to promote was one repealing the Trades Disputes Act passed by the Conservatives in the hour of reaction that followed upon the General Strike. A Bill was, in fact, introduced legalising the sympathetic strike, peaceful picketing, contracting out and affiliation of Civil Service unions with the T.U.C. The Liberals, with Conservative support, side-tracked this Bill by carrying an amendment under which the legality of strikes was drastically circumscribed. Similarly, an excellent Education Bill broke down over its financial provisions; and an Electoral Reform Bill, providing for the introduction into our honoured but eccentric system of an American device known as 'the alternative vote', was

437

sterilised by the House of Lords, who insisted that it should apply only to London and the larger boroughs.

As in 1924, it was in external rather than in domestic policy that the Labour Government were best able to display their strength and talents. Mr Arthur Henderson, the new Foreign Secretary, was at first overshadowed by the Prime Minister and by his Chancellor of the Exchequer, Mr Philip Snowden.

Mr MacDonald had made it known that he would keep within his own hands the conduct of Anglo-American relations, and that, so soon as a favourable opportunity offered, he would visit President Hoover in Washington. It was not his intention to discuss the embarrassing matter of finance: his aim was, in anticipation of the Naval Conference that had been planned for 1930, to prevent the misunderstanding that had rendered the Geneva discussion of 1927 so deplorable a fiasco.[1] On June 15, 1929, the King received the new American Ambassador, General Dawes, who expressed himself as strongly opposed to the proposition that the British Prime Minister should visit the United States:

'He (General Dawes) was the mouthpiece in England of the President of the American Government and, were the Prime Minister to go to America, it would arouse all sorts of suspicions, especially among the anti-English parties, who would raise scares in the Press and by other means, that pressure was being put upon the President and that America, as usual, would give way to England etc. etc. . . . The King dwelt on the absurdity of talking, or even thinking, of war between our two countries; we must maintain the closest friendship,'[a]

The King, none the less, with his unflagging interest in Naval matters remained uneasy and distressed:

[1] The Washington Treaty of 1921 had established parity between the United States and British navies in so far as battleships and battle cruisers were concerned. Nothing had been laid down about cruisers other than battle cruisers. Thereafter the British had constructed a large number of light cruisers, a perfectly legitimate action, which was much resented in the United States. In 1927, therefore, a Conference took place at Geneva between representatives of Great Britain, the United States and Japan in the hope of reaching agreement regarding the ratio of construction in all types of vessels. The Americans wanted to restrict *all* cruiser construction, whereas we wanted freedom to construct as many *light* cruisers as we wished. The discussions ended in vituperation, lies and turmoil. President Coolidge then asked Congress for an enormous and preponderant American programme of naval construction. It was to prevent a similar situation arising in 1930 that Mr MacDonald was so anxious to visit America in person.

438

'It seems to the King', wrote Sir Clive Wigram[1] to the Prime Minister, 'that the President and his advisers are trying to bully us into accepting *their* interpretation of the word "parity", by which the American Navy, with its great preponderance of heavy cruisers, could blow our greater number of light cruisers out of the water, according to the experiences of the last war.

There is no "give and take" about such a solution. His Majesty earnestly trusts that you will not venture upon a visit to Washington unless the President can produce some fairer and more reasonable proposals as a basis for negotiation.'[b]

In spite of all this Mr MacDonald persisted in his decision to visit the United States and to thresh the matter out in private conversation with President Hoover. He crossed the Atlantic in the early autumn of 1929 and, after the 'splendid dramatics' of a visit to New York, had a long and intimate talk with the President, seated upon a log beside the Rapidan River. He was then able to narrow down the differences between Great Britain and the United States to the single question whether the latter should construct eighteen or twenty-one cruisers armed with eight inch guns.

The Five Power Naval Conference was opened by the King in the fog-darkened Gallery of the House of Lords on January 21, 1930. Mainly owing to the entrancing and resourceful personality of Mr Dwight Morrow, the dominating figure on the American Delegation, a Three Power Settlement was on April 22 signed between Great Britain, the United States and Japan, establishing an accepted ratio of construction. A Five Power Agreement was also signed embodying those points on which all the Five Powers were unanimous. Italy and France were, however, unable to agree on the relative strength of their respective navies, and agreement between them was only reached in March of 1931. Mr MacDonald could certainly congratulate himself on having by personal influence achieved a solution which, apart from the diplomatic benefits involved, saved Great Britain an expenditure of sixty million pounds and the United States an expenditure of five hundred million dollars:

'The results of the Conference', the Prime Minister wrote to the King on April 12, 'will be of great benefit, if they are allowed to mature, and one of the greatest of these will be our improved relations with the United States. From beginning to end the two delegations worked in complete harmony.'[c]

---

[1] Colonel Wigram had received the K.C.V.O. in the New Year Honours of 1928.

The King, who had followed the negotiations with expert understanding, was delighted by this settlement:

> 'I rejoice', he wrote to Mr MacDonald on April 13, 'that in spite of all the difficulties, intricacies and delicate situations which confronted the Naval Conference, a partial Five Power Agreement, and a complete Three Power Settlement, have been secured. These satisfactory results are, I feel sure, due to your untiring labours, patience and tact, and I offer you my warmest congratulations.'[d]

A more popular success was that secured by the Chancellor of the Exchequer at the Hague Conference. The Dawes plan had been replaced by the Young Plan, under which Germany was to pay in reparation an average of £100 million a year for fifty-nine years. The distribution of these payments between the several allies was to be decided at a Conference of Finance Ministers to be held at the Hague. The preliminary allocation departed flagrantly from the original Spa percentages: of the unconditional annuities, France was allotted as many as five-sixths: and recommendations were made for payments in kind, a method regarded as odious by all healthy-minded British civil servants. Thus when the Conference opened at the Binnenhof in August, Mr Snowden startled his colleagues and the world by announcing that the British experts who had signed the Young Report did not represent their Government and that the latter was in no sense bound to accept their recommendations. He repeated that His Majesty's Government would prefer to see the complete cancellation of all debts and reparations whatsoever, as advocated in the Balfour Note; but that so long as these Shylock calculations were indulged in by others, Great Britain also must demand her pound of flesh. M. Chéron, the venerable Minister of France, sought to confute Mr Snowden, who in his most asperous voice responded by saying that the arguments of M. Chéron were 'grotesque and ridiculous'. The word 'grotesque', when translated into the French language, sounds most ill. Indignation was aroused and it was whispered immediately (and not without some reason) that Mr MacDonald was about to repudiate his Chancellor of the Exchequer. Mr Snowden, on hearing these rumours, demanded from the Prime Minister, and with an implied threat of resignation, a public expression of full support. Mr MacDonald, much as he detested diplomatic methods other than his own, was obliged to give way:

> 'The Chancellor', wrote Mr MacDonald to the King on August 14, 1929, 'has a stiff back and when in debate his words are well known to be seasoned by mustard. The incident between the French Finance

Minister and him showed the danger of a House of Commons style in an International Conference.'⁶

Mr MacDonald's criticisms may well have been justified; diplomacy by insult is seldom an efficacious means of conducting negotiations between Sovereign States. Yet the fact remains that Mr Snowden did obtain from the Conference an increase in the annuities allocated to Great Britain up to an average of two millions a year for thirty-seven years: that he did obtain a revision of the priorities: and that he did persuade the Conference to make some concessions as to deliveries in kind. More important than all these (since only a short time later reparations themselves died a natural death) was the promise obtained by Mr Snowden that the allies would evacuate the Rhineland five years before the date laid down in the Treaty of Versailles. This certainly was an important achievement. Mr Snowden returned to England to receive a popular ovation and the freedom of the City of London.

> 'I warmly congratulate you', wrote the King to Mr Snowden, 'on an achievement which has earned for you the gratitude and admiration of your fellow countrymen.'

The activities of Mr Arthur Henderson, who in later years was acclaimed by the Labour Party as the greatest of British Foreign Secretaries, seem drab in comparison to such coruscations. He renewed with Soviet Russia the official contacts that had been sundered since the Arcos raid of 1927; it was agreed that Mr Brilliant (who had adopted the name of Sokolnikov) should be appointed Russian Ambassador to the Court of St. James's. On March 27, 1930, the King was obliged to undergo the ordeal of personally receiving an envoy of the U.S.S.R.[1]

For all his frantic efforts Mr Henderson failed, as other men had failed before him, and were to fail thereafter, to secure any final

---

[1] The King, through Lord Stamfordham, had on October 12, 1929, made a final protest to the Foreign Secretary against the indignity of 'having to receive Letters of Credence from the Ambassador of a Government which, if it did not connive at, did not disapprove of, the brutal murder of his favourite first cousins; and to receive him with the other Ambassadors at a Levée, shake hands with him, and that he should remain in the Presence Chamber looking on at a ceremony which, it is fair to assume, he would regard with contempt'. Mr Henderson replied that, much as he sympathised with the King in 'what must naturally be a painful situation', he feared that it was unavoidable. (R.A., M. 2229. 38.)

settlement of the Egyptian problem.[1] The King had from the outset doubted whether, in the existing ferment of Egyptian nationalism, it would be possible to secure a reliable Treaty with Egypt, except at a price higher than we ought to pay. On reading the draft agreement reached between Sir Austen Chamberlain and Sarwat Pasha in 1927 he had in his own hand minuted as follows:

> 'The weak places are that the Egyptian Army is not limited & that in future it is possible that the League of Nations might tell us to clear our troops out of Cairo & Alexandria & go to the Canal, or might tell us to take our troops away from Egypt altogether.'*

It was not surprising therefore that, when he learnt that the Labour Government had decided to resume negotiations at the point left by the abortive draft treaty of 1927, the King should have manifested some disquiet. His anxiety was increased by the overt impatience of Mr Henderson to secure the resignation of Lord Lloyd from his post of High Commissioner at Cairo.

It was felt in Labour circles (as also in the Foreign Office) that Lord Lloyd was too reticent in expressing his admiration for the Egyptian character and too outspoken in contending that our only possible policy was to stand firmly and silently upon the reserved points of the 1922 declaration. It was hoped that the presence in Cairo of a more pliant and less proconsular representative might induce the change of climate that was so ardently desired. The methods by which Lord Lloyd's resignation were extorted appeared to the King to have been unduly abrupt:

> 'His Majesty feels', wrote Lord Stamfordham to the Foreign Office on July 22, 1929, 'that it would be right and just to any public servant,

---

[1] On Feb. 28, 1922, Lord Allenby the High Commissioner had issued a Declaration by which Great Britain recognised Egypt as a Sovereign Independent State, subject to certain 'reserved points'. Great Britain, that is, reserved responsibility for the security of the Suez Canal, the defence of Egypt from foreign invasion or interference, the protection of foreigners in Egypt, and the Sudan. In October 1925 Lord Allenby was succeeded as High Commissioner by Lord Lloyd. In November 1927 Sir Austen Chamberlain negotiated a draft Treaty of Alliance with Sarwat Pasha, the main provision of which was that the location of the British forces in Egypt would be reconsidered in ten years, and Great Britain would support Egypt's desire for admission to the League of Nations and for the abolition of the capitulations. The Sudan, under this arrangement, was reserved for future settlement. The Wafd, or Nationalist Party, refused to accept this treaty, and after Sarwat's resignation Mohammed Pasha Mahmoud was appointed Prime Minister.

holding a high and responsible position, that, if the Government consider his resignation is necessary in the best interests of the country, he should be given adequate reasons for this grave decision; and that every consideration should be shown to render his compliance with the Government's wishes easy, and so enable him to lay down his work with due self-respect.'*g*

The draft agreement reached on August 3, 1929, between Mr Henderson and Mohammed Pasha Mahmoud represented a marked advance upon that initialled by Sir Austen Chamberlain and Sarwat Pasha in 1927. It provided for the cessation of all British intervention in Egyptian affairs, the withdrawal of the British troops from Cairo and Alexandria to the canal zone, and the replacement of the British High Commissioner in Egypt by an Ambassador. It also permitted the despatch to the Sudan of a token Egyptian battalion to represent the forces that had been withdrawn at the time of the murder of the Sirdar, Sir Lee Stack, in 1924.

'The King', wrote Lord Stamfordham to the Foreign Office on July 24, 1929, 'has seen the draft Anglo-Egyptian Treaty and there is no use disguising the fact that His Majesty is somewhat concerned at the important changes in our policy on the Egyptian question which it will entail. But there is one point which His Majesty asks you will specially mention to the Prime Minister, viz: the return of one Egyptian battalion to the Sudan, which, having regard to all that led up to the withdrawal of the Egyptian army from the Sudan in 1924, will be in His Majesty's opinion a retrograde step, and will encourage the Egyptian Government to hope that we are weakening in our resolve that the Sudan shall never come under Egyptian rule. It was British lives and British money that rescued the Sudan from tyranny and barbarism and surely we shall see to it that the sacrifice was not made in vain.'*h*

The Foreign Office, in their battle for the conciliation of Egypt, obtained an unexpected ally in the person of Sir John Maffey, Governor General of the Sudan, and an unexpected adversary in the person of Mr Ramsay MacDonald:

'The Prime Minister', Lord Stamfordham wrote to the King on July 31, 1929, 'has written to Mr Henderson, Secretary of State for Foreign Affairs, criticising the handling by the Foreign Office of the negotiations with Mahmud, which, I gather from Mr Ramsay MacDonald, he did not consider had been skilful; and he evidently strongly questions the wisdom or advisability of any Egyptian troops being allowed to return to the Sudan, all of whom had been got rid of in 1924. . . .
The impression given me by the Prime Minister was that he had been beaten by the Foreign Office and that the alternative would be the

resignation of Mr Henderson, although he did not say this in so many words. . . . From all the Prime Minister told me, and from all I have heard, I am convinced that he is not happy at what has been done.'¹

As Mr MacDonald had foreseen, Mohammed Pasha Mahmoud, on his return to Egypt, was unable to induce the Wafd to regard the great concessions that had been made as providing more than a lively expectation of even further gifts to come. His successor Nahas Pasha, in the spring of 1930, resumed negotiations, but was unable to reach agreement on the question of the Sudan. The Anglo-Egyptian problem remained unsolved through the rest of King George's reign.

The indignation aroused in Conservative circles by the Government's apparent surrender to Egyptian nationalism; the deep sympathy that was felt with Lord Lloyd, the last of our great imperialists, for the scurvy treatment he had received at the hands of Sir Austen Chamberlain, Mr Arthur Henderson and the officials of the Foreign Office; all these might have combined to create a major political crisis. As the year 1930 lengthened, irritants such as these became no more than remote ticklings. The great grey shadow of economic eclipse began to stalk with shuddering strides across the world.

(3)

In forming his administration in June 1929, Mr Ramsay Mac-Donald had allotted to Mr J. H. Thomas the post of Lord Privy Seal, with the special task of reducing the heavy and rising figures of unemployment. In the course of the election campaign many Labour candidates, relying upon the brave promises contained in the Party's manifesto, *Labour and the Nation*, had expressly promised that, once the country could be freed from the blight of Tory misrule, the numbers of unemployed workers would rapidly recede.¹ On returning from a visit to Canada, Mr Thomas informed an expectant world that he 'had many things up his sleeve', and even that he had re-

¹ The figures did not recede. The percentage of insured persons out of employment rose as follows:

1926.	13·5%.	1929.	9·8%.
1927.	9·2%.	1930.	17·3%.
1928.	11·1%.	1931.	22·3%.

It should be realised, however, that this rise in unemployment was a world phenomenon. In Germany unemployment rose from 1,919,917 in 1929 to 4,618,537 in 1931 and 5,703,088 in 1932. Even in France, a country less exposed to unemployment waves, the figure rose from 10,052 in 1929 to 308,096 in 1932. (I.L.O. figures.)

turned possessed 'of the complete cure'. The highest expectations were aroused by this prophecy.

For the execution of his gigantic task Mr Thomas had been accorded three gifted or prominent assistants, Mr George Lansbury, Mr Tom Johnston and the new Chancellor of the Duchy of Lancaster, Sir Oswald Mosley. From the very outset it became apparent that the exuberant dynamism of the Chancellor of the Duchy was ill-attuned to the cheerful lethargy of the Lord Privy Seal. Having battled for months in the hope of interesting his chief in his schemes for state-aided public works, Sir Oswald resigned his appointment in despair:

> 'Sir Oswald Mosley', the King noted in his diary for May 24, 1930, 'gave up his seal of the Duchy of Lancaster, he having resigned the Chancellorship. Major Attlee was sworn as Chancellor in his place.'

It was not long before Mr Thomas also relinquished his task as Minister of Unemployment and restricted himself thereafter to the more sedative functions of Secretary of State for the Dominions. The ordinary honest socialist was distressed to observe that so little was being done to redeem the promises made at the election, whereas so much was being done to encourage the heresies of those deviationists who contended that employment or unemployment had less to do with capitalism than with trade cycles; and that these inhuman cycles were as tides, waning or waxing to the dictates of some occult economic moon. The feeling within the rank and file became manifest at the annual conference of the Labour Party held at Llandudno in October 1930. Mr James Maxton brought forward a motion to the effect that 'This Conference views with alarm the failure of the Government to apply the bold unemployment policy outlined in *Labour and the Nation*'. Mr MacDonald, in a speech vibrant with emotion, was able to swing the Conference to his side. 'My friends', he pleaded, in that wonderful voice that seemed to blend all the veracity of a Scottish engineer with all the self-pity of a Welsh revivalist:

> 'My friends, *we* are not on trial; it is the system under which we live. It has broken down, not only in this little island, it has broken down in Europe, in Asia, in America; it has broken down everywhere, as it was bound to break down. And the cure, the new path, the new idea, is Organization.'

Sir Oswald Mosley, whose words had a great effect upon the Conference, replied that it was this very Organisation that he had

445

sought so desperately to obtain from Mr J. H. Thomas and the Cabinet; that it was this very incapacity to organise firmly that had convinced him that the present Cabinet were too ignorant, too lazy, or too timid, to take the drastic measures by which alone the rising wave of unemployment could be checked. The Llandudno Conference remained loyal to Mr MacDonald; yet those who were present were well aware that a gulf had been disclosed between the leaders and the ranks. Significantly enough, it was Sir Oswald Mosley who at the conclusion of the Conference was elected to the National Executive: not Mr J. H. Thomas.

On his retirement from the Duchy of Lancaster, Sir Oswald Mosley had prepared a formidable indictment of Mr Thomas, together with a memorandum setting out his own ideas as to the action that ought immediately to be taken. This memorandum was, on January 27, 1931, considered at a special meeting of the Parliamentary Labour Party, held in Committee Room 14 of the House of Commons. The speech which Sir Oswald delivered on that occasion was valorous and forceful. Had he not, encouraged by the cheers with which he had been greeted, insisted upon putting the issue to a vote—thereby arousing all the inhibitions of party loyalties and discipline—he might well have rallied the bulk of the meeting to his side. As it was, Mr Arthur Henderson was able, by deft compliments and appeals to solidarity and common sense, to undo some at least of the damage that Sir Oswald had occasioned. Yet had the latter been less easily swept away by his own impatience, he might have forced the Government to accept his terms. His error, at that crucial moment, deprived him of an unrepeated opportunity; and the country of a great Parliamentarian. The incident was important, since it served to emphasise what had already become apparent at the Llandudno Conference, namely an ever-widening divergence between the lonely, if somewhat muddled, thoughts of Mr Mac-Donald and the passionate, sincere and decent unhappiness of the ordinary member of the Party.

(4)

Even if Great Britain had been isolated from all outside contagion, it would have been difficult for her to afford without disturbance the rising cost of unemployment. The world depression that coincided with, and to a great extent was the cause of, our own financial crisis, rendered septic wounds that might otherwise have quickly healed. Men felt that external forces, of which they had no knowledge, and over which they had no possible control, were whirling them towards some unknown abyss. When human beings are alarmed by something that they cannot identify, they tend to transfer their apprehensions to causes or agencies which are familiar. The bewilderment created by the 1931 crisis led to much suspicion, rancour, and that most pestilential of all symptoms of frightened ignorance, the attribution of false motive. Some of the poisons generated by the dreadful illness that assailed us in 1931 still linger in our memories. If therefore the crisis is to be described objectively, it will be necessary to devote some space to an examination of what were its real causes, and what the veritable motives that inspired the statesmen of that time. Since it was in connection with this crisis that King George assumed the greatest responsibility of his reign; since the solution of that crisis was largely due to the influence which he was personally able to exercise; it is all the more essential to approach that disordered and still prejudiced controversy in a mood of calm. The reader must therefore submit to a momentary suspension of the narrative; and forgive the tedium entailed.

The conditions which, between 1929 and 1931, led to a general lowering of the financial and economic vitality of Europe can be shortly summarised. The delicate, almost thermostatic, instruments, which before 1914 had adjusted the flow of supply and demand, had been completely shattered by the war; the old automatic regulators had ceased to function, whereas the idea of a planned and controlled international economy was not yet taken seriously. After 1919, a wave of economic nationalism had swept the world and resulted in tariff barriers which, as the Economic Conference of 1927 pointed out, created the greatest single obstacle to any general or lasting revival. A debilitating influence was also exercised by the tumour of war-debts and reparations. The United States and France were the two main beneficiaries from reparation and debt payments, and since their tariff policies did not permit payment in goods and services, a vast amount of gold accumulated in New York and Paris, where it remained frozen and stored. This world shortage of circulating gold, led to a fall in prices, restricted production and thereby caused unemployment. The gravity of the real situation was for a while concealed owing to the fact that the United States, between 1924 and 1929, indulged in an orgy of lending to Europe, and especially to Germany. When in 1929, the first signs of approaching depression became apparent, the flow of loans ceased suddenly, and the stark realities of an utterly unbalanced situation were revealed.

447

In October 1930 Sir Arthur Balfour, a member of the Economic Advisory Council, wrote to the Prime Minister forecasting an impending economic collapse and stating that grave measures, including some reduction in the unemployment benefit, as well as a 10 to 20% tariff on manufactured goods, would be essential if national bankruptcy were to be averted. He doubted whether any but a Coalition Government would be powerful enough to impose on the country the sacrifices that would be required. His letter was circulated to the King and Cabinet and caused a shock:

'The King feels', wrote Lord Stamfordham to the Prime Minister on October 11, 1930, 'that his Ministers will recognise with him the gravity of our industrial and commercial situation. Sir Arthur Balfour speaks as one of almost unique experience; also as a Member of your Advisory Council and one who, the King believes, has been a staunch Free Trader. His review of the critical state of affairs will, in His Majesty's opinion, bring home to his Ministers that the time has come when even emergency measures may be necessary in order to avert a calamity which, as Sir Arthur Balfour states, is not altogether incomparable with that of the Great War.'*

In Great Britain the situation had, in the opinion of some economists, been unnecessarily complicated by our return to the Gold Standard in 1925.[1] Our unfavourable trade balance, coupled with the vast sums being expended on unemployment relief, combined to diminish foreign confidence in the stability of the pound sterling. Depositors who, in reliance on the Gold Standard, had placed their money in London, began, at the first signs of approaching depression, to withdraw their deposits in gold. At the same moment the American bankers began to call in the loans which, with reckless optimism, they had for years been making to Germany.

The first clap of thunder which presaged the impending storm echoed across the world on June 18, 1931. On that day the Credit Anstalt of Vienna closed its doors. The Bank of England came to the

---

[1] In a pamphlet which he published in 1925 and which, with some asperity, he called *The Economic Consequences of Mr Churchill*, Mr J. M. Keynes had warned his readers that this defiant action would seriously weaken our competitive position in the world market. In his *Treatise on Money* (Volume II, pp. 377–87) he analysed the situation as it stood in 1930. The wholesale indexes had dropped by 20% during the last twelve months; the prices of the world's staple commodities had dropped by half; Europe had borrowed from America some five hundred million pounds for unproductive purposes; and, as a result, the unemployment figures in the United States, Germany and Great Britain stood at ten million.

rescue by making an immediate advance to the Austrian Government of £5,285,000. The panic, in spite of this quick action, spread to Berlin, where the main banking houses also suspended payment. Again the Bank of England strove to stem the tide by placing an advance of twenty-five million dollars at the disposal of the Reichsbank. The panic continued. At 6.0 p.m. on June 20 President Hoover hurriedly suggested a moratorium on war debts and reparations. This suggestion was immediately accepted by the British Government: the French Government delayed their acceptance for fourteen days, a postponement of assent that some authorities regard as having been disastrous.

The threatened crash in the value of the German mark was felt almost immediately in the City of London. Sir Clive Wigram, on July 11, wrote to the King, who had the day before opened the George V dock at Glasgow, warning him to expect the gravest developments:

'Your Majesty will have read the attached telegrams with some concern. If there is a collapse in Germany, the repercussion in this country will be awful. We are sitting on the top of a volcano, and the curious thing is that the Press and the City have not really understood the critical situation. The Governor of the Bank of England is very pessimistic and depressed. . . . If a crash comes in Germany we shall have a financial situation something like that at the outbreak of war, and there will be a demand for a moratorium all round. A Minority Government will hardly be able to deal with the situation, and it is quite possible that Your Majesty might be asked to approve of a National Government.

However, these awful storms have a way of blowing over and I trust that this one may just circle around and pass away without any ill effects.'*k*

Throughout July there were further withdrawals by foreigners of their deposits in London which led to a drain of gold from the Bank of England. The Prime Minister sought to internationalise the situation by summoning a Seven Power Conference urgently to London.[1] In his opening speech he stated that the purpose of the Conference was 'to restore the confidence of the foreign investor in Germany'.

[1] Few Conferences have united around one table men of such eminence for so short a time. The United States were represented by Mr Stimson and Mr Mellon: Germany by Dr Brüning and Dr. Curtius: Italy by Signor Grandi: France by MM. Briand and Laval: Japan by Mr Matsudaira: Great Britain by Mr Ramsay MacDonald, Mr Philip Snowden and Mr Arthur Henderson.

He was warmly supported by the United States delegation, but the French representatives refused to grant any further credits to Germany except on conditions that were unacceptable. The Seven Power Conference thus ended in overt failure, and rendered it clear to the world that the two Powers who owned the gold were not agreed on the necessity of making immediate sacrifices in order to save the German currency and to prevent a resultant panic flight from the pound sterling.

From that moment, and with ever-increasing velocity, the full force of the storm hurled itself upon the City of London.

(5)

Europe, for the reasons that have been stated, was not at the time in a condition of financial health. The local infection created by the failure of the Credit Anstalt on June 18 spread rapidly to the central banks in Austria and Germany; the Bank of International Settlements at Basle was unable to arrest the contamination; the Hoover moratorium proved but a momentary palliative; the Seven Power Conference achieved nothing; the only question that remained was whether the City of London retained or could command sufficient resources to defend the pound sterling and thus once again to prove itself the inner keep of stability in a situation in which all outer defences had been already overwhelmed.

The problem, once it became centred in London, ceased to be a purely monetary or banking problem and became political. The following harsh syllogism was imposed. The Bank of England could not save the pound sterling unless it could obtain large credits in New York and Paris: it would fail to obtain those credits unless the British Government produced a balanced budget: it would be impossible to balance that budget unless drastic economies were made: and if the world were to be convinced of the sincerity and efficacy of our policy of retrenchment, it was essential that among our economies should figure prominently some reduction of the benefits paid to the unemployed.

Looking back to the crisis of 1931 across a gulf of twenty terrible years, it may seem to younger readers that the panic aroused by what to them may appear a purely monetary difficulty was hysterical and disproportionate. The emotions experienced by each side in the controversy were, however, neither egoistic nor superficial. The one side honestly believed that the collapse of the pound sterling would entail inflation on the German scale, the liquidation of all investments,

450

savings, annuities and pensions, and the consequent ruin of several million deserving citizens. The other side were convinced that it would be a spiritual impossibility for the Labour Party to remain in power and impose sacrifices upon the most indigent section of the working class. It was not, as was often said at the time, that the puritans of the Labour movement 'put Party above country': their obstinacy was more honourable than that; it was simply that if cuts had to be made in the dole, they preferred that they should be made by someone else. It would be a grave error of comprehension to underestimate the actual anguish that was felt by both sides at the time.

In the next chapter an account will be given, in the shape almost of a day to day narrative, of the stages by which the financial emergency developed into a political crisis of such magnitude that the King was obliged, in the exercise of his constitutional duty, to assume a fearful responsibility. The degree of strain imposed upon him by the resultant conflict of duties cannot rightly be estimated unless it be realised that during that period he was suffering from nervous depression. Before, therefore, embarking upon the political narrative, it is necessary briefly to recount the personal misfortunes and distresses that assailed the King in the course of that same year.

He had not fully recovered from his grave illness, and in April he had a renewed attack of bronchitis which confined him to his room for four weeks,

'The Doctors', he wrote irritably in his diary for April 9, 'again appeared & said I was better, but I don't feel so.'

He was exposed, moreover, during the year to a series of personal bereavements and worries that increased his depression.

On January 4, 1931, his eldest sister, the Princess Royal, Duchess of Fife, died in London. 'A bad beginning', the King wrote in his diary, 'for a New Year. I feel very depressed.' Only a fortnight later, came the sudden death of Sir Charles Cust, the King's oldest and most intimate friend. They had been fellow cadets in the *Britannia* in 1877: they had been shipmates in the Mediterranean: Sir Charles Cust had served as the King's equerry for as long as thirty-nine years. With him alone had the King been able to preserve the stark intimacy of naval companionship; with him alone could he revive the memories, the banter and the squabbles of his gun-room days. Alone of the Household, Sir Charles Cust was oblivious of, or perhaps impervious to, the King's increasing dislike of being contradicted or questioned. 'Never heard such nonsense in my life', Sir Charles would grumble when the King embarked upon one of his not infrequent tirades. The other courtiers would sit aghast. The King, secure in his friend's devotion, would either laugh loudly, or retort with added vehemence.

'That brute Charles Cust', he had written as long ago as 1888, 'is sitting on the deck of my cabin behind me, because I have got no other chair, abusing both me & my cabin.'

There was nobody now who would ever dare to abuse. A void was left.

The third misfortune was even more crushing. Lord Stamfordham died on Tuesday, March 31, at the age of eighty:

'Dear Bigge', the King noted in his diary, 'passed peacefully away at 4.30 today. I shall miss him terribly. His loss is irreparable. I shall now make Wigram my Private Secretary.'

Protective, cautious, imaginative and stimulating had been the guidance which, for more than thirty years, King George had obtained from this wise man. There was no exaggeration at all in the obituary tribute which his Sovereign paid: 'He taught me how to be a King.' It was indeed a harsh blow of fate that, on the eve of his greatest trial, deprived the King of a counsellor of such unequalled authority and experience; of a friend so devoted, so sagacious and so vastly esteemed. 'He was', the King wrote to Princess Louise on April 14, 1931, 'the most loyal friend I have ever had.'

On April 15 the King was much distressed to learn that a revolution had broken out in Spain and that King Alfonso and Queen Ena had been obliged to leave the country. On April 24 King Alfonso, who had crossed to England, came down to Windsor:

'Alfonso came to see us this afternoon. He is wonderful—so plucky & cheery, in spite of his future. I fear he will be very badly off. I am sorry for him. He has tried to do his duty & to serve his country.'

With the summer there came a further blow. In his diary for June 20 the King wrote: 'Dear old Dalton came to see me today; he is ageing a good deal now. He is 91½ years old.' On July 28 there is another entry:

'Got the sad news that dear old Dalton passed away in the night. He was nearly ninety two & came to Eddy & me as our tutor in 1871, just sixty years ago. I have always been devoted to him.'

The King was thus in a mood of dejection, and not in a robust state of health, when called upon to assume personal responsibility in the crisis which, with ever intensifying ferocity, developed during the summer and autumn of 1931.

CHAPTER XXVII

NATIONAL GOVERNMENT

1931

The May Report—The Economic Committee of the Cabinet known as the 'Big Five'—Mr MacDonald returns to London—The Big Five recommend stringent economies, including a cut in unemployment relief—The Cabinet approve these recommendations, except as regards Transitional Benefit—The Prime Minister meets the T.U.C.—They refuse to consent to any reduction in the dole or in the pay and salaries of the lower income groups—Mr MacDonald angered by the interference of the T.U.C.—The Cabinet change their attitude and scale down the economies to which they had previously agreed—The 'enquiry' addressed to the bankers of New York—The King leaves Balmoral for London—He consults Sir Herbert Samuel and Mr Baldwin—Sir Herbert Samuel's advice—Mr Baldwin agrees to serve under Mr MacDonald—The Cabinet await the reply from the New York Bankers—The telegram arrives—It shocks some Labour Ministers—The King appeals to Mr MacDonald not to resign—The Buckingham Palace Conference—Mr MacDonald consents to form a National Government—The scene in Downing Street—Mr MacDonald resigns as Labour Prime Minister and then kisses hands as Prime Minister in a National Government.

(1)

ON February 11, 1931, the Conservative Opposition in the House of Commons had called attention to the state of the national finances and to the need for stringent and immediate economies. Mr Snowden in reply had admitted that, if an increasing deficit were to be avoided, 'drastic and disagreeable measures' would have to be imposed. The Liberals had then moved and carried an amendment providing for the appointment of an independent Committee to make recommendations for 'effecting forthwith all practicable and legitimate reductions in the national expenditure'. On March 17 the Government had constituted such a Committee under the chairmanship of Sir George May.[1] The Committee did not present their report to the Chancellor of the Exchequer until July 31.

[1] Sir George May had been secretary of the Prudential Assurance Co., and was regarded as one of the leading actuaries of the day. He was created Lord May of Weybridge in 1935. His colleagues on the Economy Committee were Lord Plender, Sir Thomas Royden, Mr Ashley Cooper, Sir Mark Webster Jenkinson, Mr Charles Latham and Mr Arthur Pugh.

On that day Mr Snowden informed the House of Commons that he had now received the report of the May Committee and that it would be published immediately. Its contents, he added, would come as a shock to public opinion both at home and abroad. The economies recommended by the Committee would be so unpopular that they could not possibly be enforced by a minority Government unless they had behind them the backing of the House as a whole. On the same day Mr MacDonald set up a special Committee of the Cabinet, under his own chairmanship, to consider how far the recommendations of the May Report could in practice be applied. This Committee, which played an important part in the crisis that ensued, became known as 'The Cabinet Economy Committee' or more succinctly as 'The Big Five'.[1] Parliament then dispersed for the summer holidays. The Prime Minister went to Lossiemouth, Mr Neville Chamberlain to Scotland, and Mr Baldwin to Aix-les-Bains. These holidays did not remain undisturbed.

The May Report disclosed the fact that, in order to produce a properly balanced Budget in 1932, it would be necessary to provide for a deficit of some £120 million. This deficit would have to be met by economies and fresh taxation. At present, the report added, the country was living beyond its income. The expenditure, for instance, on social services and unemployment relief, which in 1911 had amounted to approximately sixty-two million, had by 1922 reached the huge figure of nearly three hundred and forty-two million. Drastic cuts would be instantly required. The report recommended therefore a general reduction in salaries, including those of Ministers, Judges and Civil Servants. The pay of the members of the Fighting Services was to be reduced to the rates obtaining in 1925; the pay of the police was to be cut by 12½% and the salaries of teachers by 20%. Most important of all, the unemployment benefit was to be reduced by 20%, that is from 30/- a week to 24/- a week. This reduction, the Report stated, was justified by the fact that, owing to the fall in the cost of living since 1922, a rate of 14/4 a week would now possess the same purchasing power as a rate of 22/- nine years ago; thus under the proposed reductions the unemployed would, in terms of actual purchasing power, be getting only 10d. a week less than in 1928.

These several economies, the Report estimated, would produce a

[1] This Cabinet Committee was composed of the Prime Minister, Mr Philip Snowden, Mr J. H. Thomas, Mr Arthur Henderson and Mr William Graham.

total saving of £96,578,000. There would still be a gap between revenue and expenditure of between twenty and thirty million pounds. It was for the Chancellor of the Exchequer to decide by what means this perfectly manageable gap could be closed.

In a minority report Mr Charles Latham and Mr Arthur Pugh dissented from the recommendations of their colleagues on the ground that these economies would impose 'an unfair measure of sacrifice upon certain large sections of the community . . . while not imposing comparable sacrifices upon those more favourably situated'. The rank and file of the Labour Party agreed whole-heartedly with Mr Latham and Mr Pugh: Mr MacDonald and Mr Snowden did not.

(2)

Between July 13 and July 30 foreign deposits to the value of some thirty-four million pounds had been withdrawn from London. The Bank of England was obliged to obtain a credit in dollars from the Federal Reserve Bank of New York and a credit in francs from the Banque de France, to a combined value of some fifty million pounds. Mr Montagu Norman, the Governor of the Bank of England, was absent throughout this critical period, having been ordered by his doctors to take a long sea voyage. The Bank was represented during the negotiations that ensued by Sir Ernest Harvey, the Deputy Governor, and by Mr Edward Peacock, one of the Directors.[1] It was soon realised that the credits already obtained in New York and Paris would not be sufficient to meet the increased drain on gold which had been caused by the revelations of the May Report and that further loans would be required. Such supplementary loans could not, however, be raised as purely banking transactions and would, in the circumstances, have to be sponsored by the Government themselves. In that the charter of the Federal Reserve Bank of New York did not permit them to make loans to foreign Governments, Mr Harrison, the chairman of that Bank, advised Sir Ernest Harvey to negotiate any further credits through Messrs J. P. Morgan and Co., the British Government agents. From that point onwards, therefore, Mr Harrison and the Federal Reserve Bank of New York acted as friendly advisers only; the main negotiations were conducted with a consortium of New York Bankers, through the agency of J. P. Morgan.

On Saturday, August 8, Mr Ramsay MacDonald was warned

[1] Mr Edward Peacock was also a Director of Baring Brothers, and in that capacity had succeeded Lord Revelstoke as private financial adviser to the King. He received the G.C.V.O. in 1934.

that a situation of immediate gravity was impending. He left Lossie-mouth on the night of Monday, August 10, and reached King's Cross on the following morning. Mr Baldwin, who had started wandering slowly towards Aix-les-Bains, was recalled when half-way there. Mr Neville Chamberlain, who was establishing himself as the Opposi-tion's financial expert, was summoned back from Scotland. Mr Lloyd George was at the time recovering from an operation; the leadership of the Liberal Party had therefore devolved upon Sir Herbert Samuel.

The Prime Minister, on reaching Downing Street on the morning of Tuesday, August 11, entered into immediate conference with the officials of the Bank of England. The situation they disclosed was, with its implication of immediate bankruptcy, so serious that he at once telegraphed to the four other members of the Cabinet Economy Committee, asking them to come to London urgently and to meet him in Downing Street on the following day.

The Big Five gathered together on the afternoon of Wednesday, August 12, and sat all through Thursday, August 13. Mr Snowden divulged to them that the budget deficit for 1932 would be in the region of one hundred and seventy million, representing an increase of fifty million on that foreshadowed in the May Report. He added that if the flight from the pound were to be checked and bankruptcy averted, the Government would have to raise further large credits in New York and Paris; but that such credits would not be obtained unless immediate plans were formulated, accepted and published for balancing both the current and the 1932 Budget by making drastic economies on the principle of equal sacrifice for all.

The Big Five, after painful discussion, agreed that there was no alternative but to accept something like the economies suggested in the May Report, even if those economies were to include the odious necessity of a cut in unemployment benefit.[1] That the Big Five, with all their immense influence in the Labour Party, should have accepted these sacrifices filled the hearts of the Treasury officials with sweet, short-lived joy.

[1] The figures provisionally agreed to by the Big Five to meet the estimated deficit in the financial year April 1932–April 1933 were as follows:

Estimated Deficit	-	-	-	£170,000,000
Suggested Economies	-	-	-	78,575,000
Leaving a deficit of -	-	-	-	91,425,000
To be raised by taxation	-	-	-	88,500,000

(3)

The full Cabinet met in Downing Street at 11 a.m. on Wednesday, August 19, to consider the report submitted by the Big Five. The majority, with great reluctance, agreed to the economies advocated, with the important exception of the suggested cuts in Transitional Benefit. A minority insisted that there must be no reduction whatsoever in the doles being paid to the unemployed and that additional revenue must be created by imposing a general Revenue Tariff of 10%. It was decided to refer the problem of Transitional Benefit to a Sub-Committee.[1] All the latter could do was to propose some slight rearrangement of contributions, producing a saving of four million pounds in place of the twenty million that the Big Five had recommended. The Prime Minister made it clear that such a saving could not be regarded as adequate and that all idea of a Revenue Tariff must be abandoned, since it would be obnoxious to the Liberal Party.

On Thursday, August 20, the Prime Minister met the General Council of the Trades Union Congress and made them a full statement of the position, together with an outline of the economies that had been proposed. The Council refused to agree to any alteration

The suggested economies were to be composed as follows:

Unemployment Benefit -	-	-	-	£48,500,000
Composed of			
(a) on Unemployment Insurance			28,500,000
(b) on Transitional Benefit			20,000,000

(The savings on (a) were to be secured by 15M. increased contributions, 8M. by reduction to 26 weeks, 2¼M. by premium, and 3M. by removal of anomalies.)

Other Economies.

Teachers' Salaries	-	-	-	-	11,400,000
Reduction in Service Pay	-	-	-	9,000,000
Reduction in Police Pay	-	-	-	500,000
Roads	-	-	-	-	-	7,800,000
Other economies	-	-	-	-	5,350,000

Mr Arthur Henderson and Mr William Graham stated subsequently that they had only agreed to these cuts on the express condition that the scheme was to be approved by the whole Cabinet, due to meet on August 19.

[1] This Sub-Committee was composed of Mr Arthur Greenwood, Mr William Graham, Mr Tom Johnston and Miss Margaret Bondfield.

of the existing terms and conditions of the Unemployment Insurance scheme, or to contemplate any reduction whatsoever in unemployment benefit. They were also opposed to any cut in teachers' salaries or in the pay of the lower ranks of the services. Nor would they agree to any suspension of existing relief works, especially road building, since this would throw more labour out of work. The Prime Minister, on receiving these grim decisions, returned to Downing Street in a mood of furious despair.

It is impossible not to feel sympathy for Mr Ramsay MacDonald in the dilemma by which he was at that hour confronted. Every fibre of his complex temperament was torn and jangled by clashing emotions: patriotism and vanity, loyalty and resentment, impatience and irresolution, scorn and sentiment, pride and self-pity, disdain coupled with seething Celtic rage. He was frightened by the prospect of estranging himself from people whom he had served or led all his life, from friends whose loyalty he had commanded for thirty-seven years. He was too imaginative, and at the same time too realistic, not to foresee the wild charges of betrayal, the fierce misrepresentations, the cold accumulating cruelty, the terrible loneliness, to which he would expose himself if, in this crisis, he decided to separate from his Labour colleagues, associates and clients. Yet he was too proud to bow to the dictates of men whom he regarded as his intellectual and moral inferiors; too pugnacious not to court political suicide rather than to surrender tamely to the line of least resistance; too vain, perhaps, to sacrifice without deep mortification the pomps of power.[1] There is no evidence at all to suggest that by the night of August 20 he had already made up his mind to form and lead a Coalition Government: it is far more probable that, had it not been for the obstinate intransigeance of the T.U.C., he would immediately have resigned with his Ministers and allowed Mr Baldwin to impose the economies required. The refusal of the T.U.C. to move one inch to ease his difficulties, their overt attempt to dictate terms to an elected Government, outraged his political conscience, aroused his personal vindictiveness, and steeled his resolve.

The Cabinet met again in the morning of Friday, August 21.

---

[1] Mr Sidney Webb, in analysing this great political drama, did not hesitate to describe Mr Ramsay MacDonald as 'its author, its producer and its principal actor' (*Political Quarterly*, Vol. III, No. 1). Lord Parmoor contended that Mr MacDonald's failure to consult the Cabinet before accepting office was 'unconstitutional'. This seems a daring statement on the part of a lawyer (*Retrospect*, p. 317).

While asserting that no Government worthy of the name could for one instant submit to dictation from an outside body such as the T.U.C., they proceeded at once to scale down the economies to which they had previously agreed.[1] At 5.0 that evening the Prime Minister interviewed the leaders of the Opposition. They informed him that the economies as now amended were not sufficient to stem the flight from the pound, and that he must either persuade his colleagues to consent to more effective retrenchments, or place the resignation of his Government in the King's hands. The Cabinet resumed its discussion on the morning of Saturday, August 22, when the Prime Minister informed them of the stark alternatives presented to him on the previous evening by the Conservative and Liberal leaders. Mr Snowden then made to his colleagues a passionate appeal, pointing out that if, as a result of their blindness, the pound dropped suddenly to half its value, it would be every class in the community that would suffer from the resultant doubling of the cost of living.[2] Grudgingly the Cabinet agreed to allow the Prime Minister to 'enquire' of the Opposition whether, if the economy figure were raised from £56,375,000 to £76,000,000, including a 10% cut in unemployment relief, the Government could then count on Conservative and Liberal support. This suggestion was to be put to the Opposition solely and simply as an 'enquiry' and without in any way implying that the Cabinet as a whole had agreed to such increases. The Opposition leaders, when approached with this enquiry, replied, sensibly enough, that it was for the bankers to say whether such a scale of economies would suffice to convince the investing public of New York and Paris that it would be safe to sub-

---

[1] The difference between the economies accepted on August 20 and those adopted on August 21 after the intervention of the T.U.C. can be summarised as follows:

Adopted on August 20.		*As revised on August 21.*	
Unemployment -	- £48½ M.	Unemployment -	£22 M.
Other economies -	- £30 M.	Other economies -	£34,375 M.
Leaving £91 M. to be raised by taxation.		Leaving £113,635,000 to be raised by taxation.	

[2] Those who recall the fact that, when a few weeks later we were driven off the gold standard, nothing very dreadful resulted, may be inclined to believe that in so arguing Mr Snowden was not being sincere. Such hindsight is not intelligent. Mr Snowden, the Treasury and the City of London were obsessed by the terrible consequences that had accompanied inflation in Germany, when the whole middle class had been ruined and a situation of deep social and moral degradation created.

scribe to further immense loans to London. Sir Ernest Harvey and Mr Peacock, when consulted, replied that they would immediately put the case to the New York bankers and obtain their opinion. The Cabinet then adjourned.

(4)

Since August 11 the King had been at Sandringham, keeping in touch by telephone with the hourly developments of the crisis. It had already been announced in the Press that he would be leaving for Balmoral on the night of Friday, August 21. Having some suspicion that there existed within the Cabinet a greater conflict of opinion than the Prime Minister had been willing to divulge, the King suggested that it might be preferable if he were to postpone his visit to Scotland. Mr MacDonald replied that there was no reason why he should not go to Balmoral as originally planned, and that to cancel his journey at the last moment might give rise 'to alarming rumours and cause consternation'. Scarcely, however, had the King arrived at Balmoral in the early morning of Saturday, August 22, when a telephone message was received from Downing Street stating that his presence in London might after all become necessary. The King at once decided that 'there was no use shilly-shallying on an occasion like this', and that he would return to London that very night. His Majesty reached Euston shortly after eight on the morning of Sunday, August 23 : two hours later he received the Prime Minister at Buckingham Palace.

Mr MacDonald explained that the Government were urgently seeking to obtain further loans or credits in New York and Paris to a total of one hundred million pounds. They were informed that no such credits could be obtained unless it were clear that the estimated budget deficit of £170 millions would be met, not merely by increased taxation, but also by a severe programme of economies. They had the night before asked New York whether confidence would be restored if economies in the region of £76 million, including a 10% cut in the unemployment dole, were introduced, concurrently with additional taxes to the round figure of £50 million. They were expecting to receive a reply to this enquiry before midnight.

Mr MacDonald at the same time warned the King that it was possible that certain of his most influential colleagues in the Cabinet, and notably Mr Arthur Henderson and Mr William Graham, would not consent to these economies now tentatively put to New York. If
460

they were to resign from the Government it would not be possible for him to carry on the administration without their assistance. The resignation of the Labour Government as a whole would then become inevitable.

The King, on receiving this intimation, decided that the correct constitutional course was immediately to consult the leaders of the Conservative and Liberal Oppositions. Mr Baldwin, who had a second time been recalled from Aix-les-Bains and who had reached London the night before, had strayed off into the streets and could not be located: it was thus by one of the chances of history that Sir Herbert Samuel was the first of the two leaders to furnish His Majesty with advice. Sir Herbert, who reached the Palace shortly after noon, told the King that, in view of the fact that the necessary economies would prove most unpalatable to the working class, it would be to the general interest if they could be imposed by a Labour Government. The best solution would be if Mr Ramsay MacDonald, either with his present, or with a reconstituted Labour Cabinet, could propose the economies required. If he failed to secure the support of a sufficient number of his colleagues, then the best alternative would be a National Government composed of members of the three parties. It would be preferable that Mr MacDonald should remain Prime Minister in such a National Government. Sir Herbert made it clear at the same time that such a non-party Government should only be constituted 'for the single purpose of overcoming the financial crisis'.[a]

'Some time after the crisis', Sir Clive Wigram records,[b] 'in discussing it with the King, I was impressed by the fact that His Majesty found Sir Herbert Samuel the clearest-minded of the three and said that he had put the case for a National Government much clearer than either of the others. It was after the King's interview with Sir Herbert Samuel that His Majesty became convinced of the necessity for the National Government. It was quite by luck that Mr Baldwin did not come to see the King before Sir Herbert Samuel. I tried to catch the former, but found he was out and so summoned Sir Herbert Samuel instead. Consequently by the time the King saw Mr Baldwin, His Majesty had had his talk with Sir Herbert Samuel.'

At 3.0 that afternoon, Mr Baldwin in his turn came to Buckingham Palace. The King asked him whether he would be prepared to serve in a National Government under Mr Ramsay MacDonald. Mr Baldwin answered that he would be ready to do anything to assist the country in the present crisis. Even if Mr MacDonald insisted on resigning, he, Mr Baldwin, would be ready to carry on the Government if he could be assured of the support of the Liberal Party in effecting the necessary economies. In that event, once the crisis had been surmounted, he would ask His Majesty for a dissolution and go to the country. To this the King agreed:

> 'The King', wrote Sir Clive Wigram,^c 'was greatly pleased with Mr Baldwin's readiness to meet the crisis which had arisen, and to sink Party interests for the sake of the Country.'[1]

(5)

The Cabinet met again at 7.0 p.m. that Sunday evening. The Prime Minister informed them that no reply had yet been received to the enquiry addressed the night before to the New York bankers, but that a telegram was expected to arrive at any moment. He suggested that the Cabinet should adjourn until this telegram arrived. For more than an hour in the summer twilight the Ministers strolled about the garden of Downing Street discussing the terrible decision with which they were all faced. There are some who contend that it was during this anxious interlude that Mr Arthur Henderson was able finally to persuade a majority of his colleagues to resign their offices rather than consent to any reduction in unemployment relief.

At 8.45 a telephone message was received from the Bank of England to the effect that the telegram from New York had at last arrived and that the Deputy Governor, Sir Ernest Harvey, was bringing it with him to Downing Street. The Ministers then left the garden and gathered together in the Cabinet room. A few minutes later Mr C. P. Duff, the Prime Minister's Private Secretary, came in to announce that Sir Ernest Harvey had arrived. The Prime Minister dashed out, snatched the telegram from Sir Ernest's hand and

---

[1] The documents in the Royal Archives at Windsor that bear upon the 1931 crisis have been bound together in chronological order under the general File number K.2330. They are so easy to identify that detailed reference numbers have, in this chapter, been reduced to a minimum.

It should also be explained that, in describing the events that led to the formation of a National Government in 1931, the author has to some extent abandoned his general principle of only recording such facts or opinions as can be confirmed by documentary evidence. In the present narrative he has been much assisted by verbal discussions with Lord Wigram, Lord Hardinge of Penshurst, Lord Samuel, Sir Ernest Harvey, Sir Edward Peacock and Mr Herbert Morrison. He must also express indebtedness to Mr H. C. B. Mynors of the Bank of England for his courtesy in consenting to verify certain facts and figures.

returned with it to the Cabinet room. He read the telegram slowly to his assembled colleagues, and when he reached the concluding sentence loud protests were raised. To Sir Ernest Harvey, waiting in the adjoining room, it seemed that 'pandemonium had broken loose'.

On the previous morning Messrs J. P. Morgan and Co. had already hinted that the American investing public might be reluctant to subscribe to so enormous a loan, in view of the lack of confidence felt by the ordinary United States citizen in Europe in general, as well as in the willingness of a Socialist Government to balance budgets or adopt 'sound' fiscal policies. In this second telegram, while expressing every desire to assist, Messrs J. P. Morgan foresaw that there was but little prospect of the American public being willing to take up a public loan, unless and until Parliament had already passed the necessary economy legislation. It would be easier to arrange some short-term Treasury transaction than to coax the public into absorbing a large loan. In their concluding paragraph Messrs J. P. Morgan and Co. enquired whether they were correct in assuming that the economy proposals now tentatively put forward by the Cabinet had the sincere approval and support of the Bank of England and the City generally, and whether the latter regarded them as sufficient to re-establish confidence. It was, it seems, this last sentence that caused Ministers to cry aloud in pain.

Having read to the Cabinet the telegram from J. P. Morgan and Co., the Prime Minister made a strong personal appeal to his colleagues to accept the revised schedule of economies even though they comprised a 10% cut in the dole. Mr MacDonald stated that he was all too well aware that to reduce unemployment benefit would cause much resentment in Labour circles and was in fact a denial of much that the Labour movement had always stood for. Yet he was confident that the majority of the Party would support him were he able to lay the whole facts before them. Moreover, if a scheme that imposed such grave sacrifices on other sections of the community left the unemployed in a privileged position, the Labour Party might lose moral prestige. He must therefore ask the Cabinet here and now to agree to a cut of 10% in unemployment relief and, if any senior Ministers felt it necessary to resign rather than to consent to such a measure, then the Government must resign as a whole.

It was immediately evident that many important Ministers, with Mr Arthur Henderson at their head, were determined never to consent to any reduction in the benefit. The Prime Minister then stated that he proposed immediately to inform the King of what had passed in Cabinet and to advise His Majesty to summon a conference between Mr Baldwin, Sir Herbert Samuel and himself for the following morning. The Cabinet authorised the Prime Minister to inform His Majesty that they had placed their resignations in his hands. At 10.10 p.m. Mr MacDonald left the Cabinet room in a state of extreme agitation. 'I am off to the Palace', he flung at Sir Ernest Harvey in passing, 'to throw in my hand.'

Mr Peacock that evening was dining with the King. He recalls that the political crisis was not mentioned during the dinner and that the conversation turned upon fluctuations in the prices of wheat and barley. The King, with his amazing memory, was able accurately to quote those prices over the last ten years. At 10.15 a message was received at the Palace from Downing Street announcing that the Prime Minister was on his way. Mr Peacock had a short telephone conversation with Sir Ernest Harvey in Downing Street, who told him that during the last hour loud protests had been proceeding from the Cabinet room and that the Prime Minister on leaving had appeared distraught.

Mr MacDonald reached the Palace at 10.20:

'The Prime Minister', wrote Sir Clive Wigram,[d] 'looked scared and unbalanced. He told the King that all was up and that at the Cabinet 11 had voted for accepting the terms of the Bankers and 8 against. The opposition included Henderson, Graham, Adamson, Greenwood, Clynes, Alexander, Addison and Lansbury. In these circumstances the Prime Minister had no alternative than to tender the resignation of the Cabinet.

The King impressed on the Prime Minister that he was the only man to lead the country through this crisis and hoped he would reconsider the situation. His Majesty told him that the Conservatives and Liberals would support him in restoring the confidence of foreigners in the financial stability of the country.

The Prime Minister asked whether the King would confer with Baldwin, Samuel and himself in the morning. His Majesty willingly acceded to this request. The Prime Minister telephoned to Downing Street to ask his Private Secretary to arrange for Baldwin and Samuel to meet him as soon as possible.'

The Cabinet by then had dispersed, expecting to learn the next morning that the Labour Government had resigned and that the King had sent for Mr Baldwin and entrusted him with the task of forming a Conservative Government with Liberal support. Even Mr Snowden had retired to bed that Sunday night with the impression that all was over. He had at the time no suspicion at all that Mr

464

Ramsay MacDonald would ever contemplate heading a National Government with the assistance of the two leaders of the Opposition. The Prime Minister, so Mr Snowden asserts, came to that decision 'without a word of previous consultation with his Labour colleagues'. Nor, once the decision had been come to, did the prospect of breaking with past associations appear to cause him anguish, or even regret. 'On the contrary', writes Mr Snowden, 'he set about the formation of the National Government with an enthusiasm which showed that the adventure was highly agreeable to him.' This may be no more than one of Mr Snowden's mustard phrases. Mr MacDonald always asserted in later years that he had foreseen from the first moment the rancorous hostility with which he would thereafter be pursued: that he had taken his decision fully conscious that he was committing political suicide.

(6)

The King's diary for Monday, August 24, is written with his habitual avoidance of exaggeration:

'*Buckingham Palace*. Cold N.E. wind, below 50 degrees, no sun. Had another strenuous day. At 10.0 I held a Conference here in Indian room with the Prime Minister, Baldwin & Samuel & we discussed the formation of a National Government composed of all three Parties, with Ramsay MacDonald as P.M., as a temporary measure to pass the necessary Economy and Finance Bill through the House of Commons, when there would be a dissolution followed by a General Election, & this we agreed to. . . . The Prime Minister came at 4.0 and tendered his resignation. I then invited him to form a National Government, which he agreed to do.'

Sir Clive Wigram's memorandum of what happened during the Conference is more detailed and informative: '

'At 10. a.m. the King held a Conference at Buckingham Palace at which the Prime Minister, Baldwin and Samuel were present. At the beginning, His Majesty impressed upon them that before they left the Palace some communiqué must be issued, which would no longer keep the country and the world in suspense. The Prime Minister said that he had the resignation of his Cabinet in his pocket, but the King replied that he trusted there was no question of the Prime Minister's resignation: the leaders of the three Parties must get together and come to some arrangement. His Majesty hoped that the Prime Minister, with the colleagues who remained faithful to him, would help in the formation of a National Government, which the King was sure would be supported by the Conservatives and the Liberals. The King assured the Prime Minister that, remaining at his post, his position and reputation would be much more enhanced than if he surrendered the government of the country at such a crisis. Baldwin and Samuel said that they were willing to serve under the Prime Minister, and render all help possible to carry on the Government as a National Emergency Government until an emergency bill or bills had been passed by Parliament, which would restore once more British credit and the confidence of foreigners. After that they would expect His Majesty to grant a dissolution. To this course the King agreed. During the Election the National Government would remain in being, though of course each Party would fight the Election on its own lines.

At 10.35 a.m. The King left the three Party leaders to settle the details of the communiqué to be issued, and the latter said they would let His Majesty know when they were ready.

About 11.45 the King was requested to return to the Conference, and was glad to hear that they had been able to some extent to come to some arrangement. A Memorandum had been drawn up which Baldwin and Samuel could place before their respective colleagues, but the Prime Minister said that he would not read this out in Cabinet as he should keep it only for those who remained faithful to him. Probably the new National Government would consist of a small Cabinet of 12. It is quite understood that, up to now, the Cabinet had not resigned. His Majesty congratulated them on the solution of this difficult problem, and pointed out that while France and other countries existed for weeks without a Government, in this country our constitution is so generous that leaders of Parties, after fighting one another for months in the House of Commons, were ready to meet together under the roof of the Sovereign and sink their own differences for a common good and arrange as they had done this morning for a National Government to meet one of the gravest crises that the British Empire had yet been asked to face.

At the end of the Conference the following communiqué was issued to the Press:

"His Majesty the King invited the Prime Minister, Mr Stanley Baldwin and Sir Herbert Samuel to Buckingham Palace this morning, and the formation of a National Government is under consideration. A fuller announcement will be made later." "[1]

---

[1] It was suggested in some quarters that the King, in urging the leaders of the three Parties to unite in forming a National Government, had gone beyond his constitutional powers. This legend has been disposed of by Sir Herbert Samuel and others. On pages 221–222 of his Memoirs the present Lord Samuel writes as follows: 'Mr MacDonald's resignation was the necessary consequence of an irreconcilable division in his Cabinet. The King then acted in strict accordance with precedent in following the advice of the outgoing Premier: that was to bring into consultation the spokesmen of the two Parties which together could furnish a majority in the House of Commons able to sustain a new Administration. The invitation to the

A Memorandum written by Sir Herbert Samuel while the Conference was still sitting emphasises some of the points in the above record. It was clearly understood that the National Government now agreed to be formed would not be a Coalition in the ordinary sense, 'but a co-operation of individuals': it was agreed that, when the emergency had been dealt with, the respective Parties would return to their ordinary positions: the ensuing election would not be fought by the National Government as a Coalition, but by each of the three Parties, acting independently. On such conditions a National Government would be formed under Mr Ramsay Mac-Donald to impose economies to the amount of £70 million, which would include a cut of 10% in unemployment benefit and increased contributions to the Unemployment Insurance Fund of about fourteen million pounds.

Mr Ramsay MacDonald left Buckingham Palace at 11.55 and his last meeting with his colleagues took place at noon. He entered the Cabinet room with a confident, or as one of his colleagues described it, a 'jaunty' air, and at once informed the assembled Ministers that it had been decided to form a 'Cabinet of Individuals' to deal with the emergency. He himself was to be one of these 'individuals'; he invited any who so desired, to join him in this patriotic act of self-sacrifice. There was a hush when he made this astounding announcement. Mr Arthur Henderson flung himself back in his chair and emitted a low whistle. Mr Herbert Morrison, at that date a very junior Minister, broke the silence with the words: 'Well, Prime Minister, it is very easy to get in to such a combination: you will find it very difficult to get out of it. And I for one am not coming with you.' One by one around the table each of the Ministers signified his unwillingness to join. Mr Ramsay MacDonald found himself deserted, except by Mr Thomas, Lord Sankey and a most unwilling Philip Snowden. The Cabinet dispersed at 12.25.

At 2.30 that afternoon Mr Ramsay MacDonald received the junior Ministers in the Labour Government. He addressed them 'very earnestly and impressively'.[g] He assured them that he had no wish that they should accompany him into the wilderness; they were

Prime Minister to return to office, and to form a new Administration on an all-party basis, was the course advised by them. So far as I was myself concerned, neither directly nor indirectly, did any expression reach me of any personal opinion or wish of His Majesty. In every particular the principles and practice of our democratic constitution were scrupulously observed.'

young men, with their lives before them; they must consider their future careers; it would in the end be more profitable for them to dissociate themselves from himself and the National Government and to join what would now become the Labour Opposition in the House. Most of the junior Ministers followed, but without much subsequent gratitude, this unselfish advice.

At 4.0 p.m. Mr Ramsay MacDonald again drove to Buckingham Palace:

> 'The Prime Minister', wrote Sir Clive Wigram,[h] 'arrived looking worn and weary and was received by the King. The Prime Minister tendered his resignation as Prime Minister of the Labour Government which the King accepted. The King then invited him to form a National Administration. Mr Ramsay MacDonald accepted the offer, and kissed hands on his appointment as the new Prime Minister.'

By the evening of the following day, Tuesday, August 25, Mr MacDonald was able to submit to the King the names of those whom he proposed to include in his new Government.[1] That evening he broadcast a message and an explanation. He stated that the National Government had been formed to do a definite job of work:

> 'Once that work is finished', he said, 'the House of Commons and the general political situation will return to where they were last week. Those of us who have taken risks will receive either our punishment or our reward. The Election that will follow will not be fought by the Government: there will be no coupons. . . .'

At 10.30 on the morning of Wednesday, August 26, the members of the outgoing Cabinet came to surrender their seals of office:

> 'When we went to the Palace', wrote Mr Clynes,[i] 'to hand in our seals of Office to George V the atmosphere was solemn and funereal. There was no talk. We entered His Majesty's study one by one carrying our seals in small red boxes. The King stood beside a table, one hand resting upon it. His face looked grey and lined. I placed my seal on the table, bowed, and silently took my leave.'

---

[1] The new Government was constituted as follows: Mr Ramsay MacDonald, Prime Minister; Mr Baldwin, Lord President; Lord Sankey, Lord Chancellor; Sir Herbert Samuel, Home Secretary; Lord Reading, Foreign Secretary; Mr J. H. Thomas, Dominions and Colonies; Sir Samuel Hoare, India; Lord Amulree, Air Minister; Mr Philip Snowden, Chancellor of the Exchequer; Sir Archibald Sinclair, Scotland; Sir Austen Chamberlain, Admiralty; Sir P. Cunliffe-Lister, Board of Trade; Mr Neville Chamberlain, Health; Sir Donald MacLean, Education; Sir John Gilmour, Agriculture; Lord Lothian, Duchy of Lancaster.

An hour later, at 11.30, the new Cabinet were sworn in. That night Mr Ramsay MacDonald returned to Lossiemouth and the King to Balmoral.[1]

[1] One of the King's first acts on returning to Balmoral was to instruct Sir Frederick Ponsonby, Keeper of the Privy Purse, to inform the Prime Minister that he had decided that, while the emergency lasted, the Civil List should be reduced by £50,000. 'His Majesty', Sir F. Ponsonby wrote, 'desires personally to participate in the movement for the reduction of national expenditure.' The Prince of Wales at the same time contributed £50,000 to the National Exchequer.

CHAPTER XXVIII

THE STATUTE OF WESTMINSTER

1931

The 'colonial' theory of Empire—The Dominions achieve autonomy—The Balfour Formula adopted by the 1926 Conference—The 1930 Conference and the resultant Statute of Westminster—The seven 'vestiges of subordination'—Five of these abolished by the Statute—The King's close interest in Commonwealth affairs and his regret at the loosening of former ties—The exercise of the Royal Prerogative in the Dominions—Two examples of difficulty—The case of Lord Byng of Vimy—The case of Mr Scullin—Recommendations made by the 1930 Conference as a result of these two controversies—Problem of the Royal Title—Problem of the co-ordination of foreign policy—The loose ends left over by the Statute of Westminster—Is the Monarchy divisible?—Two South African Bills raise this question in a difficult form—How can Dominion Ministers furnish His Majesty with 'advice'?—The latter problem remained unsolved during King George's reign.

(1)

THE National Government inaugurated under Mr Ramsay Mac-Donald on August 26, 1931, survived, at least in name, for fourteen dangerous years. In the next chapter an account will be given of the strains and dissensions to which this Coalition was at first exposed: thereafter, relying upon a solid Conservative majority, the National Government enjoyed three years of deceptive tranquillity.

The present chapter will be devoted to a summary of the changes made between 1926 and 1931 in the structure of the British Commonwealth. These changes will be examined mainly in so far as they affected the prerogative, functions and status of the Crown.[1]

It is sometimes assumed that the old 'colonial' theory did not survive the death of Queen Victoria. This is an incorrect assumption. At the time of King George's accession in 1910, the sovereignty of the British Crown and Parliament over the whole Empire was still unimpaired. It was on the advice of British Prime Ministers alone that the King appointed his Viceroys, Governors-General and other representatives: it was from Downing Street that foreign policy was framed and executed: an appeal from the highest colonial courts

---

[1] Any more extended examination of constitutional developments in the Dominions would throw this biography out of scale. The student is referred to the works of Berriedale Keith, Wheare, Evatt and Noel Baker.

470

still lay with the King in Council: and the Monarch retained in theory, and sometimes exercised in practice, the prerogative of withholding his assent to colonial legislation. This system, inherited by King George on his accession, was fundamentally changed during the twenty-five years of his reign.

The principal landmarks on the road from partial dependence to complete autonomy can shortly be enumerated. The contribution made by the Empire during the 1914–1918 war, the part played by the Imperial War Cabinet, the separate status accorded to the Dominions and India at the Paris Peace Conference, their individual membership of the League of Nations, the right exercised by the Dominions of appointing their own diplomatic missions abroad:[1] all these innovations gradually habituated public opinion at home and overseas to the then novel conception that an Empire could become a free association of equal partners. The difficulty was to devise some formula to define this unprecedented relationship between a mother-country and her colonies. The required definition was provided by Lord Balfour, who, in his capacity as chairman of the Inter-Imperial Relations Committee, presented to the Imperial Conference held in London in 1926 a report of creative effect.

While contending characteristically that 'nothing was to be gained by attempting to lay down a Constitution for the British Empire', Lord Balfour defined the status both of the Dominions and of the mother-country in the following important words :

> 'They are autonomous communities within the British Empire, equal in status, in no way subordinate one to another in any aspect of their domestic or external affairs, though united by a common allegiance to the Crown, and freely associated as members of the British Commonwealth of Nations.'

The 1926 Conference adopted the report of Lord Balfour's Committee and directed that the above formula should be studied by legal experts in relation to existing statutes. A sub-conference met in

[1] In October 1918 Canada announced her intention of appointing a Canadian Minister in Washington. Although realising that this would lead to similar demands from other Dominions, the King wrote that 'effect must be given to Canada's wishes' (R.A., L. 1561. 3). When in November 1927 the Canadian Government proposed to accredit diplomatic missions on a reciprocal basis to France and Japan, Lord Stamfordham wrote that the proposal had 'rather taken H.M.'s breath away', and suggested that it would not be long before the Dominions started to appoint their own Ambassadors. As so often, Lord Stamfordham was correct in his forecast (R.A., L. 1561. 14).

1929, examined the reports of the legal experts, and recommended to the Imperial Conference of 1930 that the Balfour formula should be given statutory effect. A Bill, later known as 'The Statute of Westminster', was introduced into the House of Commons on November 12, 1931, and became law on December 11. Parallel legislation was passed by some Dominion Parliaments. The fundamental principle was thus established that a Dominion Parliament could legislate without reference to the laws of the United Kingdom, and that the British Parliament could not legislate for a Dominion without the consent, previously given, of the Dominion concerned.

Autonomy could scarcely be defined in more succinct terms.

(2)

After the acceptance of the Balfour formula by the 1926 Conference, the Dominion Ministers had returned to their own countries and had instructed their legal experts to draw up a list of the reserved powers and prerogatives still possessed by the British Crown and Parliament in regard to the self-governing communities overseas. The catalogue of these 'vestiges of subordination' was not a long one and can be reproduced in summary form:

(1) The prerogative of 'disallowance and reservation', by which was meant the right of the Crown, under the Colonial Laws Validity Act of 1865, to 'disallow' Dominion legislation when in conflict with that of the United Kingdom; and the right of Governors General to withhold their consent to Dominion legislation on the ground that they must 'reserve' it for His Majesty's pleasure. In practice this right had only been exercised in regard to minor legislation, such as shipping and currency laws.

(2) The denial to the Dominion Parliaments of the right to make laws 'repugnant' to the laws of Great Britain.

(3) The denial to Dominion Parliaments of the right to pass laws having extra-territorial effect.

(4) The right of appeal from the highest Dominion courts to the King in Council.

(5) The right of the King to appoint Governors General solely on the advice of the Prime Minister in the United Kingdom.

(6) The wording of the Royal Title. This wording was regarded as offensive to the Irish Free State.

(7) The almost exclusive right hitherto exercised by the British Cabinet to frame foreign policy and to sign treaties on behalf of the Empire.

Of these vestiges of subordination, the first four were explicitly or implicitly abolished by the Statute of Westminster in 1931. By Article II of that instrument the Colonial Laws Validity Act was no longer to apply to Dominion Legislation, and the prerogative of disallowance

472

and reservation was thus implicitly surrendered. Dominion Parliaments were at the same time permitted to pass legislation 'repugnant' to the laws of Great Britain. By Article III of the Statute, Dominion Parliaments were authorised to pass laws having extra-territorial operation. Under Article IV no law passed in the United Kingdom was to apply to any Dominion, except with the consent of that Dominion. Implicit in these provisions was the right of a Dominion Legislature, if it so desired, to abrogate the right of appeal from a Dominion Court to the Privy Council in London.

The preamble of the Statute of Westminster provided that 'inasmuch as the Crown is the symbol of the free association of the members of the British Commonwealth of Nations, and as they are united by common allegiance to the Crown', any alteration in the Royal succession or title shall 'require the assent of the Parliaments of all the Dominions, as of the Parliament of the United Kingdom'. So much for legal forms.[1]

The Statute of Westminster, as the ensuing India Act of 1935, solemnised the renunciation by England of an imperial mission, which in the course of centuries had brought much benefit to herself, her dependencies and the world. These two instruments did not, however, give fixed or final form to a process which, by its very nature, was bound to be evolutionary. It was fully realised at the time that a development of such originality, compass and significance could not be subjected to the constants of detailed enactment, but that it must depend upon such variants and imponderables as interest, tradition and sentiment. The difficulty of reconciling dissimilar feelings, and of applying the principles of the Statute of Westminster to the existing machines of government, will be apparent from even a slight account of the diverse problems of

---

[1] Article I of the Statute of Westminster recognised the term 'Dominion' as applying to Canada, Australia, New Zealand, South Africa, Newfoundland and the Irish Free State.

The original membership of the British Commonwealth of Nations was altered in the years that followed. In 1933 Newfoundland, owing to budget difficulties, renounced her Dominion status and in 1949 became the tenth Province of the Dominion of Canada. Ceylon became a Dominion on February 4, 1948. The Irish Free State, having successively divested herself of the obligations assumed under the 1921 Treaty, finally quitted the association in April 1949. In August 1947 India and Pakistan became independent members of the Commonwealth, owing allegiance to the Sovereign. On January 26, 1950 India became a Republic within the Commonwealth.

adjustment that confronted the King, his advisers and his representatives, during the ensuing years.

King George on his accession had decided not to emulate his father's specialisation in foreign affairs, but to devote his influence to encouraging ever-closer connections between the United Kingdom and the Empire overseas. With this in mind he had decided to crown himself at Delhi and to revisit each of the Dominions in turn. Circumstances prevented the full execution of this programme;[1] yet throughout his reign he maintained a special interest in the affairs of India and the Commonwealth; he instructed the Viceroys and the Governors General to write him regular private letters regarding the politics, economics and personalities of the several countries; the replies that he caused to be returned to these reports show that he had given them his closest scrutiny; he never failed to receive Dominion and Indian statesmen on their visits to England, and his relations with many of them were intimate and continuous. No British monarch has ever acquired so extensive a knowledge of the principles and details of Empire; his exceptionally retentive memory enabled him to astonish overseas visitors by his acquaintance with the problems, ambitions and rivalries that marked the political struggle in their own lands. It was a sad destiny that imposed upon a King, whose most ardent hope it had been to signalise his reign by creating a more intimate association between Great Britain and the Empire, the necessity of approving processes of change, which, by some authorities, are still regarded as processes of disintegration.

(3)

The Balfour formula had emphasised that common allegiance to the Crown would constitute the central factor unifying and integrating the disparate elements of which the Commonwealth was composed.[2] It was taken for granted that the relations between the King

[1] See also pages 141 and 218. Every Prime Minister in turn advised His Majesty that it would be impossible for him to visit one Dominion without visiting all the others; and that in view of the political situation at home and abroad it would not be right for him to absent himself for such long periods from England. In 1924, for instance, his brother-in-law, Lord Athlone, at ·that date Governor-General of the Union of South Africa, begged him to visit 'this priceless jewel of a country with its vast territories', 'Any move', Lord Stamfordham was instructed to reply, 'out of these islands is out of the question' (R.A., P. 474. 76).

[2] It was not at that date regarded as conceivable that any member or prospective member of the Commonwealth could renounce that allegiance

and his Ministers in the Dominions would be governed by the same general principles and conventions as had for so long regulated the relations between the King and successive Prime Ministers and Cabinets in the United Kingdom. It was soon realised that the circumstances were not identical, or even analogous. When transplanted in a different soil and climate, the seedling did not produce the same sort of tree.

In Great Britain, the balance between the rights of the Sovereign and the rights of Ministers, rests upon congenital experience, acquired tradition, instinctive feeling, frequent personal contact and unreserved mutual confidence. It was a physical impossibility for the King to establish with overseas Ministers the intimate personal relations that he had always maintained with successive Cabinets in London. His own representatives in the Dominions, the Governors-General, did not possess comparable prestige: few of them were gifted with his instinct for the possible, or possessed his sensitive antennae. On the other hand, the Dominion Ministers, having been nurtured in a distinct political atmosphere, were not always endowed with a natural understanding of the dignity and difficulty of the King's position, such as had enabled statesmen as diverse as Mr Asquith and Mr Ramsay MacDonald to achieve their objectives without provoking either conflict or offence.

It was soon discovered that the exercise of the Royal Prerogative in the Dominions was a delicate operation, subject to all manner of strains and misunderstandings. The inexperience or impulsiveness of a Governor-General, the intransigeance or suspicion of a Dominion Prime Minister, might at any moment upset the equilibrium which in England had been so ingeniously preserved. The difficulty of adjusting an English convention to the political climate of a Dominion can best be illustrated by taking, as exhibits, two special cases. The first concerns the right of the King, or his representative, to grant or refuse a dissolution; it can be illustrated by the difference uf opinion that arose between Mr Mackenzie King and the Governor-General of Canada, Lord Byng of Vimy, in June 1926. The second created a most unfortunate precedent: it concerned the right of the Sovereign to disapprove the appointment of a Governor-General. As

or join as a Republic. 'Because', writes Mr John Coatman on p. 254 of his *British Family of Nations*, 'the Crown is the strongest, the most natural and the most enduring of all ties which join the member countries of the Commonwealth to each other, any country which snaps that tie *ipso facto* forfeits its membership of the Commonwealth. '

the classic instance of this problem will be taken Mr Scullin's insistence in 1930 on 'advising' the King to approve, against His Majesty's
expressed wishes, the appointment of Sir Isaac Isaacs as Governor-
General of the Commonwealth of Australia.

In September 1925 Mr Mackenzie King, the Liberal Prime
Minister of Canada, asked Lord Byng for a dissolution which was
immediately granted. At the ensuing election the Conservative
Party, under Mr Meighen, gained a majority of fifteen seats. Mr
King contended that he could remain in power by relying on the
votes of the Labour and Progressive Parties: Lord Byng had no
alternative but to accept this advice. In June 1926 Mr Mackenzie
King was threatened with a vote of censure and asked Lord Byng
for another dissolution. Lord Byng rejected this advice, on the ground
that Mr Meighen, as leader of the largest single party in the House,
would be able to form a government without the necessity of exposing the country to a second general election in nine months. Mr
Mackenzie King thereupon resigned and Lord Byng entrusted Mr
Meighen with the formation of a new Government. Three days later
Mr Meighen was defeated by one vote in the House of Commons.
He in his turn asked the Governor-General for a dissolution, which
was at once accorded. At the ensuing election the Liberal Party were
returned with a majority and Mr Mackenzie King triumphantly
resumed office. Lord Byng was criticised for having granted to a
Conservative Prime Minister the dissolution which only a week before
he had refused to a Liberal Prime Minister. There was substance in
this criticism; but, if Lord Byng erred, he did so with excellent intentions. His motives in refusing a dissolution to Mr Mackenzie King
were admirably explained in a letter which, on June 29, 1925, he
addressed to the King:[a]

'Your Majesty, Sir,

I very much regret to tell you that another crisis took place with the
Prime Minister and myself last Saturday. . . . I had three interviews
with Mr King, at each one of which I appealed to him not to put the
King's representative in a position of appearing unconstitutional, and
that another election was at the moment not warranted by the state of
affairs. He refused all pleadings and took the line that he was entitled
to it (the dissolution) and to my support in having it. I still refused.
Thereupon he resigned and I asked Mr Meighen to form a government, which he has done.

Now this constitutional, or unconstitutional, act of mine seems to
resolve itself into these salient features. A Governor-General has the
absolute right of granting or refusing dissolution. The refusal is a very

dangerous decision. It embodies the rejection of the advice of an accredited Minister, which is the bed-rock of constitutional government. Therefore nine times out of ten a Governor-General should take his Prime Minister's advice on this as on other matters. But if the advice offered is considered by the Governor-General to be wrong and unfair, and not for the welfare of the people, it behoves him to act in what he considers the best interests of the country. This is naturally the point of view I have taken.

Mr King in our final interview requested me to consult the Government in London. While recognising to the full the help that this might afford me, I flatly refused—telling Mr King that to ask advice from London, where the conditions were not so well known as they were to me, was to put the British Government in the unfortunate position of having to offer a solution which might give people out here the feeling of a participation in their politics, which is to be strongly deprecated. . . . There seemed to be one person, and one alone, who was responsible for the decision, and that was myself. I should feel that the relationship of the Dominion to the Old Country would be liable to be seriously jeopardised by involving the Home Government, whereas the incompetent or unwise action of a Governor-General can only involve himself. . . .

Mr King, whose bitterness was very marked yesterday, will probably take a very vitriolic line against myself, in spite of his protestations of friendship—this seems only natural. But I have to await the verdict of history to prove my having adopted a wrong course, and this I do with an easy conscience that, right or wrong, I have acted in the interests of Canada and have implicated no one else in my decision.

I can only assure Your Majesty of my deepest regret for this incident towards the end of my period out here.

I have the honour to be, Sir,
Your obedient servant
(Signed) Byng of Vimy.'

It was largely as a result of this incident that the Imperial Conference of 1926 resolved that a Governor-General's functions in a Dominion were 'similar in all essentials' to those of the Sovereign in the United Kingdom. Whether this apophthegm implied that the King no longer possessed the prerogative of refusing a dissolution was not stated: in dealing with something so empirical as the British Constitution it was considered wiser to leave every possible 'i' undotted and every possible 't' uncrossed.

(4)

The King was more directly implicated in the dispute that arose owing to the insistence of Mr Scullin, the Commonwealth Prime

Minister, on the appointment of Sir Isaac Isaacs[1] as Governor-General of Australia. Prior to the Imperial Conference of 1926, the customary procedure had been for the Prime Minister in the United Kingdom, after informal consultation with the Dominion concerned, to submit to the King the names of candidates for the post of Governor-General. The individuals chosen had hitherto been natives of Great Britain, either members of the Royal Family, patricians, or men who, whether in the armed forces or elsewhere, had rendered distinguished public service. It was now contended—and notably by General Hertzog in South Africa and by Mr Scullin in Australia—that the principles accepted by the Imperial Conference of 1926 implied that in future these appointments should be made solely on the advice of the Dominion Cabinets.[2] When therefore, in March 1930, Lord Stonehaven's term as Governor-General of Australia was drawing to its close, Mr Scullin announced that he intended to advise the King to approve the appointment of Sir Isaac Isaacs as Lord Stonehaven's successor.

On March 31 the King saw Lord Passfield, Secretary of State for the Dominions and Colonies, and informed him that such an appointment could not be approved. His Majesty pointed out that, since Ministers in the United Kingdom were precluded by the 1926 resolutions from advising the Crown in a matter concerning a Dominion, it was for the Sovereign, in such circumstances to act on his own initiative. Lord Passfield feared that this would create an impossible situation and involve the Crown in political controversy. The only hope was to postpone the issue until further consideration could be given to it. He therefore begged Mr Scullin not to force a decision, but to await the next Imperial Conference which was to be held that autumn. With some reluctance Mr Scullin agreed.[b]

[1] Sir Isaac Isaacs was born in Melbourne in August 1855, and was thus verging upon seventy-six years of age. After a legal and political career in the Commonwealth he had in 1930 been appointed Chief Justice of Australia.

[2] In 1929 General Hertzog, being desirous that Lord Clarendon should succeed Lord Athlone as Governor-General of the Union, proposed to approach him direct. 'The King', wrote Lord Stamfordham to the Dominions Office on November 9, 1929 (R.A., L. 226. 37), 'most strongly objects to anything being said to Lord Clarendon except by the Secretary of State.' A compromise was reached under which General Hertzog was to make the formal submission direct, but the Prime Minister in the United Kingdom was to write to the King 'advising' him to approve General Hertzog's submission. This compromise, as will be seen, did not create a precedent for future practice.

The resolutions of the 1926 Conference had in fact been so ambiguous as to leave the position much confused:

> 'I cannot', wrote Lord Stamfordham to the Prime Minister's Private Secretary on June 19, 1930, 'for the life of me understand from anything that was passed at the last Imperial Conference that the Dominion Governments have the right to advise the King on the appointment of Governors-General, or indeed upon any other point.'[c] `

The Law Officers of the Crown, when consulted, failed to simplify the problem. It was their contention that, since the constitution of the Commonwealth of Australia did not permit Australian Ministers to advise the King, and since the 1926 resolutions did not permit British Ministers to tender advice on Dominion matters, there was nobody who could constitutionally tender advice. It was therefore incumbent on the King to act in this matter on his own initiative. Lord Stamfordham, with his uncanny instinct for awkward consequences, did not at all relish the prospect of the Crown assuming so uncovered a responsibility.[d]

In October Mr Scullin arrived in London to attend the Conference. In the interval, news of the proposed appointment of Sir Isaac Isaacs had 'unaccountably' leaked out, and the King had received protests and petitions from his Australian and Tasmanian subjects. It was evident that the appointment so ardently desired by Mr Scullin would not be warmly welcomed in the Commonwealth. On October 30 Mr Ramsay MacDonald begged Mr Scullin not to press his project; the latter replied that he would be unable to return to Australia if the appointment of Sir Isaac Isaacs were refused. The British Prime Minister feared that, if the King insisted on withholding his assent, 'a very dangerous agitation' might be started by Mr Scullin's supporters in Australia.[e] On the same day Mr Scullin had an interview with Lord Stamfordham:[f]

> 'He continued', the latter recorded, 'to state his case and I then explained that the King did not object to the fact of Mr Scullin's nominee being an Australian, but upon the principle that any local man, whether in politics or not, must have local political predilections, political friends and political opponents—whereas a nominee from England had no local politics and would therefore, as the King's representative, stand aloof from all politics as much as the Sovereign does at home. If this appointment were made and another Party was in office when a vacancy occurred as Governor-General, the same procedure would follow, and the selection would be made from the friends of the Party in office.'

The dispute was referred to the Imperial Conference, who considered it at their morning session of November 4. It was resolved that in making an appointment of Governor-General, the King 'should act on the advice of His Majesty's Ministers in the Dominion concerned'. But it was also resolved that Dominion Ministers should only make their formal submission 'after informal consultation with His Majesty'. By this means the King would be given the opportunity to dissuade a Minister from submitting a name that was manifestly undesirable.

In view of these resolutions, the King received Mr Scullin in private audience on November 29 and, after appealing in vain to him to reconsider his recommendation, was obliged formally to approve the appointment of Sir Isaac Isaacs:

> 'Received Mr Scullin', the King wrote in his diary that evening, '& he told me he wished to appoint Sir Isaac Isaacs as the new Governor-General of Australia. He argued with me for some time ... & with great reluctance I had to approve of the appointment. I should think it would be very unpopular in Australia.'

Lord Stamfordham's record of this audience is more detailed:[9]

> 'The King pointed out to Mr Scullin that ... he had departed from the time-honoured custom of informally suggesting names to the Sovereign in order to ascertain whether such persons were likely to be acceptable: and, moreover, that in the history of this country there was no record of the King's wishes in such cases being ignored. The King added that Sir Isaac Isaacs, who would be more than ever His Majesty's representative, was personally unknown to him: that he was 75 years of age and that no Australian could be selected without having some party bias, local or social, from which a Governor-General coming from some other part of the Empire would be free. ...
> Mr Scullin referred to Ireland: but the King in effect said that Ireland was a spoilt child and, after making a Treaty with the Free State, she had to be humoured. But does Australia, with her traditional loyalty to the Throne, wish to be compared with Ireland, where, alas! a considerable element of disloyalty exists?'[1]

---

[1] Since the passing of the Constitution of October 25, 1922, the Irish Free State had pursued an eccentric course, designed to remove all limitations and restrictions left over from the Treaty of 1921. Although the relation between Ireland and Great Britain bore no analogy to that existing between the mother-country and the Dominions, the success of Mr De Valera in eliminating all vestiges of the Prerogative often provided Dominion statesmen with arguments, examples and temptations. After the triumph of the Fianna Fail Party in 1932 Mr De Valera held supreme

The King further pointed out that, now that the Governor-General was appointed on the advice of the Prime Minister of the Dominion, it was possible, that with a change of Government, the new Prime Minister might wish to have a new Governor-General; but at the very possibility of such an eventuality, Mr Scullin expressed himself horrified.

The King asked how it was proposed that in future the Prime Minister in Canberra should tender advice to the King in London? Mr Scullin admitted this difficulty, which, he said, would have to be well considered.

Neither the King nor Lord Stamfordham had any illusions as to the serious nature of the precedent established by the King's surrender to Mr Scullin on the morning of November 29:

> 'It seems to me', Lord Stamfordham minuted to the King,[h] 'that this morning's incident was one of the most important political and constitutional issues upon which Your Majesty has had to decide during Your twenty years of reign.'

In their view, the appointments of local politicians to the posts of Governors-General would impair the association between the Empire and the mother-country, damage the prestige and dignity of these high offices, and above all compromise the neutrality of the immediate representative of the Crown:

> 'Needless to say', wrote Lord Stamfordham to the Prime Minister on that morning, 'the King fully realizes the supreme importance of his action in this question, the decision of which may have far-reaching reactions throughout the Empire. He recognizes that he was well

---

power for sixteen years. In 1933 he abolished the oath of allegiance and the appeal to the Privy Council: the Irish Nationality Act of 1935 established a distinction between Irish and British nationality: in 1936 the office of Governor-General, which had for long been a farce, was reduced to that of 'Seneschal' and the Senate was abolished. The Constitution of 1922 was replaced by that of 1937 under which Ireland was constituted 'a sovereign, independent and democratic State'. In 1938 Great Britain surrendered to Ireland the three naval bases that had been retained under the Treaty. On April 18, 1949, the 'Republic of Ireland Act', drafted by the Costello Government, brought about the final severance of the Irish Free State from the British Commonwealth.

The King, unlike so many of his subjects, did not allow his old affection for the Irish people to sink into bored indifference. 'Would you', he once asked the Irish High Commissioner in London, 'convey to Mr De Valera a personal message from myself?' 'Certainly, Sir', replied Mr Dulanty. 'Well, tell him from me not to make so many promises. They become so horribly difficult to carry out.'

within his right to refuse Mr Scullin's demand with (what he is assured would be the case) the warm support of the people of Australia.

But on the other hand His Majesty is well aware how easy it is to light and fan the flame of agitation by an ill-disposed minority— especially when, as in this case, constituted of Trades Unions, Communists and Irish, not of the highest class. And, as the King himself told Mr Scullin, he would not give him the opportunity of executing any such manœuvre.'*

It was unusual for Lord Stamfordham, even when indignant, to employ intemperate terms. That afternoon he sent a further letter across to the Prime Minister:

'I wish to add a postscript to my letter of this morning to say that, while I gather the King frankly told Mr Scullin that he did not intend to refuse the latter's advice, and thereby give opportunity for possible agitation in Australia against His Majesty, he did not, of course, refer in detail to the probable composition of the minority which I sketched at the beginning of the sentence.'*

The veteran Sir Isaac Isaacs was thus installed as Governor-General. Within a few weeks he was sending the King private letters of immense length, describing his own benevolent activities, and the party dissensions which rendered federal politics of such interest to an outside observer.[1]

When in 1935 Sir Isaac Isaacs, having reached the age of eighty, contemplated retirement, the problem of his successor arose. Mr Lyons, at that date Commonwealth Prime Minister, informed the King that he 'was most anxious that the next Governor-General should come from Great Britain and be of distinguished lineage'.*k* Sir Alexander Hore-Ruthven, subsequently Lord Gowrie, was therefore appointed: he proved one of the most wise and popular Governors-General that Australia had ever known.

(5)

In section 2 of this chapter it was stated that five out of the seven 'vestiges of subordination' were removed, either by resolutions of the

---

[1] Another, and more extreme, illustration of the conflict between local autonomy and the continuance of the Royal Prerogative, could be provided by the long-drawn, and extremely interesting, controversy between Mr Lang of New South Wales and successive State Governors from 1926 to 1932. This controversy turned upon the prerogative of dismissal, but (since the King was in no way directly concerned in the attitude adopted by Governors de Chair and Philip Game), the student is referred for this fascinating story to the textbooks on the subject.

Imperial Conferences of 1926 or 1930, or by the Statute of West-minster itself. There remain the two questions of the Royal Title and the co-ordination of foreign policy.

The question of the Royal Title, although subsidiary in itself, illustrates the importance attached by some Dominions to verbal formulas and the difficulty of adjusting those formulas to the pre-judices or desires of the Commonwealth as a whole. The Dominion Prime Ministers were often found in such matters to be curiously sensitive and suspicious. 'These gentlemen', wrote Mr Ramsay Mac-Donald to Lord Stamfordham at the time of the 1930 Conference,[l] 'are very kittle cattle and have to be handled very carefully'. It was the Irish representatives who raised, and not without justification, the question of the Royal Title. Under the Act of 1901 the King was styled 'of the United Kingdom of Great Britain and Ireland, and of the British Dominions beyond the Seas, King, etc. . . .' The Irish representatives pointed out that the expression 'United Kingdom' no longer corresponded to the facts. A Cabinet Committee was appointed and recommended two alternative formulas:

A. 'King of Great Britain and Ireland and of the British Dominions beyond the Seas etc. . . .'
B. 'King of Great Britain, of Ireland, and of the British Dominions beyond the Seas etc. . . .'

These two formulas, apparently so similar, in fact embodied a distinction which Mr Cosgrave, the leader of the Free State delega-tion, regarded as important. Formula A might imply that the rela-tion between the Free State and the King was in some way different from that between the King and the other Dominions. Formula B was less unacceptable, since the word 'Ireland', as it appeared in the context, could be taken to apply to Northern Ireland only, whereas the Free State could adhere to the formula under the heading of a Dominion. The King, when consulted, minuted as follows:[m]

'It is a bore having to change one's title, but I suppose it is inevitable. I prefer A, but if Cosgrave makes difficulties I would agree to B. A is much the best in every way.'

On November 17, 1926, the Prime Minister's Private Secretary informed Lord Stamfordham[n] that the Imperial Conference had finally agreed to the following title:

'George V, by the Grace of God, King of Great Britain, Ireland and the British Dominions beyond the Seas, Defender of the Faith, Em-peror of India.'

Some gremlin at this stage seems to have taken charge of the proceedings. Although the King stated expressly that he would accept no further change in the formula agreed to on November 17, in the text as published in the Press on November 21 the word 'British' was omitted before the word 'Dominions' and the word 'King' was, as in the original Act of 1901, placed after the word 'Seas'. Moreover, the expression 'United Kingdom' obstinately refused to be abolished; it crept back, without attracting attention, even into the Bill as presented to Parliament. To this day the British Government is referred to, even in official documents, as 'His Majesty's Government in the United Kingdom'. It was to such confetti of confusion that Imperial Conferences, despite Sir Maurice Hankey's vigilance and indignation, were constantly exposed.

The last remaining 'vestige of subordination', namely the pre-ponderant part played by the British Government in the framing and execution of foreign policy, has not, even to this day, been wholly abolished. So long as the British Commonwealth of Nations exists even as a theoretical entity, a major responsibility for external policy, as for Imperial defence, must rest with London. It is not merely that the influence, joint and several, of the Dominions would be much impaired if they were always, on every occasion, to speak with different voices: it is also that foreign countries, if our Union were rendered too fictitious, might ignore its existence and even claim that Imperial Preference constituted a violation of the Most Favoured Nation Clause. On the other hand, successive Imperial Conferences have given full recognition to the fact that the geo-graphical interests and dangers of the several Dominions are not always identical; that a self-governing community cannot without consultation and consent be committed to treaties concluded by another self-governing community; and that better machinery must be devised for liaison between the Dominions and the mother-country in regard to problems of foreign policy and defence affecting the Commonwealth as a whole.[1]

[1] The discussions that took place at the 1926 and 1930 Conferences established the principle that no member of the Commonwealth was bound by any treaty which had not been negotiated by its own repre-sentatives and ratified by its own Parliament. The Dominions thus did not regard themselves as bound by the Locarno Treaties, and could, if they so desired, declare their neutrality in the event of Great Britain or some other Dominion being involved in war. At the same time the British Government contended that the Dominions were not foreign countries, in the sense that agreements between Dominions need not be registered with

484

The Imperial prerogatives inherited by the Crown in 1910 were in this manner either abolished or profoundly modified in 1931. Yet, even after the passage of the Statute of Westminster, many points of uncertainty and embarrassment remained.

(6)

The King watched this process of quick decentralisation with anxiety. He was specially perturbed when the sub-conference of 1929–30 recommended separate legislation by each Dominion Parliament regarding the Royal Title and the Succession to the Throne. As eventually embodied in the preamble to the Statute of Westminister, this provision does not appear today as very dangerous. At the time, the King seems to have apprehended that it might lead to diversity of legislation and even affect the Act of Settlement:

> 'I much regret', His Majesty wrote to the Prime Minister on November 30, 1929, 'that it has been found necessary for the conference to deal with anything regarding legislation with respect to the Crown. . . . Would it not be better to allow the conference to break up, rather than consent to the abolition of the Colonial Laws Validity Act, without any provision to ensure no tampering with the Settlement Act? After following the proceedings of the conference, and estimating the spirit in which the views of some of the Dominions have been expressed, I cannot look into the future without feelings of no little anxiety as to the continued unity of the Empire.'[0]

The Dominion Ministers and jurists, being justifiably anxious to know exactly where they stood under the new dispensation, were inclined to ask embarrassing questions and to press for too precise definitions. Did the resolutions of 1926 and 1930 accord to each Dominion the right of secession from the Commonwealth? Mr

the League of Nations or referred to the Hague in cases of dispute. It was also assumed that Dominions could negotiate agreements direct with foreign countries, provided only that they notified their fellow members of the Commonwealth that they intended to do so.

During these years many important improvements were made in establishing better liaison in foreign affairs between Great Britain and the several Dominions. Mr R. G. Casey, for instance, did useful work as liaison between the British Foreign Office and the Australian Government. Similar methods of maintaining contact and exchanging information have since been adopted by other Dominion Governments, acting through their High Commissioners in London.

Ramsay MacDonald begged them not to emphasise so awkward a point. What happened in the event of the illness or incapacity of the Sovereign and under what terms and conditions would a Regency be appointed? It would, Mr MacDonald replied, be in that event incumbent on each Dominion to pass such legislation as was considered necessary.[1] Was the Monarchy divisible? Was the King to be regarded as personifying the sovereignty of the Commonwealth as a single entity, or was he in fact seven Kings, being concurrently, but separately, King of Great Britain, King of Canada, King of Australia, and so on? The British jurists regarded as dangerous the theory of a divisible Monarchy, since such multiplicity of function might impair the position of the Sovereign as the unique element of cohesion.

This problem was raised in a most complicated form when in 1934 the Government of the Union of South Africa produced two unexpected Bills entitled respectively the 'Status of the Union Bill' and the 'Royal Executive Functions and Seals Bill'. The former Bill, after declaring that the Union of South Africa possessed the status of a 'Sovereign and Independent State', added that the Executive Government of the Union was vested in the King 'acting on the advice of his Ministers of State for the Union' and could be administered, either by His Majesty in person, or by the Governor-General as his representative.

The Royal Executive Functions and Seals Bill, the purpose of which was stated to be to 'regulate the King's acts as head of the Executive of the Union' contained a clause providing that, if the inevitable delay in obtaining the King's sign manual would, in the opinion of the Prime Minister of the Union, 'retard the despatch of public business', then the Governor-General, if so advised by his Ministers, could sign documents on the King's behalf.

The King, and not without success, endeavoured tactfully to induce General Hertzog to modify some of the expressions in these enactments. It was agreed that the word 'regularize' would be substituted for the too peremptory 'regulate' in the preamble to the Royal Executive Functions Bill; and that the Governor-General should not sign documents without first obtaining the King's approval. The King also tried to persuade General Hertzog to sub-

---

[1] Mr De Valera was positive that he at least would pass no such legislation. 'As you are aware', he wrote to Mr MacDonald on June 26, 1935, 'the sole and exclusive right to enact any law in respect to Saorstat Eireann is vested in the Oireachtas' (R.A., M. 2460. III. 2).

stitute the phrase 'sovereign and independent status' for the words 'Sovereign and Independent State'.[p] The Union Prime Minister replied that any deviation from the original wording—which, he contended, was no more than a corollary of the 1926 resolutions—would create in South Africa 'the gravest possible political difficulties'.[q] The two Bills were eventually passed by the South African Parliament and received the King's Assent on June 22, 1934.

Implicit in this dispute was the vexed question whether, and if so how, Dominion Ministers should tender 'advice' to the Sovereign. Professor Berriedale Keith had stated that for the King to act directly on the advice of Dominion Ministers was a 'constitutional monstrosity'.[r] There were others who held the somewhat eccentric view that if the Sovereign were advised by seven different Governments, it would be impossible for any one of those Governments to advocate measures incompatible with the interests of the Commonwealth as a whole. The fact remained that the Imperial Conferences of 1926 and 1930, without fully considering the practical difficulties involved, had asserted the 'right of the Government of each Dominion to advise the Crown'. Yet how was that advice to be conveyed? If in every case the advice were to be given to the Governor-General, and if the latter were in every case to be an appointee of the Dominion Government in office, then the spirit of 'common allegiance' might be progressively diluted. The most convenient method would be for the Dominion Prime Ministers to advise His Majesty through the British Prime Minister or the Secretary of State for Dominion Relations. Such a procedure would, however, have been obnoxious to all the Dominion Governments as a vestige of subordination. The Dominion High Commissioners in London could, of course, furnish explanations as to the wishes and intentions of their home Governments: but obviously they could not tender 'advice' in the constitutional sense of that term. The problem, with all its implications, was not settled during King George's reign.

It was only gradually that the custom was established by which, in ordinary circumstances, the Dominion Prime Minister tenders advice to the Governor-General. In matters affecting the King personally, or in regard to which His Majesty's name is used or his Sign Manual required, the Dominion Prime Minister corresponds directly, either by letter or cable, with Buckingham Palace. The High Commissioners in London are there to furnish explanations if required, and are sometimes the channel of submission; in general, however, the correspondence is carried on through the Governor-General.[1]

This procedure is not laid down by statute, and cannot even today be said to have been established by custom and usage. The resolutions of 1926 and 1930 and the Statute of Westminster itself left King George with a number of loose ends. He did not like loose ends.

[1] Even today the practice for submission varies in different Dominions and under different Dominion Prime Ministers. Sometimes the Governor-General is the normal channel; sometimes he is almost entirely short-circuited; sometimes the existence of the High Commissioners is ignored; sometimes they are brought directly into the picture.

RACING IN THE 'BRITANNIA'

SANDRINGHAM, 1934

CHAPTER XXIX

HOME POLITICS AND INDIA

1931–1935

The Invergordon incident—A further run on gold—The National Government forced to suspend the Gold Standard—The Conservatives want an Election but the Liberals do not—Shall there be a common Manifesto?—The King returns to London—His interview with Sir Herbert Samuel—The Prime Minister's pessimism—The King's encouragement—A formula found—The General Election of October 27, 1931—Mr MacDonald's difficulty in distributing posts among the three Parties—Sir Austen Chamberlain's self-sacrifice—The 'agreement to differ'—The Ottawa Conference—Resignation of Lord Snowden and Sir Herbert Samuel—Mr Ramsay MacDonald's isolation—The King's sympathy—Foreign situation—Russia—Manchukuo—Disarmament—The World Economic Conference—The American Debt—President Roosevelt and the King—The Indian problem—Montagu-Chelmsford Reforms—Amritsar—Appointment of Lord Irwin—The Simon Commission—The King's influence invoked—The Simon Report—The Round Table Conference—Lord Irwin and Mr Gandhi—The Government of India Act 1935.

(1)

IMMEDIATELY on his return to Balmoral after the formation of the National Government, the King addressed to Mr Ramsay MacDonald a letter of thanks, written in his own hand:[a]

'Balmoral Castle
August 27, 1931

My dear Prime Minister,
    After the momentous times through which we have been passing, I should like to assure you how much I appreciate & admire the courage with which you have put aside all personal & party interest in order to stand by the country in this grave national crisis. By this proof of strength of character & devotion to duty your name will always hold an honoured place among British Statesmen.'

The admiration felt by His Majesty for Mr MacDonald's conduct was not shared by most members of the Labour Party. When the House of Commons met on September 8 it became evident that the Prime Minister's former colleagues were in a critical mood. The new Government rushed through their emergency Budget and their

Economy Bill.[1] The drain on gold ceased immediately: it seemed, for a day or two, that the crisis had in fact been surmounted.

On observing, however, the numbers and vitality of the Labour Opposition, foreign investors began to lose this initial confidence: their doubts were increased when, while the Economy Bill was still being debated, some naval ratings stationed at Invergordon refused, largely owing to a misunderstanding, to obey orders. This incident was magnified to the proportions of a naval mutiny, prelude to a national revolution. The withdrawals of gold began again. On September 16 the Bank of England had to part with five million, with ten million on the day following, with eighteen million two days later. The Directors informed the Government that they must immediately be relieved of their obligation to sell gold under the Gold Standard Act of 1925. On September 21 a Bill suspending the Gold Standard was passed by 271 votes to 148 in a single day. Internal prices, in spite of this disaster, remained fairly stable: the external depreciation of the pound sterling gave a much-needed stimulus to our export trade.

The question was not unnaturally asked why such great sacrifices had been imposed upon all sections of the community, why the Labour Government had been broken and the Socialist Party rent— merely in order to avert a measure which, when passed less than four weeks later, proved a benefit rather than a catastrophe. The answer was of course that, had it not been for the existence of a National Government, pledged to the most galling economies, our departure from the Gold Standard would have been followed by an avalanche of inflation, similar to that which had overwhelmed Germany after 1921. Yet the fact that the Government had been forced to pass the very measure which they had been created to prevent, undoubtedly weakened their position in the House of Commons. It was felt that the situation could only be regularised, and lasting confidence established, by a Government confirmed in full power by the votes of the people. The question then arose, whether the National Government should go to the country as a Coalition, and on the basis of a joint appeal, or whether each of the three sections should fight the battle as a separate and independent unit.

[1] The 'National Economy Bill' was introduced by the Prime Minister on September 11 and passed on September 14 by 309 votes to 249. Mr Philip Snowden was able to meet the deficit of £170 million, by imposing £70 million cuts in salaries and benefits, by raising a further £81 m. by fresh taxation, and by suspending debt redemption to meet the balance.

The Conservatives, scenting victory, were determined on an early General Election: their only doubt was whether it was really necessary for them to appear before their constituents under the aegis of a former Labour Prime Minister. The Liberals were uneasy. They foresaw that an Election held in the present public mood would give the Conservative section of the Coalition a great preponderance; they doubted whether Mr MacDonald, with his tiny cohort of personal supporters, would be strong enough to withstand the right-wing legions and resist their insistence that Free Trade principles must now be abandoned. Mr MacDonald himself was divided in mind. On the one hand, he felt that an Election was in fact essential and believed that it would prove to the world that in making his difficult decision he had correctly interpreted the wishes of the nation as a whole. On the other hand, it was repugnant for him to fight the friends with whom he had been associated all his life:

> 'He does not', wrote Sir Clive Wigram to the King on September 28, 'like the idea of smashing up the Labour Party at the head of a Conservative association. He does not know how to run with the hare and hunt with the hounds. He has hopes of sitting tight now and attracting a following of the Labour Party. This may take a long time.'[b]

Mr MacDonald must have known that the mass of the Labour members regarded him as a traitor to the cause: nor, in any case, would the Conservatives have permitted him to sit tight.

The Liberals contended, and with justice, that at the Buckingham Palace Conference they had only agreed to join a Coalition Government on the express understanding that, once the necessary emergency legislation had been passed, each of the three Parties would resume its former independence of action.[1] Their difficulties were not diminished by the fact that their titular leader, Mr Lloyd George, was still an irritable and puckish convalescent at Churt: the varied emissaries who visited his bedside brought back the dreadful

[1] An announcement had, as stated in Chapter XXVII, been issued from Downing Street on August 28 to the effect that, once the crisis was over, the situation would revert to what it had been in the previous July and that the three Parties 'would resume their respective positions'. Moreover, Mr Ramsay MacDonald had himself stated in a broadcast that any ensuing Election would 'not be fought by the Government: there will be no coupons'.

It was now argued that, since we had left the Gold Standard, the crises had *not* been surmounted, and that any promises made in August no longer applied.

news that his real sympathies were with Mr Arthur Henderson and the Labour Opposition; to the horror of all concerned, Mr Lloyd George suggested at one moment that he should be conveyed to Buckingham Palace in an ambulance, there to confer with the King, the Prime Minister and Mr Baldwin. He refused in any case to associate his name with a joint Electoral manifesto, such as might commit the National Government, if returned to power, to the introduction of protective tariffs. It seemed as if another deadlock had been reached. On the one hand, it appeared essential, if confidence were to be restored, that the leaders of the three Parties should appeal to the country as a Coalition possessing a common programme. On the other hand, the Conservatives would sign no joint manifesto that did not at least envisage protection, whereas the Liberals would not touch a programme that might compromise the principle of Free Trade.

(2)

On September 29 the King returned to London from Balmoral and immediately sent for the Prime Minister. The latter explained that a deadlock had arisen, and added that it might become necessary for him to ask His Majesty to summon, and preside over, another Buckingham Palace Conference. The King answered that he would be glad to do so, but that such a Conference would have to 'come out with a settled policy'. 'The Country', he said, 'had to be saved and there should be a combination of all decent-minded politicians towards this end: Party differences should be sunk.'ᶜ

The King had always been abundantly aware of every shade of Conservative opinion: he also possessed an instinctive understanding of the Socialist, even of the extreme Socialist, point of view. 'I should have felt exactly as he does', he once remarked after a long conversation with Mr Wheatley, 'if I had had his sort of childhood.' What he sometimes failed to understand was the doctrine of pure Liberalism, especially the deep religious sentiments that affected the Liberal attitude towards Protection and Free Trade. He did not fully realise that what to him appeared mere fussiness about some customs regulation was for them a crucial article of faith, loyalty and honour. The King's reception of Sir Herbert Samuel during those trying days was therefore unsympathetic:

'Received', he wrote in his diary for October 2, 'Sir Herbert Samuel at 10.30. He was quite impossible, most obstinate, & said he would not look at tariffs & that there was a deadlock as regards Conservatives and Liberals in the Govt.

God knows what can be done! ... Am much worried by the political situation & can't see a way out.'

The King's anxiety was not caused by any personal feelings about Free Trade or Protection. What worried him was the prospect that, if the Liberals left, Mr MacDonald also would resign and that the whole apparatus of National Government would then come crashing down. On October 3 Mr MacDonald told the King that 'he was beginning to feel that he had failed and had better clear out'. The King urged him to 'brace himself up to realise that he was the only person to tackle the present chaotic state of affairs': that it was his positive duty to find a solution; and that even if Mr MacDonald were to tender his resignation he, the King, would refuse to accept it.[d] Thus galvanised, the Prime Minister returned to battle with his colleagues. By midnight on October 5 a magic formula was discovered. The National Government was to go to the country and demand 'a doctor's mandate', meaning thereby that every possible remedy was to be applied to cure our maladies, even, if necessary, a cautious dose of tariffs. The word 'tariffs' was not, however, to be stressed in any joint appeal that the Government might address to the electorate.[1]

The King was profoundly relieved by this solution of the difficulty:

'P.M. came at 9.15. today to say that at last the Government have found a formula on which they can make an appeal to the Country. He has worked hard and shown great patience. Lloyd George, as usual, has been impossible. The Prime Minister asked for a dissolution which will take place tomorrow & the General Election on October 27. I am very pleased and congratulated him. Had an interesting talk with General Smuts. He is a very sound man.'

The ensuing campaign was one of unexampled acerbity. At the polls on October 27 the supporters of the National Government secured an overwhelming victory: those Labour Ministers and mem-

[1] Mr Lloyd George refused to countenance a joint manifesto which was in his memory unpleasantly associated with the Coupon Election. When the day came, he addressed to the electors of Carnarvon a manifesto that was entirely his own. Thereafter the Liberal Party tended, in spite of temporary reconciliations, to split into three sections. There were the pure free-traders headed by Sir Herbert Samuel: there were the Liberal Nationals under Sir John Simon: and there were the Lloyd George family who, possessed of ample funds, followed their own whims and convictions.

bers who had opposed Mr Ramsay MacDonald suffered almost universal defeat.[1]

The Prime Minister could be in no doubt that the nation, for the moment at least, approved by a vast majority the decision he had taken on August 26. What tortured him thereafter was that he was never wholly certain whether he approved of it himself.[2]

(3)

The new Parliament was to be opened by the King on November 10, and in the interval the Prime Minister was much harassed by the problem of allocating the posts at his disposal among the three Parties:

'The King', recorded Sir Clive Wigram on November 2, 'saw Mr Baldwin, who told His Majesty that the Prime Minister was inclined to be wobbly and unable to make up his mind over the new Cabinet and had not advanced very far in its composition. Every new-comer was inclined to sway him. . . . The King thought that Neville Chamberlain was so good as Minister of Health that it would be a pity to make him Chancellor of the Exchequer, where he would be suspected of ultra-protectionist views. His Majesty said that he thought he, Mr Baldwin, should go as Chancellor of the Exchequer, but the latter said he had asked for no portfolio. He intimated that there would be plenty for him to do, as the Prime Minister knew nothing of his new Party, especially the Conservatives—many of them young, impetuous and ambitious men—who had no chance of making reputations with no Opposition to speak against. . . . Mr Baldwin was afraid his Party might kick if they did not have some of the key positions—such as Exchequer, Home Office, Foreign Office and Dominions Office. Mr Baldwin advocated Mr Neville Chamberlain being at the Foreign Office.'[e]

----

[1] The final figures were: National Government supporters 558, Labour Opposition 56—Government majority 502. The Government supporters consisted of 471 Conservatives, 35 Liberal Nationals, 33 Pure Liberals, 13 National Labour, 2 'National'. The Opposition mustered 52 Labour members and four Lloyd George family. The Conservatives did not lose a seat at the election and gained 200. The followers of Mr Arthur Henderson did not win a single seat and lost a similar number of 200. Except for Mr Lansbury, every single member of the former Labour Government who stood in opposition to the National Government lost his seat. Mr MacDonald won a personal triumph at Seaham by securing a 5000 majority.

[2] Many years later, Mr MacDonald, discussing the 1931 crisis with the author, said: 'Any man in my position at the time, knowing all that I did, would have acted as I acted. However, I wish sometimes that someone else had been in my position at the time.'

The tangle was to some extent eased by the voluntary retirement of such veterans as Sir Austen Chamberlain, Lord Reading, Lord Crewe and Lord Amulree. The King was specially moved by Sir Austen Chamberlain's willingness to renounce office in order that 'younger men, who must bear the burden of responsibility in the future, should gain experience for their tasks'.*f*

'You may be assured', the King wrote to Sir Austen, 'that after your devoted service during the last 36 years in Conservative and National Administrations, I feel that I am parting from, though not losing, an old and valued friend. Today, as you say, circumstances are wholly abnormal, and I know that your present action in voluntarily withdrawing in order to make way for younger men, in order to further the best interests of your country and your colleagues, is in harmony with the public spirit and self-sacrifice which have always characterised your career. You have set a fine example and I trust that you may be given health and strength for many years to continue to help your Sovereign and your country.'*g*

On November 3 the King invited the Prime Minister to luncheon at Buckingham Palace in order that they might discuss the appointments still to be filled. His Majesty was delighted by the suggestion that Sir Bolton Eyres-Monsell should become First Lord of the Admiralty, remarking that 'he could not think of a better man'. The King advised the Prime Minister to make certain, before inviting Sir Herbert Samuel or Mr Philip Snowden to join the Cabinet, that they would not 'break it up when the question of tariffs were raised'. Mr MacDonald said that he would prefer for the moment to allow this sleeping dog to lie; if he pressed Sir Herbert Samuel to give advance pledges, the latter might demand pledges in return. The Prime Minister would not be able to give such pledges and Sir Herbert might then walk out, 'taking with him his 35 supporters'. It would be therefore preferable to postpone raising the issue until a later date, when Sir Herbert would 'probably not have so many followers'.*h*

The list of Government appointments was finally completed on November 9.[1] The Prime Minister's first action, on meeting the new

[1] The main posts were allocated as follows: Prime Minister, Mr Ramsay MacDonald: Lord President of the Council, Mr Stanley Baldwin: Chancellor of the Exchequer, Mr Neville Chamberlain: Lord Chancellor, Lord Sankey: Home Secretary, Sir Herbert Samuel: S. of S. for War, Lord Hailsham: Foreign Secretary, Sir John Simon: S. of S. for India, Sir Samuel Hoare: Dominions, Mr J. H. Thomas: Colonies, Sir P. Cunliffe-Lister: Air, Lord Londonderry: Scotland, Sir Archibald Sinclair: Health, Sir Edward Hilton Young: Board of Trade, Mr Runciman: Lord Privy

House of Commons, was to secure the passage of an 'Abnormal Importations Bill', designed to check the flood of goods which foreign exporters, anticipating early tariffs, were pouring into the country. The Free Traders, on being assured that this was but a temporary measure, accorded wary acquiescence. Early in the new year, the Prime Minister was able to assure the King that his Cabinet were 'in good spirits and working harmoniously'.[*i*] Such optimism was ill-founded.

A Committee had been appointed, under the chairmanship of Mr Neville Chamberlain, to consider the existing trade balance. The majority of this Committee recommended to the Cabinet that a general 10 % duty should be imposed on all imported goods, other than those scheduled on a 'free list'. Imports from the Dominions would be considered at a special conference to be held at Ottawa later in the year. The report of this Committee came before the Cabinet on January 21. Lord Snowden,[1] Sir Herbert Samuel, Sir Donald Maclean and Sir Archibald Sinclair stated that they could not accept these recommendations in that they amounted to full protection; they would be obliged therefore to resign from the National Government. All morning and all afternoon the argument continued; the Prime Minister even followed the dissentients to Lord Snowden's flat and

Seal, Viscount Snowden: First Lord of the Admiralty, Sir Bolton Eyres-Monsell: Education, Sir Donald Maclean: Labour, Sir Henry Betterton: Minister of Works, Mr Ormsby-Gore.

The following posts were given to the coming men: Mr Kingsley Wood, Postmaster General: Mr Walter Elliot, Financial Secretary to the Treasury: Mr Malcolm MacDonald, Parliamentary Secretary for the Dominions: Captain R. A. Eden, M.C., Parliamentary Under-Secretary, Foreign Office: Mr Oliver Stanley, Parliamentary Under-Secretary, Home Office: Lord Lothian, Parliamentary Under-Secretary India Office: Mr R. Hudson, Parliamentary Secretary, Ministry of Labour: Mr Hore Belisha, Parliamentary Secretary, Board of Trade: Mr Duff Cooper, Financial Secretary to the War Office.

The following changes took place in subsequent years: in 1932, on the death of Sir Donald Maclean, Lord Irwin took over the Board of Education: in 1933 Mr Stanley became Minister of Transport: in December 1933 Mr Anthony Eden became Lord Privy Seal, with the task of specialising on League of Nations affairs: in June 1934, Mr Stanley became Minister of Labour, Mr Hore Belisha Minister of Transport, Mr Duff Cooper Financial Secretary to the Treasury, and Mr H. Crookshank Under-Secretary at the Home Office. In 1935 Lord Cranborne was attached to Mr Eden as additional Under-Secretary.

[1] On the formation of the new Government in 1931 Mr Philip Snowden had been created Viscount Snowden of Ickernshaw.

sat late into the night urging them to reconsider their decision. He proved unable to move them, and telephoned to Sandringham warning the King's Private Secretary that he might have to ask for an immediate audience in order to tender the resignation of the National Government. The Cabinet met again on the morning of January 22 and Lord Hailsham then blandly suggested that, rather than destroy the National Government so early in its life, it would be better to sacrifice the rule of collective Cabinet responsibility, to accept a majority decision, and to allow those who disagreed with this decision, to speak, and even to vote, against it. This 'agreement to differ' was accepted by Sir Herbert Samuel and Lord Snowden, and for the second time disruption was postponed:

> 'It was a great relief to me', the King wrote to the Prime Minister on January 23, 'to receive your letter and to learn that the unfortunate events, which you feared would necessitate your coming to Sandringham, had not materialised—though, needless to say, I should have been pleased to see you.
> I share to the full your forebodings as to the disastrous effect both at home and abroad of the resignation of Members of your Cabinet at the present juncture. I heartily congratulate you on staving off what might have been a national crisis, and feel that the greatest credit is due to you and Lord Hailsham for your patience and wisdom in formulating conditions which in the end proved acceptable to the dissentients.
> Time alone will show what will be the outcome of this departure from the long-established practice of collective Cabinet responsibility. A National Government with an overwhelming majority, of which you are now the leader, is totally different to the ordinary Party system, and I recognize that, in these abnormal circumstances, you took the only possible course to maintain a united front.'*

The breach had not, however, been for long averted. For a short time the 'agreement to differ' maintained the Coalition intact; but with summer came the Ottawa Conference and the prospect of Imperial Preference. No formula could now disguise the fact that Mr Neville Chamberlain was about to deal a death-blow to Free Trade. Lord Snowden, Sir Herbert Samuel and their immediate supporters announced that this time their resignations must be final. In vain were such elder Liberal statesmen as Lord Reading, Lord Grey of Fallodon and Lord Crewe, invited to use their influence in favour of reconciliation: instead of curbing the zeal of Sir Herbert, they signed a letter to the Press, publicly approving the attitude he had adopted. The Prime Minister was in despair:

'I cannot hide from Your Majesty', he wrote on September 11, 'my apprehensions of the result of resignations at this time. The patched-up Government will in reality be a new Government and it will not be the one brought into being by the General Election. The country will have a shock; the Opposition Parties a score; and the outside world will see cracks in the national unity.

The new Government will also be, to all intents and purposes, a single-party administration, and I think Your Majesty will find that a Prime Minister who does not belong to the Party in power will become more and more an anomaly, and, as policy develops, his position will become more and more degrading.'[k]

Sir Herbert Samuel at the same time wrote to Sir Clive Wigram, asking him to assure the King that he and his colleagues were not resigning from narrow motives, but from a profound conviction that the Ottawa policy would 'be injurious to this country and the Empire'. The King, while expressing his deep regret that the National union should in this manner be disturbed, referred gratefully to the assistance and advice that Sir Herbert Samuel had accorded him in August 1931. The resignations were announced on September 28. When the House of Commons reassembled in October Mr Ramsay MacDonald, as he informed the King, was welcomed by 'an ovation from all sections of the supporters of Your Majesty's Government that delighted and deeply touched him'.

(4)

The stresses to which the National Government were at first exposed, the shocks occasioned by the resignations of Lord Snowden and the pure Liberals, have been considered in some detail, since they mark the last serious internal crisis of King George's reign. Thereafter, in effect, the Conservative Party assumed control. The Liberal Nationals, under Sir John Simon, the dozen or so National Labour members, became as the years passed indistinguishable, except to the eye of an expert, from their Conservative allies. Mr Ramsay MacDonald endured with tragic dignity the degradation which he had foretold. Shunned and vituperated by his former colleagues, accorded polite tolerance by his present allies, progressively weakened by ill-health, he faded off into an autumn haze, lost his powers of concentration, and was finally obliged in June 1935 to surrender his nominal leadership to Mr Stanley Baldwin. Unlike many of Mr MacDonald's admirers, the King did not cease to esteem him when misfortune came. He would visit the stricken Prime Minister in hospital; write him frequent personal letters of encouragement; and strive, whenever opportunity offered, to protect him from the poisons of former friends. In his last sad years Mr MacDonald found solace in the thought that, in one Englishman at least, he had found unswerving faithfulness.[1]

Under the deft quietism of Mr Stanley Baldwin, who from 1933 onwards was in fact in command, Great Britain settled down to a period of illusive calm. With the re-establishment of financial stability, trade improved; it was not a mere Party vaunt that England, under Conservative guidance, was the first of the great industrial countries to emerge from the great depression of 1929–1932.[2] Although the unemployment figures remained obdurate, although both in 1933 and 1934 there were impressive 'hunger-demonstrations' in London, the internal situation was sufficiently stable to allow the introduction of some most useful measures of social and agricultural reform.

The foreign situation also provided ground for optimism. The old quarrels with France had been allayed; the reparations problem had been removed by the decisions of the Lausanne Conference; Germany was resuming her lawful place in the councils of Europe; Mussolini's Italy appeared wholly occupied with internal betterment; Russia, although she behaved very oddly in arresting some British engineers, was busy with her five-year plan; Japan, although tiresome, was very far away. It seemed indeed that, with the encouragement of an enlightened and progressive British Government, the League of Nations would succeed in imposing the rule of law, and according to the peoples of the world the blessing of disarmament, an equalised wage system, and hope. It was with pleasure that the British delegates

[1] In February 1933 a Sunday newspaper published an article by Lord Snowden attacking the Prime Minister. This article was illustrated by a snapshot of Mr Ramsay MacDonald lying recumbent upon the down at Chequers in an attitude indicative of sloth. The King was incensed by this mean photograph. Sir Clive Wigram was instructed to write to Lord Snowden stating that in the King's opinion an article by a former member of Mr MacDonald's Cabinet should not be illustrated by anything so 'invidious and undignified'. Lord Snowden replied that he had of course no previous knowledge that the newspaper was going to print so insulting a photograph and that, when they saw it, both he and Lady Snowden had been aghast (R.A., K. 2363. 5).

[2] Mr Neville Chamberlain as Chancellor of the Exchequer was able without difficulty to balance the budgets of 1932 and 1933. By 1934 the budget showed a surplus of 31 million; the cuts in unemployment benefit were abolished and so also were half the cuts in the salaries of State employees. In 1935 all cuts imposed in 1931 were removed.

pranced along the wide corridors of the Palais des Nations at Geneva. But there were difficulties all the same.

In September 1931 the Japanese invaded Manchuria and the League proved wholly unable either to stop or punish this aggression. An attempt at Anglo-American intervention was frustrated by what now seems undue hesitation on the part of the British Government. The League could do no more than pass a unanimous resolution recording that Japan had violated the articles of the Covenant. The Japanese, at that, resigned their membership: a bad precedent was created.

In February 1932 the World Disarmament Conference failed to justify the expectations that it had aroused. Germany announced that she would be unable to accept any scheme for general disarmament that did not accord her equality of status. The Conference, as its successor in 1933, petered out in a series of propositions. Thereafter, with the advent of Adolf Hitler, disarmament became a lost cause.

Hopes of universal recovery were renewed when, on June 12, 1933, the King opened the World Monetary and Economic Conference in the Geological Museum at South Kensington. The British Government were hampered by the Ottawa agreements; nor did President Roosevelt, who was absorbed by his own programme of reconstruction, give to the Conference the inspiring impetus that his early attitude had led men to hope. The Conference, after passing some anodyne resolutions, adjourned indefinitely on July 27.

A further problem that shadowed the sunshine of the National Government was our war debt to the United States. In June 1932 the Lausanne Conference had, to all intents and purposes, relieved Germany of further liability to make reparation payments. Mr MacDonald on that occasion had pleaded most eloquently for what he called 'a clean slate'. The King, who preferred to base his conclusions upon ascertainable facts, did not seek to imitate the graceful if undulating movements of the League of Nations mind. 'The difficulty', His Majesty wrote to Mr MacDonald, 'of the "clean slate" policy seems to me that, unfortunately, America holds the sponge'.[1] The American public did not agree with the policy expressed in the Balfour Note that Great Britain was not in honour bound to pay the United States more than she received from her enemy and allied creditors. President Hoover refused to extend the moratorium. The payments of interest on our debt, having dribbled on sulkily, having thereafter produced a few drops in the nature of 'token' payments, ceased completely. It was hoped that the new President, Mr. Franklin Roosevelt, who assumed office on March 4, 1933, would be more urbane.

President Roosevelt, as Assistant Secretary to the Navy Department, had met King George during the war. He now suddenly addressed to him a curious letter, the exact purpose of which is still unclear:*ᵐ*

'The White House
Washington.

My dear King George,   November 5 1933.
    I have long remembered your telling me about your stamps and I thought that perhaps you would be amused at seeing the strange ways in which some of your loyal subjects insist upon addressing me. It is bad enough to have my American responsibilities without the addition of Indians, Canadians, Australians etc. to add to my woes at the rate of at least a score of letters a day. The stamps are without value but perhaps the addresses will make up for that—and it is very delightful for me to know that you and I have in common the interest in stamps and in the Navy. Your Admiral Drax is coming to tea with us in a few days.
    I am deeply sorry that the debt negotiations have got nowhere *this time*, but at least I am confident that little or no ill-feeling has been engendered on either side, and I am sufficient of an optimist to believe very deeply that both our peoples will reach an agreement when this nightmare of currency and "stabilization" is more permanently settled.
    I hope you will like our Ambassador Bingham. He is an old friend of mine and incidentally he is, like you, a good shot.
    With my sincere regards, believe me,
                            faithfully yours,
                            (Signed) Franklin D. Roosevelt.'

Before answering this letter the King considered it would be wise to consult the Foreign Office.[1] His reply, when eventually despatched, was polite but vague.*ⁿ* The King had been impressed by the argument that, since American tariffs prevented our transferring pay-

[1] The Foreign Office had already been alarmed by President Roosevelt's tendency to ignore the usual channels. On May 16, 1933, the President had sent a telegram to the King, and to other Heads of States, suggesting that the World Disarmament Conference should aim at the elimination of all 'offensive' weapons and the conclusion of a Pact of universal non-aggression. The King was advised merely to acknowledge the telegram, adding that he had referred it to his Government for careful consideration. The considered reply, when eventually despatched, was addressed to the State Department in Washington through the British Ambassador (R.A., K. 2378).

ments in the form of goods and services, it was wrong to say that we had defaulted: all that had happened was that we had been precluded by circumstances from meeting the interest on our debt. He emphasised this view in conversation at Windsor with the United States Ambassador: Mr Bingham, a most genial man, signified assent.⁰

Yet if Great Britain were to establish more sympathetic relations with the United States, it was essential that we should remove, or at least mitigate, what was proving an increasing source of misrepresentation. It was essential that the Indian problem should be handled in such a manner as to convince world opinion that we were prepared to practise what we preached; and that our oft-repeated assertion that we had all the time been educating the Indian peoples for self-government was not a mere evasive formula of postponement, but a serious statement of purpose.

(5)

The emergence of Indian[1] nationalism as a potent political force is usually dated from the year 1905. In that year the partition of Bengal aroused deep and wide resentment, while the defeat of Russia by Japan suggested that European dominance over Asia need not for ever remain unquestionable. In the ten years that followed, the younger generation of Indians became infected with hopes and hatreds that had been unknown before. By 1917 the British Government realised that something must be done to allay this effervescence: they also realised that India's conduct during the first world war merited some substantial gesture of recognition and reward. On August 20, 1917, therefore, Mr Edwin Montagu, at that time Secretary of State for India, made the following pronouncement:

'Our policy is not only the increasing association of Indians in every branch of the administration, but also the greatest possible development of self-governing institutions, with a view to the progressive realization of responsible government in India, as an integral part of the British Empire.'

If this statement meant anything, and the sincerity of Mr Montagu was never doubted—it meant that India was gradually to be prepared for Dominion status. The Viceroy, Lord Chelmsford,

[1] The expressions 'India' and 'Indians' are used in this chapter to designate the whole sub-continent and its 400 million inhabitants. The distinction between 'India' and 'Pakistan' dates only from 1947.

shared these ideas. In co-operation with the Secretary of State he elaborated what became known as the 'Montagu-Chelmsford Report', the main recommendations of which were embodied in the Government of India Act of 1919:[1]

> 'We have', wrote Lord Chelmsford to the King on October 4, 1918, 'an educated class here, 95% of whom are inimical to us, and I venture to assert that every student in every University is growing up with a hatred of us. These are, of course, at present a mere fraction of the population, but each year sees the numbers augmented, and it may well be imagined that their potentialities for mischief are infinite. If we can win these men over to our side, I am convinced that we can only do it by inviting and enlisting their co-operation. And this is the aim and object of the recommendations of our joint report.'[D]

The 1919 Act and the resultant Indian Constitution might have marked a new state in Anglo-Indian relations, had it not been for the effect upon Mohandas Gandhi of the Rowlatt Acts and the Amritsar shootings of the same year.[2] From that moment Mr Gandhi decided that there was little more to be secured from co-operation. By applying the simple axioms of the *Bhagavad Gita* and *Sesame and Lilies* to what until then had been a riot of emotional conceptions, he succeeded within a few years in transforming an intellectual agitation into a mass revolutionary movement. His was an achievement

[1] Under the 1919 Act a central legislature was established, with 70% of its members elected by an extended franchise. The executive was, however, to remain under the control of the Viceroy, who was responsible to London alone. In the provinces, the novel experiment of 'dyarchy' was introduced. Certain departments, such as education and public works, were 'transferred' to Ministers responsible to the local legislatures. Others, such as defence and internal order, were 'reserved' for the Governor-General, who remained responsible in such matters to London. A Chamber of Princes was established at Delhi for the discussion of matters of common interest.

After the lapse of ten years a Commission was to visit India to report on the working of the Act and if necessary to make recommendations for an extension of responsible government.

[2] In March 1919 the Rowlatt Acts were passed, providing that those accused of political crimes could be tried without a jury. Although these Acts were never in fact put into force, they led Mr Gandhi to lose all faith in the justice of the British Raj and to declare the first of his *hartals* or boycotts.

On April 13, General Dyer, fearing riots, ordered his troops to open fire on an unarmed crowd that had gathered in the Jallianwala Bagh at Amritsar. 379 were killed and 1200 wounded. The resentment caused by this deplorable act throughout India was deep, wide and lasting.

of rare political genius combined with almost supernatural spiritual force.

A relaxation of tension marked the five years of Lord Reading's Viceroyalty between 1921 and 1926. Mr Gandhi during those years was able to extend his influence, improve his organisation, and perfect his two almost unanswerable weapons, the boycott and non-co-operation. The choice of Lord Reading's successor presented the Cabinet with a difficult problem in personalities. The King first suggested the name of Lord Haig, but it was felt that a civilian would be better adapted to the situation. The King then suggested Mr Edward Wood,[1] at that time Minister of Agriculture and Fisheries. The suggestion met with the warm approval of the Cabinet, and Mr Wood, having adopted the title of Lord Irwin of Kirkby Underdale, reached India in April 1926.

Under the Government of India Act 1919 it had been provided that, when ten years had elapsed, a Commission would be appointed to examine the working of the new Constitution and to report whether any further reforms should now be introduced. In the autumn of 1927 the Government decided to anticipate the appointed date and to ask Sir John Simon immediately to become Chairman of a Commission of Enquiry, composed of representatives of all shades of British opinion. No Indian was included among the members of the Commission, and Mr Gandhi decided therefore that it should be boycotted by all good nationalists. The Commission none the less proceeded to India, conducted their investigations with industry and calm, and returned to England. Sir John Simon hoped to complete his report by February of 1930, and was much distressed when, in the autumn of 1929, there were signs that the Government were becoming bored by the Commission and that certain important members of the latter might decide to resign. Sir John Simon appealed to the King for assistance:

'My duty', he wrote to Lord Stamfordham on November 1, 1929, 'to

---

[1]'His Majesty', wrote Lord Birkenhead to Lord Stamfordham, 'was more responsible than anyone else for the most admirable appointment of Lord Irwin·as Viceroy.'

Mr Wood entered Parliament in 1910 as Conservative member for Ripon and became Under-Secretary for the Colonies in 1921. He was President of the Board of Education from 1922 to 1924 and Minister of Agriculture from 1924 to 1926. He succeeded his father as 3rd Viscount Halifax in 1934. After holding several posts in the National Government he succeeded Mr Anthony Eden as Foreign Secretary on February 25, 1938.

the King and the Empire is *at all costs* to keep the Indian Commission going (as I have done for 2 years) without internal rupture. We have been good colleagues and know nothing in the Commission of Party differences. . . . We can report in February if we are left alone and alive. There is a *great* danger—perhaps a certainty—that Lord Burnham will insist on resigning at once. That will be the climax of my difficulties. I believe that there is no way of stopping it, save a personal appeal from His Majesty . . . a private appeal from the Sovereign might save him. I cannot be without *all* my colleagues and his continued service would in my judgment be an act of true patriotism. It is excessively urgent.'*q*

Lord Stamfordham replied that, although the King could hardly send for Lord Burnham and make a personal appeal to him, since that would 'bring His Majesty too much into the controversy', he would himself, on his own responsibility, let Lord Burnham know that 'the King would deprecate beyond words anything like a disruption of the Simon Commission' and would much regret it were Lord Burnham to resign. Lord Burnham, on being informed of this, immediately cancelled his resignation. The incident has been cited as typical, both of the unseen influence that the King was able to exercise, and of the tact and wisdom of Lord Stamfordham's every intervention.*r*

Lord Irwin, in his anxiety to create a better atmosphere for the report of the Simon Commission, issued a message to the peoples of India to the effect that the natural issue of India's constitutional progress must be the attainment of equal Dominion status.

This statement caused some perturbation in London:

'Oh! What a hubbub', Lord Stamfordham wrote to the Viceroy on December 2, 1929, 'about your statement about "equal Dominion status" and how much talk in both Houses of Parliament! I listened to Reading, Birkenhead, Parmoor and Passfield. Poor old Parmoor—he got so mixed, referred to Ramsay MacDonald as "Lord MacDonald", and more than once spoke of *"Her* Majesty's Government", which rather touched me, as I fancied his mind was like mine, often wandering back to the much despised Victorian period! . . . However mercifully the whole thing quickly fizzled out, and I am sure at the back of everyone's mind was the desire not to embarrass you.'*s*

The Simon Report was published in June 1930.[1] It was much

1 The main proposals of the Simon Report were as follows: (1) The system of dyarchy was to be abolished and Ministers responsible to the elected legislatures were now to have charge of all departments. The Governors in extreme emergency could, however, veto a Ministerial decision. (2) The ultimate destiny of India was envisaged as a Federation

disliked by Indian nationalist opinion and the Viceroy, in view of the impending Round Table Conference, was anxious that it should not be represented as being our last word. 'There will', he had written to the King,[t] 'be a growing tendency here to contest the right of a British Parliament to be the arbiter of Indian progress'. The King, for his part, was anxious that the Simon Report should form the basis of discussions at the Conference. He much admired the Report, regarding it as the 'most accurate, faithful picture ever portrayed of that wonderful country',[u] He was worried by the tendency of the Government to damn the report with civil leer by calling it 'a thoughtful and constructive contribution to a very difficult problem':

> 'As to the Simon Report', Lord Stamfordham wrote to the Viceroy on July 6, 1930, 'the King shares the general view . . . that it is a very remarkable achievement. . . . His Majesty trusts that the Government here will regard it as the core of their policy and not allow the Round Table Conference to tear it to bits.'[v]

Mr MacDonald and Mr Wedgwood Benn, the Secretary of State for India, were anxious none the less to enter the Conference with completely free hands.

(6)

The First Round Table Conference was opened by the King in the Royal Gallery of the House of Lords on November 12, 1930. Mr Gandhi refused to attend this Conference, which was therefore boycotted by the Congress Party. The Government had been in some doubt whether to advise the King to perform the opening ceremony, since they did not wish him to be associated with something that might fail. Lord Stamfordham held the view that, if the King-Emperor were to absent himself, many of the Indian delegates would imagine that he disapproved of the whole proceedings.[w] The Viceroy was obliged to the King for the decision he had taken:

> 'It is not necessary', wrote Lord Irwin, 'for me to say how grateful I have been to you, Sir, for the immense help that your personal action

of Self-governing Provinces on the analogy of Canada. There was to be a Federal Assembly elected by members of the Provincial Assemblies. Matters affecting defence, foreign policy, financial stability, and the treatment of minorities were to remain with the Viceroy in Council. (3) The Federation was to comprise not British India only, but also the Indian States. (4) The new constitution was to be flexible and capable of development.

in opening its proceedings will have been, or for the great trouble which Your Majesties have taken to do everything possible by way of reception and entertainment of the various delegates from India.'[x]

The First Round Table Conference adjourned in January 1931, after having accepted three main principles, namely that future development must be on a Federal basis, that certain safeguards regarding defence and financial stability must be retained, and that, subject to these reservations, responsibility must be placed in Indian hands. Lord Irwin entered into communication with Mr Gandhi, who accepted these three principles, called off the civil-disobedience movement, and even agreed that he would himself attend the Conference when its meetings were resumed. The King entirely approved of these conversations between the Viceroy and Mr Gandhi and was annoyed with those who, in the House of Commons and elsewhere, contended that we were appeasing the instigator and champion of lawlessness:

'The King', wrote Sir Clive Wigram to Lord Irwin on March 27, 1931, 'deprecates as much as you do the attitude which the Conservatives, egged on by the retired die-hards from India, are adopting. . . . The King is full of admiration for the patience and forbearance you have shown in dealing with Mr Gandhi. Indeed, His Majesty feels that you deserve the very greatest credit for bringing about this temporary truce with Gandhi and the Congress, which, in the King's opinion, no one but you could have achieved.'[y]

The Viceroy's own impression of these conversations, and of the personality of the leader of Indian nationalism, were recorded in a long letter addressed by him to the King on March 13, 1931:[z]

'. . . I think most people meeting him would be conscious, as I was conscious, of a very powerful personality, and this, independent of physical endowment, which indeed is unfavourable. Small, wizened, rather emaciated, no front teeth, it is a personality very poorly adorned with this world's trimmings. And yet you cannot help feeling the force of character behind the sharp little eyes and immensely active and acutely working mind. I kept asking myself all the time was the man completely sincere, and I think as our conversations went on that I came to feel about this in rather double fashion. I came to have no doubt whatever that, if Mr Gandhi gave me his word on any point, that word was absolutely secure, and that I could trust it implicitly. On the other hand, I found what had always been my impression being confirmed, namely, that though intentionally he was completely sincere, yet in some matters he was the victim of unconscious self-deception. The tendency to this showed itself in the importance he attached to different matters, and the weight that he seemed prepared to give to different kinds of evidence. . . . Gandhi I am sure wants to find the way to peace, but it is very important that English opinion should be brought to realise exactly what he is after. I believe it, Sir, to be definitely untrue to suggest, as I see it suggested from time to time, that he is out to break the unity of Your Majesty's Empire. I discussed this with him a week or so ago and he said, as nearly as I could remember this: "I want to see India established in her own self-respect and in the respect of the world. I therefore want to see India able to discuss with Great Britain on terms of equality, and Great Britain willing to discuss with India on such terms. I know perfectly well that we want British help in many things for a long time yet—defence, administration and so on—and I am prepared to have safe-guards, or as I prefer to call them, adjustments, provided these are really in the interests of India and you will allow us to discuss them with you on equal terms. If we can reach an agreement on those lines, I shall be satisfied that I have got *Purna Swaraj* or *complete independence*, and India will have got it in what to me is the highest form in which it can be attained, namely, in association with Great Britain. But if Great Britain will not help me in this way, and if this achievement in partnership cannot be brought about, then I must pursue my end of *Purna Swaraj* or *complete independence* in isolation from Great Britain, and this I definitely regard as the second best."

The point of view will I think interest Your Majesty, and Your Majesty will observe how very far removed it is from what is probably held to be implied by him and others when they speak about complete independence, as they no doubt will do at the Congress at Karachi at the end of this month. Moreover, in judging of what will there be said, it is well to remember that they, not less than any other party, are greatly embarrassed and hampered by past commitments of writing and speech. I do not for a moment wish to suggest to Your Majesty that the difficulties are not very great; they clearly are; but I do not think that they need necessarily bring our efforts to find a solution of them to failure. . . .'

In September 1931 was held the Second Round Table Conference, this time attended by Mr Gandhi and representatives of the Congress Party. The hopes that had been aroused by this second Conference were frustrated by dissensions between the Indians themselves. The Moslems advanced extreme pretensions, the Princes became suspicious, and the Congress Party began to fear that, in any all-Indian Federation, the Princes and the Moslems might combine against them. The second Conference therefore reached a deadlock and Mr Gandhi returned to India resolved to start his civil disobedience campaign all over again. During his presence in London Mr Gandhi, with other delegates, was received at Buckingham Palace:

508

'His Majesty', wrote Sir Clive Wigram to the new Viceroy, Lord Willingdon, 'was, as is his custom, very nice to (Mr Gandhi), but ended up by impressing on him that this country would not stand a campaign of terrorism and having their friends shot down in India. His Majesty warned Gandhi that he was to put a stop to this. . . . Gandhi spluttered some excuse, but H.M. said he held him responsible.'[2a]

On the failure of the Second Round Table Conference, the British Government reverted to the principles foreshadowed by the First Conference in January. A White Paper was issued and referred to a Select Committee of both Houses, presided over by Lord Linlithgow. In November 1934 the Committee furnished a long and impressive report. It was on this report that Sir Samuel Hoare, as Secretary of State for India, based the Government of India Bill which he introduced into the House of Commons on February 6, 1935.

The Bill provided that the Provinces, now numbering eleven, should be accorded full self-government, subject to certain safeguards. A central Government was to be created, so soon as a prescribed number of States had agreed to join the Federation. The Indian Princes had by then become even more suspicious of Federation, fearing that they might be swamped by the politicians. At a Conference of Princes held in Bombay on February 25 a resolution was passed denouncing the Government of India Bill. The King, who had always hoped that the Princes would constitute an element of reason and stability, expressed himself to the India Office as 'disgusted by their vacillation'. He went so far as to say that it would be better if, instead of flocking to London for the Jubilee celebrations, they were to stay in their own countries and look after the needs of their own subjects.[2b] As a result of the attitude of the Princes, the prescribed quorum was not obtained and the provisions for the establishment of a Central Federal Government were never, most unfortunately for India, brought into operation.

Sir Samuel Hoare, with the able assistance of his Under-Secretary, Mr R. A. Butler, steered his Bill through forty sittings of the House of Commons and sixty-one days of detailed, and sometimes acrimonious, debate. The Bill passed its third reading on June 5, 1935, by a majority of 264 to 122. It received the Royal Assent on August 2.[1]

[1] King George remained Emperor of India all his life. It was not until August 1947 that India and Pakistan became independent members of the Commonwealth.

CHAPTER–XXX

JUBILEE

1935

Honours and distinctions—The Prime Minister responsible for all recommendations—The Dunedin Commission and the 1925 Honours Act —The King's way of life in London and Sandringham—Changes that had occurred since 1910—The approach of old age—The King and his Ministers—The Foreign situation—Herr Hitler establishes his despotism—Sir John Simon's visit to Berlin—Anxiety caused by the failure of these Conversations—The Silver Jubilee—The King's popularity—His broadcasts—The sunset of the League of Nations— The Abyssinian crisis—The Hoare-Laval agreement—The King's failing health—He spends his last Christmas at Sandringham—His final illness—He dies on January 20, 1936.

(1)

KING GEORGE, as has already been emphasised, preferred the usual to the unusual, the familiar to the unaccustomed, the old to the new. Yet he saw clearly that the Monarchy could not remain the sole static institution in a dynamic world; he accepted as necessities of evolution the many changes in the functions and privileges of the Sovereign which he witnessed during the quarter century of his reign. He had trained himself to draw a distinction between his responsibilities as a Monarch and his feelings, prejudices or affections as an individual. He never sought to disguise his personal opinions: indeed, he would express them with a vigour that sometimes caused dismay: yet the moment it became necessary for him to operate a⁻ a constitutional factor, individual considerations would at once be banned. Those who, whether as Cabinet Ministers or in some other capacity, had access to the King during the last decade of his reign, can still recall the smile and gesture with which, after indulging in some criticism, he would brush aside his own views as crumbs from the table, exclaiming: 'But all that, of course, is not for *me*.'

Although he accepted with acquiescence—if not always with uncomplaining acquiescence—the larger transformations of those twenty-five years, he remained suspicious of such small encroachments on the Prerogative as appeared to him to detract from the repute of the Crown. It was thus with watchfulness that he would examine the recommendations made to him for ecclesiastical appoint-
510

ments.[1] And he was often angered by the necessity of approving honours conferred upon individuals whom he himself considered unworthy, or whose sole claim to distinction was that they had proved useful, or inconvenient, to the Party in power.

The bestowal of distinctions for scientific, artistic or literary services might provoke a short discussion, but never aroused controversy, between No. 10 Downing Street and Buckingham Palace. When, for instance, Dr Bridges died early in 1930, an interesting exchange of views took place as to who should succeed him as Poet Laureate. The King was anxious that Mr Rudyard Kipling should be appointed, but it was understood that the offer, if made, would be declined. Others suggested the name of Sir Henry Newbolt, whereas the Prime Minister was believed to favour the claim of Professor A. E. Housman. But here again a refusal was to be anticipated. In the end, therefore, Mr John Masefield, with the King's warm approval, was offered and accepted the post.[a]

Far more complicated and distressing were the constant difficulties that arose over the bestowal of political honours. Ministers were inclined to make promises to individuals before His Majesty's pleasure had been obtained. A flagrant case of such disregard occurred in 1916. Mr Lloyd George and Mr Bonar Law, desiring to obtain a seat in the House of Commons for one of the new Ministers, offered a peerage to a Conservative Member representing a safe constituency. The King, when asked for his consent, replied that he did not 'see his way' to approve of this honour, since he did not consider that the 'public services' of the individual in question 'called for such special recognition'.[b] Mr Lloyd George replied that any refusal

---

[1] It is only fair to say that successive Prime Ministers—including Palmerston, Disraeli and Lloyd George—were extremely scrupulous in advising the Crown on candidates eligible for church preferment. As an example of the great care taken, may be cited the appointment in 1924 of the Vicar of St Margaret's Altrincham, as Dean of Manchester. On the death of Dr McCormick, Lord Stamfordham wrote both to the Prime Minister and the Archbishop of Canterbury giving a list of possible successors. The Archbishop then consulted Dr Temple, Bishop of Manchester, asking whether he had any special candidate to propose. The Prime Minister's Private Secretary then visited the Archbishop at Lambeth and informed him that the Prime Minister, if there were no other special candidate in the field, would like to suggest the name of the Vicar of St Margaret's Altrincham. Both the Archbishop and Dr Temple thought the Prime Minister's candidate wholly suitable. 'He always', wrote the Archbishop, 'carries weight with thoughtful people' (R.A., I. 1961).

would place him in a position of great embarrassment' and begged
Lord Stamfordham to discuss the matter with Mr Bonar Law. The
latter divulged that, not only had the individual himself been informed of his intended elevation, but that the Conservative Association in his constituency had been told that their Member was about
to move to a higher place and that a by-election would be held
immediately:

> 'I cannot conceal from you', wrote Lord Stamfordham to Mr Lloyd
> George, 'that His Majesty was surprised and hurt that this honour
> should have been offered without first obtaining his consent. . . . The
> King recognizes (in view of the promises made and information given)
> that it is impossible for him now to withhold his approval. But, in thus
> signifying his acquiescence, His Majesty commands me to say that he
> feels that the Sovereign's Prerogative should not be disregarded; and
> he trusts that in future no honours whatever will be offered by any
> Minister until his approval has been informally obtained. His Majesty
> further asks that this be made clear to your Colleagues.'[c]

Mr Lloyd George returned no reply to this protest. Lord Stamfordham therefore embodied it in a formal memorandum which he
sent to the Prime Minister on January 9, 1917. In this memorandum
Lord Stamfordham pointed out that 'the Crown is the fountain of
honour, and grants and honours can only be made by the King, acting with the advice of his Ministers'. It was only right therefore that
the King should be informally consulted before an honour was
actually promised to an individual or that promise was divulged.[d]
Mr Lloyd George still refused to put his views in writing, but
promised the King, in private audience, that he would not fail to
communicate His Majesty's views verbally to the members of the
Cabinet.[e]

An even more unfortunate incident occurred in 1922, when peerages were offered to two individuals, whose integrity had become a
matter of public questioning. The matter was raised in the House of
Lords and some strong criticism made. The King was incensed:[f]

> 'Dear Prime Minister', he wrote to Mr Lloyd George on July 3, 1922,
> 'I cannot conceal from you my profound concern at the very disagree-
> able situation which has arisen on the question of Honours.
>   The Peerages which I was advised to confer upon Sir . . . and Sir
> . . . have brought things rather to a climax: though for some time
> there have been evident signs of growing public dissatisfaction on
> account of the excessive number of honours conferred; the personality
> of some of the recipients; and the questionable circumstances under
> which the honours in certain instances have been granted.

You will remember that both in conversation and in written communications I have deprecated the ever increasing number of those submitted for the half yearly Honours Gazette: and in recent years there have been instances in which honours have been bestowed where subsequent information has betrayed a lack of care in the enquiries made as to the fitness of the persons selected for recognition.

The case of Sir . . . and all that it has evoked in the Debates of the House of Lords and in the newspaper reports of interviews given by him to Press representatives, must be regarded as little less than an insult to the Crown and to the House of Lords and may, I fear, work injury to the Prerogative in the public mind at home and even more in South Africa.

I fully recognise that the inordinate demands upon your time make it impossible for you, in spite of your marvellous capacity for work, personally to investigate the claims and qualifications of those persons whose names you submit for my approval for honours and rewards.

But I do appeal most strongly for the establishment of some efficient and trustworthy procedure in order to protect the Crown and the Government from the possibility of similar painful if not humiliating incidents, the recurrence of which must inevitably constitute an evil, dangerous to the social and political well being of the State.'

Mr Lloyd George replied immediately[g] that he entirely shared His Majesty's concern and was anxious to provide all possible safeguards against accident or abuse. He proposed therefore, in view of the publicity unfortunately given to recent errors, to suggest the appointment of a Royal Commission to enquire into the principles involved and the procedure followed. This Commission was established under the chairmanship of Lord Dunedin. One of the first acts of the Commission was to ask Lord Stamfordham whether in fact the King ever conferred an honour except upon the advice of a responsible Minister:

I replied "never" ', Lord Stamfordham recorded,[h] 'and that the King was most punctilious, even when applications came from Members of the Royal Family, that these should be made through the Prime Minister, as the King himself never initiated honours. Of course this ruling does not refer to the Royal Victorian Order; also the Sovereign maintains the right of personally selecting Members for the Order of Merit.'[1]

---

[1] The Victorian Order and the Order of Merit have always been in the personal gift of the Sovereign, and can be awarded without Ministerial advice. So, also, since December 1946, can the Orders of the Garter and the Thistle.

The report of the Dunedin Commission, when eventually published, emphasised that the Prime Minister was responsible for the names he submitted for Royal approval and that such names, therefore, should be 'unassailable'. The Commission also suggested that candidates for honours who were, or had been, domiciled in a Dominion should not be recommended until the consent of the Dominion Prime Minister had also been obtained. Their recommendation was that, in making submissions for 'political' honours, the Prime Minister should be protected against any suspicion of having been influenced in his judgment by contributions to Party funds. A Committee of Three Privy Councillors might be chosen to examine submissions before they were actually made to the Crown.[1]

Inevitably the bestowal of honours upon men of Dominion origin, who did not always possess in their home country the esteem that they had since acquired in England, aroused much criticism overseas. The Canadian House of Commons went so far as to pass a resolution that no titles should be conferred upon persons resident in Canada and that any titles already so conferred should be cancelled. In South Africa a motion was passed that no honours at all should be bestowed upon South Africans. These self-denying ordinances have not been consistently applied. But the principle could now be said to be established that, in ordinary circumstances, no honour would be conferred upon a person ordinarily resident in a Dominion, except upon the recommendation of the Prime Minister in that Dominion.

These scandals, questionings and resolutions were most unwelcome to the King, who felt that it was unfair that he should be regarded as the Fountain of Honour, and given no real opportunity to see that the waters were kept clean. In the masses of documents bearing on the bestowal of honours now stored in the Archives at Windsor, there are many instances when the King protested, often in vain, against the abuses of the system. The number of occasions when a Prime Minister was deterred, from fear of Royal displeasure, from submitting a really disgraceful name remains unrecorded. Only one instance can be found of King George himself writing to ask that an honour be conferred. In November 1930 he suggested through Lord Stamfordham that an inventor of flying boats, who was personally known to him, should be recommended for a Knighthood. The Prime Minister's Private Secretary replied that there were other in-

---

[1] The Report of the Dunedin Commission led to the passage of the 'Honours (Prevention of Abuses) Act 1925'. It was under this Act that in 1933 Mr J. Maundy Gregory was convicted of 'touting' for honours.

ventors who had prior claims, and that in any case No. 10 Downing Street was 'snowed under' with applications:

'I only hope', minuted the King, 'that the spade used will be a large one and the snow not too deep. As I so seldom ask for a knighthood, I 1   iy think that I might be treated with anyhow some consideration occasionally.'¹

In submitting the names of those who, for political services, were regarded as meriting distinction, Ministers did not always accord to the King the same suave frankness as they showed when dealing with their other encroachments on the Prerogative. It may have been shame that dimmed their candour.

(2)

As the internal situation improved, as Great Britain struggled heavily out of the great depression, the King was able once more to relax from anxiety and to resume, in more equable conditions, the recurrent cycle of his public and private life.

The organisation of his household had by then reached such a pitch of naval exactness, that not even the faintest purr of the distant engines penetrated the long corridors or stirred the silks and tapestries in the rooms. When at Buckingham Palace, he would work all morning in his writing room, the walls of which were decorated by Sir David Wilkie's *Letter Writer of Seville* and Frith's *Ramsgate Sands*. Audiences would take place, either in the India Room—with its display of oriental shields and daggers, glittering with jade, emeralds and rubies, or in the small Audience Room next door. In the afternoon he would walk quickly round the lake, accompanied by the Queen or an equerry, and often joined by Miss Agnes Keyser, who had been accorded the rare privilege of possessing a key to the palace garden.¹ In warm weather he would do his work in the summer house, or more frequently in a tent erected on the lawn. When at Windsor, he would go for long rides in the Great Park, pick daffodils on the slopes, or make expeditions to Virginia Water and Adelaide

¹ Miss Agnes Keyser was the founder and Matron of 'King Edward VII's Hospital for Officers', then established, in the vicinity of the Palace, at 17 Grosvenor Crescent. She had been a friend of King Edward's and was generally referred to as 'Sister Agnes'. Her brother was Consul General at Marseilles; her sister Fanny assisted her in managing the nursing home. She specialised in patients from the Household Cavalry and the Brigade of Guards, and enjoyed repeating to the King, not always with useful results, the talk of the town.

Cottage. Balmoral had its own special atmosphere. When in the *Victoria and Albert* a different time-table, a more marine procedure, was prescribed.

On all the mantelpieces, in all the rooms, in all the palaces and castles, the clocks ticked in exact unison. Only at Sandringham were they precisely thirty minutes in advance of their thousand colleagues; but Sandringham had always been the home apart. When there, he would rise early, greet his parrot Charlotte, take her upon his wrist when he went to tap the barometer, and allow her to accompany him into breakfast. Swaying thoughtfully from foot to foot, she would pick her delicate way among the saucers and the plates. In later years it was mounted upon his white pony 'Jock' that he would visit the old shooting haunts: the duck-ponds, Captain's Close or Dersingham Wood. Year by year there came an increasing number of grand-children to lighten his old age.[1]

Until the end of his life he never failed to attend the regatta week at Cowes, where, with the assistance of Sir Philip Hunloke, he would sail the *Britannia* in race after race along the scudding Solent, and round the swaying buoys.[2] Almost on the same day in every August he would embark at Portsmouth in the *Victoria and Albert* and anchor in Cowes Roads. Those woods and lawns and waters were evocative of many memories. Memories of past regattas, of the German Emperor's noisy touchiness, of King Edward's embarrassed indignation: memories of Queen Victoria, leaning forwards in her canopied pony-carriage, and the sound of her little laugh; memories of heartrending farewells when bound on distant voyages: memories of Mr Dalton, of

---

[1] The King was fond of children, would greet them hilariously, and ask them so many, and such rapid, questions that they sometimes became shy. They soon recovered from their embarrassment. His diary references to his grandchildren are numerous. He records every visit by the Princess Royal's two sons either to Buckingham Palace or to Windsor. Less than a fortnight before he died he noted in his diary for January 7, 1936: 'Saw my Kent grandson in his bath.' The two daughters of the Duke and Duchess of York were his favourites. The following entries are typical of many: 'Feb. 18. 1932. Lilibet and Margaret came after luncheon. My new little cairn, "Bob", was fairly friendly to them.' 'July 8 1935. All the children looked so nice, but none prettier than Lilibet and Margaret.'

[2] The *Britannia* was designed by George Watson and built by D. & W. Henderson on the Clyde. She was launched in 1893. By 1934, when she was more than 40 years old, she had sailed in 569 races and won 231 first prizes and 124 other prizes. She did not long survive her master. On July 10, 1936, she was towed out to a point south of the Isle of Wight and given naval burial in deep water.

Mr Lawless, of the excellent Fuller: memories of two small and tear-stained cadets climbing in apprehension up the gangway of the *Bacchante*.

King George always retained the habit of noting anniversaries in his diary. On August 6, 1935, on his last visit to Cowes: 'We joined the *Bacchante*', he wrote, '56 years ago today.'

Much had happened in the half century since then. The King was frequently heard to deplore post-war habits, manners and conduct, recognising in them the symptoms of a deeper alteration. Even as the incidence of power had shifted after 1870 from the territorial aristocracy to the urban middle classes: so also, from 1914 onwards, power began to slide, with ever-increasing velocity, into the hands of the industrial proletariat. The focus of attention was transferred from external and imperial affairs, from political personalities and even parliamentary debates, to new and perplexing conceptions of economic and social justice. As class distinctions began to lose their former inevitability, class enmities arose. The King realised with displeasure that new methods of visual and oral communication, new means of transport, new educational systems and opportunities, were creating a younger generation possessing different eyes, different ears and different minds.[1] No longer would any adolescent be taught, or inclined, to take his status for granted. All too clearly did the King recognise the chaotic elements in this confused transition. They seemed to him elements of moral disorder; he did not realise that they were also elements of creative vitality. More than most of his associates he earnestly desired a world of social justice: but all that he could see around him was a new world of vituperation and disobedience that was destroying everything that he had known and respected since 1879.

He was conscious, pathetically conscious, of the passing of the years. 'My old birthday (68)', he wrote in his diary for June 3, 1933. 'Received at Ballater', he commented on August 24 of the same year, 'by Ld Huntly (aged 87), Ld Aberdeen (aged 86) and Ld Dunedin

[1] Statistics emphasise these changes. In 1910 the total expenditure on social services was £55 million. In 1932 it was £430 million. In 1910 the number of those attending secondary schools was 163,221. By 1933 the figure had risen to 527,598. Of the 335 scholarships awarded by Oxford and Cambridge Universities as much as 69·3% were won by pupils who had held free places in grant-aided schools. In 1910 it was estimated that 10,500 motor vehicles were produced; by 1934 the production figure was 342,499. In 1912 there were 180,000 driving licences; in 1934 there were 3,197,000.

(aged 85).' From the following January onwards, the entry 'I only shot in the morning' becomes more frequent. Yet always he struggled to fulfil his ceremonial duties. The summer of 1934 was exacting. On June 4 he took the salute at the Trooping of the King's Colour at his Birthday Parade, and rode back to Buckingham Palace at the head of the Guards. On June 11 he received the Amir Abdullah of Transjordan in the India Room, and found him 'a very nice man & very intelligent'. On July 9 he went to Edinburgh for a week of residence in the Palace of Holyroodhouse; there were investitures, levées, drawing-rooms, garden parties or inspections every day. On July 18 he travelled to Liverpool and opened the Mersey Tunnel. By the end of that month he was back in London and gave a garden Party at Buckingham Palace on July 26. 'Rather tired', he wrote that evening, 'but did my work before dinner as usual.' On September 26 he attended the launching of the *Queen Mary* on Clydeside. In the autumn he was back in London, occupied with the preparations for the wedding of the Duke of Kent to Princess Marina of Greece:

'I was photographed by three different photographers in three different rooms; very tiring and a great bore.'

Throughout these twenty-five years there occur in his diaries these recurrent entries: 'Worked before breakfast'; 'Did my boxes as usual'; 'Got back to find many boxes waiting.' Wherever he happened to be, whatever he happened to be doing, these red despatch boxes would follow him remorselessly, piling up, one above the other, upon his desk. They contained Cabinet minutes, memoranda, circulated despatches and reports; they contained departmental statements, letters from Ministers, Governors-General and Ambassadors; documents for signature, programmes of impending functions, suggestions for engagements almost a year ahead; petitions, appeals, messages, ideas and protests from every quarter of the globe. The King would read these papers with exact attention. He was apt, in his desire that such assiduity should not pass unnoticed, to explain to Ministers in considerable detail the work of their own Departments. It was sometimes only at the end of His Majesty's monologue that Ministers were able, if courageous, to insert a few words of their own, edgeways.[1]

[1] One summer morning Mr Anthony Eden, on his way to Geneva, had an audience with the King at Buckingham Palace. The King's private apartments were then under repair, and Mr Eden was received in the North East corner room, hung with relics of the Royal Pavilion, and situated immediately above the band-stand in the forecourt. The King,

In recalling these audiences today, the survivors of King George's successive Governments will smile with affectionate reminiscence.

During the years between 1931 and 1935 the Government managed to persuade themselves and others that, even as they had led England out of the slough of the Great Depression, so also would it be vouchsafed to them to lead Europe from the dark valley of dissension up and up and up towards the bright meadows of eternal peace. The Covenant of the League of Nations was the Law: the Assembly and the Council were there to interpret the Law and to pass judgment: aggressors would be deterred by the spectre of collective security and law-breakers punished by the application of economic sanctions. The British public shared these illusions. It was with enthusiasm that they participated in the pious orgies recommended and arranged by the League of Nations Union. In vain did a few wise men, such as Mr Winston Churchill, seek to refute these illusions by pointing out that criminal lunatics cannot be restrained by incantations, but only by strength greater than their own. Such prophets were denounced as cynical, selfish, out-of-date, militaristic and anxious to promote the very conflict against which, in agonised impotence, they sought to warn their countrymen. By the end of 1935 Hitler and Mussolini had slashed and trampled these curtains of silk and muslin: through stark windows now, we recognised the opaque cloud of confusion, egoism and panic that hung over Geneva: to attentive ears there came, in the last months of King George's life, the distant grumble of the thunder of a second war.

(3)

Sir Clive Wigram,[1] who in 1931 had succeeded that remarkable man Lord Stamfordham as Private Secretary to the King, was also inclined to take an optimistic view of the world situation. He felt, as so many felt at the time, that the National Government in Great

on entering, apologised to Mr Eden for having to receive him in this unfamiliar drawing room. 'It is all right, however', His Majesty added, 'I have told the band not to play till I give the word.' The King then furnished Mr Eden with a *catalogue raisonné* of all the subjects which, at Geneva, he would have to discuss. At last he reached a conclusion, and Mr Eden, in the few minutes that remained, started to make some observations on his own. 'Just one second', said the King, as he rang the small gold hand-bell at his side. A page appeared. 'Tell the bandmaster that he can start playing now. . . . You were saying . . .?'[1]

[1] In January 1935 Sir Clive Wigram was raised to the peerage as Baron Wigram of Clewer.

519

Britain should persuade other countries to cease being discontented, unreasonable or restless; and should impose upon them the habit of peace:

> 'The King', he wrote to the Duke of Connaught on March 14, 1932, 'never had such a good set of Ministers & it is wonderful how we can put a strong team into the field whenever required. . . . Geneva, India, Round Table Conference, Lausanne, Ottawa, Paris—even our second eleven would defeat most other countries. At the present time I do not think the prestige of our country has ever stood so high.'[k]

Signor Mussolini and Herr Hitler did not envisage their own ambitions or requirements in cricketing terms.[1] They were perfectly prepared to use the League of Nations, so long as it served their purposes; the moment it became inconvenient, they were resolved to defy its mandates, calculating that such defiance would not, owing to the pacific intentions of the European Powers, and the isolationism of the United States, expose them to any very serious danger. They proved, for a while, correct in this calculation.

There were a few who, even in 1933, were alert to the coming danger. In the House of Commons, on May 26, Sir Austen Chamberlain expressed the view that internal developments in Germany might constitute 'a menace to the whole world'. On June 13 Mr Attlee pleaded that some assistance should be accorded to Austria to enable her to resist an inevitable German aggression. Mr Robert

---

[1] After the fiasco of the Ludendorff *putsch* in November 1923, and after his release from the fortress of Landsberg, Herr Hitler concentrated upon the organisation of his Party and the perfectioning of his propaganda. The economic crisis of 1930, with the terror of a second inflation that it aroused in Germany, gave him his opportunity. Although in the 1928 election the Nazi Party had only secured 12 seats, in the election of September 1930 they secured 104 seats. On January 30, 1933, President Hindenburg invited Herr Hitler to form a 'National Government'. The Reichstag fire of February 1933 enabled Herr Hitler to arrest all the left wing deputies, to obtain exceptional powers from the surviving members of the Reichstag, and thereafter to proclaim the Nazi Party as the only legitimate Party in the State. Having on June 30, 1934, eliminated by assassination all possible rivals within his own Party, he established a complete dictatorship and, on the death of President Hindenburg on August 2 of that year, succeeded him as Head of the State. In March of 1935, in defiance of Articles 198 and 173 of the Treaty of Versailles, he announced his intention of introducing conscription. In March 1936 Herr Hitler occupied the Rhineland with only verbal opposition from France and Great Britain. From that moment, all hope of a peaceful solution had to be abandoned.

JUBILEE SERVICE IN ST PAUL'S

'THE VIGIL OF THE PRINCES' BY F. E. BERESFORD
(King Edward VIII, the Duke of York, the Duke of Kent, the Duke of
Gloucester)

Boothby had already, in a prophetic speech, warned the House of Commons that, in view of Germany's military revival, and her clandestine Luftwaffe, our air estimates were ridiculously inadequate. On February 7, 1934, and again on March 8, Mr Winston Churchill forecast that before long Herr Hitler would possess a powerful German Air Force, and added that he 'dreaded the day when the means of threatening the heart of the British Empire should pass into the hands of the present rulers of Germany'. 'The support that Mr Winston Churchill received', the Prime Minister reported blandly to the King, 'came only from a very small group of Members'.

The first serious shock to public complacency occurred in the autumn of 1933, when Herr Hitler, not meeting with the deference that he desired, ordered his delegation to leave the Disarmament Conference and to shake the dust of Geneva from their feet. Sir John Simon, the British Foreign Secretary, did not at the time take this episode too tragically:

'It would be reckless', he wrote to the King on October 23, 1933, 'to declare that Germany's withdrawal has destroyed all prospect of a Disarmament Convention. It would be foolish to pretend that her withdrawal makes no difference and that Geneva can go on as though nothing had happened. The latest telegram from Rome shows that Signor Mussolini takes the strongest view that the German with-drawal is without excuse and it may be hoped that out of this will result even closer Anglo-Italian co-operation. . . . Sir John feels that Herr Hitler's theatrical action in withdrawing from Geneva is an attempt to introduce into the international field the methods by which he has attained power inside Germany, and that time must be given to see how this works out. Fortunately time is available, for Germany is at present quite incapable of undertaking aggression. Europe fore-warned is, in a sense, Europe forearmed.'[l]

Sir Horace Rumbold, British Ambassador in Berlin, had always taken a gloomy view of the German situation. 'I now feel', he had written to Sir Clive Wigram as early as March 29, 1933, 'that we are getting back to the pre-war atmosphere and mentality'.[m]

On April 24, 1934, the King seized the opportunity of a visit paid to Windsor by the German Ambassador to utter an outspoken warning. Some record of this conversation was preserved by Sir Clive Wigram:[n]

'His Majesty did not repeat his exact words but said that he had started by telling the Ambassador that at the present moment Germany was the peril of the world, and that, if she went on at the present rate, there was bound to be a war within ten years. The King asked what

Germany was arming for? No one wanted to attack her, but she was forcing all the other countries to be prepared for an attack on her part. The Ambassador tried to excuse Germany by saying that the French fortifications were impregnable and that Germany had no fortifications on her side. His Majesty ridiculed this idea, and said that in the last war fortifications were useless and would be even more so in the next.'

Throughout 1934, while Herr Hitler was consolidating his despotism, British and French Ministers continued to believe, and then to hope, that time was on their side:

'It is becoming more and more clear', wrote Sir John Simon to the King on January 14, 1935, 'that the early months of the present year may offer the opportunity for a definite improvement in European relations, in which there is every reason to believe that Your Majesty's Government will be able to play an important, and indeed the leading, part. . . . The coming year is likely to be a vital year in the sense that if European improvement is *not* secured, and some element of German reconciliation effected, the world may enter into a most dangerous future. . . . The point which Sir John has been pressing is that the practical choice is between a Germany which continues to re-arm without any regulation or agreement, and a Germany which, through getting a recognition of its rights and some modification of the Peace Treaties, enters into the comity of nations, and contributes, in this and other ways, to European stability. As between these two courses, there can be no doubt which is the wiser.'*o*

The King was not reassured by this argument:

'His Majesty feels', wrote Lord Wigram to our Ambassador in Berlin on January 16, 'that we must not be blinded by the apparent sweet reasonableness of the Germans, but be wary and not taken unawares.'*p*

Early in February, the French Ministers came to London. It was announced that the two Governments were agreed that nothing would contribute more effectively to world peace than 'a general settlement, freely negotiated between Germany and the other Powers'. When such a settlement had been reached, Germany might consent to resume the seat which she had so abruptly vacated at Geneva. Sir John Simon offered to go to Berlin in person, in order to discuss with Herr Hitler the basis of some such settlement. On March 16, 1935, a week before Sir John Simon and Mr Eden were due to leave London for their visit to Germany, Herr Hitler announced that he intended immediately to introduce military conscription, create

522

an overt Air Force, and increase the peace basis of the German Army
to thirty-six divisions. Sir John Simon was perturbed:

> 'There may be a certain advantage', he wrote to the King two days
> later, 'in the German Goverment having come out into the open.
> But it is Sir John's view that the German Government do not really
> want to make an agreement or at least only wish to do so on German
> terms which would be intolerable for others. It must not be assumed
> that the present demand for conscription and a large army is the end
> of the list: on the contrary, the demilitarised zone, the navy, Memel,
> Danzig, and the former German colonies, may be expected to be
> within the ultimate German programme.
> But Sir John feels that there is no advantage in refusing to go to
> Berlin, small though the prospects are of any positive results.'[q]

The result, as Sir John Simon reported to the King on his return,[r]
was in fact negative. Although Herr Hitler had spoken of the Locarno
Treaties, including the demilitarisation of the Rhineland, as 'binding obligations'; although he had again and again expressed his
earnest desire for better relations with Great Britain and for 'her
good opinion'; yet he had, at no point, expressed a view 'which was
promising for future agreement'.

The introduction by Herr Hitler of compulsory military service,
coupled with the failure of the Berlin conversations, caused disquiet
in Great Britain. Mr Baldwin, in the House of Commons, agreed that
'a measure of re-equipment' must now be undertaken. Lord Cranborne, at that date Mr Eden's Parliamentary Private Secretary,
shocked the House by stating that, if we assumed the leadership and
took a clear and firm line, war might possibly be averted; but that if
we continued to hesitate and 'shilly-shally', then nothing remained
but 'disaster complete and irrecoverable'. Mr Winston Churchill in
solemn words warned an uneasy Parliament that we were entering 'a
corridor of deepening and darkening danger along which we should
be forced to move, perhaps for months, perhaps for years'.

In May of 1935 Lady Snowden sent to Lord Wigram, for communication to the King, a letter addressed by Herr Hitler to Lord
Rothermere, in which the Führer expressed the view that, if 'the two
Germanic nations' could co-operate together on land and sea, the
peace of the world would be secure. The King was unimpressed by
this suggestion and instructed Lord Wigram to reply to Lady
Snowden in chilly terms:

> 'The French are not mentioned in the letter from start to finish and it
> seems to me, reading between the lines, that Hitler's object is to form

523

a block against the French and other countries in Europe, which is entirely contrary to our present Foreign Policy. . . . It came as a great surprise to me that Lord Rothermere was carrying on such a correspondence, and the King (who, as you know, is always most open with his Ministers and loyal to them) certainly thinks that the Prime Minister and Foreign Secretary should read Hitler's letter.'[8]

In making this proposal Herr Hitler was sincere. There was nothing that he desired more consistently than that Germany should be given a free hand to deal with the land-mass of Europe, while England was given a free hand to pursue her imperial and oceanic ambitions elsewhere. When people assured him that England no longer possessed these ambitions and was interested only in social welfare at home, he derided such assertions as typical of British cant.

It is easy, so long after the event, to accuse British Ministers of blindness and vacillation. Theirs was a tremendous responsibility: they represented a pacific people and were themselves bound to be pacific; it would have been difficult indeed for any British Cabinet to proclaim, in that spring of 1935, that the only method of dealing with Germany was the method of force.

In any less optimistic, phlegmatic or self-confident country anxiety regarding the intentions of Nazi Germany might have cast a gloom over the celebrations of the twenty-fifth anniversary of King George's accession. In Britain, no gloom was cast.

(4)

On Monday, May 6, 1935, King George and Queen Mary went to St Paul's Cathedral to attend a Thanksgiving Service on the occasion of their Silver Jubilee:

'A never to be forgotten day', the King wrote in his diary, 'when we celebrated our Silver Jubilee. It was a glorious summer's day: 75° in the shade. The greatest number of people in the streets that I have ever seen in my life. The enthusiasm was indeed most touching.'

Every night of that exacting week the King and Queen appeared upon the flood-lit balcony of Buckingham Palace and were cheered with rapture by crowds who had waited there all day. On Thursday, May 9, in Westminster Hall, they received addresses from both Houses of Parliament. 'The Members', the King wrote in diary, 'sang the National Anthem and then cheered; which moved me much.' On the following days, wearing Field Marshal's uniform and drawn by four greys with postilions, the King, accompanied by Queen Mary, drove through the poorer quarters of London. Through

Battersea, Kennington and Lambeth they drove; through Lime-house, Whitechapel and the dock area; through the slums and tene-ments to the North and the South-west. In each street they were greeted by hordes of children shouting lustily and waving flags; the elder people grinned delightedly and clapped their hands. From house to house there hung little flags and streamers, and banners bearing messages, and swags of green. The King was fascinated by these decorations: 'all put up', he wrote in his diary, 'by the poor.' His satisfaction was intense:

> 'His pleasure', wrote Sister Catherine Black, 'at the wonderful evidence of the people's love and regard during the Jubilee was touching. I can remember him coming back from a drive through the East End, very tired but radiantly happy. "I'd no idea they felt like that about me", he said with his usual frankness. "I am beginning to think they must really like me for myself." '*t*

Students of mass behaviour were fascinated and perplexed by these popular rejoicings. How would the historian account for the spontaneous hilarity of the celebrations and the note of direct personal affection by which they were inspired? How came it, they asked, that the King, who possessed no demagogic graces, had been able to convey to all those millions so exact an impression of his character? How came it that the populace really did regard him as the friend whom they had known for all their adult lives? Of the authenticity of this emotion there could—as they saw for themselves on those hot May nights—be no doubt whatsoever. How was this pheno-menon explained?

Ever since December 25, 1932, when the King, seated at a table in Lord Knollys's ugly little room underneath the staircase at Sandring-ham, had broadcast his first Christmas message to the peoples of the Commonwealth and Empire, his annual talks had exercised a wide and intimate influence. On the night of May 6, after an exhausting day of ceremony, the King broadcast a message of thanks:

> 'At the close of this memorable day, I must speak to my people every-where. How can I express what is in my heart? . . . I can only say to you, my very very dear people, that the Queen and I thank you from the depths of our hearts for all the loyalty—and may I say so?—the love, with which this day and always you have surrounded us. I dedi-cate myself anew to your service for all the years that may still be given me. . . .'

Surely there was magic in all this? The King, an unreal incred-ible personage, a resplendent hierophant bowing rhythmically in a golden coach, with diamond orb and sceptre in his hands, suddenly became a human voice—intimate and paternal—speaking to them in their own living-rooms, speaking to them from a box on the table between the sewing machine and the mug. 'I am speaking', the voice continued, 'to the children above all. Remember children, the King is speaking to *you*.' His was a wonderful voice—strong, emphatic, vibrant, with undertones of sentiment, devoid of all condescension, artifice or pose. The effect was wide and deep.

Yet there were other, older, deeper causes that explain the phenomenon of May 1935. Broadcasting had merely intensified a feeling that was already there: during his illness of 1928, there had been a similar sudden surge of solicitude and affection; yet in 1928 the millions had never heard his voice.

The nation as a whole, joining with the nations of the Commonwealth, were, during that week of thanksgiving, paying homage to the Monarchy as an institution of which, for diverse reasons, they were fond. There was pride in the first place, pride in the fact that, whereas the other thrones had fallen, our own monarchy, unimpaired in dignity, had survived for more than a thousand years. Reverence in the thought that in the Crown we possessed a symbol of patriotism, a focus of unison, an emblem of continuity in a rapidly dissolving world. Satisfaction in feeling that the Sovereign stood above all class animosities, all political ambitions, all sectional interests. Comfort in the realisation that here was a strong benevolent patriarch personifying the highest standards of the race. Gratitude to a man who by his probity had earned the esteem of the whole world.

The proletariat welcomed the Jubilee as a public festival, deriving pleasure from this accorded carnival. It was right that the King and Queen should visit them in their own streets and admire the decorations that they had stitched and sewn and gathered in his honour. He was just as much King in Whitechapel as King in Whitehall; he was just as much their King as he was King of all the others. So they bought flags for the children; and stood there in their millions smiling affectionately as the King and Queen drove by.

Yet behind it all, behind all this thanksgiving and rejoicing, there lay another sentiment. In those twenty-five years his subjects had come to recognise that King George represented and enhanced those domestic and public virtues that they regarded as specifically British virtues. In him they saw, reflected and magnified, what they cherished as their own individual ideals—faith, duty, honesty, courage, common sense, tolerance, decency and truth.

The people of Britain turned from these celebrations to the contemplation of the quick decay in Europe of order, humanity and hope.

(5)

Since the end of the First World War, successive British Governments had founded their foreign policy upon the Covenant of the League of Nations and the theory of Collective Security: in so doing they were reflecting the beliefs and wishes of 95% of the electorate. The theory was that the old conception of a Balance of Power, by which violence was to be restrained by strength, was dangerous and outmoded; under the new dispensation international order was to be maintained, not by compulsion, but by consent. If, as at first seemed inconceivable, any single Government were to defy the assembled conscience of mankind and commit an act of aggression, then they would find arrayed against them all the other Members of the League and would, in the last resort, be coerced by the imposition of collective, and therefore irresistible, sanctions. This pooling of power would, moreover, enable the separate governments to relax their own defence programmes and to devote what they economised in armaments to schemes of social betterment. This magnificent theory did, however, contain a grub of fallacy; it assumed a degree of unanimity and unselfishness among the nations of the world which, if it had really existed, would have rendered the whole apparatus of Geneva unnecessary.

The British Government could certainly claim that they had set an example of conciliation and had always proved consistent advocates of League diplomacy. The Assembly, it is true, had failed at the time of the Corfu incident and had failed in regard to Manchukuo. Yet it was not until Signor Mussolini decided to conquer Abyssinia that the Members of the League were presented with an issue of such magnitude that the whole future of the Covenant, and the theories that it represented, became dependent upon failure or success.

On June 7, 1935, Mr Ramsay MacDonald resigned for reasons of failing health and was succeeded as Prime Minister by Mr Stanley Baldwin. In the resultant Cabinet reshuffle, Sir Samuel Hoare became Foreign Secretary in place of Sir John Simon. Ever since the previous autumn it had been realised that Italy had designs on Abyssinia, and that the latter, weak in the face of such an aggressor, would appeal to the League. Signor Mussolini, ever since his early experience at Corfu, did not regard the League as a serious champion of the existing order, or even of its own Covenant; he had assured himself of the tacit approval of Monsieur Laval; the fact that at the Stresa Conference in April 1935 neither Mr Ramsay MacDonald nor Sir John Simon had even mentioned the word 'Abyssinia', suggested to him that Great Britain also would turn a blind eye to his adventure. He was not incorrect in this calculation. He knew that Great Britain, with her lamentable air defences, was much alarmed by the increasing might of Nazi Germany; he knew that she would refrain, at almost any cost, from throwing him into the arms of Herr Hitler; and he calculated that, apart from a few speeches at Geneva, he could annex Abyssinia without serious difficulty. This was no fantastic diagnosis:

> 'Italy', Sir John Simon had written to the King on February 21, 1935, 'is at present occupied with the Abyssinian question, as to which Sir John greatly fears that a serious outcome is probable. But this must be handled in a way which will not affect adversely Anglo-Italian relations.'[u]

There was much to be said for a League of Nations policy, even as there was much to be said for a rapid return to the Balance of Power. But the two policies were mutually exclusive; to seek to combine them was to create disaster.

On September 11, 1935, Sir Samuel Hoare at Geneva delivered a speech that stirred the hearts of all true believers:

> 'Great Britain', he said, 'stands for the collective maintenance of the Covenant in its entirety; and particularly for steady, collective resistance to all acts of unprovoked aggression.'

In October Signor Mussolini, having rejected a League compromise, declared war and invaded Abyssinia. The League of Nations pronounced him an aggressor within the meaning of the Covenant, and proceeded to impose sanctions. These sanctions were sufficiently irritating to drive Signor Mussolini and the Italian people into a state of frenzy: they were not sufficiently compulsive to impede him seriously in the conduct of his campaign.

On November 14, 1935, the National Government, under Mr Stanley Baldwin, were returned to power at a General Election; they only lost 79 seats after four arduous years in office; they faced the new Parliament on December 3 with a majority of 245.[1] Their appeal

---

[1] The figures were Government 425: Opposition 180. The Government supporters were composed of 32 National Liberals, 8 National Labour, and 385 Conservatives. The Opposition supporters were composed of Labour 154, Liberals 17, Independent Liberals 4, I.L.P. 4, Communist 1. The Liberal Nationals had lost 3 seats, National Labour 7 seats, the opposition Liberals 9 seats, the Independent Liberals 2 seats. The Labour Party increased its representation from 95 seats to 154.

to the electorate had been largely based upon a League of Nations programme; all Government candidates had pledged themselves to resist to the death any violation of its principles. It was thus with shocked indignation that the country learnt on December 10 that Sir Samuel Hoare, in passing through Paris on his way to a holiday in Switzerland, had come to an arrangement with M. Laval, whereby, behind the back of the League, a peace settlement was to be proposed, on the basis of the surrender to Italy of enormous tracts of Abyssinian territory. The indignation was such that Sir Samuel Hoare was obliged to interrupt his holiday and resign his seal as Foreign Secretary. He was succeeded by Mr Anthony Eden.

The League of Nations had been dealt a blow from which it never recovered: the theory of Collective Security had been proved fallacious; it was now realised that France and Great Britain would have to face the resurgent strength of Germany, relying upon their own resources alone.

The last weeks of King George's life were saddened by these perplexities. He consulted Sir Robert Vansittart,[1] Permanent Under-Secretary at the Foreign Office, as to whether there was in fact any possibility of our being able to reach a firm understanding with Nazi Germany. Sir Robert's views were not encouraging:

'I do not think', he wrote to Lord Wigram on November 7, 1935, 'it would be profitable to undertake any serious attempt for an agreement with Germany until our own national re-equipment is well under way. . . . Secondly it would be essential that any such exploration should be undertaken in concert with the French. . . . Any arrangement with Germany will have to be paid for and handsomely paid for . . . I am convinced that modern Germany is highly expansive and will become highly explosive if it is sought to cramp her anywhere. . . . Any attempt at giving Germany a free hand to annex other people's property in central or Eastern Europe is both absolutely immoral and completely contrary to all the principles of the League which form the backbone of the policy of this country. Any British Government that attempted to do a deal would almost certainly be brought down in ignominy—and deservedly. . . . Any suggestion that a British Government contemplates leaving, let alone inviting, Germany to satisfy her land-hunger at Russia's expense, would quite infallibly split this country from top to bottom.'[v]

---

[1] Sir Robert Vansittart, after a varied diplomatic and literary career, had been appointed Permanent Under-Secretary at the Foreign Office in 1930. During the appeasement period he was regarded as too anti-Nazi to

Such were the clouds that shadowed the King's last days.

(6)

For some time the King's health had been causing anxiety. In February 1935 there had been a sharp renewal of his bronchial trouble, and he had been obliged to spend most of March convalescing at Compton Place, Eastbourne. He had survived the exacting ceremonies of the Silver Jubilee with astonishing resilience, and when he went down to review the fleet at Spithead in July, it seemed that he had wholly recovered. On his return from Balmoral that autumn, those closest to him noticed a serious deterioration. On December 3 the death of his favourite sister, Princess Victoria, was a shattering blow:

'How I shall miss her', he wrote in his diary, '& our daily talks on the telephone. No one ever had a sister like her.'

On December 9 he was still in London. 'Received Anthony Eden', he notes, '& had a long talk with him about Italy & Abyssinia & possible war.'

On December 21 he went down to Sandringham with Queen Mary. The usual Christmas festivities were observed and the King delivered his last broadcast to the Empire. On January 15 he was feeling unwell, but went for a short ride upon his white pony in the park. On Friday, January 17, he made the last, and almost illegible, entry in his diary. 'A little snow', he wrote, '& wind. Dawson arrived this evening. I saw him & feel rotten.'

On Monday, January 20, a few chosen Members of the Privy Council gathered in the King's bedroom.[1] The Lord President read aloud the proclamation constituting a Council of State. The King answered in a clear voice, 'Approved'. He experienced great difficulty in signing the document. Lord Dawson knelt beside him and tried to guide his hand. The King did not feel it right that a subject should thus direct the sign manual. He made several attempts. He looked up at the Privy Councillors standing around him. 'Gentlemen', he said,

be convenient, and was relegated to the decorative post of Chief Diplomatic Adviser to the Foreign Secretary. He was raised to the peerage as Baron Vansittart of Denham in 1941.

[1] The Privy Councillors present at King George's last Council were The Archbishop of Canterbury, Lord Hailsham the Lord Chancellor, Sir John Simon the Home Secretary, Mr Ramsay MacDonald, the Lord President, Lord Dawson and Lord Wigram. Sir Maurice Hankey attended as Clerk to the Council.

with the faintest flash of his old smile, 'I am sorry for keeping you waiting like this—I am unable to concentrate.' In the end he succeeded in marking his initials on the paper. The Privy Councillors bowed and withdrew.

That afternoon his condition worsened. At 9.25 that night Lord Dawson drafted the bulletin that informed the world that no hope remained. 'The King's life', he wrote, 'is moving peacefully to its close.'

The final entry in the diary that he had kept so carefully since May 3, 1880, is written in the handwriting of Queen Mary:

'My dearest husband, King George V, was much distressed at the bad writing above & begged me to write his diary for him next day. He passed away on January 20th at 5 minutes before midnight.'

APPENDIX II

THE FAMILY OF QUEEN ALEXANDRA

(This Table does not carry the genealogy beyond January 1936)

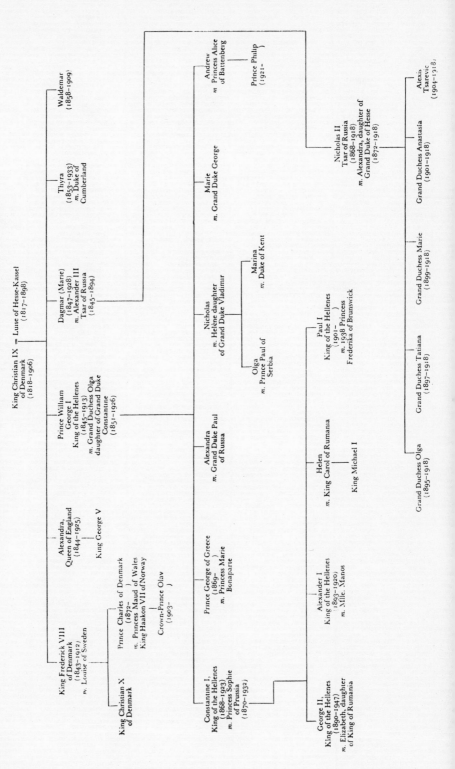

APPENDIX III

REFERENCE NOTES

THE initials 'R.A.' stand for 'Royal Archives' and designate the official and private papers correspondence and diaries preserved in the Round Tower at Windsor Castle. The initial immediately following these (K, P, Q, etc.) indicate the series under which the documents have been classified. The figures that follow indicate the number of the file itself and, when necessary, the actual number of the document in that file.

Chapter I

[a] R.A. Z.452, Dalton to Stahl, April 11, 1877—[b] Recorded by Sir Owen Morshead in January 1932, quoted by John Gore, *King George V: A Personal Memoir*, John Murray, 1941, pp. 32-33.

Chapter II

[a] R.A. Z.453, (10), Lord Beaconsfield to Queen Victoria, May 19, 1879—[b] Ponsonby, Lord, *Henry Ponsonby*, p. 105—[c] R.A. Z.453, (65), Lord Napier to General Dillon—[d] R.A. Z.453, (118)—[e] R.A. Z.453, (121)—[f] Gore, John (quoted), *King George V: A Personal Memoir*, p. 47.

Chapter III

[a] In this connection see letters from the Prince of Wales to Prince George dated respectively August 13 and 26, 1887—[b] Lee, Sir Sidney, *King Edward VII: A Biography*, Vol. I, p. 661—[c] Letter from Queen Victoria to the Empress Frederick, July 2, 1891—[d] Lee, Sir Sidney, *King Edward VII: A Biography*, Vol. I, p. 605.

Chapter IV

[a] Gore, John, *King George V*, p. 99, note—[b] Baring, Maurice, *The Puppet Show of Memory*, pp. 124-126, 163-164—[c] Letter of August 24, 1892—[d] Gore, John, *King George V*, pp. 128-129—[e] R.A. Z.477, (261)—[f] R.A. W.77.

Chapter V

[a] Bagehot, Walter, *The English Constitution*, the World's Classics edition, p. 53—[b] ibid., p. 35—[c] ibid., p. 34—[d] ibid., p. 63—[e] ibid., p. 48—[f] R.A. W.6, (2)—[g] R.A. I. a A.7—[h] R.A. W.6, (3).

Chapter VI

[a] R.A. Confidential Register, G.V., O.2570—[b] Bülow, Prince, *Deutsche Politik*, p. 25—[c] *Grosse Politik der Europaischen Kabinette*, Vol. XVII, No. 4984—[d] R.A. W.42, (58)—[e] Bülow, Prince von, *Memoirs*, 4 vols., Vol. I, pp. 545-550—[f] Interview in *The Times*, Dec. 22, 1920—[g] R.A. X.28, 37b—[h] R.A. W.4, (24)—[i] R.A. W.4, (29)—[j] Quoted by J. Gore, *King George V*, p. 207. [k] Abbott, G. F., *Through India with the Prince*, p. 196—[l] R.A., 6a A.3—[m] R.A. Additional MS. T.113.

Chapter VII

[a] Lee, Sir Sidney, *King Edward VII: A Biography*, p. 447—[b] Mr Balfour to Lord Knollys, Jan. 17, 1906 (quoted by Sir Sidney Lee, *King Edward VII*), p. 449—[c] Dugdale, E. T. S., *Maurice de Bunsen*, pp. 220-221—[d] R.A. W.57, (89)—[e] R.A. A.40, b.1—[f] R.A. W.40, (108)—[g] R.A., Letters on the death of King Edward—[h] R.A. W.45, (147)—[i] R.A. W.8, (38)—[j] R.A. W.77, (123).

Chapter VIII

[a] Anson, Sir William, *The Law and Custom of the Constitution*, Vol. 1, p. 1—[b] Bagehot, Walter, *The English Constitution*, World's Classics edition, Introduction, pp. xxxv-xxxvi—[c] Anson, Sir William, *The Law and Customs of the Constitution*, Vol. II, Part I, p. 142—[d] ibid., Vol. II, Part I, p. 56—[e] Dicey, A. V., *Introduction to the Study of the Law of the Constitution*, p. 360—[f] R.A. K.2552, (10)—[g] Anson, Sir William, *The Law and Custom of the Constitution*, Vol. II, Part I, p. 61—[h] Laski, Harold J., *Parliamentary Government in England*, p. 388—[i] ibid., p. 396.

Appendix III

Chapter IX

[a] Oxford and Asquith, The Earl of, *Fifty Years in Parliament*, pp. 86-88—[b] Gwynn, Denis, *The Life of John Redmond*, pp. 166-167—[c] Spender, J. A., and Cyril Asquith, *Life of H. H. Asquith, Lord Oxford and Asquith*, Vol. 1, p. 282—[d] Petrie, Sir Charles, *Life and Letters of Austen Chamberlain*, Vol. I, p. 381—[e] Dugdale, Mrs Edgar, *Arthur James Balfour*, Vol. II, p. 74 ff—[f] Lloyd George, The Right Hon. David, *War Memoirs*, Vol. I, pp. 34-40 —[g] R. A. K.2552, (I), 44, contains a memorandum by Balfour on the causes of the failure of the Conference with marginal notes by Asquith—[h] R.A. K.2552, (1), 41—[i] R.A. K.2552, (1), 43, and Spender and Asquith, Vol. 1, p. 296—[j] R.A. K.2552, (1), 49—[k] R.A. K.2552, (1), 54—[l] R.A. K.2552, (1), 60—[m] R.A. K.2552, (1), 63—[n] Murray, Col. the Hon. Arthur, *Master and Brother*—[o] R.A. K.2552, (2)—[p] Spender and Asquith, *Life of H. H. Asquith, Lord Oxford and Asquith*, Vol. I, p. 296—[q] R.A. K.2552, (2), 94—[r] Note by Lord Stamfordham contained in Red volume—[s] Esher, Viscount, *Journals and Letters*, Vol. III, p. 65.

Chapter X

[a] Esher Viscount, *Journals and Letters*, Vol. III, p. 17—[b] Esher, Viscount, ibid., Vol. III, p. 17—[c] Esher, Viscount, ibid., Vol. III, p. 49—[d] Lockhart, J. G., *Cosmo Gordon Lang*, p. 143—[e] Windsor, H.R.H., The Duke of Article in Life Magazine—[f] Newton, Lord, *Lord Lansdowne*, pp. 407-408—Esher, Viscount, *Journals and Letters*, Vol. III, p. 40; and R.A. K.2552, (1), 76—[g] R.A. K.2552, (2), 25—[h] Newton, Lord, *Lord Lansdowne*, pp. 404 and 410—[i] Spender and Asquith, *Life of H. H. Asquith*, Vol. 1, p. 310—[j] R. A. K.2552, (2), 1—[k] Petrie, Sir Charles, *Life and Letters of Austen Chamberlain*, Vol. I, pp. 280-282—[l] R.A. K.2522, (2), 68—[m] Morley, Viscount, *Recollections*, Vol. II, pp. 350 ff.—[n] Bigge papers.

Chapter XI

[a] Spender, J. A., 'British Foreign Policy in the Reign of King George' (*International Affairs*, Vol. XIV, 4)—[b] Macready, General Sir Nevil, *Annals of an Active Life*, Vol. I, p 155—[c] R.A. B.246—[d] R.A. B.246, (20)—[e] Bell, G. K. A. (Bishop of Chichester), *Randall Davidson*, Vol. 1, Chap. XXXVI—[f] R.A. O.1608 A, (2)—[g] R.A. N.293—[h] R.A. P. 522, (5) [i] Fortescue, Hon. John, *Narrative of the Visit to India of Their Majesties King George V and Queen Mary*, p. 121—[j] Fortescue, Hon. John, ibid., p. 155—[k] R.A. N.293— [l] Fortescue, *Narrative of the Visit to India of Their Majesties King George V and Queen Mary*, p. 244.

Chapter XII

[a] Oesterreich-Ungarn's *Aussenpolitik*, Vol. II, p. 817—[b] William II, *My Memoirs*, p. 49 —[c] ibid., p. 225—[d] Tirpitz, Admiral von, *My Memoirs*, Vol. I, p. 197—[e] Fisher, Lord, *Memories*, pp. 4, 18, 19; Bacon. Admiral Sir R. H., *The Life of Lord Fisher of Kilverstone* Vol. II, pp. 75 ff.—[f] Churchill, the Rt. Hon. Winston, *The World Crisis*, Vol. I, p. 114— [g] *Grosse Politik der Europaischen Kabinette*, Vol. XXIV, p. 104—[h] Kühlmann, Richard von, *Erinnerungen*, pp. 335 and 346—[i] *Grosse Politik*, Vol. XXIX, p. 230—[j] William II, *My Memoirs*, p. 125—[k] *Grosse Politik*, Vol. XXVII, p. 793; XXIX, p. 120. *O.U.A.*, Vol. III, p. 778—[l] Caillaux, Joseph, *Mes Memoires*, Vol. II, p. 55, and *Agadir*, p. 39—[m] *Grosse Politik*, Vol. XXIX, pp. 101-108—[n] William II, *My Memoirs*, pp. 140-142—[o] *Grosse Politik*, Vol. XXIX, No. 10562—[p] Oesterreich-Ungarn's *Aussenpolitik*, pp. 364-369— [q] *Grosse Politik*, Vol. XXIX, No. 10592—[r] Grey, Viscount Grey of Fallodon, *Twenty-Five Years*, Vol. II, p. 63—[s] Churchill, the Rt. Hon. Winston, *The World Crisis*, Vol. I, p. 67— [t] Tirpitz, Admiral von, *My Memoirs*, Vol. I, p. 211—[u] Rosen, Friedrich von, *Aus einem diplomatischen Wanderleben*, p. 350—[v] R.A. O.1608 A.I.

Chapter XIII

[a] R.A. M.230, 9 and 10—[b] R.A. M.230, I.B—[c] William II, *My Memoirs*, p. 143— [d] Bethmann-Hollweg, Th. von, *Betrachtungen zum Weltkriege*, Vol. I, p. 50—[e] Oesterreich-Ungarn's *Aussenpolitik*, Vol. IV, p. 26—[f] R.A. M.450, 8—[g] Churchill, The Rt. Hon. Winston S., *The World Crisis*, Vol. I, p. 96—[h] Tirpitz, Admiral von, *My Memoirs*, Vol. I, pp. 234-235—[i] Bigge papers—[j] Esher, Viscount, *Journals and Letters*, Vol. III, p. 117— [k] Chamberlain, Sir Austen, *Politics from Inside*, pp. 486-487—[l] R.A. K.2553, (I), 2— [m] Ullswater, Viscount, *A Speaker's Commentaries*, Vol. II, pp. 131-132—[n] R.A. K.404, 12 —[o] R.A. Private Letter File—[p] Grey, Viscount Grey of Fallodon, *Twenty-Five Years*, Vol. II, pp. 130-139—[q] R.A. M.456, 9—[r] Oesterreich-Ungarn's *Aussenpolitik*, Vol. IV, 1069— [s] R.A. M.520, A, (I)—[t] Oesterreich-Ungarn's *Aussenpolitik*, Vol. V, p. 214—[u] R.A. M.520 A, (2)—[v] *Grosse Politik*, Vol. XXXIX, p. 119 note—[w] R.A. M.520, A, (2a)

Chapter XIV

a R.A. Lord Stamfordham's Manuscript Diary—*b* R.A. O.417—*c* R.A. O.459—
d R.A. M.421, (3)—*e* Grey, Viscount Grey of Fallodon, *Twenty-Five Years*, Vol. II, p. 98—
f ibid., Vol. II, p. 109—*g* Oesterreich-Ungarn's *Aussenpolitik*, Vol. VI, p. 267—*h* *Grosse Politik*, Vol. XXXIV, p. 760—*i* R.A. M.421, (25)—*j* Benckendorff, Count, *Graf Benckendorff's Diplomatischer Schriftwechsel*, Vol. II, p. 17—*k* R.A. M.481, 2—*l* *Grosse Politik*, XXXVIII, p. 216; and *Graf Benckendorff's Schriftwechsel*, Vol. III, pp. 204-205—*m* R.A. M.590, (18)—*n* Poincaré, Raymond, *Au Service de la France*, Vol. III, p. 242—*o* Hendrick, Burton K., *The Life and Letters of Walter H. Page*, p. 275—*p* ibid., p. 173—*q* Macready, General Sir Nevil, *Annals of an Active Life*, Vol. I, p. 173—*r* R.A. K.2553, (I), 45—*s* R.A. K.2553, (I), 52—*t* R.A. K.168, A, (2)—*u* R.A., K.2553, (I), 57—*v* R.A. K.2553, (I), 70 —*w* R.A. K.2553, (I), 68—*x* R.A. K.2553, (II), 10—*y* R.A. K.2553, (II), 22—*z* R.A. K.2553, (II), 26—*za* R.A. K.2553, (II), 45.

Chapter XV

a R.A. K.2553, (II), 30—*b* R.A. K.2553, (II), 43—*c* R.A. K.2553, (II), 46 and 53—
d R.A. K.2553, (II), 60—*e* Oesterreich-Ungarn's *Aussenpolitik*, Vol. VII, No. 8818—
f R.A. K.2553, (II), 79—*g* Chamberlain, Sir Austen, *Politics from Inside*, p. 611—*h* R.A. K.2553, (III), 47—*i* R.A. K.2553, (III), 83—*j* R.A. K.2553, (III), 87—*k* R.A. K.2553, (III), 93—*l* R.A. K.2553, (III), 100—*m* R.A. K.2553, (IV), 33—*n* R.A. F.674, (83)—*o* R.A. K.2553, (V), 58—*p* R.A. K.2553, (V), 48—*q* R.A. K.2553, (VI), 13—*r* R.A. K.2553, (VI), 16—*s* R.A. K.2553, (VI), 14—*t* R.A. K.2553, (VI), 49; and Denis Gwynn, *Life of John Redmond*, p. 342—*u* Ullswater, Viscount, *A Speaker's Commentaries*, Vol. II, p. 193—*v* Haldane, Viscount Haldane of Cloan, *An Autobiography*, p. 283—*w* R.A. M.624 (3)—*x* Tirpitz, Admiral von, *My Memoirs*, Vol. I, p. 275—*y* R.A. Q.1167, (15)—*z* R.A. Q.1549, (12)—*za* R.A. Q.2, (7)—*zb* R.A. Q.2, 1549, (19)—*zc* Poincaré, Raymond, *Au Service de la France*, Vol. IV, pp. 437 ff..

Chapter XVI

a R.A. Q.685, (2), 1—*b* R.A. Q.685, (2), 43—*c* R.A. Q.711, 1—*d* Esher, Viscount, *Journals and Letters*, Vol. III, p. 207—*e* R.A. Q.832, 59—*f* R.A. Q.705, (2), 26—*g* Esher, Viscount, *Journals and Letters*, Vol. III, p. 207—*h* R.A. Q.998, (2), 7—*i* R.A. P.S. papers, 547—*j* R.A. P.S. papers, 5125—*k* Spender and Asquith, *Life of Lord Oxford and Asquith*, Vol. II, p. 109—*l* R.A. P.522, 58—*m* R.A. Q.832, 406—*n* Cooper, Sir Duff, *Haig*, Vol. I, p. 147—*o* R.A. Q.725, A, (2), 5—*p* R.A., Q.832, 72—*q* Crutwell, *History of the Great War*, p. 31—*r* R.A. Q.832, 74—*s* Grey of Fallodon, Viscount, *Twenty-Five Years*, Vol. III, p. 225 —*t* Haldane, Viscount, *Autobiography*, p. 279—*u* Lloyd George, David, *War Memoirs*, Vol. I, p. 499—*v* Arthur, Sir George, *Life of Lord Kitchener*, Vol. III, p. 323—*w* Esher, Viscount, *Journals and Letters*, Vol. III, pp. 207 and 235—*x* R.A. letter of June 20, 1916—*y* R.A. Q.762, 14—*z* R.A. Q.762, 15—*za* French, Viscount *1914*, p. 356—*zb* Churchill, Winston, *The World Crisis*, Vol. II, p. 169—*zc* R.A. K.770, 3—*zd* R.A. K.770, 11—*ze* Oxford and Asquith, Earl of, *Memories and Reflections*, Vol. II, p. 107

Chapter XVII

a Churchill, Winston, *The World Crisis*, Vol. II, p. 17—*b* R.A. Q.832, 276—*c* Bigge papers—*d* Watson, Francis, *Dawson of Penn*, pp. 138-140—*e* R.A. Q.838, 47—*f* Lloyd George, David, *War Memoirs*, Vol. I, pp. 317 ff.—*g* Oxford and Asquith, Earl of, *Memories and Reflections*, Vol. II, p. 109—*h* R.A. K.869, 3—*i* Oxford and Asquith, Earl of, *Memories and Reflections*, Vol. II, p. 54—*j* R.A. Q.760, 4—*k* R.A. Q.760, 31—*l* R.A. K.951, 1—*m* R.A. K.951, 2—*n* R.A. K.951, 4—*o* R.A. K.951, 10—*p* R.A. K.951, 12—*q* R.A. Q.832, 112—*r* R.A. Q.832, 118—*s* Cooper, Sir Duff, *Haig*, Vol. II, p. 154—*t* Cooper, Sir Duff, *Haig*, Vol. I, p. 290—*u* R.A. F.983, 1—*v* R.A. Q.832, 464—*w* R.A. Q.832, 367—*x* R.A. Q.832, 435—*y* R.A. Q.832, 366—*z* Churchill, Winston, *The World Crisis*, Vol. III, p. 214—*za* R.A. Q.832, 369—*zb* R.A. Q.832, 370—*zc* Grey of Fallodon, Viscount, *Twenty-Five Years*, Vol. III, p. 214—*zd* The King's Diary for October 18, 1916—*ze* R.A. Q.838, 106—*zf* R.A. Q.1550, (I), 15—*zg* R.A., Q.1550, 13.

Chapter XVIII

a Spender and Asquith, *Life of Lord Oxford and Asquith*, Vol. II, p. 270—*b* R.A. K.1048, A. I—*c* Maurice, Sir Frederick, *Haldane*, Vol. II, p. 44—*d* R.A. K.1263, 2—*e* R.A. K.1048, A. I—*f* R.A. K.1048, A. I—*g* Spender and Asquith, *Life of Lord Oxford and Asquith*, Vol. II, p. 275—*h* ibid., p. 278—*i* R.A. Q.1085, 3, A—*j* R.A. Q.1085, 3, C—*k* Seymour, Charles, *The Intimate Papers of Colonel House*, Vol. II, p. 125—*l* ibid., p. 194—

Appendix III

[m] Statement made to the author by Colonel House in 1930—[n] Seymour, Charles, *Intimate Papers of Colonel House*, Vol. II, p. 409; and Hendrick, *Life and Letters of W. H. Page*, Vol. II, p. 207—[o] R.A. M.1067, 29—[p] Buchanan, Sir George, *My Mission to Russia*, Vol. II, p. 103 —[q] R.A. M.1067, 37—[r] R.A. M.1067, 29—[s] R.A. M.1067, 39—[t] R.A. M.1067, 44— [u] R.A. M.1067, 61—[v] R.A. Q.832, 130—[w] R.A. Q.832, 134.

Chapter XIX

[a] Told to the author by Lord Carnock—[b] Lloyd George, David, *War Memoirs*, Vol. IV, p. 1947—[c] R.A. O.1106, 65—[d] Lloyd George, David, *War Memoirs*, Vol. IV, 1961–1963 —[e] R.A. O.1106, 40—[f] Account written by Lady Maud Warrender (unpublished)— [g] R.A. K.1080, 5—[h] R.A. O.1153, XXII, 425—[i] R.A. O.1153, XXII, 425—[j] R.A. O.1231, 3—[k] R.A. Q.1550, XVIII, 200—[l] R.A. Q.1085, 20—[m] R.A. Q.1085, 22— [n] R.A. Q.1085, 41—[o] Hendrick, B. J., *Life and Letters of Walter H. Page*, Vol. II, p. 141— [p] Letter of November 18, 1917—[q] R.A. Q.989, (2), 15—[r] R.A. Q.989, (2), 18—[s] R.A. Q.989, (2), 15—[t] R.A. O.1537, 10—[u] Pershing, General, *My Experiences in the World War*, p. 55—[v] R.A. K.1340—[w] *Hansard*, XCV, 2210–2234—[x] R.A. Separate letter box— [y] R.A. K.1135, 5—[z] R.A. K.1135, 7—[za] Dugdale, Mrs Edgar, *Arthur James Balfour*, II, 243—[zb] R.A. F.1259, 4—[zc] Churchill, Winston, *The World Crisis*, Vol. IV, pp. 386 ff.— [zd] Painlevé, Paul, *Comment j'ai nomme Foch et Pétain*, p. 245—[ze] Churchill, Winston, *The World Crisis*, Vol. IV, p. 387—[zf] R.A. F.1259, 32—[zg] Callwell, Major-General Sir C. E., *Field Marshal Sir H. Wilson*, Vol. II, p. 76—[zh] ibid., p. 103—[zi] Rosner, Karl, *Der König*, pp. 159–160.

Chapter XX

[a] R.A. K.1348, 11—[b] Keith, A. Berriedale, *The King and the Imperial Crown*, p. 168— [c] R.A. Q.1098, 2, 72—[d] R.A. Q.1098, 2, 74—[e] Spender and Asquith, *Life of Lord Oxford and Asquith*, Vol. II, p. 313—[f] R.A. P.474, 56—[g] R.A. O.1419, 8 and 9—[h] R.A. Q.1098, 79—[i] R.A. M.1380, 1—[j] R.A. M.1380, 2—[k] R.A. Q.1550, XVII, 181—[l] R.A. Q.1556, 1 —[m] R.A. Q.1555, 1—[n] R.A. K.1387, 15—[o] R.A. Q.1560, 25—[p] Bigge Papers—[q] R.A. K.1740, 1—[r] R.A. K.1740, 5—[s] R.A. O.1650, 1—[t] R.A. O.1470, 1—[u] R.A. O.1637, 2.

Chapter XXI

[a] R.A. K.1514, 1—[b] R.A. K.1514, 3—[c] R.A. K.1514, 9—[d] R.A. K.1514, 13—[e] R.A. K.1593, a—[f] R.A. K.1593, a, 9—[g] R.A. K.1514, 17—[h] R.A. K.1593, a, 19—[i] See, for instance, Pakenham, *Peace by Ordeal*, p. 77—[j] Millin, Sarah Gertrude, *Smuts*, Vol. II, pp. 319 ff.—[k] R.A. K.1702, 3—[l] R.A. K.1702, 5—[m] R.A. K.1702, 6—[n] R.A. K.1702, 8— [o] R.A. K.1702, 11—[p] R.A. K.1702, 27—[q] R.A. K.1702, 38—[r] R.A. K.1702, 41—[s] R.A. K.1702, 43—[t] R.A. K.1702, A 9—[u] R.A. K.1702, A 26—[v] R.A. K.1702, A 25—[w] R.A. K.1702, A 52.

Chapter XXII

[a] Bigge Papers—[b] Gore, John, *King George V: A Personal Memoir*, pp. 365 ff.—[c] Watson, Francis, *Dawson of Penn*, p. 285—[d] R.A. M.1811, 25—[e] R.A. M.1730, 4—[f] R.A. M.1811, 51—[g] R.A. M.1811, 91—[h] R.A. K.1814, 3—[i] R.A. K.1814, 4—[j] R.A. M.1618, 2— [k] R.A. M.1618, 8—[l] R.A. M.1811, 107—[m] R.A. P.1659, 15—[n] R.A. K.1834, 2—[o] R.A. M.1856, 15—[p] R.A. M.1856, 21—[q] R.A. M.1809, 1—[r] R.A. M.1908, 9—[s] R.A. K.1853, 1—[t] R.A. K.1853, 10—[u] R.A. K.1853, 12 and 13—[v] R.A. K.1853, 21—[w] R.A. K.1853, 35—[x] R.A. K.1894, 2.

Chapter XXIII

[a] R.A. K.1918, 14—[b] R.A. K.1918, 30—[c] R.A. K.1918, 34 and 54—[d] R.A. K.1918, 114—[e] R.A. K.1918, 154—[f] R.A. K.1918, 60—[g] R.A. K.1958, 32—[h] R.A. K.1918, 164 —[i] Clynes, Rt. Hon. J. R., *Memoirs*, pp. 343–344—[j] R.A. K.1919, 126—[k] R.A. K.1918, 207—[l] R.A. K.1918, 208—[m] R.A. K.1957, 3—[n] R.A. K.1858, 4—[o] R.A. K.1958, 14— [p] R.A. K.1958, 22—[q] R.A. K.1958, 34—[r] R.A. K.1958, 42—[s] R.A. K.1958, 40—[t] R.A. K.1958, 44.

Chapter XXIV

[a] Petrie, Sir Charles, *Life and Letters of Austen Chamberlain*, Vol. II, p. 227—[b] R.A. M.1974, 3—[c] R.A. P.586, 100—[d] R.A. M.1974, 6—[e] R.A. M.1974, 7—[f] R.A. M.1974, 53—[g] Petrie, Sir Charles, *Life and Letters of Austen Chamberlain*, Vol. II, p. 290—[h] R.A. M.2042, 6—[i] R.A. M.2061, 3—[j] R.A. M.2061, 8—[k] R.A. M.2061, 12—[l] R.A. M.2061, 15a—[m] R.A. K.2004, 1—[n] R.A. B.2015, 22—[o] Weir, L. MacNeill, *The Tragedy of Ramsay MacDonald*, p. 206—[p] R.A. B.2020, 1—[q] R.A. B.2052, 13—[r] R.A. B.2052, 23—[s] R.A. B.2052, 24—[t] R.A. M.2056, 4.

Appendix III

Chapter XXV

a R.A. O.2150, 5—*b* R.A. O.2150, 26—*c* Keith, A. Borriedale, *The King and the Imperial Crown*, Chap. XIV—*d* R.A. K.2097, 2—*e* R.A. K.2011, 2—*f* R.A. K.2011, 4—*g* R.A. K.2011, 3—*h* R.A. K.2011, 5— R.A. K.2003, 1—*j* R.A. O.1797, 1—*k* R.A. O.2193, 3—*l* Watson, Francis, *Dawson of Penn*, p. 209—*m* R.A. P.474, 97—*n* R.A. K.2223, 32—*o* R.A. K.2223, 38—*p* R.A. K.2223, 45—*q* R.A. K.2223, 87.

Chapter XXVI

a R.A. M.2217—*b* R.A. K.2231, 17—*c* R.A. G.2258, 18—*d* R.A. G.2258, 19—*h* R.A, K.2231, 8—*f* R.A. M.2130, 35—*g* R.A. M.2226, 4—*h* R.A. M.2226, 13—*i* R.A. M.2226. 26—*j* R.A. K.2301, 4—*k* R.A. M.2329, 2.

Chapter XXVII

a Samuel, Viscount, *Memoirs*, p. 204—*b* R.A. K.2330—*c* R.A. K.2330—*d* R.A. K.2330 —*e* Snowden, Viscount, *An Autobiography*, pp. 952–953—*f* R.A. K.2330—*g* Weir, MacNeill, *The Tragedy of Ramsay MacDonald*, p. 387—*h* R.A. K.2330—*i* Clynes, the Rt. Hon. J. R., *Memoirs*, p. 198.

Chapter XXVIII

a R.A. P.633, 78—*b* R.A. L.2293, 37—*c* R.A. L.2293, 148—*d* R.A. L.2293, 176—*e* R.A. L.2293, 274—*f* R.A. L.2293, 276—*g* R.A. L.2293, 338—*h* R.A. L.2293, 336—*i* R.A. L.2293, 340—*j* R.A. L.2293, 341—*k* R.A. L.2488, 39—*l* R.A. L.2314, 90—*m* R.A. K.2077, 2—*n* R.A. K.2077, 11—*o* R.A. L.2266, 90—*p* R.A. L.2403, 13—*q* R.A. L.2403, 16—*r* Keith, A. Berriedale, *Responsible Government in the Dominions*, p. xiii.

Chapter XXIX

a R.A. K.2330—*b* R.A. K.2331, 18—*c* R.A. K.2331, 20—*d* R.A. K.2331, 29—*e* R.A. K.2331, 48—*f* R.A. K.2331, III, 4—*g* R.A. K.2331, III, 5—*h* R.A. K.2331, 49—*i* R.A. K.2344, 2—*j* R.A. K.2340, 3—*k* R.A. L.2357, 1—*l* R.A. L.2357, 5—*m* R.A. M.2388, 2—*n* R.A. M.2388, 10—*o* R.A. M.2546—*p* R.A. P.522, 105—*q* R.A. N.2335, 15—*r* R.A. N.2335, 17—*s* R.A. N.2335, 21—*t* R.A. P.522, 240—*u* R.A. P.522, 294—*v* R.A. P.522, 291—*w* R.A. P.522, 296—*x* R.A. P.522, 298—*y* R.A. P.522, 308—*z* R.A. P.IV, 522, 307 —*za* R.A. P.IV, 522, 326 and 342—*zb* R.A. N.2485 and P.522, V. 398.

Chapter XXX

a R.A. K.2260, 8—*b* R.A. J.1041, 3—*c* R.A. J.1041, 4—*d* R.A. J.1041, 8—*e* R.A. J.1041, 21—*f* R.A. J.1785, A, 18—*g* R.A. J.1785, A, 19—*h* R.A. J.1785, A, 25—*i* R.A. J.2309, 59 and 61—*j* Private Information—*k* R.A. O.2079, 12—*l* R.A. K.2343, 12—*m* R.A. P.586, 170—*n* R.A. M.2545—*o* R.A. M.2445, 9—*p* R.A. P.586, II, 216—*q* R.A. M.2458, 1—*r* R.A. M.2458, 3—*s* R.A. M.2472, 2—*t* Black, Sister Catherine, *King's Nurse, Beggar's Nurse*, p. 170—*u* R.A. M.2456, 4—*v* R.A. M.2498.

INDEX

Abbas Hilmi, Khedive of Egypt: 374
Abdul Karim, 'Munshi' to Queen
  Victoria: 86
Abdullah, the Emir: 518
Aberdeen, Lord: 517
Aboukir, H.M.S.: 257
Abyssinia: 527–9
Acres, Mr B.: 58
Adamson, Mr W.: 436 n, 464
Addison, Rt Hon. C. (1869–1950):
  293 n, 464
Adly Pasha: 375 n
Aehrenthal, Count von (1854–
  1912): 102
Afghanistan, King of: 427
Africa, Union of South: first visit to,
  25–6; official visit in 1901, 66,
  70–1, 474 n, 486, 487
Agadir: *see under* Moorish Question
Aisne, Battle of the: 259
Aitken, Sir Max: *see under* Beaver-
  brook, Lord
Akers-Douglas, A. (1st Lord Chil-
  ston, 1851–1926): 132
Albany, Charles Duke of (Duke of
  Saxe Coburg-Gotha) (1884–):
  37 n
Albert Edward, Prince of Wales: *see*
  Edward VII
Albert, Prince: *see* York, Duke of
Albert Victor, Duke of Clarence:
  King George's brother (1864–
  1892), 5 n; Mr Dalton urges that
  he should accompany Prince
  George to the *Britannia*, 12, 13;
  his backwardness, 17, 23; accom-
  panies Prince George to Laus-
  anne, 34; created Duke of Clar-
  ence, 42; engaged to Princess
  Mary of Teck, 45; death of, 45;
  letters from, 35, 38
Alcock, Miss M.: vi
Alexander, Mr A. V.: 436 n, 464
Alexander, King of the Hellenes:
  312 n, 368 n, 372

Alexander, Prince (b. and d. 1871):
  6
Alexandra, Queen (1844–1925):
  her parentage and family, 3 n;
  early life, 4; her dislike of William II, 40; disapproves of Prince
  George becoming Colonel of a
  Prussian regiment, 42; on his becoming Duke of York, 47; her
  Mediterranean cruise, 48; attitude to his engagement, 49, 50;
  death of King Edward, 105; lives
  at Sandringham, 142; urges the
  King not to overwork, 316; her
  death, 410; her charm and
  beauty, 5; her domestic affections, 5, 52; her sense of humour,
  22
    Letters from, 23, 38, 42, 59,
  143
    Letters to, 24, 26, 38, 39, 40,
  172, 204, 316, 323, 341, 389
Algeciras Conference: 101, 184
Alice, Princess (1843–1878): Grand
  Duchess of Hesse-Darmstadt, 4,
  55
Allenby, Lord: 374 n, 375, 442
Ambassadors' Conference (1913):
  213
Amery, Rt. Hon. L. S.: 371 n, 376,
  403 n
Ammon, Mr C. J. (Lord Ammon):
  427
Amulree, Lord: 468 n, 495
Andersen, Mr H. N.: 294, 313
Anderson, Sir John, 68
Anglo-Egyptian negotiations: 374 n
Anglo-French Entente: 78–9, 101
Anglo-French staff talks: 190 and n
Anglo-Japanese Alliance: 189 and n
Anglo-Russian Entente: 101, 203 n,
  204
Anne, Queen: 110, 116, 130, 234
Anson, Sir William: 106, 114, 118,
  119

Index

Index

Bigge, Sir Arthur: *see* Stamfordham, Lord

Bigge, Miss Margaret: vii

Bill of Rights: 109

Bingham, Mr: 501, 502

Birkenhead, Earl of (Mr F. E. Smith, 1872–1930): 153; Attorney General, 293 n; and Irish Treaty negotiations, 360–2; remains loyal to Mr Lloyd George, 371; apprehensions in regard to Labour intentions, 383; at India Office, 403 n; and the reporting of divorce cases, 429; on appointment of Lord Irwin, 504 n

Birrell, Mr Augustine (1850–1933): President of Board of Education, 92; his Education Bill, 99; becomes Irish Secretary, 100 n; and Parliament Bill, 131; underestimates danger of Civil War in Ireland, 220, 223; tried to persuade Mr Redmond to agree to the exclusion of Ulster, 235; resigns after Easter rising, 276

Bismarck, Prince (1815–1898): disliked by Queen Alexandra, 40; Prince George's visit to, 42

Björkö, Emperors meeting at: 101

Black, Sister Catherine: 433 n, 525

'Black and Tans', the: 346, 347, 348

Blackburn, Mrs Mary: 6

Blenheim Rally, the: 199

Blessington, Countess of: 51

Blow, Mr Edward: 183

Boer War, the: 58–9; effect of, on British opinion, 72; end of, 80

Bognor: 432

Bolton Abbey: 56, 197

Bondfield, Miss Margaret: 435, 436 n, 457 n

Boothby, Mr Robert: 521

Bor, Major: 69 n, 76 n

Bosnian Crisis, 1908: 102

Botha, General: 81, 218

Bottomley, Mr Horatio: 250

Bourbon-Parma, Prince Sixte of: 313, 314

Bowes-Lyon, Lady Elizabeth: *see* York, Duchess of

Bradlaugh, Charles (1833–1891): 121 n

Briand, M. Aristide (1862–1932): 303, 367, 408, 411, 449 n

Bridges, Dr: 511

Bridgeman, Mr W. (Lord Bridgeman): 376, 403 n

Brilliant, Mr: 441

Britannia, R.Y.S.: 222, 516

Brook, Sir Thomas: 183

Brocket: 56

Brodrick, St John: *see* Midleton, Lord

Brown, Miss: 6

Brüning, Dr: 449 n

Brunswick, Duke of: 261, 250 n

Brusilov, General: 271

Bryce, James (Viscount Bryce, 1838–1922): Irish Secretary, 92, 100 n; Chairman of Committee on reform of the Second Chamber, 219 n; Chairman of Committee on Foreign Princes, 250

Bryce, Mrs Annan: 347

Buccleuch, John Scott, VII Duke of: 22 n, 363 n

Buchanan, Sir George: 300, 301, 302

Bucharest, Treaty of (1913): 212 n

Buckingham Palace Conference, 1914: 241–3

Buckmaster, Lord: 264 n, 293

Bulgaria, King Boris of: 427

Bulgaria, King Ferdinand I of (1861–1948): 212 n

Bülow, Prince: 76, 77, 78, 180

Bunsen, Sir Maurice de: 95

Burke, Edmund: 107 n

Burke, Mr F.: 309

Burnham, Lord: 315, 505

Burns, Mr John (1858–1943): enters Liberal Government, 92, 93, 94 n, 100 n; resigns, 256

Burt, Thomas: 93 n

Butler, Dr (Master of Trinity): 197

Butler, Mr R. A.: 509

Buxton, Mr Noel: 436 n

Byng of Vimy, Viscount (1862–1932): 116 n, 475–7

Byron, Colonel: 68 n

Cabinet Minutes: 293 n

'Cabinet Responsibility': 110, 111

Cadeby Colliery disaster: 196